Lecture Notes in Computer Science　　10602

Commenced Publication in 1973
Founding and Former Series Editors:
Gerhard Goos, Juris Hartmanis, and Jan van Leeuwen

Editorial Board

More information about this series at http://www.springer.com/series/7409

Xingming Sun · Han-Chieh Chao
Xingang You · Elisa Bertino (Eds.)

Cloud Computing and Security

Third International Conference, ICCCS 2017
Nanjing, China, June 16–18, 2017
Revised Selected Papers, Part I

Springer

Editors
Xingming Sun
Nanjing University of Information Science
  and Technology
Nanjing
China

Han-Chieh Chao
National Dong Hwa University
Shoufeng
Taiwan

Xingang You
China Information Technology Security
  Evaluation Center
Nanjing
China

Elisa Bertino
Department of Computer Science
Purdue University
West Lafayette, IN
USA

ISSN 0302-9743   ISSN 1611-3349 (electronic)
Lecture Notes in Computer Science
ISBN 978-3-319-68504-5   ISBN 978-3-319-68505-2 (eBook)
https://doi.org/10.1007/978-3-319-68505-2

Library of Congress Control Number: 2017956776

LNCS Sublibrary: SL3 – Information Systems and Applications, incl. Internet/Web, and HCI

Printed on acid-free paper

This Springer imprint is published by Springer Nature
The registered company is Springer International Publishing AG
The registered company address is: Gewerbestrasse 11, 6330 Cham, Switzerland

Preface

The two-volume set of proceedings (LNCS 10602 and 10603) contains the papers presented at ICCCS 2017: the Third International Conference on Cloud Computing and Security held during June 16–18, 2017, in Nanjing, China. The conference was hosted by the College of Computer and Software at the Nanjing University of Information Science and Technology, who provided the wonderful facilities and material support. We made use of the excellent EasyChair submission and reviewing software.

The aim of this conference is to provide an international forum for the latest results of research, development, and applications in the field of cloud computing and information security. This year we received more than 391 submissions from 15 countries and regions, including USA, UK, France, Australia, Ireland, South Korea, South Africa, India, Iraq, Kazakhstan, Indonesia, Vietnam, Ghana, China, and Taiwan. Each submission was allocated to three Program Committee (PC) members and each paper received on average three reviews. The committee decided to accept 116 papers, yielding an acceptance rate of 29.7%.

The program also included six distinguished talks. "Green Networking and Computing: New Perspectives and Challenges Within Energy-Oriented Infrastructures and Devices" by Dr. Aniello Castiglione, University of Salerno, Italy; "Content-Based Search over Encrypted Text Data in Cloud" by Dr. Zhangjie Fu, Nanjing University of Information Science and Technology, China; "Error Correcting Codes in Data Hiding and Secret Image Sharing" by Dr. Ching-Nung Yang, National Dong Hwa University, Taiwan; "Cloud-of-Things and Edge Computing: Recent Advances and Future Trends" by Dr. Mohammad Mehedi Hassan, King Saud University (KSU), Kingdom of Saudi Arabia; "SDN-Enabled Cloud Data Center" by Prof. Ren-Hung Hwang, National Chung Cheng University, Taiwan; and "Exploring the Geospatial Data: When Visualization Meets Query Processing" by Dr. Zhifeng Bao, RMIT University, Australia.

We would like to extend our sincere thanks to all authors who submitted papers to ICCCS 2017 and to all PC members. It was a truly great experience to work with such talented and hard-working researchers. We also appreciate the external reviewers for assisting the PC members in their particular areas of expertise. Finally, we would like to thank all attendees for their active participation and the organizing team who nicely managed this conference. We look forward to seeing you again at next year's ICCCS.

June 2017

Xingming Sun
Han-Chieh Chao
Xingang You
Elisa Bertino

Organization

General Chairs

Xingming Sun — Nanjing University of Information Science and Technology, China
Han-Chieh Chao — National Dong Hwa University, Taiwan
Xingang You — China Information Technology Security Evaluation Center, China
Elisa Bertino — University of Purdue, USA

Organizing Committee Chairs

Jian Shen — Nanjing University of Information Science and Technology, China
Kuan-Ching Li — Providence University, Taiwan
Chih-Hsien Hsia — Chinese Culture University, Taiwan
Shuangkui Xia — Beijing Institute of Electronics Technology and Application, China

Technical Program Committee Chairs

Chin-Feng Lai — National Cheng Kung University, Taiwan
Yang Xiao — The University of Alabama, USA
Aniello Castiglione — University of Salerno, Italy
Yunbiao Guo — China Information Technology Security Evaluation Center, China
Zhangjie Fu — Nanjing University of Information Science and Technology, China

Steering Committee Chairs

Xingming Sun — Nanjing University of Information Science and Technology, China
Han-Chieh Chao — National Dong Hwa University, Taiwan
Alex Liu — Michigan State University, USA
Yang Xiao — The University of Alabama, USA
Zhiqiu Huang — Nanjing University of Aeronautics and Astronautics, China

Technical Program Committee

Ming Yin	Harvard University, USA
Saeed Arif	University of Algeria, Algeria
Zhifeng Bao	Royal Melbourne Institute of Technology University, Australia
Hanhua Chen	Huazhong University of Science and Technology, China
Jie Chen	East China Normal University, China
Xiaofeng Chen	Xidian University, China
Ilyong Chung	Chosun University, South Korea
Jintai Ding	University of Cincinnati, USA
Zhangjie Fu	Nanjing University of Information Science and Technology, China
Jinguang Han	Nanjing University of Finance and Economics, China
Jiguo Li	Hohai University, China
Kuan-Ching Li	Providence University, Taiwan, China
Zhe Liu	University of Waterloo, Canada
Sungyoung Lee	Kyung Hee University, South Korea
Mohammad Mehedi Hassan	King Saud University, Saudi Arabia
Debiao He	Wuhan University, China
Wien Hong	Nanfang College of Sun Yat-Sen University, China
Qiong Huang	South China Agricultural University, China
Xinyi Huang	Fujian Normal University, China
Yongfeng Huang	Tsinghua University, China
Zhiqiu Huang	Nanjing University of Aeronautics and Astronautics, China
Patrick C.K. Hung	University of Ontario Institute of Technology, Canada
Hai Jin	Huazhong University of Science and Technology, China
Sam Tak Wu Kwong	City University of Hong Kong, SAR China
Xiangyang Li	Illinois Institute of Technology, USA
Yangming Li	University of Washington, USA
Quansheng Liu	University of South Britanny, France
Junzhou Luo	Southeast University, China
Yonglong Luo	Anhui Normal University, China
Sangman Moh	Chosun University, South Korea
Yi Mu	University of Wollongong, Australia
Zemin Ning	Wellcome Trust Sanger Institute, UK
Shaozhang Niu	Beijing University of Posts and Telecommunications, China
Jeff Z. Pan	University of Aberdeen, UK
Wei Pang	University of Aberdeen, UK
Rong Peng	Wuhan University, China
Jiaohua Qin	Central South University of Forestry and Technology, China
Yanzhen Qu	Colorado Technical University, USA
Kui Ren	State University of New York, USA
Shengli Sheng	University of Central Arkansas, USA

Robert Simon Sherratt	University of Reading, UK
Jianyong Sun	Xi'an Jiaotong University, China
Tsuyoshi Takagi	Kyushu University, Japan
Xianping Tao	Nanjing University, China
Yoshito Tobe	Aoyang University, Japan
Pengjun Wan	Illinois Institute of Technology, USA
Jian Wang	Nanjing University of Aeronautics and Astronautics, China
Honggang Wang	University of Massachusetts-Dartmouth, USA
Liangmin Wang	Jiangsu University, China
Xiaojun Wang	Dublin City University, Ireland
Q.M. Jonathan Wu	University of Windsor, Canada
Shaoen Wu	Ball State University, USA
Zhihua Xia	Nanjing University of Information Science and Technology, China
Yang Xiang	Deakin University, Australia
Naixue Xiong	Northeastern State University, USA
Aimin Yang	Guangdong University of Foreign Studies, China
Ching-Nung Yang	National Dong Hwa University, Taiwan
Ming Yang	Southeast University, China
Qing Yang	Montana State University, USA
Xinchun Yin	Yangzhou University, China
Yong Yu	University of Electronic Science and Technology of China, China
Mingwu Zhang	Hubei University of Technology, China
Wei Zhang	Nanjing University of Posts and Telecommunications, China
Xinpeng Zhang	University of Science and Technology of China, China
Yan Zhang	Simula Research Laboratory, Norway
Yao Zhao	Beijing Jiaotong University, China
Yun Q. Shi	New Jersey Institute of Technology, USA
Eric Wong	University of Texas at Dallas, USA
Frank Y. Shih	New Jersey Institute of Technology, USA
Haixiang Lin	Leiden University, The Netherlands
Haoran Xie	The Education University of Hong Kong, SAR China
Xiaodong Lin	University of Ontario Institute of Technology, Canada
Joseph Liu	Monash University, Australia
Jieren Cheng	Hainan University, China
Linna Zhou	University of International Relations, China
Bing Chen	Nanjing University of Aeronautics and Astronautics, China
Ruili Geng	Spectral MD, USA
Ding Wang	Peking University, China

Organizing Committee

Baowei Wang	Nanjing University of Information Science and Technology, China
Jielin Jiang	Nanjing University of Information Science and Technology, China
Leiming Yan	Nanjing University of Information Science and Technology, China
Lizhi Xiong	Nanjing University of Information Science and Technology, China
Qing Tian	Nanjing University of Information Science and Technology, China
Xianyi Chen	Nanjing University of Information Science and Technology, China
Yadang Chen	Nanjing University of Information Science and Technology, China
Yan Kong	Nanjing University of Information Science and Technology, China
Zilong Jin	Nanjing University of Information Science and Technology, China
Zhaoqing Pan	Nanjing University of Information Science and Technology, China
Zhiguo Qu	Nanjing University of Information Science and Technology, China
Zhili Zhou	Nanjing University of Information Science and Technology, China
Le Sun	Nanjing University of Information Science and Technology, China
Jian Su	Nanjing University of Information Science and Technology, China

Contents – Part I

Cloud Computing

IoT Applications

Contents – Part II

Multimedia Applications

Optimization and Classification

Information Hiding

Print-Scan Resilient Binary Map Watermarking Based on Extended Additive Noise Model and Scrambling

Fei Peng[1(✉)], Shuai-ping Wang[1], Gang Luo[1], and Min Long[2]

[1] School of Computer Science and Electronic Engineering,
Hunan University, Changsha 410082
Hunan Province, People's Republic of China
eepengf@gmail.com
[2] School of Computer and Communication Engineering,
Changsha University of Science and Technology,
Changsha 410082, Hunan Province, People's Republic of China

Abstract. As binary map has the characteristics of less and uneven distributed black pixels, the existing print-scan resilient watermarking cannot be well suited for it. In this paper, a novel blind print-scan resilient watermarking scheme for binary map is proposed based on extended additive noise model and scrambling. Firstly, the flipping probability of each pixel is calculated. After that, the binary map is scrambled and partitioned into blocks. Finally, based on the extended additive noise model of print-scan process and the number of the corresponding pixels, the watermark information is embedded. Experimental results show that the proposed scheme can not only provide large watermark capacity and good imperceptibility, but also can resist the impact of print-scan on the image, and has strong robustness.

Keywords: Binary map · Print-scan resilient watermarking · Image scrambling · Print-scan additive noise model

1 Instruction

With the development of information technology, the application of digital resources has gradually penetrated into various fields, and it is becoming one of the main means of communication. However, its convenience and fast implementation also provide opportunity for illegal use by criminals. Therefore, the security of digital resources has become the focus of academia and industry. In recent years, as an effective means of protection, digital watermarking has been rapidly developed. It can hide some information into a digital host, but it doesn't affect the use of the original host at the same time. Furthermore, it cannot be easily perceived or noticed by the human vision system (HVS). Through the important embedded information, the ownership or the integrity of the host can be determined.

In the real application, paper documents are important carriers for information exchange and sharing. With the rapid development of printing, scanning and copying technology, the problem of infringement of paper document copyright has also

X. Sun et al. (Eds.): ICCCS 2017, Part I, LNCS 10602, pp. 3–15, 2017.
https://doi.org/10.1007/978-3-319-68505-2_1

occurred. When computer technology is implemented to authenticate the copyright of a paper document, the printed or copied paper document needs to be scanned into a digital resource. Comparing with the original digital version, pixel distortions and geometric distortions are unavoidable. Thus, the application of digital watermarking in copyright protection of paper documents requires that the watermarking algorithm is more robust than that for the original digital document. In military and architectural design, the military maps and designing schemes are generally binary images. Comparing with grayscale or color images, HVS is more likely to find the distortion in binary images. Therefore, the requirements of imperceptibility for binary images watermarking is more restricted. So the enhancement of robustness and image fidelity are two key points for print-scan resilient watermarking for binary image.

Presently, the existing researches are mainly concentrated in the scope of the traditional digital watermarking [1–4, 7–11], and relatively few have been performed to print-scan resilient watermarking [12]. Although the method in [7] can solve problems of imperceptibility and watermark capacity, the robustness is still poor. The additive noise model proposed in [12] solves the problem of robustness, but the watermark capacity is small and the image fidelity is low.

In order to authenticate the source of the paper map, a blind watermarking scheme based on flippable pixels, image scrambling and extended print-scan additive noise model is presented. The main contributions of this paper include:

- The additive noise model of the print-scan process is extended, and it exactly reflects the real situation in the application.
- The application of image scrambling improves the watermark capacity, and facilitate the use of print-scan resilient watermarking for binary map.
- The capacity, imperceptibility and robustness of the proposed scheme is significantly improved compared with the existing schemes.

The rest of the paper is organized as follows: the proposed print-scan resilient watermarking scheme is described in Sect. 2. Experimental results and its comparative analyses are provided in Sect. 3. Finally, some conclusions are drawn in Sect. 4.

2 Description of the Proposed Scheme

The framework of the proposed scheme are shown in Fig. 1. Pixel flipping, image scrambling and print-scan extended additive noise model are three main components of it. Pixel flipping can effectively solve the problem of poor imperceptibility. Image scrambling can solve the problem of non-uniform distribution of black pixels such as military maps, engineering drawings and other binary images. It not only increases the watermark capacity of the algorithm, but also widens the range of the carrier image type. Print-scan extended additive noise model guarantees the strong robustness of the print-scan resilient watermarking.

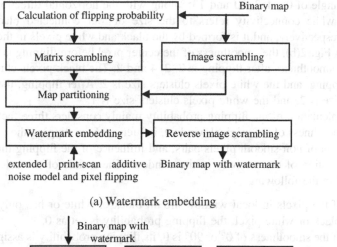

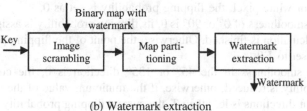

(a) Watermark embedding

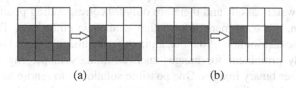

(b) Watermark extraction

Fig. 1. The framework of the proposed scheme

2.1 Flippable Pixels

A flippable pixel is a pixel whose flipping probability is greater than or equal to a certain threshold. The flipping probability refers to the apparent degree of distorting the image after a certain pixel is flipped. The larger flipping probability is, the less distortion brought to the image is. For Fig. 2(a) and (b), the image distortion induced from flipping the center pixel of Fig. 2(a) is significantly smaller than that of Fig. 2(b).

Fig. 2. A window with a size of 3×3 in a binary image

The calculation of flipping probability needs to consider the smoothness and connectivity of the local 3×3 window formed by the pixel and the adjacent 8 pixels. However, not all pixels are surrounded by 8 pixels. For example, the outermost pixels of the image. In this situation, the pixel's flipping probability is set to 0. Smoothness refers to the number of pairs of pixels of different pixel values in the adjacent positions with the angle of 0°, 45°, 90°and 135°along with the horizontal direction in the local window, while connectivity refers to the size of four connected black and white clusters, respectively, and it is formed by the black and white pixels in the window. As seen from Fig. 2(b), the smoothness of the center pixel before flipping is 0, 4, 6 and 4, while the smoothness after flipping is 2, 2, 4 and 2. The black pixels clusters size is 1 before flipping, and the white pixels clusters size is 2. After flipping, the black pixels clusters size is 2, and the white pixels clusters size is 1.

The calculation of the flipping probability mainly considers three factors, and they are the smoothness of the original window, influence of the flipping the center pixel on the variation of non-smooth pixels pairs, and influence of the flipping the center pixel on the variation of connectivity in the window. The details of the calculation [7] is described in the following.

Step 1. If the pixels in local window are all black or white or has only one isolated black or white pixel, the flipping probability is set as 0.

Step 2. If the smoothness of 0° or 90° is 0, its flipping probability is assigned to 0, and the calculation is finished. Otherwise, the point of the flipping probability can be preset to *FP*.

Step 3. If the smoothness in the 45° or 135° direction is 0, the current flipping probability is reduced; otherwise, if the minimum value of the smoothness of the four directions is less than T, the current flipping probability of the pixel is reduced.

Step 4. If the flipping of the center pixel does not change the smoothness of the current window, the current flipping probability is increased. Otherwise, if the smoothness increases, the current flipping probability is decreased.

Step 5. If the connectivity of the center pixel is changed due to the flipping of the center pixel, the current flipping probability is reduced.

2.2 Image Scrambling

When the watermark is embedded by using image block and pixel flipping, it is possible that there are few flippable pixels in some blocks, which will result in the failure of watermark embedding. For example, if it needs to flip 100 white flippable pixels to embed watermark 1, and there are only 90 corresponding pixels in the block. For this situation, the watermark information cannot be embedded. The root of the problem is that the distribution of the black pixels in the image's blocks is not balanced. This is especially prominent for images such as military maps, engineering design drawings, and other binary images. One possible solution is to ignore those blocks, but it needs extra auxiliary information to mark the corresponding blocks, which will reduce the watermark capacity and increase implementation complexity. To solve this problem, the image scrambling proposed in [5–7] is implemented to solve this problem.

2.3 Extension of the Print-Scan Additive Noise Model

As indicated in [12], in addition to geometric distortion, the main effect of the print-scan operation to the image is the diffusion of the boundary error, that is, the increase of black pixels at the edge of image. The number of black pixels in the image before and after the print-scan operation are represented by N and N', respectively, and the increment in the number of black pixels caused by the print-scan operation is ΔN. The following Eq. (1) can be obtained.

$$N' = N + \Delta N \tag{1}$$

However, in the process of model derivation, the definite integral operation used in [12] is ambiguous in comprehension and the conclusion is disputed. Here, improvements are made in the following. Assuming that the number of black pixels in the ith block before and after the print-scan are denoted by N_i and N'_i, and the mean value of the number of black pixels in all image's blocks before and after print-scan are denoted by $\overline{N}$ and $\overline{N'}$, respectively. The increment of the number of black pixels in the ith block is ΔN_i, and the increment of the mean value of the number of black pixels in the image is $\Delta \overline{N}$. According to Eqs. (1), (2) and (3) can be obtained.

$$N'_i = N_i + \Delta N_i \tag{2}$$

$$\overline{N'} = \overline{N} + \Delta \overline{N} \tag{3}$$

Since the image is scrambled before embedding, it can be assumed that the black pixels added by the print-scan operation are evenly distributed in each block. Then, Eq. (4) can be obtained.

$$\Delta N_i = \Delta \overline{N} \tag{4}$$

Substitute Eq. (4) into the difference between Eqs. (2) and (3). Then Eq. (5) can be obtained.

$$N'_i - \overline{N'} = N_i - \overline{N} \tag{5}$$

As seen from Eq. (5), the difference between the number of the black pixels in the block and the mean value of the black pixels in all image's blocks before and after print-scan doesn't change. Equation (5) only holds in the ideal case, while in reality, the distribution of the number of newly added black pixels tends to be affected by the performance of the image scrambling and the image correction algorithm. That is to say, Eq. (5) is not absolutely true.

According to the above analyses, experiments were carried out to observe the characteristics of the difference between the number of black pixels in the block and the mean value of black pixels in the image's blocks before and after print-scan operation.

The results are shown in Fig. 3(a), (b) and (c), and they are corresponded to three binary maps in Fig. 4. In Fig. 3, PS represents print-scan operation. As seen from Fig. 3(a), (b) and (c), the positive or negative sign of the differences of 85.23%,

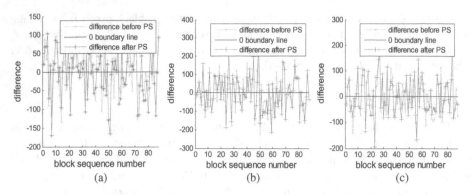

Fig. 3. The difference of the number of black pixels in image blocks and the mean number of black pixels in all image's blocks before and after print-scan

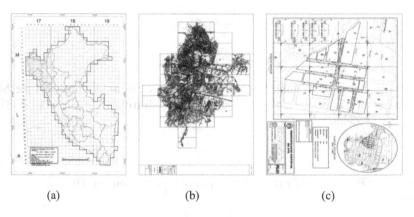

(a)　　　　　　　　(b)　　　　　　　　(c)

Fig. 4. Original binary maps

86.36% and 81.82% in image's blocks are kept, respectively. Therefore, an extended relation can be obtained:

$$\text{sgn}(N_i' - \overline{N}') = \text{sgn}(N_i - \overline{N}), \tag{6}$$

According to the above analyses and statistics, Eq. (6) holds with a high probability. The watermarking scheme proposed in this paper is based on this characteristic.

2.4　Description of the Proposed Watermarking Scheme

Watermark Embedding

Presuming that the embedded watermark information is a binary pseudorandom sequence with a length of L and it is represented as $w = \{w_i | w_i \in \{0, 1\}\}$, $i = 1, 2, 3, \ldots, L$. The details of watermark embedding is:

Step 1. Compute a flipping probability for each pixel, and obtain a flipping probability matrix.

Step 2. Scramble the original image and the flipping probability matrix, respectively.

Step 3. According to L and the size of the image, determine the size of the block, partition the scrambled image and flipping probability matrix with a predefined block size.

Step 4. Divide all blocks of the scrambled image into two categories: watermark embedding blocks and adjustment blocks.

Step 5. For each embedding block, calculate the difference Δ_i of N_i and N'_i, and modify the sign of Δ_i to embed watermark information. The rule of modification is as follows:

$$\Delta' = \begin{cases} \Delta_i \ w_i = 1, \Delta_i \geq blkDiff \\ blkDiff \ w_i = 1, \Delta_i < blkDiff \\ \Delta_i \ w_i = 0, \Delta_i \leq -blkDiff \\ -blkDiff \ w_i = 0, \Delta_i > -blkDiff \end{cases}, \qquad (7)$$

where Δ'_i is the difference after watermark embedding, and $blkDiff(>0)$ is an empirical value obtained by multiple experiments. $blkDiff$ represents the minimum absolute value of Δ'_i. Presuming that W, B represents the flipped white and black pixels, respectively, the total number of pixels which is flipped is C. Equation (8) can be obtained.

$$C = \begin{cases} \Delta'_i - \Delta_i \ (W), w_i = 1 \\ \Delta_i - \Delta'_i \ (B), w_i = 0 \end{cases} \qquad (8)$$

Step 6. For the adjustment block, the total number of pixels for flipping in the $(i+L)^{th}$ bock is:

$$C' = \begin{cases} \Delta'_i - \Delta_i \ (B), w_i = 1 \\ \Delta_i - \Delta'_i \ (W), w_i = 0 \end{cases}. \qquad (9)$$

Step 7. Repeat Step 5 to Step 6 until all watermark information are embedded.

Step 8. Inverses scrambling is performed to the embedded binary image, and the image with watermark is obtained.

Watermark Extraction

To extract the watermark, it needs to know the length of the watermark information and the image scrambling key in advance. The extraction process is as follows:

Step 1. Obtain the corrected and embedded binary image after print-scan operation.

Step 2. Scramble corrected and embedded binary image with the scrambling key.

Step 3. According to L and the size of the image, determine the size of the block, and partition the scrambled and corrected and embedded image with the predefined block size and obtain $\overline{N'}$.

Step 4. Calculate the number of black pixels in the ith block N_i' $(1 \leq i \leq L)$, and obtain the difference between the number of black pixels in the block and the mean value number of black pixels in all blocks Δ_i''. The watermark information w_i' of the current block is extracted according to the sign of Δ_i'', and it is represented as:

$$w_i' = \begin{cases} 0 & \Delta_i'' < 0 \\ 1 & \Delta_i'' > 0 \end{cases} \qquad (10)$$

Step 5. Repeat Step 4 until all L bits of watermark information are extracted.

3   Experimental Results and Analysis

In general, the binary map can be divided into three types. Firstly, the distribution of black pixels is relatively uniform but the number is small, as shown in Fig. 4(a). Then the distribution of black pixels is uneven, as shown in Fig. 4(b). Finally, the distribution of black pixels is relatively uniform and the number is large, as shown in Fig. 4(c). In order to verify the effectiveness and versatility of the proposed scheme, three binary maps are selected as the host of watermark embedding according to the above three types. In the experiments, the printer and scanner are Canon PIXMA iX6580 and Canon PIXMA MP259, respectively. The size of the images used here are all in A4.

3.1   Experimental Results

To evaluate the performance of the proposed scheme, experiments are done to test the robustness and imperceptibility of it. Its robustness is measured by watermark extraction accuracy when the carrier undergoes the print-scan operation. The higher the watermark extraction accuracy is, the stronger the robustness is. The measure of the imperceptibility is based on the method of measuring binary image distortion proposed in [13]. The Distance-Reciprocal Distortion (DRD) is a positive number. The larger the value is, the more serious the distortion is.

In the experiments, three images shown in Fig. 4(a), (b) and (c) are used for watermark embedding. The embedded binary maps are illustrated in Fig. 5(a), (b) and (c).

As seen from Fig. 5(a), (b) and (c), the embedded binary maps are very similar to the original binary maps illustrated in Fig. 4(a), (b) and (c), which indicate the good performance of the imperceptibility.

At the same time, experiments are done to test the influence of embedding threshold on the watermark extraction accuracy and the value of DRD when watermark capacity is fixed, and the results are listed in Table 1.

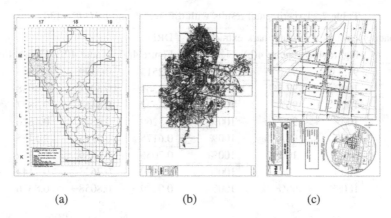

    (a)   (b)   (c)

Fig. 5. The watermarked binary maps ($L = 100$, $blkDiff = 170$)

Table 1. Experimental results with different $blkDiff$ and $L = 100$

blkDiff	Accuracy of watermark extraction			DRD		
	Figure 4(a)	Figure 4(b)	Figure 4(c)	Figure 4(a)	Figure 4(b)	Figure 4(c)
30	65%	72%	76%	0.1243	0.1284	0.1268
50	72%	81%	87%	0.1794	0.1717	0.1713
70	84%	88%	93%	0.2403	0.2230	0.2236
90	88%	87%	99%	0.3054	0.2803	0.2728
110	96%	94%	99%	0.3712	0.3404	0.3365
130	100%	96%	100%	0.4376	0.4022	0.3958
150	100%	99%	100%	0.5064	0.4643	0.4568
170	100%	100%	100%	0.5782	0.5244	0.5190

According to the watermark embedding process, the watermark extraction is based on the sign of $N_i - \overline{N}$ and $N_i' - \overline{N}_i'$, which is determined by the embedding threshold. It will finally influence the watermark extraction accuracy. Generally, the smaller the threshold is, the higher the probability of changing the sign of $N_i' - \overline{N}_i'$ is. As seen from Table 1, with the increase of embedding threshold, the watermark extraction accuracy and DRD are all increased.

Meanwhile, experiments are done to test the influence of watermark capacity on the watermark extraction accuracy and the value of DRD when the embedding threshold is fixed, and the results are presented in Table 2.

As seen from Table 2, it can be seen that with the increase of watermark capacity, the DRD is increased, which is coincided with the common sense. The experimental results indicate that the watermark extraction accuracy of proposed method is high and stable.

Table 2. Experimental results with different L and $blkDiff = 130$

Capacity	Accuracy of watermark extraction			DRD		
	Figure 4(a)	Figure 4(b)	Figure 4(c)	Figure 4(a)	Figure 4(b)	Figure 4(c)
60	98.33%	96.67%	100%	0.2515	0.2899	0.2343
80	100%	97.5%	100%	0.3361	0.3092	0.3088
100	100%	96%	100%	0.4332	0.4464	0.3877
120	100%	98.33%	100%	0.5269	0.4828	0.4626
140	100%	97.86%	100%	0.6175	0.5714	0.5355
160	100%	100%	100%	0.7056	0.6489	0.6479
180	100%	100%	100%	0.7970	0.7623	0.7144
200	100%	99%	100%	0.9279	0.8058	0.8356

3.2 Performance Analysis

Here, the performance of the proposed scheme is compared with those of the methods in [7, 12] from the aspects of watermark capacity and embedding threshold. For the method in [12], the difference between the number of black pixels in the block and the mean value of the black pixels in the image's blocks significantly fluctuates due to no scrambling is performed to the binary image. When the embedding intensity is unreasonably set, it may cause the watermark embedding to fail. For the method in [12], the number of pixels that will be flipped is calculated by multiplying the embedding intensity by the number of black pixels in current thumbnail. While for the proposed method, the number of pixels to be flipped is determined by the threshold, which represents the minimum absolute value of Δ'_i. To compare these methods under the same conditions, the number of pixels to be flipped in the current thumbnail of the method in [12] is determined in the same method as the proposed method. This will lead to higher the watermark extraction accuracy and DRD value for the method in [12].

Analysis of Performance of Watermark Extraction Accuracy
Experiments are done to compare the watermark extraction accuracy of the methods in [7, 12] with the proposed method when the embedding threshold and the watermark capacity are varied. The results are shown in Figs. 6 and 7, respectively.

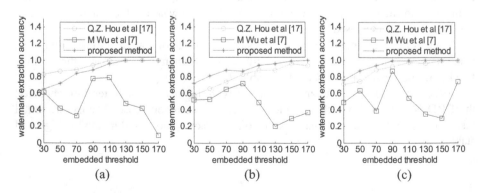

Fig. 6. Comparison of influence of the threshold on the watermark extraction

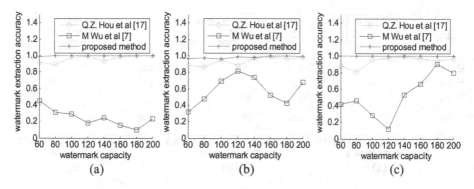

Fig. 7. Comparison of influence of the watermark capacity on the watermark extraction

As seen from Fig. 6, except the condition when the thresholds are small for the first binary map, the watermark extraction accuracy of the proposed method is better than those of the other two methods in the most of situations. In addition, it can be found that the watermark extraction accuracy of the proposed method and the method in [12] is positively proportional to the embedding threshold. However, this kind of regulation cannot be found in the method [7]. The main reason is that the characteristics chosen for watermark embedding cannot resist the dramatic changing of the number of black pixels caused by print-scan operation and image correction.

As seen from Fig. 7, with different watermark capacity, the watermark extraction accuracy of proposed method outperforms those of the other methods in [7, 12], and it is relatively stable. For the method in [7], the block size is related with the watermark capacity, and the difference of block size will cause drastic change in the pixel number. Therefore, the watermark extraction accuracy in method [7] is significantly affected by the watermark capacity.

Analysis of the Performance of Imperceptibility

Experiments are done to compare the imperceptibility of the methods in [7, 12] with the proposed method when the embedding threshold or the watermark capacity are varied. The results are shown in Figs. 8 and 9, respectively.

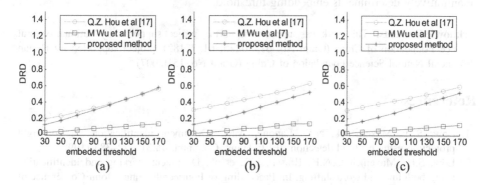

Fig. 8. Comparison of influence of the threshold on the imperceptibility

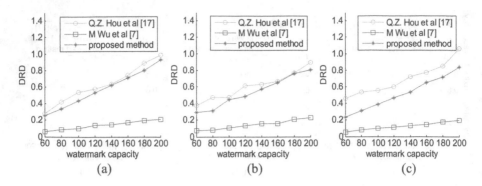

Fig. 9. Comparison of influence of the watermark capacity on the imperceptibility

From Figs. 8 and 9, it can be seen that with the increase of embedding threshold or watermark capacity, the DRD values of the three methods show a trend of gradual increase, that is, the imperceptibility decreases gradually. When the embedding threshold or watermark capacity is fixed, the method in [7] can obtain the best imperceptibility, while the method in [12] is the worst. The reason is that the increase of the embedded threshold or watermark capacity will result in the increase of the number of pixels for modifying. Thus, the imperceptibility will be gradually reduced.

4 Conclusion

In this paper, a novel print-scan resilient watermarking algorithm for binary map is proposed by using flippable pixels, image scrambling and print-scan extended additive noise model. Experimental results and comparisons show that the proposed scheme can effectively resist the impact of the print-scan operation on the embedded binary map. Comparing with the method in [12], image scrambling and different blocking method are introduced, and the performance of the proposed scheme has been greatly improved in watermark capacity, imperceptibility and robustness. The main defect is that it cannot adaptively determine its embedding threshold. Our future work will be concentrated on the additive noise model to building a complete mathematical model to quantitatively determine its embedding threshold.

Acknowledgements. This work was supported in part by project supported by National Natural Science Foundation of China (Grant No. 61370225, 61572182), project supported by Hunan Provincial Natural Science Foundation of China (Grant No. 15JJ2007).

References

1. Low, S.H., Maxemchuk, N.F., Lapone, A.M.: Document identification for copyright protection using centroid detection. IEEE Trans. Commun. **46**(3), 372–383 (1998)
2. Low, S.H., Maxemchuk, N.F., Brassil, J.T., et al.: Document marking and identification using both line and word shifting. In: Proceeding of Fourteenth Annual Joint Conference of the IEEE Computer and Communications Societies, pp. 853–860 (1995)

3. Yang, J., Zhang, M.R.: Document marking technique based on both line and word shifting. J. Xian Univ. Post Telecommun. **11**(3), 101–105 (2006)
4. Wu, M., Tang, E., Lin, B.: Data hiding in digital binary image. In: Proceeding of IEEE International Conference on Multimedia and Expo, vol. 1, pp. 393–396 (2000)
5. Wu, M., Liu, B.: Digital watermarking using shuffling. In: Proceeding of the International Conference on Image Processing, pp. 291–295 (1999)
6. Wu, M.: Multimedia data hiding, Ph.D. dissertation. Princeton Univ., Princeton, NJ (2001). http://www.ece.umd.edu/~minwu/research/phd_thesis.html
7. Wu, M., Liu, B.: Data hiding in binary image for authentication and annotation. IEEE Trans. Multimedia **6**(4), 528–538 (2004)
8. Lu, H., Kot, A.C., Cheng, J.: Secure data hiding in binary document images for authentication. In: Proceeding of the 2003 International Symposium on Circuits and Systems, vol. 3, pp. III-806–III-809. IEEE (2003)
9. Zhou, B., Chen, J.: A digital watermarking algorithm for binary image. J. Shanghai Jiaotong Univ. Chin. Ed. **38**, 1509–1514 (2004)
10. Liu, C., Dai, Y., Wang, Z.: A novel information hiding method in binary images. J. Southeast Univ. **S1**, 98–101 (2003)
11. Lu, H., Shi, X., Shi, Y.Q., et al.: Watermark embedding in DC components of DCT for binary images. In: Proceeding of the 2002 IEEE Workshop on Multimedia Signal Processing, pp. 300–303 (2002)
12. Hou, Q., Junping, D., Li, L., et al.: Scanned binary image watermarking based on additive model and sampling. Multimedia Tools Appl. **74**(21), 9407–9426 (2015)
13. Lu, H., Kot, A.C., Shi, Y.Q.: Distance-reciprocal distortion measure for binary document images. IEEE Signal Process. Lett. **11**(2), 228–231 (2004)

A New Universal Quantum Gates
and Its Simulation on GPGPU

Huimin Luo$^{(\boxtimes)}$, Jiabin Yuan, and Wenjing Dai

College of Computer Science and Technology,
Nanjing University of Aeronautics and Astronautics, Nanjing, China
{lhm,jbyuan,jing}@nuaa.edu.cn

Abstract. Classic quantum computer simulation will be a hotspot for years until the realistic quantum computers are available. As an essential component of quantum computers, the effects of the basic quantum gate and the equivalent relation are first briefly concluded in this paper. Base on the general-purpose graphics processing units (GPGPU) environment, the novel basic quantum gate simulation platform is achieved, on which any arbitrary quantum algorithm can be simulated. Our platform provides an user-friendly graphical interface for generating quantum circuit and observing the transformation of probability amplitude. Whats more, with the analyse of the combination of the existing universal quantum gates, a new universal quantum gates including Controlled-Z (C-Z), Hadamard (H), T is put forward. The proposed universal gates are considered to be more suitable for GPGPU, and it can be widely used to construct the quantum teleportation circuit and Grover's search algorithm. The new quantum circuit of Grover's search algorithm is conducted in our novel simulation platform. Results of the experiments show that the Grover's search algorithm will acquire quadratic acceleration when solving the search problem, which reflects the validity of the proposed gates.

Keywords: Universal quantum gates · Quantum circuit · GPGPU · Grover's search algorithm

1 Introduction

Quantum computation has attracted much attention in the last three decades [1] for its properties of the nature (superposition and entanglement of quantum states) [2]. A wide range of classical counterpart applications, such as large factor factorization, disordered database search [3] and quantum system simulation, are accelerated with quantum method.

A number of domestic and foreign scholars are devoted themselves to' quantum gates realization. Ferrando-Soria et al. introduced two schemes for implementing CNOT and $\sqrt{iSWAP}$ gates with supramolecular assemblies and perform detailed simulations, to demonstrate how the gates would operate [4]. Hu et al. proposed a set of universal quantum gates with topological bases through the developed DDM technique [5]. The companies of Google, Microsoft and

© Springer International Publishing AG 2017
X. Sun et al. (Eds.): ICCCS 2017, Part I, LNCS 10602, pp. 16–27, 2017.
https://doi.org/10.1007/978-3-319-68505-2_2

D-WAVE have announced the results of quantum computer research, but realistic quantum computers have not been built yet. Before the utilization of quantum computer, quantum simulation is a significant method to study quantum computing theory. Many different quantum computation simulations, such as Libquantum C, QuBit, jaQuzzi, have been designed till now [6]. Some of them were developed to demonstrate the most known quantum algorithms but not suitable for constructing an arbitrary quantum algorithms [7].

The quantum circuit model is the most widely used quantum computing model, which provides a basic architecture for the physical implementation of quantum computers. In the quantum computing theory of the circuit model, the basic quantum gate library is found first, and then the universal quantum computation is realized with the combination of these gates. The basic gate library, which also called universal quantum gates, that all unitary operations on arbitrarily many bits n can be expressed as compositions of these gates. In recent years, scholars at home and abroad have found common combination of quantum gates as follows: (1) All one-bit quantum gates plus CNOT, due to Barenco [8] (2) Toffoli, Hadamard, and S, due to Kitaev [9] (3) CNOT, Hadamard, and T, due to Boykin [10,11] (4) Toffoli plus any basis-changing single-qubit real gate; Toffoli, Hadamard; Toffoli and S; CNOT and T; CNOT and S, due to [12] (5) Hadamard, CNOT, S, and T, due to Kliuchnikov [13].

In this study, the novel basic quantum gate simulation platform is achieved under the GPGPU environment, on which any arbitrary quantum algorithm can be simulated. Furtherly, base on the existing universal quantum gates and the equivalently substituted relation, a new strategy for general quantum gates (C-Z, H, T) suitable for GPGPU cluster environment is designed. The search problem is widely used in practice, such as [14,15]. In order to validate our implementation, quantum teleportation [16] and Grover's search algorithm [17] are implemented on the proposed platform to demonstrate the validity of the proposed quantum gates.

The remainder of the paper is organized as follows. In Sect. 2, we describe the general form of the quantum gates and the form of the quantum circuit briefly. In Sect. 3, the novel basic quantum simulation platform is achieved, and a new universal quantum gates including C-Z, H, T was put forward, and experiments are presented in Sect. 4. Finally, the conclusion is presented in Sect. 5.

2 Background

2.1 Qubit Gates

An elementary unit of quantum information is a quantum bit [2]. The difference between bits and qubits is that a qubit can be in state other than 0, 1. It's also possible to form linear combinations of states, often called superpositions: $\alpha |0\rangle + \beta |1\rangle$, the number α and β are complex numbers and $|\alpha|^2 + |\beta|^2 = 1$. The superposition of n qubits is written as $|\varphi\rangle = \sum_{i=0}^{2^n-1} \alpha_i |i\rangle$, where $|i\rangle$ represents a specific computational basis state, and α_i means the probability amplitude of the relevant basis state.

The most useful single qubit gates include Hadamard, Pauli X, Pauli Y, Pauli Z, Phase shift, S and T. Multiple qubit gates usually include CNOT, C-Z and Toffoli. This section describes the effects of single quantum bit gates and multi-quantum bit gates.

(1) Single qubit gates

A quantum transformation is operated on the coefficient space of a quantum register [13]. The initial state vector is $|\phi\rangle$, and after unitary matrix operations state vector is $|\phi'\rangle$. More specifically, let us denote

$$|\phi\rangle = a(0...00)\,|0...00\rangle + a(0...01)\,|0...01\rangle + ... + a(1...1)\,|1...11\rangle$$
$$\left|\phi'\right\rangle = a'(0...00)\,|0...00\rangle + a'(0...01)\,|0...01\rangle + ... + a'(1...1)\,|1...11\rangle$$

In the case of H, for example, when H_j is applied to the state vector $|\varphi\rangle$, transforms the amplitudes according to

$$a'(*\cdots *0_j *\cdots *) = \frac{1}{\sqrt{2}}(a(*\cdots *0_j *\cdots *) + a(*\cdots *1_j *\cdots *))$$
$$a'(*\cdots *1_j *\cdots *) = \frac{1}{\sqrt{2}}(a(*\cdots *0_j *\cdots *) - a(*\cdots *1_j *\cdots *))$$

We use the $*$ to indicate that the bits on the corresponding positions are the same. It can be concluded that the H, X, Y, Phase shift gates act on the quantum bits of n require additional space for exchanging amplitudes, and the number of ground probabilities to be updated are 2^n. The gates of S, T, Z do not extra space, the number of amplitudes that need to be updated is 2^{n-1}.

(2) Multiple qubit gates

Multiple qubit gate acting on two qubits is expressed as U_{kj}, where $j < k$. For example, letting C_k^j denote a CNOT with control j and target k, the update of the probability of each basic state will comply with the following formula, all of other states at the input remain unchanged.

$$a'(*\cdots *0_k *\cdots *0_j *\cdots *) = a(*\cdots *0_k *\cdots *0_j *\cdots *)$$
$$a'(*\cdots *0_k *\cdots *1_j *\cdots *) = a(*\cdots *1_k *\cdots *1_j *\cdots *)$$
$$a'(*\cdots *1_k *\cdots *0_j *\cdots *) = a(*\cdots *1_k *\cdots *1_j *\cdots *)$$
$$a'(*\cdots *1_k *\cdots *1_j *\cdots *) = a(*\cdots *0_k *\cdots *1_j *\cdots *)$$

It can be concluded that the CNOT gate acting on the quantum bits of n requires additional space for exchanging amplitude, and the number of ground probabilities to be updated are 2^{n-1}. The number of ground-state probabilities of the controlled phase gate and Toffoli need to be updated is 2^{n-2}, and no extra space is required.

2.2 Circuit Model for Quantum Computation

In the framework of the quantum circuit model of quantum computation it is assumed that a memory register containing n qubits can be prepared in an arbitrary state. Quantum circuit consists of quantum gates and lines connecting the gates and showing the evolution of qubit states, and it is to be read from left-to-right [7]. In quantum computation, any unitary matrix can be decomposed into a series of gate operations. A number of gates and their arrangement in the circuit determine a quantum algorithm. Note that all quantum gates are usually denoted with some symbols, for example, H is the Hadamard gate, • and symbol ⊕ connected with a vertical line represent the control and target qubits in the CNOT.

3 Quantum Circuit Simulation Methods

3.1 The Quantum Simulation Platform Using GPGPU

In view of the fact that the simulation of quantum systems, such as quantum computers, requires computational resources that grow exponentially with the system size. Therefore, time and space overhead are important limited factors for multi-bit quantum computation simulation. GPGPU's efficient parallel computing power is well suitable for quantum simulation techniques to solve time bottlenecks. On the basis of the effects of quantum gate, we achieved a quantum simulation platform, including the basic gates mentioned in Sect. 2, and the quantum fourier transform algorithm. The platform provides an user-friendly graphical interface for generating quantum circuits and the simulation of 29-qubits quantum gates (Fig. 1).

```
yhave realized quantum gate as following:
1 QFT  2 Hadamard  3 CNOT  4 Pauli-X
5 Pauli-Y  6 Pauli-Z  7 S  8 T  9 Toffoli
input: 2
input target bit: 1
There is 4 device beyond 1.0
Threads per block is : 512
( 2.121320 +0.0000000i)|0> (|00>)
(-0.707107 +0.0000000i)|1> (|01>)
( 4.949748 +0.0000000i)|2> (|10>)
(-0.707107 +0.0000000i)|3> (|11>)
Do you want to continue?(y/n or Y/N)
```

Fig. 1. Quantum simulation platform

3.2   The Equivalence Relation Between Quantum Gates

(1) The relationship between CNOT and C-Z

$$\left(\frac{1}{\sqrt{2}}\begin{pmatrix}1 & 1\\ 1 & -1\end{pmatrix}\otimes I\right)\begin{pmatrix}1&0&0&0\\0&1&0&0\\0&0&0&1\\0&0&1&0\end{pmatrix}\left(\frac{1}{\sqrt{2}}\begin{pmatrix}1 & 1\\ 1 & -1\end{pmatrix}\otimes I\right)=\begin{pmatrix}1&0&0&0\\0&1&0&0\\0&0&0&1\\0&0&1&0\end{pmatrix} \quad (1)$$

According to Eq. (1), we can see that CNOT can be generated with C-Z plus H gates, the circuit diagram is as Fig. 2.

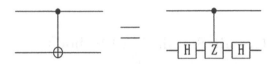

Fig. 2. The relation between CNOT and Ctrolled-Z gate

(2) The relationship between S and T

According to the metrical form of S and T can be drawn $S = T^2$, the circuit diagram is as Fig. 3.

Fig. 3. The relation between S and T gate

We use the GPGPU simulation platform to verify the correctness of Fig. 3. Like show in Fig. 4, the run time of S gate is 54654.55 (ms), and the run time of two T gates is 26677.25 (ms). We can note that T gate is better suitable to run on the GPGPU platform than the S gate. When we construct quantum circuits, two T gates are generally used to replace S gates.

(3) The equivalent relation between other gates

Implementation of the Toffoli gate using H, S, CNOT and T gates as Fig. 5. We also can use the commutation relations between CNOTs to simplify the circuit, as Eqs. 2–5. Letting C_j^i denote a CNOT with control i and target j, Z_i denote a Pauli Z gate acting on the i qubit [18].

$$C_j^i Z_i = Z_i C_j^i \quad (2)$$

$$C_j^i C_j^k = C_j^k C_j^i \quad (3)$$

$$C_k^i C_j^i = C_j^i C_k^i \quad (4)$$

$$C_j^i C_k^j = C_k^j C_k^i C_j^i \quad (5)$$

```
please input the width of qubit:1
sizeof(_cudacomplex) is 8.000000 B
Width: 1 qubits (2 states, 0.000015 MB).
way to initialize the array of amplitude:
1 one matrix  2 input interactively 3 order matrix
initialize the array of amplitude(complex numbers)
Do you want to continue?(y/n or Y/N)
y
yhave realized quantum gate as following:
0 CZ 1 QFT  2 Hadamard  3 CNOT  4 Pauli-X
5 Pauli-Y  6 Pauli-Z  7 S  8 T  9 Toffoli
10 fourcnot 11 threecz
input: 7
input target bit: 1
There is 4 device beyond 1.0
threadsPerBlock is 512
( 1.000000 +0.0000001)|0> (|0>)
( 0.000000 +1.0000001)|1> (|1>)
Do you want to continue?(y/n or Y/N)
n
nrun time is : 15039.38(ms)
```

```
irput: 8
irput target bit: 1
There is 4 device beyond 1.0
threadsPerBlock is 512
( 1.000000 +0.0000001)|0> (|0>)
( 0.707107 +0.7071071)|1> (|1>)
Dc you want to continue?(y/n or Y/N)
y
yhave realized quantum gate as following:
0 CZ 1 QFT  2 Hadamard  3 CNOT  4 Pauli-X
5 Pauli-Y  6 Pauli-Z  7 S  8 T  9 Toffoli
1C fourcnot 11 threecz
irput: 8
irput target bit: 1
Trere is 4 device beyond 1.0
threadsPerBlock is 512
( 1.000000 +0.0000001)|0> (|0>)
(-0.000000 +1.0000001)|1> (|1>)
Dc you want to continue?(y/n or Y/N)
n
nrun time is : 10689.66(ms)
```

(a) Implement S gate   (b) Implement T gate

Fig. 4. The implement of S and T gates

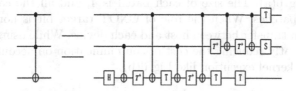

Fig. 5. The quantum circuit of Toffoli gate

3.3   The Universal Gates

In the actual design, the specific universal quantum gates can be determined according to the different quantum computers architecture and the physical realization of quantum computers. The elementary quantum gates can be used to construct an universal quantum gates, which are based on the complete, concise and easy to use three principles. The existing universal quantum gates can be listed as follows.

Table 1 shows that there are six kinds of universal quantum gates in currently, basing on the relationship between CNOT and C-Z discussed in Sect. 3.2, we

Table 1. Universal quantum gates

Index	Item
1	Toffli, H
2	Toffoli, S
3	CNOT, S
4	CNOT, T
5	CNOT, H, T
6	CNOT, H, S

propose a new general quantum gates including H, C-Z and T. The new universal quantum operators, can emulate any other operation.

Proof: First, it has defined that the H and T can approximate each single qubit operation. This is in fact easily provable, since each single qubit operation corresponds to a rotation in 3D [11]. The H operation is a rotation around of 180 around the XZ axis, the T corresponds 45° rotation. According to Ref. [19], an arbitrary unitary matrix on a d-dimensional Hilbert space may be written as a product of single qubit and CNOT gates, since C-Z can replace CNOT, so the universal gates we proposed can approximate any quantum operation.

The advantages of our new universal quantum gate can be outlined in two properties. First, in accordance with the Sect. 3.2, T gate is fit for GPGPU platform than S gate. Second, data distribution methods are discussed in Ref. [20]. An example of the simulation for 4-qubit CNOT in the case of N = 5, M = 3 is presented in Fig. 6(a). The size of each batch is 4, and all the coefficients are divided into 4 batches. When the role of CNOT target bit is non-local qubit, there needs data transfer between host and each device. While using C-Z instead of CNOT, it greatly reducing the cost of communication on account of no data transfer during kernel execution like Fig. 6(b).

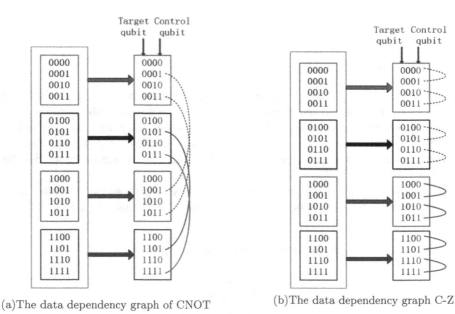

(a)The data dependency graph of CNOT   (b)The data dependency graph C-Z

Fig. 6. The data dependency graph

4 Experiments and Evaluation

4.1 Implementation of Quantum Teleportation Algorithm

To demonstrate usage of the universal gates proposed in Sect. 3.3, let us consider the quantum circuit shown in Fig. 7 that is used in quantum teleportation. Quantum teleportation is a process by which we can transfer the state of a system and can create replica of a state to another system. Quantum teleportation is the transfer of an unknown quantum state from a sender to a receiver by means of a shared bipartite entangled state and appropriate classical communication [16]. A program is simulated with successful simulation which give successful transfer of random qubit to output and which governs perfect communication between sender and receiver. The problem is to transmit an arbitrary state $|\varphi\rangle = \alpha |0\rangle + \beta |1\rangle$ of the top qubit to the bottom qubit.

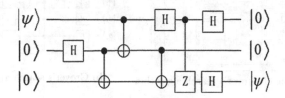

Fig. 7. Circuit implementing quantum teleportation

Input: $\{\alpha, 0, 0, 0, \beta, 0, 0, 0\}^T$ $(\alpha |0\rangle + \beta |1\rangle) |00\rangle = \alpha |000\rangle + \beta |100\rangle$

We can easily see that the final state obtained is exactly the state shown in the right-hand side of Fig. 8.

Output: $\{\alpha, \beta, 0, 0, 0, 0, 0, 0\}^T$ $\alpha |000\rangle + \beta |001\rangle = |00\rangle (\alpha |0\rangle + \beta |1\rangle)$

Base on the Sect. 3.3, we use the new universal quantum gates to construct the circuit of quantum teleportation as Fig. 8. Implementing different circuits in GPGPU simulation platform, we verified that the effect of the two circuit is the same, and we propose a new quantum teleportation circuit only need two types of gates can be achieved.

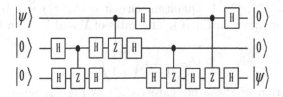

Fig. 8. New circuit implementing quantum teleportation

4.2   Implemention of Grover's Search Algorithm

Grover's search algorithm can achieve quadratic acceleration on search applications over unstructured data. There have been a wide range of generalization and applications of the algorithm, solving problems like pattern classifications and weight decision problem [21,22]. Let us simply remind the reader of the process of Grover's search algorithm. This algorithm employs pure states of n qubits which is initialized to the superposition of all computational basis state $|\psi\rangle = 1/\sqrt{2^n} \times \sum_{i=0}^{2^n-1} |i\rangle$. Then the Grover iteration can be divided into four stages which labeled as Oracle W1, R, W2, and the quantum circuit are illustrated in Fig. 9(a). Finally the measurement of the external system is followed.

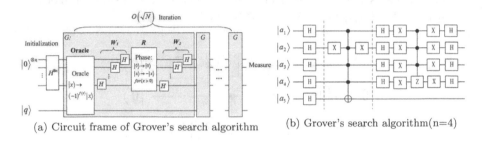

(a) Circuit frame of Grover's search algorithm   (b) Grover's search algorithm(n=4)

Fig. 9. Quantum circuit implementing Grover's search algorithm

Like Fig. 9(b), we consider the case of 4-qubits circuit and let, for instance, $k = 11$ be a hidden number, quantum memory register contain five qubits with $|a_5\rangle$ is ancillary qubit [23]. Taking into account the binary expansion (1011) of the munber 11, we can check that the function $f(a)$ outputs 1 only if its input $|a\rangle_4$ is equal to the hidden integer ($|a\rangle_4 = 1011 = |11\rangle_4$) and 0 otherwise.

To implement Grover's algorithm, the multi-bit control gate and the multi-bit control phase shift gate in Fig. 9(b) need to be decomposed into one-qubit and two-qubit quantum gates. We adopt a version of Feymans notation to denote $\wedge_4(\sigma_x)$ gate.

Theorem: For a unitary 2×2 matrix W, $W = R_z(\alpha)R_y(\theta)R_z(\beta)$, there exit matrices A, B, and C such that $ABC = I$ and $A\sigma_x B\sigma_x C = W$ [8]. When $W = \sigma_x$, let $A = V$, $B = V^+$, $C = I$. Quantum circuit of $\wedge_4(\sigma_x)$ can be described as Fig. 10, where V is shown in Eq. (6). The gates of V and V^+ can be constructed by T^2HT^2.

$$V = \frac{1}{1+i}\begin{pmatrix} 1 & i \\ i & 1 \end{pmatrix}. \tag{6}$$

The construction of the 4-bit gate $\wedge_3(Z)$ as Fig. 11, where $ABC = I$, and $A\sigma_x B\sigma_x C = Z$. A is shown in Eq. (7), $B = A^+$, $C = I$. The gates of A and B can be constructed by T^2HT^2Z.

$$A = \frac{1}{1+i}\begin{pmatrix} -i & -1 \\ 1 & i \end{pmatrix} \tag{7}$$

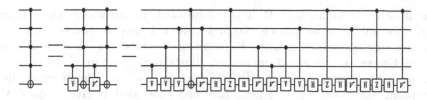

Fig. 10. Quantum circuit $\wedge_4(\sigma_x)$

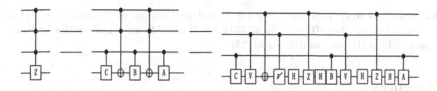

Fig. 11. Quantum circuit $\wedge_3(Z)$

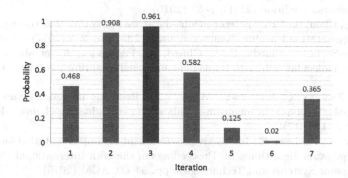

Fig. 12. Probability distribution after Grover's iterations

Base on quantum circuits described in Figs. 9(b), 10 and 11, we apply Grover's search algorithm using the new universal quantum gates on the proposed platform. Figure 12 shows that after an iterations a probability to get a correct number $k = 11$ is equal to 46.8%, while after the third Grover's iteration with probability 96.1%. However, at the six iteration, the probability decrease to 2%. The best iteration times is nearest integer to $\pi/(4 \arcsin(1/\sqrt{N}))$, where $N = 2^n$. For larger values of N this number is $O(\sqrt{N})$. Grover's algorithm provides a quadratic speed-up in solving the search problem in comparison with a classical computer which requires $O(N)$.

5   Conclusion and Future Work

In this work, we constructed an original basic quantum gate simulation platform, which can simulate any arbitrary quantum algorithm. Further, a new universal quantum gates including C-Z, H, T is put forward. To our knowledge, the proposed universal quantum gates is the first idea that uses the concept of C-Z to construct universal quantum gates. Experimental results on quantum teleportation and Grover's search algorithm circuits illustrate that the proposed universal quantum gates more suitable for GPGPU. Moreover, as an example we detailed description the Grover's search algorithm and show that it gives a quadratic speed-up in solving the search problem. In the future work, this work can be used in the simulation of more quantum algorithms.

Acknowledgments. This work was supported by Funding of National Natural Science Foundation of China (Grant No. 61571226), Natural Science Foundation of Jiangsu Province, China (Grant No. BK20140823).

References

1. Feynman, R.P.: Simulating physics with computers. Int. J. Theor. Phys. **21**(6), 467–488 (1982)
2. Nielsen, M.A., Chuang, I.L.: Quantum computation and quantum information: 10th anniversary edition. **21**(1), 1–59 (2010)
3. Tian, Q., Chen, S.: Cross-heterogeneous-database age estimation through correlation representation learning. Neurocomputing **238**, 286–295 (2017)
4. Ferrando-Soria, J., Pineda, E.M., Chiesa, A., Fernandez, A., et al.: A modular design of molecular qubits to implement universal quantum gate. Nat. Commun. **7** (2016)
5. Hu, Y., Zhao, Y.X., Xue, Z.-Y., Wang, Z.D.: Realizing universal quantum gates with topological bases in quantum-simulated superconducting chains. NPJ Quantum Inf. **3**, 1 (2017)
6. Raychev, N., Racheva, E.: Interactive environment for implementation and simulation of quantum algorithms. In: Proceedings of the 16th International Conference on Computer Systems and Technologies, pp. 54–60. ACM (2015)
7. Prokopenya, A.N.: Mathematica package "QuantumCircuit" for simulation of quantum computation. In: International Mathematica Symposium (2015)
8. Barenco, A., Bennett, C.H.: Elementary gates for quantum computation. Phy. Rev. A **52**(5), 3457 (1995)
9. Kitaev, A.Y.: Quantum computations: algorithms and error correction. Russ. Math. Surv. **52**(6), 53–112 (1997)
10. Boykin, P.O., Mor, T., Pulver, M., Roychowdhury, V., Vatan, F.: A new universal and fault-tolerant quantum basis. Inf. Process Lett. **75**(3), 101–107 (2000)
11. Raychev, N.: Universal quantum operators. Int. J. Sci. Eng. Res. (IJSR) **6**(6), 1369–1371 (2015)
12. Shi, Y.: Both Toffoli and controlled-NOT need little help to do universal quantum computing. Quantum Inf. Comput. **3**(1), 84–92 (2002)
13. Kliuchnikov, V., Maslov, D., Mosca, M.: Fast and efficient exact synthesis of single qubit unitaries generated by Clifford and T gates. Comput. Sci. **13**(7–8), 607–630 (2012)
14. Qu, Z., Keeney, J., Robitzsch, S., Zaman, F., Wang, X.: Multilevel pattern mining architecture for automatic network monitoring in heterogeneous wireless communication networks. China Commun. **13**(7), 108–116 (2016)

15. Fu, Z., Ren, K., Shu, J., Sun, X., Huang, F.: Enabling personalized search over encrypted outsourced data with efficiency improvement. IEEE Trans. Neural Netw. Learn. **27**(9), 2546–2559 (2016)
16. Sharma, M.S., De, A., Kulkarni, S.N., De, A.: Quantum teleportation circuit using Matlab and Mathematica. Int. J. Comput. Sci. Eng. (IJCSET) **2**(5), 1597–1600 (2010)
17. Xue, Y., Jiang, J., Zhao, B., Ma, T.: A self-adaptive artificial bee colony algorithm based on global best for global optimization. Soft Comput. 1–18 (2017)
18. Welch, J., Greenbaum, D., Mostame, S., Aspuruguzik, A.: Efficient quantum circuits for diagonal unitaries without ancillas. New J. Phys. **16**(3) (2013)
19. De Vos, A., De Baerdemacker, S.: The block-ZXZ synthesis of an arbitrary quantum circuit. Physics **94**(5) (2016)
20. Zhang, P., Yuan, J., Lu, X.: Quantum computer simulation on multi-GPU incorporating data locality. In: Wang, G., Zomaya, A., Perez, G.M., Li, K. (eds.) ICA3PP 2015. LNCS, vol. 9528, pp. 241–256. Springer, Cham (2015). doi:10.1007/978-3-319-27119-4_17
21. Gu, B., Sheng, V.S.: A robust regularization path algorithm for ν-support vector classification. IEEE Trans. Neural. Netw. Learn. **PP**(99), 1–8 (2016)
22. Gu, B., Sun, X., Sheng, V.S.: Structural minimax probability machine. IEEE Trans. Neural Netw. Learn. **PP**(99), 1–11 (2016)
23. Gerdt, V.P., Kragler, R., Prokopenya, A.N.: A mathematica package for simulation of quantum computation. In: Gerdt, V.P., Mayr, E.W., Vorozhtsov, E.V. (eds.) CASC 2009. LNCS, vol. 5743, pp. 106–117. Springer, Heidelberg (2009). doi:10.1007/978-3-642-04103-7_11

Data Hiding-Based Video Error Concealment Method Using Compressed Sensing

Yanli Chen[1,2], Hongxia Wang[1(✉)], and Hanzhou Wu[1,3]

[1] School of Information Science and Technology, Southwest Jiaotong University, Chengdu, Sichuan, China
yanli_027@163.com, hxwang@home.swjtu.edu.cn
[2] School of Engineering, Tibet University, Lhasa 850000, China
[3] Institute of Automation, Chinese Academy of Sciences (CAS), Beijing 100190, China
wuhanzhou_2007@126.com

Abstract. The video error concealment based on data hiding (VECDH) method aims to conceal video errors due to transmission according to the auxiliary data directly extracted from the received video file. It has the property that can well reduce the error propagated between spatially/temporally correlated macro-blocks. It is required that, the embedded information at the sender side should well capture/reflect the video characteristics. Moreover, the retrieved data should be capable of concealing video errors. The existing VECDH algorithms often embed the required information into the corresponding video frames to gain the transparency. However, at the receiver side, the reconstruction process may loss important information, which could result in a seriously distorted video. To improve the concealment performance, we propose an efficient VECDH algorithm using compressed sensing (CS) in this paper. For the proposed method, the frame features to be embedded in every video frame are generated from the frame residuals CS measurements and scrambled with other frame features as marked data. The marked data is embedded into the corresponding frames by modulating color-triples. For the receiver, the extracted data is used to reconstruct residuals to conceal errors. Error positions are located using the set theory. Since the CS has the ability to sample a signal within a lower sampling rate than the Shannon-Nyquist rate, the original signal could be reconstructed very well in theory. This indicates that the proposed method could benefit from the CS, and therefore keep better error concealment behavior. The experimental results show that the PSNR values gain about 10dB averagely and the proposed scheme in this paper improves the video quality significantly comparing with the exiting VECDH schemes.

Keywords: Video error concealment · Data hiding · Compressed sensing

1 Introduction

Video transmission is a current trend toward the provision of mobile communications. The transmission of video over wired and/or wireless channels introduces

© Springer International Publishing AG 2017
X. Sun et al. (Eds.): ICCCS 2017, Part I, LNCS 10602, pp. 28–38, 2017.
https://doi.org/10.1007/978-3-319-68505-2_3

multiple losses. These losses can propagate through inter/intra frames in a video sequence and thus the quality of video will be degraded drastically. The visual quality degradation caused by channel errors can be improved by the techniques that can be categorized into error resilience and error concealment [1]. To guarantee video quality through the error-prone network conditions, error concealment is a popular post-processing technique at the receiver side to alleviate the transmission errors.

There are two methods for error concealment. The first method is realized by concealing the error blocks using inter/intra correlation [1]. The second method is actualized by embedding frame feature information in video and also extracting data to reconstruct the original frames for error concealment [2–4]. The damaged macro-blocks are replaced with the spatially correlated macro-blocks in the previous frames/macro-blocks, and it is a simple way. However, if the reference macro-blocks are damaged, they need to be estimated from surrounding macro-blocks. So the first method may lead to distortion accumulation and produce larger distortions. Video error concealment based on data hiding(VECDH) method, which conceal errors using the reconstructed frame from extracted data, can avoid the error accumulation.

Data hiding is a technique for embedding secret data into cover media, the use of data hiding as an error control tool was first introduced by Liu and Li [5]. They embedded the direct-current (DC) components of host image into host image at the sender side, and extracted the DC components at the receiver side to reconstruct the host image and conceal the errors. The concept was extended to video coding by Bartolini et al. [6], they used data hiding DC coefficients only to increase the syntax-based error detection rate. In Ref. [2], the 2-level discrete wavelet transform (DWT) approximation coefficients are converted to halftone image which is embedded into original frame. Owing to the fact that the 2-level DWT approximation coefficients lost some approximation coefficients and detail coefficients, the concealment process may introduce distortions. In Ref. [3], the motion vectors of macro-blocks belonging to the region of interest (ROI), which is shared in a frame group, were embedded into the background region within the same frame. The ROI region sharing may lead to inaccurate motion vectors in different frames and also the concealment distortions at the receiver side may be great.

In this paper, a VECDH method using compressed sensing (CS) is proposed. CS permits, signals to be sampled at sub-Nyquist rates via linear projection onto a random basis under certain conditions [7], and the original signals can be recovered using nonlinear and relatively expensive optimization-based or iterative algorithms [8] from projection. CS is usually used to compress image and video for its low sampling rate and good reconstruction ability [9,10]. For CS, the original signal is compressed by Gaussian random matrix linearly [10], and the compressed data is Gaussian random. So, the compressed data can keep the core properties of original data and reduce the data size significantly. This is the main reason that CS is used to generate the frame features in this paper. The core idea in this paper is described as follows. The video is divided into several groups, and the first frame is considered as the background frame (BF). Since there are few differences between two near frames, the motion residuals instead of original frame are used to generate frame features. The less frames in a group makes the motion residuals more sparse. That indicates better compressive and reconstruction performance of CS may make the marked data better imperceptibility. Motion residuals between every frame and BF in a group are compressed by CS, and then the frame features in a group are scrambled and embedded into the group frames [11] by modulating color-triples [12]. At the receiver side, the frame features are extracted to reconstruct the motion residuals by generalized orthogonal matching pursuit (GOMP) [13] algorithm and the set theory is used to locate error pixels. The errors are concealed by replacing the error pixel values with the sum of background pixel values and reconstructed residual values.

The popular research on video is mainly based on the video compression standard [14,15,20], however, it may need cost energies on the standard rather than a scheme itself. In order to pay more attention to the scheme itself, a scheme is explained without considering compression standard in this paper.

This paper is organized as follows: Sect. 2 describes proposed scheme. While in Sect. 3 performance evaluation of the proposed scheme is demonstrated. Finally, conclusions are drawn in Sect. 4.

2   Proposed VECDH Scheme

All the frames in a video are divided into several groups, and the first frame in a group is considered as background frame (BF), others considered as non-background frame (NBF). The residuals, between every NBF and BF, are compressed by CS and scrambled as marked data, and then embedded into all the NBFs randomly. To distinguish BF and NBF, I-identifier, a mark of BF, is embedded into every frame. In order to keep the low distortion of BF, the data embedded in BF is less than that in NBF significantly. At the receiver side, based on the I-identifier and extracted data, groups are produced and the residuals are reconstructed to conceal errors.

2.1   Compressed Sensing

CS is a signal processing technique for efficiently acquiring and reconstructing a signal by finding solutions to under-determined linear systems. When a signal can be represented by a small number of nonzero coefficients, CS has emerged as a framework that can significantly reduce the cost at compressive side, and the original signal can be reconstructed from far fewer samples than required by the Shannon-Nyquist sampling theorem [8,13,16,17].

Let $x \in \mathbf{R}^{N \times 1}$ be a signal which can be represented as $x = \theta \cdot f$, where $\theta \in \mathbf{R}^{N \times N}$ is an orthogonal basis matrix, and $f \in \mathbf{R}^{N}$ is a K-sparse vector (K out of the N elements of f are nonzero), then a sparse representation of signal is obtained. For image, θ is usually chosen as the discrete cosine transform (DCT) matrix or discrete wavelet transform (DWT) matrix.

CS claims that a sparse signal can be retrieved from a relatively small number of measurements as follows:

$$y = \phi \cdot x = \phi \cdot \theta \cdot f, y \in \mathbf{R}^{M \times 1}, \phi \in \mathbf{R}^{M \times N}, K log_2 \frac{N}{K} \leq M < N. \qquad (1)$$

where ϕ, incoherent with θ, is a measurement matrix that satisfies restricted isometry property (RIP) [17] and y is sampled vector, [19] indicates Gaussian random matrix satisfied RIP requirement.

The reconstruction of original signal from sampled vector is based on the following optimization problem:

$$min\|f\|_0 \qquad s.t. \qquad x = \theta \cdot f \qquad (2)$$

For the l_0-norm minimization problem is an NP problem, to avoid this, the l_0-norm can be replaced by l_1-norm. The optimization problem is used to reconstruct x from y, and the algorithm GOMP (Generalized Orthogonal Matching Pursuit) in [13] is used in this proposed scheme.

For the random of measure matrix and the linear of compressive procedure, the compressed data is random and it can degrade the risk of relevance analysis attacking. CS is used to generate the frame features [17].

2.2 Proposed Error Concealment Scheme

Assuming a video with size $N_1 \times N_2$ is divided into m groups, and n frames in a group. $f_j^{(i)}$ indicates j-th frame in i-th group, $i = 1, 2, \cdots, m, j = 1, 2, \cdots, n$.

In i-th group, the marked data is obtained by compressing and scrambling the residuals. For the purpose of reducing the data amount, the residuals are performed half down-sampling both in rows and columns. The frame features are generated by measuring every color channel of down-sampled residuals.

$$W_j^i = CS(f_j^{id} - f_1^{id}), W_j^i \in \mathbf{R}^{\frac{3 \cdot N_1 \cdot N_2}{16}}. \qquad (3)$$

where CS is compressed sensing [8,13,16,17] operation with quarter compression ratio and W_j^i is the feature of down-sampled frame f_j^i. Frame features in a group are scrambled as marked data by interlacing, and the scrambled frame features are shown in Eq. (4).

$$W^i = [W_{s_2}^i, W_{s_3}^i, \cdots, W_{s_n}^i] = scramble([W_2^i, W_3^i, \cdots, W_N^i]). \qquad (4)$$

where W^i and $W_{s_j}^i$ indicate the marked data that will be embedded into i-th group and frame f_j^i.

To distinguish the BF and NBF, I-identifier is embedded into the first row of every frame as a marker of BF as the first rows are not conspicuous. For BF, the I-identifier flag is zero, and otherwise, it is 255. In order to improve the robustness, addition 2 bits are set to be redundancy bits and

I-identifier is a 10-bit number, and every two bit is embedded into one pixel. I-identifier is embedded by modulating parity of the color-triples for the parity may impact least on the carrier. Let color-triples with coordinate $(1, l)$ in BF f_1^i be $f_{1,R}^i(1, l), f_{1,G}^i(1, l), f_{1,B}^i(1, l)$, the embedding procedure is as follows:

$$f_{1,G}^i(1, l) - f_{1,B}^i(1, l) = \begin{cases} 2n + 1, n \in \mathbf{Z}, b_2 = 1 \\ 2n \quad\;, n \in \mathbf{Z}, b_2 = 0 \end{cases}. \tag{5a}$$

$$f_{1,R}^i(1, l) - f_{1,B}^i(1, l) = \begin{cases} 2n + 1, n \in \mathbf{Z}, b_1 = 1 \\ 2n \quad\;, n \in \mathbf{Z}, b_1 = 0 \end{cases}. \tag{5b}$$

For BF, the marked data is group data that indicates the group location in video. It consists of three 16-bit numbers, the total frame number in the whole video, total frame number in a group, and the group order. To extract the group data correctly for the receiver, group data is 4×4 spread spectrum and the corresponding bit is recovered by extracting majority bits from the corresponding 4×4 block. To satisfy require of transparency, green and blue color channels are selected to be embedded, the embedded positions are decided randomly by a key. The embedding process is similar with Eq. (5a). For NBF, the marked data in Eq. (4) is embedded into the corresponding frame by the same way.

Data extraction is the inverse of the embedding process. In the case that the receiver has the random key which decides the group data embedding position, the marked data can be extracted. The group is produced using group data and the recovered motion residuals are used to reconstruct by GOMP algorithm [13].

The error concealment process is implemented by locating the error positions and concealment. The set theory is used to locate the errors and the genuine residuals in received frames. The concealment process is realized using the reconstructed residuals. If the error pixels are motion pixels it is replaced by the sum of the pixel value of background and residual. Otherwise, it is replaced by background pixels.

Step (1) Calculate the residuals R_{mve}. The locations that the values are greater than a suitable threshold are judged as "errors". The "errors" may be caused by misjudging of motion residuals or error-prone channel.

$$R_{mve} = f_j^{i'} - f_1^{i'}. \tag{6}$$

Step (2) Reconstruct the original residuals R_{remv} by GOMP algorithm [13]. Limited by accuracy of reconstructing algorithm, the reconstruction introduces some noises, so the pixels in R_{remv} are made up of motion residuals and noises.

$$R_{remv} = \text{GOMP}(W_j^{i'}). \tag{7}$$

Step (3) Calculate the differences between R_{mve} and R_{remv}. The differences between original residuals and the reconstructed residuals consist of losses caused by channel and noise introduced by reconstructing.

$$d = R_{mve} - R_{remv}. \tag{8}$$

Step (4) Determine the residuals, noises and errors by suitable thresholds which are obtained from lot of experiments, and then locate the error positions by set theory.

Step (5) If error pixels are motion pixels, its value is replaced by the sum of the pixel value of background and residual value. Otherwise, it is replaced by background pixel value.

2.3   Error Concealment Analysis

The misjudging in Sect. 2.2 is mainly caused by the inaccurate judgment. To analyze the influence of misjudging expediently, the residual, noise and error pixels are converted into set, e.g., R_{mve} is converted into S_{mve} in Eq. (9).

$$if\, R_{mve}(k,l) > T, f_j^i(k,l) \in S_{mve} \tag{9}$$

where $T \in [0, 255]$ is threshold which is obtained by lots of experiments. Similarly, S_{remv} and S_d are produced, and also S_E, S_{mv} and S_N denote the errors set, residuals set and noises set. Their relations in Eq. (10a) are described as that both the noises and residuals exist incompatibly in set S_{remv}, both residuals and errors exist in S_{mve}, and both noises and errors are in S_d. The relations of S_{MV}, S_N and S_E are shown in Fig. 1.

$$S_{mve} = S_{mv} \bigcup S_E, S_{remv} = S_{mv} \bigcup S_N. \tag{10a}$$

$$S_d = S_N \bigcup S_E, S_{mv} \bigcap S_N = \phi. \tag{10b}$$

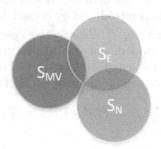

Fig. 1. The relation of S_{MV}, S_N and S_E

The sets S_E and S_{mv} can be solved using set theory as follows:

$$f_j^{i'}(k,l) \in \begin{cases} S_E, f_j^{i'}(k,l) \in S_{mve} \text{ and } f_j^{i'}(k,l) \in S_E \\ S_{mv}, f_j^{i'}(k,l) \in S_{mve} \text{ and } f_j^{i'}(k,l) \in S_{remv} \end{cases}. \tag{11}$$

Fig. 2. Simple model of error concealment

Every element in all the sets may be misjudged, and this misjudging may produce distortions. If the distortions caused by lossy channel and error concealment are considered as concealment distortions in the error concealment system, the system can be simplified as Fig. 2.

The distortion factor of concealment system in [18] is modified as Eq. (12).

$$c = \frac{D_c}{D_T}. \tag{12}$$

where D_c is concealment distortion, and D_T is transmission distortion. D_c and D_T are calculated based on the method in [18].

The misjudging is divided into two categories, correct is misjudged as error and reverse. Assuming the two probabilities are p_{ce} and p_{ec}, they are equal [19]

$$p_{ce} = p_{ec} = 0.5p. \tag{13}$$

where p is misjudging probability.

Let d_{ec} denote the distortion caused by p_{ec}, and d_{ce} denotes the distortion caused by p_{ce}, d_{ee} and d_{cc} denote the distortion caused by correct judging. Then, the distortion is calculated in Eq. (14).

$$D_c = 0.5p \cdot (d_{ec} + d_{ce}) + (1 - p) \cdot (d_{ee} + d_{cc}). \tag{14}$$

The first term in Eq. (14) are distortions introduced by incorrect judging, and the second term are distortions introduced by correct judging. Let f_j^i denote the frame before at the sender side, $f_j^{i'}$ denote the lossy frame, and $f_j^{i''}$ denote the concealed frame. The concealment distortions are calculated in Eqs. (15) and (16). While the transmission distortions are shown in Eq. (17), and the concealment distortion factor can be modified as Eq. (18).

$$d_{ec} + d_{ce} = f_j^{i'} - f_j^i, d_{ee} + d_{cc} = f_j^{i''} - f_j^i. \tag{15}$$

$$D_c = 0.5p \cdot (f_j^{i'} - f_j^i) + (1 - p) \cdot (f_j^{i''} - f_j^i). \tag{16}$$

$$D_T = f_j^{i'} - f_j^i. \tag{17}$$

$$c = \frac{0.5p \cdot (f_j^{i'} - f_j^i) + (1 - p) \cdot (f_j^{i''} - f_j^i)}{f_j^{i'} - f_j^i}. \tag{18}$$

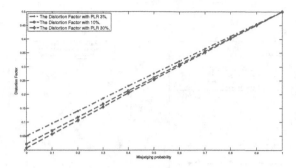

Fig. 3. The comparison of concealment distortion with different loss rates

The 2nd frame with different packet lost rate (PLR) is used to test the relationship between concealment distortions and PLR. In this paper, the 2nd frame with PLR 0.03, 0.1, 0.3 is used to calculate the concealment distortion factors. If the PLR is too great, the concealment performance is distinct in visual, and if the PLR is too small, the concealment in visual is meaningless for that the distortions caused by concealment is similar with the errors caused by channel. Also, the other similar values also can be selected as PLR. The experimental results shown in Fig. 3 illustrate that greater PLR may produce lower distortion factor.

3   Experimental Results

To describe the performance of the proposed scheme with other schemes comprehensively, Three sequences with different activities are tested, Hall (15–44 frames), Akiyo (first 30 frames) and Foreman (first 30 frames). For every sequence there are 10 frames in a frame group. The damaged frames order set is $A = \{2, 3, 5, 7, 9, 12, 15, 17, 18, 26, 27, 28\}$. The frame PLR in A is set to be $0.03, 0.05, 0.1$ cyclically.

There are few works on the VECDH schemes, we select [2,3] to be the compared literatures. Figures 4, 5 and 6 shows the experiment results,and they indicate that the scheme in [2] has the best transparency, and the proposed scheme has the best concealment performance. In Fig. 5, the PSNR-versus-frame-number curses of the two schemes are nearly coincide, because motion residuals in test video *akiyo* is little and there are nearly no differences in visual among the first 8 frames. Differently, for test video *foreman*, the motion residual is large, so there are visible difference between the curses of the two schemes. The analyses based on the results are given as follows.

Firstly, the inherent scheme is the most important reason. The embedding capacity and the marked data generation are the constraint factors. In [2], the approximation coefficients (AC) of the 2-level DWT, which is performed on the AC of first level DWT, are converted to half-toned image and then 2×2 repeated. So, the enlarged half-toned image with quarter of frame size is embedded into

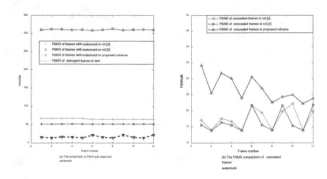

Fig. 4. The comparison of concealment performance of $hall_{c}if.yuv$

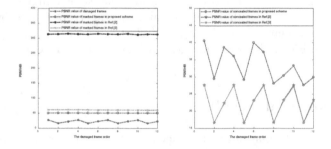

Fig. 5. The concealment performance of $akiyo_{c}if.yuv$

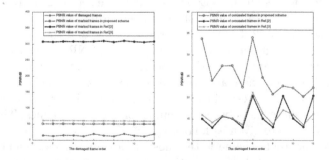

Fig. 6. The concealment performance of $foreman_{c}if.yuv$

a frame, and the binary marked data is quarter of frame size. In [3], the ROI is shared in a group, the motion vectors in ROI are embedded in the background region. The ROI is not stationary, the maximal size of ROI data is half frame size and the average size is quarter of frame size. While, in the proposed scheme, the marked data is quarter of frame size, and every data is 8-bit number. The marked data is 8 times as much in [2], and as much as in [3]. However, the inverse half-tone may introduce distortions, and the inverse DWT also may introduce greater distortions for lossy 2-level DWT in [2]. The ROI sharing in frame group may cause inaccuracy motion vectors. All of this indicate that the proposed scheme benefits from the compression performance of CS.

Secondly, the activity of selected video sequences are different. That implies the proposed scheme may be fit for different activity videos. However, the greater residuals make the more errors caused by reconstruction and the concealment performance may be decreasing. In other words, the increasing activity is directly proportional to the increasing distortions.

Thirdly, the curves in Fig. 4 are not stable, they are fluctuating. The reason is that the residuals in every frame is different. The more residual differences, the greater difference in concealment performance.

All the above makes the performance of the scheme in this paper is better.

4   Conclusion

In this paper, we have proposed a VECDH scheme using CS. At the sender side, the whole frame residual can be compressed one time by CS as marked data. For the receiver, the frame residual can be reconstructed perfectly by CS in theory for error concealment. Comparing with the related works, CS that permits a sparse signal is reconstructed from far fewer samples than sub-Nyquist sampling rate plays an important role in reconstructing the original residual. Meanwhile, locating method of the residual pixels & error pixels plays key role in concealing process. Both result in the better concealment performance in this letter.

Acknowledgements. We would like to thank all anonymous reviewers for their helpful advice and comments. This work is supported by the National Natural Science Foundation of China (NSFC) under the grant No. U1536110, and Tibet Autonomous Region Soft Science Research program under the grant No. Z2016R67F02.

References

1. Lie, W.-N., Lee, C.-M., Yeh, C.-H., Gao, X.-W.: Motion vector recovery for video error concealment by using iterative dynamic-programming optimization. IEEE Trans. Multimedia **16**(1), 216–227 (2014)
2. Adsumilli, C.B., Farias, M.C.Q., Mitra, S.K., Carli, M.: A robust error concealment technique using data hiding for image and video transmission over lossy channels. IEEE Trans. Circuits Syst. Video Technol. **15**(11), 1394–1406 (2005)

3. Yao, Y., Zhang, W., Nenghai, Y.: Adaptive video error concealment using reversible data hiding. In: Proceeding of International Conference on Multimedia Information Networking and Security (MINES), pp. 658–661 (2012)
4. Akbari, A., Danyali, H., Rashidpour, M.: Error concealment using data hiding for resolution scalable transmission. In: Proceeding of the 16th CSI International Symposium on Artificial Intelligence and Signal Processing (AISP), pp. 228–232. IEEE Press, Nanjing (2012)
5. Liu, Y., Li, Y.: Error concealment for digital images using data hiding. In: Proceeding of the 9th Digital Signal Processing Workshop Hunt, pp. 1–6 (2000)
6. Bartolini, F., Manetti, A., Piva, A., Barni, M.: A data hiding approach for correcting errors in H. 263 video transmitted over a noisy channel. In: Proceeding of IEEE Workshop on Multimedia Signal Processing, pp. 65–70. IEEE Press, Cannes (2001)
7. Mun, S., Fowler, J.E.: Residual reconstruction for block-based compressed sensing of video. In: Data Compression Conference (DCC), pp. 183–192. IEEE Press, Snowbird (2011)
8. Davenport, M.A., et al.: Signal processing with compressive measurements. IEEE J. Sel. Top. Sig. Process. **4**(2), 445–460 (2010)
9. Yang, J., Yuan, X., Liao, X., Llull, P., Brady, D.J., Sapiro, G., Carin, L.: Video compressive sensing using gaussian mixture models. IEEE Trans. Image Process. **23**(11), 4863–4878 (2014)
10. Li, S., Qi, H.: A Douglas-Rachford splitting approach to compressed sensing image recovery using low-rank regularization. IEEE Trans. Image Process. **24**(11), 4240–4249 (2015)
11. Qian, Q., Wang, H.X., Hu, Y., et al.: A dual fragile watermarking scheme for speech authentication. Multimedia Tools Appl. **75**(21), 13431–13450 (2016)
12. Wu, H.-Z., Shi, Y.-Q., Wang, H.-X., Zhou, L.-N.: Separable reversible data hiding for encrypted palette images with color partitioning and flipping verification. IEEE Trans. Circuits Syst. Video Technol. **27**, 1620–1631 (2017). doi:10.1109/TCSVT.2016.2556585
13. Wang, J., Kwon, S., Li, P., Shim, B.: Recovery of sparse signals via generalized orthogonal matching pursuit: a new analysis. IEEE Trans. Sig. Process. **64**(4), 1076–1089 (2016)
14. Pan, Z., Lei, J., Zhang, Y., Sun, X., Kwong, S.: Fast motion estimation based on content property for low-complexity H.265/HEVC Encoder. IEEE Trans. Broadcast. **62**(3), 675–684 (2016)
15. Pan, Z., Zhang, Y., Kwong, S.: Efficient motion and disparity estimation optimization for low complexity multiview video coding. IEEE Trans. Broadcast. **61**(2), 166–176 (2015)
16. Davenport, M.A., Boufounos, P.T., Wakin, M.B., Baraniuk, R.G.: Signal processing with compressive measurements. IEEE J. Sel. Top. Sig. Process. **4**(2), 445–460 (2010)
17. Zhao, H., Ren, J.: Cognitive computation of compressed sensing for watermark signal measurement. Cogn. Comput. **8**(2), 246–260 (2016)
18. Peng, Q., Deng, Y., Yang, T., Zhu, C.: A novel general end-to-end distortion estimation model for video. Transm. J. Image Graph. **11**(6), 792–797 (2006)
19. Bin, G., Sun, X., Sheng, V.S.: Structural minimax probability machine. IEEE Trans. Neural Netw. Learn. Syst. doi:10.1109/TNNLS.2016.2544779
20. Pan, Z., Jin, P., Lei, J., Zhang, Y., Sun, X., Kwong, S.: Fast reference frame selection based on content similarity for low complexity HEVC encoder. J. Vis. Commun. Image Represent. **40**(Part B), 516–524 (2016)

A Novel Robust Reversible Watermarking Scheme Based on IWT

Shuang Yu[✉], Jian Li, and Jinwei Wang

School of Computer and Software, Nanjing University of Information Science and Technology,
Nanjing 210044, China
fegxu@sina.com, ljian20@gmail.com, wjwei_2004@163.com

Abstract. This paper proposes a novel robust reversible data hiding scheme. This scheme is realized by two stages, which embed robust watermarks and fragile ones respectively. Firstly, the robust watermarks are embedded into the mid-low frequency coefficients after the image transformed from spatial domain to frequency domain. Then, side information that used to ensure the reversibility is embedded in spatial domain by the form of fragile watermarks. 5-3 integer wavelet transform (IWT) is adopted in this paper, which provides integer-to-integer transformation that ensure the low capacity of the side information. Experimental results verify high performance of robustness and image quality.

Keywords: Reversible data hiding · Robust data hiding · Integer wavelet transform · Image watermarking · Histogram shifting

1 Introduction

Reversible data hiding technology is one focus in the area of multimedia information security. This special hiding technology can not only hide information into images at the embedded terminal but also extract the information as well as restore the carrier image to the original one losslessly at the receiver. In the large number of existed reversible hiding schemes [1–10], the hidden watermarks are fragile. That is the watermarks can be extracted precisely only in the lossless environment, which means that the carrier images do not experience any attacks or alteration during the process of storage and transmission. Obviously, in the practical application, it is very difficult.

Robust reversible watermarking technology enhances the robustness which means that the data can be correctly extracted under some attacks. Vleeschouwer et al. [11] who recognized that problem early and presented a reversible watermarking scheme, which has robustness in 2003. It first divides the image into several non-overlapping blocks, then each block is grouped by two subsets that the primary histograms of them are similar. The robust data are embedded by the way of adjusting the relationship between the two histograms. The feature is that the histograms are transformed into circles. The significant limitation is that it may introduce the overflow/underflow phenomenon such as salt-and-pepper noise to reduce image quality. Aiming at this problem, Zou [12] and Ni [13] proposed different robust reversible watermarking measures respectively. Zou's method is designed for JPEG2000 compression image by

X. Sun et al. (Eds.): ICCCS 2017, Part I, LNCS 10602, pp. 39–48, 2017.
https://doi.org/10.1007/978-3-319-68505-2_4

changing the mean of the compression coefficients to embed watermarking information. Ni's method does not limit the image storage categories, as well as embeds information by the way of dividing images into blocks. However, the overflow/underflow problem is not fully resolved. Then An and Gao [14] provided a robust reversible framework based on clustering and wavelet transformation. The results show that the performance of this method is better than before. This method can not overcome shortcomings arising from side information, which needs another channel to be shared between sender and receiver. A framework for distortion-free robust image authentication was investigated by Coltuc [15] in 2007. This general framework embeds robust data and fragile ones in two stages, which provides inspiration to our work. Liu [16] adopted a intra-prediction model to provide a algorithm to embed data into integer DCT coefficients. This one is based on H.264 standard, but it achieves low robustness and still generates a large side information.

Although the most existing methods of robust reversible watermarking have made certain progress, but the indicators of robustness, data capacity and image quality are not very excellent. Beyond that, there are certain limitations of solving side information. This paper provides a new watermarking algorithm based on integer wavelet transform (IWT) and spatial domain histogram. There are relative small amounts of side information generated after embedding the robust information into the IWT coefficients. It just needs minor alterations in the spatial domain of the image, so the image quality is much better.

This article contains the following parts: The second chapter describes the related work of this algorithm. In third chapter, data embedding and extracting algorithms are addressed in detail. The experimental results are given in the fourth chapter, and the concluding remarks are employed to close this paper finally.

2   Related Work

2.1   5-3 Integer Wavelet Transform

Be different from conventional wavelet transform, IWT provides integer to integer transformation process for images. That is, images can be in the form of integers both in spatial domain and frequency domain. Besides, it provides the possibility to reduce the capacity of side information that used for the inverse process.

This paper adopts 5-3 IWT to embed watermarks. To begin with, the original carrier image is divided into non-overlapping blocks, each block is denoted by a matrix B sized $m \times n$. Then, each block B is transformed to frequency domain, as well as generates a new matrix C. This positive row-based integer wavelet transform formulas are given by (1) and (2):

$$C(i + m/2, j) = B(2i + 1, j) - \left[(B(2i, j) + B(2i + 2, j))/2 \right]. \tag{1}$$

$$C(i, j) = B(2i, j) - \left[(C(i + m/2, j) + C(i + m/2 + 1, j) + 2)/4 \right]. \tag{2}$$

The inverse of the above transform obeys Eqs. (3) and (4):

$$B(2i,j) = C(i,j) + \left[(C(i + m/2, j) + C(i + m/2 + 1, j) + 2)/4 \right]. \tag{3}$$

$$C(i,j) = B(2i,j) - \left[(C(i + m/2, j) + C(i + m/2 + 1, j) + 2)/4 \right]. \tag{4}$$

The column-based integer wavelet formulas are the same as the row-based ones which just exchange the order of the coordinates.

According to the Eqs. (1) to (4), the original block B and transformed C can be converted to each other losslessly. When we alter some coefficients of C, the alteration is recorded and the records are always called side information. C be recovered to be the original B according to these records. The alteration is used to embed robust watermarks, and the side information is embedded into each block as fragile watermarks. The embedding principle will be introduced in detail in Sects. 2.2 and 2.3 respectively.

It can be seen, the less modification to the frequency coefficients, the lower needed capacity to store side information, and the less loss of image quality.

2.2 Robust Watermarking

The robustness of a watermarking scheme is always reflected by a feature of images. In the frequency domain, the low frequency coefficients contain the most important information with high robustness, however, the visual quality is diminished rapidly after minor changes. High frequency ones are the opposite.

By 5-3 integer wavelet transform in this paper, we choose the middle-low frequency coefficients to hide robust information. A image block sized 8 × 8 which is transformed to frequency domain is shown in Fig. 1. Each image block is gone through three-step row-column 5-3 IWT. It shows that f LH2 and HL2 are related areas in the frequency block. There are two initial-related coefficients such as the red ones in Fig. 1 which the coordinates are (3, 1) and (1, 3). One bit of information can be embedded into the difference of these two coefficients. For example, if the difference is positive, one bit robust data of '1' is embed and '0' is hided otherwise. The two coefficients are

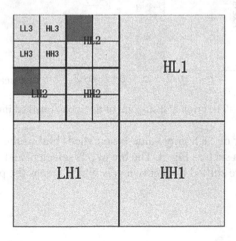

Fig. 1. The IWT coefficients of each block sized 8 × 8. (Color figure online)

swapped if the positive and negative do not agree with the bit to be encoded. Sometimes, the values of two coefficients are very close in the initial situation. The positive and negative may change after some image operations. To enhance the robustness, this algorithm adds an additional value to expand the difference. Of course, it also can choose other two related coefficients to operate this embedding process.

As it has met the robustness in the first step, the coordinates of above two coefficients and the swapping action of each block will become side information which is much less.

2.3   Fragile Watermarking

Theoretically, the second step of fragile watermarking should be used to ensure the reversibility of the watermarks and images. That is to say, it can not only extract information exactly but also reconstruct the original image perfectly when the marked images do not suffer any image operation after embedding process. Besides, the alteration caused by fragile watermarking embedding should not affect the robustness severely. Hence, the operation in the image spatial domain is selected, because the slight change of pixels value affect the visuality of images slightly.

The side information is compressed losslessly and encoded to be a binary sequence. Then the marked image which has been embedded robust watermarks in the Sect. 2.2 is mapped into its corresponding histogram such as Fig. 2. To provide enough embedding capacity for side information, it first finds some grayvalues that have much more numbers of pixels in the histogram. In Fig. 2, the value of p is a point that meet the above requirement.

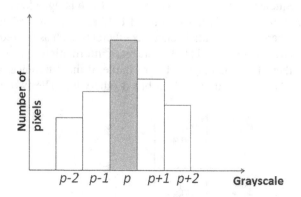

Fig. 2. The original histogram of the robust-marked image.

The pixels number of each gray value is so called 'bin' of the histogram. The bins are used to embed data such as Fig. 3. The bin of p is selected, and the other bins whose values larger than p are shifted by β gray levels which means the pixel values add β.

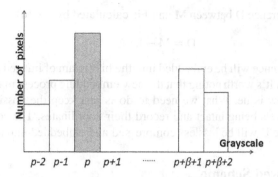

Fig. 3. Shifting of a part bins in the histogram.

Finally, we extent the bin of p to embed side information. That is, if one bit information is '1', we change one pixel from p to p + 1. As well as, if one bit information is '0',we keep the value of p being intact. This process is shown in Fig. 4. As it is shown that capacity is equal to the number of pixels in the point p. If one bin does not meet the needed capacity, we can add more bins by the same way.

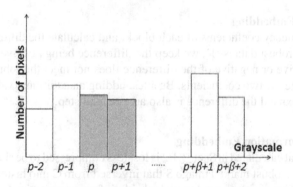

Fig. 4. Embedding by the way of extending the bin of p.

2.4 Overflow/Underflow Problem

The grayscale of gray images is 0 to 255. After embedding the robust watermarks and fragile watermarks into the image, the gray value of some pixels may be larger than 255 or less than 0, hence it may introduce overflow/underflow problem. To solve this issue, the truncation and image difference are employed. The robust-reversible marked matrix is denoted by M. Firstly, M is truncated to gray image I as Eq. (5):

$$I(i, j) = \begin{cases} 0, & \text{if } M(i,j) < 0 \\ M(i,j), & \text{if } 0 \le M(i,j) \le 255. \\ 255, & \text{if } M(i,j) > 255 \end{cases} \tag{5}$$

Then, the difference D between M and I is calculated by Eq. (6):

$$D = M - I. \tag{6}$$

Then the difference will be embedded into the histogram of image I as fragile watermarks in Sect. 2.3. It's worth noting that the new embedding process may introduce new overflow/underflow issue. What we need to do is just keep the possible overflowed/underflowered pixels being intact and record their coordinates. The coordinates along with the difference D will be lossless compressed and embedded into image I.

3 The Proposed Scheme

3.1 The Process of Embedding

3.1.1 Image Dividing and IWT
The original image is first divided into several blocks, each block sized m × n. In the meantime, each block B is transformed into frequency domain C by 5-3 integer wavelet transform.

3.1.2 Robust Embedding
Choose two frequency coefficients of each block, and calculate the difference of them. If the embedded robust data is '1', we keep the difference being positive and '0' otherwise. If the positive or negative of the difference does not meet the robust data, it just needs to exchange the two coefficients. Besides, adding an additional value into one of the two ones to expand the difference is also an essential step.

3.1.3 Side Information Embedding
The difference that calculated in Sect. 3.1.2 is lossless compressed to be side information. Then, we map the robust marked image S that inversed from C into histogram. A fewer high bins of the histogram are used to embed side information just as Figs. 2 to 4. The new generated robust-reversible marked Matrix is represented by M.

3.1.4 Solving Overflow/Underflow Problem
Matrix M is truncated into gray image Matrix I. We record the difference between M and I as well as the possible overflow/underflow coordinates. Finally, the overflow/underflow information is hided into image I by the way of fragile watermarking.

3.2 The Process of Extracting

If the carrier image does not have any attacks, it performs step Sect. 3.2.1. If not, perform step Sect. 3.2.2 to extract robust watermarks.

3.2.1 Extracting the Side Information

According to Sect. 3.1.4, the overflow/underflow information is extracted from the histogram of carrier image I. If the gray value of pixels is in the selected bins, extract data '0'. Otherwise, if the value is in the next bins of the selected ones, extract data '1'.Then, we recover I into M.

The side information is then extracted from the histogram of M just like Sect. 4.1 by the order from Figs. 4 to 2.The robust marked image S is also restored at the same time.

3.2.2 Extracting the Robust Watermarks

It divides marked image S into several blocks, each block sized m × n. In the meantime, each block B1 is transformed into frequency domain C by 5-3 integer wavelet transform.

According to the extracted side information, we recover the frequency domain block C to the original ones and extract the robust watermarks by the difference of two selected coefficients. The original image is recovered according to Eqs. (4) to (1). If the image is compressed, extract the robust watermarks according to the coefficient-difference.

4 Experimental Results

We test the performance of this scheme by using the gray image Lena sized 512 × 512. The divided size of each block is 8 × 8, so the capacity of robust embedded watermarks is 4096 bits. Test projects include robustness of the digital watermarks, invisibility and comparison with other algorithms.

4.1 Watermarking Robustness

The robust watermarks will be extracted at the receiver if the image is compressed. The extracted robust data has a litter error rate because of the embedded operation and image compression. Robustness is not the same if choose different coordinates of two frequency coefficients. Figure 5 show the precision of watermarks by different coordinates which the couples are (1, 2)-(2, 1), (1, 3)-(3, 1) and (3, 4)-(4, 3). It can be seen that the precision is more than 95% for quality factors down to 60 in the couples of (1, 2)-(2, 1) and (1, 3)-(3, 1). That is because their coordinates are close to low frequency bands, beyond that, there is higher correlation of two selected coefficients in initial state. However, the (3, 4)-(4, 3) couple has lower correlation and farther position away from low frequency domain.

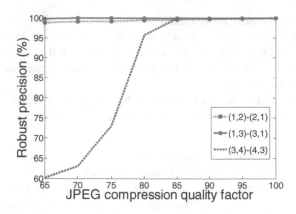

Fig. 5. Precision of robust watermarks with different JPEG compression quality factor.

4.2 Image Visibility

To a certain extent, PSNR reflects the distortion degree of the image. The larger PSNR, the less loss of images' energy, the lower distortion. The PSNR values of the image after embedding data in above three couples in Sect. 4.1 are shown on Table 1.

Table 1. PSNR of carrier image Lena after embedding in different positions.

Couples' coordinates	(1, 2)-(2, 1)	(1, 3)-(3, 1)	(3, 4)-(4, 3)
PSNR (dB)	27.26	31.59	31.62

If we connect the visibility with the robustness, the couple (1, 3)-(3, 1) is the best choice of these three ones.

4.3 Comparative Experiment

In the present technique in the field of robust watermarking, Ni et al.'s [13] method is a classic and excellent scheme on the basis of a histogram statistics that studied by a number of authors. Coltuc's [15] framework provided a new perspective for latecomers. Both of the two algorithms have advantages and shortcomings. Table 2 shows comparison between our method, Ni's and Coltuc's ones with carrier image 'Lena'. The capacity of robust watermarks in the three schemes are all 4096 bits respectively.

Table 2. Comparison wtih Ni's [13] and Coltuc's [15] methods.

	Proposed			Ni et al.'s method [13]			Coltuc's method [15]		
JPEG Factor	100	75	70	100	75	70	100	75	70
Lena	100%	99.9%	99.9%	100%	96.5%	58.5%	99.8%	99.6%	99.6%

From the third row of Table 2 we can find that the precision of extracted robust watermarks of our method is comprehensive optimal under different JPEG compression quality factor. Ni et al.'s error rate increases rapidly with lower quality factor, it is because that it is executed in the spatial domain and robustness is unstable. Coltuc's scheme and our method are operated in frequency domain. But the PSNR of Coltuc's is 24.67 dB while the proposed one is 31 dB.The better PSNR of our project is owing to the integer transformation: 5-3 IWT, which needs less side information that using for original imaging restoration.

5 Conclusions

In this paper, we proposed a novel robust reversible watermarking algorithm. It can extract robust data in the loss environment while extract information and reconstruct the original image correctly in the lossless environment. By IWT, we embedded robust watermarks into the mid-low coefficients and achieve high performance. Besides, the integer transformation provides lower side information so that it not only realizes the reversibility but also owns better image quality.

The future work is that enhance the visibility of images by trying more reversible watermarking algorithm.

Acknowledgements. This work is supported by nsfc under Grant No.61502241, Natural Science Foundation of the Universities in Jiangsu Province under Grant No.14KJB520024, Natural Science Foundation of Jiangsu Province of China under Grant No.BK20160971, BK20141006 and the Startup Foundation for Introducing Talent of NUIST under Grant No. 2241101301061.

References

1. Wang, X., Li, X., Yang, B., et al.: Efficient eneralized integer transform for reversible watermarking. IEEE Signal Process. Lett. **17**(6), 567–570 (2010)
2. Li, X., Yang, B., Zeng, T.: Efficient reversible watermarking based on adaptive prediction-error expansion and pixel selection. IEEE Trans. Image Process. **20**(12), 3524–3533 (2011). A Publication of the IEEE Signal Processing
3. Xiong, L., Xu, Z., Xu, Y.: A secure re-encryption scheme for data services in a cloud computing environment. Concurrency Comput. Pract. Experience **27**(17), 4573–4585 (2015)
4. Chen, X., Sun, X., Sunr, H.: Reversible watermarking method based on asymmetric-histogram shifting of prediction errors. J. Syst. Softw. **86**(10), 2620–2626 (2013)
5. Li, X., Wang, W., Gui, X., et al.: A Novel Reversible Data Hiding Scheme Based on Two-Dimensional Difference-Histogram Modification. IEEE Trans. Inf. Forensics Secur. **8**(7), 1091–1100 (2013)
6. Ou, B., Li, X., Zhao, Y., et al.: Pairwise prediction-error expansion for efficient reversible data hiding. J. IEEE Trans. Image Proces. **22**(12), 5010–5021 (2013). A Publication of the IEEE Signal Processing Society
7. Xia, Z., Lv, R., Zhu, Y., et al.: Fingerprint liveness detection using gradient-based texture features. Signal Image Video Process. pp. 1–8 (2016)
8. Ou, B., Li, X., Zhao, Y., et al.: Reversible data hiding based on PDE predictor. J. Syst. Softw. **86**(10), 2700–2709 (2013)

9. Gui, X., Li, X., Yang, B.: A high capacity reversible data hiding scheme based on generalized prediction-error expansion and adaptive embedding. J. Signal Process. **98**(5), 370–380 (2014)
10. Li, J., Li, X., Yang, B.: Reversible data hiding scheme for color image based on prediction-error expansion and cross-channel correlation. Signal Process. **93**(9), 2748–2758 (2013). M. Elsevier North-Holland. Inc.
11. De, V., Delaigle, J., Macq, B.: Circular interpretation of bijective transformations in lossless watermarking for media asset management. IEEE Trans. Multimedia **5**(1), 97–105 (2003)
12. Zou, D., Shi, Y., Ni, Z.: A semi-fragile lossless digital watermarking scheme based on integer wavelet transform. In: IEEE Workshop on Multimedia Signal Processing, pp. 195–198 (2004)
13. Ni, Z., Shi, Y., Ansari, N., et al.: Robust lossless image data hiding designed for semi-fragile image authentication. IEEE Trans. Circuits Syst. Video Technol. **8**(4), 497–509 (2008)
14. An, L., Gao, X., Li, X., et al.: Robust reversible watermarking via clustering and enhanced pixel-wise masking. IEEE Trans. Image Process. **21**(8), 3598–3611 (2012). A Publication of the IEEE Signal Processing Society
15. Coltuc, D.: Towards distortion-free robust image authentication. J. Phys: Conf. Ser. **77**(1), 012005 (2007)
16. Liu, Y., Ju, L., Hu, M., et al.: A robust reversible data hiding scheme for H.264 without distortion drift. Neurocomputing **151**(1), 1053–1062 (2015)

An Improved Reversible Information Hiding Scheme Based on AMBTC Compressed Images

Yi Puyang[1], Zhaoxia Yin[1,2(✉)], Guorui Feng[2], and Andrew K. Abel[3]

[1] Key Laboratory of Intelligent Computing and Signal Processing,
Ministry of Education, Anhui University, Hefei 230601,
People's Republic of China
yinzhaoxia@ahu.edu.cn

[2] School of Communication and Information Engineering, Shanghai University,
Shanghai 200072, People's Republic of China
grfeng@shu.edu.cn

[3] Department of Computing Science and Software Engineering,
Xi'an Jiaotong-Liverpool University, Suzhou, China
andrew.abel@xjtlu.edu.cn

Abstract. This paper proposes an efficient reversible information hiding method based on AMBTC compressed images. At present, most digital images are stored and transmitted in compressed form, so research and development of such a scheme is necessary. Hong et al. proposed a reversible information hiding based approach based on AMBTC compression of images to provide considerable embedding capacity and effectively reduce the bit-rate. However, it did not carry out a detailed categorization of the error value or adopt the most suitable method for category information encoding, where error value is the difference of the original quantization value and the prediction quantization value. So there's possibility to reduce the bit-rate. In this paper, we propose an Improved Centralized Error Division (ICED) technique to conduct a more detailed categorization of the error value. In addition, we also adopt an optimal Huffman code to encode category information, so as to further reduce the bit-rate. Our experimental results show that our proposed approach has an equal embedding capacity as Hong et al.'s method and is higher than other relevant work. In addition, the proposed scheme has a lower bit-rate than Hong et al.'s method.

Keywords: Reversible information hiding · AMBTC · Prediction · Low bit-rate · Huffman coding

1 Introduction

Information hiding has been the subject of extensive attention in recent years for the purpose of hiding data in cover media and transmitting it secretly to protect private data. Cover media consists of text, images, videos, audios or any other digital signals, but in this paper, we focus on information hiding technology

© Springer International Publishing AG 2017
X. Sun et al. (Eds.): ICCCS 2017, Part I, LNCS 10602, pp. 49–60, 2017.
https://doi.org/10.1007/978-3-319-68505-2_5

applied to images, with the primary challenge being to strengthen data embedding capacity while maintaining a high quality image. Combining cryptography [1,2], image processing [3,4], network technology [5,6] and machine learning [7,8], information hiding can theoretically be widely applied in many fields. In particular, reversible information hiding is an important technology, which is able to completely recover an original image after extracting encrypted data from it [9,10]. This method is mainly applied in scenarios which impose strict requirements, for example, military reconnaissance and medical imaging. Consequently, in recent years, reversible information hiding technology has become a hot topic.

Most reversible data hiding methods for images are carried out in spatial domain and compressed domain. In 2003, Barton [11] first proposed a reversible information hiding scheme in the spatial-domain. However, digital images on the internet are generally being stored in a compressed format to decrease time and data cost during transmission. Common compression methods include JPEG, JPEG2000, VQ (vector quantization) and BTC (block truncation coding). Therefore, the development of reversible information hiding in compressed images is of importance.

BTC is a block-based image compression technology, similar to JPEG and VQ, but with a lower computational cost, so it can be applied widely. 2010, Chen et al. [13] proposed a lossless information hiding scheme based on Absolute Moment BTC (AMBTC) compression. In 2013, Sun et al. [14] developed another reversible information hiding scheme base on AMBTC that effectively improved the embedding capacity. This was further optimized by Hong et al. [12] to increase the embedding capacity and lower the bit-rate by using a Median Edge Detection (MED) predictor and the Alternative Prediction (AP) technique to precisely predict the quantization value.

The rest of this paper is organized as follows. In Sect. 2, we briefly introduce the original AMBTC compression technique and Hong et al.'s method [12]. In Sect. 3, a detailed description of the proposed method is given and its operation is also being discussed. Experimental results and a comparison with other related work are given in Sect. 4. Finally, we conclude the paper in Sect. 5.

2 Related Work

2.1 Absolute Moment Block Truncation Coding (AMBTC)

AMBTC is a block-based spatial domain lossy compression technique. Before coding, the original image I must firstly be divided into non-overlapping blocks $\{X_i\}_{i=1}^{N}$ of size $v \times v$ pixels, where N is the total number of blocks. The average value for each block can be obtained by performing Eq. (1), denoted as $aver_i$, where i indicates the block number, j is the j-th pixel in the i-th block. According to the average values, a bitmap $B_i = \{\lambda_{i,j}\}_{j=1}^{v \times v}$ is then constructed to record the comparison result of $x_{i,j}$ and $aver_i$ using Eq. (2). Assume n_i is the number of 1's in the bitmap, the two quantization values q_i^{H} and q_i^{L} can be calculated with Eqs. (3) and (4), where q_i^{H} and q_i^{L} denote the high mean and the low mean of block X_i.

$$aver_i = \frac{1}{v \times v} \sum_{j=1}^{v \times v} x_{i,j} \tag{1}$$

$$\lambda_{i,j} = \begin{cases} 1, & x_{i,j} \geq aver_i, \\ 0, & x_{i,j} < aver_i. \end{cases} \tag{2}$$

$$q_i^H = \frac{1}{n_i} \sum_{x_{i,j} \geq aver_i} x_{i,j} \tag{3}$$

$$q_i^L = \frac{1}{v \times v - n_i} \sum_{x_{i,j} < aver_i} x_{i,j} \tag{4}$$

By repeating the above steps, the AMBTC-compressed code for image I can be obtained, depicted as $\{q_i^H, q_i^L, B_i\}_{i=1}^N$. After receiving the triples $\{q_i^H, q_i^L, B_i\}_{i=1}^N$, image receivers can decode the pixels with q_i^H and q_i^L if the bits in the bitmap are 1 or 0, respectively.

2.2 Hong et al.'s Method

In 2016, Hong et al. [12] proposed a reversible information hiding scheme based on the significant higher embedding capacity and lower bit-rate of AMBTC compressed images. This approach adopts a Median Edge Detection (MED) predictor based approach that calculates a prediction value for a pixel, based on adjacent pixels, and also uses the Alternative Prediction (AP) technique to shrink the prediction value range to enhance prediction precision. For embedding data, Hong et al. divide the AMBTC quantization value into two parts: reference quantization value and predicable quantization value. They choose the first row and column in the quantization table to be the reference quantization value without embedding any data, which can be used for predicable quantization value recovery when decoding.

Assume $\{q_i^H, q_i^L, B_i\}_{i=1}^N$ is the AMBTC compressed code for conducting data embed, we will choose a pair of quantization values q_i^H and q_i^L to encode. Firstly, in this approach, q_i is defined as a high or low mean value, and $q_{i,1}$, $q_{i,2}$, and $q_{i,3}$ are the three quantization values adjacent to q_i as shown in Fig. 1. The prediction value p_i of q_i is then defined by Eq. (5). Hong et al. call this prediction method an MED predictor.

$q_{i,3}$	$q_{i,2}$	
$q_{i,1}$	q_i	

Fig. 1. The neighbors of q_i

$$p_i = \begin{cases} max(q_{i,1}, q_{i,2}), & q_{i,3} \leq min(q_{i,1}, q_{i,2}), \\ min(q_{i,1}, q_{i,2}), & q_{i,3} \geq max(q_{i,1}, q_{i,2}), \\ q_{i,1} + q_{i,2} - q_{i,3}, & otherwise. \end{cases} \tag{5}$$

By conducting the above prediction process, we can separately get the corresponding prediction quantization values p_i^H and p_i^L of the high and low mean value. Next, we will do a further dispose on the obtained prediction quantization value, we will consider whether high or low mean value prediction should adopt this technology by secret key k_x. If $k_x = 1$, said the high mean value q_i^H is selected, then the final prediction quantization value is calculated by Eq. (6), otherwise, if $k_x = 0$, said the low mean value q_i^L is selected, the final prediction quantization value is calculated by Eq. (7). Hong et al. refer to this handling method as the AP technique.

$$\begin{cases} \hat{p}_i^H = max(q_i^L, p_i^H), \\ \hat{p}_i^L = p_i^L. \end{cases} \tag{6}$$

$$\begin{cases} \hat{p}_i^H = p_i^H, \\ \hat{p}_i^L = min(q_i^H, p_i^L). \end{cases} \tag{7}$$

After calculating the final prediction quantization value, the prediction error value e_i^H and e_i^L of the quantization value are calculated by using Eq. (8). A parameter m is then introduced to classify the obtained prediction error value as being one of 4 categories, and encode each prediction error value as appropriate. When $e_i = 0$, the code is empty; when $-(2^m - 1) \leq e_i < 0$ or $0 < e_i \leq 2^m - 1$, use m bits for coding; when $|e_i| > 2^m - 1$, replace e_i by the 8-bit binary code of q_i. A binary fixed length code $d_{i,1}d_{i,2}$ is used to distinguish between the four parts, as shown in Eq. (9).

$$\begin{cases} e_i^H = q_i^H - \hat{p}_i^H, \\ e_i^L = q_i^L - \hat{p}_i^L. \end{cases} \tag{8}$$

$$(e_i)_2 = \begin{cases} empty, & e_i = 0, & d_{i,1}d_{i,2} = 00_2, \\ (|e_i|, m)_2, & -(2^m - 1) \leq e_i < 0, & d_{i,1}d_{i,2} = 01_2, \\ (e_i, m)_2, & 0 < e_i \leq 2^m - 1, & d_{i,1}d_{i,2} = 11_2, \\ (q_i, 8)_2, & |e_i| > 2^m - 1, & d_{i,1}d_{i,2} = 10_2. \end{cases} \tag{9}$$

In order to embed the secret message S into an AMBTC compressed image, random bits $r_{i,1}r_{i,2}r_{i,3}r_{i,4}$ are created using a secret key k_y. Embedded bits $s_{i,1}s_{i,2}s_{i,3}s_{i,4}$ that is waiting for embedding from S, the xor-ed secret bits $s'_{i,1}s'_{i,2}s'_{i,3}s'_{i,4}$ can be obtained by conducting the bitwise xor operation on them. The final codes for q_i^H are obtained by connecting the xor-ed secret bits $s'_{i,1}s'_{i,2}$, division information $d_{i,1}^H d_{i,2}^H$, and the prediction error $(e_i^H)_2$, depicted as $C_i^H = s'_{i,1}s'_{i,2}||d_{i,1}^H d_{i,2}^H||(e_i^H)_2$, where $||$ is the concatenation operator. In the same way, the codes $C_i^L = s'_{i,3}s'_{i,4}||d_{i,1}^L d_{i,2}^L||(e_i^L)_2$ for can be obtained.

In order to extract secret data $s_{i,1}s_{i,2}s_{i,3}s_{i,4}$ and recover q_i^H and q_i^L, we read $s'_{i,1}s'_{i,2}$ and $s'_{i,3}s'_{i,4}$ from C_i^H and C_i^L. Secret data is then extracted by conducting the bitwise xor operation on it with random bits $r_{i,1}r_{i,2}r_{i,3}r_{i,4}$. Secondly, the MED predictor and AP technique are used to return the final prediction quantization value $\hat{p}_i^H$ and $\hat{p}_i^L$, continue to read category information $d_{i,1}^H d_{i,2}^H$ and $d_{i,3}^H d_{i,4}^H$ from C_i^H and C_i^L respectively. What is left is the error value $(e_i^H)_2$ and $(e_i^L)_2$. This can be converted to base-10 based on the category information, as shown in Eq. (9). Ultimately, Hong et al. can recover the quantization value q_i^H and q_i^L using Eq. (10).

$$
q_i = \begin{cases}
\hat{p}_i, & d_{i,1}d_{i,2} = 00_2, \\
\hat{p}_i - |e_i|, & d_{i,1}d_{i,2} = 01_2, \\
\hat{p}_i + |e_i|, & d_{i,1}d_{i,2} = 11_2, \\
e_i & d_{i,1}d_{i,2} = 10_2.
\end{cases}
\tag{10}
$$

3   Proposed Method

3.1   Improved Centralized Error Division (ICED) Technique

From Sect. 2.2, it can be seen that Hong et al. regard the prediction error $e_i = 0$ as an individual category without any encoding. They also introduce a parameter m, which classifies the non-zero prediction error values into 4 categories. m-bit binary coding is used for representing the two categories that are closest to $e_i = 0$. The remaining two categories are represented by 8-bit binary coding. The 5 different categories are then distinguished between with 2-bit binary coding $\{d_{i,1}d_{i,2}, d \in (0,1)\}$ for differentiating between plus and minus when recovering the prediction error value. There is scope for improving this method though. For instance, if we assume $m = 4$, then 4-bit binary coding could express the prediction error value e_i from $-(2^4-1)$ to 2^4-1. This includes the prediction error value within the range $e_i \in \{-(2^2-1), 2^2-1\}$, which could be signified by 2-bit binary coding rather than 4-bit. Hence unnecessary code could be avoided by using less bits. Similarly, for prediction error values in the ranges $e_i \in \{-(2^6-1), -(2^4-1)\}$ and $e_i \in \{2^4-1, 2^6-1\}$, we should use 6-bit binary coding rather than 8-bit, to express the prediction error value. Therefore in this research, we propose a carry out a more precise classification of the prediction error value e_i, and divide it into one of eight categories $\{area_1, area_2, area_3, area_4, area_5, area_6, area_7, area_8, \}$. The specific classification is given in Eq. (11). According to this partition method, every error value e_i could be expressed by x-bit binary coding, and x may be 0, 2, 4, 6 and 8.

$$(e_i)_2 = \begin{cases} empty, & e_i = 0, & area_1, \\ (|e_i|, 2)_2, & -(2^2 - 1) \le e_i < 0, & area_2, \\ (e_i, 2)_2, & 0 < e_i \le 2^2 - 1, & area_3, \\ (|e_i|, 4)_2, & -(2^4 - 1) \le e_i < -(2^2 - 1), & area_4, \\ (e_i, 4)_2, & 2^2 - 1 < e_i \le 2^4 - 1, & area_5, \\ (|e_i|, 6)_2, & -(2^6 - 1) \le e_i < -(2^4 - 1), & area_6, \\ (e_i, 6)_2, & 2^4 - 1 < e_i \le 2^6 - 1, & area_7, \\ (q_i, 8)_2, & |e_i| > 2^6 - 1, & area_8. \end{cases} \quad (11)$$

3.2   Binary Huffman Coding (BHC)

We replace the original fixed-length encoding with Binary Huffman coding (BHC) for error value category information coding. Since BHC is the optimal code for this work, it will improve coding efficiency.

As mentioned previously, the prediction error value is divided into 8 categories. But when decoding the prediction error value, it is not possible to distinguish which category the current prediction error value belongs to. We therefore need to use an adapted BHC method to identify the 8 areas using binary codes. Firstly we count the appearance probability of prediction error value e_i in the 8 categories $\{p_1, p_2, p_3, p_4, p_5, p_6, p_7, p_8\}$, and then begin encoding on the basis of BHC to get the Huffman code corresponding to the 8 categories: $\{area_1, area_2, area_3, area_4, area_5, area_6, area_7, area_8\}$. These categories cover the ranges shown in Fig. 2.

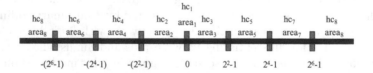

Fig. 2. Assignment of division information for ICED

During decoding, we confirm which category the prediction error belongs to according to the Huffman coding. After that we recover the quantization value q_i based on Eq. (12), where $\hat{p}_i$ is the final prediction quantization value of q_i, the length of $[d_{i,1} d_{i,2} \dots d_{i,x}]$ is not unknown.

$$q_i = \begin{cases} \hat{p}_i, & [d_{i,1} d_{i,2} \dots d_{i,x}] = hc_1, \\ \hat{p}_i - |e_i|, & [d_{i,1} d_{i,2} \dots d_{i,x}] = hc_2, \\ \hat{p}_i + |e_i|, & [d_{i,1} d_{i,2} \dots d_{i,x}] = hc_3, \\ \hat{p}_i - |e_i|, & [d_{i,1} d_{i,2} \dots d_{i,x}] = hc_4, \\ \hat{p}_i + |e_i|, & [d_{i,1} d_{i,2} \dots d_{i,x}] = hc_5, \\ \hat{p}_i - |e_i|, & [d_{i,1} d_{i,2} \dots d_{i,x}] = hc_6, \\ \hat{p}_i + |e_i|, & [d_{i,1} d_{i,2} \dots d_{i,x}] = hc_7, \\ e_i, & [d_{i,1} d_{i,2} \dots d_{i,x}] = hc_8. \end{cases} \quad (12)$$

3.3   Embedding Process

In order to embed secret message S into a AMBTC compressed image I, assume that compression triples $\{q_i^H, q_i^L, B_i\}_{i=1}^{Nr \times Nc}$ of image I have already been obtained, where Nr and Nc respectively stand for the block rows and columns. The size of each block is $v \times v$. We build the high mean value table $\{q_i^H\}_{i=1}^{Nr \times Nc}$ and low mean value table $\{q_i^L\}_{i=1}^{Nr \times Nc}$ individually. The quantization value of the first row and first column will not be used for embedding, and the 8-bit binary code will be used to represent quantization value for reference. All of the remaining quantization value is predictable and can be embedded into a 2-bit secret message. The final code of an AMBTC compressed image embedded with a secret message is expressed by C. The detailed embedding process is as follows:

Input: AMBTC triples $\{q_i^H, q_i^L, B_i\}_{i=1}^{Nr \times Nc}$, secret data S, keys k_1, k_2.

Output: The AMBTC marked codes C.

Step 1: Scan high mean value table $\{q_i^H\}_{i=1}^{Nr \times Nc}$ and low mean value table $\{q_i^L\}_{i=1}^{Nr \times Nc}$ from top to bottom and left to right. Encode the reference quantization value in the first row and column of every table by 8-bit binary coding. Mark R as the final coding result of the reference quantization value.

Step 2: Scan predictable quantization value, following the MED prediction method can be used to calculate q_i^H and q_i^L. Secret key k_1 is used to choose to apply the AP technique to either q_i^H or q_i^L, and $\hat{p}_i^H$ and $\hat{p}_i^L$ will express the final prediction result, as discussed in Sect. 2.2.

Step 3: Random bits $r_{i,1}, r_{i,2}, r_{i,3}, r_{i,4}$ are calculated using secret key k_2 and 4 bits s_1, s_2, s_3, s_4 from secret message S. The bitwise xor operation is then carried out on $r_{i,1}, r_{i,2}, r_{i,3}, r_{i,4}$ and s_1, s_2, s_3, s_4 to create s_1', s_2', s_3', s_4'.

Step 4: Calculate the prediction error $e_i^H = q_i^H - \hat{p}_i^H$ and $e_i^L = q_i^L - \hat{p}_i^L$, and classify the prediction error into 8 categories, as discussed previously. This results in $(e_i^H)_2$ and (e_i^L), which are found by representing the prediction error with x-bit binary coding.

Step 5: Count the error value probability of every category $\{p_1, p_2, p_3, p_4, p_5, p_6, p_7, p_8\}$, then code and mark every area by Huffman coding to get the remarked Huffman code of each area $\{hc_1, hc_2, hc_3, hc_4, hc_5, hc_6, hc_7, hc_8\}$. According to the category $area_x$ and $area_y$ that error values (e_i^H) and e_i^L belong to, we can respectively obtain the corresponding Huffman codes hc_x and hc_y.

Step 6: Combine the xor-ed secret message s_1', s_2' with the Huffman coding message hc_x and the prediction error code $(e_i^H)_2$ to obtain the final coding structure $C_i^H = s_1', s_2'||hc_x||(e_i^H)_2$ of the quantization value q_i^H. Use a similar process to get the final coding structure $C_i^L = s_3', s_4'||hc_y||(e_i^L)_2$ of quantization value q_i^L.

Step 7: Repeat steps 2–6 above until all of the predictable quantization value is embedded into the secret message. Connect R, bitmap code $\{B_i\}_{i=1}^{Nr \times Nc}$ and $\{C_i^H\}_{i=1}^{Nr \times Nc}, \{C_i^L\}_{i=1}^{Nr \times Nc}$, to produce the final AMBCT marked codes C.

In order to accurately extract the embedded secret message S and recover the original AMBTC compressed image, we need to know the parameters Nr, Nc, v for accurately recovering the reference quantization value R and the bitmap message $\{B_i\}_{i=1}^{Nr \times Nc}$. In addition, the secret keys k_1, k_2 and partition Huffman code message $\{hc_i\}_{i=1}^8$ are the key of acquiring secret data and recovering original image. The receiver therefore needs Nr, Nc, v and $k_1, k_2, \{hc_i\}_{i=1}^8$ when decoding and recovering the AMBTC compressed image.

3.4 Decoding and Extraction Process

After receiving the AMBTC marked codes C, the receiver can extract the embedded secret message S and successfully recover the AMBTC compression triple. This process is as follows:

Input: AMBTC marked codes C, keys $k_1, k_2, Nr, Nc, v, \{hc_i\}_{i=1}^8$.

Output: AMBTC triples $\{q_i^H, q_i^L, B_i\}_{i=1}^{Nr \times Nc}$ and secret data S.

Step 1: Read $2 \times (Nr + Nc - 1) \times 8$ bits from the C in-sequence to re-build the reference quantization value R, which will be used to create the first row and column of the quantization matrix. Next $Nr \times Nc \times v^2$ bits are read, bitmap message $\{B_i\}_{i=1}^{Nr \times Nc}$ can be rebuilt, then read the rest to get $\{C_i^H\}_{i=1}^{Nr \times Nc}$ and $\{C_i^L\}_{i=1}^{Nr \times Nc}$.

Step 2: Extract s_1', s_2' and s_3', s_4' from $\{C_i^H\}_{i=1}^{Nr \times Nc}$ and $\{C_i^L\}_{i=1}^{Nr \times Nc}$, create $r_{i,1}, r_{i,2}, r_{i,3}, r_{i,4}$ with secret key k_2. Conduct bitwise xor operation on s_1', s_2', s_3', s_4' and $r_{i,1}, r_{i,2}, r_{i,3}, r_{i,4}$ to get the embedded secret message s_1, s_2, s_3, s_4.

Step 3: Conduct prediction on quantization value q_i^H and q_i^L by using the MED predictor to find the prediction quantization values p_i^H and p_i^L. Decide whether q_i^H or q_i^L should adopt the AP technique during prediction, based on secret key k_1, to obtain prediction quantization value $\hat{p}_i^H$ and $\hat{p}_i^L$.

Step 4: The rest of $\{C_i^H\}_{i=1}^{Nr \times Nc}$ and $\{C_i^L\}_{i=1}^{Nr \times Nc}$ will read the bit message $[d_{i,1} d_{i,2} \ldots d_{i,x}]$ that has the same length as partition message code $\{hc_i\}_{i=1}^8$ to compare with the Huffman code. If equal, it belongs to the corresponding category. Hence we can acquire $area_x, area_y$, which prediction value $(e_i^H)_2$ and $(e_i^L)_2$ belongs to, that will be recovered next. As shown in Eq.(11), we can keep on reading x bits to get prediction values $(e_i^H)_2$ and $(e_i^L)_2$, and transfer binary values $(e_i^L)_2$ and $(e_i^L)_2$ into decimal integers $|e_i^H|$ and $|e_i^L|$.

Step 5: Recover quantization values q_i^H and q_i^L base on Eq. (12).

Step 6: Repeat steps 2–5 until all of the secret message are extracted. And all of the quantization value $\{q_i^H\}_{i=1}^{Nr \times Nc}$ and $\{q_i^L\}_{i=1}^{Nr \times Nc}$ should recover.

4   Experimental Results

We used six 8-bit grayscale images (512×512) during our experiments, Lena, Jet, Peppers, Baboon, Tiffany, and House. In the AMBTC compression process, every block is of dimension 4×4. We assess the performance of our proposed scheme with a number of experiments, and compare it with relevant existing research.

There are two types of performance indictors used. The first are embedding performance indicators, which includes the hiding capacity, bit-rate and embedding efficiency (EF). The hiding capacity is the amount of total embedded secret data in the AMBTC compressed image; the bit-rate is the number of bits when store each pixel, a low bit-rate image is capable of occupying less space in memory; the EF represents the code utilization rate. In our experiments, we aim for a high hiding capacity and EF and a low bit-rate. With regard to the image quality indicators, these experiments use the peak signal-to-noise ratio (PSNR) to describe AMBTC compressed image quality, with a larger PSNR indicating a higher quality image. For instance, given a $h \times w$ 8-bit grayscale image, the PSNR value is calculated as shown in Eq. (13). The bit-rate is calculated as shown in Eq. (14), and the EF is found by Eq. (15), all where $x_{i,j}$ and $x'_{i,j}$ are the original and marked grayscale pixel values located at (i,j) respectively, and L is the codestream length.

$$PSNR = 10 \cdot \log_{10} \frac{255^2 \times h \times w}{\sum_i^h \sum_j^w (x_{i,j} - x'_{i,j})^2} \tag{13}$$

$$bit\text{-}rate = \frac{L}{h \times w} \tag{14}$$

$$EF = \frac{Payload}{L} \tag{15}$$

4.1 Performance of Proposed Method

To show the embedding performance in our proposed scheme, we plot a bit-rate column diagram with the 6 test images embedded with the same bits of secret data (64516 bits) as shown in Fig. 3. A standard 4×4 AMBTC compressed image has a bit-rate of 2 bits per pixel (bpp) as given by the straight line in Fig. 3. Figure 3 shows clearly that the bit-rate of five of the test images (all except Baboon) are lower than 2 bpp, which means that after embedding 64515 bits of secret data, our proposed approach can still maintain a smaller bit-rate than an original AMBTC compressed image. The reason that Baboon's bit-rate is higher than 2 bpp is due to the inaccuracy of the prediction value and the

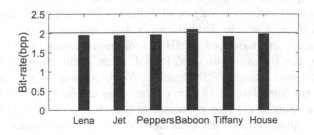

Fig. 3. Bit-rate values for six test images

Baboon image containing the richest image texture. The results show that the proposed scheme can not only embed secret data, but also maintain a lower bit-rate than the original AMBTC compressed image.

4.2   Comparison of the Proposed Method with Others

In this section, we first compare the bit-rate between our proposed scheme and Hong et al. [12] as shown in Fig. 4. Using the same secret data, we use test image Lena as an example. Figure 4(a) of Hong et al.'s method shows that when $m = 3$, Lena's bit-rate can reach the lowest value (1.98 bpp). However in our approach, there is no control parameter, resulting in a stable bit-rate. Lena's bit-rate is 1.95 bpp with our method, which is lower than Hong et al. The same results were found with the other test images, as shown in Fig. 4(b) to (f). This shows that when embedding the same amount of secret data, our proposed approach improves on work by Hong et al.

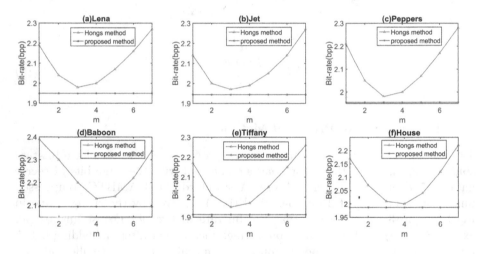

Fig. 4. The bit-rate comparison with Hong et al.'s scheme

We also compare our proposed approach with other research by with Chen et al. [13], Sun et al. [14] and Hong et al. [12]. We focus on the PSNR, Bit-rate, Payload and EF as shown in Table 1. Since both our proposed approach and the other methods are based on AMBTC-compressed images' reversible data hiding scheme, the recovered images' PSNR value is the same as the original AMBTC-compressed images' PSNR value. With respect to the payload, our method offers the joint largest capacity (the same as Hong et al.), higher than Chen et al. and Sun et al. The proposed approach can embed 2-bits of secret data into every quantization value. Table 1 also shows that compared to Hong et al. when embedding the same amount of secret data, the bit-rate of our scheme is lower but the EF is higher. In addition, the EF of the proposed scheme is about three times that of Chen et al. Compared to Sun et al. it is higher by approximately 1%, as also shown in Table 1. In summary, the results demonstrate that our scheme successfully improves embedding performance and reduces the bit-rate to an extent.

Table 1. Performance comparisons of the proposed method and other related works

Performance	Methods	Lena	Jet	Peppers	Baboon	Tiffany	House
PSNR(dB)	AMBTC	33.237	31.974	33.424	26.980	35.769	30.892
	Chen et al.	33.237	31.974	33.424	26.980	35.769	30.892
	Sun et al.	33.237	31.974	33.424	26.980	35.769	30.892
	Hong et al.	33.237	31.974	33.424	26.980	35.769	30.892
	Proposed	33.237	31.974	33.424	26.980	35.769	30.892
Bit-rate(bpp)	AMBTC	2.00	2.00	2.00	2.00	2.00	2.00
	Chen et al.	2.00	2.00	2.00	2.00	2.00	2.00
	Sun et al.	2.10	2.09	2.09	2.18	2.07	2.14
	Hong et al.	1.98	1.97	1.98	2.13	1.95	2.00
	Proposed	1.95	1.94	1.95	2.09	1.91	1.98
Payload(bits)	Chen et al.	16384	16384	16384	16384	16384	16384
	Sun et al.	64008	64008	64008	64008	64008	64008
	Hong et al.	64516	64516	64516	64516	64516	64516
	Proposed	64516	64516	64516	64516	64516	64516
EF	Chen et al.	0.042	0.042	0.042	0.042	0.042	0.042
	Sun et al.	0.116	0.117	0.117	0.112	0.118	0.114
	Hong et al.	0.124	0.125	0.124	0.116	0.126	0.123
	Proposed	0.126	0.127	0.126	0.118	0.129	0.124

5 Conclusions

This paper proposes a high embedding capacity and low bit-rate reversible information hiding scheme based on AMBTC compressed images. In Hong et al.'s scheme, the embedding capacity and bit-rate shows a good performance, but still has room for further improment. We improved on limitations with the work of Hong et al. by introducing two techniques, ICED and BHC. The proposed ICED technique divides the error value into more detailed categories, so the encoding length is reduced effectively. In addition, the BHC technique is capable to reduce the length of coding either. The experimental result shows that the performance of proposed scheme is better than Hong et al.'s approach and other relevant works with regard to bit-rate and embedding efficiency.

Acknowledgements. This research work is partly supported by National Natural Science Foundation of China (61502009, U1536109), China Postdoctoral Science Foundation (2016M591650), Anhui Provincial Natural Science Foundation (1508085SQF216)

and Key Program for Excellent Young Talents in Colleges and Universities of Anhui Province (gxyqZD2016011).

References

1. Yuan, C., Xia, Z., Sun, X.: Coverless image steganography based on SIFT and BOF. J. Internet Technol. **18**(2), 435–442 (2017)
2. Chen, X., Chen, S., Wu, Y.: Coverless information hiding method based on the Chinese character encoding. J. Internet Technol. **18**(2), 313–320 (2017)
3. Li, J., Li, X., et al.: Segmentation-based image copy-move forgery detection scheme. IEEE Trans. Inf. Forensics Secur. **10**(3), 507–518 (2015)
4. Zhou, Z., Wang, Y., et al.: Effective and efficient global context verification for image copy detection. IEEE Trans. Inf. Forensics Secur. **12**(1), 48–63 (2017)
5. Guo, P., et al.: A variable threshold-value authentication architecture for wireless mesh networks. J. Internet Technol. **15**(6), 929–935 (2014)
6. Xie, S., Wang, Y.: Construction of tree network with limited delivery latency in homogeneous wireless sensor networks. Wireless Pers. Commun. **78**(1), 231–246 (2014)
7. Chen, B., Shu, H., et al.: Color image analysis by quaternion zernike moments. J. Math. Imaging Vis. **51**(1), 124–144 (2015)
8. Wang, B., Gu, X., Ma, L., Yan, S.: Temperature error correction based on BP neural network in meteorological WSN. Int. J. Sensor Netw. **23**(4), 265–278 (2017)
9. Tsai, C.L., Chiang, H.F., et al.: Reversible data hiding and lossless reconstruction of binary images using pair-wise logical computation mechanism. Pattern Recogn. **38**(11), 1993–2006 (2005)
10. Shiu, C.W., Chen, Y.C., Hong, W.: Encrypted image-based reversible data hiding with public key cryptography from difference expansion. Signal Process. Image Commun. **39**, 226–233 (2015)
11. Barton, J.M.: Method and apparatus for embedding authentication information within digital data. US, US6523114 (2003)
12. Hong, W., et al.: An efficient reversible data hiding method for AMBTC compressed images. Multimedia Tools Appl. **76**(4), 5441–5460 (2016)
13. Chen, J., et al.: Steganography for BTC compressed images using no distortion technique. Imaging Sci. J. **58**(4), 177–185 (2010)
14. Sun, W., et al.: High performance reversible data hiding for block truncation coding; compressed images. Signal Image Video Process. **7**(2), 297–306 (2013)

An Efficient Copy-Move Detection Algorithm Based on Superpixel Segmentation and Harris Key-Points

Yong Liu[1], Hong-Xia Wang[1(✉)], Han-Zhou Wu[2], and Yi Chen[1]

[1] School of Information Science and Technology,
Southwest Jiaotong University, Chengdu 611756, China
liuymy@my.swjtu.edu.cn, hxwang@swjtu.edu.cn
[2] Institute of Automation, Chinese Academy of Sciences (CAS),
Beijing 100190, People's Republic of China

Abstract. Region duplication is a commonly used operation in digital image processing. Since region duplication could be utilized to easily tamper the raw content by intentional attackers, it has become a very important topic in image forensics. Most of the existing detection methods designed to region duplication are based on the exhaustive block-matching of image pixels or transformed coefficients. They may be not efficient when the duplicate regions are relatively smooth, or processed by some geometrical transformations. This has motivated us to propose a reliable copy-move forgery detection algorithm based on super-pixel segmentation and Harris key-points to improve the detection accuracy due to these specified attacks. For a given image, the proposed method first uses SLIC super-pixel segmentation and cluster analysis technique to partition the image content into complex regions and smooth regions. Then, a region description method based on sector mean is introduced to represent the relatively small image regions around each Harris point by adopting a well-designed feature vector. Thereafter, for both complex regions and smooth regions, we perform the feature matching operation, which is finally exploited to locate the tampered region. Experimental results have shown that, our algorithm significantly outperform some related works in terms of the detection accuracy when the test images are processed by blurring, adding noise, JPEG compression and rotating, which has shown the superior of our work.

Keywords: Copy-move forgery detection · Image segmentation · Cluster analysis · Harris points · Sector mean

1 Introduction

An image with copy-move forgery contains a couple of local regions whose contents are often identical. Copy-move forgery could be performed by a forger aiming either to cover the truth or to enhance the visual effect of the image. Normal people might neglect this malicious operation when the forger hides the tampering trace. However, we are in urgent need of an effective copy-move forgery detection method to automatically point out the clone regions in the image [1], since the copy-move operation

© Springer International Publishing AG 2017
X. Sun et al. (Eds.): ICCCS 2017, Part I, LNCS 10602, pp. 61–73, 2017.
https://doi.org/10.1007/978-3-319-68505-2_6

may result in security problems such as content integrity, authenticity. It can be said that, copy-move forgery detection has been becoming one of the most important yet challenging topics in the field of digital forensics currently.

In the literature, there are mainly two types of copy-move forgery detection algorithms. One is based on block division, and the other uses key point extraction.

The detection method based on block division, it can be roughly generalized as follows: a test image is partitioned into overlapping or non-overlapping blocks and the features of each block are extracted and sorted, and then, cloned blocks could be detected by matching the features of each image blocks. Reference [2] first suggested such method. In Ref. [2], the quantified DCT coefficients of each block were used as features. The features of all blocks were sorted lexicographically, and then they checked whether the adjacent blocks were similar or not by matching their features. This method can detect cloned regions in image, however, due to high computational complexity, many subsequent works such as [3–8] focused on improving calculation efficiency. Reference [3] employed the principle component analysis (PCA) to reduce the feature dimension. Reference [4] combined discrete wavelet transformation with singular value decomposition (SVD) to generate feature vectors, and then the feature vectors were matched to detect clone regions. Recent research, Ref. [9] presented an efficient expanding block algorithm for image copy-move forgery detection. This method primarily uses direct block comparison rather than indirect comparisons based on block features. The advantage of direct block comparison is that it can be done without a large sacrifice in performance time. Reference [10] compared four block-based detection methods for copy-move forgery detection, which are based on PCA, DCT, spatial domain, and statistical domain. It is concluded that the PCA method outperforms the others in terms of time complexity and accuracy. Blocks matching techniques really provide an efficient approach to detect cloned image regions, but most of them have some common shortages such as high computational complexity and weaker robustness for rotating and scaling.

The key-point based algorithms depend on the extraction of local interest points (key-points) from local interest regions with high entropy without any image sub-blocking. Huang [11] proposed a method by matching the SIFT key points to display the tampered area. In [12], the BOW matching method is used to obtain the SIFT matching, and then a global context descriptor (OR-GCD) based on the overlapping region is extracted to test the matching pairs. Amerini [13] proposed to use G2NN to deal with multiple copics, the hierarchical clustering and Random Sample Consensus (RANSAC) were employed to filter out outliers and significantly improved the detection accuracy. In Ref. [14], a hybrid approach was proposed, where SURF was used to detect the key points in the image and Binary Robust Invariant Scalable Keypoints (BRISK) features were used to represent corresponding features at these keypoints. In Ref. [15], Chen is used to extract the Harris points of the image, and then the feature vectors are matched by the step sector statistical information. Recently, in Ref. [16], image segmentation and an EM (Expectation-Maximization)-based stage are proposed in order to reduce the affine estimation error. This technique can reduce the errors, but the imposed computational cost is unaffordable on large-scale images. In Ref. [17], the paper first extract the image Harris, then feature matching by each Harris point average DC coefficient and AC DCT coefficients of the center of the square, can greatly reduce the complexity of the algorithm, but it cannot detect smooth tampered regions. Although key point-based methods are robust to geometric transformation and keep computational cost low, they may not work well in dealing with smooth regions. In summary, key point-based methods may fail to work for copied smooth regions. On the contrary, block-based methods work well in such cases yet it will bring high computation cost and some block-based methods weaker robustness for rotating.

In this paper, we propose a new method to deal with the above problem. Our method can not only detect the copy-move forgery in smooth regions, but also resist against rotation tampering. The flowchart of the proposed method, as shown in Fig. 1. In Fig. 1, a test image is first adaptively divided into non-overlapped region, using simple linear iterative clustering (SLIC) algorithm, and we partition these regions into two categories according to the mean and standard deviation. Two categories are called as smooth regions and non-smooth (i.e., complex) regions. Then, we extract the dense points of the Harris corner in the test image, an image region description method based on sector mean is developed to represent the small circle image region around each Harris point by adopting a feature vector. Afterwards, RANSAC is used to prune outlier after getting all matching feature points. Finally, we obtain the detection result. Experiments results have shown our method can achieve a better detection performance when compared with some related works.

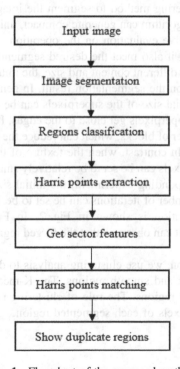

Fig. 1. Flowchart of the proposed method

The rest of this paper are organized as follows. Section 2 describes image segmentation and cluster analysis. In Sect. 3, the Harris corner detection is described in detail. Then, the image region description based on sector mean and detection in complex region and smooth region are introduced in Sects. 4 and 5. Section 6 gives some experimental results and analysis. Finally, we conclude this paper in Sect. 7.

2 Image Segmentation and Cluster Analysis

In order to separate the copying source region from the pasting target region, the image should be segmented into small patches, each of which is semantically independent to the others. The concept of superpixel is a kind of irregular pixel block which is composed of adjacent pixels with similar texture, color and brightness. It makes use of the similarity of the features between pixels to group the pixels, and uses a small number of pixels instead of a large number of pixels to express the image features. To a great extent, it reduces the complexity of image post-processing.

We firstly segment the image into semantically independent non-overlapping regions by using the segmentation algorithm, such as simple linear iterative clustering (SLIC) algorithm [18] and generalized FCM (GFCM) algorithm [19]. Here we choose SLIC due to its low computational complexity, which allows us to employ the simple and efficient K-means clustering method to segment the image into visually homogeneous regions. The SLIC algorithm can generate compact, uniform and uniform pixels, and has a high comprehensive evaluation on the operation speed, the object contour and the shape of the pixels, it also meet the desired segmentation effect.

In practice, images have different content and size, the initial size of the superpixels has considerable influence on the segmentation result. In general, when the texture of the image is simple, the initial size of the superpixels can be set to be relatively large, which can ensure that the superpixels get close to the edges. Furthermore, larger initial size implies a smaller number of blocks, which can reduce the computational cost when processing smooth region. In contrast, when the texture of the image is complicated, the initial size of the superpixels can be set to be relatively small to ensure good forgery detection results. By corresponding experiment, the initial size of the superpixels can be set to be 200 and the number of iterations can be set to be 10. An example of image SLIC superpixels segmentation is shown in Fig. 2. In Fig. 2, the two trees are copy-move forged regions. It can observed that the forged region is divided into several patches.

After image segmentation, we use clustering analysis to divide the image into two categories, complex regions and smooth regions. The K-mean cluster is used for the clustering of the segmented regions. The rule of clustering is based on the mean and standard deviation of the pixels of each segmented region.

(a)   (b)

Fig. 2. Example of image SLIC super-pixels segmentation: (a) The forgery image, (b) The result after SLIC super-pixels segmentation.

3 Harris Corner Detection

The proposed method employs Harris corners as a key-points based method for region duplication forgery detection after converting colored images into gray images. The Harris corner detector is an invariant to rotation technique that identifies corners of an image. Harris corner detection is based on the second moment auto correlation matrix [20]. This matrix describes the Gradient distribution of input images at point x, weighted by Gaussian $G(x, \sigma)$ as the following:

$$M(x,y) = G(x, \sigma) \begin{bmatrix} I_x^2(x, \sigma) & I_x I_y(x, \sigma) \\ I_x I_y(x, \sigma) & I_y^2(x, \sigma) \end{bmatrix} \tag{1}$$

where $I_x^2, I_y^2, I_x I_y$ are square derivatives of input image I.

The traditional Harris corner response need to choose the appropriate empirical constant, it can be measured using Eq. (2).

$$R(x,y) = det(M(x,y)) - k * tr^2(M(x,y)) \tag{2}$$

where k is the empirical constant which choose from the range [0.04, 0.06].

In order to avoid choosing the empirical constants k, here we choose the improved method [21] of the Harris corner response, it can be measured using Eq. (3).

$$R(x, y) = det(M(x, y))/(trace(M(x, y)) + \varepsilon) \tag{3}$$

where $R(x, y)$ is the response value of the Harris corner, ϵ is any small positive number. Corner points have large positive eigenvalues and hence a large Harris measure response. Thus, corner points that are greater than a specified threshold are identified as local maxima of the Harris measure response, i.e.,

$$\{(x_c, y_c)\} = \{(x_c, y_c) | R(x_c, y_c) \rangle R(x_i, y_i), \forall (x_i, y_i) \in W(x_c, y_c), R(x_c, y_c) > t_{th}\} \quad (4)$$

where $\{(x_c, y_c)\}$ is the set of all corner points, $R(x, y)$ is the Harris measure response calculated at point (x, y), $W(x_c, y_c)$ is setting centered around the point (x_c, y_c), and t_{th} is a specified threshold. Obviously, the number of detected Harris corner points depends on the threshold t_{th}. By changing the threshold of the Harris extracted values, we can get enough Harris corner points in smooth region, here we choose the threshold as $t_{th} = 10^{-5}$, the result of extracting Harris corner points, as shown in Fig. 3.

(a)　　　　　　　　　　　　　　(b)

Fig. 3. The detected Harris corner points: (a) The test image, (b) The result of extracting Harris points.

4　Image Region Description Based on Sector Mean

We use Chen's method [15] to construct the sector, an image region description method based on sector statistics is introduced to represent the small circle regions around the Harris corner interest points. As we know, an image is rotated around a center just like a wheel turning around an axis. If a fixed point is marked on the wheel, then any other point on the wheel can be located according to this marked point. In a similar way, we can make a sector mask to extract the image feature along the radial direction. After the image features of all directions are extracted, their location relationship can be determined through a marked direction [15]. Thus, the image region description method based on sector statistics is constituted as the following steps.

4.1　Creating the Sector Mask

For each Harris corner point, a representation will be given to the small circle region around it. We take the Harris corner point as the center, then the sector is derived from the circle of Harris corner points, the created sector masks are shown in Fig. 4. We get

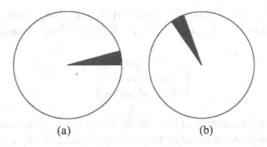

(a)   (b)

Fig. 4. The sector masks: (a) The sector mask in direction of 10°, (b) The sector mask in direction of 120°.

36 sector masks labeled as $S_1, S_2, \ldots, S_{36}$ will be obtained after dividing the circle into 36 equal parts. The radius of the sector mask is 16, and the angle is 10° these parameters are determined through lots of experiments.

4.2 Extracting the Sector Mask Features

After we getting the sector masks, the sector masks $S_k (k = 1, 2, \ldots, 36)$ are used to constitute the sector mask feature by computing the mean of the pixels within each sector mask S_k, e.g., $M_{S_1} = mean(S_1)$. Finally, a vector of 36 dimensions is obtained, i.e. $(M_{S_1}, M_{S_2} \ldots, M_{S_{36}})$.

No matter how many degrees the circle image region has been rotated, the sectors in the circle image region have the same location relationship. Therefore, the sector with the largest mean can be set as the direction mark of the circle image region, and then all the other sectors are just rearranged in a preset direction (clockwise or counterclockwise). Thus, the sector mask is arranged according to the content of the circle image region, which is barely affected by rotation [15]. In this way, the image region description method based on sector mask features can be rotation-robust.

If the element with the largest mean in the aforementioned 36 dimensional feature vector is M_{S_i}, the elements in the vector can be rearranged as

$$\left(M_{S_i}, M_{S_{i+1}}, \ldots, M_{S_{36}}, M_{S_1}, M_{S_2}, \ldots, M_{S_{i-1}}\right)$$

5 Detection in Complex Region and Smooth Region

After the Harris corner points are obtained, the small circle region around each Harris point is represented with a feature vector using the image region description method based on sector statistics described. We set the Harris corner points as $P = \{P_1, P_2, \ldots, P_n\}$, the corresponding vector is labeled as $X = \{x_1, x_2, \ldots, x_n\}$. Then, the detected Harris points are matched based on their representation feature vectors using the G2NN algorithm [22].

We find the matching points by using G2NN algorithm in complex region and smooth region respectively. We calculate the Euclidean distances between

$x_i(i = 1, 2, \ldots, n)$ and the others. We then sort the resulting distances in ascending order and label them as $D = \{d_1, d_2, \ldots, d_{n-1}\}$. If the resulting distances can satisfy the formula:

$$\begin{cases} d_k/d_{k+1} < T \\ d_{k+1}/d_{k+2} > T \end{cases} \tag{5}$$

where T is the appropriate threshold (in default, $T = 0.5$), we think that the Harris point x_i matches with these points that the corresponding distance is $\{d_1, d_2, \ldots, d_k\}$. In order to avoid searching the nearest neighbors of a Harris point from its adjacent region, the distance between two matched Harris points should be larger than a certain distance such as 2R (R is the radius of the sector region). In order to avoid searching the nearest neighbors of a Harris point from its adjacent region, every two matched Harris points should not be in the same segmented region.

All the matched Harris interest point pairs are displayed by circles of radius 16 (same as the radius of the sector mask), with a line connecting them. Thus, the duplicate regions can be revealed through these circles and relation lines. However, the number of matched pairs will vary among different images. When there are two or more matched pairs that cluster to show a certain kind of affine transformation, the regions they cover can be considered as duplicate regions. When there is only one matched pair or several matched pairs but distributing randomly, false matching may occur. Since the Harris points are almost uniformly distributed in the image, when there is one matched pair, there is a high probability that the Harris points nearby will be matched, and thus the single matched pair may be false matching. However, this single matched pair may also be correct matching of small duplicate regions as small duplicate regions give limited information in the detection process. While in most region duplications, the duplicate regions are large enough to offer more information. Therefore, we use RANSAC algorithm [23] to filter outliers and remove the false match points. Figure 5 (a) and (b), illustrate the comparison of the matching keypoints before and after filtering, respectively.

(a)   (b)

Fig. 5. The result of matching keypoints before and after using RANSAC algorithm: (a) The matching key-points before using RANSAC algorithm, (b) The matching key-points after using RANSAC algorithm.

6 Experimental Results

In this section, we discuss the performance of the proposed algorithms via experiments. Our method is implemented and tested using MATLAB2013a. We run programs in the computer with Inter(R) Core(TM) i5-2430M CPU @ 2.40 GHz, 4.00 GB RAM (Table 1).

Table 1. Setting of the attacks

Attack	Parameters
Blurring	Filter radius: 0.5, 1.5, 2.5
Noise	Zero mean, variance: 0.001, 0.002, 0.003
JPEG compression	Quality: 70, 80, 90, 100
Rotation	Angle: 10, 30, 50, 70, 90

We evaluate the reliability and efficiency of the proposed method using SBU-CM16 [24] image databases and 24 uncompressed PNG images released by the Kodak Corporation for unrestricted research use. This database contains 24 original images and 240 forged images, each image in this dataset has one forged part. Forged images created by coping one part and pasting it on another part of the same image. After that, one attack is performed on the copied region or on the whole image. The details of the utilized attacks are summarized in the following table:

Figures 6, 7, 8 and 9 are the detection result of the proposed method in different tampering attacks, Figs. 6, 7, 8 and 9 show that the proposed method can detect the forged images, in which the tampering region occurs in the smooth region or complex region, and it also robust for the manipulation such as blurring, adding noise, JPEG compression, and rotation.

    (a)   (b)

Fig. 6. The detection result after the attack of blurring: (a) The forged image, (b) The detected result.

(a)   (b)

Fig. 7. The detection result after the attack of adding noise: (a) The forged image, (b) The detected result.

(a)   (b)

Fig. 8. The detection result after the attack of JPEG compression: (a) The forged image, (b) The detected result.

(a)   (b)

Fig. 9. The detection result after the attack of rotation: (a) The forged image, (b) The detected result.

In this paper, we adopt True Positive Rate (T_{PR}) and False Positive Rate (F_{PR}) as evaluation metrics which are often used in the field of forgery detection and information retrieval. True Positive Rate (T_{PR}) and False Positive Rate (F_{PR}) are also called true positive and false positive. They are defined as follows:

$$T_{PR} = \frac{No.\ of\ forged\ images\ detected\ as\ forged}{No.\ of\ forged\ images} \quad (6)$$

$$F_{PR} = \frac{No.\ of\ original\ images\ detected\ as\ forged}{No.\ of\ original\ images} \quad (7)$$

The robustness performance of the proposed method is evaluated against sets of various kinds of post-processing operations including blurring, adding noise, JPEG compression and rotation. We evaluate the robustness of the proposed method using SBU-CM16 image databases, and compared with the algorithm of Refs. [15] and [17]. The correct detection rate of comparison experiment is shown in Table 2. The results of comparison experiment are shown in Table 3.

Table 2. The correct detection rate of comparison experiment

	Blurring	Noise	JPEG compression	Rotation
Ref. [15]	64.58%	68.75%	70.31%	72.50%
Ref. [17]	52.00%	68.75%	71.88%	2.50%
Proposed method	83.30%	75.00%	85.93%	97.50%

Table 3. Detection results of comparison experiment

Measures	Ref. [15]	Ref. [17]	Proposed method
T_{PR}	69.58%	44.16%	87.08%
F_{PR}	12.50%	4.17%	8.33%

As shown in Table 2, the proposed method has a good performance, the proposed method have a higher correct detection rate when compared with the Refs. [15] and [17]. It can resist against some content-preserving manipulations such as blurring, adding noise, JPEG compression and rotating. Table 3 shows that the proposed method have a lower False Positive Rate compared with the Ref. [15].

7 Conclusion

In this paper, we present a copy-move detection algorithm for digital images in which the tampered regions are relatively smooth. We use the SLIC super-pixel segmentation to divide the test image content into different disjoint regions, and further employ the

K-mean cluster to classify these regions as smooth or complex. Moreover, an image region description method based on sector mean is developed to represent the small circle image region around each Harris point by using a feature vector. For experiments, we use the database of SBU-CM16 to evaluate the reliability and efficiency of the proposed method. Detection performance of the proposed method is demonstrated to be excellent, namely, the proposed method has a better ability to resist against some content-preserving manipulations such as blurring, adding noise, JPEG compression and rotating, when compared with some related works. In addition, for the proposed method, when to detect forgery in smooth regions, the initial size of the superpixels and the sort numbers of the cluster analysis has a great influence on the detection results. In future, we will aim to find the appropriate parameters to improve the detection speed and accuracy.

Acknowledgments. This work is supported by the National Natural Science Foundation of China (NSFC) under the grant No. U1536110.

References

1. Christlein, V., Riess, C., Jordan, J., Riess, C., Angelopoulou, E.: An evaluation of popular copy-move forgery detection approaches. IEEE Trans. Inf. Forensics Secur. **7**(6), 1841–1854 (2012)
2. Fridrich, J., Soukal, D., Lukas, J.: Detection of copy-move forgery in digital images. In: Proceeding on Digital Forensic Research Workshop, August 2003
3. Popescu, A.C., Farid, H.: Exposing digital forgeries by detecting duplicated image regions in computer science. Dartmouth College, Technical Report TR2004-515 (2004)
4. Li, G., Wu, Q., Tu, D., Sun, S.J.: A sorted neighborhood approach for detecting duplicated regions in image forgeries based on DWT and SVD. In: Proceeding of IEEE International Conference on Multimedia Expo (ICME), Beijing, 1750–1753, July 2007
5. Bayram, S., Sencar, H.T., Memon, N.: An efficient and robust method for detecting copy-move forgery. In: IEEE International Conference on Acoustics, Speech and Signal Processing, 1053–1056. IEEE (2015)
6. Mahdian, B., Saic, S.: Detection of copy-move forgery using a method based on blur moment invariants. Forensic Sci. Int. **171**(2–3), 180–189 (2007)
7. Luo, W., Huang, J., Qiu, G.: Robust detection of region-duplication forgery in digital image. Chin. J. Comput. **4**(11), 746–749 (2007)
8. Khan, E.S., Kulkarni, E.A.: An efficient method for detection of copy-move forgery using discrete wavelet transform. Int. J. Comput. Sci. Eng. **2**(5), 1801–1806 (2010)
9. Shih, F.Y., Yuan, Y.: A comparison study on copy-cover image forgery detection. Open Artif. Intell. J. **4**(1), 49–54 (2010)
10. Lynch, G., Shih, F.Y., Liao, H.Y.M.: An efficient expanding block algorithm for image copy-move forgery detection. Inf. Sci. **239**(4), 253–265 (2013)
11. Huang, H., Guo, W., Zhang, Y.: Detection of copy-move forgery in digital images using sift algorithm. In: The Workshop on Computational Intelligence & Industrial Application, pp. 272–276. IEEE (2008)
12. Zhou, Z., Wang, Y., Wu, J.Q.M., Yang, C.N., Sun, X.: Effective and efficient global context verification for image copy detection. IEEE Trans. Inf. Forensics Secur. **12**(1), 48–63 (2017). doi:10.1109/TIFS.2016.2601065

13. Atnerini, I., Ballan, L., Caldelli, R., et al.: A SIFT-based forensic method for copy-move attack detection and transformation recovery. IEEE Trans. Inf. Forensics Secur. 6(3), 1099–1110 (2011)
14. Kumar, S., Desai, J., Mukherjee, S.: A fast keypoint based hybrid method for copy move forgery detection. Int. J. Comput. Digital Syst. 4(2), 91–99 (2015)
15. Chen, L., Lu, W., Ni, J.: Region duplication detection based on Harris corner points and step sector statistics. J. Vis. Commun. Image Present. 24(3), 244–254 (2013)
16. Li, J., Li, X., Yang, B., Sun, X.: Segmentation-based image copy-move forgery detection scheme. IEEE Trans. Inf. Forensics Secur. 10(3), 507–518 (2015). doi:10.1109/TIFS.2014.2381872
17. Wang, X., He, G., Tang, C.: Keypoints-based image passive forensics method for copy-move attacks. Int. J. Pattern Recognit. Artif. Intell. 30(3), 304–308 (2016)
18. Achanta, R., Shaji, A., Smith, K., Lucchi, A., Fua, P., Susstrunk, S.: SLIC super pixels compared to state-of-the-art superpixel methods. IEEE Trans. Pattern Anal. Mach. Intell. 31(11), 2274–2282 (2012)
19. Zheng, Y., Jeon, B., Xu, D., Wu, J.Q.M., Zhang, H.: Image segmentation by generalized hierarchical fuzzy C-means algorithm. J. Intell. Fuzzy Syst. 28(2), pp. 961–973 (2015). DOI:10.3233/IFS-141378,2015
20. Harris, C.; Stephens, M.: A combined corner and edge detector. In: Proceedings of the Alvey Vision Conference, Manchester, UK, 2 September 1988
21. Yan-Ming, M., Mei-Hui, L., Yun-Qiong, W., Qiao-Sheng, F.: An improved corner detection method based on Harris. Comput. Technol. Develop. 19(5), 130–133 (2009)
22. Atnerini, I., Ballan, L., Caldelli, R., et al.: A SIFT-based forensic method for copy-move at tack detection and transformation recovery. IEEE Trans. Inf. Forensics Secur. 6(3), 1099–1110 (2011)
23. Fischler, M.A., Bolles, R.C.: Random sample consensus: a paradigm for model fitting with applications to image analysis and automated cartography. Commun. ACM 24(6), 381–395 (1981)
24. Zandi, M., Mahmoudi-Aznaveh, A., Mansouri, A.: Adaptive matching for copy-move forgery detection. In: IEEE International Workshop on Information Forensics and Security (WIFS), 119–124 (2014)

Improved CMD Adaptive Image Steganography Method

Yingbo Yu[1] and Xin Liao[1,2(✉)]

[1] College of Computer Science and Electronic Engineering, Hunan University,
Changsha 410082, China
[2] Shenzhen Key Laboratory of Media Security, Shenzhen University,
Shenzhen 518060, China
xinliao@hnu.edu.cn

Abstract. With the rapid development of information communication, information security is becoming more and more important. As an important technology in the field of information security, image steganography has attracted wide attention. CMD (clustering modification directions) steganographic strategy has high security performance. The cover image is decomposed into several sub-images, and then the costs of pixels are updated dynamically and the pixel modification directions are clustered. However, the sub-image cannot completely exploit mutual embedding impacts. In this paper, we propose a new steganography method based on patched block. This strategy can make the post-processing sub-image be influenced by all the sub-images which have already embedded. The experimental results show that the proposed method is more secure than CMD image steganographic method.

Keywords: Adaptive image steganography · Patched block · Clustering Modification Directions (CMD)

1 Introduction

With the rapid development of Internet communication technologies and the arrival of the big data, it has been challenged to ensure the correctness of the multimedia information and the security of personal information. The technology of image copy detection [1–3] can effectively guarantee the correctness of the image, and researchers focus on privacy-preserving content-based image retrieval in cloud computing [4–11]. Therefore, multimedia security plays an increasingly important role in our life.

Steganography is a new approach of information security to hide secret messages into innocuous digital media without drawing suspicion [12]. In spatial domain image steganography, the secret messages are usually embedded into cover image by modifying the pixel values. LSB (least significant bit) is the simplest steganography that secret messages are embedded by changing the least significant bit of the pixel. LSB matching (LSBM) [13] is a similar method that

© Springer International Publishing AG 2017
X. Sun et al. (Eds.): ICCCS 2017, Part I, LNCS 10602, pp. 74–84, 2017.
https://doi.org/10.1007/978-3-319-68505-2_7

randomly increases or decreases the pixel value by one to match the LSB of stego pixel with the message bit. Both LSB and LSBM adopt a single pixel as an embedding unit to carry k bits of information. Though LSB and LSBM can easily cheat our human eyes, it is easy to be detected even at a low payload by using some statistical steganalytic methods. In order to improve the security, some adaptive embedding methods have been proposed. The most effective steganographic schemes are based on minimizing a distortion function correlated with statistical detectability [14]. A distortion function is considered additive when it is expressed as a sum of costs, which element-wisely evaluate the effect of respective embedding modification, and then combine with the advanced Syndrome-Trellis Codes (STCs) coding technique [15] to minimize the overall distortion of the stego image. The popular schemes include HUGO (highly undetectable stego) [16], WOW (wavelet obtained weights) [17], improved WOW [18], S-UNIWARD (spatial-universal wavelet relative distortion) [19], HILL (high-pass, low-pass, and low-pass) [20], and so on. While the distortion introduced by data embedding is non-additive in essence, because there are inter-pixel correlations and interactions among embedding changes.

Recently, Li et al. proposed a non-additive steganography algorithm CMD (clustering modification directions) [21]. The cover image is decomposed into several sub-images, in which message segments are embedded with well-known schemes using additive distortion functions. It can exploit mutual embedding impacts in order to reduce the risk of detection. However, the sub-image of post-processing can not fully exploit the interactions among the embedding changes of former sub-image. In this paper, we will improve CMD adaptive image steganography method to solve this problem. We adopt a new manner to decompose the cover image. This manner is called patched block which is similar to PRT (patched reference table) [22]. The secret message segments are embedded by using the well-known additive distortion functions. The merits of our work are demonstrated experimentally by comparing with CMD and showing an improvement in statistical detectability.

The rest of this paper is organized as follows. The next section briefly reviews CMD embedding method and PRT embedding method. Section 3 presents the improved CMD adaptive image steganography method. The experimental comparisons and analyses are presented in Sect. 4. Finally, the conclusions are made in Sect. 5.

2   Previous Works

In this section, we give a brief overview of CMD embedding method and PRT embedding method.

2.1   CMD Embedding Method

CMD exploits the mutual embedding impacts of pixels to reduce the risk of detection. Suppose the size of an original cover image is 4×4 as Fig. 1(a).

Firstly, the cover image is decomposed into 4 sub-images and each pixel of 2×2 neighboring pixels is assigned to different sub-images. We can acquire 4 sub-images like Fig. 1(b). Suppose the red sub-image as S_1, the green sub-image as S_2, the yellow sub-image as S_3, the blue sub-image as S_4. Message segments are embedded into sub-images by the well-known schemes with additive distortion functions according to the embedding sequence $S_1 \rightarrow S_2 \rightarrow S_3 \rightarrow S_4$ in Fig. 1(c). The costs of pixels are updated dynamically to take mutual embedding impacts into account. Specifically, when the neighboring pixels are changed toward a positive/negative direction, the cost of the considered pixel is biased toward the same direction. Figure 2(a) shows that the four-neighboring of a pixel in image. Based on the embedding sequence, we can get the four-neighboring of the pixel in sub-image S_2, S_3, S_4 as shown in Figs. 2(b), (c) and (d), respectively. Thus, the sub-image S_2 can exploit the embedding impacts of sub-image S_1 and S_3.

However, the sub-image S_2 is prior to the sub-image S_3 in the embedding sequence, the embedding changes of the sub-image S_2 is only affected by sub-images

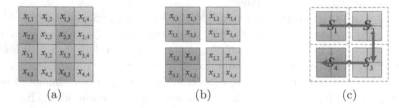

(a)   (b)   (c)

Fig. 1. A sample example of the pre-processing for CMD. (a) A sample image of size 4×4 pixels. (b) Four sub-images. (c) Embedding order for the four sub-images with horizontal zig-zag scan.

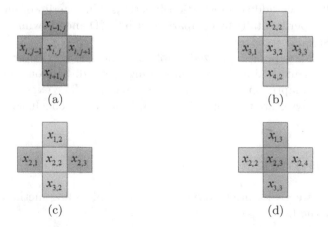

(a)   (b)

(c)   (d)

Fig. 2. The four-neighboring pixels of sub-image in CMD. (a) The four-neighboring $N_{i,j}$ of the pixel at location (i, j). (b) The four-neighboring of the pixel $x_{3,2}$ in sub-image S_2. (c) The four-neighboring of the pixel $x_{2,2}$ in sub-image S_3. (d) The four-neighboring of the pixel $x_{2,3}$ in sub-image S_4.

S_1. Similarly, the embedding changes of the sub-image S_3 is only affected by sub-image S_2, and the embedding changes of the sub-image S_4 is affected by sub-image S_1 and sub-image S_3. Therefore, according to the above analysis, the way of decomposing cover image into sub-images can not completely exploit the mutual embedding impacts of pixels.

2.2   PRT Embedding Method

PRT (patched reference table) embedding method uses a patched reference table as a guide and provides a better image quality and extendable embedding capacity.

The PRT is composed by many patches. The patch consists of 2^{2k} search positions and arranges non-repeating integers ranging from 0 to $2^{2k} - 1$ in it. Thus, all $2^k \times 2^k$ search positions in the PRT include non-repeating integers ranging from 0 to $2^{2k} - 1$. The simplest patch is shown in Fig. 3(a) and the center is the green position. These positions are designed by minimizing the MSE (mean square error) in the center position. Then, the embedding sequence is constructed by scanning every position in the cover image with raster scan order, and the embedding units are randomly combined with one of the four embedding directions. The four embedding directions are the right, bottom right, bottom, and left bottom of the current position. We could select a pixel pair (r, c) in embedding sequence and calculate the absolute difference of the pair to determine a threshold value. Please see Ref. [22] for more details.

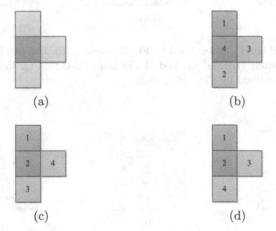

Fig. 3. An example of the arranged of number $1 \sim 2^{2k}$ into a patch with 2^{2k} pixels. (a) A simple patch with 2^2 pixels. (b) A choice arranged the number $1 \sim 2^2$. (c) A choice arranged the number $1 \sim 2^2$. (d) A choice arranged the number $1 \sim 2^2$. (Color figure online)

3   Improved CMD Image Steganography Method

According to the analysis in Sect. 2.1, the way of decomposing cover image into sub-images can not completely exploit the mutual embedding impacts of pixels. Thus, we design a method called patched block to decompose the cover image. The patch of Fig. 3(a) is utilized in the proposed method. We fill the patch with non-repeating integers ranging from 1 to 4 as shown in Figs. 3(b), (c) and (d). Then, we apply the patch to compose a patched block table. Figure 4 shows three different patched block tables. The numbers in the patched block table denote that the cover image pixel in this position will be decomposed into corresponding sub-image. For different patched block tables, the four-neighboring pixels in the sub-image S_2, S_3, S_4 are shown as Figs. 5, 6 and 7, respectively. According to the embedding sequence $S_1 \rightarrow S_2 \rightarrow S_3 \rightarrow S_4$, each sub-image can exploit the embedding impacts of all previous embedded sub-images. Combining the proposed patched block and CMD, we design an improved CMD adaptive image steganographic method, which can completely exploit the mutual embedding impacts of pixels and achieve higher security performance.

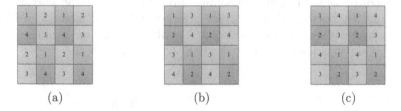

Fig. 4. The patched blocks tables filled by Fig. 3 patches. (a) The patched blocks table filled by Fig. 3(b) patch. (b) The patched blocks table filled by Fig. 3(c) patch. (c) The patched blocks table filled by Fig. 3(d) patch.

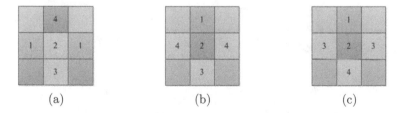

Fig. 5. The four-neighboring of the sub-image S_2 blocked by Fig. 3 patches. (a) The four-neighboring of the sub-image S_2 blocked by Fig. 3(b) patch. (b) The four-neighboring of the sub-image S_2 blocked by Fig. 3(c) patch. (c) The four-neighboring of the sub-image S_2 blocked by Fig. 3(d) patch.

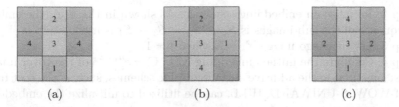

(a)   (b)   (c)

Fig. 6. The four-neighboring of the sub-image S_3 blocked by Fig. 3 patches. (a) The four-neighboring of the sub-image S_3 blocked by Fig. 3(b) patch. (b) The four-neighboring of the sub-image S_3 blocked by Fig. 3(c) patch. (c) The four-neighboring of the sub-image S_3 blocked by Fig. 3(d) patch.

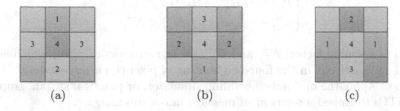

(a)   (b)   (c)

Fig. 7. The four-neighboring of the sub-image S_4 blocked by Fig. 3 patches. (a) The four-neighboring of the sub-image S_4 blocked by Fig. 3(b) patch. (b) The four-neighboring of the sub-image S_4 blocked by Fig. 3(c) patch. (c) The four-neighboring of the sub-image S_4 blocked by Fig. 3(d) patch.

3.1 The Embedding Processes

The detailed steps of the embedding processes in the proposed adaptive image steganographic method are as follows.

Step 1: Decompose the cover image **X** with the size of $n_1 \times n_2$ into 2×2 disjoint sub-images, and ensure the adjacent 2×2 pixels in cover image belonging to different sub-images. The index set of the pixels in a sub-image can be represented by

$$I_{a,b} = \begin{cases} \{(i,j) \mid i = a + 2k_a, j = b + 2k_b\}, & i \% 4 = 1 \ or \ 2 \\ \{(i,j) \mid i = a + 2k_a, j = (b+1) \% 2 + 2k_b\}, & i \% 4 = 0 \ or \ 3 \end{cases} \quad (1)$$

where $a, b \in \{1, 2\}$, $k_a \in \{0, 1, \cdots, \lfloor \frac{n_1}{2} \rfloor - 1\}$, $k_b \in \{0, 1, \cdots, \lfloor \frac{n_2}{2} \rfloor - 1\}$, $(i,j) \in \{1, \cdots, n_1\} \times \{1, \cdots, n_2\}$, $\lfloor . \rfloor$ denotes the floor operator.

For convenience, the pixel in cover image **X** which corresponds to the number l in patched block table composed by the patch[1] as Fig. 3(b) is divided into sub-image S_l. We can acquire that $S_1 = I_{1,1}$, $S_2 = I_{1,2}$, $S_3 = I_{2,2}$, $S_4 = I_{2,1}$. Divide the m bits message into four equal segments.

---

[1] If the patch as Fig. 3(c) is adopted, we can acquire that $S_1 = I_{1,1}$, $S_2 = I_{2,1}$, $S_3 = I_{1,2}$, $S_4 = I_{2,2}$. If the patch as Fig. 3(d) is used, we can acquire that $S_1 = I_{1,1}$, $S_2 = I_{2,1}$, $S_3 = I_{2,2}$, $S_4 = I_{1,2}$.

Step 2: Initialize an embedding sequence. As shown in Fig. 1(c), the embedding sequence of the sub-images is $S_1 \rightarrow S_2 \rightarrow S_3 \rightarrow S_4$ is used.

Step 3: Let the stego image $\mathbf{Y} = \mathbf{X}$ when $t = 1$.

Step 4: Compute the initial embedding costs $\mathbf{C} = c_{i,j}^{n_1 \times n_2}$ of the cover image. The cost functions in the additive steganographic schemes, such as the cost functions of WOW, S-UNIWARD, HILL, can be utilized to initialize the embedding costs.

Step 5: Compute the embedding modification $\mathbf{D}$ between $\mathbf{X}$ and $\mathbf{Y}$, $\mathbf{D} = \mathbf{Y} - \mathbf{X} = (d_{i,j})^{n_1 \times n_2}$. Update costs. If $t = 1$, set $\boldsymbol{\rho}^+ = \boldsymbol{\rho}^- = \mathbf{C}$. Otherwise, update the costs according to $\mathbf{D}$. Specifically, we use

$$\begin{cases} \rho_{i,j}^+ = c_{i,j}/\alpha & if \ N_{i,j}^+ > N_{i,j}^- \\ \rho_{i,j}^- = c_{i,j}/\alpha & if \ N_{i,j}^+ < N_{i,j}^- \end{cases} \tag{2}$$

where α is a scaling factor, $N_{i,j}^+$ and $N_{i,j}^-$ are the numbers of pixels which adds one and subtracts one in the four-neighboring of pixel (i, j), respectively.

Step 6: Apply the optimal embedding simulator, or practical steganographic codes STCs to embed a segment of message into a sub-image.

Step 7: Repeat the algorithm from Step 5 until all sub-images are embedded.

Since the proposed steganographic method is based on patched block and CMD, the proposed steganographic method is abbreviated to PCMD. If the additive distortion functions in HILL and WOW are utilized, we call it PCMD-H and PCMD-W, respectively.

3.2   The Extracting Processes

The patch used in the steganographic method is shared between the sender and the receiver. The receiver uses the patch to divide the stego image into four sub-images. Then the remaining extracting processes are the same as that of CMD. Please see Ref. [21] for more details.

4   Experimental Results

In this section, some experiments are carried out. All experiments are conducted on BOSSBase (v1.01) image database [23] which contains 10,000 gray-scale images of size 512×512 pixels. The scaling factor is set as $\alpha = 9$ in this paper. The optimal embedding simulator is used for embedding. The steganalyzer using the 34,671-dimensional SRM feature set [24] with the ensemble classifiers [25] is applied to evaluate the performance. A number of 5,000 randomly selected cover images and their stego images are used for training, and the remaining 5,000 image pairs are utilized for testing. The testing classification error is computed as the mean value of the false positive rate and the false negative rate, which is averaged over ten random splits of the data set. PCMD-W and PCMD-H is used in this section, and they are compared with the original CMD methods (CMD-W and CMD-H), respectively.

4.1 Impact of Patched Blocks

We fill the patch with non-repeating integers ranging from 1 to 4, and obtain three different kinds of patched blocks as shown in Figs. 3(b), (c) and (d). In this subsection, we compare the performance of PCMD-H with three different kinds of patched blocks. The experimental result of three patched blocks as shown in Table 1.

Table 1. The testing classification errors of PCMD-H1, PCMD-H2, PCMD-H3

Payload	0.05bpp	0.1bpp	0.2bpp	0.3bpp	0.4bpp	0.5bpp
PCMD-H1	0.4783	0.4522	0.3962	0.3437	0.2976	0.2552
PCMD-H2	0.4782	0.4512	0.3967	0.3426	0.2989	0.2566
PCMD-H3	0.4766	0.4540	0.3947	0.3456	0.2949	0.2537

PCMD-H1, PCMD-H2, PCMD-H3 represent PCMD-H are applied with different patched blocks, respectively. It can be observed that the experimental results of PCMD-H1, PCMD-H2 and PCMD-H3 are very similar. For example, when the embedding payload is 0.2 bpp, the testing classification errors of PCMD-H1, PCMD-H2 and PCMD-H3 are 0.3962, 0.3967 and 0.3947 respectively. Therefore, in the following experiments, we exploit the patched blocks as shown in Fig. 3(b).

4.2 Comparison of Statistical Detectability

In this section, we compare testing classification error of CMD method with our proposed method by using the SRM (spatial rich model) steganalyzer features. The experimental results are shown in Fig. 8. The X-axis represents different embedding payloads, and the Y-axis represents the relative testing error ratio (by percentage) increased by the proposed PCMD method. For each embedding payload, the incremental testing error ratio E_r is computed as

$$E_r = \frac{E_{PCMD} - E_{CMD}}{E_{CMD}} \times 100\% \tag{3}$$

where E_{PCMD} is the testing error value of ours proposed method, and E_{CMD} is the testing error value of the original CMD method.

In general, the testing errors against SRM steganalysis of our propose method is better than CMD as shown in Fig. 8. The red bars represent the testing error of PCMD is better than CMD, while the blue bars show the testing error of PCMD is a litter bit worse than CMD. Figure 8(a) shows that the performance of PCMD-W against SRM steganalysis is better than CMD-W as a whole. For instance, when the payload is 0.3 bpp, the testing classification error of PCMD-W is 0.301 and the testing classification error of CMD-W is 0.296. The proposed method could improve the anti-steganalysis performance by about 1.69%. From

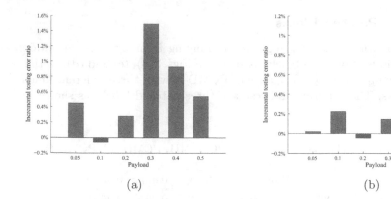

(a)   (b)

Fig. 8. Comparison of the relative testing error based on the BOSSBase image set against SRM steganalysis. The red bars represent the testing error of PCMD is better than CMD, while the blue bars show the testing error of PCMD is a litter bit worse than CMD. (a) Comparison of the testing errors between PCMD-W with CMD-W. (b) Comparison of the testing errors between PCMD-H with CMD-H. (Color figure online)

Fig. 8(b), it is show that the detection error of PCMD-H is generally higher than the detection error of CMD-H. For example, when the payload is 0.4 bpp, the detection error of CMD-H against SRM steganalysis is 0.295, while the testing classification error of PCMD-H is 0.298. The anti-steganalysis performance is improved 1.02% by using our proposed PCMD method. Through the above analysis, the proposed PCMD method can effectively resist steganalysis, and improve the security performance.

5   Conclusions

In this paper, an improved CMD adaptive image steganography method based on patched block is proposed, so that the mutual impacts of data embedding can be exploited completely. The cover image is decomposed into sub-images by the patched block firstly, thus sub-images can exploit the embedding impacts of the previous embedded sub-images. Experimental results show that the proposed image steganography method could perform better than the original CMD method.

Acknowledgments. This work is supported by National Natural Science Foundation of China (Grant Nos. 61402162, 61572182, 61370225, 61472131, 61272546), Hunan Provincial Natural Science Foundation of China (Grant No. 2017JJ3040), Specialized Research Fund for the Doctoral Program of Higher Education (Grant No. 20130161120004), Science and Technology Key Projects of Hunan Province (Grant Nos. 2015TP1004, 2016JC2012), Opening Project of Shanghai Key Laboratory of Integrated Administration Technologies for Information Security (Grant No. AGK201605).

References

1. Zhou, Z., Wang, Y., Wu, J., Yang, C., Sun, X.: Effective and efficient global context verification for image copy detection. IEEE Trans. Inf. Forensics Secur. **12**, 48–63 (2017)
2. Zhou, Z., Yang, C., Chen, B., Sun, X., Li, Q., Wu, J.: Effective and efficient image copy detection with resistance to arbitrary rotation. IEICE Trans. Inf. Syst. **99**(6), 1531–1540 (2016)
3. Pan, Z., Lei, J., Zhang, Y., Sun, X., Sam, K.: Fast motion estimation based on content property for low-complexity H.265/HEVC encoder. IEEE Trans. Broadcast. **62**, 675–684 (2016)
4. Xia, Z., Xiong, N., Vasilakos, A.V., Sun, X.: EPCBIR: an efficient and privacy-preserving content-based image retrieval scheme in cloud computing. Inf. Sci. **387**, 195–204 (2017)
5. Xia, Z., Wang, X., Zhang, L., Qin, Z., Sun, X., Ren, K.A.: Privacy-preserving and copy-deterrence content-based image retrieval scheme in cloud computing. IEEE Trans. Inf. Forensics Secur. **11**, 2594–2608 (2016)
6. Xia, Z., Zhu, Y., Sun, X., Qin, Z., Ren, K.: Towards privacy-preserving content-based image retrieval in cloud computing. IEEE Trans. Cloud Comput. **99**, 1–1 (2015)
7. Xiong, L., Xu, Z., Xu, Y.: A secure re-encryption scheme for data services in a cloud computing environment. Concur. Comput. Pract. Exp. **27**, 4573–4585 (2015)
8. Fu, Z., Sun, X., Ji, S., Xie, G.: Towards efficient content-aware search over encrypted outsourced data in cloud. In: IEEE International Conference on Computer Communications, pp. 1–9. IEEE Press, Brest (2016)
9. Xia, Z., Lv, R., Zhu, Y., Ji, P., Sun, H., Shi, Y.Q.: Fingerprint liveness detection using gradient-based texture features. Sig. Image Video Proc. **11**, 381–388 (2017)
10. Chen, X., Sun, X., Zhou, Z., Zhang, J.: Reversible watermarking method based on asymmetric-histogram shifting of prediction errors. J. Syst. Softw. **86**, 2620–2626 (2013)
11. Liao, X., Shu, C.: Reversible data hiding in encrypted images based on absolute mean difference of multiple neighboring pixels. J. Vis. Commun. Image Representation **28**, 21–27 (2015)
12. Anderson, R.J., Petitcolas, F.A.: On the limits of steganography. IEEE J. Sel. Areas Commun. **16**, 474–481 (1998)
13. Cox, I.J., Miller, M.L., Bloom, J.A., Fridrich, J., Kalker, T.: Digital Watermarking and Steganography, 2nd edn. Morgan Kaufmann, San Francisco (2008)
14. Fridrich, J.: Minimizing the embedding impact in steganography. In: 8th ACM Workshop Multimedia Secur, Geneva, Switzerland, pp. 2–10 (2006)
15. Filler, T., Judas, J., Fridrich, J.: Minimizing additive distortion in steganography using syndrome-trellis codes. IEEE Trans. Inf. Forensics Secur. **6**, 920–935 (2011)
16. Pevný, T., Filler, T., Bas, P.: Using high-dimensional image models to perform highly undetectable steganography. In: Böhme, R., Fong, P.W.L., Safavi-Naini, R. (eds.) IH 2010. LNCS, vol. 6387, pp. 161–177. Springer, Heidelberg (2010). doi:10.1007/978-3-642-16435-4_13
17. Holub, V., Fridrich, J.: Designing steganographic distortion using directional filters. In: 2012 IEEE International Workshop on Information Forensics and Security, pp. 234–239. IEEE Press, Tenerife (2012)
18. Liao, X., Chen, G., Li, Q.: Improved WOW adaptive image steganography method. In: 15th IEEE International Conference on Algorithms and Architectures for Parallel Processing, pp. 685–702. IEEE Press, ChangSha (2015)

19. Holub, V., Fridrich, J., Denemark, T.: Universal distortion function for steganography in an arbitrary domain. EURASIP J. Inf. Secur. **2014**, 1–13 (2014)
20. Li, B., Wang, M., Huang, J., Li, X.: A new cost function for spatial image steganography. In: IEEE International Conference on Image Process, pp. 4026–4210. IEEE Press, Paris (2014)
21. Li, B., Wang, M., Li, X., Tan, S.: A strategy of clustering modification directions in spatial image steganography. IEEE Trans. Inf. Forensics Secur. **10**, 1905–1917 (2015)
22. Hong, W.: Adaptive image data hiding in edges using patched reference table and pair-wise embedding technique. Inf. Sci. **221**, 473–489 (2013)
23. Bas, P., Filler, T., Pevný, T.: "Break Our Steganographic System": the ins and outs of organizing BOSS. In: Filler, T., Pevný, T., Craver, S., Ker, A. (eds.) IH 2011. LNCS, vol. 6958, pp. 59–70. Springer, Heidelberg (2011). doi:10.1007/978-3-642-24178-9_5
24. Fridrich, J., Kodovsk, J.: Rich models for steganalysis of digital images. IEEE Trans. Inf. Foren. Secur. **7**, 868–882 (2012)
25. Kodovsk, J., Fridrich, J., Holub, V.: Ensemble classifiers for steganalysis of digital media. IEEE Trans. Inf. Foren. Secur. **7**, 432–444 (2012)

Quantum Computer Simulation on GPU Cluster Incorporating Data Locality

Zhen Li$^{(\boxtimes)}$ and Jiabin Yuan

College of Computer Science and Technology,
Nanjing University of Aeronautics and Astronautics, Nanjing, China
{cristianlee,jbyuan}@nuaa.edu.cn

Abstract. Quantum computer simulation provides researchers with tools for verification of quantum algorithms. GPU (Graphics Processing Units) cluster is an advisable platform for this task. However, the high cost of communication between GPUs makes the simulation inefficiency. To overcome this drawback, we propose the following two methods. (1) A method for GPU cluster quantum simulation to improve the data locality is introduced, and two schemes for data exchanging are proposed. (2) A novel data distribution method for quantum computer simulation on GPU cluster is proposed. Experimental results show that the simulation of 33-qubit Quantum Fourier Transform algorithm using 4 nodes outperforms the serial program of the CPU cluster with a speedup of 129 times.

Keywords: Quantum computer simulation · GPU cluster · High performance computing · CUDA

1 Introduction

In recent years, more and more researchers focused on quantum computation [1], especially on quantum computer physics implementation and quantum algorithm. However, existing technology can't construct a physically stable general purpose quantum computer of large dimensions. Quantum computer simulator on classical computer provides researchers an effective tool for validation of quantum algorithms. But there are bottlenecks in the simulation, due to the exponential increase in the cost of time and space with the growing scale of quantum system [2].

Due to the huge computation ability in GPGPU (General Purpose Graphics Processing unit), several implementations of quantum simulation based on GPGPU have been proposed in the past several years [3–7], these implementations have obtained considerable acceleration compared to the sequential program. However, despite the strong computing power of GPU, memory capacity of GPU limits the scale of the quantum computer simulation. Multi-GPU system can break the bottleneck of memory capacity, but the number of devices on the PCI-E buses in a single-node is limited. Hence, quantum computer simulation based on GPU cluster is proposed in this paper.

© Springer International Publishing AG 2017
X. Sun et al. (Eds.): ICCCS 2017, Part I, LNCS 10602, pp. 85–97, 2017.
https://doi.org/10.1007/978-3-319-68505-2_8

The main bottleneck of GPU cluster computing is communication overhead, the main purpose of our research is to reduce communication frequency and the amount of communication data during the simulation, this is the major challenge of our research too.

The main contribution of this paper is: We show that quantum computers can be efficiently simulated on GPU cluster. To achieve this goal, we introduce a data locality method for GPU cluster and propose two schemes for exchanging qubits. Then we propose a novel data distribution method, which can reduce the communication frequency.

This paper is organized as follows. In Sect. 2, the related work is described. We introduce the reader to the fundamentals of quantum computing in Sect. 3. We present the method and implementation of the simulator in Sect. 4. Section 5 presents our experiments to evaluate our design. Conclusions are summarized in Sect. 6.

2 Related Work

A wide list of quantum computer simulators has been developed, there are also some significant works of quantum computer simulation based on GPUs. The following is a brief introduction of some prominent work [8–10].

Simulations proposed in [6] run over a single GPU with a number of optimizations for Quantum Fourier Transform (QFT) against CUDA architecture. They obtained speedup of about 160 times compared with CPU implementation. In [4], simulations were executed in NVIDIA GeForce 8800 GTX GPU and Intel Core2 6400@2.13 GHz, a speed up of 95 times at most against sequential code was achieved, a register up to 26-qubit can be simulated. In [3], two workflows for Grover algorithm are proposed and four versions of simulations were implemented on a NVIDIA Tesla C2050 GPU and CUDA 3.2 programming model, experimental results showed that the distinguished program on CUDA obtained a speedup of up to 23 times against the serial program. More recently, in [7], several simulations are tested and compared on one node using four NVIDIA K20c GPUs gains a performance ratio of 358, compared to serial implementation of libquantum [11], the parallel efficiency is 0.92. Restricted by the storage space of a single node, the prior works have limitations in simulation scale.

3 Background

3.1 Quantum Computing

The qubit is the elementary storage unit of a quantum computer, which can be described by a two-dimensional state vector in Diracs notation [12]:

$$|\psi> = \alpha|0> + \beta|1> \tag{1}$$

Where the coefficients represent the amplitudes of the states, and α and β verify

$$|\alpha|^2 + |\beta|^2 = 1. \tag{2}$$

The coefficients are complex numbers that indicate the probability of measuring $|0>$ or $|1>$. The state of a quantum system with W qubits is described by a state vector, which can be written as

$$|\Psi> = \sum_{i=0}^{2^W-1} \alpha_i |i> verify \sum_{i=0}^{2^W-1} |\alpha_i|^2 = 1 \tag{3}$$

A quantum algorithm is corresponding to a set of unitary transformations (quantum gates) on Ψ, the unitary transformation is defined by square matrices of order W, each unitary transformation U operating on Ψ will lead to a transformation of the amplitudes of the states in Ψ, we can denote the transformation as

$$|\Psi'> = U \otimes \Psi = \sum_{i=0}^{2^W-1} \alpha_i' |i> \tag{4}$$

Detailed introduction to quantum gates refers to [1, 12]. We implement the simulator base on the fact that singe qubit gates and the CNOT gate can construct a universal quantum computer [1].

From the previous study [2], considering the operation of a single-qubit gate on qubit j, the amplitude of $|k> \alpha_k'$ can be computed from α_k and $\alpha_{k\oplus2^j}$, a two-qubit operation on control qubit j and target qubit t, the amplitude α_k' can be computed with α_k and $\alpha_{k\oplus2^t}$, similarly, three-qubit gates where qubit j and qubit l are the control bit and qubit t is the target bit, the amplitude α_k is also determined by α_k and $\alpha_{k\oplus2^t}$.

3.2 GPU Cluster

A GPU cluster is a computer cluster in which each node is equipped with several GPUs, the types of interconnects include Gigabit Ethernet and InfiniBand etc. [13]. In this paper, the type of interconnect we studied is InfiniBand. We employ the Message Passing Interface (MPI) [14] for data transfer between nodes, and Compute Unified Device Architecture (CUDA) [15] for GPU computing, in this model, CPU is in charge of control and computations are performed on GPU. Data transmission inside node is much faster than between nodes, despite the use of Infiniband.

4 Quantum Computer Simulation on GPU Cluster

Different from the traditional cluster, GPU cluster is a heterogeneous system in which there are several types of communication modes. In response to this feature, we propose a new method to reduce the communications and data transfer frequencies.

4.1   Data Locality Method

We assume that the GPU cluster consists of 2^M nodes and 2^D GPU devices in each node and each device can store 2^L amplitudes of the states. We allocate one MPI process for each node, then each node has a MPI rank $a_m(m \subseteq (0, M-1), m \subseteq Z)$ and each GPU device in the node has a device rank a_{d_n} $(d_n \subseteq (0, D-1), d_n \subseteq Z)$, then each device has a global rank $a_d = a_m * 2^D + a_{d_n}$ throughout the system. In binary notation, the address of a amplitude consists of its local address $L = (x_{L-1}...x_0)$ and the rank of GPU where it stored $R = (x_{(M+D-1)}...x_0)$.

As can be seen from Sect. 3.1, performing a quantum gate on qubit j requires to update 2^{L+D+M} amplitudes. If $j < L$ we call qubit j a local bit and there are no communication during the operation. If $j \geq L$ and $j < L + D$, the operation requires communication between GPUs, we call qubit j an inside-node nonlocal (IN) qubit. Similarly, if $j \geq L + D$, communication between MPI processes is required, we call qubit j a outside-node nonlocal (ON) qubit. As shown in Sect. 3.2, data transfer speed of IN is much faster than ON. A simple method of communication is that each pairs of GPUs interchange one half of their data, then perform the quantum gate and interchange one half of their data again, an obvious drawback of this method is that half of the amplitudes has to be interchanged twice for performing a quantum gate on a nonlocal qubit. An example of a GPU cluster in the case of L = 2, M = 1, D = 2 is shown in Fig. 1. Each node has 2^2 GPU, then qubit 3 and qubit 2 is an inside-node nonlocal qubit and qubit 4 is an outside-node nonlocal qubit, the others are local qubit.

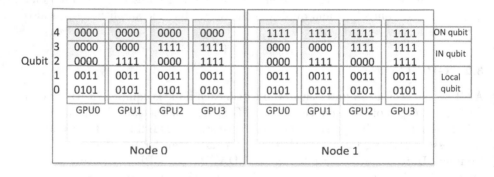

Fig. 1. A GPU cluster of 2 nodes and 8 GPU devices

In order to reduce the communications of the GPU cluster, we expand the method used in the supercomputer [2] to GPU cluster. We apply the method that swapping the nonlocal qubits with local qubits. The method is to swap k local qubits in $L = \{l_0, l_1...l_k\}$ with k nonlocal qubits in $R = \{r_0, r_1...r_k\}$ and the other qubits remain unchanged. Due to the differences between GPU cluster and supercomputer, the process of swap local and nonlocal qubits on GPU cluster is quite different from supercomputer. More specifically, we assume exchange k pairs of local and nonlocal qubits, and the k nonlocal qubits consist of k_n ON qubits and $k - k_n$ IN qubits, we need to interchange amplitudes at

$(*...*l_0...*1...*k...*)$ of GPU with rank $(*...*r_0*...*r_1*...*r_{k-k_n-1}*...*)$ in node with rank $(*...*r_{k-k_n}*...*r_k*...*)$

with amplitudes at

$(*...*r_0*...*r_1*...*r_k*...*)$ of GPU with rank $(*...*l_0*...*l_1*...*l_{k-k_n-1}*...*)$ in node with rank $(*...*l_{k-k_n}*...*l_k*...*)$ where $(l_0l_1...l_k) \neq (r_0r_1...r_k)$.

We perform the exchanging of qubits in three steps. Step 1, copy data from devices to hosts. Step 2, reorder and package the data, then transfer data between nodes. Step 3, distribute data from hosts to devices. After step 1, the amplitudes will be stored in memory sequentially. Hence, in step 2, the node with rank $(*...*r_{k-k_n}*...*r_k*...*)$ need to send 2^{L+D-k_n} amplitudes to the node with rank $(*...*l_{k-k_n}*...*l_k*...*)$ where $(l_{k-k_n}...l_k) \neq (r_{k-k_n}...r_k)$, the nodes, where the corresponding positions of the asterisks are the same, are divided into a group, each node is required to communicate with the others in the group, so $2^{k_n} - 1$ buffer of 2^{L+D-k_n} size is required, each buffer needs to be sent to a node in the group. And the data need to be reordered, exactly, host address of amplitude at $(*...*l_0*...*l_k*...*r_0*...r_{k_{n-1}}**)$ should be changed to $(*...*r_0*...*r_k*...*l_0*...l_{k_{n-1}}*...*)$. Two schemes of step 2 are proposed in this paper.

- Scheme A.
  - Compute the rank of nodes in the group.
  - Reorder the amplitudes in the host by exchange the amplitudes at $(*...*l_0*...*l_1*...*l_{k-k_n-1}*...*r_0*...*r_1*...*r_{k-k_n-1}*...*)$ with the amplitudes at $(*...*r_0*...*r_1*...*r_{k-k_n-1}*...*l_0*...*l_1*...*l_{k-k_n-1}*...*)$ where $(l_0l_1...l_{k-k_n-1}) \neq (r_0r_1...r_{k-k_n-1})$.
  - Store the amplitude in the buffer corresponds to the target node, the amplitude is stored sequentially.
  - Send the buffer and each node receive the data from the others in the group, put the amplitudes to corresponding place where they should be.
- Scheme B.
  - Compute the rank of nodes in the group.
  - In host with rank $(*...*r_{k-k_n}*...*r_k*...*)$, store the amplitudes at $A = (*...*l_0*...*l_k*...*r_0*...*r_{k-k_n-1}*...*)$ in the buffer $(r_{k-k_n}...r_k)$ at address $S = (*...*r_0*...*r_{k-k_n-1}*...*l_0*...*l_{k_{n-1}}*...*)$, the bits $(r_{k-k_n}...r_k)$ of A' are directly removed from the address, and the other bits remain unchanged.
  - Send the buffer and each node receive the data from the others in the group, the amplitude at address S in the receive buffer with rank $(r_{k-k_n}...r_k)$ should be copied to local address $A' = (*...*r_0*...*r_k*...*l_0*...*l_{k_{n-1}}*...*)$.

Scheme B has eliminated the induction variable, so we can use GPUs to accelerate the major computation steps and the process can be executed parallel.

Exchanging k pairs local and nonlocal qubits sequentially needs each GPU to send $k2^{L-1}$ amplitudes to another GPU. Exchanging k pairs nonlocal and local qubits at once needs each GPU to send $(2^k - 1)2^{(L-k)}$ amplitudes to another GPU, the larger the k is, the communication is less.

4.2 Improved Data Distribution Method

At the beginning of simulation, the simulator will read the quantum circuit of the quantum algorithm to be simulated. We will improve the data distribution according to the quantum circuit. After swapping local and nonlocal qubits, the nonlocal qubits are local, so we consider the continuous operations on the same qubit as a single access to the qubit. Thus, we can get an access list of the quantum algorithm. An example of quantum circuit to perform a quantum Fourier transform (QFT) on five qubits is illustrated in Fig. 2. In this case, the access list will be $AL = \{4, 3, 2, 1, 0\}$. On the basis of this, we propose a method to improve the data distribution. We go through the access list $AL = \{x_k...x_0\}$ and localize the first accessed L qubits $FAL = \{x'_{L-1}...x'_0\}$ in initialization, we assume that original mapping of the qubits is $\{x_{M+D+L-1}...x_{L-1}...x_1, x_0\}$, and $\{x_{L-1}...x_1x_0\}$ are local qubits and the others are nonlocal, after the exchange of qubits, the mapping will be $\{x'_0x'_{L-1}x'_{M+D+L-1}\}$, so the permutation of qubits is

$$\varphi = \begin{pmatrix} x'_0 & ... & x'_{L-1} & ... & x'_{M+D+L-1} \\ x_0 & ... & x_{L-1} & ... & x_{M+D+L-1} \end{pmatrix} \tag{5}$$

then we will initialize data on each GPU according to the permutation φ, the amplitude $(x'_0...x'_{M+D+L-1})$ is distributed to GPU with rank $(x'_L...x'_{M+D+L-1})$ at address$(x'_0...x'_{L-1})$.

Use Fig. 2 as an example for L = 3, M = 1, D = 1, the qubits $\{0, 1, 2\}$ are local qubits, and others are nonlocal qubits, we can get the first accessed 3 qubits $FAL = \{4, 3, 2\}$, and the permutation of qubits is $\varphi = \begin{pmatrix} 1\,0\,2\,4\,3 \\ 4\,3\,2\,1\,0 \end{pmatrix}$, so we distribute amplitude $\{x_4x_3x_2x_1x_0\}$ to address $\{x_3x_4x_2\}$ on GPU with rank $\{x_0\}$ on node with rank $\{x_1\}$ as shown in Fig. 3, the dotted line in the figure indicates the association between data while a gate is performed on qubit 4, so operation of qubit 4 can be performed without communications.

During the simulation, every time a quantum gate operates on a nonlocal qubit, an exchange of local and nonlocal qubits is required, similarly, we traverse the rest of the access list and localize the first accessed L qubits. There are two cases when swapping local and nonlocal qubits. 1. The swap list contains ON qubits. Communications between nodes are required. 2. The swap list contains only IN qubits. We need to transfer data from devices to host and reorder the data, then distribute data to devices. After that, the nonlocal qubit will be localized.

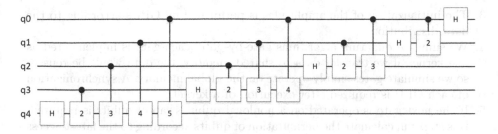

Fig. 2. Quantum circuit of QFT on five qubits

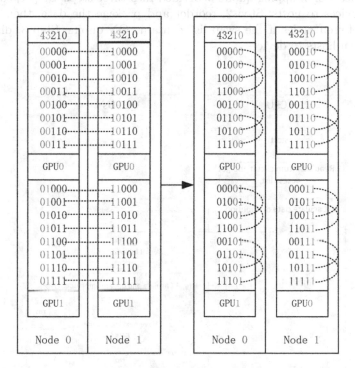

Fig. 3. Initial data distribution for L = 3, M = 1, D = 1

4.3   Workflow of the Simulator

Our implementation is based on the method proposed in Sect. 4. The workflow of the quantum simulator is illustrated in Fig. 4.

The key steps with sequence number in the figure are explained as follows:

1. We use a formatted file that contains pseudocode of quantum circuit as an input of the simulator. We will calculate the access list while reading the circuit, the list will be updated throughout the simulation process.
2. The data distribution is got from the access list.

3. The initialization of the amplitudes is performed on GPUs according to the data distribution.
4. We simulate quantum algorithms gate-by-gate, each gate is implemented as one kernel, if we transfer data to shared memory, the data won't be reused, so we simulate gates simply operate on the global memory. A synchronization of each GPU is required after execution of a kernel.
5. If the next gate is operated on a nonlocal qubit, swap of qubits is required, this step will calculate the permutation of qubits according to the latest access list.
6. The process of swapping qubits is divided into three steps. Step 1, copy data from devices to hosts. Step 2, reorder and package the data, then transfer data between nodes if the swap list contains ON qubits. Step 3, distribute data from hosts to devices.

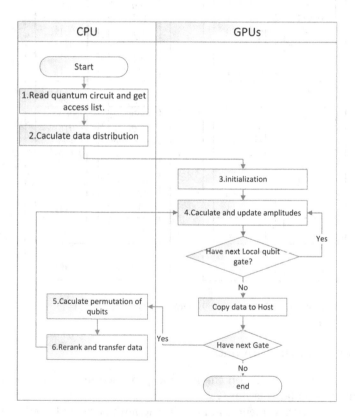

Fig. 4. Workflow of the quantum simulator

5 Experiments

In this section, we present and analyze the experimental results of the quantum computer simulator based on a GPU cluster with 4 nodes. Tables 1 and 2 show the hardware configurations. The CUDA version is 7.5.

Table 1. Hardware configurations (one node)

	Model	Memory	Device num
CPU	Intel(R) Xeon(R) CPU E5-2609 v2 @ 2.50 GHz	64 GB	2
GPU	Nvidia Tesla K20 m	4.68 GB	4

Table 2. Bandwidth

	Bandwidth
Device to device	146774.3 MB/s
Device to host	6553.6 MB/s
Host to device	6104.8 MB/s
Host to host (Infiniband)	1473.44 MB/s

5.1 Experimental Programs

We use Quantum Fourier Transform to evaluate the simulator, we implemented the following 3 programs to evaluate the method described above.

- Program 1(P1). The simulator is implemented without the improved data distribution according to data reorder scheme A.
- Program 2(P2). The simulator is implemented with the improved data distribution according to data reorder scheme A.
- Program 3(P3). The simulator is implemented with the improved data distribution according to data reorder scheme B.

The block sizes of the three programs are 512. In order to achieve a high bandwidth of the Infiniband, we split and send the buffer in a fixed size (2 GB in our experiments) each time when the buffer is too large.

5.2 Performance Comparisons

In this section, we analyze the performance of the three programs through the runtime and speed-up radio compared to the serial code on a CPU cluster, the steps of each program are the same.

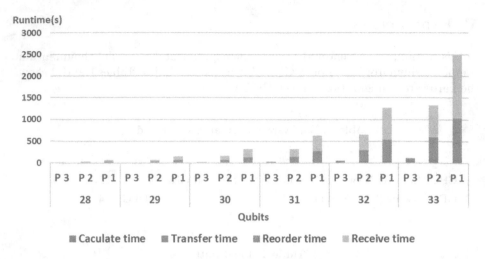

Fig. 5. Runtime of three programs on 4 nodes.

We mainly focus on the simulation above 28 qubits, Fig. 5 shows the runtime of the three programs on a GPU cluster with 4 nodes, the runtime is divided into four parts: computing time, data transfer, data reorder and data receive. As shown in Fig. 5, simulations with GPU cluster cannot change the fact that cost of time grows exponentially with the growth of the simulation scale. Due to the limitation of memory size on GPU, the largest size of qubits can be simulated on one node is 31. With the improved data distribution method, simulation of QFT algorithm requires only one time of swap of qubits but P1 requires twice, so P2 has a performance advantage over P1, as we can see from Fig. 5, data reorder and data receive are bottlenecks of P2 and P1, however, scheme B has eliminated the bottleneck, so P3 has the best performance.

Speed-up radio is computed by T_{CPU}/T_{GPU}, T_{CPU} is the runtime of serial codes on CPU cluster, and T_{GPU} is the runtime of GPU programs. Table 3 shows the runtime of CPU and GPU programs. As shown in the table, the speed-up radio of P3 on 4 nodes reaches 129 for the simulation of 33 qubits.

5.3   Parallel Efficiency

The Parallel efficiency is computed by $\eta = T_{time}(1)/(T_{time}(N) \times N)$, $T_{time}(1)$ represents the runtime on 1 node, and $T_{time}(N)$ is the runtime on N nodes. As shown in Fig. 6, the parallel efficiency of 4 nodes is lower than 2 nodes, due to the increase of communication, and despite the calculate time is reduced, but the other overheads are still equal.

Table 3. Runtime of CPU and GPU (P3)

Qubits	N_{node}	$T_{CPU}(s)$	$T_{GPU}(s)$	Speed-up (T_{CPU}/T_{GPU})
28	1	1084.797	8.55	126.87
	2	712.8	5.13	138.94
	4	359.57	2.98	120.66
29	1	2304	17.85	129.07
	2	1537.4	10.9	141.04
	4	750.4	6.15	122.01
30	1	4897.3	37.18	131.71
	2	3119.7	22.1	141.16
	4	1575.96	12.4	127.09
31	1	10423.5	79.5	131.11
	2	6714.02	46.7	143.76
	4	3463.9	26.4	131.20
32	1	-	-	-
	2	14533.8	98.8	147.10
	4	7241.76	55	131.66
33	1	-	-	-
	2	-	-	-
	4	15468.56	119.6	129.33

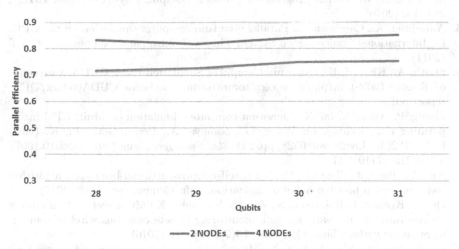

Fig. 6. Parallel efficiency on GPU cluster

6 Conclusion

Approaches to the simulation of a universal quantum computer using GPU cluster with NVIDIA GPUs have been proposed and analyzed in this paper.

We introduce a method for GPU cluster quantum simulation to improve the data locality, and two schemes for data exchanging are proposed. Afterwards we propose a novel data distribution method for quantum computer simulation on GPU cluster, which can reduce the communication frequency, then we put forward an implementation scheme for GPU cluster. The experimental results show that the proposed methods are able to obtain a better performance. An ideal quantum computer simulator of up to 33 qubits can be simulated on the GPU cluster, the performance radio of performing the Quantum Fourier Transform algorithm achieves 129 on 4 nodes.

Acknowledgments. This work was supported by Funding of National Natural Science Foundation of China (Grant Nos. 61571226), Natural Science Foundation of Jiangsu Province, China (Grant Nos. BK20140823).

References

1. Nielsen, M.A., Chuang, I.L.: Quantum Computation and Quantum Information. Cambridge University Press, Cambridge (2000)
2. De Raedt, K., et al.: Massively parallel quantum computer simulator. Comput. Phys. Commun. **176**(2), 121–136 (2007)
3. Lu, X., Yuan, J., Zhang, W.: Workflow of the Grover algorithm simulation incorporating CUDA and GPGPU. Comput. Phys. Commun. **184**(9), 2035–2041 (2013)
4. Gutirrez, E., Romero, S., Trenas, M.A., Zapata, E.L.: Quantum computer simulation using the CUDA programming model. Comput. Phys. Commun. **181**(2), 283–300 (2010)
5. Amariutei, A., Caraiman, S.: Parallel quantum computer simulation on the GPU. In: International Conference on System Theory, Control, and Computing, pp. 1–6 (2011)
6. Smith, A., Khavari, K.: Quantum Computer Simulation Using CUDA. University of Toronto (2009). http://www.eecg.toronto.edu/*moshovos/CUDA08/arx/QFT_report.pdf
7. Zhang, P., Yuan, J., Lu, X.: Quantum computer simulation on Multi-GPU incorporating data locality. In: Wang, G., Zomaya, A., Perez, G.M., Li, K. (eds.) ICA3PP 2015. LNCS, vol. 9528, pp. 241–256. Springer, Cham (2015). doi:10.1007/978-3-319-27119-4_17
8. Xue, Y., Jiang, J., Zhao, B., Ma, T.: A self-adaptive artificial bee colony algorithm based on global best for global optimization. Soft. Comput. pp. 1–18 (2017)
9. Qu, Z., Keeney, J., Robitzsch, S., Zaman, F., Wang, X.: Multilevel pattern mining architecture for automatic network monitoring in heterogeneous wireless communication networks. China. Commun. **13**(7), 108–116 (2016)
10. Fu, Z., Ren, K., Shu, J., Sun, X., Huang, F.: Enabling personalized search over encrypted outsourced data with efficiency improvement. IEEE. Trans. Parallel Distrb. **27**(9), 2546–2559 (2016)
11. Butscher, B., Weimer, H.: Libquantum library. http://www.libquantum.de
12. Deutsch, D.: Quantum computational networks. In: Proceedings of the Royal Society of London A: Mathematical, Physical and Engineering Sciences, vol. 425, pp. 73–90. The Royal Society (1989)

13. Kindratenko, V.V., Enos, J.J., Shi, G., Showerman, M.T.: GPU clusters for high-performance computing. In: IEEE International Conference on CLUSTER Computing and Workshops, pp. 1–8. IEEE Press (2009)
14. Message Passing Interface Forum. http://www.mpi-forum.org
15. NVIDIA CUDA: programming guide, and SDK. http://www.nvidia.com/cuda

Tampering Detection in Oral History Video Using Watermarking

Jianfeng Lu, Peng Gao, Shanqing Zhang, Li Li, Wenqiang Yuan,
and Qili Zhou$^{(\boxtimes)}$

School of Computer Science and Technology, Hangzhou Dianzi University,
Hangzhou 310018, China
{jflu,sqzhang,lili2008,wqyuan,zql}@hdu.edu.cn, 67222166@163.com

Abstract. The oral history videos present highly cultural and historical values. The protection of its authenticity and integrity are important. A lot of video watermarking schemes are proposed to prevent malicious attacks in recent years. An innovative algorithm is proposed in
this work to resist key frames dropping and detect the subtitle tampered. Firstly, Simple Linear Iterative Clustering (SLIC) Superpixels are
used to extract the natural codes of the video. Meanwhile, the targeting
codes are obtained from the natural codes which are modified by the
(7, 4) Hamming code error correction for identifying the watermarked
frame. Secondly, the text region is located accurately by structure tensor
and subtitle segmentation. Furthermore, the watermark information is
composed of stroke and structural characteristic of Chinese characters.
Finally, the watermark is embedded into the oral history videos based
on Discrete Cosine Transform (DCT) and Singular Value Decomposition
(SVD) robustly. The experimental results show the algorithm is against
to several attacks including tampering texts, frames dropping and compression.

Keywords: Video watermarking · SLIC · Structure tensor

1 Introduction

Video has become a part of our lives. At the same time, some serious problems
are exposed in the video application field, such as the copyright infringement
and content tampering by changing the subtitles of the video. Specifically, the
Chinese oral history video is for storage and inheritance of intangible cultural
heritage. These videos have taken much time and money of the interviews and
are precious because some of the entertainers have been dead. The watermarking
is an effective method for the copyright protection and detection of malicious
tampering.

Nowadays, many methods related to video watermarking are designed. Mehdi
et al. [1] proposed a method to detect video tampering. The watermarks consist of the indexes of macro-blocks and frames are embedded into the nonzero
quantized DCT value of blocks. This strategy is useful to distinguish malicious

X. Sun et al. (Eds.): ICCCS 2017, Part I, LNCS 10602, pp. 98–109, 2017.
https://doi.org/10.1007/978-3-319-68505-2_9

tampering. Antonio et al. [2] designed a video watermarking scheme based on Human Visual System (HVS). It is robust to Gaussian noise contamination, impulsive noise contamination, Gaussian low-pass filter and volumetric scaling attacks. Xu et al. [3] proposed a content-based authentication watermarking scheme. The authentication code is embedded into the DCT coefficients in diagonal positions using a modulation method. It is robust to some attacks such as recompression, Gaussian noise, brightness increase and robust to spatial tampering. Chen et al. [4] proposed a slope-based video watermarking algorithm. The four values are found from four consecutive frames to denote a vector. A watermarking algorithm is presented based on 1D DFT along temporal direction and Radon transform [5].

The aforementioned methods are robust to video compression, geometric transformation, frame swapping and frame lost etc. However, they cannot be used to detect subtitle tampering. Actually, Existing methods for subtitle detection can be roughly categorized into three major groups: connected component (CC) based methods, edge characteristics-based methods and texture characteristics based methods. Jie et al. [6] propose a novel subtitle lines detection method based on Maximal Stable Extremal Region (MSER), CC based methods usually perform well for subtitle that have uniform color and regular spacing; However, CCs may not preserve the full shapes of characters due to color bleeding and the low contrast of subtitle lines [7]. Lyu et al. [8] detected video subtitle using Sobel edge features and Chen et al. [9] used Canny edge features and a morphological close operation to detect video subtitle. But they produce many false positives when the background is complex. To overcome this problem, texture features are utilized to detect text in video frames [10], Traditional subtitle detection schemes based on texture feature mainly through the DCT, the wavelet transform and Gabor filter [11–13] to describe texture feature of video subtitle. However, these methods have the decisive drawback to induce a lot of redundancy and produce many feature channels. To overcome these problem, subtitle detection method by texture descriptor based on structure tensor has proposed [14,15].

With the purpose of detecting subtitle tampering, a novel video watermarking algorithm is proposed in this work. The contributions of this work are mainly two points. Firstly, to resist temporal tampering the frame location method based on Hamming code correction is proposed. This approach guarantees that the watermark information can be extracted by identifying watermarked frame. Secondly, the tampering detection method based on subtitle has been proposed to protect video copyright, which utilizes structure tensor and subtitle segmentation to extract stroke and structural characteristic of Chinese characters.

2   Related Works

In the field of computer vision, Superpixels division is typically used for edge detection. (7, 4) Hamming code in the tradition is mainly applied to parity when errors occur during transmission and reception. In this work, we use SLIC Superpixels to extract natural codes X. Then we use X and Hamming error correction mechanism to embed targeting codes for resisting temporal tampering.

2.1 SLIC Superpixels

In this section, Superpixels [16] take a series of adjacent position and the color, brightness, texture into consideration. The cluster centers of segmentations regions are stable by SLIC Superpixels algorithm. Compared with K-means, SLIC Superpixels have a significant speed advantage. In this paper, we use SLIC method to extract its natural codes X (X is a 7-bit sequence with 0 and 1) of video frames. This method is effective to resist attacks of frame dropping, frames insertion and recoding.

2.2 (7, 4) Hamming Coding

Hamming codes are used to detect and correct one error in a block of bits. The (7, 4) Hamming code encodes four data bits $d = (d_1, d_2, d_3, d_4)$ into seven cover bits X (also called a code) by adding three parity bits (c_1, c_2, c_3). The general algorithm positions the parity bits behind the data bits. So, the formed transmitted code can be $(d_1, d_2, d_3, d_4, c_1, c_2, c_3)$. In this work, the targeting codes are embedded with Hamming error correction mechanism.

3 Targeting Codes for Identification the Watermarked Frames

SLIC Superpixels and (7, 4) Hamming code are used to resist compression, temporal tampering such as frame insertion, recoding, frame rate changing and so on. The targeting codes are used to identify the watermarked frame to guarantee that the watermark information can be extracted.

3.1 Generation of Targeting Code

Figure 1 shows the detailed flowchart of the generation process of targeting code, which mainly consists of the following steps:

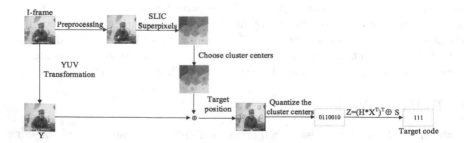

Fig. 1. Flowchart of the generation process of targeting code.

Step 1. Image preprocessing and the SLIC Superpixels to get cluster center.

Conduct a simple pretreatment process in order to promote the subsequent segmentation process. Then the chosen frame is decomposed into 9 segmentations and 7 cluster centers chosen according to sample rules by SLIC Superpixels.

Step 2. Quantized coordinates and get natural codes X.

Quantize the coordinates of seven cluster centers in order to improve the robustness. Then the seven pixel values with the mean of the luminance channel is com-pared, if the former is larger the result is 1, otherwise is 0. The feature sequence X is obtained.

Step 3. Combination of X and Hamming codes to embed targeting codes.

Combine (7, 4) Hamming code with the computed (0–1) sequence in Step 2 to form targeting codes S.

An example is used to show the embedding of targeting code S. Firstly, the natural codes X (i.e. $X = (1010111)$) is computed by image preprocessing, SLIC Superpixels and quantization. The parity check matrix H of the Hamming code and the column vector X^T with entries modulo 2, and then the result is transposed to compute the syndrome vector. The parity check matrix H is known, as shown below. The targeting code S is self-defined for identifying the watermarked frame, i.e. $S = (011)$.

$$H = \begin{pmatrix} 0\,0\,0\,1\,1\,1\,1 \\ 0\,1\,1\,0\,0\,1\,1 \\ 1\,0\,1\,0\,1\,0\,1 \end{pmatrix}$$

According to Eq. 1 calculate the syndrome vector:

$$z = (H \times X^T)^T \oplus S = \left(\begin{pmatrix} 0\,0\,0\,1\,1\,1\,1 \\ 0\,1\,1\,0\,0\,1\,1 \\ 1\,0\,1\,0\,1\,0\,1 \end{pmatrix} \times \begin{pmatrix} 1 \\ 0 \\ 1 \\ 0 \\ 1 \\ 1 \\ 1 \end{pmatrix} \right)^T \oplus (0\,1\,1) = (1\,0\,1) = 5 \quad (1)$$

According to Eq. 1, the syndrome vector is converted to decimal, change one bit of X according to the value of decimal. After the modification X is changed from $X = (1010111)$ to $X = (1010011)$. So that the video frame targeting codes S is embedded.

3.2   Effectiveness of Targeting Code

The bit rate of original video is set 80%, 60%, 40% and 20% in four group experiments. Table 1 shows the correct ratio of targeting code extraction before and after the operations of compression, quantization and Gaussian smoothing.

For attacks of frame insertion, frame rate changing and recoding, without any temporal tampering manipulation, the extracted frame number versus the

Table 1. Experimental comparison without and with related attack operations.

Videos	Bit rate	Correct ratio before the operations	Correct ratio before the operations
Sample 1	Original	100%	100%
	80%	83.5%	100%
	60%	76%	100%
	40%	69%	99%
	20%	66%	98.5%
Sample 2	Original	100%	100%
	80%	93.5%	100%
	60%	85.5%	98%
	40%	65.5%	96.5%
	20%	26.5%	96.5%
Sample 3	Original	100%	100%
	80%	92.5%	100%
	60%	57.5%	100%
	40%	55.5%	100%
	20%	32%	95%
Sample 4	Original	100%	100%
	80%	95%	100%
	60%	79%	99%
	40%	50%	98.5%
	20%	24%	95%

observed frame number is shown in Fig. 2. Frame insertion test is performed by inserting 20 frames. There is a jump from 41 to 60 in Fig. 2(a). After the changing process of frame rate, the result is displayed in Fig. 2(b). After recoding process, the result is dis-played in Fig. 2(c).

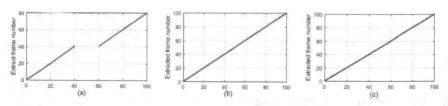

Fig. 2. Temporal tampering: (a) Frame insertion, (b) Frame rate changing, (c) Recoding.

4   Tampering Detection Watermarking Algorithm

In our watermarking scheme, the stroke and structure character of subtitle information extracted by text detection and segmentation are used to generate stability watermark information (Fig. 3).

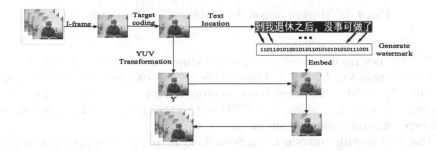

Fig. 3. Flowchart of the watermark embedded

4.1   Watermark Information Generation

The watermark information is based on the stroke feature and structural feature of the Chinese characters. It is necessary to accurately locate the subtitle area in the video and remove background interference by subtitle area segmentation. The accurate subtitle detection method based on structural tensor and morphological operation has been proposed.

Detection and Segmentation of Subtitle Regions

Subtitle Regions Detection. In order to reduce the dimensions of traditional structure tensor (ST), the structure tensor based scalar texture descriptor proposed in [15] is used to represent subtitle regions of video.

For a scalar image, the classical structure tensor is obtained by Gaussian smoothing of the tensor product of the image gradient, i.e.

$$I^{''} = K_\sigma * (\nabla I \nabla I^T) = \begin{pmatrix} K_\sigma * I_x^2 & K_\sigma * I_x I_y \\ K_\sigma * I_x I_y & K_\sigma * I_y^2 \end{pmatrix} \qquad (2)$$

Where K_σ is a Gaussian kernel with standard deviation σ, and subscripts x and y denote the partial derivatives. In [15] proposed a scalars texture descriptor based on eigenvalues of ST as the following:

$$T = \frac{1}{1 + B(\lambda_1 - \lambda_2)^n} \qquad (3)$$

(a)   (b)   (c)

Fig. 4. (a) Original image, (b) ST image, (c) Binarization ST.

T is the descriptor applied to represent video subtitle. B is constant. λ_1 and λ_2 are eigenvalues of I''. $n = 1$. The subtitle regions can be roughly and quickly described by scalar texture descriptor. In order to remove interference of nonsubtitle regions of low gray value, the OTSU method has been used for binarization. The experimental results are shown in Fig. 4.

The final subtitle components are obtained by the horizontal morphological opera-tion open and close which is used to remove isolated points in roughly results.

Subtitle Segmentation. In order to ensure the integrity and quality of subtitle segmentation, the OTSU method is used to segment subtitle on global image and the block is divided into $w \times w$ size. Our method are compared with Qians [11] and Lis [12] methods. Figure 5 shows that our method is more accurate.

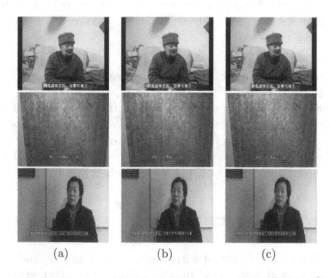

(a)   (b)   (c)

Fig. 5. The results of different methods. (a) Results of Qian's [11], (b) Results of Li's [12], (c) Results of our method

The recall R and the precision P are computed by [12]:

$$R = N_c(N_c + N_m) \tag{4}$$

$$P = N_c(N_c + N_f) \tag{5}$$

where N_c denotes correct detection number, N_m denotes missed detection number and N_f denotes false detection number. The performance comparisons results compared with Qians [11] and Lis [12] method are show in the Table 2. The split comparison results are shown in Table 3. (The results of Table 3 demonstrate our text segmentation method is applicable in video with complex back-grounds.)

Table 2. The performance comparisons between our algorithm and others method.

		Qian's [11]	Li's [12]	Our method
Image1	R(%)	68.56%	95.26%	100.00%
	P(%)	100.00%	91.18%	100.00%
Image2	R(%)	90.63%	63.80%	100.00%
	P(%)	82.80%	100.00%	100.00%
Image1	R(%)	91.67%	93.55%	100.00%
	P(%)	68.46%	46.09%	100.00%

Table 3. The comparisons of different text segmentations.

Original gray image	到我退休之后，没事可做了
Qians [11]	到我退休之后，没事可做了
Lis [12]	到我退休之后，没事可做了
Our algorithm	到我退休之后，没事可做了

Watermarking Generation. The text result obtained by the above detection and segmentation methods can be used to generate the video watermarking information. Each Chinese character generated with above segmentation method in the text regions will be normalized to a block that is 24×24. Each Chinese character is signed by 34 bits with the rule as follow:

Step 1. The percentage of Chinese character in the block is used to generate 2 bits (00 under 25%; 01 under 26%–50%; 10 under 51%–75%; 11 under 75%–100%);

Step 2. The block is divided into 4 sub-blocks. The mean value of every sub-blocks is compared with the mean value of block to generate 4 bits ($w = 1$ when value in sub-blocks is bigger; $w = 0$ when otherwise);

Step 3. The sub-blocks are compared with each other in the block. It generates 4 bits;

Step 4. The sub-blocks is divided into 4 micro-blocks. Every micro-blocks is operated as Step 1 and Step 2 to generate 24 bits;

Step 5. Every Chinese character is signed by 34 bits that is generated above;

The watermarking that include all Chinese characters in the frame.

4.2   Watermarking Embedding and Extraction

Watermarking Embedding. To enhance the watermarking robustness, watermarking is embedded into DCT coefficients of luminance channel, which is embedded by the following steps:

Step 1. I frame of GOP is chosen to embed watermark.

Step 2. I frame is divided into channels Y, U, V. The watermark is embedded in Y channel.

Step 3. Y is divided into $8 * 8$ blocks B. A macro-block (MB) includes four blocks.

Step 4. The watermarking bit is embedded into the block whose DC coefficient is biggest of four. The rule of embedding is as follows.

The matrix A is structured as follows.

$$A = \begin{pmatrix} B(0,0) & B(0,1) \\ B(1,0) & B(1,1) \end{pmatrix} \tag{6}$$

$B(x, y)$ is the element of matrix B.

The matrix A is processed according to SVD decomposition, and $A = USV^T$. $S(2 \times 2)$ is a diagonal matrix that is sorted by value. The watermark information is embedded into the biggest element $S(0,0)$, which is given by

$$C(0,0) = S(0,0)/\lambda \tag{7}$$

$$\begin{cases} C(0,0) = C(0,0) + 1 & w = 0, C(0,0)\%2! = 0 \\ C(0,0) = C(0,0) + 1 & w = 0, C(0,0)\%2 == 0 \\ C(0,0) = C(0,0) & else \end{cases} \tag{8}$$

w is one watermarking bit. λ is the quantization step. According to experimental results, the optimum value of λ is 15.

Watermarking Extraction. Extraction is opposite processing of embedding.

Step 1. I frame of GOP is chosen to extract watermarking.

Step 2. I frame is divided channels Y, U, V. The watermarking is extracted in Y channel.

Step 3. Y is divided into 8×8 blocks B. A macro-block (MB) includes four blocks.

Step 4. Repeat processing steps to find $C(0,0)$. Watermarks are detected as following:

$$w = \begin{cases} 0, & C(0,0)\%2 = 0 \\ 1, & C(0,0)\%2 = 1 \end{cases} \tag{9}$$

Watermarks are compared with the information generated by text region in current frame to detect the tampered subtitles.

5 Experimental Results and Analysis

Some experiments are performed to evaluate the robustness of our algorithm. The experiment data that is from the videos (see Fig. 6) are analyzed as follows. Three groups of data are listed for different compression rates in Table 4. BCR (bit correct rate) is to measure that the amount of data of watermarking is extracted successfully. When video is compressed to 80%, the extracted watermarking is close to100%. Even if the compression rate is 60%, the extracted watermarking is close to 95%.

The BCR of tampering detection is 100%. But when tampering proportion is less than 15%, the word that was not tampered is detected. Average FDR (false detection rate) of tampering detected is listed in Table 5. Moreover, some experiments are conducted to analyze the influence of temporal tampering. For watermarking video, temporal tampering can cause serious consequences. Specific temporal tampering are frame dropping, frame adding. After frame alignment operation is executed, the watermarking video can resist temporal tampering in this algorithm. 10 videos are used to experiment about temporal tampering. Table 6 show the average of 10 videos data for frame dropping. Every

Fig. 6. Videos for experiment.

Table 4. BCR of extracted watermarking after compression.

Compression rate	Sample 1	Sample 2	Sample 3
100.0%	100.0%	100.0%	100.0%
80.0%	100.0%	99.6%	100.0%
60.0%	94.7%	93.7%	96.3%
40.0%	59.3%	46.0%	57.3%

Table 5. FDR of tampering detected.

Area of tampering	5%	10%	15%
FDR	48.41%	35.0%	0%

Table 6. Frame dropping.

Dropping rate	Drop I, B, P		Drop B, P	
	BCR of frame alignment mark	BCR of extracted watermarking	BCR of frame alignment mark	BCR of extracted watermarking
0%	100%	100%	100%	100%
5%	94.76%	94.76%	100%	100%
10%	90.71%	90.71%	100%	100%
15%	84.52%	84.52%	100%	100%
20%	80.48%	80.48%	100%	100%
25%	77.38%	77.38%	100%	100%
30%	73.10%	73.10%	100%	100%

video has 500 frames. The related frames executing the operations of frame dropping and adding are randomly selected. All watermarking in a frame that the alignment mark is detected is extracted manually. Thus, BCR of frame alignment mark and BCR of extracted watermarking are the same.

6   Conclusions

This paper proposes a robust watermarking algorithm that is preprocessed by SLIC Superpixels and (7, 4) Hamming coding to resist temporal tampering. The characteristic of subtitle is used to be watermarking that can detect malicious tampering in this algorithm. The experimental results have demonstrated the effectiveness and robustness of the proposed algorithm, which can resist frame dropping and adding.

Acknowledgments. This work was mainly supported by National Natural Science Foundation of China (no. 61370218).

References

1. Fallahpour, M., Shirmohammadi, S., Semsarzadeh, M.: Tampering detection in compressed videos using watermarking. IEEE Trans. Instrument. Measur. **63**, 1057–1072 (2014)
2. Hernandez, A.C., Hernandez, M.C., Vazquez, M.G.: Transcoding resilient video watermarking scheme based on spatio-temporal HVS and DCT. Sig. Process. **97**, 40–54 (2014)
3. Xu, D.W., Wang, R.D., Wang, J.C.: A novel watermarking scheme for H.264/AVC video authentication. Sig. Process. Image Commun. **26**, 267–279 (2011)
4. Chen, H., Zhu, Y.: A robust video watermarking algorithm based on singular value decomposition and slope-based embedding technique. Multimed Tools Appl. **71**, 991–1012 (2014)
5. Liu, Y., Zhao, J.Y.: A new video watermarking algorithm based on 1D DFT and radon transform. Sig. Process. **90**, 626–639 (2010)
6. Yuan, J., Wei, B., Liu, Y.: A method for text line detection in natural images. Multimed Tools Appl. **74**, 859–884 (2015)
7. Yin, X.C., Zuo, Z.Y., Tian, S., Liu, C.L.: Text detection, tracking and recognition in video: a comprehensive survey. IEEE Trans. Image Process. **25**, 2752–2773 (2016). A Publication of the IEEE Signal Processing Society
8. Lyu, M.R., Song, J., Cai, M.: A comprehensive method for multilingual video text detection, localization, and extraction. IEEE Trans. Circ. Syst. Video Technol. **15**, 243–255 (2005)
9. Chen, D., Bourlard, H., Thiran, J.P.: Text identification in complex background using SVM. In: IEEE Computer Society Conference on Computer Vision & Pattern Recognition, pp. 621–626 (2001)
10. Shivakumar, P., Pha, T.Q., Tan, C.L.: Texture-based approach for text detection in images using support vector machines and continuously adaptive mean shift algorithm. IEEE Trans. Pattern Anal. Mach. Intell. **25**, 1631–1639 (2003)
11. Qian, X., Liu, G., Wang, H., Su, R.: Text detection, localization, and tracking in compressed video. Sig. Process. Image Commun. **22**, 752–768 (2007)
12. Li, Z., Liu, G., Qian, X., Guo, D.: Effective and efficient video text extraction using key text points. Let Image Process. **5**, 671–683 (2011)
13. Yi, C., Tian, Y.: Text detection in natural scene images by Stroke Gabor words. In: International Conference on Document Analysis & Recognition, pp. 177–181 (2011)
14. Bigun, J., Granlund, G.H., Wiklund, J.: Multidimensional orientation estimation with applications to texture analysis and optical flow. IEEE Trans. Pattern Anal. Mach. Intell. **13**, 775–790 (1991)
15. Zhang, S.Q., Zhang, K.L.: Texture image segmentation model based on eigenvalues of structure tensor. Acta Electronica Sin. **41**, 1324–1328 (2013)
16. Achanta, R., Shaji, A., Smith, K.: SLIC superpixels compared to state-of-the-art superpixel methods. IEEE Trans. Pattern Anal. Mach. Intell. **34**, 2274–2282 (2012)

Steganalysis with CNN Using Multi-channels Filtered Residuals

Yafei Yuan[1], Wei Lu[1,3(✉)], Bingwen Feng[2], and Jian Weng[2]

[1] School of Data and Computer Science, Sun Yat-Sen University, Guangzhou 510006, China
yuanyaf@mail2.sysu.edu.cn, luwei3@mail.sysu.edu.cn
[2] College of Information Science and Technology, Jinan University, Guangzhou 510632, China
bingwfeng@gmail.com, crytpjweng@gmail.com
[3] State Key Laboratory of Information Security,
Institute of Information Engineering, Chinese Academy of Sciences, Beijing 100093, China

Abstract. In the current study of steganalysis, Convolutional Neural Network (CNN) have attracted many scholars' attention. Recently, some effective CNN architectures have been proposed with better results than traditional Rich Models with Ensemble Classifiers. Inspired by the idea that Rich Models use various types of sub-models to enlarge different characteristics between cover and stego features, a scheme based on multi-channels filtered residuals is proposed for digital image steganalysis in this paper. This paper mainly focus on the stage of image processing, 3 high-pass filtered image residuals are fed to a deep CNN architecture to make full use of the great nonlinear curve fitting capability. As known, deep learning is powerful in pattern recognition, most previous networks only use single type of filtered residuals in steganalysis, varied high-pass filtered residuals can offer stronger features for CNN in this paper. After filtering, the residuals are superposed into a multi-channels residual map before training, this measure can involve a joint optimization of CNN's parameters. But single residual map has no such effect. The experiment results prove that it's an efficient way to provide a better detection performance, achieving an accuracy of 82.02% on Cropped-BOSSBase-1.01 dataset.

Keywords: Steganalysis · CNN · Multi-channels · Residual

1 Introduction

Steganography is an efficient method in the field of information hiding due to hardly detection. Among all the mediums, digital image is the most common and fundamental one, because images always contain massive redundant information where is ideal for embedding secret messages. Steganography can be harmful with the rapid development of Internet, it is more convenient for data sharing and exchange with the help of cloud services [1], therefore, developing some effective steganalysis methods is of great significance.

In the early work of digital image steganography, obvious information disturbance can be produced, such as LSBM [2], make it easy to detect. In order to improve the security,

© Springer International Publishing AG 2017
X. Sun et al. (Eds.): ICCCS 2017, Part I, LNCS 10602, pp. 110–120, 2017.
https://doi.org/10.1007/978-3-319-68505-2_10

some adaptive embedding schemes are proposed [3–7]. EA [3] is one kind of content-adaptive steganographic algorithms, the secret messages are embedded in the edge regions considering visual quality and security. Some adaptive steganographic algorithms with distortion function are proposed after EA, such as HUGO [4], S-UNIWARD [5] and HILL [6]. The distortion function is defined to measure the costs of all changed elements between cover and stego images. These schemes improve the security through minimizing the distortion function, without changing the original images' information as far as possible. It can narrow the difference of features. In addition, adaptive steganographic algorithms seem to embed messages in the region with complex texture where is hard for detection.

Steganalysis has attracted a large amount of attention to against steganography [8, 9]. Traditional machine learning approaches consist of feature extraction and classification, this method is also used in other related fields [10, 11]. Feature extraction is the key to steganalysis, appropriate features can help make a distinction between cover and stego images. SPAM [12], one of the most effective feature extraction algorithms, based on different directions and orders Markov chains, its theorem makes a significant impact on the later algorithm design. In order to resist adaptive steganographic algorithms, Fridrich et al. [13, 14] proposed Rich Models using large amount of sub-features to increase diversity of features to improve detection results. In this kind of features, various image filtered residuals are generated from minmax and spam filters, followed by truncation and quantization operation. After that, co-occurrence matrices from several directions are computed as the final features. During the procedure of feature extraction, the stego noise is easy to disappearbecause of a shortage of enough image representations, Rich Models can compensate for this by catching various types of relationships among neighboring pixels. The adaptive steganographic algorithms are always tend to embedding secret information in complex texture areas, however, it may alter relationships included with Rich Models.

Deep learning has made great success in the field of computer vision due to deep architecture and back-propagation optimization, besides, the help of powerful floating-point computing ability provided by high-performance GPUs. It is based on large data sets, generating millions of neurons to fit samples information. One of the most effective tools of deep learning is CNN [15], which has been introduced in steganalysis [16–23] recently. We propose a new image processing scheme in this paper, introduce multi-channels filtered residuals as the input of CNN.

2   Multi-channels Filtered Residuals in CNN

In 2012, Krizhevsky et al. [15] got a best classification result in the ImageNet competition at that time using a deep CNN architecture and two GPU cards. CNN attracted a lot of attention once again, it was adopted many other fields afterwards. Qian et al. [16] proposed a CNN architecture with five convolutional layers, three fully connected layers and Gaussian activation function, it was the first time for CNN used in steganalysis task. In their network, they adopted a handcraft image processing layer which is not optimized during the training period before the first convolutional layer, it is a kind of high-pass filtering operation. In [21, 22], Shi et al. constructed another CNN with deep architecture and BN (batch normalization) layers [24], whose performance surpass SRM [14].

2.1 Deep CNN Architecture

The framework Shi proposed is shown in Fig. 1. The methods based on CNN combine the traditional handcraft feature extraction and classification, and improve the classification result using back-propagation mechanism. And the scheme of Shi can get a good detection result for the following reasons:

(i) a large number of convolution kernels and deep architecture can hold a good fitting ability. Unlike traditional methods based on image features, CNN prefer to learn structures of image. The networks can hardly converge due to the steganographic message is too weak, deep CNN can detect the message more effectively.

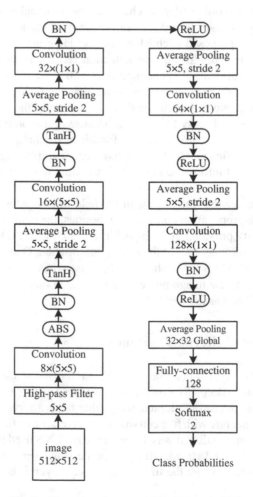

Fig. 1. The network proposed by Shi et al. [21].

(ii) batch normalization layers. Batch normalization constraints the range of feature map as well as accelerates the convergence. The steganographic message is so weak that it doesn't work well in the classification, it can react well with compressing the range of data because batch normalization restrains strong but maybe useless information, the weak information can play a role.

2.2 Filtered Residuals

Traditional image features used in steganalysis are almost based on statistical information, such as Rich Models, containing various kinds of co-occurrence matrices, which is not appropriate for CNN. CNN can be seen as powerful classifier, just like advanced SVM [25, 26]. SVM seems to find a best hyperplane to distinguish between different types of data, it takes features of samples as input. So we conducted extensive

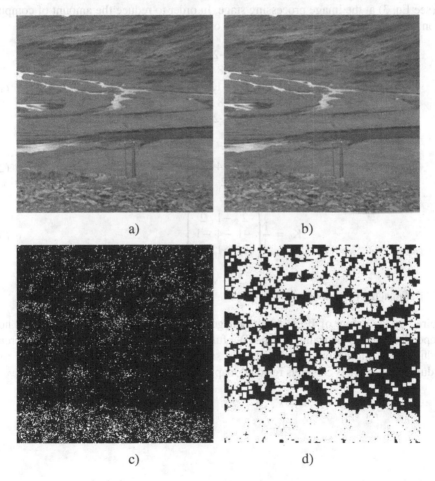

a)   b)

c)   d)

Fig. 2. (a) cover image. (b) stego image. (c) difference between cover and stego images before filtering. (d) difference between cover and stego images after filtering.

experiments on traditional features with CNN, but the results were not satisfied. Compared to SVM, CNN is more like a kind of learners, and have powerful responses to image content, it can fit object's structures with large-scale parameters or neurons. Besides, CNN can take sample data as input, without feature extraction. In previous works, here is image processing before sending to the CNN, it is a high-pass filter also used in SRM. Its kernel can suppress the content of images, enhance the difference between cover and stego images, just as Fig. 2, the white points are the different area. We conclude that the traditional image features are not suitable for CNN to learn, filtered residual can be a good option for steganalysis problem.

As has been proved in [13, 14, 23], various filtered residuals can offer more useful information in classification, helping to improve the result. We introduce various filtered residuals in the image processing stage, the first filter kernel, K_0 (see Eq. 1), was obtained in [27], it has been used in many works [16–19, 21, 22] as well as Rich Models. We selected another high-pass filter kernel K_1 (see Eq. 2) used in SRM and its one variant K_2 (see Eq. 3) at the image processing stage. In order to reduce the amount of computation and promote detection efficiency, we only use 3 residual maps in our works.

$$K_0 = \frac{1}{12} \begin{pmatrix} -1 & 2 & -2 & 2 & -1 \\ 2 & -6 & 8 & -6 & 2 \\ -2 & 8 & -12 & 8 & -2 \\ 2 & -6 & 8 & -6 & 2 \\ -1 & 2 & -2 & 2 & -1 \end{pmatrix} \tag{1}$$

$$K_1 = \frac{1}{4} \begin{pmatrix} -1 & 2 & -1 \\ 2 & -4 & 2 \\ -1 & 2 & -1 \end{pmatrix} \tag{2}$$

$$K_2 = \frac{1}{4} \begin{pmatrix} 2 & -1 & 2 \\ -1 & -4 & -1 \\ 2 & -1 & 2 \end{pmatrix} \tag{3}$$

2.3   Proposed Framework

Inspired by the nature of JPEG format images, we think that the feature maps are not independent during the training stage. We fully take the relationship between different residual maps into account, and propose a scheme to generate a superposition of the residual maps into a 3-channels residual map as the input of CNN (see Fig. 3).

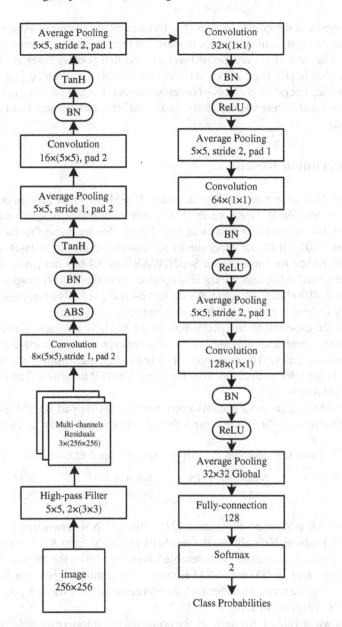

Fig. 3. Proposed CNN architecture using multi-channels filtered residuals.

In our network, the 3 high-pass kernels mentioned in Sect. 2.2 are used to produce different kinds of filtered residuals with size of 256 × 256. The residual maps are superposed into one residual map with 3 channels, followed by a deep learning network. The residuals are not independent at the training stage, multi-channels residuals can involve a joint optimization in the whole stage together, far more effective than one residual map.

As have been mentioned in Sect. 2.1, large number of neurons is one of the keys to good classification results. In order to maintain the number of neurons in our network, the strikes in the first convolutional layer and the first pooling layer are set to 1. Batch normalization is also used in our network, but the bias is disabled just same as Shi's work. Padding operation is involved in certain layers. The last convolutional layer output 128 dimensional feature vector, a fully connected layer and softmax loss function is used afterwards.

3   Experiment Results

We conduct our experiments on the database BOSSBase v1.01 [28], in order to enlarge the dataset, we take the measure in [17], where each image is split into four images. After that, we have 40,000 images of size 256×256, we name this dataset Cropped-BOSSBase-1.01, all of our experiments are conducted on this dataset. In our experiments, we embed the images with S-UNIWARD at 0.4 bits per pixel, the embedding key is not reused. After that, the training database contains 80,000 images (40,000 cover images and 40,000 stego images). We choose 64,000 (32,000 cover/stego pairs) images randomly for training, and the left 16,000 images for validation.

All of the experiments are performed on the publicly available Caffe toolbox [29]. Minibatch gradient descent is used in our experiments, the minibatch size is 128 images (64 cover/stego pairs). The momentum is fixed to 0.9, the learning rate is initialized to 0.001 and scheduled to decrease 10% for every 100,000 iterations. The CNN is trained for 200,000 iterations.

We conduct a 2 cross-validation experiment on the Cropped-BOSSBase-1.01 dataset using 3-channels residuals, the mean value of accuracies is given in Table 1.

Table 1. Accuracies of experiments on Cropped-BOSSBase-1.01 (%)

3-channels CNN	6-channels CNN	Shi et al. [21]	SRM [14] + EC [30]
82.02	80.73	78.56	76.15

We reworked Shi et al. experiment [21] with our CNN network on Cropped-BOSS-Base-1.01 database, but only use the residuals produced from K_0, under the same environment. Besides, we trained an Ensemble Classifier [30] on the training 64,000 images and tested another 16,000 with SRM features. The results are given in Table 1.

In addition, we created another 6-channels residuals CNN using K_0–K_5 (see Eq. 1–6), the result is also given in Table 1.

As shown in Table 1, the network we proposed can improve the detection efficiently, multi-channels CNN can get better results than Shi's works and SRM. Especially, the 3-channels CNN get a 3.46% higher accuracy compared with Shi's works. The reason that 6-channels CNN get a lower performance maybe that the parameters is not enough for this 6-channles residuals. More residuals call for more convolutional kernels to fit the data, it will increase the amount of calculation. Moreover, K_3–K_5 maybe not effective as others, redundancy in the 6-channels residual cause a decrease in accuracy. But the result of 6-channels CNN still shows that multi-channels residuals san effectively improve CNN's classification performance compared to Shi's works and SRM.

We also make some experiments to demonstrate the effectiveness of our proposed method. We split the center of each image in BOSSBase v1.01, and name it Center-BOSSBase-1.01. We embed the Center-BOSSBase-1.01 with S-UNIWARD at 0.4 bits per pixel, so we have 10,000 cover images and 10,000 stego images. We test our model trained from the 3-channels CNN using the Center-BOSSBase-1.01 and its stego images, the results are given in Table 2. To compare the results, we also test models trained from Shi's network (see Table 3) and our 6-channels CNN network (see Table 4).

$$K_3 = \frac{1}{4}\begin{pmatrix} -1 & 2 & -4 & 2 & -1 \\ 2 & -6 & 8 & -6 & 2 \\ -4 & 8 & -4 & 8 & -4 \\ 2 & -6 & 8 & -6 & 2 \\ -1 & 2 & -4 & 2 & -1 \end{pmatrix} \tag{4}$$

$$K_4 = \frac{1}{4}\begin{pmatrix} 0 & 1 & 0 \\ 1 & -4 & 1 \\ 0 & 1 & 0 \end{pmatrix} \tag{5}$$

$$K_5 = \frac{1}{4}\begin{pmatrix} 1 & 0 & 1 \\ 0 & -4 & 0 \\ 1 & 0 & 1 \end{pmatrix} \tag{6}$$

Table 2. Accuracies of testing 3-channels CNN model on Center-BOSSBase-1.01 (%)

Cover	Stego	Total
79.03	80.18	79.61

Table 3. Accuracies of testing 6-channels CNN model on Center-BOSSBase-1.01 (%)

Cover	Stego	Total
80.79	75.54	78.17

Table 4. Accuracies of testing Shi's network on Center-BOSSBase-1.01 (%)

Cover	Stego	Total
76.32	73.07	74.70

As shown in Tables 1, 2, 3 and 4, the accuracy of testing 3-channels CNN model is decreased by 2.41% compared to the training accuracy. The 6-channels CNN model can get an accuracy of 78.17%, 2.56% lower than the training accuracy. Shi's work get the biggest loss, decreases by 3.86%. The experiment results demonstrate the effectiveness and robustness of our approach sufficiently. Multi-channels residuals can capture diversity between cover and stego effectively, it can help CNN to fit the regular pattern of steganography better. Single type of residual get the biggest drop in accuracy due to the lack of valid steganographic rules.

4   Conclusions

In this paper, we propose to use multi-channels residuals to improve the results of CNN used in steganalysis. As known, CNN is good at learning strong features, we use various filtered residuals to enhance the diversity between the cover and the stego since the embedding message is weak, which is helpful to reduce the classification error. Moreover, we generate a superposition of the residual maps before feeding the CNN, it's helpful for joint optimization in CNN. We also test our networks using different datasets, and obtain similar results with training accuracies. Our future studies will concentrate on looking for more effective filter kernels during the image pre-processing stage. Furthermore, we will try some new CNN architecture.

Acknowledgments. This work is supported by the Natural Science Foundation of Guangdong (No. 2016A030313350), the Special Funds for Science and Technology Development of Guangdong (No. 2016KZ010103), the Fundamental Research Funds for the Central Universities (No. 16lgjc83), and Scientific and Technological Achievements Transformation Plan of Sun Yat-sen University.

References

1. Fu, Z., Huang, F., Sun, X., Vasilakos, A. and Yang, C.-N.: Enabling semantic search based on conceptual graphs over encrypted outsourced data. IEEE Trans. Serv. Comput. 1, **PP** (2016). 5555, doi:10.1109/TSC.2016.2622697
2. Sharp, T.: An implementation of key-based digital signal steganography. In: Moskowitz, I.S. (ed.) IH 2001. LNCS, vol. 2137, pp. 13–26. Springer, Heidelberg (2001). doi: 10.1007/3-540-45496-9_2
3. Luo, W., Huang, F., Huang, J.: Edge adaptive image steganography based on lsb matchingrevisited. IEEE Trans. Inf. Forensics Secur. **5**(2), 201–214 (2013)
4. Pevný, T., Filler, T., Bas, P.: Using high-dimensional image models to perform highly undetectable steganography. In: Böhme, R., Fong, P.W.L., Safavi-Naini, R. (eds.) IH 2010. LNCS, vol. 6387, pp. 161–177. Springer, Heidelberg (2010). doi:10.1007/978-3-642-16435-4_13
5. Holub, V., Fridrich, J., Denemark, T.: Universal distortion function for steganography in an arbitrary domain. EURASIP J. Inf. Secur. **2014**(1), 1 (2014)
6. Li, B., Wang, M., Huang, J., Li, X.: A new cost function for spatial image steganography. In: IEEE International Conference on Image Processing, pp. 4206–4210 (2014)
7. Yuan, C., Xia, Z., Sun, X.: Coverless image steganography based on SIFT and BOF. J. Internet Technol. **18**(2), 435–442 (2017)
8. Xia, Z., Wang, X., Sun, X., Wang, B.: Steganalysis of least significant bit matching using multi-order differences. Secur. Commun. Netw. **7**(8), 1283–1291 (2013)
9. Xia, Z., Wang, X., Sun, X., Liu, Q., Xiong, N.: Steganalysis of LSB matching using differences between nonadjacent pixels. Multimedia Tools Appl. **75**(4), 1947–1962 (2014)

10. Zhou, Z., Yang, C., Chen, B., Sun, X., Liu, Q., Wu, Q.: Effective and efficient image copy detection with resistance to arbitrary rotation. IEICE Trans. Inf. Syst. **E99-D**(6), 1531–1540 (2016)

11. Zhou, Z., Wang, Y., Wu, Q., Yang, C., Sun, X.: Effective and efficient global context verification for image copy detection. IEEE Trans. Inf. Forensics Secur. **12**(1), 48–63 (2017)

12. Sullivan, K., Madhow, U., Chandrasekaran, S., Manjunath, B.S.: Steganalysis of spread spectrum data hiding exploiting cover memory. In: Proceedings of Security, Steganography, and Watermarking of Multimedia Contents VII, San Jose, California, USA, 17–20 January 2005, pp. 38–46 (2005)

13. Fridrich, J., Kodovský, J., Holub, V., Goljan, M.: Steganalysis of content-adaptive steganography in spatial domain. In: Filler, T., Pevný, T., Craver, S., Ker, A. (eds.) IH 2011. LNCS, vol. 6958, pp. 102–117. Springer, Heidelberg (2011). doi: 10.1007/978-3-642-24178-9_8

14. Fridrich, J., Kodovsky, J.: Rich models for steganalysis of digital images. IEEE Trans. Inf. Forensics Secur. **7**(3), 868–882 (2012)

15. Krizhevsky, A., Sutskever, I., Hinton, G.E.: Imagenet classification with deep convolutional neural networks. In: International Conference on Neural Information Processing Systems, pp. 1097–1105 (2012)

16. Qian, Y., Dong, J.,Wang,W., Tan, T.: Deep learning for steganalysis via convolutional neural networks. In: Proceedings of SPIE, vol. 9409, pp. 94090J-1–94090J-10 (2015)

17. Pibre, L., Pasquet, J., Ienco, D., Chaumont, M.: Deep learning is a good steganalysis tool when embedding key is reused for different images, even if there is a cover sourcemismatch. In: Media Watermarking, Security, and Forensics, pp. 79–95 (2016)

18. Qian, Y., Dong, J., Wang, W., Tan, T.: Learning and transferring representations for image steganalysis using convolutional neural network. In: IEEE International Conference on Image Processing, pp. 2752–2756 (2016)

19. Qian, Y., Dong, J., Wang, W., Tan, T.: Learning representations for steganalysis from regularized CNN model with auxiliary tasks. In: Liang, Q., Mu, J., Wang, W., Zhang, B. (eds.) Proceedings of the 2015 International Conference on Communications, Signal Processing, and Systems. LNEE, vol. 386, pp. 629–637. Springer, Heidelberg (2016). doi: 10.1007/978-3-662-49831-6_64

20. Couchot, J.F., Couturier, R., Guyeux, C., Salomon, M.: Steganalysis via a convolutional neural network using large convolution filters for embedding process with same stego key (2016)

21. Xu, G., Wu, H.Z., Shi, Y.Q.: Structural design of convolutional neural networks for steganalysis. IEEE Signal Process. Lett. **23**(5), 708–712 (2016)

22. Xu, G., Wu, H.Z., Shi, Y.Q.: Ensemble of CNNs for steganalysis: an empirical study. In: ACM Workshop on Information Hiding and Multimedia Security, pp. 103–107 (2016)

23. Zeng, J., Tan, S., Li, B., Huang, J.: Large-scale JPEG steganalysis using hybrid deep-learning framework (2016)

24. Ioffe, S., Szegedy, C.: Batch normalization: Accelerating deep network training by reducing internal covariate shift. In: Computer Science (2015)

25. Cortes, C., Vapnik, V.: Support-vector networks. Mach. Learn. **20**(3), 273–297 (1995)

26. Lyu, S., Farid, H.: Detecting hidden messages using higher-order statistics and support vector machines. In: Petitcolas, F.A.P. (ed.) IH 2002. LNCS, vol. 2578, pp. 340–354. Springer, Heidelberg (2003). doi:10.1007/3-540-36415-3_22

27. Kodovsky, J., Fridrich, J., Holub, V.: On dangers of overtraining steganography to incomplete cover model. In: ACM Multimedia and Security Workshop, pp. 69–76 (2011)

28. Fridrich, J., Kodovský, J., Holub, V., Goljan, M.: Breaking HUGO – the process discovery. In: Filler, T., Pevný, T., Craver, S., Ker, Andrew (eds.) IH 2011. LNCS, vol. 6958, pp. 85–101. Springer, Heidelberg (2011). doi:10.1007/978-3-642-24178-9_7
29. Jia, Y., Shelhamer, E., Donahue, J., Karayev, S., Long, J., Girshick, R., Guadarrama, S., Darrell, T.: Caffe: Convolutional architecture for fast feature embedding. In: Proceedings of the 22nd ACM International Conference on Multimedia, MM 2014, pp. 675–678. ACM, New York (2014)
30. Kodovsky, J., Fridrich, J., Holub, V.: Ensemble classifiers for steganalysis of digital media. IEEE Trans. Inf. Forensics Secur. 7(2), 432–444 (2012)

Coverless Text Information Hiding Method Using the Frequent Words Distance

Jianjun Zhang[1,2($\boxtimes$)], Yicheng Xie[2], Lucai Wang[2], and Haijun Lin[2]

[1] College of Computer Science and Electronic Engineering,
Hunan University, Changsha 410080, China
jianjun998@163.com
[2] College of Engineering and Design,
Hunan Normal University, Changsha 410081, China
1431330481@qq.com, wlucai9776@vip.sina.com,
linhaijun801028@126.com

Abstract. The attackers may discover the existence of the secret information or even get it by analyzing the cover's statistical characteristics, changes of which often occur due to the embedding. In this paper, a novel coverless text information hiding method was proposed. By using the words rank map and the frequent words distance, normal texts containing the secret information could be retrieved from the text database, and will be sent to the receiver without any modification. Because the embedding is not needed, the proposed method could be able to escape from almost all state-of-the-art steganalysis methods.

Keywords: Coverless information hiding · The rank map · The frequent words distance · The big data

1 Introduction

Information Hiding, also known as Steganography, can be informally defined as an application that is not detectably passing secret information in a carrier object [1]. This technology mainly uses the redundancy of the digital signal such as texts [2], images [3, 4], and videos [5] to achieve information hiding. Steganography can be used for intellectual property protection [6]. For example, Refs. [7, 8] introduced two methods of detecting illegal copies of copyrighted images. Since the text is frequently used in people's daily lives, text information hiding has attracted many researchers' interest [9]. Classified by the covers, text steganography could be put into main three types: text format-based [10–12], generating-based and embedding-based natural language information hiding. For text format-based information hiding, the embedded information will no longer exist if the document is generated without format after extracting the text content. Generating-based natural language information hiding methods can fool the computer statistical analysis, but is relatively easy to be identified by people [13]. Embedding-based natural language information hiding methods have more robust and better concealment than text format-based information hiding, but the hiding algorithm is difficult to implement, and there are some deviations and distortions in the statistic and linguistics because of the limitation of the natural language processing [14].

Once the information hiding algorithm is public, the steganalysis methods will be appearing. If there is information embedding in the steganography process, then the attacker will have the means to find the existence of hidden information or even get it. Be there an algorithm with which the secret information could be hidden without any modification of the covers. Coverless information hiding [15, 16], firstly proposed by Xingming Sun et al. is the best answer to the above question. Its main idea is to retrieve the stego-vector (texts or images) that contains the secret message by directly traversing the covers in the big data environment [17]. Although coverless information hiding is a new branch of the steganography, it has attracted many researchers' interest because it requires no modification on covers and could resist various steganalysis methods. Reference [15] presented the first coverless image steganography framework, and Ref. [16] proposed the first coverless text information hiding method based on the Chinese Mathematical Expression. These two methods can directly retrieve the stego-images (stego-texts) that contain secret information in the big data environment. The covers could be sent to the receiver without any modification. A coverless information hiding method using Chinese character encoding technology is proposed in [17, 18] proposed a text coverless information hiding method based on multi-keywords, [19] proposed a coverless image steganography scheme based on scale invariant feature transform and bag of feature, and [20] utilized the text coverless information hiding by introducing the active learning based named entity recognition.

In this paper, a novel coverless text information hiding method is proposed. Firstly, a text database is constructed by collecting a large number of texts from the Internet. Then the word rank maps of the words will be calculated by statistically analyzing the text big data, meanwhile, the frequent words distance of every text is calculated. When the secret information will be transmitted, some normal texts, which contain the secret information, will be retrieved from the text database by using the frequent words distance and the word rank maps, and sent to the receiver without any modification.

The remainder of this paper is organized as follows. In Sect. 2, we introduced the proposed text coverless information hiding method in detail. The example verification and security analysis were discussed in Sect. 3, and the paper is concluded in the last section.

2   Proposed Method

2.1   Preparation of the Text Database

We constructed a natural text database by fetching the news from the normal news web sites. For each word of the vocabulary, we calculate the frequency of its occurrence, and then rank the words with the descending way (Most frequent word has rank 1, next frequent word has rank 2 …). Figure 1 shows the ranking result of words in a text database.

In order to make good use of the information of the words' occurrence in a text database (or in a text), the **Word Rank Map** of a text database (or a text) is defined as

$$RM = \{(w_i, f_i) | i = 1, 2, 3, \ldots, U\}. \tag{1}$$

```
the number of words is 1282023
the number of unique words is 33268

RANK    WORD        :    FREQUENCY :

1       the         :    85042     :
2       of          :    35709     :
3       to          :    35441     :
4       in          :    31856     :
5       and         :    31335     :
6       a           :    26815     :
7       on          :    15521     :
8       said        :    14452     :
9       that        :    11644     :
10      for         :    10688     :
11      is          :    8758      :
12      with        :    8203      :
13      as          :    7633      :
14      at          :    7185      :
15      -           :    6716      :
16      was         :    6698      :
17      by          :    6661      :
18      from        :    5851      :
19      has         :    5688      :
20      he          :    5590      :
21      it          :    5242      :
22      us          :    5210      :
23      will        :    5193      :
24      have        :    4849      :
25      china       :    4811      :
26      an          :    4797      :
27      be          :    4530      :
28      are         :    4082      :
29      its         :    3929      :
30      his         :    3812      :
```

Fig. 1. Part of a text collection's word rank map.

Where U is the number of unique words in a text database (or in a text), i is the rank of a word w_i, and f_i is the frequency of w_i. Figure 1 shows the word rank map of a text database. For the example in the Fig. 1, we can obtain

$$RM = \left\{ \begin{array}{l} (the, 85042), (of, 35709), \\ (to, 35441), (in, 31856), \ldots \end{array} \right\}. \tag{2}$$

Obviously, the top frequent words are: the, of, to, in, and, a, on, etc.

For each text in a text database, we can calculate its word rank map defined as the formula (1). Figure 2 shows the rank map of a text named as "2 abducted Italians freed

```
the number of words   211
the number of unique words 130

RANK    WORD        :         REQUENCY:

1       the         :         8    :
2       a           :         8    :
3       of          :         6    :
4       to          :         5    :
5       in          :         5    :
6       been        :         5    :
7       and         :         5    :
8       were        :         4    :
9       two         :         4    :
10      on          :         4    :
11      men         :         3    :
12      for         :         3    :
13      after       :         3    :
14      have        :         3    :
15      said        :         3    :
16      italian     :         2    :
17      tripoli     :         2    :
18      released    :         2    :
19      three       :         2    :
20      libya       :         2    :
21      abducted    :         2    :
22      by          :         2    :
23      militia     :         2    :
24      who         :         2    :
25      gaddafi     :         2    :
26      libyan      :         2    :
27      snatched    :         2    :
28      political   :         2    :
29      is          :         2    :
30      its         :         2    :
```

Fig. 2. Part of an article's word rank map.

in Libya.txt", in which there are 211 words, 130 unique words. From the rank map, we learn that the top frequent words are: the, a, of, to, in, been, and, etc.

For the top frequent words in the text database, we can calculate their occurrences in a text in the same collection. So, the **Frequent Words Hash Function** is defined as

$$H_k(t) = \{h_1 h_2 h_3 \cdots h_k\}. \tag{3}$$

Where k is the number of the top frequent words that were chose from the vocabulary of a text database, t is a text in the text database, and h_i is defined by

$$h_i = \begin{cases} 1, & the\ i-th\ frequent\ word\ appears\ in\ text\ t \\ 0, & the\ i-th\ frequent\ word\ does\ not\ appear\ in\ text\ t \end{cases} \tag{4}$$

For the top 30 frequent words shown in Fig. 1, we can calculate the hash value of a text named as "2.1 million Audi cars affected by emissions cheating scandal.txt". The hash value is

$$H_{30}(t) = \{111111101110111101001010010010\}. \tag{5}$$

So, we map a text into a 30 bits string. Figure 3 shows the hash values of some texts in a text database. In order to measure the occurrence of the frequent words in a text t, we define the **Frequent Words Distance** of a text as:

$$DFW_k(t) = HD(H_k(t), (b_1, b_2, b_3, \cdots, b_k)), \ b_i = 0, \ i = 1, 2, 3, \cdots k. \tag{6}$$

Where k is the number of the top frequent words, t is a text in the text database, and HD is Hamming Distance calculating operation.

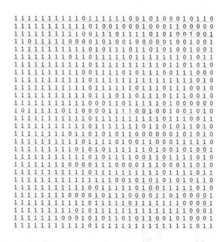

Fig. 3. The hash values of some texts in a text database.

By statistical analyzing the occurrence of each word in the text database, we can calculate the word rank map of each word. For each word w_i in the vocabulary of the text database, its word rank map is defined as

$$RMW_i = \{(rw_{ij}, fw_{ij}, wt_{ij}) | i = 1, 2, 3, \ldots, U; j = 1, 2, 3, \ldots N\}. \tag{7}$$

Where rw_{ij} is the rank of the word w_i in a text wt_{ij} according to its occurrence, fw_{ij} is the frequency of w_i's occurrence in wt_{ij}, and N is the number of the texts in which w_i appears. Figure 4 shows the word rank map of "by", whose rank is 17 in the word rank map shown in Fig. 1.

RANK	FREQUENCY	:	RESOURCE TEXT
2	2	:	7 killed, 11,000 displaced as floods hit Indonesia
4	7	:	US intelligence suggests Russian plane crash caus
4	4	:	Yemen Suicide car bomb, assault kill 52
4	5	:	S
4	8	:	Russian airstrikes destroy IS command center Defense M
4	4	:	Yemen Suicide car bomb, assault kill 5
5	9	:	First planeload of Syrian refugees arrives in Canad
5	6	:	UK advertising up almost 20 pct on mobile video
5	7	:	MH17 hit by Buk missile system Dutch Safety Boar
5	4	:	Iran's Guardian Council passes nuclear bill into la
5	3	:	'In' leads by 7 percentage points ahead of Britain's E
5	4	:	Measures aim to tackle tax evasio
5	8	:	WH releases NSA review by outside pane
5	10	:	UN Security Council adopts resolution to cut off Islam
5	8	:	WH releases NSA review by outside panel
6	4	:	Russia fires missiles at IS positions from submarine d
6	4	:	Turkish PM says drone downed recently Russian-mad
6	3	:	Radio broadcaster shot dead in Philippines
6	8	:	Japan to revive Fukushima operator
6	5	:	US can't rule out terrorism in Russian plane crash in
6	8	:	US caution urged over missile mov
6	7	:	Islamic State is prime suspect in Turkey bombing, as p
6	8	:	Japan to revive Fukushima operato
6	7	:	US woos Malaysia in TPP talks
6	4	:	Nearly 3
6	7	:	Abe's official website latest to come under possible A
7	9	:	Thousands of guns sold illegally online in US
7	17	:	China reiterates emission cut goal, reassures world
7	5	:	Hundreds to march in new anti-Park rall

Fig. 4. Part of the rank map of "by".

2.2 Information Hiding

The information hiding process is shown in Fig. 5. Detail procedures are introduced as follows.

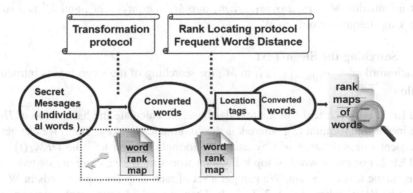

Fig. 5. The process of information hiding

Suppose the constructed text database is T, and the communication key is k. The key can be generated by running the synchronization function between communication parties. We can calculate the word rank map of T by using the formula (1), and get the vocabulary of T, and let it be $W = \{w_i | i = 1, 2, 3, \cdots U\}$ where i is the rank of w_i, and U is the number of unique words in T. For each text t_i in T, we can calculate its word rank map by using the formula (1), and let it be RM_{t_i}

Because the key is k, we arrange the top frequent $k \times k$ words in W as the right part of Fig. 6. Suppose the hidden message is $M = m_1, m_2, m_3, \ldots, m_n$ where m_i is a word, and n is the number of words in the hidden message. For each word m_i in M, it is chosen from the top frequent $k \times k$ words in W. Obviously, the selection range of m_i depends on k. Therefore, both sides of communication can choose larger k so that m_i has more options.

w_1		w_1	w_{k+1}	w_{2k+1}	$\cdots$	$w_{(k-1)\times k+1}$
w_2		w_2	w_{k+2}	w_{2k+2}	$\cdots$	$w_{(k-1)\times k+2}$
$\vdots$		$\vdots$	$\vdots$	$\vdots$	$\vdots$	$\vdots$
w_{k-1}		w_{k-1}	$w_{k+(k-1)}$	$w_{2k+(k-1)}$	$\cdots$	$w_{(k-1)\times(k+1)}$
w_k		w_k	w_{k+k}	w_{2k+k}	$\cdots$	$w_{k \times k}$

Fig. 6. The words conversion table.

2.2.1 Words Conversion

In order to enhance the security of the secret message, we convert each word in M into one of the top frequent k words in W before the information hiding. The conversion rule is shown in Fig. 6. For each word in $\{w_1, w_{k+1}, \cdots w_{(k-1)\times k+1}\}$, it will be converted into w_1. For each word in $\{w_2, w_{k+2}, \cdots w_{(k-1)\times k+2}\}$, it will be converted into w_2. And so on.

For each word m_i in M, we can get its rank by using the word rank map of T, and let it be R_{m_i}. Then, it is located in the $((R_{m_i} - 1)\%k + 1)$ row, $((R_{m_i} - 1)/k + 1)$ column in the word conversion table shown in Fig. 6, where "%" is a remainder operation. Therefore it will be converted into $m_i' = w_{((R_{m_i}-1)\%k+1)}$. In this way, we can convert the secret information $M = m_1, m_2, m_3, \ldots, m_n$ into $M' = m_1' m_2' \ldots m_n'$, and M' is a subset of the k top frequent words in W.

2.2.2 Searching the Stego-Text

For each word $m_i' = w_{((R_{m_i}-1)\%k+1)}$ in M', the searching of the stego-text is introduced as follows.

> **STEP 1.** For each text t in the text database, we calculate the hash value of $H_k(t)$, defined as the formula (3), where k is the communication key. Then, we can get the frequent words distance of t by using the formula (6), ant let it be $DFW_k(t)$.
> **STEP 2.** For every word of top k frequent words in W, we compute its word rank map in the text collection. We can get a set of rank map for top k words in W, and let it be RMW_i where $i = 1, 2, 3, \ldots, k$. Then, we calculate the rank intersection of

$RMW_i(i = 1, 2, 3, \ldots, k)$, and let it be IR. So $IR = \{\bigcap_{i=1}^{k} f_i | f_i \in RMW_i\}$. Because these words are top k words in W, the intersection is not null, and the values of elements in IR are integers. For m_i', we choose a rank number from the intersection *IR* by implementing the rank location protocol agreed upon by communication parties, and assume the chose rank of m_i' is $R_{m_i'}$.

STEP 3. Because m_i' is in the top k frequent words in W, we can get the rank map of m_i' by using the formual (7), and let it be $RMW_{m_i'}$.

STEP 4. By using the word rank map $RMW_{m_i'}$, we retrieve all texts containing m_i' to search a text t in which the rank of m_i' is equal to $R_{m_i'}$, and the frequent word distance of t is equal to $((R_{m_i} - 1)/k + 1)$. There may be some texts satisfying this condition, then, we can select a text from those texts as the stego-text for m_i'.

Finally, as described above, we can search a stego-text for each m_i' in M'. These stego-texts is a normal text set that contains the converted secret message, and they can be sent to the receiver without any modifying.

2.3   Information Extraction

The process of extraction is shown in Fig. 7. Suppose the stego-text is S, so S is a set of normal texts. The number of texts in S is the number of words in M. Let k be the communication key. Because the text database T is open for all users, receiver can calculate the word rank map of T, and get the top k frequent words in W by using the communication key k. Certainly, receiver can get the same word conversion table shown in Fig. 6.

For each stego-text t in *S*, the details of information extraction will be introduced as follows.

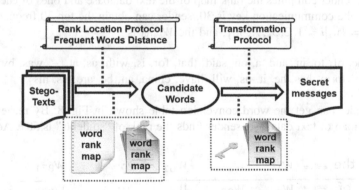

Fig. 7. Secret message extracting process

2.3.1   Get the Candidate Word

Firstly, For each word of the top k frequent words in W, receiver calculates its rank map set $RMW_i(i = 1, 2, 3, \ldots, k)$. So, receiver can get the rank intersection

$IR = \{\bigcap_{i=1}^{k} f_i | f_i \in RMW_i\}$, and the rank tab by implementing the rank location protocol and let it be R_r. R_r is obviously equal to the rank tab $R_{m_i'}$ computed by the sender.

Then, Receiver calculates the word rank map of t by using the formula (1). By retrieving the word rank map of t, receiver can get the candidate word whose rank is equal to $R_{m_i'}$ in text t. Obviously, the candidate word is $m_i' = w_{((R_{m_i}-1)\%k+1)}$.

2.3.2   Get the Secret Message

Receiver calculates the frequent words distance of t by using formula (6) and let it be $DFW_k(t)$. Obviously, $DFW_k(t)$ is equal to $((R_{m_i}-1)/k+1)$. Receiver can find the secret message m_i that is located in the "$w_{((R_{m_i}-1)\%k+1)}$" row, the $((R_{m_i}-1)/k+1)$ column in the word conversion table shown in Fig. 6.

So, receiver can get every word m_i in M, and then get the secret message $M = m_1, m_2, m_3, \ldots, m_n$.

3   Discussion

3.1   Example Verification

In order to clearly explain the above coverless text information hiding process, we illustrate it by a simple example. We have constructed a text database which can be expanded constantly, and it is open for all users. Suppose the communication key is 30 and the secret M is only one word "students". For more than one word in the secret message, the operation procedure is same. It is worth mentioning that, however, M is a subset of the top 900 frequent words in the text database. Both sides of communication may choose larger k, so that words of M have more options. The operating procedure of information hiding is introduced as follows.

Firstly, sender computes the rank map of the text database and ones of each text in it. Because the communication key is 30, sender can obtain the top 30 frequent words set $W_{top30} = \{w_i | i = 1, 2, 3, \ldots, 30\}$, and the W_{top30} is

$\{$the, of, to, in, and, a, on, said, that, for, is, with, as, at, $-$, was, by, form, has, he, it, us, will, have, china, an, be, are, its, his$\}$

So, sender can get the word conversion table shown in Fig. 8. By retrieving the word rank map of text database, sender finds the rank of "students" is 587. According

the	w_1	w_{31}	w_{61}	$\cdots$		w_{871}
of	w_2	w_{32}	w_{62}	$\cdots$		w_{872}
$\vdots$	$\vdots$	$\vdots$	$\vdots$	$\vdots$		$\vdots$
its	w_{29}	w_{59}	w_{89}	$\cdots$		w_{899}
his	w_{30}	w_{60}	w_{90}	$\cdots$		w_{900}

Fig. 8. The words conversion table when k is 30.

to the word conversion table shown in Fig. 8, therefore, "students" is located in 17th row, 20th column. Hence, "students" will be converted into "by".

Secondly, sender computes the word rank map of the 30 frequent words, and get the rank intersection of them. The intersection is {5 6 7 8 9 10 11 13 14 15 16 17 18 19 20 22 23 24 26 31 35 36 37 42}. By implementing the rank tab location protocol, sender choose a rank tab for "by", and suppose the rank tab is 36. Next step is to find a text in which the rank of "by" is 36 and its frequent words distance is 20.

Thirdly, sender calculates the word rank map of "by". By retrieving the word rank map, sender can find a text named "5 aims to follow in star's footstep.txt", and let it be t_s. The word rank maps of t_s is shown in Fig. 9. From Fig. 9, we learn that the rank of "by" is 36 in text t_s whose frequent words distance is 20, and the frequent words are {the, of, to, in, and, a, on, said, is, with, as, –, was, by, he, china, an, its, his} in it.

RANK	WORD	:	FREQUENCY:
1	the	:	13	:
2	a	:	12	:
3	of	:	9	:
4	his	:	9	:
5	in	:	9	:
6	to	:	7	:
7	with	:	6	:
8	and	:	6	:
9	star	:	5	:
10	shirt	:	5	:
11	on	:	5	:
12	murtaza	:	5	:
13	from	:	5	:
14	messi	:	5	:
15	messi's	:	4	:
16	one	:	4	:
17	day	:	4	:
18	ahmadi	:	4	:
19	brother	:	3	:
20	boy	:	3	:
21	afghan	:	3	:
22	soccer	:	3	:
23	like	:	3	:
24	him	:	3	:
25	plastic	:	3	:
26	bag	:	3	:
27	lionel	:	2	:
28	5	:	2	:
29	makeshift	:	2	:
30	made	:	2	:
31	fan	:	2	:
32	it	:	2	:
33	dreams	:	2	:
34	hamayon	:	2	:
35	becoming	:	2	:
36	by	:	2	:
37	facebook	:	2	:
38	photos	:	2	:
39	said	:	2	:
40	is	:	2	:

Fig. 9. The word rank map of a stego-text.

Finally, sender sends t_s as the stego-texts to the receiver without any modification.

Because the text database is open to all users, receiver can calculate its word rank map, the top 30 frequent words and the word conversion table shown in Fig. 8 by using the communication key k = 30. Then, he (or she) calculates the word rank map of stego-text t_s. By implementing the rand tab location protocol, receiver can get the rank tab is 36, and find that the candidate word is "by" by retrieving the word rank map of t_s. Then, receiver calculates the frequent words distance of t_s and finds that it is 20. Finally, receiver can obtain the secret message "students" located in "by" row, 20th column in the word conversion table shown in Fig. 8. Hence, receiver successfully extract the secret message "students" from the stego-text.

3.2   Security Analysis

Steganalysis is usually performed through the use of irrelevance between the embedded information and the carriers. Attackers often make steganalysis by analyzing the difference of their statistical distributions [21]. In our proposed hiding method, however, the carriers are normal pure text and the secret information is not been embedded in the carriers. The carriers can be sent to receiver without any modification. So the information hiding does not change the probability distribution of the carriers. According to the definition of the security of an information hiding system in [22], the proposed information hiding method is theoretically safe. At the same time, the proposed approach is also followed the Kerckhoffs Principle [23] in cryptography, and detail of information hiding is open. If he does not know the communication key, the attacker cannot gain any information about the hidden information [24]. Therefore, the proposed method could resist almost all kinds of current steganalysis method.

3.3   The Importance of Big Data

However, it is worth mentioning that, in order to enhance security, there are two works must be done: one is to change periodically the communication key to ensure that the secret message may be converted into different subsets of the top frequent words in the text database. The second is to establish a large text database (text big data) to make sure that the rank tab has more choices [9]. For example, in the chose text database, there are some subset including a small number of texts. For the same communication key 30, the rank intersection of the word rank map of the top 30 frequent words in one subset is {5 6 7 8 9 10 12 13 17 22 28 34}, one of the other subset is {6 7 8 9 10 11 12 13 14 15 16 18 19 20 21 24 30 32 40}, and one of the whole text collection is {5 6 7 8 9 10 11 13 14 15 16 17 18 19 20 22 23 24 26 31 35 36 37 42}. Obviously, the number of the rank intersection is becoming small when the number of texts is small. Moreover, we analysis the correlation between the number of elements in the rank

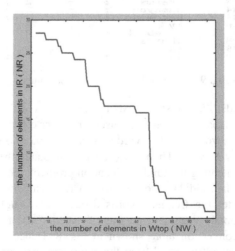

Fig. 10. The correlation between IR and Wtop.

intersection *IR* named as NR and the number of elements in the top frequent words W_{top} named as NW. The result is shown in Fig. 10. From Fig. 10, we learn that NR is becoming smaller with the increasing of NW. For example, NR is 27 when NW is 10, and NR is 1 when NW is 99. So NR is smaller means that the choice of rank tab is less. Therefore, the text big data is necessary to ensure the smoothly implement of the proposed method, and some search methods, which could be implemented in the big data environment, were proposed [25–27].

4 Conclusions

This paper presented a coverless text information hiding method based on the frequent words distance. By using the words rank map and the frequent words distance, normal texts containing the secret information could be retrieved from the text database, and will be sent to the receiver without any modification. Because there is no embedding, the information hiding does not change the probability distribution of the covers. Therefore, the proposed method is theoretically safe, and could be able to escape from almost all state-of-the-art steganalysis methods.

Acknowledgments. This work is supported by National Natural Science Foundation of China (61304208), Open Fund of Demonstration Base of Internet Application Innovative Open Platform of Department of Education (KJRP1402), Open Fund of China-USA Computer Science Research Center (KJR16239), Hunan Province Science And Technology Plan Project Fund (2012GK3120), Scientific Research Fund of Hunan Province Education Department (13CY003, 14B106), Changsha City Science and Technology Plan Program (K1501013-11), Hunan Normal University University-Industry Cooperation.

References

1. Fridrich, J.: Steganography in Digital Media – Principle, Algorithms, and Application. National Defense Industry Press, Beijing (2014)
2. Por, L.Y., Ang, T.F., Delina, B.: WhiteSteg: a new scheme in information hiding using text steganography. WSEAS Trans. Comput. **7**(6), 735–745 (2008)
3. Xia, Z., Lv, R., Zhu, Y., Ji, P., Sun, H., Shi, Y.: Fingerprint liveness detection using gradient-based texture features. Sig. Image Video Process. **11**(2), 381–388 (2017)
4. Huang, L., Tseng, L., Hwang, M.: The study on data hiding in medical images. Int. J. Netw. Secur. **14**(6), 301–309 (2012)
5. Wang, S., Xiao, C., Lin, Y.: A high bitrate information hiding algorithm for video in video. In. J. Comput. Electr. Autom. Control Inf. Eng. **3**(11), 2572–2577 (2009)
6. Liu, T.Y., Tsai, W.H.: A new steganographic method for data hiding in microsoft word documents by a change tracking technique. IEEE Trans. Inf. Forensics Secur. **2**(1), 24–30 (2007)
7. Zhou, Z., Wang, Y., Wu, Q.M.J., Yang, C., Sun, X.: Effective and efficient global context verification for image copy detection. IEEE Trans. Inf. Forensics Secur. (2016). doi:10.1109/TIFS.2016.2601065
8. Xia, Z., Wang, X., Zhang, L., Qin, Z., Sun, X., Ren, K.: A privacy-preserving and copy-deterrence content-based image retrieval scheme in cloud computing. IEEE Trans. Inf. Forensics Secur. **11**(11), 2594–2608 (2016)

9. Zhang, J., Shen, J., Wang, L., Lin, H.: Coverless text information hiding method based on the word rank map. In: Sun, X., Liu, A., Chao, H.-C., Bertino, E. (eds.) ICCCS 2016. LNCS, vol. 10039, pp. 145–155. Springer, Cham (2016). doi:10.1007/978-3-319-48671-0_14

10. Low, S.H., Maxemchuk, N.F., Brassil, J.T.: Document marking and identification using both line and word shifting. In: Proceedings of INFOCOM 1995, vol. 2007, pp. 853–860. IEEE (1995)

11. Low, S.H., Maxemchuk, N.F., Lapone, A.M.: Document identification for copyright protection using centroid detection. IEEE Trans. Commun. **46**(3), 372–383 (1998)

12. Brassil, J.T., Low, S.H., Maxemchuk, N.F.: Copyright protection for the electronic distribution of text documents. Proc. IEEE **87**, 1181–1196 (1999)

13. Bo, S., Hu, Z., Wu, L., Zhou, H.: Steganography of Telecommunication Information. National Defense University, Beijing (2005)

14. Meng, P., Huang, L., Chen, Z., Yang, W., Yang, M.: Analysis and detection of translation based steganography. Acta Electronica Sinica **38**(8), 1748–1852 (2012)

15. Zhou, Z., Sun, H., Harit, R., Chen, X., Sun, X.: Coverless image steganography without embedding. In: Huang, Z., Sun, X., Luo, J., Wang, J. (eds.) ICCCS 2015. LNCS, vol. 9483, pp. 123–132. Springer, Cham (2015). doi:10.1007/978-3-319-27051-7_11

16. Chen, X., Sun, H., Tobe, Y., Zhou, Z., Sun, X.: Coverless information hiding method based on the Chinese mathematical expression. In: Huang, Z., Sun, X., Luo, J., Wang, J. (eds.) ICCCS 2015. LNCS, vol. 9483, pp. 133–143. Springer, Cham (2015). doi:10.1007/978-3-319-27051-7_12

17. Chen, X., Chen, S., Wu, Y.: Coverless information hiding method based on the Chinese character encoding. J. Int. Technol. **18**(2), 313–320 (2017)

18. Zhou, Z., Mu, Y., Yang, C., Zhao, N.: Coverless multi-keywords information hiding method based on text. Int. J. Secur. Its Appl. **10**(9), 309–320 (2016)

19. Yuan, C., Xia, Z., Sun, X.: Coverless image steganography based on SIFT and BOF. J. Int. Technol. **18**(2), 435–442 (2017)

20. Sun, H., Grishman, R., Wang, Y.: Active learning based named entity recognition and its application in natural language coverless information hiding. J. Int. Technol. **18**(2), 443–451 (2017)

21. Xia, Z., Wang, X., Sun, X., Liu, Q., Xiong, N.: Steganalysis of LSB matching using differences between nonadjacent pixels. Multimedia Tools Appl. **75**(4), 1–16 (2014)

22. Cachin, C.: An information-theoretic model for steganography. In: Aucsmith, D. (ed.) IH 1998. LNCS, vol. 1525, pp. 306–318. Springer, Heidelberg (1998). doi:10.1007/3-540-49380-8_21

23. Katzenbeisser, S., Petitcolas, F.A.P.: Information Hiding Techniques for Steganography and Digital Watermarking. Artech House Publishers, Boston (1999)

24. Petitcolas, F.A., Anderson, R., Kuhn, M.: Information hiding - a survey. Proc. IEEE **87**(7), 1062–1078 (1999)

25. Zhang, J., Lin, H., Wang, L.: Coverless text information hiding method based on the rank map. J. Int. Technol. **18**(2), 427–434 (2017)

26. Fu, Z., Huang, F., Sun, X., Vasilakos, Athanasios V., Yang, C.: Enabling semantic search based on conceptual graphs over encrypted outsourced data. IEEE Trans. Serv. Comput. (2016). doi:10.1109/TSC.2016.2622697

27. Fu, Z., Sun, X., Ji, S., Xie, G.: Towards efficient content-aware search over encrypted outsourced data in cloud. In: Proceedings of the 35th Annual IEEE International Conference on Computer Communications (IEEE INFOCOM), San Francisco, CA (2016). doi:10.1109/INFOCOM.2016.7524606

Improved STDM Watermarking Using Semantic Information-Based JND Model

Chunxing Wang[1], Teng Zhang[1], Wenbo Wan[2,3(✉)], Jiande Sun[2,3], Jing Li[4], and Meiling Xu[1]

[1] School of Physics and Electronics, Shandong Normal University, Jinan 250014, China
cxwang@sdnu.edu.cn
[2] School of Information Science and Engineering, Shandong Normal University, Jinan 250014, China
wanwenbo@sdnu.edu.cn
[3] Institute of Data Science and Technology, Shandong Normal University, Jinan 250014, China
[4] School of Mechanical and Electrical Engineering, Shandong Management University, Jinan 250100, China

Abstract. The perceptual just noticeable distortion (JND) model has attracted increasing attention in the field of the quantization-based watermarking framework. The JND model can provide a superior trade-off between robustness and fidelity. However, the conventional JND models are not fit for the quantization-based watermarking, as the image has been altered by watermarking embedding. In this paper, we present an improved spread transform dither modulation (STDM) watermarking scheme, which is based on the image primitive features produced according to JND mechanism. The procedures include the contrast masking effect by utilizing a new measurement of edge strength which represent semantic information. What's more, the proposed semantic information-based JND model can be theoretically invariant to the changes in the watermark-embedding processing. The newly proposed JND model is very simple but more effective in the STDM watermarking. Experiments results demonstrate that the proposed watermarking scheme can bring about better performance compared with previously proposed perceptual STDM schemes.

Keywords: Watermarking · JND Model · STDM · Semantic information

1 Introduction

With the development of the imaging devices, such as digital cameras, smartphones, and medical imaging equipments, our world has been witnessing a tremendous growth in quantity, availability, and importance of images. Image recognition, image retrieval, image search, fingerprint detection and watermarking have caused more and more scholars concern [1–6].

X. Sun et al. (Eds.): ICCCS 2017, Part I, LNCS 10602, pp. 133–142, 2017.
https://doi.org/10.1007/978-3-319-68505-2_12

Digital watermarking has been attracting much researchers attention because of its importance in copyright protection, image authentication and anti-counterfeiting. It is the technology of embedding and identifying information into an original image without degrading the perceptual quality and simultaneously ensuring robust resistance to common attacks [7]. So how to maintain a balance between imperceptibility and robustness is important for a sophisticated watermarking framework. With the development of the imaging devices, such as digital cameras, smartphones, and medical imaging equipments, our world has been witnessing a tremendous growth in quantity, availability, and importance of images.

Spread transform dither modulation (STDM), proposed by Chen and Wornel [8], is a typical one owing to its advantages in implementation and computational flexibility. To achieve a better rate-distortion-robustness tradeoff the researchers proposed various STDM watermarking algorithms based on the just noticeable distortion (JND) models to various factors of HVS, such as brightness, contrast sensitivity, etc. In 2006, Derrerr et al. [9] first proposed a new STDM watermarking using Watson's perceptual JND model [10]. In their framework, the projection vectors used in STDM are assigned as the slacks computed by Watson's perceptual model, so as to ensure that more changes are directed to coefficients with larger perceptual slacks. But it is not robust enough for valumetric scaling attack. Subsequently, an improved method was proposed [11], where the perceptual model is not only used to determine the projection vector but also used to select the quantization step size. But it must use lots of DCT coefficients for one bit embedding and a low embedding rate can be resulted. Ma proposed to compute the quantization step size by adopting the projection vector and the perceptual slacks from Watson's JND model [12]. But Watson's perceptual model is image-dependent and relies on adapting to local image properties. Based on the luminance effect which was only part of Watson's model, Li et al. [13] proposed a step-projection based scheme that can ensure the values of quantization step size used in the watermark embedder and detector. More recently, Tang [14] presented an improved STDM watermarking scheme based on a more sophisticated luminance-based JND model [15]. Nevertheless, the luminance-based JND model, without the contrast masking, cannot be better correlated with the real visual perception characteristics of HVS.

Lin's recent work shows that edge is the most important feature which carrying most of the semantic information in an image [16–18]. Motivated by that we provide a novel STDM watermarking scheme using semantic information-based JND model in this paper. The rest of this paper is organized as follows. Section 2 provides a brief introduction to STDM. Semantic information-based JND model for STDM watermarking framework is detailed in Sect. 3. Section 4 incorporates the proposed model to design an improved STDM watermarking scheme. In Sect. 5, experimental results are provided to demonstrate the superior performance of the proposed scheme. Finally, Sect. 6 summarizes the paper.

2 Spread Transform Dither Modulation (STDM)

As an important extension of quantized index modulation, STDM uses dither modulation (DM) to modulate the projection of host vector along a given direction [8]. It can provide the superior performance compared to DM.

As we all know, the host vector x is projected onto the random direction vector u in the STDM algorithm. And then the dither modulation is performed to realize the embedding of the watermark. The distortion caused by the watermark essentially occurs only in the random direction u. The perceptual slack s also needs to be projected onto the random direction u.

STDM differs from regular DM. The host vector x is first projected onto the random direction vector u to obtain the projection x_u. So we can use the traditional dither modulation to embed the watermark bit m to modulate x_u. Finally, we get the watermarking information y:

$$y = x + (Q(x^T u, m, \Delta, \delta) - x^T u) \cdot u, m \in (0,1) \tag{1}$$

where the quantization modulation $Q(\cdot)$ is expressed as

$$Q(x^T u, m, \Delta, \delta) = \Delta \cdot round\left(\frac{x_u + \delta}{\Delta}\right) - \delta, m \in (0,1) \tag{2}$$

where Δ is the quantization step and δ is the dither signal corresponding to the message bit m [14].

In the extraction procedure, the received vector y' can be attacked and projected onto the direction vector u, we can get y'_u. Then the watermark m' is detected according to the minimum distance detector as follows:

$$m' = \arg \min_{b \in \{0,1\}} | y'_u - Q(y'_u, b, \Delta, \delta) | \tag{3}$$

3 Semantic Information-Based JND Model for STDM Watermarking

In the STDM watermarking, the perceptual JND model is introduced not only to perceive a variety of perceptual changes, including the spatial contrast sensitivity function (CSF), the luminance adaption effect and the contrast masking effect, but also remains invariant with watermark embedding procedure. Consequently, the error due to watermark embedding can not exceed the JND slack in case the watermark becomes perceptible.

Recently, a new luminance-based JND model is employed as a product of the spatial contrast sensitivity function and the luminance adaption effect [15]. The simple perceptual model relies not only on the background luminance of an image but also on DCT frequency. It is well known that the contrast masking effects reflect the edge complexity in the HVS perception. The CM effects indicate that the HVS is less sensitive to distortion in highly textured regions than edge or plain regions. As discussed in Ref. [18], edge is the most important feature carrying most of the semantic information in an image. So the CM effects can be measured by the semantic information. Considering that, an improved JND model is presented to incorporate the CM effects. The overall JND profile in DCT domain can be expressed as

$$JND(n, i, j) = s \cdot N \cdot J_{base} \cdot M_{LA} \cdot M_{SI} \qquad (4)$$

where s is intended to account for summation effect of individual JND thresholds over a spatial neighborhood for the visual system and is set to 0.14. N is the dimension of DCT. n is the index of a DCT block and (i, j) is the position of $(i, j) - th$ DCT coefficient. The parameters J_{base}, M_{LA} and M_{SI} will be detailed later.

3.1   Spatial CSF Effect

The human visual system is a multi-channel structure that breaks the input image into different sensory components. Each sensory channel has its own threshold (called the visual threshold). If the excitation value is lower than the visual threshold of the channel, the human eye can not feel the incentive. The visual threshold prevents the damage below the threshold from being perceived. On the other hand the masking increases the visual threshold. The main features of the HVS show that HVS has a band-pass property. It is more sensitive to the noise injected in the DCT basis function along the horizontal and vertical directions than the diagonal direction in spatial frequency. The spatial CSF model describes the sensitivity of human vision for each DCT coefficient.

The base threshold J_{base} is generated by spatial CSF based on a uniform background image [15] and can be given by considering the oblique effect [16] as

$$J_{base}(\omega_{i,j}, \varphi_{i,j}) = (J_d(\omega_{i,j}) - J_v(\omega_{i,j})) \cdot \sin(\varphi_{i,j})^2 + J_v(\omega_{i,j}) \qquad (5)$$

where $J_d(\omega_{i,j})$ and $J_v(\omega_{i,j})$ is found as

$$\begin{cases} J_d(\omega_{i,j}) = 0.0293 \cdot \omega_{i,j}^2 + (-0.1382) \cdot \omega_{i,j} + 1.75 \\ J_v(\omega_{i,j}) = 0.0238 \cdot \omega_{i,j}^2 + (-0.1771) \cdot \omega_{i,j} + 1.75 \end{cases} \qquad (6)$$

where $\omega_{i,j}$ is cycle per degree (cpd) in spatial frequency for the $(i, j) - th$ DCT coefficient and is given by

$$\omega = \sqrt{i^2 + j^2}/2N\theta \qquad (7)$$

$$\theta = \tan^{-1}[\frac{1}{2} \cdot R_{VH} \cdot H] \qquad (8)$$

where θ indicates the horizontal/vertical length of a pixel in degrees of visual angle [19], R_{VH} is the ratio of the viewing distance to the screen height, H is the number of pixels in the screen height, and $\varphi_{i,j}$ stands for the direction angle of the corresponding DCT component, which is expressed as

$$\varphi_{i,j} = \sin^{-1}(2 \cdot \omega_{i,0} \cdot \omega_{0,j}/\omega_{i,j}^2) \qquad (9)$$

3.2 Luminance Adaptation Effect

The LA factor remains sensitive to valumetric scaling since the average intensity does not scale linearly with amplitude scaling, so we need the average intensity to scale linearly with valumetric scaling for robustness. We introduce μ_p to describe the pixel intensity and it is expressed as

$$\mu_p = \frac{\sum\limits_{x=0}^{N-1}\sum\limits_{y=0}^{N-1} I(x,y)}{KN^2} \cdot \frac{128}{C_0} \tag{10}$$

where N is the DCT block size. $I(x,y)$ is the pixel intensity at the position (i,j) of the block. K is the maximum pixel intensity and C_0 denotes the mean intensity of the whole image.

A novel empirical luminance adaptation factor M_{LA} that employed both the cycles per degree (cpd) $w_{i,j}$ for spatial frequencies and the average intensity value of the block μ_p can be formulated as

$$M_{LA}(w_{i,j},\mu_p) = \begin{cases} 1 + (M_{0.1}(w_{i,j}) - 1) \, | \, \frac{\mu_p - 0.3}{0.2} \, |^{0.8} & \mu_p \leq 0.3 \\ 1 + (M_{0.9}(w_{i,j}) - 1) \, | \, \frac{\mu_p - 0.3}{0.6} \, |^{0.6} & \mu_p > 0.3 \end{cases} \tag{11}$$

where the $M_{0.1}(w_{i,j})$ and $M_{0.9}(w_{i,j})$ are empirically set as

$$\begin{cases} M_{0.1}(w_{i,j}) = 2.468 \times 10^{-4} w_{i,j}^2 + 4.466 \times 10^{-3} w_{i,j} + 1.14 \\ M_{0.9}(w_{i,j}) = 1.230 \times 10^{-3} w_{i,j}^2 + 1.433 \times 10^{-2} w_{i,j} + 1.34 \end{cases} \tag{12}$$

3.3 Semantic Information-Based Contrast Masking Effect

As we know, the LOG operator is a power edge detector, which can detect the edge pixels for a given image. For a given block, if it contains very sparse edge pixels, it can be considered as a flat block. On the other hand, if it contains many edge pixels, it means that this block has higher edge strength and more semantic information, thus it can be considered as a high detail block. In this paper, we propose to use the semantic information, more specifically, the edge strength only to measure the contrast masking effects of the original image.

In the JND model-based watermarking framework, the blind watermark detector must derive the edge strength from the watermarked image. However, since the watermark embedding alters the original image, the edge strength in the detector is not the same as that in the embedder. The mismatch problem can dramatically affect robustness. Here, we introduce the AC coefficients $AC_{0,1}$ and $AC_{1,0}$ (in which the subscripts refer to the row and column indices of the block, which have been regard as an effective measurement for the edge strength in both horizontal and vertical directions [20]. And what's more important, it can avoid the edge computation using LOG operator. Therefore, the semantic information metric can be described by the edge strength of the block, which is defined as

$$S_{AC}(i,j) = |AC_{0,1}(i,j)| + |AC_{1,0}(i,j)| \tag{13}$$

When the S_{AC} is lower than the threshold T, the corresponding block is considered as a flat block; otherwise it is considered as a high detail block. In our experiments, it is found that $T = 180$ works well for most images.

For the high detail block, eyes are less sensitive to the low frequency distortion, such as blocky artifacts, but the high detail frequency information should be reserved [18]. Based on the above considerations, the CM effects (M_{SI}) can be determined by

$$M_{SI} = \begin{cases} 1.05, & \text{for flat block} \\ 1.35, & \text{for high detail block} \end{cases} \qquad (14)$$

4 Proposed Scheme

As illustrated in Fig. 1, our proposed scheme consists of two parts, the embedding procedure and the detection procedure. The embedding procedure of the proposed scheme can be described as Fig. 1.

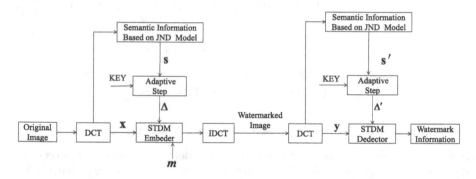

Fig. 1. Block diagram of proposed STDM watermarking using semantic information-based JND model

4.1 Watermark Embedding Procedure

As shown in Fig. 1, a new method is adopted in this section. Improved STDM watermarking using semantic information-based JND model is composed of embedding and detection procedures.

The watermark embedding process as follows:

(1) Divide the carrier image into 8×8 blocks and perform DCT transform to determine the DCT coefficients. The coefficients are scanned by zig-zag arrangement. Then select a part of these coefficients which range from the third to the next $L - th$ zig-zag-scanned DCT coefficients to form a single vector which denoted as the host vector x.

(2) The proposed perceptual JND model is calculated to get the perceptual slack vector s.

(3) The host vector x and the perceptual slack vector s are projected onto the given projection vector u, which is set as the Key, to generate the projections x_u and s_u. Then we can obtain the quantization step size Δ via s_u, which can be multiplied by the embedding strength in practice.

(4) One bit of the watermark m is embedded in the host projection x_u.

(5) Finally, the modified coefficients are transformed to obtain the watermarked image.

4.2   Watermark Extraction Procedure

The watermarked image may sustain certain attacks during transmission. The received image is used to detect the watermark as follows:

(1) The vector y of the sub-blocks of the detected image is obtained by the same manner as in the embedding step (1).

(2) The perceptual slack vector s' is calculated by the proposed perceptual JND model.

(3) The host vector y and the perceptual slack vector s' are projected onto the given projection vector u, which is set as the Key, to generate the projections x_{u}' and s_{u}'. Note that we can obtain the quantization step size Δ via s_{u}', which can be multiplied by the factor.

(4) Use the STDM detector to extract the watermark message m according to Eq. (3).

5   Experimental Results and Analysis

To evaluate the performance of our proposed scheme, we used standard images with dimensions of 256×256 from the USC-SIPI image database [21]. A random binary message of length 1024 bits was embedded into each image. Specifically, we selected the 4 to 10 DCT coefficients (in zig-zag-scanned order after 8×8 block DCT on each image) to form the host vector and embedded one bit in it. The test images were watermarked with a uniform fidelity, a fixed SSIM of 0.982. The bit error rate (BER) was computed for comparison purposes.

The experiments were conducted to compare the performance of the proposed scheme and other proposed STDM improvements, termed as STDM-RW [9], STDM-AdpWM [12], STDM-RDMWm [13] and STDM-JNDC [14]. Meanwhile, three kinds of attacks, Gaussian noise with mean zero variance ranging from 0 to 25; JPEG compression, where the JPEG quality factor varies from 20 to 100 valumetric scaling attacks that can reduce the image intensities as scaling factor varies from 0.1 to 1.5, were used to verify the performance of the proposed models.

Figure 2 shows the response to additive white Gaussian noise. The STDM-RW and STDM-AdpWM perform significantly worse because of the mismatch problem. Our proposed scheme does not exceed 22% for the Gaussian noise with variance $2.5 \times 10^{-3}v$. Our proposed scheme has average BER values 5%

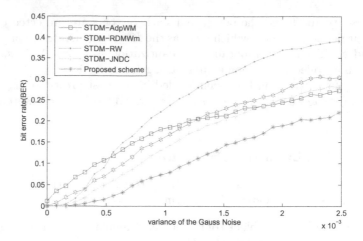

Fig. 2. BER versus Gaussian noise for different watermarking algorithms

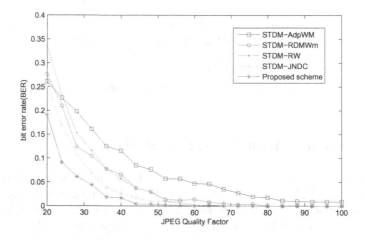

Fig. 3. BER versus JPEG compression for different watermarking algorithms

lower than STDM-AdpWM and 8% lower than STDM-RDMWm. Obviously, our scheme outperforms others in the noise-adding attacks-in particular.

The sensitivity to JPEG compression is demonstrated in Fig. 3. From the robustness results, STDM-AdpWM has average BER values 5% higher than the STDM-RW and STDM-RDMWm schemes, which have similar results. And the STDM-JNDC has average BER values 4% lower than the STDM-RW and STDM-RDMWm schemes. Our proposed scheme, on the other hand, has average BER values 2% lower than the STDM-JNDC The superior performance of the proposed scheme is achieved by the superior robustness properties of our proposed STDM scheme using Semantic information-based JND Model.

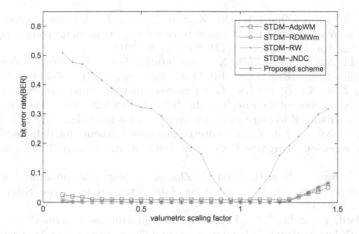

Fig. 4. BER versus valumetric scaling factor for different watermarking algorithms

As shown in Fig. 4, all the schemes except STDM-RW, do have robustness to valumetric scaling due to the mismatch problem within the watermark embedding. Although the other three algorithms showed passable robustness to this attack, our proposed scheme has the best performance.

6   Conclusion

In this paper, we propose an improved STDM watermarking scheme based on the perceptual JND model, which operates on the semantic information feature, more specifically edge strength according to JND mechanism. The framework of the proposed JND model is straightforward and robust to watermark embedding. In this way, a better tradeoff between robustness and fidelity is obtained. Experimental results show that the proposed scheme provides powerful resistance against common attacks compared to state-of-the-art STDM watermarking algorithms. The work in this paper reveals the high correlation between visual perception of the image and the watermarking scheme.

Acknowledgments. This work is partially supported by the Natural Science Foundation of China (No. 61601268), Natural Science Foundation of Shandong Province (ZR2016FB12, ZR2014FM012), Key Research and Development Foundation of Shandong Province (2016GGX101009) and Scientific Research and Development Foundation of Shandong Provincial Education Department (J15LN60).

References

1. Wang, J., Li, T., Shi, Y.-Q., Lian, S., Ye, J.: Forensics feature analysis in quaternion wavelet domain for distinguishing photographic images and computer graphics. Multimedia Tool Appl. 1–17 (2016)

2. Xia, Z., Wang, X., Zhang, L., Qin, Z., Sun, X., Ren, K.: A privacy-preserving and copy-deterrence content-based image retrieval scheme in cloud computing. IEEE Trans. Inf. Forensics Secur. **11**(11), 2594–2608 (2016)

3. Li, J., Li, X., Yang, B., Sun, X.: Segmentation-based image copy-move forgery detection scheme. IEEE Trans. Inf. Forensics Secur. **10**(3), 507–518 (2015)

4. Fu, Z., Sun, X., Ji, S., Xie, G.: Towards efficient content-aware search over encrypted outsourced data in cloud. In: IEEE INFOCOM 2016 - The 35th Annual IEEE International Conference on Computer Communications, pp. 1–9 (2016)

5. Xiong, L., Xu, Z., Xu, Y.: A secure re-encryption scheme for data services in a cloud computing environment. Concurr. Comput. Pract. Exp. **27**(17), 4573–4585 (2015)

6. Chen, X., Sun, X., Sun, H., Zhou, Z., Zhang, J.: Reversible watermarking method based on asymmetric-histogram shifting of prediction errors. J. Syst. Softw. **86**(10), 2620–2626 (2013)

7. Abdullatif, M., Zeki, A.M.: Properties of digital image watermarking. In: 2013 IEEE 9th International Colloquium on Signal Processing and its Applications, pp. 235–240 (2013)

8. Chen, B., Wornell, G.: Quantization index modulation: a class of provably good methods for digital watermarking and information embedding. IEEE Trans. Inf. Theor. **47**(4), 1423–1443 (2001)

9. Doerr, G., Li, Q., Cox, I.J.: Spread transform dither modulation using a perceptual model. In: Proceedings of IEEE International Workshop on Multimedia Signal Processing, pp. 98–102 (2006)

10. Watson, A.B.: DCT quantization matrices optimized for individual images. In: Proceedings of Human Vision Processing and Digital Display IV, vol. 1913, pp. 202–216. SPIE (1993)

11. Li, Q., Cox, I.J.: Improved spread transform dither modulation using a perceptual model: robustness to amplitude scaling and JPEG compression. In: Proceedings of IEEE ICASSP, vol. 2, pp. 185–188 (2007)

12. Ma, L.: Adaptive spread-transform modulation using a new perceptual model for color image. IEICE Trans. Inf. Syst. **E93–D**(4), 843–856 (2010)

13. Li, X., Liu, J., Sun, J., Yang, X., Liu, W.: Step-projection-based spread transform dither modulation. IET Inf. Secur. **5**(3), 170–180 (2011)

14. Tang, W., Wan, W., Liu, J., Sun, J.: Improved spread transform dither modulation using luminance-based JND model. In: Zhang, Y.-J. (ed.) ICIG 2015. LNCS, vol. 9218, pp. 430–437. Springer, Cham (2015). doi:10.1007/978-3-319-21963-9_39

15. Bae, S.H., Kim, M.: A novel DCT-based JND model for luminance adaptation effect in DCT frequency. IEEE Sig. Process. Lett. **20**, 893–896 (2013)

16. Rust, B., Rushmeier, H.: A new representation of the contrast sensitivity function for human vision. In: Proceedings of the International Conference on Image, Science System, Technology, pp. 1–15 (1997)

17. Wei, Z., Ngan, K.N.: Spatio-temporal just noticeable distortion profile for grey scale image/video in DCT domain. IEEE Trans. Circ. Syst. Video Technol. **19**(3), 337–346 (2009)

18. Qi, H., Jiao, S., Lin, W.: Content-based image quality assessment using semantic information and luminance differences. Electron. Lett. **50**(20), 1435–1436 (2014)

19. Ahumada, A.J., Peterson, H.A.: Luminance-model-based DCT quantization for color image compression. In: Proceedings of SPIE, vol. 1666, pp. 365–374 (1992)

20. Muthuswamy, K., Rajan, D.: Salient motion detection in compressed domain. IEEE Sig. Process. Lett. **20**(10), 996–999 (2013)

21. USC-SIPI Image Database. http://sipi.usc.edu/database/

The Categories of Quantum Information Hiding Protocol

Shujiang Xu[✉], Lianhai Wang, Guangqi Liu, Xiaohui Han,
Dawei Zhao, and Lijuan Xu

Shandong Provincial Key Laboratory of Computer Networks, Shandong Computer Science
Center (National Supercomputer Center in Jinan), Jinan 250014, China
{xushj,wanglh,liuguangqi,hanxh,zhaodw,xulj}@sdas.org

Abstract. Quantum information hiding, which is a popular topic in quantum information, can be chosen as an alternative method for privacy protection. As the latest developments of classical information hiding in quantum scenario, quantum information hiding employs the effects of quantum information and quantum computation to achieve the target of information hiding by utilizing quantum states as the carriers of information transmission. Since it was first proposed in 2001, quantum information hiding has been developed very fast. In this paper, quantum information hiding protocols are divided into three categories, including quantum steganography, quantum covert channel and quantum watermarking, according to the application purpose. And then every class of the quantum information hiding protocols are described respectively. At the end of the paper, the new trends on the quantum information hiding research and the perspective of quantum information hiding research are given.

Keywords: Quantum information hiding · Quantum steganography · Quantum covert channel · Quantum watermarking

1 Introduction

Quantum secret communication, which transmits classical or quantum information through the quantum channel, achieves an unconditional secure communication between two legitimate parties without being eavesdropped. Because the uncertainty principle requires anyone measuring a quantum system to disturb it, the disturbance inevitably alerts legitimate users to the eavesdropper's presence. Quantum secret communication is one of the most interesting contents of the research of quantum information. A well-known example is the quantum key distribution (QKD) protocols. In 1984, Bennett and Brassard [1] proposed the first QKD protocol (namely BB84) using two groups of orthogonal quantum states. With the rapid development of quantum information technology, the outstanding research achievements of quantum secret communication theory and technology have brought a revolutionary impact on the research of the present information science and aroused great concern. More and more researchers devote themselves to the new scientific research field. It is particularly worth mentioning that information hiding has also been introduced into this remarkable research field.

X. Sun et al. (Eds.): ICCCS 2017, Part I, LNCS 10602, pp. 143–152, 2017.
https://doi.org/10.1007/978-3-319-68505-2_13

Information hiding, as well as cryptography, is one of the important means for protecting privacy and security [2–4]. Cryptography protects the content of the secret message, while information hiding conceals the existence of the secret message. Information hiding can be used to realize covert communication, copyright protection or anti-counterfeit. Quantum information hiding, which can be considered as the latest developments of classical information hiding in quantum scenario, employs the effects of quantum information and quantum computation to achieve the target of information hiding by utilizing quantum states as the carriers of information transmission. It is also a popular topic in the study of information security. Due to quantum non-cloning theorem and quantum uncertainty principle, quantum information hiding protocols also can achieve unconditional security. Thus, quantum information hiding has more inherent advantage of security than that of the classical information hiding. The categories of quantum information hiding protocols are researched according to the application purpose in this paper. We divide quantum information hiding protocols into three categories and describe every class of the quantum information hiding protocols respectively. At the end of the paper, we will introduce the new trends in the quantum information hiding research and give the perspective of quantum information hiding research.

This paper is organized as follows. Section 2 divides quantum information hiding protocols into three categories and introduces every type of quantum information hiding protocols respectively. Section 3 concludes this paper.

2   Categories of Quantum Information Hiding

The first quantum information hiding protocol [2] was proposed in 2001. Since then, quantum information hiding has made a great progress quickly. Especially after 2010, many new quantum information hiding protocols were proposed. According to the application purpose, quantum information hiding protocols can be divided into three basic categories: quantum steganography, quantum covert communication and quantum watermarking, which is shown in Fig. 1. Below, we respectively describe every class of the quantum information hiding protocols in details.

2.1   Quantum Steganography

Quantum steganography, which is an important subdiscipline of quantum information hiding, embeds secret message into another innocuous looking quantum carrier so as to conceal the existence of the secret message. Based on the difference of the carrier medium, the quantum steganography protocols can be divided into five small classes.

The first one is physical property-based quantum data hiding protocol. In terms of this class of quantum steganography protocols, the secret bits can be hidden utilizing some physical properties of quantum states, and recovered via local operations and classical communication (LOCC) for some parties. Based on the fact that $|\Psi^-\rangle$ is spin singlet Bell state while the other three Bell states, $|\Phi^+\rangle$, $|\Phi^-\rangle$, and $|\Psi^+\rangle$ are spin triplets, Terhal et al. [5] proposed the first quantum information hiding protocol in 2001. The

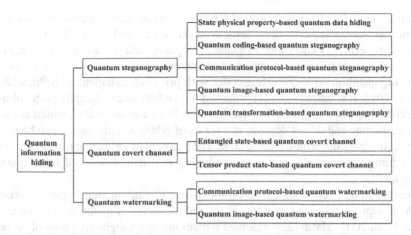

Fig. 1. The categories of quantum information hiding.

protocol was expanded by DiVincenzo et al. [6] by using superdense coding and quantum teleportation. Eggeling and Werner [7] presented a general technique for hiding a classical bit in multipartite non-entangled quantum states in 2002. In 2003, Guo et al. [8] presented a method to integrate the uncertainty of Bell state preparation into the data-hiding procedure spontaneous parameter down-conversion, and gave a quantum data hiding protocol by the extended Bell states. The scheme simplifies the encoding process of the secret messages. A multiparty data hiding protocols for quantum information was proposed by Hayden et al. [9] using all possible threshold access structures in 2005. In the protocol, one hidden qubit only needs a local physical qubit to store it. In 2007, Chattopadhyay and Sarkar [10] proved local indistinguishability of four orthogonal activable bound entangled states shared among even number of parties, and established a multipartite quantum data hiding scheme. Matthews et al. [11] research how to distinguish two quantum states under restricted families of measurements, and then they showed that protocol [5] has the best possible dimensional dependence and can be against local operations attack in 2009. In 2012, Allati et al. [12] proposed a quantum steganography protocol using GHZ_4 state, where the GHZ_4 state can be rewritten into four different forms by two groups of different orthogonal basis. Because all the given 8 groups of unitary transformations that the sender applied can change a GHZ_4 state into 6 instead of 8 different states when the global phase is not considered, Xu et al. [13] analyzed and improved this protocol. Because the large amount of the quantum states consumed necessarily, even if they have remarkable quantum physical property and very suit for quantum data hiding, this class of quantum steganography is develops slowly and the number of achievements is limited.

The second one is quantum coding-based quantum steganography protocol. The secret message can be taken as redundant codeword of the quantum code to achieve the target of information hiding. Gea-Banacloche [14] gave an idea for hiding quantum information by disguising it as noise in a codeword of a quantum error-correcting code in 2002. However, he did not give the hiding and extraction scheme of the secret message. In 2010, Shaw and Brun [15, 16] proposed the detailed scheme by sharing a random quantum (or classical) key, in which the secret messages are disguised as channel error into a error-coding code or its' error syndromes. Cao and Song [17–19] introduced the quantum secret key encryption to quantum steganography protocol to avoid the large number of key distribution. A quantum steganography algorithm was proposed by combining quantum error-correcting codes with prior entanglement by Mihara [20] in 2015. In 2012, Basharov et al. [21] proposed a quantum steganography protocol using the decoherence free w states. The decoherence free quantum states, which are decoherence immune and do not degrade in a series of relaxation processes, can be used to construct the quantum error-avoiding code. The protocol has a leading role for the design of quantum steganography protocols employing the redundancies of other quantum coding methods.

The third one is communication protocol-based quantum steganography protocol which attempts to take the secret bits as the redundancies of quantum communication protocols. In 2007, Matin [22] presented a quantum steganography protocol based on the BB84-QKD protocol [1], in which the secret bit is took as a bit of the eavesdropping detection sequence of QKD protocol. In 2010, Liao et al. [23] proposed a multipartite quantum steganography protocol that hides the secret bit in the eavesdropping detection sequence of a quantum secret sharing (QSS) protocol. Gao et al. [24] pointed out that QKD and QSS can be used for deterministic secure communication, and believed they are not suitable for steganography based classical prisoner model in 2012. However, there may be no dilemma for quantum prisoners due to the enormous computing power of quantum computers [25–27]. Therefore, it may be reasonable to believe that QKD and QSS are suitable for steganography based quantum prisoner model.

The fourth one is quantum image-based quantum steganography protocol which employs the redundancies of quantum image to hide secret message by the quantum processing technology. In 2008, Mogo [28] proposed a quantum steganography protocol by using three level quantum system to describe RGB image. Based on the novel enhanced quantum representation (NEQR), Wang et al. [29] proposed the least significant qubit (LSQb) protocol for quantum image employing the Fourier transform in 2015. In which the least significant qubit is implied to hid the secret message. Based on the (NEQR), Qu et al. [30] presented a quantum steganography algorithm in 2016. In this protocol, the second least significant qubit of quantum carrier image is replaced with the secret information, while the least significant qubit is used for quantum watermarking. With the novel quantum representation for color digital images (NCQI), a LSQb information hiding algorithm was proposed by Sang et al. [31]. Due to the widely application of digital image and the diversity of the representation method for quantum image, quantum image-based quantum steganography has a great development potential.

The last one is quantum transformation-based quantum steganography protocol, in which the secret message is hid in the redundancies of a quantum transformation. In the process of quantum Fourier Transform, Mihara [32] introduced a quantum steganography protocol which embeds secret message in the phase of quantum entangled states in 2012. Wei et al. [33, 34] proposed two quantum steganography protocols based on quantum probability measurements. Based on the NEQR of digital images, Jiang and Wang [35] presented a quantum image steganography protocol using the Moire pattern in 2015. Because of the widely application of quantum transformation in the quantum age, quantum transformation-based quantum steganography protocol is expected to develop rapidly.

2.2 Quantum Covert Channel

Quantum covert channel, which is the latest development of classical covert channel protocol in the field of quantum information, usually establishes a covert channel inside a given quantum communication channel to send a secret message. In order to keep the existence of secret messages imperceptible, the given quantum communications channel is used to transfer normal looking information. Note that quantum covert channel is distinct from, and often confused with, quantum stenography. The way for information hiding is different between them, quantum steganography takes another innocuous looking quantum states as the carrier to hiding secret messages, while quantum covert channel tunnels a covert channel inside a given quantum communication channel to send secret messages. Moreover, after embedding secret messages, the carrier of a quantum steganography protocol usually is slightly modified, while the carrier of the quantum covert channel has no perceptible change.

In 2010, Qu et al. [36, 37] first proposed the idea of quantum covert channel based on the entanglement of Bell states and χ-type quantum states, respectively. In the two protocols, covert channels are build up in the given quantum secure direct communication (QSDC) channels to send secret messages. In 2013, Ye and Jiang [38, 39] proposed two quantum covert channel protocols respectively based on the entanglement swapping of GHZ states and the entanglement swapping between one GHZ state and one Bell state in cavity quantum electrodynamics. The four protocols [37–39] have high security and good imperceptibility, but they consume some auxiliary quantum states. In 2013, Xu et al. [40, 41] formally introduced the definition of quantum covert channel, and proposed a novel quantum covert channel [41] using the tensor product of Bell states without consuming any auxiliary quantum state. The quantum covert channel protocol has a low computational complexity and a large capacity. The paper [40] showed the reason why a covert channel can be established within a given QSDC channel by analyzing the properties of the unitary transformations used in the a QSDC scheme. Because the unitary transformations in a QSDC protocol have three remarkable characteristics: information encoding, secrecy and universality, it can be again used to encode another information bits. So, the unitary transformations used in a given QSDC channels can be employed to build quantum covert channels. Compared with the first three classes of quantum steganography protocols, the quantum covert channel has a large capacity.

2.3 Quantum Watermarking

Quantum watermarking, which is the third important subdiscipline of quantum information hiding, writes and extracts quantum watermarking by means of quantum mechanism. Based on the difference of the thoughtway, the quantum watermarking protocols can be divided into two small classes.

The first one is communication protocol-based quantum watermarking protocol which can write the watermarking underlying the quantum communication channel. It is effective to keep the security of the watermarking. By the relative frequency of error in observing qubits in a dissimilar basis, Worley III [42] proposed a quantum watermarking protocol based on BB84 [1] protocol in 2004. Employing the entanglement swapping of Bell states, Fatahi and Naseri [43] presented a quantum watermarking protocol without consuming any auxiliary quantum state in 2012. Based on the entanglement swapping property of Bell dual basis, Mo et al. [44] proposed a quantum watermarking protocol in 2013. The two protocol utilized QSDC protocols, but their capacity is only 1/2 that of the given QSDC protocols.

The second one is quantum image-based watermarking protocol. In which the watermarking is written in the redundancies of quantum images or the redundancies of quantum transformation for quantum images. Since the proposal of quantum image representation method in 2010, quantum image watermarking has made a repaid progress. In recent years, some new quantum image watermarking protocols was proposed based on quantum image representation method, especially flexible representation of quantum image (FRQI). In 2011, a watermarking and authentication strategy for quantum images (WaQI) were proposed based on restricted geometric transformations and FRQI by Iliyasu et al. [45]. In 2013, Zhang et al. [46] presented a watermark strategy for quantum images based on FRQI. Compared with the the former, the later not only can be used to find out who is the real owner, but also can achieve a maximum capacity. A robust watermark strategy for quantum images was proposed based on quantum Fourier transform by Zhang et al. [47]. In the protocol, the watermarking image is embedded into the Fourier coefficients of the quantum carrier image. Because the classical simulation procedure is employed which do not observe the basic principles of quantum mechanics, Yang et al. [48] pointed out that the protocol is incorrect and gave an improved protocol for it. Using FRQI, Song et al. proposed two dynamic watermarking scheme for quantum images based on quantum wavelet transform [49] and quantum Hadamard transform [50] respectively. In which, a dynamic vector instead of a fixed parameter is utilized for controlling embedding strength. Yang et al. [51] pointed out that the protocol [49] does not observe the basic principles of quantum mechanics, and then gave an improved protocol in 2014. Shen et al. [52] proposed a quantum image watermarking scheme based on the second structure of quantum cosine transform in 2015. In 2016, Wei et al. [53] designed a quantum multi-control rotation gate, and then presented a spatial domain quantum watermarking scheme using FRQI. Some new quantum image watermarking protocols were proposed based other representation methods of quantum image. A duple watermarking strategy on multi-channel quantum images (MCQI) is proposed based on quantum Fourier transforms by Yan et al. [54]. The watermark image is embedded into both the spatial domain and the frequency domain of the MCQI. Utilizing the NEQI, Heidari and Naseri [55] presented a quantum image watermarking protocol including quantum image scrambling based on least significant bit in 2016. Using simple and small-scale quantum circuits, a new quantum gray-scale image watermarking scheme was proposed by Miyake and Nakamae [56] based on NEQI. Li et al. [57] introduced a flexible representation for quantum color image (FRQCI), and presented a quantum image watermarking protocol based on controlled rotation of qubits. The research of quantum watermarking has just started and will be make a quickly progress in the future because the wildly application of digital images.

3 Conclusion

Most of the quantum steganography protocols, belonging to the first three classes, have small capacity, and can be employed to send some short messages consequently. Due to the large redundancies of quantum image and quantum image transformation, the last two classes of quantum steganography protocols may have a large capacity than that of the first three classes. Quantum covert channel is an good choice for covert communication because of its excellent imperceptibility. In comparison, quantum watermarking will play an important role in copyright protection and anti-counterfeit.

In the future quantum information age, quantum encoding technology and quantum image will have variety of applications. Quantum encoding may have redundant encoding words, both quantum image and quantum image transformation will have some redundancies. Each of the redundancies is a chance for quantum information hiding. So the quantum encoding-based quantum information hiding and the quantum image-based quantum information hiding have great potential for development.

Acknowledgements. This work is supported by the National Natural Science Foundation of China under Grant Nos. 61602281 and 61373131, the Shandong Provincial Natural Science Foundation of China under Grant Nos. ZR2013FM025, ZR2014FM003, ZR2015YL018, ZR2016YL011 and ZR2016YL014, the Shandong Provincial Outstanding Research Award Fund for Young Scientists of China under Grant No. BS2015DX006, PAPD and CICAEET funds, and the Shandong Academy of Sciences Youth Fund Project, China under Grant Nos. 2015QN003, 2015QN011 and 2013QN007.

References

1. Bennett, C.H., Brassard, G.: Quantum cryptography: Public-key distribution and coin tossing. In: Proceedings of IEEE International Conference on Computers, Systems and Signal Processing, pp. 175–179. IEEE Press, New York (2001)
2. Fu, Z.J., Ren, K., Shu, J.G., Sun, X.M., Huang, F.X.: Enabling personalized search over encrypted outsourced data with efficiency improvement. IEEE Trans. Parallel Distrib. Syst. **27**, 2546–2559 (2016)
3. Qu, Z.G., Keeney, J., Robitzsch, S., Zaman, F., Wang, X.J.: Multilevel pattern mining architecture for automatic network monitoring in heterogeneous wireless communication networks. China Commun. **13**, 108–116 (2016)
4. Xue, Y., Jiang, J.M., Zhao, B.P., Ma, T.H.: A self-adaptive artificial bee colony algorithm based on global best for global optimization. Soft Comput. (2017) doi:10.1007/s00500-017-2547-1
5. Terhal, B.M., DiVincenzo, D.P., Leung, D.W.: Hiding bits in Bell states. Phys. Rev. Lett. **86**, 5807–5810 (2001)
6. DiVincenzo, D.P., Hayden, P.A., Terhal, B.M.: Quantum data hiding. IEEE Trans. Inf. Theor. **48**, 580–599 (2002)

150   S. Xu et al.

7. Eggeling, T., Werner, R.F.: Hiding classical data in multipartite quantum states. Phys. Rev. Lett. **89**, 097905 (2002)
8. Guo, G.C., Guo, G.P.: Quantum data hiding with spontaneous parameter down-conversion. Phys. Rev. A **68**, 044303 (2003)
9. Hayden, P., Leung, D., Smith, G.: Multiparty data hiding of quantum information. Phys. Rev. A **71**, 062339 (2005)
10. Chattopadhyay, I., Sarkar, D.: Local indistinguishability and possibility of hiding cbits in activable bound entangled states. Phys. Lett. A **365**, 273–277 (2007)
11. Matthews, W., Wehner, S., Winter, A.: Distinguishability of quantum states under restricted families of measurements with an application to quantum data hiding. Commun. Math. Phys. **291**, 813–843 (2009)
12. El Allati, A., Ould Medeni, M.B., Hassouni, Y.: Quantum steganography via Greenberger-Horne-Zeilinger GHZ$_4$ state. Commun. Theor. Phys. **57**, 577–582 (2012)
13. Xu, S.J., Chen, X.B., Niu, X.X., Yang, Y.X.: Steganalysis and improvement of a quantum steganography protocol via GHZ$_4$ state. Chin. Phys. B **22**, 060307 (2013)
14. Gea-Banacloche, J.: Hiding messages in quantum data. J. Math. Phys. **43**, 4531–4536 (2002)
15. Shaw, B.A., Brun, T.A.: Quantum steganography with noisy quantum channels. Phys. Rev. A **83**, 022310 (2011)
16. Shaw, B.A., Brun, T.A.: Hiding quantum information in the perfect code. arXiv:quant-ph/1007.0793v2
17. Cao, D., Song, W.L.: A novel quantum steganography with optimal private-key scheme. J. Inf. Comput. Sci. **8**, 1793–1800 (2011)
18. Cao, D., Song, W.L.: Multi-party quantum steganography with GHZ private-key. J. Inf. Comput. Sci. **8**, 2703–2709 (2011)
19. Cao, D., Song, W.L.: Multi-party quantum covert communication with entanglement private-keys. J. Appl. Sci. Electron. Inf. Eng. **30**, 52–58 (2012)
20. Mihara, T.: Quantum steganography using prior entanglement. Phys. Lett. A **379**, 952–955 (2015)
21. Basharov, A.M., Gorbachev, V.N., Trubilko, A.I.: A quantum steganography protocol based on W class entangled states. Opt. Spectrosc. **112**, 323–326 (2012)
22. Martin, K.: Steganographic communication with quantum information. In: Furon, T., Cayre, F., Doërr, G., Bas, P. (eds.) IH 2007. LNCS, vol. 4567, pp. 32–49. Springer, Heidelberg (2007). doi:10.1007/978-3-540-77370-2_3
23. Liao, X., Wen, Q.Y., Sun, Y., Zhang, J.: Multi-party covert communication with steganography and quantum secret sharing. J. Syst. Softw. **83**, 1801–1804 (2011)
24. Gao, F., Liu, B., Zhang, W.W., Wen, Q.Y., Chen, H.: Is quantum key distribution suitable for steganography? Quantum Inf. Process. **12**, 625–630 (2012)
25. Collins, G.P.: Schrodinger's games: for quantum prisoners, there may be no dilemma. Sci. Am. **282**, 28–29 (2000)
26. Du, J., Li, H., Xu, X., Shi, M., Wu, J., Zhou, X., Han, R.: Experimental realization of quantum games on a quantum computer. Phys. Rev. Lett. **88**, 137902 (2002)
27. Chen, K.Y., Hogg, T.: How well do people play a quantum prisoner's dilemma. Quantum Inf. Process. **5**, 43–67 (2006)
28. Mogos, G.: Stego quantum algorithm. In: International Symposium on Computer Science and its Applications, pp. 187–190. IEEE Press, New York (2008)
29. Wang, S., Sang, J., Song, X.H., Niu, X.M.: Least significant qubit (LSQb) information hiding algorithm for quantum image. Measurement **73**, 352–359 (2015)

30. Qu, Z., He, H., Ma, S.: A novel self-adaptive quantum steganography based on quantum image and quantum watermark. In: Sun, X., Liu, A., Chao, H.-C., Bertino, E. (eds.) ICCCS 2016. LNCS, vol. 10040, pp. 394–403. Springer, Cham (2016). doi: 10.1007/978-3-319-48674-1_35
31. Sang, J.Z., Wang, S., Li, Q.: Least significant qubit algorithm for quantum images. Quantum Inf. Process. **15**, 4441–4460 (2016)
32. Mihara, T.: Quantum steganography embedded any secret text without changing the content of cover data. J. Quantum Inf. Sci. **2**, 10–14 (2012)
33. Wei, Z.H., Chen, X.B., Niu, X.X., Yang, Y.X.: The quantum steganography protocol via quantum noisy channels. Int. J. Theor. Phys. **54**, 2505–2515 (2015)
34. Wei, Z.H., Chen, X.B., Niu, X.X., Yang, Y.X.: A novel quantum steganography protocol based on probability measurements. Int. J. Quantum Inf. **11**, 1350068 (2013)
35. Jiang, N., Wang, L.: A novel strategy for quantum image steganography based on Moire Pattern. Int. J. Theor. Phys. **54**, 1021–1032 (2015)
36. Qu, Z.G., Chen, X.B., Zhou, X.J., Niu, X.X., Yang, Y.X.: Novel quantum steganography with large payload. Opt. Commun. **283**, 4782–4786 (2010)
37. Qu, Z.G., Chen, X.B., Luo, M.X., Niu, X.X., Yang, Y.X.: Quantum steganography with large payload based on entanglement swapping of χ-type entangled states. Opt. Commun. **284**, 2075–2082 (2011)
38. Ye, T.Y., Jiang, L.Z.: Quantum steganography with large payload based on dense coding and entanglement swapping of Greenberger-Horne-Zeilinger states. Chin. Phys. B **22**, 050309 (2013)
39. Ye, T.Y., Jiang, L.Z.: Large payload quantum steganography based on cavity quantum electrodynamics. Chin. Phys. B **22**, 040305 (2013)
40. Xu, S.J., Chen, X.B., Niu, X.X., Yang, Y.X.: A novel quantum covert channel protocol based on any quantum secure direct communication scheme. Commun. Theor. Phys. **59**, 547–553 (2013)
41. Xu, S.J., Chen, X.B., Niu, X.X., Yang, Y.X.: High-efficiency Quantum Steganography Based on the Tensor Product of Bell States. Sci. China Phys. Mech. Astron. **56**, 1745–1754 (2013)
42. Worley III, G.G.: Quantum watermarking by frequency of error when observing qubits in dissimilar bases. arXiv:quant-ph/0401041v2
43. Fatahi, N., Naseri, M.: Quantum watermarking using entanglement swapping. Int. J. Theor. Phys. **51**, 2094–2100 (2012)
44. Mo, J., Ma, Z.F., Yang, Y.X., Niu, X.X.: A quantum watermarking protocol based on Bell dual basis. Int. J. Theor. Phys. **52**, 3813–3819 (2013)
45. Iliyasu, M., Le, P.Q., Dong, F., Hirota, K.: Watermarking and authentication of quantum images based on restricted geometric transformations. Inf. Sci. **186**, 126–149 (2012)
46. Zhang, W.W., Gao, F., Liu, B., Jia, H.Y., Wen, Q.Y., Chen, H.: A quantum watermark protocol. Int. J. Theor. Phys. **52**, 504–513 (2013)
47. Zhang, W.W., Gao, F., Liu, B., Wen, Q.Y., Chen, H.: A watermark strategy for quantum images based on quantum fourier transform. Quantum Inf. Process. **12**, 793–803 (2013)
48. Yang, Y.G., Jia, X., Xu, P., Tian, J.: Analysis and improvement of the watermark strategy for quantum images based on quantum Fourier transform. Quantum Inf. Process. **12**, 2765–2769 (2013)
49. Song, X.H., Wang, S., Liu, S., El-Latif, A.A.A., Niu, X.M.: A dynamic watermarking scheme for quantum images using quantum wavelet transform. Quantum Inf. Process. **12**, 3689–3706 (2013)
50. Song, X.H., Wang, S., Liu, S., El-Latif, A.A.A., Niu, X.M.: Dynamic watermarking scheme for quantum images based on Hadamard transform. Multimedia Syst. **20**, 379–388 (2014)

51. Yang, Y.G., Xu, P., Tian, J., Zhang, H.: Analysis and improvement of the dynamic watermarking scheme for quantum images using quantum wavelet transform. Quantum Inf. Process. **13**, 1931–1936 (2014)
52. Wang, S., Song, X.H., Niu, X.M.: Quantum cosine transform based watermarking scheme for quantum images. Chin. J. Electron. **24**, 321–325 (2015)
53. Wei, Z.H., Chen, X.B., Xu, S.J., Niu, X.X., Yang, Y.X.: A spatial domain quantum watermarking scheme. Commun. Theor. Phys. **66**, 66–76 (2016)
54. Yan, F., Iliyasu, A.M., Sun, B., Venegas-Andraca, S.E., Dong, F.Y., Hirota, K.: A duple watermarking strategy for multi-channel quantum images. Quantum Inf. Process. **14**, 1675–1692 (2015)
55. Heidari, S., Naseri, M.: A novel LSB based quantum watermarking. Int. J. Theor. Phys. **55**, 4205–4218 (2016)
56. Miyake, S., Nakamae, K.: A quantum watermarking scheme using simple and small-scale quantum circuits. Quantum Inf. Process. **15**, 1849–1864 (2016)
57. Li, P., Xiao, H., Li, B.: Quantum representation and watermark strategy for color images based on the controlled rotation of qubits. Quantum Inf. Proc. **15**, 1–26 (2016)

Coverless Information Hiding Technology Research Based on News Aggregation

Conghua Liu[1]([⊠]), Gang Luo[1], and Zuwei Tian[2]

[1] College of Computer Science and Electronic Engineering,
Hunan University, Changsha 410082, China
lchzls@163.com, luo.g@qq.com
[2] School of Information Science and Engineering,
Hunan First Normal University, Changsha 410205, China
tianzuwei@126.com

Abstract. This paper proposes a novel coverless information hiding method based on news aggregation. It converts the secret message M to a large integer N, and hides N in a news web by changing the order of news headlines. Experimental results and analysis show that this method is robust for any current steganalysis algorithm, and effective for stego-message delivery.

Keywords: Coverless information hiding · News aggregation · Change the order · News headlines

1 Introduction

In recent years, with the rapid development of network and multimedia technologies, information hiding technology has become a research hotspot in the field of information security. As a result, more and more people have devoted themselves to research on information hiding methods. Information hiding technology means utilizing the redundancy of the host signal and then embedding the secret data in a host signal under the premise that the secret data is not easy to be perceived by people [1]. It is applied in the fields of digital media and copyright protection. The method of information hiding can be divided into four types according to the kinds of covers: information hiding based on image [2], information hiding based on video [3], information hiding based on audio [4], information hiding based on text [5]. There is a big shortcoming among these traditional information hiding methods, i.e., they make some modification in the carrier according to certain instructions in order to embed the information to be hidden. Therefore, most existing information hiding approaches are also difficult to resist the detection of various types of steganalysis algorithms [6, 7]. The coverless information hiding technology has become a new research trend.

Coverless information hiding is a new concept which was first proposed by Sun X to resist steganalysis tools. Instead of conventional information hiding that needs to search an embedded carrier for the secret information, coverless information hiding requires no other carriers. It is driven by the secret information to generate an encryption vector. The coverless information hiding technology uses the big data to construct the database, dividing the secret message to be hidden into keywords [8–10].

© Springer International Publishing AG 2017
X. Sun et al. (Eds.): ICCCS 2017, Part I, LNCS 10602, pp. 153–163, 2017.
https://doi.org/10.1007/978-3-319-68505-2_14

What's more, it sets the characteristic tags to guide the extraction of the keywords and searches natural texts including "tag + keyword" in the database to send the receiver. Eventually, the receiver will extract the secret message from the texts they have received.

Combined with the characteristics of the news, the paper proposes a novel coverless information hiding method based on news aggregation. The proposed method converts the secret message M to a large integer N, and hides N in a news web by changing the order of news headlines. As a whole, the algorithm is relatively simple to implement. Moreover, because any modification trace will not be left in the news texts, our method is robust for any current steganalysis algorithm and effective for stego-message delivery.

The paper is structured as follows: the 1st Sect. is a brief introduction to the coverless information hiding; the 2nd Sect. is related to the relevant work; the 3rd Sect. presents coverless information hiding and extraction algorithms; the 4th Sect. is devoted to the experimental results and analysis; the 5th Sect. is a summary of the paper.

2   Related Works

Coverless information hiding technology, as an important branch of multimedia information hiding technology, has attracted more and more scholars' attention. The main purpose of coverless information hiding research is to resist steganography detection fundamentally. So far, we have obtained some good results. After a careful study, coverless information hiding technology can be mainly divided into text-based coverless information hiding and image-based coverless information hiding.

Chen et al. [11] first presented a coverless information hiding method based on the Chinese mathematical expression. The proposed algorithm directly generates a stego-vector from the hidden information at first, and then based on text big data, a normal text that includes the stego-vector will be retrieved, which means that the secret message can be send to the receiver without any modification for the stego-text. However, its implementation is a little complex and the hidden capacity is not large enough. In order to further improve the hidden capacity, Zhou et al. [12] proposed a coverless information hiding method based on multi-keywords. The main idea of the method is that the number of keywords will be hidden in the text where keywords have been hidden. However, there are few numbers in one text, so the success rate of the method is low. Zhang et al. [13] proposed a coverless text information hiding method based on the word rank map. Firstly, stego-vectors are directly generated from the secret message by using the rank map. Secondly, some normal texts, stego-texts including the generated stego-vectors, will be searched from the text big data. Finally, the secret information can be sent to the receiver without any modification of the stego-texts. The proposed algorithm is robust for almost all current steganalysis methods, but only 1 word can be hidden in each English text. Based on the big data of texts, Chen et al. [14] proposed a coverless information hiding method using Chinese character encoding technology. In the proposed method, the tags which are based on binary numbers and transformed by Chinese characters, are designed to locate the secret information and meet the requirements of both randomness and universality.

Then the receiver would extract the secret information according to several certain tags, which are selected based on an independent secret key of the receiver. The experimental results show that the success rate of hiding could reach up to about 95.25%.

Zhou et al. [15] proposed a coverless image steganography framework in which the secret data can be communicated by sending a series of images which already contain the secret data. The method can be robust to various typical image attacks. However, only 8-bit data can be hidden in each original image. Zhou et al. [16] introduced a coverless information hiding method based on the bag-of-words model. To hide text information into an image, visual words are extracted to represent the text information. The proposed method has good performance in anti-steganalysis capability, robustness against common attacks, and security, but because each image only selects a location label to hide, the hidden capacity of each image is limited. Yuan et al. [17] proposed a novel coverless image steganography scheme based on scale invariant feature transform and bag of feature. Firstly, the robust feature hash sequences are constructed with our protocol of feature. Secondly, the secret message is converted into bitstreams. Finally, these images with the secret information are chosen and sent to receivers through using inverted index. The method can resist the analysis of existing steganalysis tools and have a desirable robustness to the common image attacks.

In order to resist all of the existing steganalysis tools and improve the capacity of information hiding in natural text, this paper proposes a novel coverless information hiding method based on news aggregation. It converts the secret message M to a large interger N, and hides N in a news web by changing the order of news headlines. Experimental results and analysis show that this method is robust for any current steganalysis algorithm, and effective for stego-message delivery. It is of utmost significance both in theoretical and practical value.

3 Information Hiding and Extracting

3.1 Basic Definitions

Definition 1. $W(t_1, t_2 \ldots, t_n)$ indicates that there are n news subjects in the news web W, where t_i represents the subject numbered i. The number of subjects in news web W is increasing sequentially.

Definition 2. $T_{jk}(a_1, a_2, \ldots, a_n)$ indicates that there are n news headlines in the k-th div block of the j-th subject in the news web W, among which j represents the number of subject, k represents the total number of the current subject's div blocks, a_i represents every news headline in the current div block.

Definition 3. $|W|$ indicates the total number of news subjects in news web W, $|T_j|$ represents the total number of div blocks in the j-th subject, $|T_{jk}|$ represents the total number of news headlines in the k-th div block of the j-th subject.

Nature 1. $T_{jk}(a_1, a_2, \ldots, a_n)$ has n! permutations.

Suppose that $Z(T) = \{z | z \in Z, 0 \leq z \leq n! - 1\}$, and then $T_{jk}(a_1, a_2, \ldots, a_n)$ can generate n! permutations according to the dictionary ordered method [18]. Suppose that $s(a_1, a_2, \ldots, a_n)$ is the corresponding sequence in the permutations for $T_{jk}(a_1, a_2, \ldots, a_n)$, and $s(a_1, a_2, \ldots, a_n) \in Z(T)$.

Definition 4. Define the mapping relationship $f : E(T) \rightarrow Z(T)$.

For $\forall T_{jk}(a_1, a_2, \ldots, a_n), \exists p \in Z(T)$, when $p = s(a_1, a_2, \ldots, a_n)$, the function $f(T_{jk}(a_1, a_2, \ldots, a_n)) = p$ is established; For $\forall p \in Z(T), \exists s(a_1, a_2, \ldots, a_n)$, the inverse function $f^{-1}(p) = (T_{jk}(a_1, a_2, \ldots, a_n))$ is established. Thus, the mapping relationship f is one-to-one mapping.

3.2 Hiding and Extraction Algorithms

In order to ensure the security of hidden information, $(h_1, h_2, \ldots, h_n)$ is used to replace $(a_1, a_2, \ldots, a_n)$ to generate n! permutations, among which $h_i = h(a_i \circ key)$, $h(\circ)$ is a hash function, $\circ$ is the join operator and key is the receiver's ID.

Algorithm 1: hiding algorithm.
Input: the secret message and the private key.
Output: a news web containing secret message.
The process of information hiding is shown as follows:

1. Convert secret message M to a large integer N.
2. Initialize $i = 1$, where $1 \leq i \leq |W|$.
3. If $i \leq |W|$, go step 4; Otherwise, go step 5.
4. Count the total number of news headlines in the subject t_i, denoted as S_i. Select the former S_i news headlines in the subject t_i from the database order by news time. Use these news headlines as pre-display content for the subject t_i. Compute $i = i + 1$, return to step 3.
5. Initialize $i = 1, j = 1, k = 1$, where $1 \leq j \leq |W|, 1 \leq k \leq |T_j|$.
6. Compute $N' = N/|T_{jk}|!$, $p_i = N mod |T_{jk}|!$, then we can get $T_{jk}(a_1', a_2', \ldots, a_n') = f^{-1}(p_i)$ and rename $T_{jk}(a_1', a_2', \ldots, a_n')$ as T_{jk}'. Besides, $T_{jk}(a_1, a_2, \ldots, a_n) = T_{jk}'$.
7. Compute $N = N'$. If $N = 0$, go step 8; Otherwise, $i = i + 1, k = k + 1$. If $k > |T_j|$, $k = 1$, $j = j + 1$, and return to step 6.
8. Get all $T_{jk}(a_1, a_2, \ldots, a_n)$, and news headlines are showed in the corresponding div block in the news web W in turns according to the sequence of $a_1, a_2, \ldots, a_n$.

Figure 1 shows the process of information hiding.

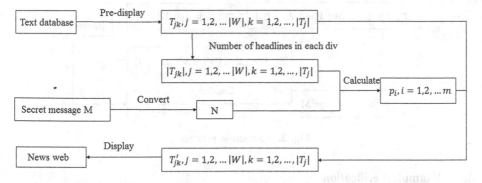

Fig. 1. Hiding process

Mapping process from T_{jk} to T'_{jk} is shown in Fig. 2.

Algorithm 2: extraction algorithm.
Input: news web, the private key.
Output: the hidden secret message.
The process of information extraction is shown as follows:

1. Read the content of each div block in turns according to the number of news subjects. Combined with the private key, compute $p_i = f(T_{jk}(a_1, a_2, \ldots, a_n))$ and get the collection $p\{p_1, p_2, \ldots, p_m\}$.
2. Initialize $N_{m+1} = 0$ and calculate the value of N_1 by the iteration formula $N_i = N'_{i+1} * |T_{jk}|! + p_i$.
3. Convert N_1 to the hidden secret message.

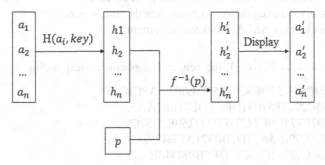

Fig. 2. Mapping process from T_{jk} to T'_{jk}

Figure 3 shows the process of information extraction.

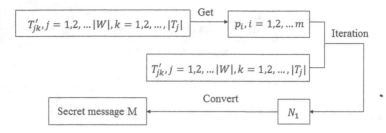

Fig. 3. Extraction process

3.3   Example Verification

In order to clearly describe the above coverless text information hiding process, it is illustrated by a simple example. For example, let the secret information M be 信息隐藏. Suppose there are 3 subjects in the news web, each subject has 3 div blocks and each div block has 5, 5, 5, 5, 5, 5, 5, 5, 6 news headlines respectively. The operating procedure of the information hiding is shown as follows:

Firstly, the secret information M can be converted to a large integer N 5755987831139894735. The sender computes p_i continuously and get the collection P. The P is:

$$P = \{95, 82, 12, 74, 49, 81, 108, 103, 133\}$$

Secondly, the sender selects the news headlines in each subject from the database order by news time and makes them as pre-display content. Suppose the news headlines in a div block are as follows:

a_1 :   First China-Britain freight train arrives back in China;
a_2 :   Xi's poverty alleviation drive helps ethnic groups in Yunnan;
a_3 :   Beijing court sees surge in unfair competition cases;
a_4 :   China's big data regulation to boost health care, security;
a_5 :   China welcomes ASEAN summit statement;

According to $h_i = h(a_i^\circ key)$, the sender can obtain corresponding h_i:

h_1:   A0ADD9C61D57D80C21150DE694AA8C87;
h_2:   7E82D95C2725851081DDE5DF71687AA3;
h_3:   9FBDFD7F775D9DFC37FFAD769E2952C9;
h_4:   9B44A450099085A31D2B0371AEE429D5;
h_5:   BE6BA06E69592C53F2D7FFB98D48E9E9;

After sorting, the sequence is changed to be $h_2h_4h_3h_1h_5$. The sender sets it as the initial permutation sequence and finally obtains 120 permutations. For each div block, the sender repeats the above operation. Obviously, for every h_i in P, the sender can get the corresponding permutation. Because the map relation is one to one between a_i and h_i, the map matrix between p_i and permutation is shown as follows:

$$95 \qquad 82 \qquad 12 \qquad 74 \qquad 49$$
$$a_1 a_4 a_3 a_2 a_5 \quad a_3 a_5 a_2 a_4 a_1 \quad a_5 a_3 a_1 a_4 a_2 \quad a_2 a_1 a_4 a_4 a_3 a_5 \quad a_2 a_3 a_1 a_4 a_5$$
$$81 \qquad 108 \qquad 103 \qquad 133$$
$$a_4 a_2 a_5 a_3 a_1 \quad a_1 a_2 a_3 a_5 a_4 \quad a_2 a_1 a_4 a_5 a_3 \quad a_2 a_5 a_1 a_3 a_4 a_6$$

Finally, the news headlines are shown in the corresponding div block in the news web according to the new permutation sequence in which each news headline is not be modified. Then the sender sends the web site to the receiver.

Because the private key is the receiver's ID, the receiver can easily get the collection P and we will not repeat the process of computing. According to the collection P and the iterative formula, the receiver can compute the value of N, i.e. 5755987831139894735. Finally, the receiver converts N to the hidden secret information 信息隐藏.

3.4 Correctness Proof

3.4.1 Algorithm 1 Proof

Assuming that in the ideal case, the pre-displayed content in the news web is sufficiently rice, i.e., the value of $T_{jk}(a_1, a_2, \ldots, a_n)$ is always available under the conditions of $1 \leq j \leq |W|$, $1 \leq k \leq |T_j|$. In addition, the $|T_{jk}|!$ is changed with the increase of the number of cycles i in Algorithm 1. The proof of Algorithm 1 is described as follows:

For any secret message M, it can be converted to a large integer N. Rename N as N_1.

1. Initialize $i = 1, k = 1, j = 1$. If $N_1 < |T_{11}|!$, then $N'_1 = N_1/|T_{11}|! = 0, p_1 = N_1 mod |T_{11}|$, $T_{11}(a'_1, a'_2, \ldots, a'_n) = f^{-1}(p_1)$. So,we can get $T_{11}(a_1, a_2, \ldots, a_n) = T_{11}(a'_1, a'_2, \ldots, a'_n)$. Because $N_2 = N'_1 = 0$, the whole cycle can be terminated. The news web can generate news headlines containing secret information according to news headlines sequence in $T_{jk}(a_1, a_2, \ldots a_n)$.

2. According to Algorithm 1, if $N_1 \geq |T_{11}|!$, then $N_i = N_{i+1} * |T_{ij}|! + P_i$. Assume Algorithm 1 is cycled m times altogether, there must be the following results: $N_m < |T_{jk}|!$, $P_m = N_m mod |T_{jk}|!$, $N_{m+1} = 0$. If $N_{m+1} \neq 0$ when it is cycled m-th time, $N_m = N_{m+1} * |T_{jk}|! + P_m$, and it can be inferred that $N_m > |T_{jk}|!$. This contradicts $N_m < |T_{jk}|!$, so there must be $N_m < |T_{jk}|!, P_m = N_m mod |T_{jk}|!$, $N_{m+1} = 0$ in the implementation process of algorithm 1. In other words, Algorithm 1 can terminate the loop normally. According to the above steps, we can get the collection P. Combined with the Definition 4, we can get the new order of news headlines after rearranging in each div block. Ultimately, all news headlines containing secret information are displayed on the news web. So, Algorithm 1 is correct and the proof is finished.

3.4.2 Algorithm 2 Proof

The proof of Algorithm 2 is described as follows:

In the premise of the correctness of the Algorithm 1, the receiver reads the content of the news web in accordance with the order of the news subject number. Combined with the private key and the Definition 4, we can obtain the collection P successfully. The size of P is m. Thus, according to Algorithnm 1, $N_{m+1} = 0$. So we can get the following process by the iterative formula $N_m = N_{m+1} * |T_{jk}|! + P_m$:

1. If $m = 1$, then $N_1 = P_1$.
2. If $m \neq 1$, the iteration process of algorithm 2 is as follows:

$$N_m = N_{m+1} * |T_{jk}|! + P_m = 0$$
$$N_{m-1} = N_m * |T_{jk}|! + P_{m-1}$$
$$\cdots\cdots$$
$$N_1 = N_2 * |T_{jk}|! + P_1$$

Therefore, according to the iterative formula, we can get the value of N_1. Convert N_1 into the hidden secret information, and the receiver can extracts the secret information successfully according to Algorithm 2. So, Algorithm 2 is correct and the proof is finished.

4 Experimental Results and Analysis

The news dataset of this paper is from the scroll web of Sina News by using web crawler technology. Compared with the previous coverless information hiding algorithm, this paper doesn't need to establish a large-scale database in advance, but crawls the latest news data from the Internet dynamically. Therefore, the relational database MySQL is the first choice. According to the news subject category, we store them in the corresponding database table. Besides, we update the database at regular intervals by using the above method, that is, we delete the oldest news data while inserting the lasted news data in the database. What's more, there are three important experimental parameters: the number of news subjects, the number of div blocks in each news subject and the number of news headlines in each div block. The three parameters determine the maximum hiding capacity.

4.1 Hiding Capacity

The permutation number of news headlines in a div block represents the capacity of information that the div block can hides, so it can be defined as the maximum of hiding capacity corresponding to the div block [19]. Suppose that $|T_{jk}| = n$, indicating that the total number of news headlines in the div block is n, and that M_{jk} represents $T_{jk}(a_1, a_2, \ldots, a_n)$ corresponding to the maximum hiding capacity in the div block. According to the Nature 1, we learn that $M_{jk} = n!$. Suppose that N_{jk} is the maximum of bits that can be hidden in $T_{jk}(a_1, a_2, \ldots, a_n)$, then $N_{jk} = [log_2(n!)]$ where [] represents rounding down operation. Suppose that C is the maximum hiding capacity of news web

W, we can see that the integer N is decremented when it is constantly divided by the permutations number of news headlines in div blocks according to Algorithm 1. Therefore, $C = \Pi(|T_{jk}|!)$. Suppose that W_b is the maximum of bits which can be hidden in the news web, then $W_b = [log_2(\Pi(|T_{jk}|!))]$. We use W_b to represent the capacity in our experiment. In order to clearly learn that the changing process of the maximum of bits when we hide the secret information in news headlines, we illustrate it by a simple example. Figure 4 demonstrates that the maximum of bits which can be hidden in the case of 100 news headlines, where the number of news headlines are the largest average under the condition of the different number of div blocks.

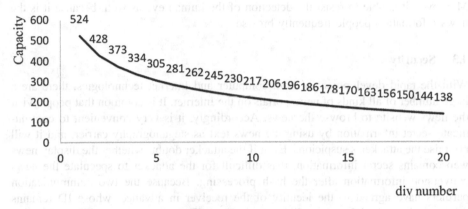

Fig. 4. The different div capacity distribution when total number of news headlines is 100

As can be seen from Fig. 4, in the case of a given total number of news headlines, there is a gradually declination in the maximum of bits that can be hidden with the number of div blocks increasing. Experimental results in [12] show that an average of 1 KB file can hide 1 keyword in [11] whereas it can hide 1.57 keywords. If the average length of the keyword is 2, combined with the Chinese character coding and redundancy analysis [11], [20] can hide 10.08 bits, [12] can hide 15.82 bits. In this paper, the average 1 KB file size is equivalent to 20 news headlines. If we use two div blocks to hide secret information, the max bits of secret information is 43 in hiding. Therefore, compared with the [11, 12], the method in our paper improves the hidden capacity to a certain extent. In addition, the paper just give experimental results about mean capacity in the [11, 12], so the comparative extraction performance is not discussed there. The experimental results are shown in Table 1:

Table 1. Experimental results

Method	The maximum of hidden bits
Literature [11]	10.08
Literature [12]	15.82
Our method	43

4.2   The Resistance to Steganalysis Tools

Although the text information hiding has attracted the attention of many scholars and made a lot of achievements, there are a common ground that these traditional methods have a weak ability in anti-statistical analysis. Furthermore, as long as the carrier is modified, the secret information will certainly be detected and it can hardly escape from steganalysis. Therefore, the existing steganography technology is need to be improved. In this paper, the secret information M is converted into a large integer N and then N is hidden in a news web by changing the order of news headlines. Fundamentally, it is resistant to various steganalysis algorithms based on statistics because it doesn't leave any modification trace in the cover news text during conveying secret information. Moreover, it is able to resist the detection of the human eye as well, because it is the news information people frequently browse.

4.3   Security

With the rapid development of both computer and Internet technologies, there are a large number of all kinds of news portals on the Internet. It is common that people visit the news website to browse the news. Accordingly, it is very convenient to communicate secret information by using the news text as steganography carrier, and it will not raise the attacker's suspicions. Even if the attacker doubts whether the display news web contains secret information, it is difficult for the attacker to speculate the news conversion information after the hash processing. Because the two communication partners have agreed to the identity of the receiver in advance, whose ID remains private to them. And they can utilize the receiver's ID as the parameter of hash function while communicating. At the same time, the display news information has undergone hash processing. To sum up, the algorithm also has good security even in the case of public database. It is difficult to be decoded by the malicious attacker.

5   Conclusion

With the development of computer and further research in the field of information security, coverless information hiding technology has become a hot issue. In this paper, we propose a novel coverless information hiding method based on news aggregation. The method converts the secret message M to a large integer N, and hides the large integer N in the news web by changing the order of news headlines. Compared with the previous coverless information hiding algorithm, this paper just need to establish a small dynamic database rather than a large-scale database in advance. Besides, because any modification trace will not be left in the news texts, our method is robust for any current steganalysis algorithm and effective for stego-message delivery.

Acknowledgments.   This work is supported by National Natural Science Foundation of China (61373132), Key Laboratory of Hunan Province Of Basic Education Information Technology (2015TP1017), Research Project of Teaching Reform in Colleges and Universities in Hunan (2012[528]).

References

1. Shen, C., Zhang, H., Feng, D.: A survey of information security. Sci. China **37**(2), 129–150 (2007)
2. Zhang, G., Yue, Y., Zhang, C.: Adaptive steganography algorithm of rapid wet paper code based on Hilbert. Comput. Eng. **39**(7), 161–164 (2013)
3. Budhia, U., Kundur, D., Zourntos, T.: Digital video steganalysis exploiting statistical visibilityin the temporal domain. IEEE Trans. Inf. Forensics Secur. **1**(4), 502–516 (2006)
4. Bai, Y., Bai, S., Liu, C.: Digital audio watermarking algorithm based on wavelet and cepstrum domain. Comput. Appl. Softw. **29**(3), 163–167 (2012)
5. Fu, D., Chen, G., Yang, Q.: A covert communication method based on XML documents slicing. Comput. Appl. Softw. **28**(9), 106–107 (2011)
6. Xia, Z., Wang, X., Sun, X., et al.: Steganalysis of LSB matching using differences between nonadjacent pixels. Multimed. Tools Appl. **75**(4), 1947–1962 (2016)
7. Xia, Z., Wang, X., Sun, X., et al.: Steganalysis of least significant bit matching using multi-order differences. Secur. Commun. Netw. **7**(8), 1283–1291 (2014)
8. Fu, Z., Ren, K., Shu, J., et al.: Enabling personalized search over encrypted outsourced data with efficiency improvement. IEEE Trans. Parallel Distrib. Syst. **27**(9), 2546–2559 (2016)
9. Fu, Z., Wu, X., Guan, C., et al.: Toward efficient multi-keyword fuzzy search over encrypted outsourced data with accuracy improvement. IEEE Trans. Inf. Forensics Secur. **11**(12), 2706–2716 (2016)
10. Fu, Z., Sun, X., Liu, Q., et al.: Achieving efficient cloud search services: multi-keyword ranked search over encrypted cloud data supporting parallel computing. IEICE Trans. Commun. **E98-B**(1), 190–200 (2015)
11. Chen, X., Sun, H., Tobe, Y., Zhou, Z., Sun, X.: Coverless information hiding method based on the chinese mathematical expression. In: Huang, Z., Sun, X., Luo, J., Wang, J. (eds.) ICCCS 2015. LNCS, vol. 9483, pp. 133–143. Springer, Cham (2015). doi:10.1007/978-3-319-27051-7_12
12. Zhou, Z., Mu, Y., Zhao, N., Wu, Q.M.J., Yang, C.-N.: Coverless information hiding method based on multi-keywords. In: Sun, X., Liu, A., Chao, H.-C., Bertino, E. (eds.) ICCCS 2016. LNCS, vol. 10039, pp. 39–47. Springer, Cham (2016). doi:10.1007/978-3-319-48671-0_4
13. Zhang, J., Shen, J., Wang, L., Lin, H.: Coverless text information hiding method based on the word rank map. In: Sun, X., Liu, A., Chao, H.-C., Bertino, E. (eds.) ICCCS 2016. LNCS, vol. 10039, pp. 145–155. Springer, Cham (2016). doi:10.1007/978-3-319-48671-0_14
14. Chen, X., Chen, S., Wu, Y.: Coverless information hiding method based on the chinese character encoding. J. Internet Technol. **18**(2), 91–98 (2017)
15. Zhou, Z., Sun, H., Harit, R., Chen, X., Sun, X.: Coverless image steganography without embedding. In: Huang, Z., Sun, X., Luo, J., Wang, J. (eds.) ICCCS 2015. LNCS, vol. 9483, pp. 123–132. Springer, Cham (2015). doi:10.1007/978-3-319-27051-7_11
16. Zhou, Z., Cao, Y., Sun, X.: Coverless information hiding based on bag-of-words model of image. Electron. Inf. Eng. 527–536 (2016)
17. Yuan, C., Xia, Z., Sun, X.: Coverless image steganography based on SIFT and BOF. J. Internet Technol. **18**(2), 209–216 (2017)
18. Lu, K.C.: Combination Mathematics, 2nd edn, pp. 16–18. Tsinghua University Press, Beijing (1991)
19. Sun, X., Huang, H., Wang, B., et al.: An algorithm of webpage information hiding based on equal tag. J. Comput. Res. Dev. 756–760 (2007)
20. Zhao, H., Lin, G., Chen, S., et al.: Chinese character coding and redundancy analysis. J. Dongguan Univ. Technol. 39–44 (2012)

Cloud Computing

SIEM Based on Big Data Analysis

Tianmu Li[✉] and Leiming Yan

School of Computer and Software, Jiangsu Engineering Center of Network Monitoring,
Nanjing University of Information Science and Technology, Nanjing 210044, China
l_time@163.com

Abstract. Information security problem being more and more serious, plenty of data about security being produced fast, the Security Information and Event Management (SIEM) systems have faced with diversity of Volume Big data sources, so it is necessary that big data analysis should be used. This paper presents the architecture and principle of SIEM systems which use popular big data technology. The information security data is transferred from flume to Flink or Spark Computing Framework through Kafka and is retrieved through Elastic Research. The K-means algorithm is used in analyzing the abnormal condition with spark mllib. The report of experiment and results of SIEM shows it is efficient systems process big data to detect security anomaly. In the end, the full paper is summarized and the future work should be the usage of stream computing in the SIEM to solve inform security problem in large-scale network with the continuously producing information security data.

Keywords: SIEM · Big data · Information security · K-means

1 Introduction

Nowadays Information security problem has become more and more serious, thus Security Information and Event Management (SIEM) systems have been founded, which regulate and master the security data flows in the large-scale network. SIEM technology provides real-time event management and historical analysis of security data from a wide set of heterogeneous sources [1]. Data from Intrusion Detection Systems (IDS) and Log Management software is collected to realize Security Information Management (SIM) and Security Event Managers (SEM).

Today, SIEM technology has become an essential part on the application of information security. However, there are many problem in Security Information and Event Management (SIEM), although therapy market growth and technology improvements. The SIEM systems face difficulty about data collection, storage, analysis and visualization [2]. Gogoi et al. present the huge volume of data as a key challenge for outlier detection [3]. Marchal et al. propose that current solutions realizing in-depth packet analysis are not scalable and adaptable to big network producing high quantity of data [4]. Suthaharan et al. explain problems of machine learning analysis of network intrusion-related Big Data [5].

© Springer International Publishing AG 2017
X. Sun et al. (Eds.): ICCCS 2017, Part I, LNCS 10602, pp. 167–175, 2017.
https://doi.org/10.1007/978-3-319-68505-2_15

In this paper, the prototype of a SIEM system based on big data is described, which includes the most progressive big data technologies being used in data processing and analysis. The SIEM systems realize the following functions. First, Logstash is used to collect all log messages coming to our system from heterogeneous sources for big data analysis better than other existing formats [6–9]. Second, security analytic include signatures, query-based analytic and machine learning. Third, both monitoring algorithm and unsupervised algorithm is used to analyze both numeric and textual data. Finally, the architecture of SIEM systems is constructed as real-time computing using spark or flink computing framework.

The paper is organized as follows. Section 2 discusses the Related work about SIEM and Big data. Section 3 presents the architecture and principle of SIEM systems based on big data. Section 4 reports the experiment and results of SIEM and then Sect. 5 end with concluding the paper and demonstrate some preliminary ideas for future work.

2   Related Work

Now there are a lot of researches on information security. Encryption and watermarking techniques are used to privacy-preserve and copy-detect, which is one aspect of information security [10, 11]. In the current cloud computing scenario to solve security problem encrypted outsourced data is searched based on key word [12–14]. In order to realize secret communication, the secret message is converted into bit streams then secret information are chosen and sent to receivers through using inverted index [15]. Although information security have made great progress, it is necessary that big data is used in information security. In recent years, the achievement about big data is abundant, and big data has been applied in business, social, financial, education, industry, agriculture and so on all walks of life [15–17]. But it has only just begun that the big data are applied in information security [5]. The heterogeneous nature of data coming from all possible sources for high speed security analysis, which traditional SIEM systems cannot accommodate [18]. High data volumes are generated daily, Therefore, modern SIEM systems should be capable of collecting and analyzing these data in real-time [2].

Many different anomaly detection algorithms suitable for security analytics were developed within the last decades for the traditional SIEM systems can only discover security attack based on Existing rules, but new security attack need be found through machine learning [19]. Papalexakis et al. apply anomaly detection with k-means on the KDD Cup 1999 dataset [20], one-class SVM can also be used in security data [21]. Alshammari and Zincir-Heywood, tested Support Vector Machines (SVM), Naive Bayes, RIPPER, and C4.5 algorithms using three publicly available data sets, focusing on classifying encrypted traffic [22]. P. Casas etc. build an anomaly detection sys-tem using machine learning techniques, which is meant to detect anomalies within the traffic in a cellular network and it is built using Random Neural Networks [23].

All in all, to apply detection of information security, the solutions which can process huge volumes of data, calculate the log messages, efficient clustering and so on should be designed [24]. Andrey Sapegin etc. also point that SIEM can be used in analysis of security events in large-scale networks, but advanced big data technologies are not employed [25]. This paper, The architecture of SIEM systems based on big data is presented in the section below.

3   Architecture of SIEM Systems Based on Big Data

The SIEM system based on Big data is presented in Fig. 1. The SIEM system collect of security data from any sources, including network devices, HTTP server, data base SQL log, File systems and other syslog. The collected data is received by Flume. The middleware Kafka transfer security data from flume to Flink or Spark Computing Framework which can analyze security data. The result of analysis may store in Hive, HBase or Elastic. The user of SIEM can interview the data through Web or Analytic Tools.

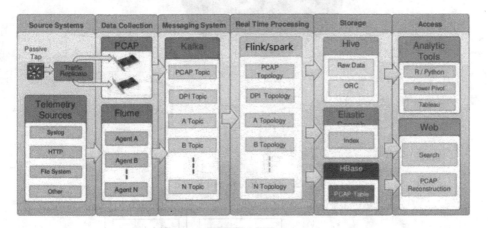

Fig. 1. SIEM system based on Big data

Kafka is an open-source stream processing platform developed by the Apache Software Foundation, which is used for building real-time data pipelines and streaming applications in Fig. 2. In SIEM systems, Kafka links Flume and Flink/Spark as real-time information is delivered.

The construction of SIEM system can be demonstrated as Fig. 3 concisely. The spark and flink in the system are fast and general engine for large-scale data processing, which can be applied in the analysis the data from Kafka. The result can be retrieved through Elastic Research.

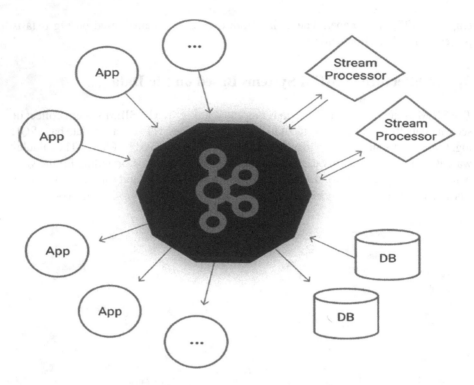

Fig. 2. The structure of Kafka

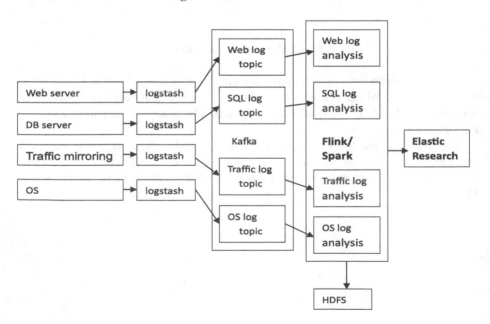

Fig. 3. The construction of SIEM system

4   Application Case of SIEM Systems

Some security information data should been collected by SIEM Systems from net-work device mainly for analysis. In this paper, we use a public dataset, the KDD Cup 1999 data was an annual data mining competition organized by a special interest group of the ACM. In experiment, the data is collected into SIEM which detect anomalous network traffic using Spark millib. The KDD Cup 1999 data is shown as Fig. 4.

0, tcp, http, SF, 230, 46187, 0, 0, 0, 0, 0, 1, 0, 0, 0, 0, 0, 0, 0, 0, 0,
0, 1, 1, 0. 00, 0. 00, 0. 00, 0. 00, 1. 00, 0. 00, 0. 00, 0, 0, 0. 00, 0. 00
, 0. 00, 0. 00, 0. 00, 0. 00, 0. 00, 0. 00, normal.

Fig. 4.   The sample of log

The sample express that a TCP connection to an HTTP service. 230 bytes were sent and 46187 bytes were received. The SIEM Systems have collected millions of samples from which spark can be used to detect anomaly. Anomaly detection is often used to find fraud, detect network attacks, or discover problems in servers or other sensor-equipped machinery.

In anomaly, some attacks attempt to flood a computer with network traffic to crowd out legitimate traffic. But in other cases, attacks attempt to exploit flaws in networking software in order to gain unauthorized access to a computer. But some attacks are unknown and the biggest threat may be the one that has never yet been detected and classified. Through machine learning, the SIEM Systems can detect attacks which have not been known.

Here, unsupervised learning techniques like K-means can be used to detect anomalous network connections. K-means can cluster connections based on statistics about each of them. Anything not close to a cluster could be anomalous.

The K-means algorithm *is* explained as follows. Given an initial set of k-means $m_1^{(1)}, \ldots, m_k^{(1)}$ (see below), the algorithm proceeds by alternating between two steps:

Assignment step: Assign each observation to the cluster whose mean yields the least within-cluster sum of squares. Since the sum of squares is the squared Euclidean distance, this is intuitively the "nearest" mean.

$$S_i^{(t)} = \left\{ x_p : ||x_p - m_i^{(t)}||^2 \leq ||x_p - m_j^{(t)}||^2 \forall j, 1 \leq j \leq k \right\}$$

Where each x_p is assigned to exactly one $S^{(t)}$, even if it could be assigned to two or more of them.

Update step: Calculate the new means to be the centroids of the observations in the new clusters.

$$m_i^{(t+1)} = \frac{1}{\left|S_i^{(t)}\right|} \sum_{x_j \in S_i^{(t)}} x_j$$

Since the arithmetic mean is a least-squares estimator, this also minimizes the within-cluster sum of squares objective.

The data would apply k-means algorithm in spark mllib for cluster analysis, whose Features are normalized using following formula normalize di $= \dfrac{feature_i - \mu_i}{\sigma_i}$

To produce a better clustering, k should be chose. Then the distance among clustering may be least. The consequence of experiment is shown as follow (Table 1).

Table 1. The number and distance

Number k	Distance
80	0.0388
90	0.0363
100	0.0255
110	0.0234
120	0.0157
130	0.0111
140	0.0102
150	0.0087
160	0.0090
170	0.0100
180	0.0101
190	0.0103
200	0.0104
210	0.0106
220	0.0109
230	0.0110
240	0.0112
250	0.0113
260	0.0114
270	0.0116
280	0.0117
290	0.0119
300	0.0120

The result of experiment means that k = 150 is optimal choice. And the most anomalous in the data can be found according to this model, which involved over two hundred different connections to the same service in a short time and ended in an unusual TCP state, S1 (Figs 5 and 6).

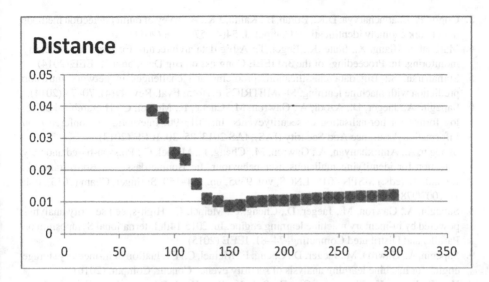

Fig. 5. The relationship between k and distance

0, tcp, http, S1, 299, 26280, 0, 0, 0, 1, 0, 1, 0, 1, 0, 0, 0, 0, 0, 0, 0, 0, 0, 15, 16, 0. 07, 0. 06,
0. 00, 0. 00, 1. 00, 0. 00, 0. 12, 231, 255, 1. 00, 0. 00, 0. 00, 0. 01, 0. 01, 0. 01, 0. 00, 0. 00

Fig. 6. The most anomalous sample

From experiment, we can see that SIEM systems based on big data are practicable, which can find the abnormal station of network efficiently.

5   Conclusions and Future Works

This paper indicates big data analysis should be used in SIEM systems to solve increasingly serious information security problem, presents the architecture and principle of SIEM systems, reports experiment and results of SIEM through machine learning algorithm K-means, which show that the SIEM systems are efficient to process big data for detection of security anomaly.

Information security condition is changing fast with the development information technology. Information security data is produced continuously, thus the future work is the usage of stream computing in the SIEM to solve inform security problem in large-scale network.

References

1. Zuech, R., Khoshgoftaar, T.M., Wald, R.: Intrusion detection and big heterogeneous data: a survey. J. Big Data **2**(1), 1–41 (2015)
2. Bhatt, S., Manadhata, P.K., Zomlot, L.: The operational role of security information and event management systems. IEEE Secur. Priv. **12**(5), 35–41 (2014)

3. Gogoi, P., Bhattacharyya, D.K., Borah, B., Kalita, J.K.: A survey of outlier detection methods in network anomaly identification. Comput. J. **54**(4), 570–588 (2011)
4. Marchal, S., Jiang, X., State, R., Engel, T.: A big data architecture for large scale security monitoring. In: Proceedings of the 3rd IEEE Congress on Big Data, 56–63. IEEE (2014)
5. Suthaharan, S.: Big data classification: problems and challenges in network intrusion prediction with machine learning. SIGMETRICS Perform Eval. Rev. **41**(4), 70–73 (2014)
6. Sapegin, A., Jaeger, D., Azodi, A., Gawron, M., Cheng, F., Meinel, C.: Hierarchical object log format for normalisation of securityevents. In: 2013 9th International Conference on Information Assurance And Security (IAS), IAS 2013, 25–30. IEEE (2013)
7. Sapegin, A., Amirkhanyan, A., Gawron, M., Cheng, F., Meinel, C.: Poisson-based anomaly detection for identifying malicious user behaviour. In: Boumerdassi, S., Bouzefrane, S., Renault, É. (eds.) MSPN 2015. LNCS, vol. 9395, pp. 134–150. Springer, Cham (2015). doi: 10.1007/978-3-319-25744-0_12
8. Sapegin, A., Gawron, M., Jaeger, D., Cheng, F., Meinel, C.: High-speed security analytics powered by in-memory machine learning engine. In: 2015 14th International Symposium on Parallel and Distributed Computing, 74–81. IEEE (2015)
9. Sapegin, A., Gawron, M., Jaeger, D., Cheng, F., Meinel, C.: Evaluation of in-memory storage engine for machine learning analysis of security events. Concur. Comput. (2016)
10. Xia, Z., Wang, X., Zhang, L., Qin, Z., Sun, X., Ren, K.: A Privacy-preserving and Copy-deterrence Content-based Image Retrieval Scheme in Cloud Computing. IEEE Trans. Inf. Forensics Secur. **11**(11), 2594–2608 (2016)
11. Chen, X., Chen, S., Yulei, W.: Coverless information hiding method based on the Chinese character encoding. J. Internet Technol. **18**(2), 313–320 (2017)
12. Zhangjie, F., Xinle, W., Guan, C., Sun, X., Ren, K.: Toward efficient multi-keyword fuzzy search over encrypted outsourced data with accuracy improve-ment. IEEE Trans. Inf. Forensics Secur. **11**(12), 2706–2716 (2016)
13. Xia, Z., Wang, X., Sun, X., Wang, Q.: A secure and dynamic mul-ti-keyword ranked search scheme over encrypted cloud data. IEEE Trans. Parallel Distrib. Syst. **27**(2), 340–352 (2015)
14. Fu, Z., Sun, X., Liu, Q., Zhou, L., Shu, J.: Achieving efficient cloud search services: multi-keyword ranked search over encrypted cloud data sup-porting parallel computing. IEICE Trans. Commun. **E98-B**(1), 190–200 (2015)
15. Yuan, C., Xia, Z., Sun, X.: Coverless image steganographybased on SIFT and BOF. J. Internet Technol. **18**(2), 435–442 (2017)
16. Tian, Q., Chen, S.: Cross-heterogeneous-database age estimation through correlation representation learning. Neurocomputing **2**(38), 286–295 (2017)
17. Cavallaro, G., Riedel, M., Richerzhagen, M., Benediktsson, J.A., Plaza, A.: On understanding big data impacts in remotely sensed image classification using support vector machine methods. IEEE. J. Sel. Top. Appl. Earth Obs. Remote Sens. **8**, 4634–4646 (2015)
18. Sapegin, A., Jaeger, D., Cheng, F., Meinel, C.: Towards a system for complex analysis of security events in large-scale networks. Comput. Secur. **67**, 16–34 (2017)
19. Ahmed, M., Mahmood, A.N., Hu, J.: A survey of network anomaly detection techniques. J. Netw. Comput. Appl. **60**, 19–31 (2016)
20. Papalexakis, E.E., Beutel, A., Steenkiste, P.: Network anomaly detection using co-clustering. In: 2012 IEEE/ACM International Conference on Advances in Social Networks Analysis and Mining, 403–410 (2012)
21. Alshammari, R., Zincir-Heywood, A.N.: Machine learning based encrypted traffic classification: identifying ssh and skype. In: IEEE Symposium on Computational Intelligence for Security and Defense Applications (CISDA 2009), 1–8 (2009)

22. Casas, P., D'Alconzo, A., Fiadino, P., Callegari, C.: Detecting and diagnosing anomalies in cellular networks using random neural networks In: International Wireless Communications and Mobile Computing Conference (IWCMC), 351–356 (2016)
23. Song, J., Takakura, H., Okabe, Y., Nakao, K.: Toward a more practical unsupervised anomaly detection system. Inf. Sci. **231**, 4–14 (2013)
24. Gottwalt, F., Karduck, A.P.: SIM in light of big data. In: 2015 11th International Conference on Innovations in Information Technology (IIT), 326–31. IEEE (2015)
25. Sapegin, A., Jaeger, D., Cheng, F., Meinel, C.: Towards a system for complex analysis of security events in large-scale networks Comput. Secur. **67**, 16–34 (2017)

Workload-Aware VM Consolidation in Cloud Based on Max-Min Ant System

Hongjie Zhang, Guansheng Shu, Shasha Liao, Xi Fu, and Jing Li[✉]

School of Computer Science and Technology,
University of Science and Technology of China, Hefei, China
{zhanghongjie,sgs2012,lss1017,fuxi}@mail.ustc.edu.cn, lj@ustc.edu.cn

Abstract. With the increasing consumption of energy in cloud data center, the cloud providers pay more attention to the green cloud computing for saving energy. The most effective way in green cloud computing is using virtual machine (VM) consolidation to pack VMs into a smaller amount of physical machines (PMs), which can save energy by switching off the idle PMs. However, in traditional static workload approach, VMs are over-provisioned with a static capacity to guarantee peak performance, which increases the unnecessary energy consumption. In this paper, we propose an innovative approach WAVMC to achieve efficient VM consolidation by using multi-dimensional time-varying workloads based on the Max-Min Ant System (MMAS). In the MMAS, we employ the complementary of both workload patterns and multi-dimensional resources usage as heuristic factors. Extensive simulations on production workloads demonstrate that the proposed model outperforms state-of-the-art baselines in active server counts and resources wastage.

Keywords: Cloud computing · VM consolidation · Workload patterns · Multi-dimensional resources · Max-Min Ant System

1 Introduction

Cloud computing [1] has become a popular computing paradigm for hosting and delivering services over the internet. In order to meet the growing users' demands for computing resources, cloud providers have been expanding the size of the data centers. However, the issue of increasing energy consumption has become more serious. From the provider's perspective, energy costs for operating the equipment in such large-scale data centers have increased significantly. According to the statistics [2], the electricity consumed for powering the data centers already exceed \$7B per year since 2011 in the USA. The key factor that costs high energy consumption is hardware over-provisioned, which in order to guarantee the services' peak performance. In the traditional data center, servers use only 10–15% resources of its capacity in most cases [3]. Virtualization technology allows multiple VMs to be placed on a single physical server to improve resource utilization. But consolidating resources will increase the risk of violating the Service Level Agreement (SLA), which needs to compensate to customer.

© Springer International Publishing AG 2017
X. Sun et al. (Eds.): ICCCS 2017, Part I, LNCS 10602, pp. 176–188, 2017.
https://doi.org/10.1007/978-3-319-68505-2_16

There have been previous efforts to solve this consolidation problem. On the one hand, the work of [4–6] evaluated virtual machine's historical workloads and calculated a static capacity of the virtual machine. The virtual machine consolidation problem is solved as a multi-dimensional bin packing problem according to the static capacity. But workload is not a static value, which is changing over time. So, summarizing historical workloads with a single value can lose too much information [7]. On the other hand, the work of [7,8] proposed a virtual machine multiplexing technique based on the correlation of workloads. Multiplexing two negatively correlated virtual machines into one super virtual machine and placing on the physical machine. Compared to the provision of two separate virtual machines, it saves about 40% of the resources. However, the work of [7,8] only considers the workload of CPU, while ignores other resources usage. Imbalanced usage of resources can lead to a large amount of resource fragmentation. Moreover, their approaches rely on simple greedy algorithms which perform resource-dissipative VM placement.

Our approach WAVMC (Workloads-Aware VM Consolidation) overcomes these drawbacks in previous works by abstracting VM consolidation as a multi-dimensional stochastic bin packing problem where object sizes are multidimensional and follow a distribution forecasted by time series technique. When placing the next VM to current PM, we prefer to choose the VM which is complementary to current PM. On the one hand, we take into account the complementary of workload patterns, which is estimated by time series analysis techniques. On the other hand, we consider the complementary of multi-dimensional resources usage (e.g. CPU, memory, IO) based on the variance in statistics. Since the bin packing problem is strictly NP-hard, we employ the Max-Min Ant System (MMAS) [9] to solve it by minimizing the active server counts and resources wastage. Our approach places the same number of virtual machines onto fewer physical servers under the restriction of SLA. Furthermore, our approach uses multi-dimensional resources more balanced which reduces the waste of resources.

To summarize, this paper makes the following contributions:

(1) Introducing SLA into our model, which maps the quality of service requirements to the resource requirements of the virtual machine across its life cycle.
(2) Integrating the correlation of workload patterns and the imbalanced usage of resources into the MMAS, which makes minimize the number of physical machines and the waste of resources as the optimize targets to perform the VM consolidation.
(3) We conduct simulations to evaluate the proposed algorithm by using massive dataset collected by the google data center [10]. Compared with state-of-the-art baselines, the results show that the metrics of active server counts, resources wastage and median utilization have been considerable improved.

2   Related Research

Dynamic VM placement has been studied ever since dynamic VM migration became available to data centers. The work of [11,12] proposed a multi-objective optimization approach for VM placement in cloud data center based on Ant Colony Optimization (ACO), that effectively reduced the resource wastage and power consumption, and minimized violation of SLA. Farahnakian et al. [13] proposed an approach to solve VM consolidation problem which aims to reduce the energy consumption. Mishra et al. [14] proposed an innovative multi-dimensional resource deployment strategy based on vector arithmetic, that aims to balance multi-dimensional resource usage. Using greedy algorithm to choose the best VM whose resources are complementary with physical machines. Ferdaus et al. [15] improved the algorithm in [14], using ACO to consolidate VMs for minimizing the number of physical machines. It improves about 40% in resource wastage than [14]. These algorithms regard the virtual machine's workload as a static value and ignore workload changing over time, that will lead to a large amount of resource fragmentation in VM.

To overcome the above problem, many researchers propose VM multiplexing algorithm based on the correlation between VM's workloads. The work of [7,8,16] proposed an algorithm to calculate the correlation between VMs. These algorithms, firstly, predict the resources demand of the VMs. And then using the Pearson correlation coefficient to find the best negative correlation VMs as complementary VMs. Multiplexing the complementary VMs to a super VM. At last, using FFD to place them onto physical machines. Lin et al. [17] improved [7,8,16], proposed a workload-driven VM consolidation algorithm, which not only considered the correlation between VMs but also the correlation between VM and PM. However, these algorithms ignore the multi-dimensional resource balanced usage, that will lead to large amount waste of resources. Moreover, their approaches rely on simple greedy algorithms which perform resource-dissipative VM placement.

3   VM Consolidation Problem Based on Workload

The demand of resources for a service running in a virtual machine changing over time. We abstract the VM consolidation problem as a multi-dimensional stochastic bin packing problem where object sizes are multi-dimensional and follow a distribution forecasted by time series technique. On the one hand, placing virtual machines which are complementary in different type resources onto the same physical machine, could reduce the waste of resources. For example, there are two types of resources (CPU and memory) on the physical server. Some memory will be wasted for insufficient CPU available after placing the similar VMs onto PM. On the other hand, the resource demand of a service is changing over time. If we place the VMs with positive correlation will increase the resource fragmentation in VM. We could place the VMs which have the negative correlation in workload patterns onto the same physical machine, that will reduce the resource fragmentation in VM.

3.1   Modeling SLA of VM

We cite the SLA model defined in [7,17].

Definition 1. *Suppose VM i is allocated a fixed capacity within a time frame [1, L]. Let $x_i(t)$ denote VM i's workload volume in time slot t. A constraint on the capacity of VM i is expressed as*

$$\frac{1}{k_i} \sum_{s=0}^{k_i-1} I\left(\frac{\sum_{t=sk_i+1}^{(s+1)k_i} x_i(t)}{T_i} > c_i \right) \leq \theta_i \qquad (1)$$

where $T_i \in \{1, 2, 4, \ldots\}$, $k_i = \frac{L}{T_i}$ is an integer, $0 \leq \theta_i \leq 1$

The inequality (1) means that the probability of average workload in time slot exceeds capacity no more than the threshold θ_i. In inequality (1), $\frac{\sum_{t=sk_i+1}^{(s+1)k_i} x_i(t)}{T_i}$ represents the average workload during T_i. The parameters T_i and θ_i depend on specific applications. The value of T_i should be close to the normal response time experienced by the application [7]. And the c_i represents the minimum static capacity that satisfied SLA. Given the T_i and θ_i, we could calculate the minimum static capacity c_i of VM i that satisfied it's SLA.

3.2   Modeling Dynamic Workload

In this paper, we use the Autoregressive Integrated Moving Average (ARIMA) model to forecast the workload. The ARIMA(p, d, q) model is defined as follow.

$$\Phi(B) \bigtriangledown^d x_t = \Theta(B)\epsilon_t \qquad (2)$$

In the equality (2), $\Phi(B) = 1 - \phi_1 B - \cdots - \phi_p B^p$ and $\Theta(B) = 1 - \theta_1 B - \cdots - \theta_q B^q$. The x_t represents the time series of workload. And the B represents delay of x_t, which means $B^p x_t = x_{t-p}$. The ϵ_t represents the white noise. The other parameters need to be fitted by historic workload of VM.

Using ARIMA model, we could predict the mean and variance of future workload $x(t)$, where t is any future time point. We assume that future workload $x(t)$ follows a normal distribution $N(\mu, \sigma^2)$. For calculating the SLA and correlation coefficient, we need a deterministic workload $\hat{x}(t)$ which need to meet $P(x(t) \leq \hat{x}(t)) \geq p$. The p represents the confidence level. The inequality means that the $\hat{x}(t) \geq \phi^{-1}(1 - p)$ must be true, where ϕ^{-1} is the quantile-function of $x(t)$. It is obviously that a higher p leads to a higher predicted value and a lower SLA violation.

3.3   Modeling Correlation Based on Workload Patterns

Modeling Correlation Between VMs. The correlation between VMs is estimated by analyzing the time series of workload patterns. The target is to find the best complementary VMs. Think about it, an approach that multiplexes VMs with similar peak and trough in workload patterns cannot achieve resource savings compared to an approach that multiplexes VMs with complementary workload behavior. We reference the correlation coefficient in [17] which is defined as follow.

$$r[X^1, X^2] = \frac{\sum_{t=1}^{L} \left(X_t^1 - \overline{X^1}\right)\left(X_t^2 - \overline{X^2}\right)}{\sqrt{\sum_{t=1}^{L} \left(X_t^1 - \overline{X^1}\right)^2}\sqrt{\sum_{t=1}^{L} \left(X_t^2 - \overline{X^2}\right)^2}} \qquad (3)$$

In the above equality, $\{X^1\}$ and $\{X^2\}$ represent the time series of resource requirements for VM1 and VM2, respectively.

Modeling Correlation Between VM and PM. The physical machine's workloads at each moment are equal to the sum of the workloads of all the VMs which running on it. So, the correlation between VM and PM can be estimated by using the correlation between VM and VM. But whenever we place a VM onto a PM, the correlation between next VM and the PM must be recalculated. This is a very time-consuming method when the number of VMs grows larger. The authors of paper [17] proposed a good approach to reduce the time-consuming when calculate the correlation coefficient. Firstly, we need some attributes of the correlation coefficient. We can obtain Pearson correlation coefficient from covariance of VMs. The following equality exhibits the covariance.

$$cov[X^1, X^2] = \frac{\sum_{t=1}^{L} \left(X_t^1 - \overline{X^1}\right)\left(X_t^2 - \overline{X^2}\right)}{L-1} \tag{4}$$

In the above equality, $\{X^1\}$ and $\{X^2\}$ represent the time series of resource requirements for VM1 and VM2, respectively.

Suppose that we already placed k VMs onto a PM and calculated the workloads of the PM which is marked as $\{X_t^{old}\}$. And $\{X_t^{old}\}$ can be expressed as the sum of the first $k-1$ virtual machines and the k-th virtual machine, which means $X_t^{old} = X_t^{old-1} + X_t^{last}$. The X_t^{old-1} represents the sum of the first $k-1$ virtual machines. And X_t^{last} represents the k-th virtual machine. Now, we can calculate the correlation between the current physical machine and the virtual machine to be placed. The following equality exhibits the approach which is defined in [17].

$$r[X^{old}, X^{new}] = \frac{cov[X^{old-1}, X^{new}] + cov[X^{last}, X^{new}]}{\sqrt{cov[X^{old}, X^{old}]cov[X^{new}, X^{new}]}} \tag{5}$$

In the above equality (5), X^{new} represents the virtual machine to be placed. By this way, our algorithm could save large amount of time to finish consolidation.

3.4   Modeling Multi-dimensional Resource Imbalanced Usage

Balancing the usage of multi-dimensional resources can effectively improve the utilization of resources. In order to take into account the balanced resource usage, we reference the Variance into our model. We use a random variable called Multiple Resources Variance (MRV) to represent the difference between resources. The formal definition of MRV is $MRV = \frac{\sum_{i=1}^{N}(r_i - r)^2}{N}$, where r_i is the i-th resource usage, and r is the mean of all r_i.

In order to avoid the impact of the capacity of PM on MRV, we need to normalize the MRV. The magnitude of MRV of PM v is $MRV_v = \left|\ln\sqrt{MRV}\right|$. The greater the MRV is, the more balanced the resource usage is. When selecting a VM to place, we prefer to select VM that makes the MRV of PM as high as possible.

3.5   Modeling Resource Wastage in Data Center

Physical machine's multi-dimensional resource imbalanced usage will lead to waste resources. According to the definition in [11], we define the waste of resources as follow.

$$W = \sum_{p \in P} \sum_{r \in R} \left[(1 - U_p^r) - (1 - U_p^{max}) \right] \tag{6}$$

In the above equality (6), P is the set of all physical machines. R is all resource types. U_p^r represent the r-th resource utilization of the p-th PM, which belongs to $[0, 1]$. So the $(1 - U_p^r)$ is the remaining amount of this dimension resource. max represents the resource, that has the highest utilization.

3.6   Modeling Power Consumption in Data Center

The energy consumption of PM is directly proportional to its CPU utilization [18]. Our algorithm calculates the energy consumption of data center during time frame $[1, L]$. According to the energy consumption in [18], we extend it by adding time frame $[1, L]$. The energy consumption of a data center is defined as follow.

$$E = \sum_{p=1}^{P} \sum_{t=1}^{L} \left[(E_{full} - E_{idle}) U_{p,t}^{CPU} + E_{idle} \right] \tag{7}$$

We can conclude the following formula according to the above equality.

$$E = (E_{full} - E_{idle}) \sum_{i=1}^{m} \sum_{t=1}^{L} u_{i,t}^{CPU} + P L E_{idle} \tag{8}$$

In the above equality, $u_{i,t}^{CPU}$ represents the CPU utilization of VM i at time t. So, the $\sum_{i=1}^{m} \sum_{t=1}^{L} u_{i,t}^{CPU}$ represents that the sum of CPU utilization of all VMs in time frame $[1, L]$, which is a constant static value. The formula (8) implies that the energy consumption of a data center is proportional to the number of active physical machines.

3.7   Formal Problem Definition

We abstract the consolidation problem as a multi-dimensional stochastic bin packing problem. The capacity of PM is represented as a d-dimensional vector, which means $P_j = [C_1, C_2, \ldots, C_d]^T$. Each element in the vector represents the capacity of one type resource. In this paper, we only consider CPU, memory and disk IO. The resources demand of VM is represented by a $d \times L$ matrix $[r_{i,j}]$ which means the i-th type of resource at time j.

The target is to minimize the number of PM and the waste of resources. The formal problem definition is shown as follow.

Target:

$$\min \left(w_1 \sum_{p \in P} y_p + w_2 W \right) \tag{9}$$

Constraint:

$$\frac{1}{L}\sum_{t=1}^{L} I\left(\left(\sum_{i=1}^{n} r_{cpu,t}^{(i)} a_{ij}\right) > p_j^{cpu}\right) \leq \theta, j = [1, \ldots, m] \tag{10}$$

$$\frac{1}{L}\sum_{t=1}^{L} I\left(\left(\sum_{i=1}^{n} r_{mem,t}^{(i)} a_{ij}\right) > p_j^{mem}\right) \leq \theta, j = [1, \ldots, m] \tag{11}$$

$$\frac{1}{L}\sum_{t=1}^{L} I\left(\left(\sum_{i=1}^{n} r_{io,t}^{(i)} a_{ij}\right) > p_j^{io}\right) \leq \theta, j = [1, \ldots, m] \tag{12}$$

$$\sum_{j=1}^{m} a_{ij} = 1, i = [1, \ldots, n] \tag{13}$$

In the above equations, the target is to minimize the number of PM and the waste of resources. The y_p is the indicator function which represents the state of physical server. The parameters w_1 and w_2 are used to balance the relative importance between targets. Parameter m represents the number of PMs and n represents the number of VMs. The constraints mean that the probability of the resource requirements of virtual machines exceed the PM's capacity no more than θ. The constraint (13) means that one VM is placed on one PM.

4 Proposed Solution

4.1 Multi-objective Optimization for VM Consolidation

Our approach employs the MMAS [9] to solve the multi-dimensional stochastic bin packing problem. We use the linear weighting to transform the multi-objective into a single-objective problem. The WAVMC algorithm pseudo-code is shown in Algorithm 1. The algorithm takes a set of VMs and PMs as input, and returns global best solution which contains VM-PM pairs.

Firstly, the algorithm calculates the covariance for each VM-VM pair according to formula (4) and saves them to matrix cov (line 2). For each ant, it opens an empty PM p randomly and starts building a solution S_a. The ant's solution S_a is a $n \times m$ matrix, which each element x_{ij} is a binary value to represents VM i placed onto PM j. After initialization, the algorithm starts assigning the VMs to PMs until there is no free VM left (lines 6 to 18). The *allowed* set contains all VMs which are not yet assigned to any PM and do not violate the capacity constrains of the current PM. If the *allowed* set is not empty, the Pearson correlation coefficient and MRV will be calculated for each VM in *allowed* to current PM (line 9). And then the heuristic information is calculated according to equality (15). Then the probabilistic decision rule is used to select one VM v out of the set to place onto current PM p, stochastically (line 13). The ant's solution S_a is updated by setting x_{vp} equal to 1 (line 14). Afterward, when the capacity of current PM is saturated, the next PM will be opened and starts to place VM as

Algorithm 1. WAVMC for VM Consoliation.

Input: The set of VMs, V; The set of PMs, P; The vector of capacity of PM, C; The
$d \times L$ matrix of requirements of VMs, r; {nCycleTerm,nAnts,α,β,γ_{min},γ_{max},e,w}

Output: Global best solution GBS

1: Initialize, $[\tau_{i,j}] = \gamma_{max}$, GBS:=$\varnothing$, $[cov_{i,j}] = 0$.
2: calculate the $cov[v_1, v_2]$ $\forall(v_1, v_2) \in V$ accord. to Eq. 4.
3: **for all** $k \in \{0, \ldots, nCycleTerm - 1\}$ **do**
4:     **for all** $a \in \{0, \ldots, nAnts - 1\}$ **do**
5:         VMs:=V; p:=random(P); $S_a := [x_{ij} := 0]$
6:         **while** $VMs \neq \varnothing$ **do**
7:             allowed:=$\{i|meet\ the\ constraints\ 18 - 20\}$
8:             **for all** $i \in allowed$ **do**
9:                 calculate the Pearson correlation coefficient and MRV.
10:                 calculate the Heuristic information accord. to Eq. 15.
11:             **end for**
12:             **if** $allowed \neq \varnothing$ **then**
13:                 Choose vm $v \in allowed$ stochastically according to Eq. 14.
14:                 $x_{vp} := 1; VMs := VMs - \{v\}$; Update the PM p's rest capacity.
15:             **else**
16:                 p:=p+1
17:             **end if**
18:         **end while**
19:     **end for**
20:     Compare all S_a to get S_{cycle} based on f
21:     **if** k=0 $\vee$ IsGlobalBest(S_cycle) **then**
22:         Save cycle best solution as new GBS
23:     **end if**
24:     Update pheromone $\tau_{v,p}$ accord. to Eq. 16.
25: **end for**

before (line 16). When all ants finished their solutions, the algorithm will choose
the cycle best solution according to the objective function f and save the cycle
best solution to S_{cycle} (line 20). Compare the S_{cycle} to GBS and choose the best
solution as the new GBS (lines 21 to 23). And then the algorithm updates the
pheromone level for each VM-PM pair according to equality (16). If the level
greater than γ_{max}, it will be set to γ_{max} and vice versa. Finally, the algorithm
gets the global best solution GBS.

4.2 Pseudo-random Decision Rule

Our Pseudo-random Decision Rule is defined as follows.

$$p_v^i = \frac{[\tau_{i,v}]^\alpha \times [\eta_{i,v}]^\beta}{\sum_{u \in N_v} [\tau_{u,v}]^\alpha \times [\eta_{u,v}]^\beta}, \forall i \in N_v \quad (14)$$

In the above equality, v represents the v-th PM. And the N_v represents the
not deployed VMs which meet the constraints. The matrix $[\tau_{i,v}]$ represents the
pheromone level of the pair of VM i and PM v. The heuristic information $\eta_{i,v}$
is defined at the follow subsection, which represents a measure of benefit of
selecting a solution component VM-PM. The p_v^i represents the probability that
an ant to choose a VM i as the next one to pack in its current PM v.

4.3   Heuristic Information

We define the heuristic value favoring both balanced resource utilization in all dimensions and higher overall resource utilization:

$$\eta_{i,v} = w \times \sum_{r=1}^{R} \frac{(1-\rho_{i,v}^r)X_i^r}{C_v^r} + (1-w) \times MRV_v \tag{15}$$

In the above equality, the $\rho_{i,v}^r$ represents the Pearson correlation coefficient between VM i and PM v in resource r. X_i^r is the PM's static workload in resource r after place VM i onto it. C_v^r is the capacity of resource r of PM v. So, the $\sum_{r=1}^{R} \frac{(1-\rho_{i,v}^r)X_i^r}{C_v^r}$ is a variant of FFD, which uses the Pearson correlation coefficient as weights of size.

4.4   Pheromone Trail Update

The formula (16) defines the pheromone trail update rule, which is used to simulate pheromone evaporation and reinforce. The pheromone update rule is defined as follows.

$$\tau_{i,u} = (1-e) \times \tau_{i,u} + e \triangle \tau_{i,u}^{best} \tag{16}$$

In the above equalities, $\triangle \tau_{i,u}^{best} = f(S_{cycle})$ whenever $x_{i,u} = 1$. And the e represents pheromone evaporation coefficient and $0 \le e \le 1$. And $f = \frac{nVMs}{nPMs \times W}$, that the $nVMs$ represents the number of VMs to be placed and the $nPMs$ represents the number of PMs used in the solution. The W is the resource wastage.

5   Experimental Evaluation

5.1   Experimental Setup

This paper compares the performance of our algorithm to the following existing works: (1) First Fit (FF), (2) Best Fit (BF), (3) FFD, (4) the VectorDot [19], (5) the Multiplexing approach [7], (6) the AVVMC [15], (7) the Workload-Driven [17]. All of the existing algorithms are implemented according to their papers.

To evaluate WAVMC, the production workloads of Google data center [10] are collected and used. Google recorded more than 670,000 jobs which include 40 million task events across about 12,000 machines at minute resolution in a production system in 2011 over a one-month period. The PM's workload at a given time point is a total load of all running tasks on that particular machine. We assume that each PM in the data center has the same capacity vector.

We use three metrics to evaluate the quality of our consolidation algorithm: the number of active PMs, the waste of resources and the median utilization of each algorithm. In the experiments, we repeat each algorithm for 15 times, and each time we use different VMs. Finally, we use the average value as the performance metric. We conducted the experiment with 400, 500, 600, 700, 800, 900 VMs and time frame is one day. The capacity vector of each PM is $(6.0, 6.0, 6.0)$. $nCycleTerm = 5, nAnts = 15, \alpha = 2, \beta = 5, e = 0.7, w = 0.8$.

5.2   Evaluation Results

When we use the forecasted value to consolidate VM, the original SLA might
be violated. We use the upper bound of workload $\hat{x}(t)$ with confidence level p
which meets $P(x(t) \leq \hat{x}(t)) \geq p$. Figure 1 shows the real θ by using different
confidence level p. The X-axis is given θ and the Y-axis is the percentage of less
than the corresponding given θ. Figure 1a shows that more than 80% of VM have
their real θ less than the given θ. Figure 1b shows the Mean Absolute Percentage
Error (MAPE) of predicted and real VM capacity c which is defined in (1) with
different confidence level p. It shows that if we use $p = 0.7$, the SLA of VM will
be satisfied about 80% of the time and the MAPE of VM capacity c no more
than 10%.

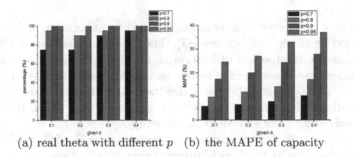

(a) real theta with different p (b) the MAPE of capacity

Fig. 1. The influence of different confidence level

Figure 2a shows the number of PMs used by the eight algorithms with different numbers of VMs (400 to 900) on Google data. It shows that our approach
uses a smaller number of PMs. The Workload-Driven algorithm is close to our
approach in terms of the number of PMs, because that both of us considered
the correlation of workloads. We outperform the Workload-Driven by 8% for
server counts, because that we consider the balanced usage of multi-dimensional

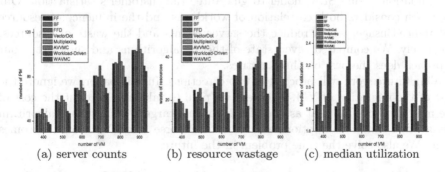

(a) server counts   (b) resource wastage   (c) median utilization

Fig. 2. The comparison between all methods with prediction error is 0

resources when choosing the VM. And we outperform the others by 20% for server counts.

Figure 2b shows that our approach has the lowest waste of resources. The AVVMC algorithm is close to our approach in terms of waste of resources, because that reducing the waste of resource is the target of their algorithm and take into account the resource imbalance vector to reduce the waste of resources. On the one hand, the AVVMC has a good performance on the waste of resources but bad performance on server counts. On the other hand, the Workload-Driven algorithm has a good performance on server counts but bad performance on the waste of resources. We outperform the Workload-Driven by 40% for the waste of resources. With the Workload-Driven approach it is more likely to choose the VM with imbalanced resource usage, leading to waste a lot of resources. It is obviously, our approach has a good performance on both server counts and resource wastage.

The utilization of servers is measured by median utilization, or 50% quantile of utilization of all physical servers [17]. The median utilization is the median of workloads. So, the median utilization should be as high as possible. In this experiment, we use three types of resources which means the median utilization belongs to $[0.0, 3.0]$. Figure 2c shows the median utilization of servers for the eight algorithms with different numbers of VMs on Google data. It shows that our approach utilizes the servers more efficiently.

We also evaluated the time-consuming performance. For 900 VMs, we spend 10 min just the same as Workload-Driven approach [17]. There are two ways to reduce the cost of WAVMC. First, we could increase the time frame $[1, L]$. Our algorithm will be sure that there is no migration during time frame $[1, L]$, which could reduce the influence of WAVMC. Second, we could split the data center into some small data centers which contain small number of VMs. Each part can consolidate in parallel.

6   Conclusion

In this paper, we analysed several aspects of server resource utilization and consolidation. Using SLA model to guarantee the customer's satisfaction. Our approach considers both correlation of workloads and the influence of resource imbalanced usage, which reduce the server counts and the waste of resources, effectively. We compared seven state-of-the-art algorithms and shows that our approach does the best on three metrics.

Our future work will proceed in two directions. In this paper, we ignore the cost of the migration of VM. The next we plan to take into account the cost of the migration of VM, that as one of the optimal targets. At last, our algorithm has a large time-consumption, which become worse when VM count becomes large. We also solve the time problem in the future.

Acknowledgments. This work was supported by National Key Research and Development program under grant No. 2016YFB0201402.

References

1. Armbrust, M., Fox, A., Griffith, R., Joseph, A.D., Katz, R.H., Konwinski, A., Lee, G., Patterson, D.A., Rabkin, A., Stoica, I., et al.: Above the clouds: a Berkeley view of cloud computing (2009)
2. Meisner, D., Gold, B.T., Wenisch, T.F.: PowerNap: eliminating server idle power. In: ACM SIGPLAN Notices. vol. 44, pp. 205–216. ACM (2009)
3. Barroso, L.A., Hölzle, U.: The case for energy-proportional computing (2007)
4. Viswanathan, B., Verma, A., Dutta, S.: Cloudmap: workload-aware placement in private heterogeneous clouds. In: 2012 IEEE Network Operations and Management Symposium, pp. 9–16. IEEE (2012)
5. Feller, E., Rilling, L., Morin, C.: Energy-aware ant colony based workload placement in clouds. In: Proceedings of the 2011 IEEE/ACM 12th International Conference on Grid Computing, pp. 26–33. IEEE Computer Society (2011)
6. Chen, M., Zhang, H., Su, Y.Y., Wang, X., Jiang, G., Yoshihira, K.: Effective VM sizing in virtualized data centers. In: 12th IFIP/IEEE International Symposium on Integrated Network Management (IM 2011) and Workshops, pp. 594–601. IEEE (2011)
7. Meng, X., Isci, C., Kephart, J., Zhang, L., Bouillet, E., Pendarakis, D.: Efficient resource provisioning in compute clouds via VM multiplexing. In: Proceedings of the 7th International Conference on Autonomic Computing, pp. 11–20. ACM (2010)
8. Zhao, C., Liu, J., Li, Y.: Virtualization resource management tool based on improved virtual machine consolidation algorithm. J. Univ. Electron. Sci. Technol. China 45(3), 356 (2016)
9. Stützle, T., Hoos, H.: Improvements on the ant-system: introducing the Max-Min Ant System. In: Smith, G.D., Steele, N.C., Albrecht, R.F. (eds.) Artificial Neural Nets and Genetic Algorithms, pp. 245–249. Springer, Vienna (1998). doi:10.1007/978-3-7091-6492-1_54
10. Reiss, C., Wilkes, J., Hellerstein, J.L.: Google cluster-usage traces: format + schema. White Paper, pp. 1–14. Google Inc. (2011)
11. Fei, M., Feng, L., Zhen, L.: Multi-objective optimization for initial virtual machine placement in cloud data center. J. Inf. Comput. Sci. 9(16), 5029–5038 (2012)
12. Gao, Y., Guan, H., Qi, Z., Hou, Y., Liu, L.: A multi-objective ant colony system algorithm for virtual machine placement in cloud computing. J. Comput. Syst. Sci. 79(8), 1230–1242 (2013)
13. Farahnakian, F., Ashraf, A., Pahikkala, T., Liljeberg, P., Plosila, J., Porres, I., Tenhunen, H.: Using ant colony system to consolidate VMs for green cloud computing. IEEE Trans. Serv. Comput. 8(2), 187–198 (2015)
14. Mishra, M., Sahoo, A.: On theory of VM placement: anomalies in existing methodologies and their mitigation using a novel vector based approach. In: 2011 IEEE International Conference on Cloud Computing (CLOUD), pp. 275–282. IEEE (2011)
15. Ferdaus, M.H., Murshed, M., Calheiros, R.N., Buyya, R.: Virtual machine consolidation in cloud data centers using ACO metaheuristic. In: Silva, F., Dutra, I., Santos Costa, V. (eds.) Euro-Par 2014. LNCS, vol. 8632, pp. 306–317. Springer, Cham (2014). doi:10.1007/978-3-319-09873-9_26
16. Wan, J., Pan, F., Jiang, C.: Placement strategy of virtual machines based on workload characteristics. In: 2012 IEEE 26th International Conference on Parallel and Distributed Processing Symposium Workshops and PhD Forum (IPDPSW), pp. 2140–2145. IEEE (2012)

17. Lin, H., Qi, X., Yang, S., Midkiff, S.: Workload-driven VM consolidation in cloud data centers. In: 2015 IEEE International Conference on Parallel and Distributed Processing Symposium (IPDPS), pp. 207–216. IEEE (2015)
18. Fan, X., Weber, W.D., Barroso, L.A.: Power provisioning for a warehouse-sized computer. In: ACM SIGARCH Computer Architecture News, vol. 35, pp. 13–23. ACM (2007)
19. Singh, A., Korupolu, M., Mohapatra, D.: Server-storage virtualization: integration and load balancing in data centers. In: Proceedings of the 2008 ACM/IEEE Conference on Supercomputing, p. 53. IEEE Press (2008)

Parallel Service Selection Method
Based on Adaptive Cloud Model
for Mobile Application

Longchang Zhang[1(✉)], Yanhong Yang[2], and Decai Sun[1]

[1] College of Information Science and Technology, Bohai University,
No. 19, Keji Road, Songshan New District, Jinzhou, China
zlc_041018@163.com
[2] Library, Bohai University,
No. 19, Keji Road, Songshan New District, Jinzhou, China

Abstract. The service selection based on QoS is very important in mobile Web service computing, because QoS is highly uncertain in service providing for mobile applications. From the uncertain QoS data described, a parallel service selection method based on adaptive cloud model (PSSM_ACM) is presented for the first time. First, PSSM_ACM employs cloud model to portray QoS to solve the QoS's uncertainty in mobile applications. Then, 2 kinds of backward QoS cloud generator are introduced to convert big QoS data to QoS cloud model, and a QoS cloud model adaptive adjustment mechanism is introduced too. Next, by reference the technique for order preference by similarity to an ideal solution (TOPSIS) theory, 2 kinds of service selection algorithm are designed to obtain the optimal service reflecting user's QoS needs. The last, some experiments demonstrate the superiority and efficiency of our approach.

Keywords: Cloud model · mobile web service · Service selection · TOPSIS

1 Introduction

Recently, the mobile service has received much attention since it can provide various and powerful applications for the mobile user. The optimal Web service selection based on Quality of Service (QoS) is still a hot issue, especially for mobile applications. For mobile users, the following three factors caused the QoS's dynamic and uncertainty: (1) the network environment of mobile terminal, the hardware and software environment of mobile terminal; (2) the service provider behavior, software and hardware environment of servers, network environment of servers; (3) transmission network status. To obtain precise QoS of mobile Web service, above factors need to be considered. However, currently more feasible approach is to obtain QoS information from mobile users' terminal, such as WS-Dream [1] dataset.

The QoS Web service was investigated in WSDream data set. The following problems need to be solved. (1) The QoS attributes depict problem. In order to obtain more accurate QoS that researchers have conducted some contribution to describe QoS, such as real number [1], interval number [2], fuzzy number [3], the mean standard

X. Sun et al. (Eds.): ICCCS 2017, Part I, LNCS 10602, pp. 189–200, 2017.
https://doi.org/10.1007/978-3-319-68505-2_17

deviation [4] and some QoS prediction based on real number [5]. The response time of mobile service from 10 mobile users feedback are 5352, 5516, 598, 406, 420, 506, 447, 311, 408, 405, and converted it into the mean, the interval number and the mean standard deviation are 1436.9, (311, 5516) and (1436.9, 2108.3) (Because the fuzzy number is facing to linguistic variable, it is not considered). The real number (the mean value is 1436.9) can not reflect the distribution and fuzzy characteristics of the 10 user feedback; the interval number (311, 5516) is lower accuracy and cannot reflect distribution characteristics; the mean standard deviation (1436.9, 2108) can not reflect the uncertainty of the degree of standard deviation. Another example, the response time from 10 users feedback are 5452, 5416, 498, 406, 420, 606, 447, 311, 408, 405, the mean standard deviation is (1436.9, 2108), both have the same mean value and standard deviation, but the standard deviation of the first example is more stable. Existing methods have problem in portraying QoS data sequence uncertainties although which can well portray some aspects of QoS. Cloud model [6] than above method can be a good description for above QoS data, which uses expectation, entropy and hyper entropy to describe sample set. Where expectation represents the whole sample, entropy reacts the discrete degree of sample, hyper entropy reacts the uncertainty of discrete degree. (2) Constantly getting QoS information from mobile user clients engenders big QoS data. In mobile service selection, taking into account all the history QoS information not only is unreality but also can not reflect the current QoS status. Taking some most recent feedbacks to establish QoS model is reasonable. While the established QoS model can not reflect the current state, and the QoS model is needed to be recalculated. This is called QoS cloud model adaptive adjustment. (3) Existing research results for service selection mainly include service selection based on real QoS [7], service selection based on fuzzy QoS [3], service selection based on random QoS [8]. A novel collaborative filtering-based Web service recommender system was proposed to help users select services with optimal Quality-of-Service (QoS) performance [5, 7]. Two selection approaches are described and compared: one based on local (task-level) selection of services based on multiple attribute decision making and the other based on global allocation of tasks to services using integer programming [2]. A novel approach called combinatorial auction for service selection was proposed to support effective and efficient service selection for service-based systems based on combinatorial auction [9]. A Web services dynamic combination method which support risk appetite based on portfolio theory was proposed [10]. Both the web service selection and server dynamic speed scaling arc optimized by maximizing the quality of service (QoS) revenue and minimizing energy costs; stochastic models of web service systems were proposed, and quantitative analysis of the performance and energy consumption is carried out [11]. Uncertain multi-attribute decision making-based service selection algorithms were proposed to support hybrid QoS [2]. Almulla proposed the service selection algorithms supported fuzzy numbers based on multi-attribute decision making [3]. A systematic approach was proposed to calculate QoS for composite services with complex structures, taking into consideration of the probability and conditions of each execution path [12]. Existing service selection algorithms cannot effectively solve the service selection problem which QoS described by cloud model. So based on the new QoS model, a new efficient service selection algorithm must to be proposed.

To solve problems above, a parallel service selection method based on adaptive cloud model (PSSM_ACM) for mobile service computing is proposed. The contributions have 3 points: (1) QoS cloud model is proposed to describe the QoS status and two kinds of backward QoS cloud generator are introduced; (2) The adaptive judgment method of QoS cloud model is put forward; (3) To obtain the optimal mobile service meeting user requirements, a parallel service selection algorithm based on cloud model and TOPSIS method is proposed.

2   QoS Model

QoS can be defined as $QoS(s) = ((q_1(s), q_2(s), \ldots, q_3(s)))$, $q_i(s)$ may be response time, call failure rate, price, popularity, availability, reliability, etc. Attributes have the following characteristics: (1) Attributes have efficiency type and cost type; (2) There exist different dimension between the attributes. In order to solve problems above, the attribute values have to be standardized. The 0–1 change is used (shown in formula (1)) to normalize attribute values in this paper. Let the service decision matrix be $Y = (y)_{m \times n}$, standardized decision matrix is $Z = (z)_{m \times n}$, z_{ij} is an attribute value, set y_j^{max} and y_j^{min} are the maximum value and minimum value of the j attribute. k is the multiples relative to the user ratings. O is benefit type attributes and I is cost type attributes. For example two mobile services' QoS (the attributes include response time and availability), $s_1 = (600, 0.90)$ and $s_2 = (400, 0.95)$, and take $k = 10$ (the user scores is ten times as big as the value after changing). Using the formula (1), $s_1 = (0, 0)$ and $s_2 = (10, 10)$ can be get.

$$z_{ij} = k(\frac{y_{ij} - y_j^{min}}{y_j^{max} - y_j^{min}}), j \in O; z_{ij} = k(\frac{y_j^{max} - y_{ij}}{y_j^{max} - y_j^{min}}), j \in I \qquad (1)$$

2.1   QoS Cloud Model

Definition 1 (cloud). Set U is a quantitative domain, which is expressed by exact numerical values. C is a qualitative concept on U; For the element $x(x \in U)$, there is a random numbers $\mu(x) \in [0, 1]$ with a stable tendency, called the membership that x for C; x distributed on the domain of U called cloud, each x is called a cloud droplet.

Definition 2 (cloud model). The model, called the cloud model, is represented by (Ex, En, He), written $C(Ex, En, He)$. Where Ex is the expectation value of droplet distribution in domain space; the entropy- En is the uncertainty measurement of qualitative concept, and it can be used to describe the span of cloud and reflects the discrete degree of cloud droplets; the super entropy- He is the uncertainty measurement of entropy, which reflects the discrete degree of cloud.

Definition 3 (QoS cloud model). Each QoS attributes of mobile service using cloud model to describe is called QoS cloud model. Where the expectation- Ex expresses the expectation value of mobile user feedback distribution, it is the point that can best represent qualitative concepts; the entropy- *En* describes the span of the numerical sequence distribution, which reflects the discrete degree of mobile user feedback; super entropy- *He* is the uncertainty measurement of entropy, which reflects the stability of the mobile user feedback.

2.2   Backward QoS Cloud Model Generator

Algorithm 1. Static Backward QoS cloud model generator (S_QoS_BCG)
Input: m services, n QoS attributes, the feedback is $(x)_{m \times n \times N}$ of N mobile users
Output: Cloud model matrix is $(c)_{m \times n}$ of m services and n QoS attributes

Steps: (1) Calculate sample mean $\bar{x}_{ij} = \frac{1}{N} \sum_{k=1}^{N} x_{ijk}$, $k = 1 \cdots N$, an order absolute central moment $|\bar{x}_{ij}| = \frac{1}{N} \sum_{k=1}^{N} |x_{ijk} - \bar{x}_{ij}|$ of sample, sample variance $S_{ij}^2 = \frac{1}{N-1}$ $\sum_{k=1}^{N} (x_{ijk} - \bar{x}_{ij})^2$;

(2) The estimated value $\bar{E}x_{ij} = \bar{x}_{ij}$ of the expectations value $c_{ij}.Ex$;
(3) The estimated value $\bar{E}n_{ij} = \sqrt{\frac{\pi}{2}} |\bar{x}_{ij}|$ of the super entropy value $c_{ij}.En$;
(4) The estimated value $\bar{H}e_{ij} = \sqrt{\left| S_{ij}^2 - \bar{E}n_{ij}^2 \right|}$ of the entropy value $c_{ij}.He$;

Algorithm 2. Distributed static backward QoS cloud generator (DS_QoS_BCG)
Input: m services, n QoS attributes, the feedback is $(x)_{m \times n \times N}$ of N users
Output: Cloud model matrix is $(c)_{m \times n}$ of m services and n QoS attributes
Steps: (1) Assign mobile user feedback matrix to l processors, if $l < = m * n$, then each processor handle $\lceil \frac{m*n}{l} \rceil$ QoS attributes, and call S_QoS_BCG; If $m * n < l < 2 * m * n$, then each processor handle $\lceil \frac{m*n}{l} \rceil$ QoS attributes, and call S_QoS_BCG; If $2 * m * n < = l$, then there are $k = \lfloor \frac{l}{m*n} \rfloor$ processors to jointly compute one cloud model, execute Step (2), (3), (4).

(2) Calculating the sample mean value $\bar{x}_{ij} = \frac{1}{N} \sum_{t=1}^{N} x_{ijk}$ of this group of data by $x_{ijk}, t = 1...N$, and then gaining the estimate value of expectations Ex_{ij}.

(3) Dividing the sample $x_{ij1}, x_{ij2}, \ldots, x_{ijN}$ into k groups, and each groups have r samples ($N = r * k$), then calculating the sample variance $\bar{y}_h^2 = \frac{1}{r-1} \sum_{t=1}^{r} (x_{ijt} - \bar{E}x_h)^2$ in each group, where $\bar{E}x_h = \frac{1}{r} \sum_{t=1}^{r} x_{ijt} (h = 1, 2, \ldots, k)$. According to the forward cloud generator [6], $y_1, y_2, \ldots, y_k$ can be considered a set of samples which came from $N(En_{ij}, He_{ij}^2)$.

(4) Estimated $\bar{E}n_{ij}$ and $\bar{H}e_{ij}$ from the sample $y_1^2, y_2^2, \ldots, y_k^2$. That the calculating

formula as $\bar{E}n_{ij} = \sqrt{\frac{1}{2}\sqrt{4(\bar{E}_Y)^2 - 2\bar{D}_Y^2}}$ and $\bar{H}e_{ij}^2 = \bar{E}_Y^2 - \bar{E}n^2$, where $\bar{E}_Y^2 = \frac{1}{k}\sum_{i=1}^{k}\bar{y}_i^2$ and

$\bar{D}_Y^2 = \frac{1}{k-1}\sum_{i=1}^{k}(\bar{y}_i^2 - \bar{E}_Y^2)^2$.

2.3 QoS Cloud Model Adaptive Computing

According to the current QoS status, QoS cloud model needs to be adjusted constantly. Based on Chebyshev inequality, the QoS cloud model adaptive computing is designed. Chebyshev inequality $(P(\mu - k\sigma < X < \mu + k\sigma) \geq 1 - \frac{1}{k^2})$ describes that there are at least $1 - \frac{1}{k^2}$ samples in k standard deviation range at the average as center. Based on the definition of forward cloud generator [6], Ex and En of the cloud model respectively as the mean value and standard deviation, setting the degree of confidence as β. After calling a mobile service, supposing the mobile user's feedback QoS attribute value is x; if meet any conditions in formula 2, then the QoS cloud model must be adjust. In the formula, m_0 is the number of original samples which falls in the range of $\{Ex - \beta En, Ex + \beta En\}$, m_1 is the number of newly increased samples which falling into this range, n_0 is the number of original samples, and n_1 is the number of newly increased samples.

$$(1)\, x \notin \{Ex - \beta En, Ex + \beta En\}; (2)\, (m_0 + m_1)/(n_0 + n_1) > 1 - \frac{1}{\beta^2} \qquad (2)$$

Example 1. Samples 598,406,420,506,447,311,408,405 describe the response time, generated the cloud model as (437.625,74.6114,39.2827), set $\beta = 5$, then according to the definition of Chebyshev inequality that should be 96% of the samples fall in {64.5680,810.6820}, the cloud model can best represents the current state, after SaaS call that generated the value is $x = 5352$, sample as a whole becomes bad, by the condition (1) of formula (2) calculating that $x \notin \{64.5680, 810.6820\}$, And the original cloud model can not represent the condition of current numberical sequence, then get after 8 samples recalculate gain the cloud model is (1031.9,1353.6,1103.5).

Example 2. From the Example 2 can be obtained $m_0 = 8$, $n_0 = 8$; after the increase of the sample 450 can be obtained $m_1 = 1$, $n_1 = 1$, satisfied the condition (2) in the formula (2), and original cloud model can not represent the condition of current numberical sequence, then get after 8 samples recalculate gain the cloud model is (419.1250,55.3752).

3 Service Decision Algorithm Based on Qos Cloud Model

The backward QoS cloud model generator generates a service matrix which QoS is expressed by cloud model, set $A(c) = (c)_{m \times n}$, where $c_{ij} = (Ex_{ij}, En_{ij}, He_{ij})$. Drawn on the basic idea of TOPSIS, the service decision method based on cloud model is put forward (named SDA_CM). The process is as follows (Note: When $k = 10$ that after normalizing by the formula (1), $0 \leq Ex_{ij}, En_{ij}, He_{ij} \leq 10$ in c_{ij}.

Step 1: Construct weighted matrix.

User weights reflect the user's demand for each attribute of QoS, set user weights as $\omega = (\omega_1, \omega_2, \ldots, \omega_n)$, $\sum_{i=1}^{n} \omega_i = 1$. The weighted matrix is as follows:

$$\bar{c}_{ij} = \left(\omega_j Ex_{ij}, \omega_j Sx_{ij} \right) \tag{3}$$

Step 2: Determine the positive ideal solution and negative ideal solution.

In order to determine service is better or worse, the standard of comparison needs to be defined and the positive and negative ideal solution are calculated as formula (4).

$$A^+ = \left\{ \left(c_1^+, c_2^+, \ldots, c_n^+ \right) \right\} = \left\{ \left(c_j^+ = (1,0,0) \right) \right\}; A^- = \left\{ \left(c_1^-, c_2^-, \ldots, c_n^- \right) \right\}$$
$$= \left\{ \left(c_j^- = (0,0,0) \right) \right\} \tag{4}$$

When all attribute values are 1 that the result is the best, where $Ex = 1$, $En = 0$, $He = 0$; when all attribute values are 0 that the result is the worst, where $Ex = 0$, $En = 0$, $He = 0$. The positive ideal solution is the best solution and the negative ideal solution is the worst solution. Generally, the positive and negative ideal solution does not exist.

Step 3: Calculate the distance.

The distance of alternative service from the positive ideal solution determines its degree of better or worse. Since QoS attributes of alternatives, the positive ideal solution and negative ideal solution described by the cloud model, the distance between two clouds model need to be defined, and the follow methods are given to calculate the distance between the cloud models.

Definition 4. Given the vector c_i and c_j of cloud model i and j, then the Euclidean distance between these two cloud models i and j:

$$d(i,j) = d\left(c_i, c_j \right) = \sqrt{ \left(Ex_i - Ex_j \right)^2 + \left(En_i - En_j \right)^2 + \left(He_i - He_j \right)^2 } \tag{5}$$

Where there is $c_i = (Ex_i, En_i, He_i)$, $c_j = (Ex_j, En_j, He_j)$, and $0 \leq d(i,j) \leq 1$, the smaller the Euclidean distance, the closer the distance of i and j.

Step 4: Calculating the distance from the alternative to the positive and negative ideal solution.

We can use formula (5) to calculate the distance each alternative to the positive ideal solution and negative ideal solution, the calculation method still using n-dimensional Euclidean distance. Supposing the distance of alternative to the positive ideal solution A^+ as $d_{s_i}^+$ and the distance that alternative to the negative ideal solution A^- as $d_{s_i}^-$, computation formula is as follow.

$$d_{s_i}^+ = \left\{ \sum_{j=1}^n d\left(c_j, c_j^+\right)^2 \right\}^{\frac{1}{2}}, i = 1, \ldots, m; d_{s_i}^- = \left\{ \sum_{j=1}^n d\left(c_j, c_j^-\right)^2 \right\}^{\frac{1}{2}}, i = 1, \ldots, m \quad (6)$$

Step 5: Calculating the optimal degree of alternative.

The basic idea of TOPSIS is that the optimal alternative is the closer to positive ideal solution and the farther away from negative ideal solution. The following based on basic thought of TOPSIS gives the optimal degree calculation formula of alternative.

$$R_i = \frac{d_{s_i}^-}{\left(d_{s_i}^+ + d_{s_i}^-\right)}, i = 1, \ldots, m \quad (7)$$

Where $R_i \in [0, 1]$. While $R_i = 0$, $d_i = A^-$, the alternative is the worst one; While $R_i = 1$, $d_i = A^+$, the alternative is the optimal one. In practical multi-objective decision-making, that the possibility of existence is very small of A^+ and A^-. By sorting the value of R_i from small to big, the service is optimal one with the biggest R_i.

In SDA_CM, the alternative is regarded as basic unit to calculate optimal degree. So m alternative can form the under graph structure (shown in Fig. 1). Therefore each process of SDA_CM can be executed in parallel, called PSDA_CM.

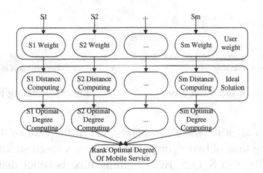

Fig. 1. Parallel processing of SDA_CM (PSDA_CM)

4 Experimental Analysis

4.1 Backward QoS Cloud Generator Analysis

Take the response time of certain mobile service and its cloud model is $C(8, 0.9, 0.3)$, run the forward cloud generator (BCG) [6] 10 times, produce n cloud droplets each times, call S_QoS_BCG and DS_QoS_BCG to calculate $\bar{En}$ and $\bar{He}$, repeat 10 times and get the absolute value of deviations and the mean run time of algorithms. Figures 2 and 3 show little difference deviations between the two algorithms, DS_QoS_BCG slightly better than S_QoS_BCG. In Fig. 4, the experiment is under the condition of ten processors (each processor is 2 GHz) and ten processors share 10G RAM; In Fig. 5, the number of samples is 1000. We can get the following experimental results: (1) the

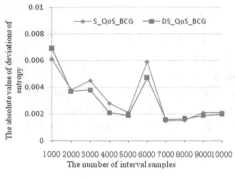

Fig. 2. Comparison of absolute value of deviations of entropy

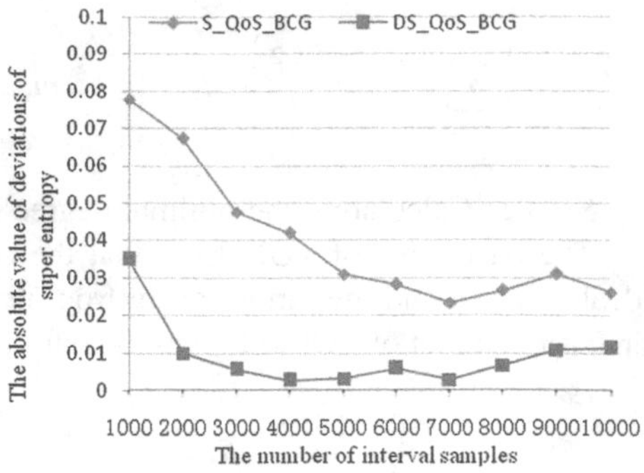

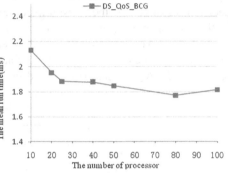

Fig. 3. Comparison of absolute value of deviations of super entropy

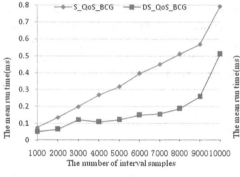

Fig. 4. Comparison of mean run time

Fig. 5. Running time curve

deviation of the two algorithms are acceptable; (2) In the case of the samples size is 1000 that the running time of two algorithms have been very close, and with the sample size becoming smaller that S_QoS_BCG running time is better than DS_QoS_BCG; (3) Unlimited increasing the number of processor cannot unlimited reduce running time of DS_QoS_BCG, while the processor number is proportional to the number of samples, the run time of DS_QoS_BCG is the shortest.

4.2   The Analysis of the QoS Cloud Model Adaptive Computing

The QoS cloud model adaptive computing is used to dynamically adjust the QoS cloud model, it is called adaptive QoS cloud model (AQoS_CM), here are two methods to generate QoS cloud model: (1) continue to collect QoS feedback, after QoS feedback of each collection reached n, calculating the QoS cloud model by taking the n QoS feedback which distance from the current time recently, this method is called n interval of QoS cloud model (NIQoS_CM). (2) As long as collected the new QoS feedback, then the QoS cloud model will be calculated by taking the n QoS feedback which distance from the current time recently, this method is called real-time QoS cloud model (RTQoS_CM). Real-time QoS model is an ideal method, but its calculation is too frequent, it is not realistic. This experiment analysis the accuracy and the execution time of AQoS_CM, NIQoS_CM and RTQoS_CM. Taking the response time data of the service number 1 in QoSDataset2 in WSDream dataset [1] and setting $\beta = 5$.

Figures 6, 7 and 8 illustrate that the accuracy of AQoS_CM is better than NIQoS_CM; Fig. 9 shows that the execution times AQoS_CM is lot less than the RTQoS_CM and gradually approaching NIQoS_CM in the execution times. In addition, AQoS_CM has completly runned before the service selection, and does not affect the user experience.

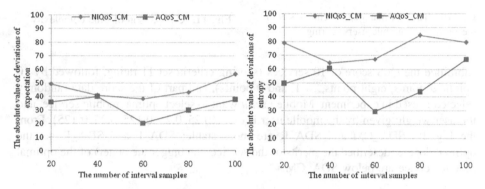

Fig. 6. Comparison of deviations of expectation

Fig. 7. Comparison of deviations of entropy

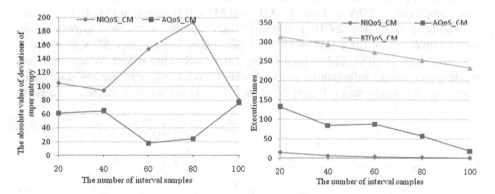

Fig. 8. Comparison of deviations of super entropy

Fig. 9. Comparison of execution times

4.3 The Application Scene Analysis

There are 10 mobile book retrieval services $(s_1, s_2, \ldots, s_{10})$ in a university library, QoS attributes include cost, response time, reliability, availability and reliability. The university has 40000 teachers and students, where 10000 teachers and students has

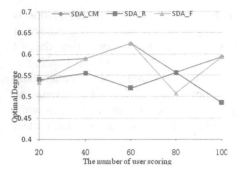
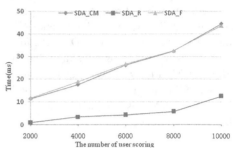

Fig. 10. The optimal degree changes with the number of mobile users scoring

Fig. 11. Comparison of time complexity

submitted the QoS score of 10 services (scoring criteria set 11 rating, followed by 10 points, 9 points, eight points,..., 1, and 0 points), and part of the score data randomly selected is used in experiment. Mobile user u want to select optimal mobile service, and the user weight given by the mobile user is $\omega = (0.25, 0.25, 0.125, 0.25, 0.125)$. From the Fig. 10, SDA_CM and SDA_R are more stable; SDA_F and SDA_R get the optimal degree (described the merits of the service, the bigger the better) of the optimal mobile service are below SDA_CM.

4.4 Algorithm Performance Analysis

Under the application scenarios in real world in the Sect. 4.4, the comparison of the time complexity of SDA_CM and SDA_R and SDA_F is shown in Fig. 11 (hardware environment: 1 G RAM, 2 GHz processor). Three algorithms are linear growth trend; time complexities of SDA_CM and SDA_F are similar and less than SDA_R method. The extra time of SDA_CM is used to engender QoS cloud model. When there are enough user ratings information, the QoS cloud model will reach steady state (it is known as the steady state). Figure 12 shows three cloud number characteristic is in

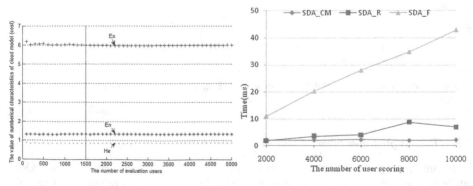

Fig. 12. Cloud model curve for Cost of S1

Fig. 13. Comparison of time complexity under steady state

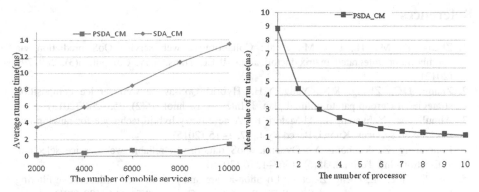

Fig. 14. Run time comparison of SDA_CM and PSDA_CM

Fig. 15. Time consumption curve of PSDA_CM

stable state which generated after about 1500 user scoring. Under steady state, the comparison of time complexity of three kinds of algorithms is shown in Fig. 13.

There are 5 QoS attributes in service, QoS value is randomly generated, user weight is $\omega = (0.2, 0.2, 0.2, 0.2, 0.2)$, and the number of processors is 10 (each processor is 2 GHz) and ten processors share 10 G RAM), comparing the time consumption of SDA_CM and PSDA_CM two algorithms (see Fig. 14). The PSDA_CM time consuming changes with the number of processors increasing, as shown in Fig. 15.

5 Conclusion

Big QoS data of mobile service from mobile users' feedback has randomness and fuzziness, so cloud model is put forward to depict the QoS attributes, and this paper has demonstrated that this method relative to the existing method has better ability to describe. The backward QoS cloud model generator is presented to convert the big QoS to QoS cloud model. Through the QoS cloud model adaptive adjustment mechanism, the QoS cloud model is dynamically adjusted. The service selection algorithm presented based on cloud model can obtain the QoS optimal service to meet mobile user demand, and the parallel algorithm designed in this paper can improve the response time of the algorithm. Experiments show that PSSM_ACM is an efficient and reliable method on dealing with the optimal service selection based on QoS with uncertain.

Acknowledgments. This work was supported in part by "Humanities and social science research Youth Fund of Ministry of Education of China" (15YJC870028), "Natural Science Foundation of Liaoning Province" (2015020009), and "Social Science Planning Fund of Liaoning Province of China" (L15BTQ002).

References

1. Zheng, Z., Ma, H., Lyu, M., et al.: Collaborative web service QoS prediction via neighborhood integrated matrix factorization. IEEE Trans. Serv. Comput. 6(3), 289–299 (2012)
2. Zhang, L.C., Zhang, X.X., Yang, Y.H.: Hybrid QoS-aware web service composition strategies for group pareto optimal plan. J. Internet Technol. 16(2), 255–266 (2015)
3. Almulla, M., Yahyaoui, H., Al-Matori, K.: A new fuzzy hybrid technique for ranking real world Web services. Knowl.-Based Syst. 77, 1–15 (2015)
4. Longchang, Z., Yanhong, Y.: Dynamic QoS data-driven reliable web service selection. J. Electron. Inf. Technol. 38(6), 1368–1376 (2016)
5. Liu, J., Tang, M., Zheng, Z., et al.: Location-aware and personalized collaborative filtering for web service recommendation. IEEE Trans. Serv. Comput. 9(5), 686–699 (2016)
6. Wang, G., Li, D., Yao, Y., et al.: Cloud Model and Granular Computing, pp. 1–22. Science Press, Beijing (2012)
7. Chen, X., Zheng, Z., Yu, Q., et al.: Web service recommendation via exploiting location and QoS information. IEEE Trans. Parallel Distrib. Syst. 25(7), 1913–1924 (2014)
8. Zheng, H., Zhao, W., Yang, J., et al.: QoS analysis for web service compositions with complex structures. IEEE Trans. Serv. Comput. 6(3), 373–386 (2013)
9. He, Q., Yan, J., Jin, H., et al.: Quality-aware service selection for service-based systems based on iterative multi-attribute combinatorial auction. IEEE Trans. Softw. Eng. 40(2), 192–215 (2014)
10. Lin, R., Chen, B., Peng, X., et al.: Web services dynamic combination method which support risk appetite. Chin. Sci. (Inf. Sci.) 44(1), 130–141 (2014)
11. Huang, J., Lin, C.: Agent-based green web service selection and dynamic speed scaling. In: 2013 IEEE 20th International Conference on Web Services (ICWS), pp. 91–98 (2013)
12. Zheng, H., Zhao, W., Yang, J., et al.: QoS analysis for web service compositions with complex structures. IEEE Trans. Serv. Comput. 6(3), 373–386 (2013)

A Hybrid Artificial Bee Colony Algorithm to Solve Multi-objective Hybrid Flowshop in Cloud Computing Systems

Jun-qing Li[1,2(✉)], Yu-yan Han[1], and Cun-gang Wang[1]

[1] College of Computer Science, Liaocheng University,
Liaocheng 252059, People's Republic of China
{lijunqing,hanyuyan,wangcungang}@lcu-cs.com
[2] State Key Laboratory of Synthetic Automation for Process Industries,
Northeastern University, Shenyang 110819, People's Republic of China

Abstract. This paper proposes a local search enhanced hybrid artificial bee colony algorithm (LABC) for solving the multi-objective flexible task scheduling problem in Cloud computing system. The task scheduling is modeled as a hybrid flow shop scheduling (HFS) problem. In multiple objectives HFS problems, three objectives, i.e., minimum of the makespan, maximum workload, and total workload are considered simultaneously. In the proposed algorithm, each solution is represented as an integer string. A deep-exploitation function is developed, which is used by the onlooker bee and the best food source found so far to complete a deep level of search. The proposed algorithm is tested on sets of the well-known benchmark instances. Through the analysis of experimental results, the highly effective performance of the proposed LABC algorithm is shown against several efficient algorithms from the literature.

Keywords: Hybrid flow shop scheduling problem · Artificial bee colony algorithm · Cloud system · Multi-objective optimization

1 Introduction

In cloud computing, a cloud is a cluster of distributed devices provides on-demand computational resources or services for potential users across the internet [1–7]. In the cloud system, several tasks are to be processed on several kinds of computational resources, such as a shared computational CPU, shared memory and shared hard disk storage. The same kind of resource constitutes a resource series. The flexible task scheduling in Cloud computing system is presented as follows: given a cloud computing environment, there are n tasks to be processed on m computational resources in a predefined order. Each task contains s operations, and should visit each stage following the same production flow: stage$_1$, stage$_2$, ..., stage$_s$. The m computational resources are grouped into s stages in series. In each stage i ($1 \leq i \leq s$), there are m_i identical or un-related computational resources in parallel, where $m_{iz} \geq 1$, and there are at least two parallel computational resources in one stage. When a task arrives at a stage i, it can select exactly one computational resource from m_i available parallel computational resources. Each computational resource in the same stage can process

© Springer International Publishing AG 2017
X. Sun et al. (Eds.): ICCCS 2017, Part I, LNCS 10602, pp. 201–213, 2017.
https://doi.org/10.1007/978-3-319-68505-2_18

only one task at a time, while each task can be operated by only one computational resource at a time. The above flexible task scheduling process is similar to the classical hybrid flow shop scheduling (HFS) problem. Indeed, the cloud system requires an optimization mechanism to minimize certain objectives. In this study, we model a HFS for the above task scheduling problem, and propose a hybrid algorithm for solving the given problem.

The HFS scheduling problem is one branch of the classical flow shop scheduling problem (FSSP), which has been verified to be an NP-hard (Non-deterministic Polynomial-time hard) problem [8, 9], that is, which is at least as hard as or harder than any problem in NP. There are two phases of tasks in HFS: (1) in the first phase, a processing device should be selected from a set of candidate devices for each waiting job; (2) in the second phase, each task should be scheduled on each selected device, which is similar to the whole task in the classical FSSP. Therefore, HFS is harder than the classical FSSP with the addition of the consideration of parallel device selection for each job. In this study, by combining with ABC and several neighborhood structures, we propose a hybrid algorithm for solving the task scheduling problems in Cloud systems. The proposed eight neighborhood structures are utilized to enhance the exploitation and exploration ability of the proposed algorithm. The rest of this paper is organized as follows: Sect. 2 gives the problem formulation. Then, the canonical ABC algorithm is presented in Sect. 3. The proposed LABC algorithm is shown in Sect. 4. Section 5 reports the experimental results and compares with other algorithms in the literature to demonstrate the performance of LABC. Finally, the last section presents conclusions of our work.

2 Literature Review

In a flexible task scheduling problem in Cloud computing system, there are n tasks to be processed on m devices in a predefined order. All tasks and devices are available at time zero. Preemption is not allowed, that is, any task cannot be interrupted before the completion of its current operation. Setup times are negligible and problem data is deterministic and known in advance. There are unlimited intermediate buffer between two successive stages. The aim of HFS is to schedule each task on each device so as to minimize the makespan or other objectives.

2.1 Hybrid Flow Shop Scheduling Problem

The first paper to solve the HFS was published in 1970 [8], with the branch and bound (B&B) algorithm. After that, many published papers have discussed the HFS with many different algorithms [8, 9].

We can classify these algorithms by the stage size of the considered problems. There are three kinds of problems, that is, two-stage, three-stage, and m-stage. The two-stage is the HFS with two consecutive stages, while the m-stage is the problem with m stage series. Table 1 briefly gives the references about the HFS problems.

Table 1. Literature about the HFS problems

Category	Features	Methods	References
2-stages	Identical machines	Branch and Bound (B&B)	Gupta [10]
	Sequence-dependent setup time	Heuristic	Lin and Liao [11]
	Setup and removal times	Heuristic algorithms	Gupta and Tunc [12]
	Minimizing total tardiness	Branch and Bound (B&B)	Lee and Kim [13]
	Dedicated machines	Heuristic	Yang [14]
3-stages	Two dedicated machines in stage two	Heuristic	Riane et al. [15]
	Identical machines	Agent cooperation method	Babayan and He [16]
	HFS in printed circuit boards	Genetic algorithms	Jin et al. [17]
m-stages	No setup effects	Lagrange method	Chang and Liao [18]
	k-stage hybrid flowshop scheduling problem	Branch and bound crossed with GA	Portmann et al. [19]
	With multiprocessor tasks	Genetic algorithm	Oguz and Ercan [20]
			Engin et al. [21]
	Makespan	Quantum-inspired immune algorithm	Niu et al. [22]
	Multiprocessor task scheduling	Ant colony system approach	Ying and Lin [23]
	With bottleneck heuristic	Particle swarm optimization and	Liao et al. [24]
	With multiprocessor tasks	Particle swarm optimization with cocktail decoding method	Chou [25]
	With total flowtime minimisation	Migrating birds optimisation	Pan and Dong [26]
	Combination of forward decoding and backward decoding	Discrete artificial bee colony algorithm	Pan et al. [27]
	A constructive heuristic called NEH heuristic is incorporated	Improved cuckoo search algorithm	Marichelvam et al. [28]
	Friedman test and Holm–Sidak test are performed	hybridizing Biogeography-Based Optimization (BBO) technique with Artificial Immune Algorithm (AIA) and Ant Colony Optimization (ACO)	Savsani et al. [29]
	Reentrant HFS with time window constraints	Genetic algorithm hybridized ant colony optimization	Chamnanlor et al. [30]

2.2 Multi-objective HFS

Compared to the research of the single-objective hybrid flow shop scheduling problem and the multi-objective optimization methods, there are less literature considering the multi-objective HFS. Table 2 gives a brief illustration about the multi-objective HFS problems.

Table 2. Literature about the multi-objective HFS problems

Objectives	Methods	References
The maximization of the utilization rate of the bottleneck and the minimization of the maximum completion time	Multi-objective genetic algorithm	Dugardin et al. [31]
Makespan and sum of the earliness and tardiness of jobs	Pareto based multi-objective method	Behnamian et al. [32]
Makespan and maximum tardiness criteria	Independent parallel genetic algorithm	Rashidi et al. [33]
Makespan and maximum tardiness criteria	Group scheduling based on Pareto archive method	Karimi et al. [34]
Makespan and mean flow time	Discrete multi-objective firefly algorithm	Marichelvam et al. [35]
Minimizing total weighted tardiness and maximum completion time	Multi-population genetic algorithm	Zandieh, and Karimi [36]
Minimization of makespan and total tardiness	Local-search based Pareto genetic algorithms	Cho et al. [37]
Minimise the unavailability of the first stage machine and to minimise the makespan	A multi-objective tabu search method	Wang and Liu [38]

3 The Proposed Algorithm

The artificial bee colony (ABC) algorithm has been investigated and applied to solve many types of scheduling problems [39–45]. In this study, we utilized and improved the canonical ABC algorithm for solving the considered multi-objective HFS problem.

3.1 Solution Representation

For solving HFS problems, the classical solution representation is mainly classified into two categories: the permutation based representation, and the representation considering both routing and scheduling parts. In the permutation based representation, each solution is represented by a string of integer. Each integer in the string corresponds to a task number. Thus, the length of the string equals to n. In this study, we conduct the permutation based solution representation, because of its simplicity and easy of implementation.

Figure 1 gives an example task scheduling problem in a Cloud system: (1) there are five tasks, seven devices, and three stages; (2) in the first stage, there are three parallel data servers to process the data from the client user; (3) in the following stage, there are two candidate diagnostic devices to analysis certain characters of the processing data; (4) in the last stage, there are two printers carrying the task to print the needed information. The processing time of each operation on each device is given in Table 3. Suppose one solution is represented by {2, 3, 1, 4, 5}, which means that in the first stage, the scheduling sequence is J_2, J_3, J_1, J_4, and J_5.

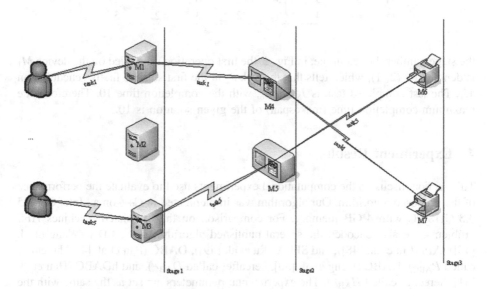

Fig. 1. An example task scheduling problem in a Cloud system

3.2   Decoding

It is notable that the solution encoding given above contains no device selection (routing) information in each stage. In this study, device selection tasks are scheduled dynamically by using the following heuristics:

Step 1: In the first stage, schedule each task one by one according to their sequence in the solution representation. For the above example solution listed in Subsect. 4.1, in the first stage, the task scheduling sequence is J_2, J_3, J_1, J_4, and J_5. When one task is to be scheduled, it will select the earliest available device. If there are several available devices with the same available time, the task will randomly select one.

Step 2: In the other stages, each task will be scheduled as soon as it completes its previous operation. The device selection strategy is the same as in the first stage, that is, select the first available device for the waiting task.

Figure 2 gives the Gantt chart for the above example solution listed in Subsect. 3.1. In Fig. 2, each operation is represented by a pair of number, i.e., the task number and

Table 3. Processing time table

	Stage1 (three parallel devices)			Stage2 (two parallel devices)		Stage3 (two parallel devices)	
	M1	M2	M3	M4	M5	M6	M7
J1	7	3	3	5	3	2	1
J2	1	5	2	3	3	3	4
J3	3	2	5	4	1	5	3
J4	3	5	3	2	6	3	2
J5	6	4	8	2	3	2	5

the stage number. For example, in Fig. 2, the first operation scheduled on the device M_1 is denoted by (2, 1), which tells that the task J_2 in the first stage is firstly scheduled on M_1. The last completed task is J_5 on M_6, with the completion time 10. Therefore, the maximum completion time (makespan) of the given solution is 10.

4   Experiment Results

This section discusses the computational experiments used to evaluate the performance of the proposed algorithm. Our algorithm was implemented in C++ on an Intel Core i5 3.3 GHz PC with 4 GB memory. For comparison on the un-related machines HFS problems, we also encoded the several published algorithms, i.e., EDA (Wang et al. [45]), AIS (Liu et al. [48]), and SFLA (Xu et al. [49]), DABC (Pan et al. [42], hereafter called P_{ABC}), DABC (Deng et al. [50], hereafter called D_{ABC}), and hDABC (Han et al. [51], hereafter called H_{ABC}). The experimental parameters are set as the same with the literature.

4.1   Comparisons of the Two Real Production Problems

In order to solve the HFS problems, we selected two kinds of benchmarks with un-related machines in each stage, i.e., the two real HFS problems in steel production [45], and the 34 new-generated benchmarks extended from the relative harder problem discussed in [24] The three objectives, i.e., the minimum of makespan, maximum workload, and total workload, are considered simultaneously. After 20 independent runs, the average computational results are collected and the average CPU times for each instance are reported as well.

The two real un-related machine HFS production problems, from [28–30], are tested and compared with the four algorithms, i.e., EDA (Wang et al. [45]), AIS (Liu et al. [48]), and SFLA (Xu et al. [49]). The processing time of the two problems are given in Tables 4 and 5, respectively. Table 6 gives the comparison results of the four compared algorithms for the two real production problems.

It can be concluded from Table 4 that: (1) for solving the two problems, the proposed LABC shows the best performance among the four compared algorithm; (2) considering the average value of makespan, the computational results due to our

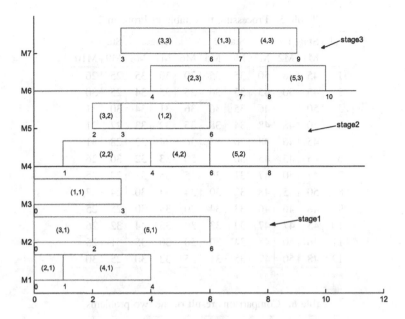

Fig. 2. Gantt chart for the example solution

Table 4. Processing time table of Problem 1

Job	Stage1			Stage2			Stage3		
	M1	M2	M3	M4	M5	M6	M7	M8	M9
1	2	2	3	4	5	2	3	2	3
2	4	5	4	3	4	3	4	5	4
3	6	5	4	4	2	3	4	2	5
4	4	3	4	6	5	3	6	5	8
5	4	5	3	3	1	3	4	6	5
6	6	5	4	2	3	4	3	9	5
7	5	2	4	4	6	3	4	3	5
8	3	5	4	7	5	3	3	6	4
9	2	5	4	1	2	7	8	6	5
10	3	6	4	3	4	4	8	6	7
11	5	2	4	3	5	6	7	6	5
12	6	5	4	5	4	3	4	7	5

proposed algorithm are the same as the best values for each instance, which shows the robustness of LABC; and (3) for solving the two different scale problems, our LABC algorithm consumed only about one second, which verifies the efficiency of the algorithm. The Gantt chart of the best solution for Problem 2 ($f_1 = 297$, $f_2 = 191$, $f_3 = 1628$) is given in Fig. 2.

Table 5. Processing time table of Problem 2

Job	Stage1			Stage2			Stage3		Stage4	
	M1	M2	M3	M4	M5	M6	M7	M8	M9	M10
1	45	48	50	35	35	30	30	35	25	26
2	45	50	45	35	36	35	35	34	25	30
3	50	45	46	35	36	36	31	34	30	31
4	50	48	48	34	38	35	32	33	27	31
5	45	46	48	30	35	50	34	32	28	31
6	45	45	45	30	35	50	33	32	30	26
7	47	50	47	31	30	35	35	31	29	25
8	50	45	48	32	30	34	34	30	24	27
9	48	46	46	33	34	30	34	30	25	25
10	45	47	47	33	33	30	35	34	32	26
11	46	50	45	34	30	50	30	35	31	25
12	48	50	47	35	31	35	32	30	25	30

Table 6. Comparisons result of the two problems

Problem	LABC						AIS		SFLA		EDA	
	f_1	f_2	f_3	Fitness value	Avg makespan	Time (s)	f_1	Avg	f_1	Avg	f_1	Avg
1	23	19	119.65	41.13	23	1.25	27	27	24	24	23	23.4
2	297	193.6	1642.7	535.12	297	0.53	-	-	297	307.3	297	297.4

4.2   Comparisons of the 34 Extended Problems

In this section, 34 extended instances are generated to make the corresponding HFS benchmarks more close to the Cloud reality. In the traditional parallel machine HFS problems, in each stage, a waiting operation can select any machine with the same processing time. Thus, the machine selection approach is simple. However, in real task scheduling of Cloud system, the distributed devices for processing tasks are different in processing ability. Therefore, in the extended problems, in each stage, a scheduling operation should consider the two key issues before the selection of the processed machine, i.e., the processing time on the machine, and the machine idle time. Given a job i, in stage j, there are k machines in the stage, the processing time is pt_{ij} in the traditional problem. Then, the extended mechanism is realized as following steps.

Step 1. Let $w = 1$;
Step 2. Randomly generate an integer value r range in [0, $pt_{ij}/2$];
Step 3. if $pt_{ij}/2 < 1$, then let $r = 0$;
Step 4. Randomly generate a processing time p range in [$pt_{ij} - r$, $pt_{ij} + r$];
Step 5. Assign p as the processing time to machine w for processing job i in stage j;
Step 6. Let $w = w + 1$; if $w < k$, go back to step 2; otherwise, stop the procedure.

The computational comparison results between LABC (hereafter called L_{ABC}), P_{ABC}, H_{ABC} and D_{ABC} are reported in Table 7.

Table 7. Comparisons results on best fitness values of the 34 un-related HFS problems

Problem	Best	Algorithm				%Deviation			
		L_{ABC}	P_{ABC}	H_{ABC}	D_{ABC}	L_{ABC}	P_{ABC}	H_{ABC}	D_{ABC}
j10c5c1	109.30	109.30	109.30	109.30	109.30	0.00	0.00	0.00	0.00
j10c5c2	102.70	102.70	102.70	102.70	102.70	0.00	0.00	0.00	0.00
j10c5c3	106.00	106.00	106.00	106.00	106.00	0.00	0.00	0.00	0.00
j10c5c4	105.40	105.40	105.40	105.40	105.40	0.00	0.00	0.00	0.00
j10c5c5	113.70	113.70	113.70	113.70	113.70	0.00	0.00	0.00	0.00
j10c5c6	101.10	101.10	101.10	101.10	101.10	0.00	0.00	0.00	0.00
j10c5d1	98.50	98.50	98.50	98.50	98.50	0.00	0.00	0.00	0.00
j10c5d2	123.80	123.80	123.80	123.80	123.80	0.00	0.00	0.00	0.00
j10c5d3	96.80	96.80	96.80	96.80	96.80	0.00	0.00	0.00	0.00
j10c5d4	105.70	105.70	105.70	105.70	105.70	0.00	0.00	0.00	0.00
j10c5d5	103.90	103.90	103.90	103.90	103.90	0.00	0.00	0.00	0.00
j10c5d6	93.40	93.40	93.40	93.40	93.40	0.00	0.00	0.00	0.00
j15c5c1	143.90	143.90	144.40	144.50	144.80	0.00	0.35	0.42	0.63
j15c5c2	160.80	161.30	160.80	160.80	161.70	0.31	0.00	0.00	0.56
j15c5c3	150.50	150.50	150.90	151.70	151.90	0.00	0.27	0.80	0.93
j15c5c4	143.50	143.50	143.80	143.80	143.50	0.00	0.21	0.21	0.00
j15c5c5	133.70	133.70	133.70	133.70	133.70	0.00	0.00	0.00	0.00
j15c5c6	155.50	155.50	155.50	156.10	156.00	0.00	0.00	0.39	0.32
j15c5d1	200.90	200.90	200.90	200.90	201.10	0.00	0.00	0.00	0.10
j15c5d2	147.40	147.40	147.40	147.40	147.40	0.00	0.00	0.00	0.00
j15c5d3	138.60	138.60	138.70	138.80	139.20	0.00	0.07	0.14	0.43
j15c5d4	148.20	148.20	148.80	148.30	148.30	0.00	0.40	0.07	0.07
j15c5d5	139.90	139.90	139.90	140.60	140.40	0.00	0.00	0.50	0.36
j15c5d6	134.00	134.00	134.00	134.40	134.30	0.00	0.00	0.30	0.22
j30c5e1	1273.80	1273.80	1286.10	1298.10	1301.20	0.00	0.97	1.91	2.15
j30c5e2	1461.70	1461.70	1469.00	1471.10	1480.30	0.00	0.50	0.64	1.27
j30c5e3	1499.10	1499.10	1502.50	1513.50	1528.10	0.00	0.23	0.96	1.93
j30c5e4	1366.80	1366.80	1382.20	1384.40	1393.40	0.00	1.13	1.29	1.95
j30c5e5	1444.80	1444.80	1453.50	1472.70	1464.50	0.00	0.60	1.93	1.36
j30c5e6	1393.50	1393.50	1408.50	1414.10	1422.20	0.00	1.08	1.48	2.06
j30c5e7	1407.80	1407.80	1418.00	1421.30	1430.10	0.00	0.72	0.96	1.58
j30c5e8	1630.70	1630.70	1638.10	1646.00	1664.10	0.00	0.45	0.94	2.05
j30c5e9	1532.30	1532.30	1547.70	1554.10	1563.00	0.00	1.01	1.42	2.00
j30c5e10	1606.40	1606.40	1608.90	1611.00	1618.60	0.00	0.16	0.29	0.76
Avg performance						0.01	0.24	0.43	0.61

There are ten columns in Table 7. The first column lists the problem name. In this study, for simplicity, the extended instances are assigned the same name with the source benchmarks. The second column collects the best fitness value for each instance found so far by the four algorithms. The following four columns report the computational result due to the four compared algorithms, i.e., L_{ABC}, P_{ABC}, H_{ABC} and D_{ABC}, respectively. The next four columns list the deviation values of the four compared algorithms to the best fitness values. The formula of the deviation is given as follows:

$$\%\text{deviation} = \frac{C_{comp} - best}{best} \times 100\% \qquad (1)$$

where, C_{comp} is the computational results collected by the corresponding compared algorithm.

It can be concluded from Table 7 that: (1) for solving the 34 extended un-related machine HFS problems, the proposed LABC obtained the best fitness value for 33 problems, except for the instance "j15c5c2"; (2) in the last line of the table, the average deviation values are reported, which verify that, in average, the proposed LABC algorithm show better performance than the other three algorithms in searching the best fitness values.

5 Conclusions

In this study, a hybrid discrete artificial bee colony algorithm is proposed for solving the flexible task scheduling problem in Cloud system. The detailed encoding and decoding mechanism is developed for the problem.

Acknowledgments. This research is partially supported by National Science Foundation of China under Grant 61573178, 61374187, 61603169 and 61503170, basic scientific research foundation of Northeastern University under Grant N110208001, starting foundation of Northeastern University under Grant 29321006, Science Foundation of Liaoning Province in China (2013020016), Key Laboratory Basic Research Foundation of Education Department of Liaoning Province (LZ2014014), Shandong Province Higher Educational Science and Technology Program (J14LN28), Postdoctoral Science Foundation of China (2015T80798, 2014M552040), and State Key Laboratory of Synthetical Automation for Process Industries (PAL-N201602).

References

1. Xia, Z., Wang, X., Sun, X., et al.: A secure and dynamic multi-keyword ranked search scheme over encrypted cloud data. IEEE Trans. Parallel Distrib. Syst. **27**(2), 340–352 (2016)
2. Fu, Z., Ren, K., Shu, J., et al.: Enabling personalized search over encrypted outsourced data with efficiency improvement. IEEE Trans. Parallel Distrib. Syst. **27**(9), 2546–2559 (2016)
3. Guo, P., Wang, J., Li, B., Lee, S.: A variable threshold-value authentication architecture for wireless mesh networks. J. Internet Technol. **15**(6), 929–936 (2014)
4. Fu, Z., Sun, X., Liu, Q., et al.: Achieving efficient cloud search services: multi-keyword ranked search over encrypted cloud data supporting parallel computing. IEICE Trans. Commun. **98**(1), 190–200 (2015)
5. Ren, Y., Shen, J., Wang, J., et al.: Mutual verifiable provable data auditing in public cloud storage. J. Internet Technol. **16**(2), 317–323 (2015)

6. Buyya, R., Yeo, C.S., Venugopal, S., et al.: Cloud computing and emerging IT platforms: vision, hype, and reality for delivering computing as the 5th utility. Future Gener. Comput. Syst. **25**(6), 599–616 (2009)
7. Li, J., Qiu, M., Ming, Z., et al.: Online optimization for scheduling preemptable tasks on IaaS cloud systems. J. Parallel Distrib. Comput. **72**(5), 666–677 (2012)
8. Ruiz, R., Vázquez-Rodríguez, J.A.: The hybrid flow shop scheduling problem. Eur. J. Oper. Res. **205**(1), 1–18 (2010)
9. Ribas, I., Leisten, R., Framiñan, J.M.: Review and classification of hybrid flow shop scheduling problems from a production system and a solutions procedure perspective. Comput. Oper. Res. **37**(8), 1439–1454 (2010)
10. Gupta, J.N.D.: Two-stage, hybrid flowshop scheduling problem. J. Oper. Res. Soc. **39**, 359–364 (1988)
11. Lin, H.T., Liao, C.J.: A case study in a two-stage hybrid flow shop with setup time and dedicated machines. Int. J. Prod. Econ. **86**(2), 133–143 (2003)
12. Gupta, J.N.D., Tunc, E.A.: Scheduling a two-stage hybrid flowshop with separable setup and removal times. Eur. J. Oper. Res. **77**, 415–428 (1994)
13. Lee, G.C., Kim, Y.D.: A branch-and-bound algorithm for a two-stage hybrid flowshop scheduling problem minimizing total tardiness. Int. J. Prod. Res. **42**, 4731–4743 (2004)
14. Yang, J.: A new complexity proof for the two-stage hybrid flow shop scheduling problem with dedicated machines. Int. J. Prod. Res. **48**(5), 1531–1538 (2010)
15. Riane, F., Artiba, A., Elmaghraby, S.E.: A hybrid three-stage flowshop problem: efficient heuristics to minimize makespan. Eur. J. Oper. Res. **109**(2), 321–329 (1998)
16. Babayan, A., He, D.: Solving the n-job three-stage flexible flowshop scheduling problem using an agent-based approach. Int. J. Prod. Res. **42**, 777–799 (2004)
17. Jin, Z.H., Ohno, K., Ito, T., Elmaghraby, S.E.: Scheduling hybrid flowshops in printed circuit board assembly lines. Prod. Oper. Manag. **11**, 216–230 (2002)
18. Chang, S.C., Liao, D.Y.: Scheduling flexible flow shops with no setup effects. IEEE Trans. Robot. Autom. **10**(2), 112–122 (1994)
19. Portmann, M.C., Vignier, A., Dardilhac, D., Dezalay, D.: Branch and bound crossed with GA to solve hybrid flowshops. Eur. J. Oper. Res. **107**, 389–400 (1998)
20. Oguz, C., Ercan, M.: A genetic algorithm for hybrid flow-shop scheduling with multiprocessor tasks. J. Sched. **8**, 323–351 (2005)
21. Engin, O., Ceran, G., Yilmaz, M.K.: An efficient genetic algorithm for hybrid flow shop scheduling with multiprocessor task problems. Appl. Soft Comput. **11**(3), 3056–3065 (2011)
22. Niu, Q., Zhou, T., Ma, S.: A quantum-inspired immune algorithm for hybrid flow shop with makespan criterion. J. Univ. Comput. Sci. **15**, 765–785 (2009)
23. Ying, K.C., Lin, S.W.: Multiprocessor task scheduling in multistage hybrid flow-shops: an ant colony system approach. Int. J. Prod. Res. **44**(16), 3161–3177 (2006)
24. Liao, C.J., Tjandradjaja, E., Chung, T.P.: An approach using particle swarm optimization and bottleneck heuristic to solve hybrid flow shop scheduling problem. Appl. Soft Comput. **12**, 1755–1764 (2012)
25. Chou, F.D.: Particle swarm optimization with cocktail decoding method for hybrid flow shop scheduling problems with multiprocessor tasks. Int. J. Prod. Econ. **141**(1), 137–145 (2013)
26. Pan, Q.K., Dong, Y.: An improved migrating birds optimisation for a hybrid flowshop scheduling with total flowtime minimisation. Inf. Sci. **277**, 643–655 (2014)
27. Pan, Q.K., Wang, L., Li, J.Q., et al.: A novel discrete artificial bee colony algorithm for the hybrid flowshop scheduling problem with makespan minimisation. Omega **45**, 42–56 (2014)
28. Marichelvam, M.K., Prabaharan, T., Yang, X.S.: Improved cuckoo search algorithm for hybrid flow shop scheduling problems to minimize makespan. Appl. Soft Comput. **19**, 93–101 (2014)

29. Savsani, P., Jhala, R.L., Savsani, V.: Effect of hybridizing Biogeography-Based Optimization (BBO) technique with Artificial Immune Algorithm (AIA) and Ant Colony Optimization (ACO). Appl. Soft Comput. **21**, 542–553 (2014)

30. Chamnanlor, C., Sethanan, K., Gen, M., et al.: Embedding ant system in genetic algorithm for re-entrant hybrid flow shop scheduling problems with time window constraints. J. Intell. Manuf. (2015). doi:10.1007/s10845-015-1078-9

31. Dugardin, F., Yalaoui, F., Amodeo, L.: New multi-objective method to solve reentrant hybrid flow shop scheduling problem. Eur. J. Oper. Res. **203**(1), 22–31 (2010)

32. Behnamian, J., Ghomi, S.F., Zandieh, M.: A multi-phase covering Pareto-optimal front method to multi-objective scheduling in a realistic hybrid flowshop using a hybrid metaheuristic. Expert Syst. Appl. **36**(8), 11057–11069 (2009)

33. Rashidi, E., Jahandar, M., Zandieh, M.: An improved hybrid multi-objective parallel genetic algorithm for hybrid flow shop scheduling with unrelated parallel machines. Int. J. Adv. Manuf. Technol. **49**(9–12), 1129–1139 (2010)

34. Karimi, N., Zandieh, M., Karamooz, H.R.: Bi-objective group scheduling in hybrid flexible flowshop: a multi-phase approach. Expert Syst. Appl. **37**(6), 4024–4032 (2010)

35. Marichelvam, M.K., Prabaharan, T., Yang, X.S.: A discrete firefly algorithm for the multi-objective hybrid flowshop scheduling problems. IEEE Trans. Evol. Comput. **18**(2), 301–305 (2014)

36. Zandieh, M., Karimi, N.: An adaptive multi-population genetic algorithm to solve the multi-objective group scheduling problem in hybrid flexible flowshop with sequence-dependent setup times. J. Intell. Manuf. **22**(6), 979–989 (2011)

37. Cho, H.M., Bae, S.J., Kim, J., Jeong, I.J.: Bi-objective scheduling for reentrant hybrid flow shop using Pareto genetic algorithm. Comput. Ind. Eng. **61**(3), 529–541 (2011)

38. Wang, S., Liu, M.: Two-stage hybrid flow shop scheduling with preventive maintenance using multi-objective tabu search method. Int. J. Prod. Res. **52**(5), 1495–1508 (2014)

39. Karaboga, D.: An idea based on honey bee swarm for numerical optimization. Technical report-TR06, Computer Engineering Department, Engineering Faculty, Erciyes University (2005)

40. Karaboga, D., Basturk, B.: On the performance of artificial bee colony (ABC) algorithm. Appl. Soft Comput. **8**(1), 687–697 (2008)

41. Karaboga, D., Akay, B.: A comparative study of artificial bee colony algorithm. Appl. Math. Comput. **214**(1), 108–132 (2009)

42. Pan, Q.K., Tasgetiren, M.F., Suganthan, P.N., et al.: A discrete artificial bee colony algorithm for the lot-streaming flow shop scheduling problem. Inf. Sci. **181**(12), 2455–2468 (2011)

43. Li, J.Q., Pan, Q.K., Gao, K.Z.: Pareto-based discrete artificial bee colony algorithm for multi-objective flexible job shop scheduling problems. Int. J. Adv. Manuf. Technol. **55**(9), 1159–1169 (2011)

44. Pan, Q.K., Wang, L., Mao, K., Zhao, J.H., Zhang, M.: An effective artificial bee colony algorithm for a real-world hybrid flowshop problem in steelmaking process. IEEE Trans. Autom. Sci. Eng. **10**(2), 307–322 (2013)

45. Wang, S., Wang, L., Liu, M., et al.: An effective estimation of distribution algorithm for solving the distributed permutation flow-shop scheduling problem. Int. J. Prod. Econ. **145**(1), 387–396 (2013)

46. Engin, O., Döyen, A.: A new approach to solve hybrid flow shop scheduling problems by artificial immune system. Future Gener. Comput. Syst. **20**(6), 1083–1095 (2004)

47. Alaykýran, K., Engin, O., Döyen, A.: Using ant colony optimization to solve hybrid flow shop scheduling problems. Int. J. Adv. Manuf. Technol. **35**(5), 541–550 (2007)

48. Liu, F., Zhang, X., Zou, F., et al.: Immune clonal selection algorithm for hybrid flow-shop scheduling problem. In: Control and Decision Conference, CCDC 2009, pp. 2605–2609. IEEE (2009). (In Chinese)
49. Xu, Y., Wang, L., Zhou, G., Wang, S.: An effective shuffled frog leaping algorithm for solving hybrid flow-shop scheduling problem. In: Huang, D.-S., Gan, Y., Bevilacqua, V., Figueroa, J.C. (eds.) ICIC 2011. LNCS, vol. 6838, pp. 560–567. Springer, Heidelberg (2011). doi:10.1007/978-3-642-24728-6_76
50. Deng, G.L., Xu, Z.H., Gu, X.S.: A discrete artificial bee colony algorithm for minimizing the total flow time in the blocking flow shop scheduling. Chin. J. Chem. Eng. 20(6), 1067–1073 (2012)
51. Han, Y.Y., Liang, J.J., Pan, Q.K., Li, J.Q., Sang, H.Y., Cao, N.N.: Effective hybrid discrete artificial bee colony algorithms for the total flowtime minimization in the blocking flowshop problem. Int. J. Adv. Manuf. Technol. 67(1–4), 397–414 (2013)

A Group-Based Replica Consistency Schema for Cloud Storage

Guoping Du[1], Wenbin Yao[1(✉)], Dongbin Wang[2], and Xiaole Wen[3]

[1] Beijing Key Laboratory of Intelligent Telecommunications Software
and Multimedia, National Engineering Laboratory for Mobile Network Security,
Beijing University of Posts and Telecommunications, Beijing 100876, China
duguoping01@163.com, yaowenbin_cdc@163.com
[2] Key Laboratory of Ministry of Education for Trustworthy Distributed
Computing and Service, Beijing University of Posts and Telecommunications,
Beijing 100876, China
dbwang@bupt.edu.cn
[3] State Key Laboratory of Networking and Switching,
Beijing University of Posts and Telecommunications, Beijing 100876, China
xiaolewen_bupt@163.com

Abstract. Replica is the most meaning of data availability, scalability and reliability in the cloud storage. There are rooms for reducing the cost of consistency by designing an effective replica management schema. To address the conflict between potential inconsistency and efficiency problem, a new group based replica consistency schema, namely GBRC, was proposed in this paper. The schema will divide replicas located on different network topology into independent replica groups and provide two kinds of consistency management mechanism for replica group and replica members of group. In the GBRC, replica group is an autonomous unit on group management level. It is an effective way to organize adjacent replica node into the same group to reduce cost of communication and complex of management. In this paper, a novel replica group construction process adapted to select adjacent nodes which meet user storage requirement to be self-consistent group. Then, all groups of the same replica consist of entire replica management system on the top level, which is effective way simplify replicas organization, management and consistency. Experiments show that replica group autonomy consistency respectively can improve consistency speed and simplify metadata management especially when replicas are geographic distributed. In addition, design a new dynamic replica consistency strategy based multi replicas consistency quality of service. The strategy dynamically adapts replica consistency number at runtime to achieve a dynamic service balance between consistency and quality of service. Evaluation results show that consistency strategy improves cloud storage responding speed while guaranteeing the user data storage's consistency requirement.

Keywords: Cloud storage · Replica management · Replica schema · Replica consistency

X. Sun et al. (Eds.): ICCCS 2017, Part I, LNCS 10602, pp. 214–225, 2017.
https://doi.org/10.1007/978-3-319-68505-2_19

1 Introduction

With the rapid development of the Internet application, these application service providers have higher demands on data storage volumes, read-write ability, effectiveness, reliability and scalability [1]. It is a general idea to solve these problems with distributed cloud storage technology [2]. Distributed multi-replica is one of the key technologies to solve these problems. Different from the previous replica schema, our schema takes replica network topology location into consideration to minimize negative impact of cross-regional replica consistency processes on storage efficiency. In addition, this paper performs qualitative analysis of the proximity characteristics and then conducts to quantify the proximity of multi replicas. Pluralities of replicas that satisfy a certain degree of proximity are assigned to the same replica group to provide uniform replicas process control. It is an effective way to avoid the impact of network communication fault on the replica communication, timely detection replica inconsistency, and to improve replica mutual transmission within the same group.

2 Related Work

Replica schema in a weak networked connection environment, especially in the unreliable environment where communication delays are uncertain, is a critical task. Multi replica grouping management, which is no longer to focus on replica, has been proved to be an effective replica organization [3]. To reduce the bandwidth consumption of replica data transition and replica access latency is purpose of these replica model [4–8]. By dividing a large number of distributed replicas into a few of replica groups, it is useful abstraction to translate complex processes between all replicas to inter-group and intra-group replicas consistency [9, 10].

Most no replica group strategy aims to optimize replica data consistency replication order. A static replica management strategy, which places file chuck replica by storage server rack position and then each replica forwards the data to the "closest" replica which haven't been updated to avoid network bottlenecks and high-latency in the network topology, was presented in HDFS [3]. However, the rack relative position information does not represent a real dynamic storage topology network and not solve the replica synchronization problem of the cross-data center or complex network environment. An adaptive replica consistency service for data grid was proposed by Chang et al. [11]. According to the replica access frequency during the consistency process, the service treats the same replicas as three kinds of different type. If access frequency exceeds a predefined threshold, first level replicas and original replica can be updated immediately with user operator as well as the second level replicas for simplicity and consistency. Otherwise, the second level replicas updating is delayed until before the replica is gonging to access. Some similar workaround were also raised in paper [12, 13]. Assuming that data update messages are propagated in order, [14] put forward a causally consistent geo-replicated data store that provides throughput comparable to eventual consistency and superior to current implementations of causal consistency by a periodic aggregation protocol to determine whether updates can be made visible in accordance with causal consistency. Moreover, all works in [12, 14, 15] assume strong consistency between any two replicas within each datacenter because that they cannot apply an easy way to guarantee causal consistency within each datacenter.

There are some replica group management proposals, which are mainly related replica group analysis, design, and performance evaluation, to improve system and cluster availability, fault-tolerant or performance [3, 16]. In the paper [17], an implementation framework, which is group-oriented and supportive of overlapping groups, to support various policies attributes and options were presented. These papers [18, 19] share a common design feature that they use multiple groups executing Byzantine replication protocols to partition the load among the system members. Douceur and Howell [20] also analyze the problem of dealing with replica groups in a large-scale system from a perspective of isolating the effects of faulty replica groups. Rodrigo Rodrigues [21] insisted that the overall correctness of large-scale systems composed of many groups of replicas executing BFT protocols scales poorly with the number of groups. This is because the probability of at least one group being compromised (more than 1/3 faulty replicas) increases rapidly as the number of groups increases. A solution that a simple modification to Castro and Liskov's BFT replication allows for arbitrary choice of replicas number and failure threshold addressed in the paper.

Compared with the existing work, our research focuses on designing a new schema to take full consideration of the replica group structure and QoS-aware replica server to improve service satisfaction in cloud storage based on geo-distributed replicas grouping consistency. Moreover, the scheme provides a more simple consistency mechanism to manage replicas inter-group and intra-group.

3   Overall of GBRC

In this section, we first present entities and measurements which are used in our schema and then illustrate the schema as well as its strategy.

3.1   Model Entities

First, some relative concepts are defined so as to further explain the detailed contents of the GBRC. The replica is the basic entity in our management schema and assigns to all nodes in storage clusters. These replicas can be distributed in different data centers as well as geo-graphical sites. A single replica group is a collection of distinguish replica entities in which each replica member entity communicates with other members by multicasting message to other members belong to the same group. Procedure of replica group initialization is the choice of replica node which meets the performance requirements of replica storage and group construction indicators. In this paper, a consistency replica group means that the percentage of the number of consistent replicas in the group is not less than weight coefficient after one replica update operator. At this point the consistency replicas within the group are called consistency replica subset S_{cr} of consistency group. It means that our strategy is not strong consistent. In addition, a consistency group subset S_{cg} is defined to describe multi replica group consistency. The status of replica, replica group and user data must belong to consistency or inconsistency shown as

$$Status(e) \in \{consistency, inconsistency\}, e \in \{r, g, d\} \tag{1}$$

where r is a replica entity, g is a single replica group entity, d is the all replica group entities of user data.

3.2 Measurements

It is effective that appropriate strategy can be adapted to control and prevent some poor performance replica nodes decreases performance of entire replica cluster at the beginning of initializing replicas. For each data node has dynamic resource utilization U and static attribute A to show the status of computing, network, storage, I/O resource. Replica r_i utilization U_i is given by $U_i = [U_{cpu}, U_{mem}, U_{net}, U_{io}]$, where U_{cpu}, U_{mem}, U_{net}, $U_{io} \in (0, 1)$ denotes utilization CPU, memory, network and I/O of node respectively. The static attribute is presented as $A_i = [A_{cpu}, A_{mem}, A_{net}, A_{io}]$. The standard of replica which can be selected to be a member of the replica group expresses $S_i = [A_{cpu}, A_{mem}, A_{net}, A_{io}]$. In this paper, if the available resource of the replica node $B_i = [A_{cpu} * (1 - U_{cpu}), A_{mem} * (1 - U_{mem}), A_{net} * (1 - U_{net}), A_{io} * (1 - U_{io})], P = B_i - A_i$ satisfies the function 1, this means the replica can join in the replica group.

$$p_{1,j} \geq 0, \forall j \in [0, 3] \tag{2}$$

The group structure indictor is presented as $Need = [N, S_i]$. The number of user data replica N and the standard requirement of group S_i present replica structure parameters.

Furthermore, we define a new 'group tightness' concept to measure the effect of distributed replica members of a group. There is a pragmatic way of reducing the impact of the adverse factor that failure in communication network and link across multiple switches or routers result in that replicas can't work cooperatively well in the complex network environment. The distance between any two replicas r which belong to the same group is expressed by communication delay t. If the communication t_{ij} between any replicas r_i and r_j, then the group tightness can be denoted as follow function 3. The function Max is used to compute the maximum delay time to communication any two in replica group. Where δ indicates the degree of the group tightness, the variable δ is smaller, the group is more compact and higher efficiency of replica interaction. In our model, the group tightness is the guiding principles to choose replica node in the storage cluster.

$$\delta = \text{Max}\left(t_{ij}\right) \tag{3}$$

In the schema, initializing the replica group is to probe neighbor area of selected replica nodes. Assuming the distance of the $i(th)$ time to probe is δ_i and having chosen N_i replica nodes, the next probe range δ_{i+1} is calculated by Eq. 4 where N is the size of

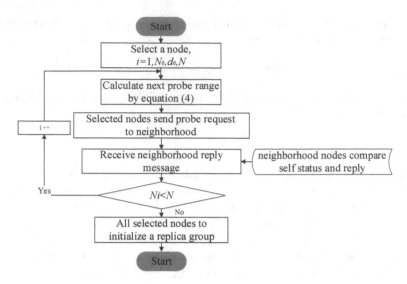

Fig. 1. The single replica group contracture process

the target group. With the concept of group tightness, the construction of replica group shows in the Fig. 1. The replica node choice scope is expanded by iteration.

$$\delta_{i+1} = \sqrt{N/N_i} * \delta_i \tag{4}$$

3.3 Schema

This section mainly states the overall structure of the model. In order to manage geo-distributed replicas distributed in different data centers effectively, our model groups all replicas into different management groups unit by topology position on network and proximity of multi replicas. One characteristic of replica management in our model is that replica grouping and group autonomy. In our paper, a hierarchical replica structure is designed as shown in Fig. 2 in which groups and replicas within group are two layer. Normally, user data will be distributed in several groups to improve data availability, but all replica member of one group will be in the same datacenter because the consistency communication delay can't be tolerated. Viewing from group layer, it is unity consistency even if there are some inconsistent replicas with other in same group avoiding the ambiguous attributes of group. Assuming the number of group member $2n + 1$, it can be said that the group status is consistency when the number of consistent replica is at least $n + 1$. Similarly, the replica status is either consistent or inconsistent.

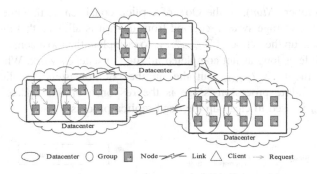

Fig. 2. The structure of GBRC

4 Replica Consistency Process

4.1 Quality of Service Determination Component

This component is in charge of collecting all replicas status and calculating the consistency of the group replicas in the same group. The main measurement in our model are counting the number of completing consistency after an update and timing the group consistency phase. Assuming the pre-set overtime is t, this component will collect the replica status and count the replicas which status are inconsistent. The group consistency is defined as

$$n > \lfloor N/2 \rfloor \tag{5}$$

where N is the size of group, and n is the number of consistency replicas which have completed the update operator within a certain time t. When the group satisfies the function 4, the group status will be updated to be consistent, otherwise should be update to be inconsistent.

The replica quality of service determination is part of the core control in our replica consistency model. Both business and users percept of cloud storage service QoS mainly includes four aspects: data storage reliability, accessibility of data services, the cost of data storage and response time. Data service reliability is the foundation of cloud storage. The reliability of the data storage service mainly has the following several aspects: the reliability of the storage service and stored data. The reliability of the storage service can be said that the normal usage probability of storage their data by service interfaces. Generally it can be presented that the ratio of success number and the total number. The accessibility of the data storage service is data storage service ability of continuous service. Data storage service fee is the cost of using storage service from services provider. However, Feeling of user quality of service is mainly influenced by the maximum response time. It is one of the core problems to solve in replica consistency. In our dynamic consistency strategy, we presuppose five variable parameter to allow users dynamically to set consistent degree to reduce the response time in data storage include user response time ($T_{userResponse}$), user response overtime ($T_{userOut}$), System response overtime (T_{sysOut}), the minim percentage of consistency replica (P_{min})

and replica number (*Num*). In the QoS of replica consistency, timeline is shown as Fig. 3. When the storage system received from user, it is allowed that the consistency component takes up the period of $T_{userResponse}$ to complete the most consistency replicas as far as possible as long as not completed all the consistency work. When processing time reached the time $T_{userOut}$ but the number of consistency replicas less than $\lceil P_{min} * Num \rceil$, failure process message is the response of this update request. The variable T_{sysOut} is used to clean up the dead replica processes.

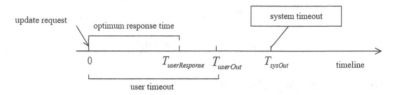

Fig. 3. Replica consistency time line

4.2 Consistency Process

The process of the replica consistency in our model is shown Fig. 4. First, the client launches the data update operator including metadata of the data object to be updated. After completing update log consistency, the current replica master group, that the leader group will receive the replica operator firstly. The replica master group distributed the update operator to the follower groups. Each follower group has its own master replica node which as administrator of this group administrates members of the

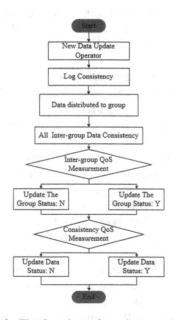

Fig. 4. The flowchart of consistency process

group include synchronizing log and data. It is clear, in our model, that each data consistency procedure only has two stage inter-group and intra-group consistency process. At the stage of inter-group replica consistency, the master replica node plays a role of managing the other replica node in the same group.

5 Simulation Results

5.1 Simulation Setup

Using a real test environment for evaluation and analysis of the proposed model of cloud storage is a significant challenge. So we evaluate the performances of our consistency model by using the open source CloudSim [22] under the Ubuntu 16.04. We define different number of storage nodes and replicate 49 replica to 7 group over 7 geo-distributed datacenter. In order to estimate the performance of our model, we define two key performance indicators (synchronization speed and responding speed) to illustrate. The indicator of synchronization speed is calculated as below:

$$Sync = \frac{N * Size}{Time} \qquad (6)$$

where N is the number of replicas which have been updated before response information. $Time$ is the process time of consistency process, and $Size$ is the size of updated data in a single operation.

$$Resp = \frac{Size}{Time} \qquad (7)$$

The responding speed is different from the synchronization speed that responding speed is shown the entire consistency speed.

5.2 Single Group Consistency Evaluation

This set of experiments is designed to measure the replica consistency within group with respect to several metrics such as replica distribute and node load. In order to estimate the single group performance of the model, we compare the manner of building group and selecting the nodes with rack induction like Hadoop. In the setting of parameters of the performance, the network speed is 2 Mb/s and the data size to be updated is 128 KB, 256 KB, 512 KB, 1 MB, 2 MB and 4 MB separately. Avoiding inaccuracy in a single test, we calculated the average in the 50 times test. The result is shown as Fig. 5. It can be said that the strategy which we proposed has better performance comparing the arbitrary strategy. The performance advantage is resulted from the shorter distance between any two replica nodes in the group.

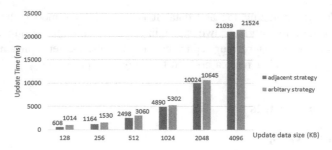

Fig. 5. Consistency time in single replica group

5.3   GBRC Evaluation

The experiment is processed under different system load to compare the performance of eventual and strong consistent strategy. In the experiment, the size of updated data is 1 MB and $T_{sysOut} = 150$ s. The synchronization speed, which is defined in Eq. 6, under different user response time and user out time is shown in the Table 1, when $P_{min} = 51\%$ and $Num = 49$. It can be seen, from an overall view, which synchronization speed is in deceasing as the increasing user response time because that more replica can be consistent before reply. The number of consistency replica illustrates the phenomenon in the Fig. 6. It means that our consistency strategy is able to adjust the consistency degree and response time.

Table 1. The synchronization speed under $T_{userResponse}$ and $T_{userOut}$

$T_{userOut}$	$T_{userResponse}$						
	20	25	30	35	40	45	50
25	1.25	1.16	1.02	0.96	0.843	0.8	0.71
30	1.21	1.216	1.01	0.95	0.86	0.81	0.74
35	1.23	1.15	1.06	0.94	0.84	0.801	0.75
40	1.24	1.12	1.05	0.91	0.82	0.813	0.72
45	1.25	1.21	1.10	0.943	0.91	0.82	0.73

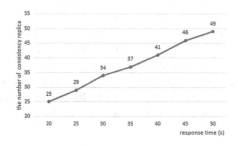

Fig. 6. The number of consistency replica and response time

In the Fig. 7, the ratio of consistency is average value using 100 times of user-stored tests under different system load. We compare the ratio consistency among the strong consistency, eventual consistency and GBRC strategy. For strongly consistent and ultimately consistent policies, the number of replicas that have completed is consistent when the user receives a reply. And our strategy according to the system load can dynamically adjust the number of copies to meet the different reliability and then to improve the response speed.

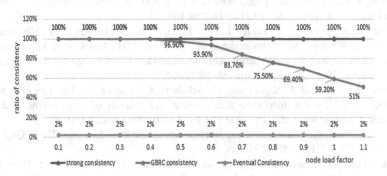

Fig. 7. Ratio of consistency and node load factor

6 Conclusion

In this paper, we present a group-based replica consistency schema (GBRC). It applies an innovative replica management schema to optimize to choose appropriate replica node according to nodes network topology locations to construct replica group. Additionally, the paper proposes the minimum response time boundary to dynamically adjust of the degree of consistency of multiple replicas. By adjusting reliability to accelerate storage response time, our current works consider only replica reliability and response time factors for cloud storage. Therefore, we did not discuss the specific scenes when server can't complete the other replica node consistence in background. In the future, we will incorporate the replication failure into our research.

Acknowledgements. This work was partly supported by the NSFC-Guangdong Joint Found (U1501254) and the Co-construction Program with the Beijing Municipal Commission of Education and the Ministry of Science and Technology of China (2012BAH45B01) and National key research and development program (2016YFB0800302) the Director's Project Fund of Key Laboratory of Trustworthy Distributed Computing and Service (BUPT), Ministry of Education (Grant No. 2017ZR01) and the Fundamental Research Funds for the Central Universities (BUPT2011RCZJ16, 2014ZD03-03) and China Information Security Special Fund (NDRC).

References

1. Armbrust, M., Fox, A., Griffith, R., Joseph, A.D., Katz, R., Konwinski, A., Lee, G., Patterson, D., Rabkin, A., Stoica, I., Zaharia, M.: A view of cloud computing. Commun. ACM **53**, 50–58 (2010). doi:10.1145/1721654.1721672
2. Greenberg, A., Hamilton, J., Maltz, D.A., Patel, P.: The cost of a cloud: research problems in data center networks. SIGCOMM Comput. Commun. Rev. **39**, 68–73 (2008). doi:10.1145/1496091.1496103
3. Birman, K.P.: The process group approach to reliable distributed computing. Commun. ACM **36**, 37–53 (1993). doi:10.1145/163298.163303
4. Chervenak, A., Deelman, E., Foster, I., Guy, L., Hoschek, W., Iamnitchi, A., Kesselman, C., Kunszt, P., Ripeanu, M., Schwartzkopf, B., Stockinger, H., Stockinger, K., Tierney, B.: Giggle: a framework for constructing scalable replica location services. In: ACM/IEEE 2002 Conference on Supercomputing, pp. 58–58 (2002)
5. Chervenak, A., Foster, I., Kesselman, C., Salisbury, C., Tuecke, S.: The data grid: towards an architecture for the distributed management and analysis of large scientific datasets. J. Netw. Comput. Appl. **23**, 187–200 (2000). doi:10.1006/jnca.2000.0110
6. Guy, L., Kunszt, P., Laure, E., et al.: Replica management in data grid. Glob. Grid Forum Inf. Doc. GGF5 **3**(1), 2–18 (2002)
7. Lamehamedi, H., Shentu, Z., Szymanski, B., Deelman, E.: Simulation of dynamic data replication strategies in data grids. In: Proceedings of the 17th International Symposium on Parallel and Distributed Processing, p. 100. IEEE Computer Society, Washington, DC (2003)
8. Ranganathan, K., Foster, I.: Identifying dynamic replication strategies for a high-performance data grid. In: Lee, C.A. (ed.) GRID 2001. LNCS, vol. 2242, pp. 75–86. Springer, Heidelberg (2001). doi:10.1007/3-540-45644-9_8
9. Ghemawat, S., Gobioff, H., Leung, S.-T.: The Google file system. In: Proceedings of the Nineteenth ACM Symposium on Operating Systems Principles, pp. 29–43. ACM, New York (2003)
10. Pitoura, E., Bhargava, B.: Data consistency in intermittently connected distributed systems. IEEE Trans. Knowl. Data Eng. **11**, 896–915 (1999). doi:10.1109/69.824602
11. Chang, R.-S., Chang, J.-S.: Adaptable replica consistency service for data grids. In: Third International Conference on Information Technology: New Generations (ITNG 2006), pp. 646–651 (2006)
12. Tang, Y., Sun, H., Wang, X., Liu, X.: Achieving convergent causal consistency and high availability for cloud storage. Future Gener. Comput. Syst. **74**, 20–31 (2017). doi:10.1016/j.future.2017.04.016
13. Bailis, P., Fekete, A., Hellerstein, J.M., Ghodsi, A., Stoica, I.: Scalable atomic visibility with RAMP transactions. In: Proceedings of the 2014 ACM SIGMOD International Conference on Management of Data, pp. 27–38. ACM, New York (2014)
14. Du, J., Iorgulescu, C., Roy, A., Zwaenepoel, W.: GentleRain: cheap and scalable causal consistency with physical clocks. In: Proceedings of the ACM Symposium on Cloud Computing, pp. 4:1–4:13. ACM, New York (2014)
15. Akkoorath, D.D., Tomsic, A.Z., Bravo, M., Li, Z., Crain, T., Bieniusa, A., Preguiça, N., Shapiro, M.: Cure: strong semantics meets high availability and low latency. In: 2016 IEEE 36th International Conference on Distributed Computing Systems (ICDCS), pp. 405–414 (2016)

16. Mishra, S., Fei, L., Xing, G.: Design, implementation and performance evaluation of a CORBA group communication service. In: Proceedings of the Twenty-Ninth Annual International Symposium on Fault-Tolerant Computing, p. 166. IEEE Computer Society, Washington, DC (1999)
17. Morgan, G., Ezilchelvan, P.D.: Policies for using replica groups and their effectiveness over the internet. In: Proceedings of NGC 2000 on Networked Group Communication, pp. 119–129. ACM, New York (2000)
18. Adya, A., Bolosky, W.J., Castro, M., Cermak, G., Chaiken, R., Douceur, J.R., Howell, J., Lorch, J.R., Theimer, M., Wattenhofer, R.P.: Farsite: federated, available, and reliable storage for an incompletely trusted environment. SIGOPS Oper. Syst. Rev. **36**, 1–14 (2002). doi:10.1145/844128.844130
19. Rodrigues, R., Liskov, B.: Rosebud: a scalable byzantine-fault-tolerant storage architecture (2003)
20. Douceur, J.R., Howell, J.: Byzantine fault isolation in the Farsite distributed file system. IPTPS (2006)
21. Rodrigues, R., Kouznetsov, P., Bhattacharjee, B.: Large-scale byzantine fault tolerance: safe but not always live. In: Proceedings of the 3rd Workshop on Hot Topics in System Dependability. USENIX Association, Berkeley (2007)
22. Calheiros, R.N., et al.: CloudSim: a novel framework for modeling and simulation of cloud computing infrastructures and services. Computer Science (2009)

A Multi-objective Optimization Scheduling Method Based on the Improved Differential Evolution Algorithm in Cloud Computing

Zhe Zheng[1], Kun Xie[1(✉)], Shiming He[2], and Jun Deng[3]

[1] College of Computer Science and Electronic Engineering, Hunan University, Changsha 410082, China
{zhezheng,xiekun}@hnu.edu.cn
[2] Computer and Communication Engineering, Changsha University of Science and Technology, Changsha 410114, China
heshiming_hsm@163.com
[3] Hunan Vocational College of Science and Tecnology, Changsha 410004, China
13786145089@163.com

Abstract. Cloud computing provides a large number of opportunities to solve large scale scientific problems. Task scheduling is important in cloud computing and attract a lot of attentions in recent years. To more efficiently scheduling the resources in cloud systems, this paper studies a novel multi-objective task scheduling problem which aims to Minimize the task's Completion Time as well as to Minimize the Resource Payment (termed as MCT-MRP problem). However, the multi-objective optimization problem for task scheduling is generally an NP-hard problem. To efficiently solve the problem, this paper proposes an improved differential evolution algorithm. With adaptive parameter setting (control parameter F and the crossover factor CR) and an novel crossover operation and selection strategy, our improved differential evolution algorithm can solve the problems faced in traditional differential evolution algorithm such as premature convergence, slow convergence rate and difficult parameter setting. We have done extensive simulations. The simulation results demonstrate the efficiency and affectivity of our proposed algorithm.

Keywords: Cloud computing · Differential evolution · Multi-objective scheduling · Cost

1 Introduction

Cloud computing has attracted great interests from both the industry and the academic [1–4]. Task scheduling is important in cloud computing [5–7]. An effective task scheduling method requires not merely meeting the needs of users but also improving the efficiency of the whole cloud system.

Originally, task scheduling in cloud computing only focuses on a single objective scheduling, such as minimize the task's completion time, minimize the cloud

© Springer International Publishing AG 2017
X. Sun et al. (Eds.): ICCCS 2017, Part I, LNCS 10602, pp. 226–238, 2017.
https://doi.org/10.1007/978-3-319-68505-2_20

center's energy consumption. However, single objective based task scheduling can not satisfy multiple requirements from both users and cloud system provider.

To more efficiently schedule the resources in cloud systems, this paper studies a novel multi-objective task scheduling problem, which aims to Minimize the task's Completion Time as well as to Minimize the Resource Payment (termed as MCT-MRP). However, the multi-objective optimization problem for task scheduling is generally an NP-hard problem [8]. Although various heuristic algorithms have been proposed to solve the task scheduling problem, current algorithms suffer from the problems such as premature convergence, slow convergence rate and difficult parameter setting [9].

Differential evolution (DE) is an efficient and powerful population-based stochastic search technique for solving optimization problems over continuous space, which has been widely applied in many scientific and engineering fields, including a variety of scheduling problems [10–13]. Differential evolution is easy to obtain a global optimal solution, and it is robust and does not rely on the strict mathematical optimization and structural features of the problem itself.

It is promising to apply differential evolution to solve our MCT-MRP. However, when using the differential evolution algorithm, it is easy to fall into a local optimum and suffers from the problems such as premature convergence and slow convergence, which makes designing efficient differential evolution based algorithm very challenge.

To conquer the problem, we propose an improved differential evolution algorithm to solve our MCT-MRP. Instead of using fix control parameter F and the crossover factor CR in the traditional differential evolution algorithm, the control parameter F and the crossover factor CR are adaptively changed to avoid premature convergence as well as to speedup the convergence process. Moreover, we also improve the crossover operation and selection strategy of differential evolution algorithm to make the new generation carry more information and thus enhances search capability of DE algorithm. We have done extensive simulations. The simulation result demonstrate the efficiency and affectivity of the proposed algorithm.

2 Problem Description

We consider a set of tasks $N = \{1, 2, \cdots, \mathcal{N}\}$ and a set of VMs $K = \{1, 2, \cdots, \mathcal{K}\}$ in the current system. Our multi-objective optimization scheduling problem is to find a solution that assigns all tasks to the VMs such that the completion time and the energy consumption of all applications is minimized. The parameter meanings are listed in following.

- N_i: The tasks i, $1 < i < \mathcal{N}$.
- K_j: The VM j, $1 < j < \mathcal{K}$.
- $\mathcal{N}, \mathcal{K}$: The amount of tasks and resources.
- t_{ij}: The time of task N_i in VM K_j.
- $\mathcal{C}_j, \mathcal{M}_j$: CPU and memory of K_j.

- C_i, M_i: CPU and memory of N_i.
- α, β: The weight factors of time and resources.
- B_i: The deadline time of task N_i.
- $\mathcal{C}_{cost}(j)$, $\mathcal{M}_{cost}(j)$: The cost of the CPU and the memory.
- $\mathcal{C}_{base}$, $\mathcal{M}_{base}$: The base cost of the CPU and the memory.
- X_{ij}: The task N_i run in VM K_j. Matrix X is the assignment matrix with its entry identifying the assignment between corresponding tasks and VMs.

Definition 1. *(Tasks): $N_i = [C_i, M_i, B_i]$ where C_i and M_i are the total amount of CPU and memory requested by the task. B_i is the deadline of the task, that is, task N_i should be executed and completed before time B_i.*

Definition 2. *(VMs): $K_j = [\mathcal{C}_j, \mathcal{M}_j]$ where $\mathcal{C}_j$ and $\mathcal{M}_j$ are the total amount of CPU and memory resources provided by VM K_j.*

In the system, a task will be matched with a single VM for resources, while one VM can be matched with multiple tasks. To use the resources in a VM, the user of a task should pay some cost. If task N_i is assigned to VM K_j, the total payments should cover both payment on CPU and memory, which are defined as follows.

CPU Cost: assign task N_i to VM K_j.

$$C_{cost}(j) = C_{base} \cdot t_{ij} \cdot C_j \tag{1}$$

where t_{ij} is the executing time that runs task N_i on VM K_j, the C_j is the amount of CPU resources, and the C_{base} the base cost of CPU. In this paper, we set $C_{base} = 0.17/h$ according to the price of Amazon.

Memory Cost: assign task N_i to VM K_j.

$$M_{cost}(j) = M_{base} \cdot t_{ij} \cdot \mathcal{M}_j \tag{2}$$

where t_{ij} is the executing time that runs task N_i on VM K_j, the $\mathcal{M}_j$ is the amount of CPU resources, and the M_{base} the base cost of memory. In this paper, we set $M_{base} = 0.05/GB/h$ according to the price of Amazon.

This paper wants to assign tasks to VMs so that minimize the total completion time of all the tasks as well as minimize the total payment for the users to use cloud resources. The problem can be formulated as Eq. (3), where $D = \sum_{i=1}^{N} C_{cost}(j) \cdot X_{ij} + \sum_{i=1}^{N} M_{cost}(j) \cdot X_{ij}$ is the total payments for all the tasks use the VMs' resources, $B = \sum_{i=1}^{N} \sum_{j=1}^{K} (t_{ij} \cdot X_{ij})$ is the total executing time of all the tasks. $\sum_{i=1}^{N} C_i \cdot X_{ij} \le C_j$ and $\sum_{i=1}^{N} C_i \cdot X_{ij} \le C_j$ are the resource constraints. For example, $\sum_{i=1}^{N} C_i \cdot X_{ij} \le C_j$ means that the total CPU resource required by the tasks should be less than the total amount of CPU resource of the VM. $\sum_{j=1}^{K} t_{ij} X_{ij} \le B_i$ is the executing time constraint, that is, the completion time of task i should less than the task's executing deadline.

$\sum_{j=1}^{K} X_{ij} = 1$ means that a task is assigned with a single VM for resources.

$$Minimize \quad \alpha \cdot B + \beta \cdot D$$

$$s.t. \quad D = \sum_{i=1}^{N} C_{cost}(j) \cdot X_{ij} + \sum_{i=1}^{N} M_{cost}(j) \cdot X_{ij}$$

$$B = \sum_{i=1}^{N} \sum_{j=1}^{K} (t_{ij} \cdot X_{ij})$$

$$\sum_{i=1}^{N} M_i \cdot X_{ij} \le M_j$$

$$\sum_{i=1}^{N} C_i \cdot X_{ij} \le C_j \quad (3)$$

$$\alpha + \beta = 1$$

$$\sum_{j=1}^{K} t_{ij} X_{ij} \le B_i$$

$$X_{ij} = 0, 1$$

$$\sum_{j=1}^{K} X_{ij} = 1$$

Equation (3) is a multi-objective optimization problem which is generally an NP-hard problem. In following section, we propose an improved differential evolution algorithm to solve the problem.

3   Detailed Solution

Differential Evolution (DE) [14–16] algorithm has successfully been applied to diverse domains of science and engineering. However, almost all the DE-related evolutionary algorithms still suffer from the problems such as premature convergence, slow convergence rate and difficult parameter setting [17]. To solve these problems, we propose an Improved Differential Evolution(IDE) algorithm, which improve the control parameters F and the crossover factor CR, at the same time improve crossover operation and selection strategy.

3.1   The Initialization

Here the focus is the encoding for queue scheduling, differential evolution using real number coding method, length coding for the number of tasks, every value is the number of occupied resources. If you have 8 tasks $(N_1, N_2, N_3, N_4, N_5, N_6, N_7, N_8)$, and there are 4 VM (K_1, K_2, K_3, K_4), the code length is 4, each bit has a value in the set $\{1,2,3,4\}$. Assume that the individual is encoded as [3,1,2,3,4,3,2,1], the first bit code is 3, it means N_1 runs on K_3, N_2 runs on K_1, and so on. Assume that population size is NP, the number of tasks is $\mathcal{N}$, the resources is $\mathcal{K}$, the random initialization described as: by the system randomly generated NP individual with the length of $\mathcal{N}$. Every one of each individual has randomly value from the set $\{1, 2, ..., \mathcal{K}\}$.

3.2   The Improved Differential Evolution Algorithm

The basic operation of DE algorithm includes mutation, crossover and evolution. We propose an improved differential evolution algorithm. Instead of using fix control parameter F and the crossover factor CR in the traditional differential evolution algorithm, the control parameter F and the crossover factor CR are adaptively changed to avoid premature convergence as well as to speedup the convergence process. Moreover, we also improve the crossover operation and selection strategy of differential evolution algorithm to make the new generation carry more information and thus enhances search capability of DE algorithm.

Firstly, random initialization population, random initialization population. Then make a mutation to the individual $x_i(t)$ of t generation in population to get $h_i(t+1)$:

$$h_i(t+1) = x_{p1}(t) + F(x_{p2}(t) - x_{p3}(t)) \quad (i \neq p1 \neq p2 \neq p3) \tag{4}$$

$x_{p1}(t)$ is the base vector of parent generation. $x_{p2}(t)$, $x_{p3}(t)$ is the difference vector of parent generation, F is the zoom factor and t is the number of iterations. The zoom factor F plays a regulatory role in local search of algorithm and global search, and its general scope in formula (5) is [0,2]. Specially, the influence of the factor F is used to control the differential vector. Bigger F is beneficial to keep the population diversity and global search, and smaller F is conducive to improve the convergence precision and local search. In this paper, we used the method of an adaptive scaling factor F.

Adaptive mutation factor F is designed as follows:

$$\lambda = e^{1 - \frac{T}{T+1-t}}$$
$$F = F_0 \cdot 2^\lambda \tag{5}$$

Here, F_0 is the mutation operator, and T represents the largest evolution algebra, t represents the current evolution algebra.

At the beginning of the algorithm, the zoom factor F general value is $2F_0$. In the initial stages of the search, we should keep individual diversity to avoid prematurity. In the late search, the zoom factor F is close to F_0, it can keep good information to avoid damage to the optimal solution, and increasing the probability to search the global optimal solution.

Next, make a crossover operation, The basic crossover operator of the differential evolution algorithm is able to generate two individuals, but actually we only use one of them. This is bound to be lost part of the genetic information, slow convergence. Therefore, in this paper we will add another discarded child to produce new individual competition.

Two individuals v_{ij} and u_{ij} formula is as follows:

$$v_{ij}(t+1) = \begin{cases} h_{ij}(t+1) & \text{If}\,(randl_{ij} \leq CR)\,\text{or}\,(j = rand(i)) \\ x_{ij}(t) & \text{otherwise} \end{cases} \tag{6}$$

$$u_{ij}(t+1) = \begin{cases} x_{ij}(t) & \text{If}\,(randl_{ij} \leq CR)\,\text{or}\,(j = rand(i)) \\ h_{ij}(t+1) & \text{otherwise} \end{cases} \tag{7}$$

Similarly, the crossover factor CR in the formulas (7) and (8) also affects the search ability and convergence of the algorithm. CR general scope is [0,1], the larger the CR is, the more benefit in accelerate convergence speed and local search, the smaller the CR is conducive to global search and keep population diversity. In this paper, we use a crossover factor increment method to improve the effectiveness of the algorithm, the factor CR is designed as follows:

$$CR = CR_{min} + (CR_{max} - CR_{min})(\frac{t}{T})^2 \tag{8}$$

Here, T is the maximum number of iterations, t is the current iteration number, CR_{min} is the smallest crossover factor, and CR_{max} is the maximum crossover factor. At the beginning of the algorithm implementation, smaller CR is conducive to global search and keep population diversity. And in the late search, bigger CR is conducive to speed up the convergence.

In order to speed up the algorithm evaluation, we use the following methods to select the new individual. With one of the first individual offspring v_{ij} and target x_{ij} competition. If v_{ij} is better than x_{ij}, without consider another individuals u_{ij}. Otherwise simulated u_{ij} and compete with the parent individual x_{ij}. This method can reduce the simulation time and keep more genetic information. The selection algorithm of the formula is as follows:

$$x_i(t+1) = \begin{cases} v_i(t+1) & \text{if}\,(f(v_i(t+1)) \leq f(x_i(t))) \\ u_i(t+1) & \text{else if}\,(f(u_i(t+1)) \leq f(x_i(t))) \\ x_i(t) & \text{otherwise} \end{cases} \tag{9}$$

3.3 The Processing of the Constraint Problem

As Mentioned in Sect. 2, the task scheduling in cloud computing is always a constrained problem, while the DE algorithm is unconstrained. To solve this problem, we process these constraints in our IDE algorithm. The target optimization problem with constraints is defined as follows:

$$\begin{aligned} Minimize \quad & f(x) \\ \text{s.t.} \quad & \begin{cases} l_i < x_i < u_i & i = 1, 2, \cdots, D \\ g_i(x) \leq 0 & j = 1, 2, \cdots, J \\ h_k(x) & k = 1, 2, \cdots, K \end{cases} \end{aligned} \tag{10}$$

Here, $f(x)$ is the objective function, $g_j(x)$ is the inequality constraints, and $h_j(x)$ is equality constraint. In general, the equality constraint $h_j(x) = 0$ can be transformed to $h_j(x) - \delta < 0$, where δ is an infinitely small number, and $\delta > 0$. To solve these optimization problems, we should find out a feasible solution that can minimize $f(x)$. The inequality constraint is expressed as follows:

$$V_j = max\{0, g_j(x)\}, j = 1, 2, \cdots, J \tag{11}$$

The equality constraint value can be formalized as follows:

$$V_{J+K} = |h_k(x)|, k = 1, 2, \cdots, K \tag{12}$$

We can get the default value of individual x:

$$V_x = \sum_{m=1}^{J+K} Violation_m(x) \tag{13}$$

Here, we can first transform the constraints of the task scheduling, then getting the cloud task scheduling default value:

$$V_x = g_1(x) + g_2(x) + g_3(x) + h_4(x) \tag{14}$$

where $g_1(x)$ is the default value of memory, $g_2(x)$ is the default value of cpu, $g_3(x)$ is the default value of delay time, and $h_4(x)$ is an indivisible default value of equality dispatch task. We present a partial order relationship in Eq. (15), which is used to compare the merits of two individuals, x_u and x_v:

$$Better(x_u, x_v) = \begin{cases} true & if\, V(x_u) < V(x_v) \\ true & if\, V(x_u) = V(x_v)\, and\, f(x_u) \leq f(x_v) \\ false & if\, V(x_u) > V(x_v) \\ false & if\, V(x_u) = V(x_v)\, and\, f(x_u) > f(x_v) \end{cases} \tag{15}$$

We take a rule-based approach to process these constraints, the idea of comparing each individual in the population can be described as follows: We first judge whether the two solutions are feasible. If both of them are feasible, we select the smaller one as the optimal solution. If only one of the them is feasible, we select the feasible one as the optimal solution. If both of them are infeasible, we select the smaller default value of function as the optimal solution. If both of them are infeasible and have the same default value, we select one smaller one as for the optimal solution.

We explain the application of our IDE algorithm in the cloud task scheduling policy through following example. Assume there are six tasks that need to be scheduled, which can be described as $(N_1, N_2, N_3, N_4, N_5, N_6)$, and four heterogeneous virtual machines (K_1, K_2, K_3, K_4), which are numbered as $(0, 1, 2, 3)$ respectively. We need to schedule these six tasks to four virtual machines, and minimize the completion time and cost. Corresponding to the above scheduling model $\mathcal{N} = 6$, $\mathcal{K} = 4$, we randomly generate the initial population (the initial solution of the task scheduling), which size is NP. If the resulting sequence is (3, 1, 2, 3, 0, 3), and the sequence corresponds to the $x_i(0)$ of IDE, that is the first generation of chromosomes, we need to find the optimal solution for these solutions. According to the procedure of our IDE algorithm, First, we mutate the population. The mutated population will evolve into the next generation to produce a new sequence $h_i(t + 1)$. Since the mutation will produce negative and decimal, we first get the absolute value of the mutation, then divided it by the number of virtual machines, 4, and get a new variant individuals $h_i(t + 1)$. Second, we crosses these new variant individual $h_i(t + 1)$, and generate two new sub-individuals $v_i(t + 1)$ and $u_i(t + 1)$. Third, we compare the new individual with the parent individual, and choose a better individual (better solution) to evolve the next generation. The detailed comparison measure can be describe as follows: we first choose a small value of default, and then get the better solution of objective function, step by step it until the iterative condition is satisfied, and find the approximate optimal solution.

The complete procedure of the IDE is formalized in Algorithm 1.

Algorithm 1. IDE algorithm

Input: $T_1, T_2, ..., T_N, K_1, K_2, ..., K_K$,
Output: value (T_i, K_j)
1: Initial Parameters: population size NP, factor F, CR, CR_{max}, CR_{min};
2: $t = 0, i = 1, j = 1$;
3: Random initialization $x_i(t) = \{x_{i1}, x_{i2}, ..., x_{ij}\}$, each individual F, CR using the formula (7), (8);
4: Calculate all individuals adaptation $x_i(t)$;
5: **while** iterations **do**
6:     Mutation: generate the variation vector $h_{ij}(t + 1)$;
7:     Crossover: generate a new individual $v_i(t + 1)$ and $u_i(t + 1)$;
8:     adaptive value $v_i(t + 1)$;
9:     **if** Better$(v_i(t + 1), x_i(t))$ **then**
10:        $x_i(t + 1) = v_i(t + 1)$
11:     **else**
12:        adaptive value $u_i(t + 1)$;
13:        **if** Better$(u_i(t + 1), x_i(t))$ **then**
14:            $x_i(t + 1) = u_i(t + 1)$
15:        **else**
16:            $x_i(t + 1) = x_i(t)$;
17:        **end if**
18:     **end if**
19: **end while**

---

4   Evaluation

In this section, some simulation experiments were designed using Cloudsim 3.0 [18] to verify the performance of IDE.

4.1   Simulation Setup

In all experiments, we generate the data center using Cloudsim 3.0 [18]. Experimental environment is as follows: with 3 hosts, 15 virtual node resources, and 600 scheduling independent tasks. Each resource node execution speed $MIPS$ and task length instruction MB random by Matlab.

Population size NP is equal to the number of tasks 600, the largest scaling factor $F_{max} = 1$, the minimum zoom factor $F_{min} = 0.5$, maximum crossover probability factor $CR_{max} = 1$, the smallest crossover probability factor $CR_{min} = 0.5$. And we set the initial value $F = 0.5$, $CR = 0.5$.

4.2   The Performance Contrast Experiment

In the process of experiment, the fitness function formula (6): When the $\alpha = 1, \beta = 0$, at this time, the task scheduling algorithm only consider the makespan, the results are shown in figure Fig. 1. When the $\alpha = 0, \beta = 1$, at this time, the task scheduling algorithm only consider the cost, the results are shown in Fig. 2.

Figure 1 shows the makespan and cost from 100 to 600 tasks, which goal is only consider the minimize time. Given the same number of tasks, Fig. 1(a) demonstrates that IDE and Min-Min spend much less time to execute scheduling than DE, while Fig. 1(b) illustrates that Min-Min consume much more cost than IDE.

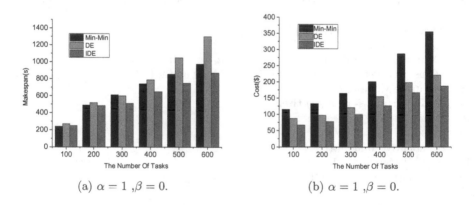

(a) $\alpha = 1$, $\beta = 0$.   (b) $\alpha = 1$, $\beta = 0$.

Fig. 1. Time and resource cost.

Figure 2 shows the makespan and cost from 100 to 600 tasks, which goal is only consider the minimize cost. The task requires better and more performance resources for completion. Therefore, the corresponding costs will be higher, which is consistent with the resource cost model. Besides, as the number of tasks increase, Min-Min and DE spend much more time and cost than IDE.

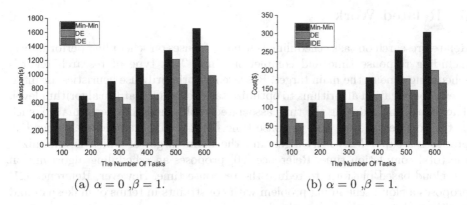

Fig. 2. Time and resource cost.

4.3 The Performance Contrast Experiment of Different Factors

In order to verify the IDE algorithm based on different factors $(\alpha, \beta) = \{(0.1, 0.9), (0.2, 0.8)...(0.9, 0.1)\}$, we compare the performance and task of Multi-Objective Optimization Scheduling algorithm.

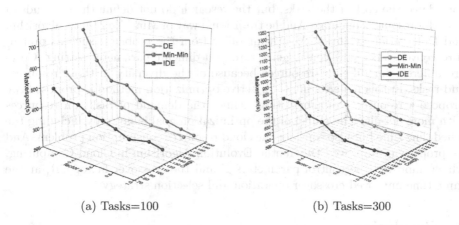

(a) Tasks=100   (b) Tasks=300

Fig. 3. Time and resource cost.

Figure 3 shows the makespan and cost of 100 and 300 tasks, which goal is consider the minimum completion time and cost. We can see that IDE has obvious advantages. It spend less time and cost than Min-Min and DE in different factors α, β. Since Min-Min hasn't considered the cost in task scheduling, it has been high resource consumption. DE and IDE consider the scheduling time and cost at the same time. However, DE is premature convergence and slow convergence rate and its performance is worse than the IDE.

5   Related Work

Related research on task scheduling is usually focuses on scheduling performance, including response time and completion time. This type of research regards scheduling time as the main target. Researchers primarily use heuristics, or intelligent optimization algorithms to optimize task scheduling at the algorithm level. The focus is on reducing the time associated with scheduling performance, such as the completion time and response time [19–21]. For example, Reference [19] proposes a super MIN-MIN algorithm the main target of which is minimized the total completion time. Reference [20] proposes an scheduling algorithm on the cloud-based platform to reduce the response time. However, Reference [21] proposes a cloud scheduling problem with constraints in terms of makespan and flowtime, they propose a genetic algorithm.

Additionally, A few researchers consider all of the targets which include the completion time and the economic cost [22]. Reference [22] proposes a differential evolution algorithm the main target of which is minimum completion time, maximum load balancing degree.

There are several problems in the existing research work using the above analysis. The papers [19–21] consider scheduling time only, while ignore the cloud resources. However, single objective based task scheduling can not satisfy multiple requirements from both users and cloud system provider. The paper [22] considered the cost of the tasks, but the research do not define the demands of tasks for resources in detail. And he traditional way of Min-Min genetic algorithm and Differential Evolution Algorithm suffer from the problems such as premature convergence, slow convergence rate and difficult parameter setting. Costs are different for different resources because of the diversity in those resources and tasks. In this paper, a multi-objective optimization method is proposed, we propose a resource cost model that defines the demand of tasks on resources with more details. The model of the optimization goal is not only including the scheduling time but also consider the cloud resources consumption problem. And we propose an Improved Differential Evolution Algorithm in Cloud Computing, which improved the control parameters F and the crossover factor CR, at the same time improved crossover operation and selection strategy.

6   Conclusion

In this paper, we study a novel multi-objective task scheduling problem, which not only minimize the tasks completion time but also minimize the resource payment. Besides, to efficiently schedule task, we propose an improved differential evolution algorithm. With adaptive parameter setting (control parameter F and the crossover factor CR) and an novel crossover operation and selection strategy, our improved differential evolution algorithm can solve the problems faced in traditional differential evolution algorithm such as premature convergence, slow convergence rate and difficult parameter setting.

Acknowledgments. The work is supported by the National Natural Science Foundation of China under Grant Nos.61572184, 61472130, and 61472131.

References

1. Zhu, C., Leung, V.C.M., Hu, X., Shu, L., Yang, L.T.: A review of key issues that concern the feasibility of mobile cloud computing. In: Green Computing and Communications, pp. 769–776 (2013)
2. Fu, Z., Sun, X., Ji, S., Xie, G.: Towards efficient content-aware search over encrypted outsourced data in cloud. In: IEEE INFOCOM 2016 - The IEEE International Conference on Computer Communications, pp. 1–9 (2016)
3. Abass, A.A., Xiao, L., Mandayam, N., Gajic, Z.: Evolutionary game theoretic analysis of advanced persistent threats against cloud storage. IEEE Access (2017)
4. Liu, X., Liu, Q., Peng, T., Wu, J.: Dynamic access policy in cloud-based personal health record (PHR) systems. Inf. Sci. **379**, 62–81 (2017)
5. Bala, A., Chana, I.: Multilevel priority-based task scheduling algorithm for workflows in cloud computing environment (2016)
6. Xie, K., Wang, X., Xie, G., Xie, D., Cao, J., Ji, Y., Wen, J.: Distributed multidimensional pricing for efficient application offloading in mobile cloud computing. IEEE Trans. Serv. Comput. **PP**(99), 1 (1939)
7. He, S., Xie, K., Zhang, D.: Completion time-aware flow scheduling in heterogenous networks. In: Wang, G., Zomaya, A., Perez, G.M., Li, K. (eds.) ICA3PP 2015. LNCS, vol. 9528, pp. 492–507. Springer, Cham (2015). doi:10.1007/978-3-319-27119-4_34
8. Ullman, J.D.: Np-complete scheduling problems. J. Comput. Syst. Sci. **10**(3), 384–393 (1975)
9. Mohamed, A.W., Sabry, H.Z., Abd-Elaziz, T.: Real parameter optimization by an effective differential evolution algorithm. Egypt. Inf. J. **14**(1), 37–53 (2013)
10. Ruben, V.D.B., Vanmechelen, K., Broeckhove, J.: Cost-efficient scheduling heuristics for deadline constrained workloads on hybrid clouds. In: IEEE Third International Conference on Cloud Computing Technology and Science, pp. 320–327 (2011)
11. Price, K.V.: Differential evolution vs. the functions of the 2nd ICEO. In: IEEE International Conference on Evolutionary Computation, pp. 153–157 (1997)
12. Prakash, T., Singh, V.P., Chauhan, D.P.S., Madariya, M.: Optimization with improved differential evolution algorithm having variable tolerance. In: Second International Conference on Computational Intelligence and Communication Technology, pp. 270–274 (2016)
13. Xue, Y., Jiang, J., Zhao, B., Ma, T.: A self-adaptive artificial bee colony algorithm based on global best for global optimization. Soft Comput. 1–18 (2017)
14. Price, K.V.: An introduction to differential evolution (1999)
15. Ilonen, J., Kamarainen, J.K., Lampinen, J.: Differential evolution training algorithm for feed-forward neural networks. Neural Process. Lett. **17**(1), 93–105 (2003)
16. Storn, R.: Designing nonstandard filters with differential evolution. IEEE Sig. Process. Mag. **22**(1), 103–106 (2005)
17. Zhu, C., Ni, J.: Cloud model-based differential evolution algorithm for optimization problems. In: Sixth International Conference on Internet Computing for Science and Engineering, pp. 55–59 (2012)

18. Calheiros, R.N., Ranjan, R., Beloglazov, A., De Rose, C.A.F., Buyya, R.: Cloudsim: a toolkit for modeling and simulation of cloud computing environments and evaluation of resource provisioning algorithms. Softw. Pract. Exp. **41**(1), 23–50 (2011)
19. Chen, H., Wang, F., Na, H., Akanmu, G.: User-priority guided min-min scheduling algorithm for load balancing in cloud computing. In: National Conference on Parallel Computing Technologies, pp. 1–8 (2013)
20. Bartolini, C., Stefanelli, C., Targa, D., Tortonesi, M.: A cloud-based solution for the performance improvement of it support organizations. In: Network Operations and Management Symposium, pp. 953–960 (2012)
21. Cui, H., Li, Y., Liu, X., Ansari, N., Liu, Y.: Cloud service reliability modelling and optimal task scheduling. IET Commun. **11**, 161–167 (2017)
22. Xue, J., Li, L., Zhao, S., Jiao, L.: A study of task scheduling based on differential evolution algorithm in cloud computing. In: International Conference on Computational Intelligence and Communication Networks, pp. 637–640 (2014)

A Network Calculus Analysis for the Baseband Processing Capacity in Cloud Radio Access Network

Muzhou Xiong, Haixin Liu, and Deze Zeng$^{(\boxtimes)}$

School of Computer Science, China University of Geosciecnes, Wuhan 430074, China
{mzxiong,deze}@cug.edu.cn, liuhaixiyan@qq.com

Abstract. Recently, cloud radio access network (C-RAN) has been widely regarded as a promising architecture for the next generation cellular networks. By separating traditional cellular base station to remote radio head (RRH) and baseband unit (BBU), C-RAN exhibits many advantages such as lower operating expenditure, higher throughput and energy efficiency. In order to understand the potential of C-RAN, much effort has been devoted to analyzing the performance of C-RAN. However, we notice that existing work usually assumes some preknown stochastic characteristics on the distribution of network traffic demands. In this paper, we would like to derive the backlog conditions in the BBU pool so as to understand how C-RAN can satisfy the real-time requirement in general cases without relying on any stochastic assumption. Specially, we build an analysis framework based on network calculus to analyze the baseband processing capacity of BBU pool in C-RAN. Then, we derive the effective bandwidth, based on the aggregated flow from RRHs, as the upper bound of the processing capacity of BBU pool. With the derived effective bandwidth, the upper bound of the number of BBUs can be also obtained accordingly. Numerical results validate the analysis result.

1 Introduction

Recent decades have witnessed the proliferation of mobile traffic volume, which is forecasted to grow 13 folds from 2012 to 2017 according to Cisco [1]. The surprising increase is driven by both the sharp increase of mobile devices (like smart phones, tablets, and wearable devices), and the wide span mobile applications (e.g. video streaming, gaming). In addition, cost will also be paid to handle the security challenges [8,18,19], which further burdens the load cost of communication infrastructure. In order to better serve mobile users and provide required Quality-of-Service (QoS), the mobile cellular communication standard has involved from the second to the fourth generation in less than two decades, and is moving towards the fifth generation, which will be 1000x times faster than the currently widely applied 4G standard.

On the other hand, the fast evolution of mobile network communication standard is approaching the Shannon limit. In order to further improve the capacity

© Springer International Publishing AG 2017
X. Sun et al. (Eds.): ICCCS 2017, Part I, LNCS 10602, pp. 239–250, 2017.
https://doi.org/10.1007/978-3-319-68505-2_21

of mobile network, novel techniques have been proposed to obtain a better multiplex gain of spectrum in space dimension, like HetSNets, MIMO, and Massive MIMO. All these techniques need base station densely deployed in the servicing area, incurring unprecedented higher cost for mobile operators, including both capital expenditure (CAPEX) and operational expenditure (OPEX).

Aiming at reducing the operation cost for mobile network operator, a novel mobile architecture, i.e., cloud radio access networks (C-RAN), has been proposed and drawn much attention from both academia and industry It was originally proposed by IBM [9] and further described by China Mobile in [3]. The basic principle of C-RAN is to decouple the analogy signal and baseband processing units in traditional base station and then to form two new network entities, i.e., remote radio header (RRH) and baseband processing unit (BBU). RRHs are scattered in the network serving area, while BBUs are virtualized as a BBU pool and serve the requests from RRHs as a cloud service. By such means, C-RAN is potential to improve the capacity of mobile network as well as to reduce the cost. It has become one of the key techniques for the evolution towards the next generation mobile cellular network [6].

Of the newly proposed architecture, one challenge is to understand the performance efficiency and energy efficiency of C-RAN. For example, it is essential to determine the least number of BBUs with the given traffic characteristic so as to minimize the energy consumption and to satisfy the requirements for QoS of mobile network link in the meantime. For example, Suryaprakash et al. [16] shows that C-RAN reduces 10–15% less capacity expenditure per square kilometer than traditional LTE architecture. The simulation results in [10] show that C-RAN can obtain at most 75% multiplex gain by centralizing the baseband processing unit. On the other hand, the traffic in mobile network is nonuniform with tilting pattern [1], which dynamically varies during different periods of daily time. The processing capacity of BBU pool should be determined based on the traffic characteristic.

In order to provide satisfied QoS for mobile devices as well as to minimize the number of BBUs to obtain energy-efficiency for C-RAN, pioneering researchers have also proposed many different optimization methods. For example, Fluid-Net [15] provides flexible configuration of front-haul network for RRH and BBU association, aiming to minimize the needed computing resources in BBU pool, with the deterministic traffic data. Assuming that RRH load follows exponential distribution with time-varying traffic rate, Mishra et al. [11] propose an load-aware algorithm to minimize the number of active BBUs. However, existing work for the analysis and optimization of required number of BBUs is based on either static RRH traffic load or assuming a specified distribution. They cannot provide an general analysis for the relationship between RRH traffic demand and BBU processing capacity. Regarding this, this paper aims to analyze the C-RAN performance under different traffic demands and to reveal the least number of required BBUs via the conclusion of Network Calculus, without any assumption for stochastic characteristics of mobile traffic demand.

Network Calculus provides a general paradigm for classical queuing problems. It is first introduced by Cruze [4,5] and further developed in [12]. By this tool, the delay and backlog bound in processing queue can be derived for applications with QoS guarantee. Network Calculus helps to convert non-linear queuing problem to traceable analysis framework with closed form expression. Such feature makes the analysis without additional assumption for the traffic distribution. In this paper, we treat the C-RAN architecture as a flow problem. The baseband processing requests sent from a RRH to BBU pool are generalized as a flow. The BBUs in the pool are abstracted as an aggregated service unit. By applying the Network Calculus, we analyze the minimum processing capacity provided by BBU in the worst case under the constraint of a given specific QoS guarantee, and thus to derive the upper bound of the number of required BBUs.

The main contributions of this paper exist in the following two folds:

- To our best knowledge, we are the first to apply network calculus to analyze the performance of C-RAN. In particular, we are interested in the processing capacity of BBU pool.
- With the proposed analysis framework, we derive a closed-form expression for the upper bound of the number of required BBUs with the given QoS guarantee. The numerical results validate the correctness of our analysis.

The rest of the paper is organized as follows: the existing related work is summarized in Sect. 2. The system and traffic model is given in Sect. 3. The analysis framework, as well as the upper bound of the number of BBUs for the C-RAN is given in Sect. 4. Evaluation and numerical results are given in Sect. 5. Finally, Sect. 6 concludes this paper.

2 Related Work

In this section, we briefly summarize the state-of-art work of C-RAN, with a special emphasis on its performance analysis.

The concept of C-RAN was proposed in 2009 and has drawn much attention from industry. Aiming at the provision of an efficient mobile network framework with less cost expenditure, it holds the advantages of adaptability to nonuniform traffic and scalability, energy and cost savings by statistical multiplexing gain in BBU pool, increase of throughput and decrease of delay, and ease in network upgrading and maintenance. The basic principle of C-RAN is the separation of traditional base station into two new networking functionality units, i.e., RRH and BBU. RRHs are densely deployed in the serving area and only process analogy signal, while BBUs are in charge of base band processing and are deployed in a centralized manner. In academia, many pioneer researchers have made contributions for the novel architecture aiming at obtaining better performance. In [17], Wu et al. propose a logical structure of C-RAN consisting of a physical plane, a control plane and a service plane, which emphasizes the how the virtualized services provide the ability for the C-RAN processing. A flexible C-RAN architecture for small cells is proposed and implemented in [15], with intelligent specification of front-haul network between the BBUs and RRHs. Detailed description of C-RAN as well as its advantages and challenges can be found in the survey [2].

The performance analysis of C-RAN has been conducted in order to obtain an insightful understanding on the performance of C-RAN for different scenarios. In [7], the outage performance and minimal number of RRHs are analyzed by modeling the RRH location as a Poisson point process. Yang et al. [20] further analyze the C-RAN performance with uniformly distributed base stations with the considerations of both small-scale Reyleigh fading and large-scale path loss. By using Gauss-Chebyshev integration, the method obtains tightly approximation of outage probability and ergodic rate. Aiming at mitigating the interior interference and improving energy efficiency in heterogeneous C-RAN, a joint energy-efficient resource assignment and power allocation optimization is proposed in [13]. Taking cooperative interference management among RRH into account, [21] gives SINR-based downlink throughput models. A formation game is formulated for the situation where RRHs can make individual decisions to cooperatively serve their mobile users so as to obtain higher throughput.

Existing work for C-RAN performance analysis usually assumes certain stochastic characteristics for RRH and BBU location distribution, as well as the traffic from user over time. There is still lack of performance analysis for the general scenarios (i.e., without the assumption of stochastic distributions). Targeting at general case analysis, our work put the emphasis on the analysis of minimum processing capacity of BBU pool constrained by the QoS guarantee. With the derived closed-form expression, the analysis reveals the relationship between processing capacity and traffic demand. The upper bound for the number of required BBUs can be further derived based on our analysis results.

3   System Model

In this section, we give the system model for our C-RAN analysis.

In this paper, we consider the mobile network is organized as illustrated in Fig. 1. The tradition base stations are separated into Remote Radio Head (RRH) and the pool of Baseband Units (BBU). Each mobile User Equipment (UE) is associated with a RRH to which it sends baseband processing request to access the mobile network. RRH performs digital processing, digital to analog conversion, analog to digital conversion, power amplification and filtering for the packets from user. RRHs are deployed in the environment and are able to serve the area exclusively by adjusting the transmission power. The basic working process for the upper link channel of the proposed architecture is that the packets are first generated at the UE and then sent to the associated RRH; the RRH resends the I-Q samples to a BBU in the pool for baseband processing via the optical fiber networks. The BBU pool assigns one of BBUs inside to handle the request and further transmits it to the mobile backhaul network to complete the communication request from UE. We also assume that RRH have enough spectrum resources and hence we simply aggregate the requests from

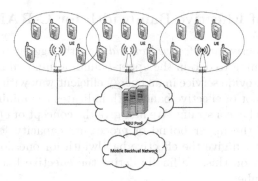

Fig. 1. System model for C-RAN

the associated UEs in RRH. The emphasis of the performance analysis is on the relationship between the requests from RRHs and the number of required BBUs.

After completing these operations, RRH sends the packets to the BBU pool via the interface to fiber. The BBU pool assigns one of BBUs inside to handle the request and further transmits it to the mobile backhaul network to complete the network request from UE.

In this analysis, we mainly consider the uplink communication of C-RAN. The goal of the performance analysis is to determine the required number of BBUs in the pool in the worse case according to different request arrival rates from RRHs. We consider the requests from a RRH to BBU pool is a flow on time domain. The flow of RRH r_i is described by a cumulative function $R_i(t), t \geq 0$ on time domain with the unit of bps to indicate how many bits are aggregated at r_i from time 0 to t. It is obvious that the cumulative function $R_i(t)$ is left continuous. We use *arrival curve* to describe the flow characteristic defined as follows.

Definition 1 (Arrival Curve). *Given wide-sense increasing function $\alpha_i(t), t \geq 0$, we say that the flow $R_i(t)$ is constrained by α_i if and only if for all $s \leq t$:*

$$R_i(t) - R_i(s) \leq \alpha_i(t - s) \tag{1}$$

We say that the flow of RRH r_i $R_i(t)$ has $\alpha_i(t)$ as an arrival curve, *or also R is α smooth.*

We assume the traffic aggregated at RRH follows the TSPEC(M, p, r, b) [14], where M is the maximum packet size, p is the peak traffic rate, r is the mean rate for the long run, and b is the burst tolerance for traffic packet, with $0 < r < p$ and $0 < M < b$. The arrival curve of the flow constrained by TSPEC(M, p, r, b) can be given as:

$$\alpha(t) = \min(M + pt, rt + b) \tag{2}$$

4   Analysis of Effective Bandwidth for C-RAN

In this section, we derive an *effective bandwidth* for the aggregated traffic for users from all RRHs, aiming to obtain the upper-bound of minimal necessary number of BBUs so as to provide service in an energy efficient way with guaranteed QoS. Actually, the concept of effective bandwidth indicates the minimum service rate to guarantee the delay constraint. We first give the concept of *effective bandwidth* and the proof for the upper bound of processing capacity for a given traffic arrival curve. We then give the effective bandwidth for one flow and two flows, respectively. Based on this, we finally derive the effective bandwidth for flows with arbitrary number.

The following proposition gives the expression for effective bandwidth. It can be used to indicate the upper bound of processing rate of the C-RAN system, with the traffic flow constrained by the arrival curve $\alpha(t)$.

Proposition 1 *[Effective Bandwidth]. The queue at a BBU with a constant processing rate C which guarantees a delay bound D for a flow from a RRH with arrival curve $\alpha(t)$ if,*

$$C \geq C_D(\alpha(t))$$

$$\text{with } C_D(\alpha(t)) = \sup_{t \geq 0} \frac{\alpha(t)}{t + D} \tag{3}$$

We call $C_D(\alpha(t))$ the effective bit rate, or effective bandwidth, *with respect to the arrival curve $\alpha(t)$ and the delay constraint D.*

It is obvious that the effective bandwidth is the slope of tangent of the arrival curve drawn from $t = -D$, if the arrival curve is differential. In the following analysis, we specify $TSPEC(p, M, r, b)$ as the arrival curve for each RRH with different parameter values. Proposition 2 derives the effective bandwidth for one RRH with $TSPEC(p, M, r, b)$.

Proposition 2. *For a flow constrained by $TSPEC(p, M, r, b)$, i.e., the arrival curve given by Eq. 2, the effective bandwidth with the burst tolerance D is*

$$C_D(\alpha(t)) = \max(\frac{M}{D}, r, \frac{px_1 + M}{x_1 + D}),$$

$$\text{with } x_1 = \frac{b - M}{p - r}. \tag{4}$$

Proof. Since the arrival curve follows the $TSPEC(p, M, r, b)$, the arrival curve can be reformulated as:

$$\alpha(t) = \begin{cases} pt + M, t \in [0, x_1], \\ rt + b, t \in (x_1, \infty), \end{cases} \text{with } x_1 = \frac{b - M}{p - r}. \tag{5}$$

The arrival curve function is not differential for $t \in (0, \infty)$. According to Eq. (3), the effective bandwidth here can be interpreted as the maximum slope of the line from $(-D, 0)$ to any point in the arrival curve. It is easy to prove whether the slope of the tangent line from $(-D, 0)$ to any point of the two lines of the arrival curve monotonically increases or decreases with time increase. For example, at any point on the line $rt + b = 0$, the slope is $\frac{pt_0 + M}{t_0 + D}$. The derivative of the slope function is $\frac{p(D-M)}{(t+D)^2}$, and therefore is positive $(D \geq M)$ or negative $(D < M)$. Regarding this, the maximum slope is determined by three points in the arrival cure, i.e., $t = 0$, $t = x_1$ and $t \to \infty$. For the former two points, the slope is $\frac{M}{D}$ and $\frac{px_1 + M}{x_1 + D}$. As $t \to \infty$, the slope can be calculated as:

$$\lim_{t \to \infty} \frac{rt + b}{t + D} = \lim_{t \to \infty} \frac{r + b/t}{1 + D/t} = r. \tag{6}$$

In summary, the effective bandwidth for the arrival curve with Eq. (4) is

$$\max(\frac{M}{D}, r, \frac{pX_1 + M}{X_1 + D}). \tag{7}$$

This concludes our proof.   □

We now derive the effective bandwidth for arbitrary number of non-identical flows, with its expression given in Theorem 1.

Theorem 1. *There are n flows, each of which is constrained by TSPEC (p_i, M_i, r_i, b_i), with $i \in \{1, 2, \cdots n\}$. The x-coordinate of the non-differentiable point for each arrival curve is $x_i = \frac{b_i - M_i}{p_i - r_i}$. It is also assumed that the index set $\{1, 2, \cdots n\}$ is sorted in ascend order with respect to x_i. All the flows hold the same burst tolerance D. The effective bandwidth for the aggregated flow composed of the n flows is*

$$C_D \left(\sum_{i=1}^{n} \alpha_i(t) \right) = \max \left(\frac{\sum_{i=1}^{n} M_i}{D}, \frac{\sum_{i=1}^{n} p_i X_1 + \sum_{i=1}^{n} M_i}{X_1 + D}, \right.$$

$$\frac{(r_1 + \sum_{i=2}^{n} p_i) x_2 + b_1 + \sum_{i=2}^{n} M_i}{x_2 + D},$$

$$\cdots, \frac{(\sum_{i=1}^{j-1} r_i + \sum_{i=j}^{n} p_i) x_j + \sum_{i=1}^{j-1} b_i + \sum_{i=j}^{n} M_i}{X_j + D}, \tag{8}$$

$$\left. \cdots, \frac{(\sum_{i=1}^{n-1} r_i + p_n) X_n + \sum_{i=1}^{n-1} b_i + M_n}{X_n + D}, \sum_{i=1}^{n} r_i \right)$$

with $j \in [3, n-1]$, and $j \in N$.

Proof. We treat the ranges of t for the following three categories:

1. At $t \in [0, x_1)$, the arrival curve of the aggregated flow first period, $x \in (0, x_1]$, we need to calculate the slope from $(-D, 0)$ to the point with x-coordinate value 0 in the arrival curve. When t in this range, the arrival curve is written as $\sum_{i=1}^{n} p_i t + \sum_{i=1}^{n} M_i$. Hence, the calculated slope in this range is

$$slope_0 = \frac{\sum_{i=1}^{n} M_i}{D} \tag{9}$$

2. As $t \to +\infty$, the aggregated arrival curve can be written as $\sum_{i=1}^{n} r_i t + \sum_{i=1}^{n} b_i$. The slope for this range can be calculated as

$$slope_n = \sum_{i=1}^{n} r_i \tag{10}$$

The proof of which is similar to the process as illustrated in Eq. (6).

3. As for $t \in [x_j, x_{j+1}]$ with $j \in \{2, 3 \cdots n - 1\}$, the aggregated arrival curve is with the formulation as

$$\alpha(t) = (\sum_{i=1}^{j-1} r_i + \sum_{i=j}^{n} p_i)t + \sum_{i=1}^{j-1} b_i + \sum_{i=j+1}^{n} M_i \tag{11}$$

The slope for each of the ranges is

$$slope_j = \frac{\alpha(x_j)}{x_j + D} = \frac{(\sum_{i=1}^{j-1} r_i + \sum_{i=j}^{n} p_i)t + \sum_{i=1}^{j-1} b_i + \sum_{i=j+1}^{n} M_i}{x_j + D} \tag{12}$$

$$\text{with } j \in [2, n - 1]$$

As the effective bandwidth is the maximum value among $slope_0$, $slope_1, \cdots$, $slope_{n-1}$, $slope_n$, it concludes the proof. $\square$

So far, we have derived the formulation of effective bandwidth for aggregated flow with arbitrary number of flows by RRH, with different arrival curves and the same burst tolerance. With the calculated effective bandwidth, we can determine the maximum number of BBUs in order to guarantee the burst tolerance. Actually, with the processing capacity R for each BBU, the maximum number of BBUs should be $\lceil C_D(\alpha(t)/R \rceil$.

5   Experiments and Evaluations

In the previous section, we derive the effective bandwidth which represents the upper bound of processing capacity provided by BBU pool. Since the processing capacity is proportional to the number of BBUs, the upper bound of required BBUs is also obtained. In this section, we evaluate the derived performance bound in different scenarios.

In the experiment configuration, we consider a C-RAN deployed with 5 RRHs, each of which has the aggregated traffic from mobile devices following $TSPEC(M, p, r, b)$, with values as $(0.1, 0.8, 0.6, 0.6)$, $(0.1, 1, 0.8, 0.9)$, $(0.1, 1.2, 1, 1.3)$, $(0.1, 1.2, 1, 1.7)$, and $(0.1, 1.6, 1.4, 3.1)$, respectively. The unit used for the parameter specification is kbps.

Hence, the aggregated arrival curve at BBU pool can be expressed as:

$$\alpha(t) = \begin{cases} 6t + 0.6, x \in (0, 2] \\ 5.8t + 1.1, x \in (2, 4] \\ 5.6t + 1.9, x \in (4, 6] \\ 5.4t + 3.1, x \in (6, 8] \\ 5.2t + 4.7, x \in (8, 10] \\ 5t + 7.7, x \in (10, +\infty) \end{cases} \tag{13}$$

We also set the communication delay requirement $D = 2\,\mathrm{s}$, the service rate for each BBU as $1.2\,\mathrm{kbps}$. Substituting the parameter values to Eq. (8), the effective bandwidth for the BBU pool can be calculated as $5\,\mathrm{kbps}$.

In the following experiments, we vary the number of BBUs in the system as 3, 4, and 5, respectively. For each experiment, the traffic flow from each RRH is generated by two ways: one way is that the traffic is *randomly* generated constrained by the arrival curves, and in another way the traffic is generated *strictly* according to the arrival curve for each RRH. If the generated traffic strictly follows the arrival curve given by Eq. (13), the traffic arrival rates at BBU are set to 6, 5.8, 5.6, 5.4, 5.2 and 5.0 kbps for time interval $(0, 2]$, $(2, 4]$, $(4, 6]$, $(6, 8]$, $(8, 10]$, and $(10, +\infty)$, respectively. As for the random generation case, the traffic arrival rate is no more than the peak rate for the corresponding period as given by the arrival curve. We compare the backlog of each flow in different traffic generation ways.

First, we set the number of BBUs to 3, and check the backlog for each RRH with the traffic generated via the aforementioned two ways. The simulation results are shown in Fig. 2. As analyzed previously, the processing capacity for 3 BBUs is less than the required effective bandwidth. Hence, the backlogs for all the 5 RRHs increase as time elapses. Figure 2(a) illustrates the backlogs for the 5 flows at different time with random traffic. Since the BBU pool can not provide enough processing capacity for the given traffic, the backlog for each flow keeps rising up. When the traffic demands are randomly generated, we can see that the backlog increases but fluctuates with the time. As for the flow generated strictly according to the given arrival curve (as illustrated in Fig. 2(b)), the backlog for each flow increases almost linearly. The reason for this is that the arrival traffic for each flow is with a fixed arrival rate in specified time interval.

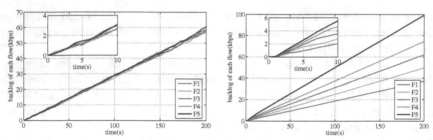

(a) Traffic randomly generated accrod- (b) Traffic strictly accoriding to arrival
ing to arrival curve   curve

Fig. 2. The backlog from each RRH with 3 BBUs

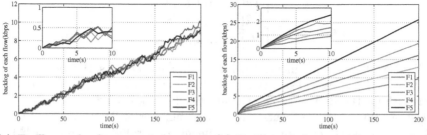

(a) Traffic randomly generated accrod- (b) Traffic strictly accoriding to arrival
ing to arrival curve   curve

Fig. 3. The backlog from each RRH with 4 BBUs

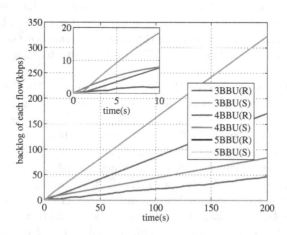

Fig. 4. The total backlog of each aggregate flow served with different number of BBUs

As the number of BBUs is set to 4, we give the backlog for each flow in Fig. 3. Due to the lack of processing capacity by BBU pool, the backlogs for both random traffic (Fig. 3(a)) and the one strictly according to the arrival curve (Fig. 3(b)) keep increasing, with similar pattern to results in Fig. 2. Thanks to the processing capacity improvement, the backlog in this experiment is less than the counter-part in the results with 3 BBU.

Next, we further set the number of BBUs to be 5. As analyzed previously, the processing rate for this experiment is larger than the derived effective bandwidth. The simulation results show that there is no backlog for either traffic generation way. It shows that the C-RAN system with 5 BBUs is enough to handle the requesting traffic to guarantee the delay tolerance. We show the simulation results for this experiment in Fig. 4, compared with the aggregated backlogs from all RRH for the previous two experiments. It is obvious that as the number of BBUs increases, the backlog for the aggregated backlog decreases. When the number reaches 5, the volume of backlog becomes 0.

6   Conclusion

As C-RAN becomes a promising candidate architecture for the next generation cellular network, the performance analysis of C-RAN is critical with dynamic traffic volume from mobile user. This paper establishes a network calculus framework to derive the effective bandwidth for the incoming traffic. The obtained effective bandwidth can describe the characteristics of incoming traffic in both real-time and long-term aspects. With a specified processing capability in BBU pool (i.e., the number of BBUs), the backlog of the traffic can be easily obtained. Simulation results show the backlog in different situations with different traffic arriving rates as well as different BBU processing capability. The results validate the feasibility and correctness of our the network calculus based framework.

Acknowledgments. This research was supported by the Key Technologies Research and Development Program of China (grant No. 2016YFB0502603), the NSF of China (Grant No. 61673354, 61672474, 61402425, 61501412), the Open Research Project of the Hubei Key Laboratory of Intelligent Geo-Information Processing (KLIGIP201603 and KLIGIP201607).

References

1. Global mobile data traffic forecast update, 2012–2017. Technical report, Cisco (2013)
2. Checko, A., Christiansen, H.L., Yan, Y., Scolari, L., Kardaras, G., Berger, M.S., Dittmann, L.: Cloud RAN for mobile networks technology overview. IEEE Commun. Surv. Tutor. **17**(1), 405–426 (2015)
3. Chen, K., Duan, R.: C-RAN the road towards green RAN. China Mobile Research Institute, White paper 2 (2011)
4. Cruz, R.: A calculus for network delay. I. Network elements in isolation. IEEE Trans. Inf. Theory **37**(1), 114–131 (1991)

5. Cruz, R.: A calculus for network delay. II. Network analysis. IEEE Trans. Inf. Theory **37**(1), 132–141 (1991)
6. Demestichas, P., Georgakopoulos, A., Karvounas, D., Tsagkaris, K., Stavroulaki, V., Lu, J., Xiong, C., Yao, J.: 5G on the horizon: key challenges for the radio-access network. IEEE Veh. Technol. Mag. **8**(3), 47–53 (2013)
7. Ding, Z., Poor, H.V.: The use of spatially random base stations in cloud radio access networks. IEEE Signal Process. Lett. **20**(11), 1138–1141 (2013)
8. Fu, Z., Ren, K., Shu, J., Sun, X., Huang, F.: Enabling personalized search over encrypted outsourced data with efficiency improvement. IEEE Trans. Parallel Distrib. Syst. **27**(9), 2546–2559 (2016)
9. Lin, Y., Shao, L., Zhu, Z., Wang, Q., Sabhikhi, R.K.: Wireless network cloud: architecture and system requirements. IBM J. Res. Dev. **54**(1), 4–12 (2010)
10. Liu, J., Zhou, S., Gong, J., Niu, Z., Xu, S.: Statistical multiplexing gain analysis of heterogeneous virtual base station pools in cloud radio access networks. IEEE Trans. Wireless Commun. **15**(8), 5681–5694 (2016)
11. Mishra, D., Amogh, P.C., Ramamurthy, A., Franklin, A.A., Tamma, B.R.: Load-aware dynamic RRH assignment in cloud radio access networks. In: 2016 IEEE Wireless Communications and Networking Conference, pp. 1–6, April 2016
12. Parekh, A.K., Gallagher, R.G.: A generalized processor sharing approach to flow control in integrated services networks: the multiple node case. IEEE/ACM Trans. Networking (ToN) **2**(2), 137–150 (1994)
13. Peng, M., Zhang, K., Jiang, J., Wang, J., Wang, W.: Energy-efficient resource assignment and power allocation in heterogeneous cloud radio access networks. IEEE Trans. Veh. Technol. **64**(11), 5275–5287 (2015)
14. Shenker, S., Partridge, C., Guerin, R.: RFC 2212: specification of guaranteed quality of service, status: Proposed Standard, September 1997. ftp://ietf.org/rfc/rfc2212.txt
15. Sundaresan, K., Arslan, M.Y., Singh, S., Rangarajan, S., Krishnamurthy, S.V.: Fluidnet: a flexible cloud-based radio access network for small cells. IEEE/ACM Trans. Networking **24**(2), 915–928 (2016)
16. Suryaprakash, V., Rost, P., Fettweis, G.: Are heterogeneous cloud-based radio access networks cost effective? IEEE J. Sel. Areas Commun. **33**(10), 2239–2251 (2015)
17. Wu, J., Zhang, Z., Hong, Y., Wen, Y.: Cloud radio access network (C-RAN): a primer. IEEE Network **29**(1), 35–41 (2015)
18. Xia, Z., Wang, X., Sun, X., Wang, Q.: A secure and dynamic multi-keyword ranked search scheme over encrypted cloud data. IEEE Trans. Parallel Distrib. Syst. **27**(2), 340–352 (2016)
19. Xia, Z., Wang, X., Zhang, L., Qin, Z., Sun, X., Ren, K.: A privacy-preserving and copy-deterrence content-based image retrieval scheme in cloud computing. IEEE Trans. Inf. Forensics Secur. **11**(11), 2594–2608 (2016)
20. Yang, Z., Ding, Z., Fan, P.: Performance analysis of cloud radio access networks with uniformly distributed base stations. IEEE Trans. Veh. Technol. **65**(1), 472–477 (2016)
21. Zhan, S.C., Niyato, D.: A coalition formation game for remote radio heads cooperation in cloud radio access network. IEEE Trans. Veh. Technol. **PP**(99), 1 (2016)

Live Migration Among CloudBased on MOOSE Address

Yubing Mao and Zhengyou Xia[✉]

College of Computer Science and Technology,
Nanjing University of Aeronautics and Astronautics, Nanjing, China
{iamandam,zhengyou_xia}@nuaa.edu.cn

Abstract. The introduction of virtualization and the expansion of scale in data center result in sharp consumption of MAC address which also expose some weaknesses in MAC address such as inefficient allocation scheme, and one-dimensional address structure, among others. Hence, we have proposed a centralized management based on MOOSE address. However, structure of MOOSE address is based on location information, MOOSE address will change after VM migration. Hence, existing schemes are not good enough to meet the demand based on these new structures of MAC address and thus we propose a thoroughly VM migration scheme in data center based on MOOSE address. We have implemented and tested our solution, and found it to be a practical and effective way of achieving migrating VMs without interrupting their network connections based on MOOSE address.

Keywords: Live migration · Cloud computing · Centralized address

1 Introduction

With the development and application of cloud computing, enterprises are adept to run their server applications in data centers, which provide them with computational and storage resources nowadays. Thereby cloud computing has become research hotspot nowadays. NIST defines cloud computing [1] as a model for enabling ubiquitous, convenient, on-demand network access to a shared pool of configurable computing resources (e.g., networks, servers, storage, applications, and services) that can be rapidly provisioned and released with minimal management effort or service provider interaction. In Wikipedia [2], cloud computing is defined as a type of Internet-based computing that provides shared computer processing resources and data to computers and other devices on demand. Furthermore, virtualization is one of fundamental technologies in architecting cloud infrastructure. By establishing a virtualized layer, such technology manages to provide system resources for higher layer while allocating various tasks to underlying physical resources [3] which tackling problem of how to allocate resources efficiently and dynamically.

However, visualization of servers, storage and network has brought exponential growth of virtual facilities, which results in sharp consumption of MAC address. The extensive use of visualization devices has exposed some defects of MAC address itself. Firstly, the life cycle of assigned MAC address is permanent. Accordingly, each physical

© Springer International Publishing AG 2017
X. Sun et al. (Eds.): ICCCS 2017, Part I, LNCS 10602, pp. 251–261, 2017.
https://doi.org/10.1007/978-3-319-68505-2_22

device can virtualized multiple virtual devices and these numerous virtualized devices in data center can occupy MAC address space rapidly. Secondly, MAC address is one-dimensional and can't provide location information. Because fast growth of virtual devices, current content addressable memory (CAM) which storing forwarding tables doesn't match the growth rate of table length [4, 5] which can cause broadcast storm once data overflow. Additionally, it is inefficient to locate where virtual machine breaks down since MAC address can't provide location information.

Many researchers proposed new MAC address structures to solve these problem, such as EUI-64 [6], Zonal [7], MOOSE [8], etc. The structure of MOOSE [8] designed by Malcolm Scott is proper to settle problems above, which is associated three bytes host identifier with a fixed three bytes switch identifier. This address structure embeds location information into the layered address, which solves explosive consumption of MAC address space. We have proposed a centralized address allocation scheme based on MOOSE address.

However, in order to make use of computing resources efficiently and achieve load balancing, it is necessary for virtual machines to migrate from one place to another place among the clouds. While simultaneously allowing for convenient deployment of services, virtualization is difficult to be realized because of the reality of complicated network environment. Several challenges need to be addressed to realize migration in cloud. Firstly, to achieve seamless migration, it is desirable to reduce data latency by minimizing application downtimes during migration in which way users can't be aware of the migration. Additionally, when migration takes place between servers in different networks, it will generally change network configuration and thus existing network connection will break which results in inaccessible situation for virtual machine. Certainly, the problem makes scheme based on MOOSE address assigned according to device's location difficult to deploy when it comes to migration. Although many researchers proposed solutions to seamless live migration, such as [10–17], those schemes are on the condition that hardware address doesn't change during migration. And since structure of MOOSE address is based on location information, MOOSE address will change after VM migration. Hence, existing schemes are not enough to meet demands based on these new structure of MAC address and thus we have proposed a thoroughly VM migration scheme in data center based on MOOSE address. We have implemented and tested the above our solution, and found it to be a practical and effective way of achieving migrating VMs without interrupting their network connections based on MOOSE address.

2 Related Work

Nowadays, to realize seamless live migration as we previously mentioned in this paper, several of researchers have proposed their own architectures from many angles. So far many studies have focused on transferring run-time memory state among cloud. However, it is crucial to not just transfer the VMs image but also transfer its on-going network connections. Hence, we concentrate on how to maintain connection during migration. Generally, we classify these scheme into four categories.

One approach to resolve disconnection during migration is flattening layer 2. VMware cooperating with cisco proposes virtual Extensible LAN (VXLAN). VXLAN [9] overlays layer 2 on the top of layer 3 network by encapsulating MAC in UDP. Hence, VM can remain the same IP address during migration since it migrates in the same VXLAN segment and packets can be delivered to destination through VXLAN tunnel. This solution expands virtualization migration beyond layer 2 and breaks bottleneck that VLAN ID using for isolating network is insufficient. In [10], Wood proposes a cross-regional migration platform in data center called CloudNet to achieve the vision of seamless connected resource pools that permit flexible placement and live migration of applications. This scheme makes use of virtual private LAN service (VPLS) to dynamically modify configurations of PE routers in order to establish a new VPN topology required by WAN migration. And this enables seamless connectivity between migrating VM and correspondent node by keeping the Virtual Machine IP address the same. The problem of these kinds of schemes is that flattening layer 2 is an expensive and complex process because it requires special routers and network configurations [11]. And [12] puts forward that reconfiguration costs plus the potential cost of new equipment makes this solution very costly for large cloud networks.

Another way analogizes network disconnection caused by migration among clouds with one in IP mobility. This is akin to problem caused by IP mobility because VM migrates between different physical devices within different networks in VM migration scenario while wireless device roams between different networks in IP mobility. Hence, in [12], they propose an architecture of Hypervisor controlled mobile IP to support live migration of virtual machine across networks. Besides, IP mobility solution is applied to solve network disconnection during migration. Hypervisor can be considered as the network attachment point to the VM. Therefore they apply hypervisor to act as network attachment point. In this solution, source hypervisor will register new VM with home agent before creating it. And when a VM migrates from one host to another, the network attachment point for the VM is also changed. Hence, destination hypervisor needs to send a request with updating information to register with home agent again. Additionally, Minxiong Wen [13] implements Proxy Mobile IP to solve the problem that VM could not communicate with correspondent nodes after it migrate from a subnet to another subnet in a like manner of [12]. They design registration and management module in foreign proxy to send a registration request when a VM migrates to foreign network. And the VM's home agent responses the foreign proxy to finish binding of the new address peer. And then home agent and foreign agent establish a new bi-directional tunnel to transfer packets for the VM. This kind of solution takes advantage of proxy mobile IP to realize VM migration without changing network configuration and it's transparent to migration VMs. However, such routing tunnels can result in triangle routing because foreign proxy intercepts and tunnels packets to home agent for VM and triangle route is often longer than optimal unicast path [15].

Additionally, there is one solution based on IP tunnel. Travostino [14] describes a solution to implement seamless live migration over wide-area network using IP tunnel. Dynamically configured IP tunnels allow connectivity from correspondent nodes to the virtual machine as it migrates across network. The IP tunnels are reconfigured with each migration event to retain layer-3 connectivity by maintaining the same IP address. This solution does not require VM to involve in the live migration process. But correspondent nodes must participate in the process. And if each correspondent node creates a tunnel on the host, the number of client that a VM can serve is greatly limited by the network tunnel resources consumed on the host, which is also a huge burden on the host itself [12].

The last way is to use dynamic DNS to redirect network connection. Authors in [15] propose an end-to-end approach for host mobility. They take advantage of the widely-deployed Domain Name System (DNS) [16] to locate mobile host's location, and propose a new migrate TCP option for connection migration. This migrate option contains a token representing a previously established connection between the same destination <address, port> peer. During migration, host may restart the previously established TCP connection using the token. And in [17], Bradford proposes an enhancement to Xen live migration. This approach combines IP tunnel with dynamic DNS to realize a temporary network redirection system which can reconfigure network configuration. The procedure establishes IP tunnel when VM is to be paused. Once migration is complete, this procedure dynamically updates DNS entries for services the VM provides while VM can respond at its new network location. Virtual machine uses two IP address after migration which can cause some problems. Firstly, source host can't free all resources used by the VM after migration, because it is responsible for forwarding the packets designated to the old address through tunnel. It is not mentioned for how long the source host should wait before it removes the tunnel, and what happens if some nodes still used the old address after the tunnel is removed [12].

Those four categories solve network disconnection problem during migration from different TCP/IP hierarchy. Solutions flattening 2 layer can provide transparent live migration, though it requires special routers and network configurations. Schemes based on proxy mobility IP or IP tunnel are easy to deploy, but it is also easy to cause triangle routing. Moreover, architectures based on dynamic DNS can preferably achieve live migration without network disconnection while the migration is visible to TCP or any other higher-layer sessions and has the same problem with IP tunnel, which is that we can't be sure when the tunnel is to be destroyed. In general, different methods have different advantages and disadvantages.

However, all of the solutions is under a premise that one of addresses between MAC and IP is fixedness. And MOOSE address is allocated based on location information, so it could happen that both of MAC and IP address change. Therefore, we propose a thoroughly VM migration scheme in data center based on MOOSE address.

3   An Approach Based on MOOSE Address

In our previous work, we propose a centralized management switch address allocation scheme based on MOOSE address. And host's MOOSE address is allocated by its direct-connected switch. Thus, when VM migrates from one switch to another switch, its MOOSE address changes based on switch it connects.

Therefore, in this section, we describe a migration scheme based on MOOSE address that can apply on our previous work. The approach this paper proposes can be divided into two situations based on location of target host. When source host and target host are in the same network segment, it only requires broadcast gratitude ARP for network reconnection because only MOOSE address changes. In another situation that source host and target host are in different network segment, both IP address and MOOSE address change. Hence, we choose to take advantage of DNS because of constancy of domain name. In this case, we not only need to send gratitude ARP but also need packet redirection and dynamically update DNS in a DNS sever. And the general procedure of migration is depicted in Fig. 1. And two situations mentioned above are described thoroughly in Sects. 3.1 and 3.2.

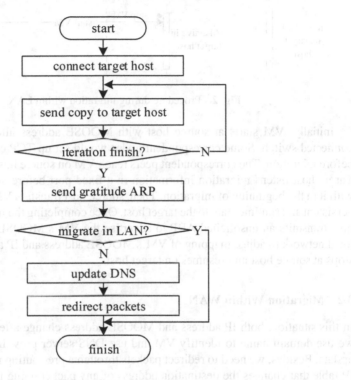

Fig. 1. General procedure

3.1 Migration Within LAN

In this situation, IP address stays the same while MOOSE address changes according to switch connected by target host. In order to bind IP address with the new MOOSE address, it is essential to update ARP table and corresponding ports of nods in network segment of source host. ARP table can be updated using Gratuitous ARP which brings no additional requirements to the VM and correspondent nodes. The procedure is depicted in Fig. 2.

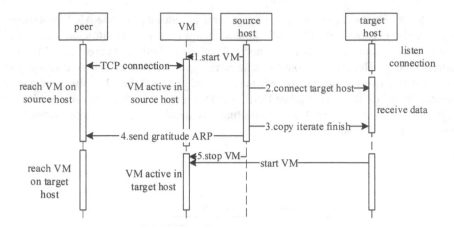

Fig. 2. Procedure during migration within LAN

Initially, VM starts at source host with MOOSE address allocated by its direct connected switch. Some correspondent nodes would set up TCP connection with VM before migration. The correspondent peers reach VM on source host during this period. Target host listens migration information in a fixed port before source host connects with it in the beginning of migration. Then, source host transfers VM's image and local persistent and runtime state to the target host. Once completing the final iteration, source host transmits an unsolicited ARP to advertise the VM's MOOSE and IP address for local network to adjust mapping of VM's MOOSE address and IP address. At last, VM stops at source host and resumes on target host.

3.2 Migration Within WAN

In this situation, both IP address and MOOSE address change after migration. Hence, we use domain name to identify VM and use DNS server providing dynamical DNS update. Besides, we need to redirect packets through a pre-routing rule to source host's IP table that changes the destination address of any packet going to the source VM to that of the destination VM. And then packets sent to source VM can be redirect to destination VM.

The whole migration procedure is shown in Fig. 3. Although former 3 steps is same with procedure in Fig. 2, it is noteworthy that gratitude ARP is not required sending to local network by source host since VM has been migrate to other network segment and IP address of VM doesn't remain the same IP address with address before migration. Additionally, target host should broadcast gratitude ARP to advertise the mapping of VM's MOOSE address and IP address. And in the meantime, VM needs to update its ARP cache after starting at target host. After stopping VM, source host trigger DSN server to update DNS and start a watchdog to monitor the old TCP connection while VM resumes at target host. In this period, correspondent peer reaches VM through source host. While all old connection is stopped, source host can stop redirecting packets.

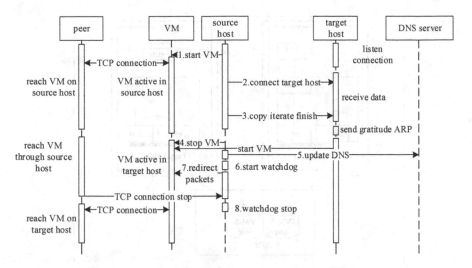

Fig. 3. Procedure during migration within WAN

4   Implementation and Performance

In this section, we evaluate the performance of the proposed migration scheme based on MOOSE address. To this end, we have implemented the solution based on the QEMU which is a generic and open source machine emulator and virtualizer. It realizes full-system emulation run operating systems for any machine, on any supported.

4.1   Emulation Setup

The implementation scenario can be described in Fig. 4.

Both source host and target host are physical connected together, and virtual machine uses bridged networking to communicate with outside world. And because we mainly focus on the virtual machine in the migration process of network connections, therefore, in order to apply the fast migration, we configure the NFS server in the network to store the virtual machine image file. The virtual machine will migrate from the source host to the target host in the emulation.

For the testing we used two hosts in the setup. Both hosts ran Ubuntu 14.04 and the version of QEMU emulator is 2.8.50. Table 1 shows some of specifications of these hosts. In the meantime, the VM being set up on source host were created with 1024 MB of RAM, 10 GB virtual disk allocated running Ubuntu. The migrated VM was provided with 1024 MB of RAM and was configured to use a single CPU. The VM used a 10 GB virtual disk allocated using NFS service with installation of Ubuntu and other essential software.

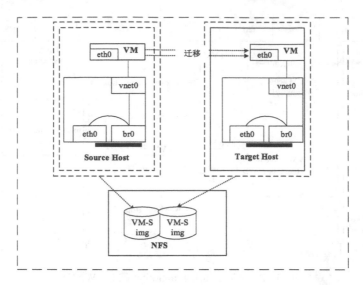

Fig. 4. Implementation scenario

Table 1. Host specification

	Source host	Target host
Operating System	Ubuntu 14.04	Ubuntu 14.04
Processor	Intel® Core™ i5	Intel® Core™ i5
Hard Drive	500 GB	150 GB
Total RAM	4 GB	4 GB
QEMU Emulator Version	2.8.50	2.8.50

In this experiment, we test the virtual machine migration process in several different performance metrics, including resolve times for total time, downtime, and network setup time along with network throughput and packet loss during the migration process. Among these indexes, total time is a time measured from beginning to end to complete the migration, and down time is a time difference between when VM being stopped on the source host and resumed at the target host. Network setup time is service response time observed by a client. At the same time, we use the ICMP packets to test packet loss.

4.2 Emulation Results Analysis

Initially, we evaluate several time metrics during migration. In Table 2, we present the comparison results of total time, downtime, and network setup time between the normal situation used MAC address and our migration scheme based on MOOSE address. The results show that the average total time is almost the same between the two schemes which indicates that our scheme does not affect the total migration time. Additionally, we observe that the down time of our scheme is only 0.3 s and network setup time is around 0.012 s while 0.2 s down time and 0.08 s setup time of default scheme in QEMU which can indicate that the disruption of break network connection is too small for clients to observe during migration. Subsequently, we evaluate the throughput in the network. The throughput in our scheme is slightly larger than that in default scheme of QEMU as presented in Table 2. Besides, throughput is mainly affected by the data transferred during the migration. In general, the throughput caused by our scheme is almost negligible.

Table 2. Average time and throughput

	Total time (milliseconds)	Down time (milliseconds)	Setup time (milliseconds)	Throughput (Mbps)
Default scheme	33034.5	260.5	8.5	94.2275
Our scheme	33642.75	355	12.5	94.14

Last, we measure packet loss number and ICMP response time in several times.

In Table 3, packets transmitted is average number of packets transmitted while packets loss is average number of packets without response. As showed in Table 3, our scheme only losses 1.2 packets in average when around 40 packets transmitted during migration procedure which indicate our scheme is acceptable and viable. And also we present sequence of response time when sending ICMP packets during one of the migration. We can see from Fig. 5 that response time of both default scheme in QEMU and our scheme is about 4 ms in the procedure of data copy iteration procedure. And after VM resumes at target host, the response time of several ICMP packets transferring subsequently in our scheme increase slightly about 4 ms, and this is because procedure of redirection is performed. And VM can be accessed quickly after this procedure.

Table 3. Average number of packets transmitted and loss

	Packets transmitted	Packets loss
Default scheme	38	0.2
Our scheme	40.6	1.2

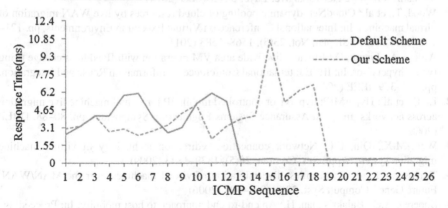

Fig. 5. Response Time of ICMP

5 Conclusion

In this paper, we have presented a migration scheme based on MOOSE address. We use gratitude ARP and update DNS dynamically to maintain network connection. We have implemented and tested the above solution. The proposed scheme can recovery network connection fast caused by migration without much effect of the transmission of other packets. In the meanwhile, a client can hardly feel the ongoing migration. Additionally, experimental results validate our scheme is a practical and effective way of achieving migrating VMs and recovering their network connections quickly. The performance degradation experienced by the VM is minimal. And the proposed scheme is viable, as confirmed by simulation results.

References

1. Mell, P., Grance, T.: The NIST definition of cloud computing. Commun. ACM **53**(6), 50 (2011)
2. Cloud_computing. https://en.wikipedia.org/wiki/Cloud_computing
3. Ren, Y., Dan, H.: KVM: Principles and Practices. China Machine Press, Beijing (2013)
4. Yu, F., Katz, R.H., Lakshman, T.V.: Efficient multimatch packet classification and lookup with TCAM. IEEE Micro **25**(1), 50–59 (2005)
5. Pagiamtzis, K., Sheikholeslami, A.: Content-addressable memory (CAM) circuits and architectures: a tutorial and survey. IEEE J. Solid-State Circuits **41**(3), 712–727 (2006)
6. Guideline for use of EUI. http://standards.ieee.org/develop/regauth/tut/eui64.pdf
7. Making Room for IEEE 802 Protocols in the Local Space. http://www.ieee802.org/1/files/public/docs2014/new-p802c-marks-LocalSpaceUse-1114.pdf
8. Scott, M., Moore, A., Crowcroft, J.: Addressing the Scalability of Ethernet with MOOSE. In: Dc Caves Workshop (2009)
9. Mahalingam, M., Dutt, D., Duda, K., Agarwal, P., Kreeger, L., Sridhar, T., Bursell, M., Wright, C.: Virtual eXtensible Local Area Network (VXLAN): A Framework for Overlaying Virtualized Layer 2 Networks over Layer 3 Networks (2014)
10. Wood, T., et al.: CloudNet: dynamic pooling of cloud resources by live WAN migration of virtual machines. In: International Conference on Virtual Execution Environments, pp. 121–132 (2011). ACM Sigplan Not. **23**(5), 1568–1583 (2015)
11. Ajila, S.A., Iyamu, O.: Efficient live wide area VM migration with IP address change using type II hypervisor. In: IEEE International Conference on Information Reuse and Integration, pp. 372–379. IEEE (2013)
12. Li, Q., et al.: HyperMIP: hypervisor controlled mobile IP for virtual machine live migration across networks. In: High Assurance Systems Engineering Symposium, pp. 80–88. DBLP (2008)
13. Wen, M.X., Qin, L.I.: Network connection redirection technology in virtual machine migration system. Appl. Res. Comput. **26**(5), 1839–1843 (2009)
14. Travostino, F., et al.: Seamless live migration of virtual machines over the MAN/WAN. Future Gener. Comput. Syst. **22**(8), 901–907 (2006)
15. Snoeren, A.C., Balakrishnan, H.: An end-to-end approach to host mobility. In: Proceedings of the 6th Annual International Conference on Mobile Computing and Networking, pp. 155–166. ACM (2001)

16. Mockapetris, P., Dunlap, K.J.: Development of the domain name system. In: Symposium Proceedings on Communications Architectures and Protocols, pp. 123–133. ACM (1988)
17. Bradford, R., et al.: Live wide-area migration of virtual machines including local persistent state. In: International Conference on Virtual Execution Environments, VEE 2007, San Diego, California, USA, pp. 169–179. DBLP, June 2007
18. Smith, T.F., Waterman, M.S.: Identification of common molecular subsequences. J. Mol. Biol. **147**, 195–197 (1981)
19. May, P., Ehrlich, H.-C., Steinke, T.: ZIB structure prediction pipeline: composing a complex biological workflow through web services. In: Nagel, W.E., Walter, W.V., Lehner, W. (eds.) Euro-Par 2006. LNCS, vol. 4128, pp. 1148–1158. Springer, Heidelberg (2006). doi: 10.1007/11823285_121
20. Foster, I., Kesselman, C.: The Grid: Blueprint for a New Computing Infrastructure. Morgan Kaufmann, San Francisco (1999)
21. Czajkowski, K., Fitzgerald, S., Foster, I., Kesselman, C.: Grid information services for distributed resource sharing. In: 10th IEEE International Symposium on High Performance Distributed Computing, pp. 181–184. IEEE Press, New York (2001)
22. Foster, I., Kesselman, C., Nick, J., Tuecke, S.: The Physiology of the Grid: an Open Grid Services Architecture for Distributed Systems Integration. Technical report, Global Grid Forum (2002)

Achieving Proof of Shared Ownership for the Shared File in Collaborative Cloud Applications

Yuanyuan Zhang[1], Jinbo Xiong[1,2(✉)], Mingwei Lin[2], Lili Wang[1], and Xuan Li[2]

[1] Faculty of Software, Fujian Normal University, Fuzhou, China
zyy837603010@163.com, jinbo810@163.com, wanglili_2004@163.com
[2] Fujian Engineering Research Center of Public Service Big Data Mining
and Application, Fuzhou, China
linmwcs@163.com, jessieli24@163.com

Abstract. Collaborative cloud applications are increasingly popular in our daily life, and generate plenty of cooperative files. The ownerships of these files are jointly shared by all participants. However, it is still a challenge to keep secure access and storage to those shared files, while ensuring the cloud storage efficiency. To tackle this problem, in this paper, we formalize a novel notion called Proof of Shared oWnership (PoSW), and propose a specific PoSW scheme to implement both secure ownership verification and data deduplication. In the PoSW scheme, we employ the convergent encryption algorithm to protect the content confidentiality of the shared file, introduce the secret file dispersal and secret sharing algorithm to implement the shared authorization and file ownership, and construct a novel interaction protocol between the file owners and the cloud server to verify the shared ownership and achieve deduplication to the shared file. Security analysis and performance evaluation show the security and efficiency of the proposed scheme.

Keywords: Proof of Shared Ownership · Secure deduplication · Shared file · Privacy protection · Collaborative cloud application

1 Introduction

Nowadays, collaborative cloud applications are increasingly popular in our daily life [19], e.g., a new technical white paper cooperatively written by scholars coming from different research institutions, a joint medical record co-signed by different doctors, a project contract co-signed by different participants, etc. These *cooperative files*, obviously, are different from a general file only owned by an individual user, have *shared ownership* belonging to all participants. To protect the security and the privacy of these *shared files*, the basic idea is to encrypt these files before outsourcing them to the cloud [20,21]. However, how to effectively access, store and manage these large-scale encrypted shared files still remains a big challenge in cloud [13,16].

In order to improve the storage efficiency, existing cloud service providers, e.g., Dropbox, Google Drive, always adopt positive storage efficiency solutions

X. Sun et al. (Eds.): ICCCS 2017, Part I, LNCS 10602, pp. 262–274, 2017.
https://doi.org/10.1007/978-3-319-68505-2_23

for user's outsourcing data [5,6]. Data deduplication [9,22], as a matter of fact, is a desirable technique to store duplicate cloud data outsourced by different users only once, thus greatly saves storage space and bandwidth overheads [11]. Harnik *et al.* [9] categorized data deduplication strategies into the file-level deduplication [1] and the block-level deduplication [3] according to the basic data unit they handled. The architectures of existing deduplication schemes can be divided into the target-based approach (or server-side deduplication) and the source-based approach (or client-side deduplication) [22]. The source-based approaches are carried out based on the convergent encryption (CE) algorithm [18] and message-lock encryption (MLE) algorithm [3]. However, the pattern that the same plaintext is able to generate the same ciphertext will be destroyed after performing data encryption using any semantic security encryption algorithm. Jiang *et al.* [10] focused on ciphertext deduplication by adding additional randomness to some certain ciphertext. Recent studies for secure data deduplication (e.g., [12,15,22]) showed that cross-user data deduplication can save storage overheads by more than 50% in the standard file systems, and even as high as 90–95% for the general back-up applications.

Despite of these advantages, data deduplication may arise some serious privacy concerns and pose a new security challenge, such as the side-channel attacks [9]. In order to resist against above attack, Halevi *et al.* [8] introduced the notion of proof of ownership (PoW), which is used in the cloud server to verify that a user who indeed owns a particular file. To improve the efficiency of PoW, Pietro *et al.* [4] proposed a s-PoW scheme, which is an enhanced PoW [8] with adding some particular random bits to the requested file. Blasco *et al.* [2] proposed a bf-PoW scheme, which is based on the bloom filter to improve the query efficiency of cloud server. Gonzalez-Manzano *et al.* [7] proposed a ce-PoW scheme based on the CE algorithm [18] and highlighted the efficiency and feasibility.

However, existing cloud applications and data deduplication schemes [2,4] still retain the file with an *individual ownership*, where each proving file uploaded by user's client is owned by an individual user, who can *unilaterally* set up access control policies to decide whether to grant permission to any access request to that file, rather than owned by all the cooperative participants. Soriente *et al.* [17] defined a notion of *shared ownership* and proposed a new access control solution named Commune to secure access the shared file. But it does not provide a proof approach to make the cloud server assure that a threshold of owners indeed own the archived shared file for secure access and deduplication.

Furthermore, the existing approaches always ignore some vital factors: (*i*) one owner unilaterally processing the shared file may result in the problem of privilege abuse; (*ii*) one owner may not be willing to represent all of the other owners to do some access control decisions; (*iii*) current methods did not consider secure deduplication for the shared files, which is a key technology to improve the storage efficiency and reduce the communication overhead.

To tackle the above problems, in this paper, we present a notion called Proof of Shared oWnership (PoSW), a novel proposal that achieves secure access and deduplication for the shared files in the cloud computing environment, which is resilient to the cloud servers and the side-channel attacks based on the CE algorithm [18], secret file dispersal [17] and secret sharing [21]. To the best of our knowledge, PoSW is the first solution to simultaneously address secure ownership verification and data deduplication for the shared files in collaborative cloud applications. The contributions of this paper are shown as follows:

- We describe a novel data deduplication problem for the shared file in collaborative cloud application, and give a formal definition of the PoSW. Furthermore, we propose a specific PoSW scheme, which employs the secret file dispersal to encode the shared file into blocks, uses the secret sharing algorithm to share the convergent key to all the shared owners, and constructs a novel challenge-response interaction protocol between the shared owners and the cloud server. Moreover, one owner is able to prove the shared ownership of the shared file to implement secure deduplication.
- The security analysis makes it clear that the proposed PoSW scheme is secure under the adversary model without requiring complex key management. The performance evaluation indicates that the computational cost of the proposed scheme is trivial and acceptable.

Organizations. The rest of the paper is organized as follows: Sect. 2 introduces some preliminaries in our work. Section 3 gives an elaborate description of the proof of shared ownership. Section 4 shows the security analysis of the proposed scheme. Section 5 demonstrates the performance analysis and evaluation of the PoSW scheme. Finally, we draw the conclusion in Sect. 6.

2   Preliminaries

In this section, we first introduce some notations and descriptions of the proposed PoSW scheme, which are shown in Table 1, and then give some basic cryptographic tools used in PoSW.

2.1   Secret File Dispersal

Secret file dispersal enables encoding a file into n blocks, and any t blocks (where $t \leq n$) are sufficient to decode the file [17], and any user with fewer than t blocks does not obtain any meaningful information about the original file. It contains the following two algorithms in our schemes.

$\{c_1, c_2, ..., c_n\} \leftarrow SF.Encode(t, n, f, k, \lambda)$. Encode a file f into n blocks, where k represents an encryption key and λ is the security parameter.

$f' \leftarrow SF.Combine(k, C, \lambda)$. Take the encryption key k, a set of blocks C, and the security parameter λ as input, and outputs a file f'. If $C \subseteq \{c_1, c_2, ..., c_n\}$ and $|C| \geq t$, then $f' = f$.

Table 1. Notations and descriptions

Notations	Descriptions
$f[i]$	The i-th block of a shared file f
k_i	The convergent key of a block $f[i]$, $k_i = H_2(f[i])$
$id[i]$	The i-th owner's identity id
$eid[i]$	The hash value of $id[i]$, $eid[i] = H_3(id[i])$
$token$	$token[i] \leftarrow H_2(E_{H_2(f[i])} f[i])$
h_f	$h_f \leftarrow H_1(token)$, the digest of the shared file
SO_j	The j-th shared owner
H_1	A cryptographic hash function, $\{0,1\}^* \rightarrow \{0,1\}^\varepsilon$, ε is a positive integer
H_2	A cryptographic hash function, $\{0,1\}^b \rightarrow \{0,1\}^l$, b and l represent the block size and the token size
H_3	A cryptographic hash function, $\{0,1\}^q \rightarrow \{0,1\}^m$, q and m represent the owner's and the encrypted id size

2.2 Secret Sharing

Secret sharing scheme includes two algorithms: *Share* and *Recover* [21]. A secret is firstly divided and shared by using *Share*, and then the secret can be recovered by using *Recover* if it is not less than the threshold shares. The two algorithms are defined as follows in our schemes.

$\{s_1, s_2, ..., s_n\} \leftarrow SF.Share(s, t, n)$. Divide a secret s into n shares of the same size using erasure code.

$s' \leftarrow SF.Recover(\{s_1, s_2, ..., s_r\})$. Input any r out of n shares and then outputs s'. If $r \geq t$, then $s' = s$.

3 Proof of Shared Ownership

3.1 Formal Description

Proof-of-shared-ownership (PoSW) is an interactive protocol between the cloud server and the shared owners on a joint input S_t (which is the input token of a shared file). At first, the verifier (cloud server) summarizes to itself the input S_t and generates a verification information *ver*. Thereafter, the prover (one of the shared owners) and the verifier engage in an interactive protocol where the prover has S_t and the verifier only has *ver*. Finally, the verifier either accepts or rejects. Remarkably, to obtain S_t, the requester (the prover) must request other pieces of the shared files from the senders (other shared owners). Hence, PoSW is specified by a summary function $F_S(\cdot)$ (which could be randomized and takes S_t and the security parameter λ as input), a function $F_V(\cdot)$ (which could be randomized and takes the shared owner's id and the security parameter γ as input), an interactive two-party protocol $\mathfrak{B}(Pr \leftrightarrow Ve)$ and an interactive multi-party protocol $\mathfrak{H}(Re \leftrightarrow Se)$, where Pr represents the prover, Ve represents the verifier, Re represents the requester, Se represents the multiple senders.

Validity. The scheme $SP = (F_S, \mathfrak{B})$ is valid if (a) F_S and $\mathfrak{B}$ are efficient, (b) for every input $id \in \{0,1\}^\gamma$ and every value of the security parameter γ, it holds that $\mathfrak{H}(Re(id, 1^\gamma) \leftrightarrow Se(F_V(id, 1^\gamma))) \Rightarrow$ token S_t with all but negligible probability in γ, (c) for every input $S_t \in \{0,1\}^\lambda$ and every value of the security parameter λ, it holds that $\mathfrak{B}(Pr(S_t, 1^\lambda) \leftrightarrow Ve(F_S(S_t, 1^\lambda))) \Rightarrow accept$ with all but negligible probability in λ.

Efficiency. The main efficiency parameters of PoSW are (a) the size of the summary information $ver = F_S(S_t, 1^\lambda)$, (b) the communication complexity of the protocols $\mathfrak{B}$ and $\mathfrak{H}$, and (c) the computation complexity of computing the function F_S and the two parties in $\mathfrak{B}$ and the participants in $\mathfrak{H}$ (all with respect to the size of S_t and the security parameter λ). In our solutions, the computation complexity of F_S and Pr grows linearly with the size of S_t, and the computation complexity of $\mathfrak{B}$ grows linearly with the number of the shared owners. Therefore, the proposed PoSW scheme is effective.

3.2 System Model

In this paper, the system model of the PoSW scheme involves a shared file creator, several shared owners and a cloud server.

The shared file creator is responsible for creating a shared file, calculating and distributing all of the key shares and token shares, and is also a special shared owner. One shared owner wants to securely access to a shared file requiring the access permissions from at least $t - 1$ other owners, and also needs these permissions to challenge to the cloud server to prove that he indeed has shared ownership of the shared file. Cloud server is responsible for creating a shared cloud repository, storing the shared files and establishing an associative array for each shared file to implement the processes of the PoSW challenge-response interactions.

3.3 Adversary Model and Design Goal

We assume that the cloud server is a "honest-but-curious" server [14,21]. The shared file creator is trusted in the PoSW system, and the other shared owners are "honest-but-curious" to the shared file, they should honestly operate the PoSW protocol, and may also utilize the limited key share and token share to collude with malicious users in attempt to obtain useful sensitive information.

Based on the above assumptions, malicious users are considered in the PoSW scheme, as users who may try to access the shared file even if fewer than t shared owners have granted the corresponding permissions. The malicious users may also collude with the cloud server to attempt to extract some useful sensitive information from the shared files.

Our main design goals are that: the probability that a malicious user runs a successful PoSW protocol must be negligible under the security parameter; and the cloud server and malicious users know nothing about sensitive information in the shared files.

3.4   Construction of the PoSW Scheme

The proposed PoSW scheme includes the following four phases, as shown in Fig. 1.

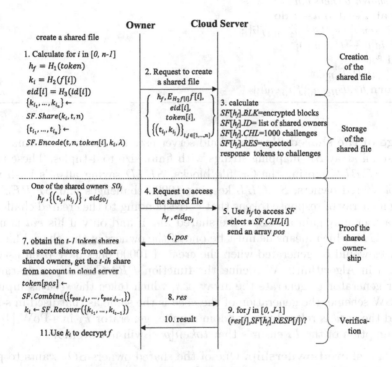

Fig. 1. The proposed PoSW scheme

Creation of the shared file. In our PoSW scheme, the "Creation of shared file" phase requires a trusted creator selecting from the shared owners [17]. Before uploading the shared file to the shared cloud repository, the creator need to divide the file into n blocks of same size and calculate the H_2 over $f[i]$ in order to get a convergent key. Furthermore, the creator gets a token array and run H_1 over the token array to obtain h_f, as shown in Algorithm 1. For each block $f[i]$, the creator runs the function $\{k_{i_1}, k_{i_2}, ..., k_{i_n}\} \leftarrow SF.Share(k_i, t, n)$ to produce n shares of the shared secret k_i, and runs $\{t_{i_1}, t_{i_2}, ..., t_{i_n}\} \leftarrow SF.Encode(t, n, token[i], k_i, \lambda)$ to obtain n shares of the $token[i]$. For one of the shared owners SO_j, the creator uploads a binary group $\{(t_{i_j}, k_{i_j})\}$ to SO_j's account in the cloud server. Moreover, each shared owner receives one piece of the *token*, and then calculates the digest value $eid[i]$ using H_3 over his own identity id, that is $eid[i] = H_3(id[i])$. Then the creator sends $\{h_f, E_{H_2(f[i])}f[i], eid[i], token[i], \{(t_{i_j}, k_{i_j})\}_{i,j \in [1,...,n]}\}$ to the cloud server for requesting to create the shared file.

Algorithm 1. Client-side: create a shared file

---

input: *the number of tokens n, a shared file f, the identity of all shared owners id*
output: *the hash value h_f, the encrypted file blocks $E_{H_2(f[i])}f[i]$, and encrypted id of the shared owners $eid[i]$*
  1: **for all** $i \leftarrow 0$ to $n - 1$ **do**
  2:    $token[i] \leftarrow H_2(E_{H_2(f[i])}f[i])$;
  3:    $eid[i] \leftarrow H_3(id[i])$;
  4: **end for**
  5: $h_f \leftarrow H_1(token)$;
  6: **return** $h_f, E_{H_2(f[i])}f[i], eid[i]$

Storage of the shared file. The cloud server uses the received information to establish an array SF mapping strings with finite size to 4-tuples. These tuples contain $SF.BLK$ storing the CE file blocks, $SF.ID$ saving all id's hash value $eid[i]$ of shared owners, $SF.CHL$ keeping 10000 challenges and $SF.RES$ containing an array of response tokens that corresponding to the created challenges. When a user may gain access to the shared file, if and only if his eid is in the array $SF.ID$, which means he must be one of the owners of this shared file, new challenges would be generated when the created 10000 ones have been used up, as shown in Algorithm 2. We define the function $PRNG$ as a pseudo-random number generator to generate the array pos, which takes the *seed* as input. In the PoSW scheme, the generation of the *seed* is the same as that used in s-PoW [4]. And the *seed* is related to a random number generator F_s in s-PoW [4], and the assumption of the F_s ensures that $token[pos]$ will not overflow.

Proof the shared ownership. One of the shared owners SO_j wants to prove that he indeed has the ownership of the shared file. Firstly, SO_j sends the $\{h_f, eid_{SO_j}\}$ to the cloud server. If h_f is found in SF, the cloud server seeks the array SF for an unused array pos of length J and the corresponding responses, then replies the challenge to this shared owner SO_j. Secondly, after receiving the pos, SO_j obtains the $t-1$ shares of the *token* from other shared owners, and gets the t-th shares from his account in the cloud server. We assume that the process of getting the permission from other shared owners is in a specific environment and has a little impact on computational overhead. Finally, according to the received pos, SO_j runs $token[pos] \leftarrow SF.Combine(\{t_{pos,j_1}, t_{pos,j_2}, ..., t_{pos,j_t}\})$ to produce res of the challenge and runs $k_i \leftarrow SF.Recover(\{k_{i_1}, k_{i_2}, ..., k_{i_t}\})$ to get the convergent key, then sends the $token[pos]$ as the res to the cloud server.

Verification. The cloud server receives the array of res and runs the function $Match$ to check if it matches the array of response *token* that the server sought

---

Algorithm 2. Server-side: the server creates an array SF for a shared file.

input: h_f, $blk[i] = E_{H_2(f[i])}f[i], eid[i]$
output: *the array* $SF[h_f]$
1: **for** $i \leftarrow 0$ to $n-1$ **do**
2:     Calculate *token* from encrypted blocks $blk[i]$;
3:     $token[i] \leftarrow H_2(blk[i])$;
4:     $eid[i] \leftarrow H_3(id[i])$;
5: **end for**
6: **for** $i \leftarrow 0$ to 9999 **do**
7:     **for** $j \leftarrow 0$ to $J-1$ **do**
8:         $pos[j] \leftarrow PRNG(seed)$;
9:         $chl[i,j] \leftarrow pos[j]$;
10:         $res[i,j] \leftarrow token[pos[j]]$;
11:     **end for**
12: **end for**
13: $SF[h_f].BLK \leftarrow blk$;
14: $SF[h_f].ID \leftarrow eid$;
15: $SF[h_f].CHL \leftarrow chl$;
16: $SF[h_f].RES \leftarrow res$; **return** $SF[h_f]$

Algorithm 3. Server-side: verification.

input: h_f *of the shared file* f, *an array res that is the client response tokens, and an array response that is the server preset response*
output: *the result of the challenge*
1: **for** $j \leftarrow 0$ to $J-1$ **do**
2:     **if** Match($res[j]$, $SF[h_f].RES[-,j]$); **then**
3: **return** true;
4:     **end if**
5: **end for**
6: **return** false

---

before. If successful, then SO_j passes the PoSW protocol and the cloud server will assign $SF[h_f].BLK[j]$ to him. Otherwise, SO_j fails, as shown in Algorithm 3.

If the verification is valid, the cloud server will return the ciphertext to the shared owner SO_j (the requester), then SO_j can use the recovered k_i to decrypt the ciphertext.

3.5   Deduplication Implementation

When one of the shared owners wants to store or access a shared file stored in the cloud server, firstly, he will send $\{h_f, eid_{SO_j}\}$ to the cloud server. The server will check whether the metadata of the shared file has been stored in the array SF. If h_f is not stored in SF, that means, the shared file is not archived in the cloud server. The server will ask the owner to upload this shared file. Otherwise, if h_f is found in SF, then the owner must enforce to process the "Proof the shared ownership" phase to interact with the cloud server to prove that he indeed has the ownership of the shared file. Therefore, the shared file deduplication is implemented without storing the shared file again.

4   Security Analysis

The security of PoSW depends on the information theoretical assumption that was created in s-PoW [4] and Commune [17], and assumed in bf-PoW [2]. Given a shared file, the main goal of an adversary is to pass the PoSW challenge without possessing the entire shared file [7]. PoSW is not designed for the adversary that makes the legitimate shared owner as a real-time Oracle to get the right responses to the PoSW challenges. However, in order to model the PoSW interaction, the adversary may collude with some malicious users, who may obtain some sensitive information from the shared file via public channels. According to the adversary model in Sect. 3.3, they can obtain fewer than t permissions granted by the shared owners to access the shared file. While in the "Proof the shared ownership" phase, if the adversary obtains less than t shares of the token, he neither run the *SF.Combine* to get *token[pos]* and *SF.Recover* to get k_i, nor obtain the correct response to the PoSW challenge. Therefore, our algorithms share the tokens and ensure that the coalition is impossible.

   In addition, we assume that the probability of the adversary knowing the target shared file is p, that means for a block $f[i]$ of size b, p means the probability of the adversary knowing a byte of the block $f[i]$ at a randomly chosen position, and also assume that if the adversary does not possess a particular byte of the shared file, he will be able to guess it with probability g. In the "Proof the shared ownership" phase, the adversary can obtain J tokens randomly, each of which is divided into n shares through secret sharing. Therefore, the adversary must obtain at least t shares to decode the correct token. Furthermore, the adversary gets a random challenge array, then we define $token_i$ as the event that adversary obtains i-th block $f[i]$ correctly, ω as the event that adversary knows a block $f[i]$ with probability p. After obtaining the $f[i]$, the adversary can run hash operation to get the corresponding token, if the adversary cannot know the whole $f[i]$ and their knowledge on file block is independent, then the probability that the adversary guessing other y unknown bytes is g^y. In other words, adversary can guess the token with length l directly, each bit is either 0 or 1, therefore, the probability of each byte being guessed is 0.5. Therefore, for a specific token, the probability of a correct guess is 0.5^l. Because l is far less than the length of file block, the probability of a direct guess is far less than the probability of obtaining file block, that is $g^y \ll 0.5^l$. Through the analysis above, the probability that the adversary obtaining a token can be described as:

$$P(token_i) = P(token_i \cap (\omega_i \cup \overline{\omega_i}))$$
$$= P(token_i \mid \omega_i)P(\omega_i) + P(token_i \mid \overline{\omega_i})P(\overline{\omega_i})$$
$$= p + 0.5^l(1 - p). \tag{1}$$

For J random independent blocks, we have:

$$P(token) = P(token_i)^J$$
$$= (p + 0.5^l(1-p))^J. \tag{2}$$

We set up the security parameter λ to derive a lower bound for J based on s-PoW [4], that is $P(token) \leq 2^\lambda$, as:

$$J \geq \lambda ln2/(1-p)(1-0.5^l). \tag{3}$$

According to the Eqs. (2) and (3), we can know that J is independent of the length of the shared file. Therefore, it can meet the security requirement of the PoSW scheme described in Sect. 3.3.

5   Performance Analysis and Evaluation

5.1   Complexity Analysis

About the computational complexity of our proposed scheme, we consider the computational cost and I/O requirements of both the shared owner's client and the cloud server, and compare our PoSW scheme with the-state-of-the-art solutions in Table 2.

Table 2. Computational complexity analysis and comparison

Scheme	Client compu.	Client I/O	Server init compu.	Server regular compu.	Server init I/O	Server memory usage
s-PoW [4]	$O(f_s) \cdot h$	$O(f_s)$	$O(f_s) \cdot h$	$O(n \cdot \lambda) \cdot PRF$	$O(f_s)$	$O(n \cdot \lambda)$
ce-PoW [7]	$O(b) \cdot CE \cdot h \cdot h$	$O(f_s)$	$O(b) \cdot h \cdot h$	$O(n \cdot l \cdot \lambda) \cdot PRNG$	$O(f_s)$	$O(n \cdot l \cdot \lambda)$
PoSW	$O(b) \cdot CE \cdot h \cdot h \cdot \psi$	$O(f_s)$	$O(b) \cdot h$	$O(n \cdot l \cdot \lambda) \cdot PRNG$	$O(f_s)$	$O(n \cdot l \cdot \lambda)$

Notes: f_s represents the size of the shared file; λ rep. the security parameter; h rep. the hash operation; n rep. the number of $tokens$; l rep. the $token$ size; b rep. the block size; ψ rep. the operations of $Encode$ and $Share$ or $Combine$ and $Recover$.

In order to make the results more intuitive, we assume the hash functions (H_1, H_2, H_3) have the same computational cost. From Table 2, on the server-side, ce-PoW and our scheme divide the file into n blocks, therefore, the unit of data processing is the file block. In terms of the server-side and bandwidth, the computational cost of s-PoW scheme is less than that of others. Compared with the other schemes, our scheme involves more complexity in computation, which is the balance between security and efficiency.

5.2   Performance Measurements

We measure the computational cost of the PoSW scheme by using the OpenSSL library for cryptographic operations. Particularly, we employ the AES-256 and the SHA-256 for symmetric encryption and hash algorithms. Our scheme uses C++ language on Linux system. Our test computer has the following configurations: CPU: Intel Core i5-4590 3.30 GHz; RAM: DDR3 8 GB; Hard disk: WDC (1 TB/7200 r/min); and OS: Ubuntu 12.04.4 LTS.

We measure the computational cost of the four phases respectively in terms of the running times of the basic cryptographic operations. All of the calculations run 200 times to get the average value. In our simulation experiments, we choose eight shared files with different size. The symmetric encryption algorithm is the standard AES algorithm with 256 bits, and Hash algorithm is with 256 bits. The measurement result is shown in Fig. 2.

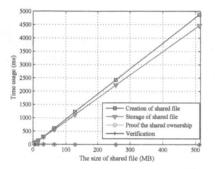

Fig. 2. Computational cost with different file size

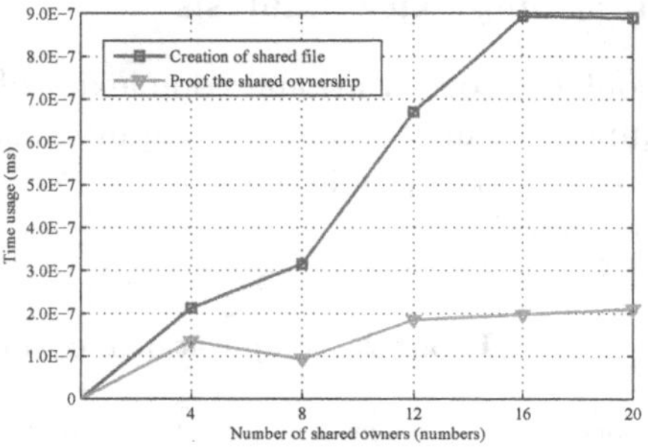

Fig. 3. Computational cost with different shared owners

It can be seen from the complexity analysis that the computational cost of the first phase is close to that of the second phase. Therefore, the two curves are almost overlap together. In the third phase, the owner's client just runs J times $SF.Combine$ and one time $SF.Recover$. In the fourth phase, the owner's client only runs one time AES decryption algorithm. Consequently, the computational cost of above two phases is not related to the size of the shared file.

We also measure the computational cost with different numbers of the shared owners in the "Creation of the shared file" phases and "Proof the shared ownership" phases, as shown in Fig. 3. Because the number of the shared owners is different, the same shared files need to be divided into different blocks, in order to prevent the block size affecting the accuracy of experimental data, we use 2 MB as the block size. All of the calculations run 200 times to get the average value. From Fig. 3, it can be seen that the computational cost of these two phases grows with the number of the shared owners increases. When the number of the shared owners goes up to 20, the encoding time for a single file block in the "Creation of the shared file" phase is about 0.9 ms, which is highly efficient.

6   Conclusion

This paper formalized the notion of proof of shared ownership (PoSW), and presented a special PoSW scheme, which is a secure protocol for the cooperative files in collaborative cloud applications. The proposed PoSW scheme can verify whether one of the owners indeed owns the shared file. Moreover, we employed convergent encryption, secret file dispersal and secret sharing scheme to avoid the possible attacks and to implement secure deduplication to the shared files in collaborative cloud applications. Security analysis and performance evaluation confirm the security and efficiency of the proposed scheme.

Acknowledgments. This work is supported by the National Natural Science Foundation of China (61402109, 61370078, 61502102 and 61502103); Natural Science Foundation of Fujian Province (2015J05120, 2016J05149, 2017J01737 and 2017J05099); Fujian Provincial Key Laboratory of Network Security and Cryptology Research Fund (Fujian Normal University) (15008); Distinguished Young Scientific Research Talents Plan in Universities of Fujian Province (2015, 2017).

References

1. Bellare, M., Keelveedhi, S., Ristenpart, T.: Message-locked encryption and secure deduplication. In: Johansson, T., Nguyen, P.Q. (eds.) EUROCRYPT 2013. LNCS, vol. 7881, pp. 296–312. Springer, Heidelberg (2013). doi:10.1007/978-3-642-38348-9_18
2. Blasco, J., Di Pietro, R., Orfila, A., et al.: A tunable proof of ownership scheme for deduplication using bloom filters. In: IEEE CNS, pp. 481–489. IEEE (2014)
3. Chen, R., Mu, Y., Yang, G., et al.: Bl-mle: Block-level message-locked encryption for secure large file deduplication. IEEE TIFS **10**(12), 2643–2652 (2015)
4. Di Pietro, R., Sorniotti, A.: Boosting efficiency and security in proof of ownership for deduplication. In: ACM CCS, pp. 81–82. ACM (2012)
5. Fu, Z., Huang, F., Sun, X., et al.: Enabling semantic search based on conceptual graphs over encrypted outsourced data. In: IEEE TSC (2016)
6. Fu, Z., Wu, X., Guan, C., et al.: Toward efficient multi-keyword fuzzy search over encrypted outsourced data with accuracy improvement. IEEE TIFS **11**(12), 2706–2716 (2016)
7. González-Manzano, L., Orfila, A.: An efficient confidentiality-preserving proof of ownership for deduplication. JNCA **50**, 49–59 (2015)
8. Halevi, S., Harnik, D., Pinkas, B., et al.: Proofs of ownership in remote storage systems. In: ACM CCS, pp. 491–500. ACM (2011)
9. Harnik, D., Pinkas, B., Shulman-Peleg, A.: Side channels in cloud services: deduplication in cloud storage. IEEE S&P **8**(6), 40–47 (2010)
10. Jiang, T., Chen, X., Wu, Q., et al.: Secure and efficient cloud data deduplication with randomized tag. IEEE TIFS **PP**(99), 1 (2016)
11. Li, J., Li, J., Xie, D., et al.: Secure auditing and deduplicating data in cloud. IEEE TC **65**(8), 2386–2396 (2016)
12. Li, J., Qin, C., Lee, P.P.C., et al.: Information leakage in encrypted deduplication via frequency analysis. In: IEEE/IFIP DSN (2017)
13. Li, Q., Ma, J., Li, R., et al.: Large universe decentralized key-policy attribute-based encryption. SCN **8**(3), 501–509 (2015)

14. Li, Q., Ma, J., Li, R., et al.: Provably secure unbounded multi-authority ciphertext-policy attribute-based encryption. SCN **8**(18), 4098–4109 (2015)
15. Liu, J., Asokan, N., Pinkas, B.: Secure deduplication of encrypted data without additional independent servers. In: ACM CCS, pp. 874–885. ACM (2015)
16. Liu, Q., Cai, W., Shen, J., et al.: A speculative approach to spatial-temporal efficiency with multi-objective optimization in a heterogeneous cloud environment. SCN **9**(17), 4002–4012 (2016)
17. Soriente, C., Karame, G.O., Ritzdorf, H., et al.: Commune: shared ownership in an agnostic cloud. In: ACM SACMAT, pp. 39–50. ACM (2015)
18. Storer, M.W., Greenan, K., Long, D.D., et al.: Secure data deduplication. In: ACM IWSS, pp. 1–10. ACM (2008)
19. Tang, B., Sandhu, R., Li, Q.: Multi-tenancy authorization models for collaborative cloud services. CCPE **27**(11), 2851–2868 (2015)
20. Wu, D., Yang, B., Wang, H., et al.: Privacy-preserving multimedia big data aggregation in large-scale wireless sensor networks. ACM TMCCA **12**(4), 60:1–60:19 (2016)
21. Xiong, J., Li, F., Ma, J., et al.: A full lifecycle privacy protection scheme for sensitive data in cloud computing. P2PNA **8**(6), 1025–1037 (2015)
22. Xiong, J., Zhang, Y., Li, F., et al.: Research progress on secure data deduplication in cloud. J. Commun. **37**(11), 169–180 (2016)

Design and Test of the Intelligent Rubber Tapping Technology Evaluation Equipment Based on Cloud Model

Jieren Cheng[1,2], Kuanqi Cai[3], Boyi Liu[1(✉)], and Xiangyan Tang[1]

[1] College of Information Science and Technology,
Hainan University, Haikou 570228, China
cjr22@163.com, liuboyilby@163.com, Tangxy36@163.com
[2] State Key Laboratory of Marine Resource Utilization in South China Sea,
Hainan University, Haikou 570228, China
[3] Mechanical and Electrical Engineering College,
Hainan University, Haikou 570228, China

Abstract. The level of rubber workers' tapping technology is the key to the impact of rubber production. Accurate rubber tapping level evaluation plays an important role in improving the level of rubber tapping teams and rubber production. We have designed and implemented an intelligent-tapping-technology learning system based on the cloud model. This paper introduces the mechanical structure of the intelligent-tapping-technology learning instrument. To evaluate the level of rubber tapping, the system combines the Delphi method and the gray correlation to determine the 10 evaluation. By using entropy weight method, the system obtains rubber tapping level quantitative function, and through combining with the inverse cloud generator, it transforms the score into the qualitative evaluation of the level of tapping. At last, it uses the k-means clustering method to determine the center points of different tapping level and completes the classification of tapping level by minimizing the European distance. The experimental results show that the accuracy of the rubber tapping level evaluation by model-based intelligent tapping technology auxiliary learning system is higher than 90%, and time cost of the real-time update performance is less than 3 s. The system is conducive to the rubber workers to improve the level of tapping, thereby advancing the rubber production and therefore it can be used and further promoted.

Keywords: Tapping gray · Relational degree · Entropy weight method · Cloud model · Learning instrument

1 Introduction

Rubber [1] is an important industrial raw material, which is important in economic construction. Because of its irreplaceability and renewable nature, the rubber industry has become an important part of the tropical countries and regional economy [2, 3]. Rubber tapping is very important in the rubber production process, and the degree of mastery of rubber workers' tapping technology determines the rubber yield during the tapping process. It is difficult for new rubber workers to master tapping technology in a

© Springer International Publishing AG 2017
X. Sun et al. (Eds.): ICCCS 2017, Part I, LNCS 10602, pp. 275–287, 2017.
https://doi.org/10.1007/978-3-319-68505-2_24

short time, which decreases the production of rubber trees even with no rubber, seriously affecting the development of rubber industry. To solve this problem, we have designed and implemented a tapping technology auxiliary learning instrument for real-time evaluation of rubber tapping technology to help beginners grasp the tapping technology quickly.

2   Research Status

At present, with the development of big data [4–9], cloud computing [10] and the base of more mature wisdom agriculture now. More and more wisdom agricultural equipment was invented, and put into various fields of agriculture, to solve the high cost of human work. Such as agricultural robot of disease control [11], quadruped wheel robot for wheat precision seeding [12] and so on. In this paper, the rubber industry is one of the important basic industries of the national economy, it also has a lot of issues, most important of all is tapping technology is difficult to grasp. After that we design an intelligent rubber tapping technology evaluation equipment based on cloud model

3   Overall Structure and Working Principle

3.1   Overall Organization

As shown in Fig. 1, the intelligent tapping technology auxiliary learning instrument is mainly composed of intelligent auxiliary learning module and tapping module. The tapping module includes the main body of the cutting knife, and the intelligent module consists of a display screen, a temperature and humidity detection device, a lighting

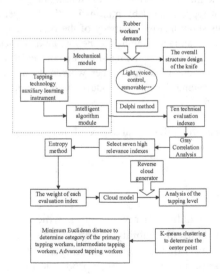

Fig. 1. Intelligent tapping technology auxiliary learning instrument machine structure and working principle diagram.

system, a detachable device, a sensor module and the internal Arduino Mega 2560 development board.

3.2   Working Principle and Technical Parameters

Combine the intelligent auxiliary learning module and the ordinary tapping knife before using, and adjust the position of the displacement sensor head ball. The worker starts the button to start working. After hearing the rear sound output device sending the MP3 tone, the screen lights up, and the sensor will send the collected data to the development board. After processing the data, the development board shows the time, temperature, humidity, the thickness of rubber which had been cut, the thickness of rubber which still needed to be cut and the score information of the worker on the screen. Then the worker only need to speak "lights" to open the LED lights. The worker should make the head ball of the displacement sensor close to the bark, and pay attention to whether the displacement sensor is parallel to the cutting knife at the beginning of the cutting. The knife cut rubber into the trunk, and the spring receives the rubber tree skin's block and compress, because the amount of compression is equal to the degree of thickness cut, and the instantaneous tapping thickness is obtained indirectly then reflected in the display screen in real time. At the same time, the machine can record the thickness in memory, evaluate it and give the opinion through the algorithm in the Arduino Mega 2560 development board, providing the visualization data for next time tapping. The sound output device will give the evaluation score to the worker to promote the growth of the level of the tapping technology, which achieves learning. When the body sensor through the microwave monitors that the rubber worker rest away from the cutter, the sensor will pass the signal to the Arduino Mega 2560 development board to control the cutting knife standby and achieve the purpose of saving energy. When the level of tapping meets the requirements, the learning module can be removed through the L-shaped sleeve, and the L-shaped sleeve size match the tapping knife in most of the market, can be modular demolition, easy maintenance. Workers can grasp the tapping technology quickly through the repeated training with the aid of learning instrument (Fig. 2).

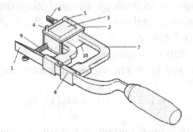

1. Cutter main body 2. Shell 3. Display screen 4. Sound sensor 5. Human body sensing device 6.LED light 7. Fixing arm 8.L Ring cover 9. Displacement sensor 10. Sound device.

Fig. 2. Three-dimensional model of the intelligent tapping technology auxiliary learning instrument

4 Tapping Level Evaluation Method

4.1 The Setting of Relevant Indexes

The degree of rubber tapping is evaluated by the benefit of information system. In order to deal with the multi-factor, ambiguous and subjective judgment of the information system, this paper quantifies the original qualitative evaluation. First of all, it is necessary to determine the evaluation index which affects the level of the tapping. Because there is no perfect and high degree of recognition evaluation system or data can be used for reference, this article uses Delphi method [13–15] to set the indexes.

We used 10 indicators to evaluate, they are average tapping thickness, tapping temperature, tapping humidity, tapping thickness fluctuation, the number of times of pauses, the proportion of the best thickness, tapping time coefficient, the number of times beyond dangerous thickness, the deepest tapping thickness and the stability.

4.2 Gray Correlation Analysis

In order to accurately grasp the key index that affect the rubber tapping technology, achieve the correct guidance of the rubber workers, and help workers grasp the tapping technology quickly, we comprehensively evaluate the above-mentioned 10 indexes. The evaluation method can be divided into subjective weighting method and objective weighting method according to the determination of the weight. At present, the mainstream comprehensive evaluation and decision-making methods include principal component analysis, TOPSIS, hierarchy analysis and so on. Because the tapping process has a lot of uncertain factors and their relationships are complex, this paper uses the gray relational analysis [16], combining the qualitative and quantitative methods, to determine whether the contact is close by calculating the geometric similarity between the reference data and the number of comparative data columns, and reflects the degree of correlation between the curves. The algorithm is simple to calculate, and it can reduce the subjective arbitrariness of decision makers to a certain extent.

In addition to the study of the mechanism, this paper analyzes the factors influencing the rubber tapping technology by analyzing the data of the influencing factors and the gray relational analysis to find out the factors that have significant influence. The steps are as follows:

Step1: determine the analysis sequence.

Set the reference sequence (also known as the parent sequence) as follows:

$$x_0 = \{x_0(k)|k = 1, 2, \cdots, n\} = (x_0(1), x_0(2), \cdots, x_0(n)) \tag{1}$$

The comparison sequence (also known as the subsequence) is:

$$x_i = \{x_i(k)|k = 1, 2, \cdots, n\} = (x_i(1), x_i(1), \cdots, x_i(n)), i = 1, 2, \cdots, m \tag{2}$$

Where the reference sequence x_0 is composed of the influence factor that may affect the level of tapping such as the tapping thickness, the tapping temperature, the degree of tapping thickness fluctuation, the number of pauses, the maximum proportion of the best thickness, the tapping time coefficient, the number of times beyond the dangerous thickness, deepest tapping thickness and stability. The comparison sequence xi is the score of the worker's tapping level.

Step2: Percent conversion of the data:

$$f(x(k)) = \frac{x(k)}{\max\limits_{k} x(k)} \tag{3}$$

In the formula of percent transformation of the data: $x(k)$ is the individual element in the sequence, and the value is the ratio of the single element to the maximum value of the row. Due to the different dimension of the data in the various columns of factors that affect the level of tapping technology, it is not easy to compare. So before the gray correlation analysis, we need to make a percentage conversion of the data.

Step3: Calculate the correlation coefficient

Calculate the correlation coefficient of the comparison sequence xi for the reference sequence x_0 at k is as follows:

$$\xi_i(k) = \frac{\min\limits_{s} \min\limits_{t} |x_0(t) - x_s(t)| + \rho \max\limits_{s} \max\limits_{t} |x_0(t) - x_s(t)|}{|x_0(t) - x_s(t)| + \rho \max\limits_{s} \max\limits_{t} |x_0(t) - x_s(t)|} \tag{4}$$

The $\min\limits_{s} \min\limits_{t} |x_0(t) - x_s(t)|$ is the minimum difference between two stages; $\max\limits_{s} \max\limits_{t} |x_0(t) - x_s(t)|$ is the two maximum difference between two stages; $\rho \in [0, 1]$ is the resolution coefficient, and the greater the resolution coefficient ρ is, the greater the resolution is. Through this formula, we can get the correlation coefficient of the sequence of tapping level scores on the sequence of impact index.

Step4: Calculate the degree of correlation

The correlation coefficient calculation formula is an index to describe the degree of correlation between the influencing factors and tapping technology. Since the different k values have a correlation number, the information is too scattered to be compared. Therefore, the formula r_i adds up the correlation coefficient of an index that affects tapping technology, and the average of the sum is used as the degree of correlation of the index that affects tapping technology to the score of the tapping level.

$$r_i = \frac{1}{n} \sum_{k=1}^{n} \xi(k), k = 1, 2, \Lambda, n \tag{5}$$

Step5: Ranking of the degree of correlation

Rank the correlation degree of each influence index according to the size. The greater the degree of correlation is, the greater the impact of the index on the level of tapping is.

4.3 Entropy Method to Determine the Weight

The current main weight determination methods include AHP method, variation coefficient method, and Delphi method and so on. In order to increase the precision, this paper chooses the objective entropy weight method [17] as the empowerment method of tapping technology influence index.

4.4 Qualitative and Quantitative Analysis of the Cloud Model

The cloud model [18] was proposed by Li from the academician of Chinese Academy of Engineering in 1995. The model was used to deal with the uncertain transformation of qualitative and quantitative descriptions [19]. Most of the cloud models are applied in data mining, decision analysis, intelligent control and many other areas. Let U be the quantitative domain of the precise numerical representation to determine advantages and disadvantages of the tapping technology. C is the fuzzy description of U, that is, the tapping level evaluation of the primary, the intermediate, and the advanced. If one of the scoring x is a stochastic realization in the score U of the tapping level, x is a random number with stable tendency respect to the C, where x is the cloud droplet, the distribution of x in the quantitative domain is cloud. Backward Cloud Generator is to realize the transformation of the concept of quantitative values to the qualitative model. We use reverse cloud generator [20] to achieve the transformation from the evaluation score of the tapping to the quality degree of the tapping technology, the steps are as follows:

Step1: Each tapping worker is a cloud droplet. The tapping technology score is the quantitative value x_i, and its membership degree is y_i. The expression of a cloud droplet is (x_i, y_i).

Step2: Calculate the mean value of the sample of the test worker's tapping level score, the first-order sample absolute center moment, and the sample variance

$$S^2 = \frac{1}{n-1} \sum_{i=1}^{n} (x_i - \overline{X})^2.$$

Step3: The mean value of the sample is the expected value, which is the most typical sample of the conversion of the tapping technology from qualitative to quantitative.

Step4: Combine the sample mean to obtain the entropy E_n from the formula $En = \sqrt{\frac{\pi}{2}} \times \frac{1}{n} \sum_{i=1}^{n} |x_i - \overline{X}|$, and the entropy value represents the degree of discretization of the tapping score, and its value also reflects the range of the tapping score that can be accepted by the concept space.

Step5: The super entropy can be obtained from the above sample variance and entropy through the formula $H_e = \sqrt{s^2 - En^2}$. The greater the super entropy, the greater the discretization degree of the tapping scores. Randomness of the membership degree also increases.

4.5   Determination of Cluster Centers and Classification of Tapping Levels

Clustering algorithm includes k-means clustering algorithm, cohesive hierarchical clustering algorithm [21] in hierarchical method, and neural network in the model [22] clustering algorithm. In order to reduce the algorithm computing complexity, we choose the efficient k-means clustering [23] method to determine the level of different tapping centers.

Step1: First we select three rubber workers as the central point of the three clusters: the primary rubber workers, the intermediate rubber workers, and the advanced rubber workers, where each center point includes the expectation of the rubber worker, entropy, and super entropy three indexes. In the case of three initial cluster centers, the expectations of each rubber worker, entropy and super entropy are grouped into the clusters represented by the nearest cluster center.

Step2: After all the scores are allocated, the center point of the cluster is recalculated according to the average of all expectations, entropy and super entropy in a cluster.

Step3: Iterate the steps to allocate points and update the cluster center points until the error is smaller than a certain value or to a certain number of iterations, when the error does not change. The score of same level of workers can get closer through the above clustering, and different levels of workers get farther. Finally form three more reasonable cluster center. Minimum Euclidean distance to determine the category [24, 25].

Step1: Enter the expectation, entropy and super entropy x ($x1$, $x2$, $x3$) of a test worker. Set up three sets of features that are primary workers, intermediate workers, and advanced workers. The vector constituted by expectation, entropy and super entropy of the primary worker is v1 expressed as v (v11, v12, v13), the vector constituted by expectation, entropy and super entropy of the intermediate worker is v2 expressed as v(v21, v22, v23), the vector constituted by expectation, entropy and super entropy of the advanced worker is v3 expressed as v (v31, v32, v33).

Step2: Find the distance between x and the three features. The formula is as follows:

Step3: The tapping level of the test worker is closer to the small distance set of features.

5   Experiment

5.1   Experimental Equipment, Environment and Data

After completing the mechanical design, algorithm design and implementation of the tapping technology auxiliary learning instrument, we completed the in-kind production of the technology validation machine of the tapping technology auxiliary learning instrument. Figure 3 is the prototype and test of machine.

After completing the learning device verification machine, we conducted a field experiment on September 15 in Dan Zhou City rubber-tapping team, Hainan Province, and some of the real-time screenshots of the experiment were shown in Figure. In the process of the experiment, a total of 24 rubber workers were tested on the technical

Fig. 3. Tapping technology auxiliary learning instrument

verification machine, including 8 primary rubber workers, 8 intermediate rubber workers and 8 advanced rubber workers. Take the verification machine tapping data of one of each level worker as sample data, and the rest as the test data. A total of 2310 data were obtained, including 330 evaluation data, which consists of 30 samples data and 300 test data.

Experiments in the Dan Zhou Hainan rubber forest is conducted amount the apprentice who just finished tapping training, rubber worker who had 3 years of work experience, tapping counselors who had 10 years tapping work experience, and each one carried out a 7 day tapping experiment. Three different kinds of workers on behalf of the tapping technology at the beginning, middle and high three levels. And the data of influencing factors were collected as shown in Table 1.

Table 1. Average tapping thickness

Average tapping thickness (mm)	13	14	14	15	17	18	10	19	21
Temperature (degrees Celsius)	17	18	19	18	18	18	17	18	18
Humidity (%)	85	86	87	86	85	86	86	88	86
Tapping thickness fluctuation degree	0	0	0	0	1	2	2	3	5
The number of times of pauses	0	1	0	1	0	1	2	2	3
The proportion of the best thickness(%)	98	97	95	93	90	92	85	70	86
Tapping time coefficient	0	0	1	0	0	1	0	1	1
The number of times beyond dangerous thickness	0	0	0	0	0	0	0	1	1
The maximum thickness of the tapping	18	17	18	19	18	19	19	20	21
Stability	1.8	1.9	2.1	2.5	3.2	2.6	4	3.2	3.5

Note: The tapping temperature and humidity data are collected by a temperature and humidity sensor (DHT11) installed on the intelligent tapping technology auxiliary learning instrument.

5.2   Evaluation Model Experiment

Step1: Based on the gray relational grade model and sample data, the correlation degree analysis of 10 tapping technology level evaluation indexes proposed in this paper is carried out. The sample data are shown in Table 2. The correlation data of each index and tapping technology level are shown in Table 3. The correlation degree of each index is shown in Fig. 4.

Table 2. Worker's score in the sample data

Primary workers	Intermediate workers	Advanced workers
8.3	8.3	2.1
8.1	6.7	1.4
7.4	5.6	1.2
6.9	5.4	5.1
8.7	7.8	7
8	4.8	2
6.2	2.5	3.6
6.9	8.2	3.8
8.1	5.2	3.6
8.3	5	4.7

Table 3. Results of the correlation analysis of each evaluation index

Average tapping thickness	Temperature	Humidity	Tapping thickness fluctuation degree	The number of times of pauses	The proportion of the best thickness	Tapping time coefficient	The number of times beyond dangerous thickness	The maximum thickness of the tapping	Stability
0.8947	0.6566	0.6162	0.8777	0.8118	0.7218	0.8115	0.8290	0.5527	0.8819

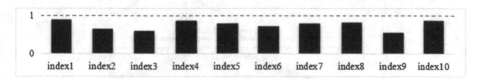

Fig. 4. Comparison of the correlation degree of each index

According to the experimental data described above, the evaluation index was selected. Finally, we selected seven evaluation indexes, which are the average tapping thickness, the degree of tapping thickness fluctuation, the number of pauses, the optimal thickness of tapping, the time coefficient of tapping, the number of times beyond dangerous thickness and stability.

Step2: Use the entropy method and sample data described above to determine the weight of each index. Table 4 shows the weight of each index. According to the weight and real-time data, rubber workers' tapping results can be obtained.

Table 4. Weight of each evaluation index

Average tapping thickness	Tapping thickness fluctuation degree	The number of times of pauses	The proportion of the best thickness	Tapping time coefficient	The number of times beyond dangerous thickness	Stability
7.5%	27%	43%	2.2%	7.7%	3.5%	9.1%

Step3: According to the experimental data of part 5.2 of the sample data, the calculation method of the rubber tapping performance can be obtained. Then, using the same data of the three rubber workers, the qualitative transformation experiment based on the reverse cloud generator was carried out. As shown in Table 5 below, it is the expectation, entropy and super entropy of the three tapping grades cloud model.

Table 5. Parameters of the cloud model of three rubber workers' grades

	Primary worker	Intermediate workers	Advanced workers
Ex	7.69	5.95	1.7797
En	0.8422	1.8048	3.4500
He	0	0.2028	0.4395

The graph of the cloud droplets generated from the parameters of the cloud model of three workers' tapping grades is shown in Fig. 5.

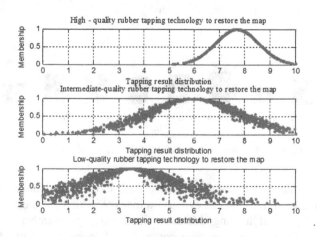

Fig. 5. The cloud map of the scores of different rubber worker's tapping level

Seen from the diagram, the advanced worker has the highest expectations, and the grade distribution is relatively concentrated. The grade distribution of the primary and intermediate worker is relatively scattered, and the performance is not stable. According to the experimental data obtained by the three rubber workers experiments, the matrix scatter plots [26] corresponding to all grades of the three different levels rubber workers are shown in the following figure.

According to the clustering, the three cluster centers are: advanced rubber workers: (7.7, 0.85, 0); intermediate rubber workers: (6, 1.8, 0.2); primary workers: (1.78, 3.45, 0.44).

Step 4: Use the cluster analysis to analyze the expectation, entropy and super entropy of the cloud model corresponding to the different unit time periods that obtained by the long-time test of the three rubber workers. We use the k-means clustering method, and the experimental results is shown in Fig. 6. After obtaining clustering centers of three levels, according to minimum Euclidean distance method, experimental data had verified the experiment in this paper.

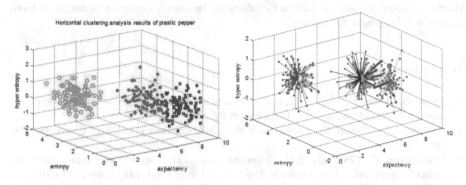

Fig. 6. Cluster diagram of cloud model parameters corresponding to different levels of tapping and experimental test results (Color figure online)

5.3 Test Experiment and Result Analysis

As shown in Fig. 6 above, there are 300 test data nodes, and lines in the color of blue, black and cyan, which indicate the correct experimental data node. The bold brown connection of the nodes indicates the data node corresponding to wrong evaluation results. There are 5 wrong data points in total, so the experimental correct evaluation rate of the tapping technology auxiliary learning instrument is 98%.

6 Conclusion

Based on Delphi method, gray relational degree analysis, entropy weight method and cloud model [5, 27, 28], this paper presents an evaluation method of tapping technology, which can display the thickness of tapping in real time, the real-time evaluation and scoring of rubber tapping technology. This technology improves rubber tapping technology. And this evaluation method has a high reference value in the field of tapping technology evaluation and it can be applied in practice. At the same time, we designed and produced a smart tapping technology auxiliary learning instrument. Not only does the learning instrument meet the structural requirements of the function required by the tapping worker, but also it has a strong real-time characteristic and a high evaluation accuracy that were all verified by the test. The production and manufacture of this machine will play a great role in promoting the level of rubber tapping and rubber production.

Acknowledgments. This work was supported by the National Natural Science Foundation of China (Project no. 61363071, 61379145, 61471169), The National Natural Science Foundation of Hainan (Project no.617048), Hunan Province Education Science Planning Funds (Project no. XJK011BXJ004), Hainan University Doctor Start Fund Project (Project no. kyqd1328). Hainan University Youth Fund Project (Project no. qnjj1444). State Key Laboratory of Marine Resource Utilization in the South China Sea, Hainan University. College of Information Science & Technology, Hainan University. Nanjing University of Information Science & Technology (NUIST); A Project Funded by the Priority Academic Program Development of Jiangsu Higer Education Institutions; and the Jiangsu Collaborative Innovation Center on Atmospheric Environment and Equipment Technology.

References

1. Spanò, D., Pintus, F., Mascia, C., et al.: Extraction and characterization of a natural rubber from Euphorbia characias latex. Biopolymers **97**, 589–594 (2012)
2. Hebbard, G.M., Powell, S.T., Rostenbach, R.E.: Rubber industry. Ind. Eng. Chem. **39**, 589–595 (1947)
3. Musikavong, C., Gheewala, S.H.: Assessing ecological footprints of products from the rubber industry and palm oil mills in Thailand. J. Clean. Prod. **142**, 1148–1157 (2016)
4. Xia, Z., Wang, X., Sun, X., et al.: A secure and dynamic multi-keyword ranked search scheme over encrypted cloud data. IEEE Trans. Parallel Distrib. Syst. **27**, 340–352 (2016)
5. Gu, B., Sheng, V.S.: A robust regularization path algorithm for v-support vector classification. IEEE Trans. Neural Netw. Learn. Syst. **28**, 1241–1248 (2016)
6. Gu, B., Sun, X., Sheng, V.S.: Structural minimax probability machine. IEEE Trans. Neural Netw. Learn. Syst. **28**, 1646–1656 (2016)
7. Zhangjie, F., Sun, X., Liu, Q., et al.: Achieving efficient cloud search services: multi-keyword ranked search over encrypted cloud data supporting parallel computing. IEICE Trans. Commun. **98**, 190–200 (2015)
8. Liu, Q., Cai, W., Shen, J., et al.: A speculative approach to spatial-temporal efficiency with multi-objective optimization in a heterogeneous cloud environment. Secur. Commun. Netw. **9**, 4002–4012 (2016)
9. Zhiguo, Q., Keeney, J., Robitzsch, S., et al.: Multilevel pattern mining architecture for automatic network monitoring in heterogeneous wireless communication networks. China Commun. **13**, 108–116 (2016)
10. You, C., Huang, K., Chae, H.: Energy efficient mobile cloud computing powered by wireless energy transfer. IEEE J. Sel. Areas Commun. **34**, 1757–1771 (2016)
11. Oberti, R., Marchi, M., Tirelli, P., et al.: Selective spraying of grapevines for disease control using a modular agricultural robot. Biosyst. Eng. **146**, 203–215 (2016)
12. Lin, H., Yi, C., Zunmin, L.: Experimental study on quadruped wheel robot for wheat precision seeding. Key Eng. Mater. **693**, 1651–1657 (2016)

13. Linstone, H.A., Turoff, M.: The Delphi method: techniques and applications. J. Mark. Res. **18**, 363–364 (1975)
14. Strand, J., Carson, R.T., Navrud, S., et al.: Using the Delphi method to value protection of the Amazon rainforest. Ecol. Econ. **131**, 475–484 (2017)
15. Weir, A., Hölmich, P., Schache, A.G., et al.: Terminology and definitions on groin pain in athletes: building agreement using a short Delphi method. Br. J. Sports Med. **49**, 825–827 (2015)
16. Rajesh, R., Ravi, V.: Supplier selection in resilient supply chains: a grey relational analysis approach. J. Cleaner Prod. **86**, 343–359 (2015)
17. Tang, P., Chen, D., Hou, Y.: Entropy method combined with extreme learning machine method for the short-term photovoltaic power generation forecasting. Chaos Solitons Fractals **89**, 243–248 (2016)
18. Wang, J., Peng, J., Zhang, H., et al.: An uncertain linguistic multi-criteria group decision-making method based on a cloud model. Group Decis. Negot. **24**, 171–192 (2015)
19. Wang, G., Xu, C., Li, D.: Generic normal cloud model. Inf. Sci. **280**, 1–15 (2014)
20. Xiahou, J., Lin, F., Huang, Q., et al.: Multi-datacenter cloud storage service selection strategy based on AHP and backward cloud generator model. Neural Comput. Appl. 1–15 (2016)
21. Lafondlapalme, J., Duceppe, M.O., Wang, S., et al.: A new method for decontamination of de novo transcriptase's using a hierarchical clustering algorithm. Bioinformatics **33**, 1293–1300 (2016)
22. Lin, J., Zhu, B.: A novel kernel clustering algorithm based selective neural network ensemble model for economic forecasting. In: Kang, L., Liu, Y., Zeng, S. (eds.) ISICA 2007. LNCS, vol. 4683, pp. 310–315. Springer, Heidelberg (2007). doi:10.1007/978-3-540-74581-5_34
23. Shahrivari, S., Jalili, S.: Single-pass and linear-time k-means clustering based on MapReduce. Inf. Syst. **60**, 1–12 (2016)
24. Bermanis, A., Wolf, G., Averbuch, A.: Diffusion-based kernel methods on Euclidean metric measure spaces. Appl. Comput. Harmon. Anal. **41**, 190–213 (2016)
25. Dokmanic, I., Parhizkar, R., Ranieri, J., et al.: Euclidean distance matrices: essential theory, algorithms, and applications. IEEE Sig. Process. Mag. **32**, 12–30 (2015)
26. Nordhausen, K., Oja, H.: Independent subspace analysis using three scatter matrices. Austrian J. Stat. **40**, 93–101 (2016)
27. Xia, Z., Wang, X., Zhang, L., et al.: A privacy-preserving and copy-deterrence content-based image retrieval scheme in cloud computing. IEEE Trans. Inf. Forensics Secur. **11**, 2594–2608 (2016)
28. Fu, Z., Ren, K., Shu, J., et al.: Enabling personalized search over encrypted outsourced data with efficiency improvement. IEEE Trans. Parallel Distrib. Syst. **27**, 2546–2559 (2016)

An Affective Computing and Fuzzy Logic Framework to Recognize Affect for Cloud-based E-Learning Environment Using Emoticons

Kyle Morton[1], Yanzhen Qu[1(✉)], and Marilyn Carroll[2]

[1] Colorado Technical University, Colorado Springs, CO, USA
k.morton15@my.cs.coloradotech.edu, yqu@coloradotech.edu
[2] Strayer University, Dallas, TX, USA
marilyn.carroll@strayer.edu

Abstract. The deficiency in the ability for instructors in the Cloud based E-Learning environments to accurately determine a student's affective status has resulted in the inability to provide effective feedback to student. Feedback is important in learning as it allows a student to learn from their mistakes and helps build their academic confidence. In this paper, we have proposed an affective based E-Learning framework that uses fuzzy logic and emoticons to determine a student's affective status in a Cloud-based E-Learning Environment. This framework uses three emotions represented using emoticons, which are "excited", "tired", and "sad" to accurately detect a student's emotion during their learning process.

Keywords: Affective computing · E-Learning · Emoticons · Fuzzy systems

1 Introduction

In any type of learning environment, effective feedback is reliant on the following: the difference in time when student posits the questions; and the time the student receives the feedback which also includes the feedback accuracy. It has been determined that students in a Cloud-based E-Learning environments do not experience the feedback effectiveness similar to that of a face-to-face setting [1]. This is largely due to delayed communication and lack of adequate knowledge on the student's learning aptitude, often reflected through cognitive capacity, study style or the real time affect, outlook [2]. Consequently, feedback cannot be effective without knowing and understanding a student's affective status.

Students build knowledge through rational evaluation of new information, and integrating with previous perceptions, which are further enhanced through observation and experimentation, as well as receiving external feedback. Researchers have identified particular trends on the impact of feedback on-learning programs, but ultimately providing feedback has obvious positive results on student achievement [3]. The use of emoticons in virtual environments is prevalent in entertainment and social networking, but its application in education is currently limited. Therefore, this paper presents an affective based E-Learning framework using fuzzy logic to incorporate a student's emotions into learning for the ability to accurately provide effective feedback.

1.1 Challenges of Sensing Affect in a Cloud-based E-Learning Environments

A successful Cloud-based E-Learning experience must engage students intellectually and emotionally in all the related activities. Currently, the ability for an online class instructor to gauge an affective status of a student is non-existent, unless the instructor inquires the student about his or her emotions. Recent research explores the relationship between effective learning and emotions, particularly in the Cloud-based E-Learning environment, with positive moods cited for increased flexibility and creativity in resolving issues, including efficiency and diligence in making decisions. Scholars are adopting Emoji's/emoticons to represent personality and emotional nuances found in face-to-face communication, aimed at improving the effectiveness and quality of text-based communication, in Cloud-based E-Learning settings [4]. But, there is not any Cloud-based E-Learning environment such as Moodle, Blackboard, or Desire to Learn (D2L), where the affective status of students are not evaluated and tracked for the system or instructors to address that student appropriately.

1.2 Affective Status and Emoticons

Emoticons have become popular digital tools for use in messaging, emailing and on social media site. Most of these pictograms reveal a light-hearted nature, but at times appear as a comical form of communication. Emoticons have a considerable influence on tone, introduce humor, and grant individuals an efficient and fast way to convey color and personality into dull networked spaces common in most texts. These symbols are creating new forms of digital feeling, while still remaining in the service of the market and can be used as accurate measurement in allowing someone to express how they feel.

According to researchers, affect is what sticks to people, objects and places, while affective impulses create emotional capacity which preserve social relations within the boundaries of economic efficiency and instrumentalism [5]. The absence of nonverbal behavior communication – hand gestures, facial expressions – which supports effective learning can be supported by emoticons, and the latter can complement learning delivery in the digital environment. This can be found in supplementing the effort in closing the transactional gap – communication and psychological – existing between students and instructors. This gap needs to be bridged so as to achieve deliberate and effective learning experiences [6].

The ability for instructors to display their mood towards a student's progress is imperative. The emoji smiley has been credited for having a strong impact on an individual's mood, with a wide range of these icons been created to realistically convey human expressions and emotions, especially when used as student feedback from an instructor. According to a study conducted on conversations on Facebook, it emerged that nearly all sentences were graced with smileys, an obvious indication of the new role of emoji in nonverbal communication [7].

The prevalent use of emoticons is influenced by the environment, from which it is applied, rather than age, gender or nationality. The nature of interaction – social or task oriented – may determine how the individual expresses the self in a nonverbal way. Students in particular are said to prefer the use of emoticon in socially emotional groups than in a task-oriented setting, these observation are a reflective of societal norms. It is often easier to express emotions among family and friends, than in professional circles. Which is important that a student's affective status is taken into consideration, as student failure is the relationship between the balance of multiple responsibilities – family, profession and family – contributed to the rise in negative emotions [8]. Overall Cloud-based E-Learning is a distinct social context, with emoticons emerging as effective tools of: improving communication; increasing social presence; and developing communities in an E-Learning environment's elements which ensure the icons are effective in delivering feedback.

The rest of this paper consists of the following content: the related work section will summarize what have been done by other researchers to the subject; the problem statement and hypothesis section will present the problem statement and the hypothesis for an assumed solution to address the root cause of the problem, as well as two research questions which can help approve or disapprove the hypothesis; the methodology section will present a framework by which we can further develop two experiments to answer the two research questions; and the experiments and results section will present the details of experiments and the results of the experiments; and the final section will conclude this paper.

2 Related Work

Chen and Lee [9] in their study concluded that, imaginative and fascinating avatars can positively impact on learner's attitudes and behaviors. Their research used animated pedagogical agents (APAs) which have characteristics similar to humans – facial expressions, gestures and emotions, to interact with students. Their findings indicated that learners were inspired to act according to the avatar's expectations, thereby putting greater effort on specific and quantitative learning activities.

The use of gaming and avatar to enhance learning activities, communications and collaborations, has been examined by [10]. The study was evaluated MARVIN, an avatar-based authoring program, adopted as a digital storytelling tool to support learning in New Zealand's educational framework. Though the study acknowledges limitations due to its "generalizability", analyzed data indicate that combining a learning model with an avatar-based virtual setting, creates an affective, effective, and valuable learning experience.

Stark and Crawford [11] delve into the relevance of emoji characters, as outlets for affective labor in relation to informational capitalism in social networks. The scholars assert that, emoji's in their form, emphasize on tone, humor, and grant users an efficient and fast way to show color and personality. Additionally, emoji characters symbolize the strains between affect in human capacities, and as productive forces which capital seeks to connect through the management of daily bio-politics. In the conclusion of their paper, Stark and Crawford, affirm that, emoji's support learners in digital environments to manage their emotion within the technological platforms operating beyond their control.

Opinion differs on whether online activities are subjected to emotions and social intelligence. According to Meyer and Jones [12] in their survey on college student's emotions and social intelligence, learners transfer their persona to class-related virtual environments. This study supports the need for the adoption of avatars to enhance the effect of learning programs. Cloud-based E-Learning is non-intrusive and instantaneous and avatars are effective tools of communicating emotions and social intelligence.

Digital literacy is dependent on the effective application of electrically-mediated communication (EMC), more so in online instructions, as the latter relies on text formats, where meaning and intent may be distorted. Dunlap and Lowenthal [13] advocate for the use of emoji's to improve on communication, while enhancing social presence. Instructors in Cloud-based E-Learning environments are always seeking out techniques to improve the effectiveness and quality of text-based communications, with emoji's emerging as resourceful alternatives.

Recognition of emotions in speech, particularly during online interactions has attracted researchers. Vogt et al. [14] developed EmoVoice, a framework for recognizing emotions in speech. EmoVoice operates with an interface which creates own personal emotion recognizer. This technology allows for online tracking of user voice emotions and can supplement Cloud-based E-Learning instructions.

Instant Messaging (IM) a prevalent feature of the Cloud-based E-Learning environment often uses graphical icons (emoji's) to portray emotions. Huang et al. [15] in exploring the effects of emoticons/emoji found that users reacted positively, viewed the experience as useful for communication. The three scholars in their research explored the following issues: personal interaction, enjoyment, perceived usefulness, and the relevance of the information. Their findings identified a correlation between information richness and emoji use, and this affects communication, particularly among peer users. Additionally, integrating emoji's within IM fosters a caring and supportive environment.

3   Problem Statement and Hypothesis

3.1   Problem Statement

In a Cloud-based E-Learning environment instructors cannot accurately observe and determine a student's affective state which in turn results to ineffective feedback because of the inability for Cloud-based E-Learning environments to collect timely and accurate metrics representing a student's affective state for instructor use in providing effective feedback.

3.2   Hypothesis

If we build a system that allows students to use and update an emoticon that represents their affective status which is associated with class assignments, discussions, and instructor's feedback; then we can accurately collect affective metrics from students to provide effective feedback resulting in a more personal online educational experience, improvement academically, and improved student engagement.

3.3 Research Questions

In order to approve or disapprove the hypothesis, we will need to answer the following two research questions:

Question 1: If students can communicate their affective status to the instructor, will instructor adjust the feedbacks to students so that students' academic performance will be impacted?
Question 2: If students can communicate their affective status to the instructor, will it help to enhance students in class engagement?

Obviously, one of the main task for this research project is to design a method by which we can develop proper experiments to make the two research questions answered.

4   Methodology

This section describes a framework for a Cloud-based E-Learning system with the ability of recognizing a student's affective status for providing effective feedback. This framework uses emoticons and fuzzy logic to determine a student's affective status, which is used by the system and instructors for providing effective feedback. This framework uses Moodle, which is a Learning Platform or course management system (CMS), as a Cloud-based E-Learning platform to integrate our framework.

4.1   Affective Based Learning Framework

This framework entails the facet that defines how a student's affective status is recognized using emoticons and how to use the collection of a student's affective data to accurately provide effective feedback. This framework focuses on tracking three different emotions from the student. The emotions are "Excited", "Tired", and "Sad". These three emotions are easily expressed using emoticons and can be recognized by self. Moreover, a student's affective status will be represented by the system as the "Affective Status Rating (ASR)". The ASR is defined as the computed affective status of a student for the duration of a course using fuzzy logic. Therefore, after each completed assignment by a student, the student's affective status is recorded and computed into the ASR. For each assignment, the student has the option of choosing an emoticon that represents excited, tired, or sad. The emoticon image and value for each affective status is denoted below in Table 1.

Table 1. Emoticon values

Affective Status	Image	Value
Excited		1.0
Tired	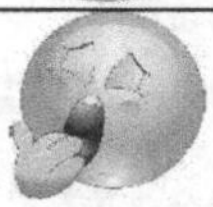	0.5
Sad		0.2

The average of all emoticon representing the three emotions for each of a student's assignments and the student's current cognitive ability, which is the grade earned on an assignment or current grade in the course are used as membership values for the membership functions that determines the student's affective status based on a defined set of fuzzy rules, which consists of an if-part (antecedent) and a then-part (conse-quence). These fuzzy rules have multiple conditions combined using conjunction (AND), which is also explained as

$$\mu_{A \wedge B}(x) := \min\{\mu_A(x), \mu_B(x)\}.$$

Min defines the conjunction of two fuzzy sets as the minimal of degrees of member ship of the fuzzy sets. Also the consequence specifies the overall affective status of the student which should be used for providing feedback. The membership functions for current affective status and current cognitive ability, which is the grade earned on an assignment or current grade in the course, are defined in Fig. 1.

$$f(x) \begin{cases} Excellent, if\, 1. \geq x > .95 \\ Good, if\, .95 \leq x \geq .80 \\ Fair, if\, .80 > x \geq .70 \\ Poor, if\, .70 > x \end{cases}$$

Membership function for Cognitive ability

$$f(x) \begin{cases} Excited, if\, 1. \leq x > .7 \\ Tired, if\, .7 \geq x > .3 \\ Sad, if\, .3 \geq x \end{cases}$$

Membership function for Affective Status

$$\mu_{A \wedge B}(x) := \min\{\mu_A(x), \mu_B(x)\}$$

Membership function for overall affective status

Fig. 1. Membership functions

Where in Fig. 2 $\mu_a(x)$ is the membership value of the cognitive ability and $\mu_b(x)$ is the membership value of the affective status.

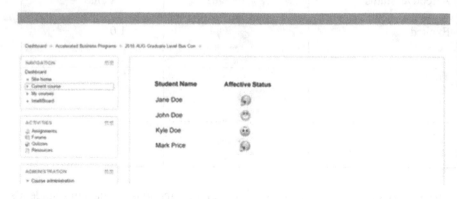

Fig. 2. Instructor's student affect list

4.2 Affective Status User Interface

We used Moodle as our course management platform. Moodle was selected because it is open source software and is a very popular online learning platform solution for universities. The user interface for the instructor to view a student's affective status is displayed in a table format in the instructor's admin, as displayed in Fig. 2. This allows an instructor to have the ability stay aware of a student's affective status at a given time. The instructor is also notified when a student's affective status changes.

In Fig. 3, an illustration of the student's user interface for selecting their affective status is shown. The student is given three options for selecting their affective status of excited, tired, and sad. The student is also given an option to express in text with more detail how they feel to the instructor. Using this approach, the system and/or the course instructor can provide effective feedback targeting a specific problem. If a student do not select or update their affective status for each assignment, then the affective status will default to the affective status of excited.

Furthermore, the student's affective status is always displayed in their course dashboard. The student always has the ability to update their affective status for an assignment. This is so, because a student may find understanding or become more confused after receiving an instructor's feedback. Figure 4 displays a student's dashboard representing their overall affective status for the course and the affective status for each individual assignment.

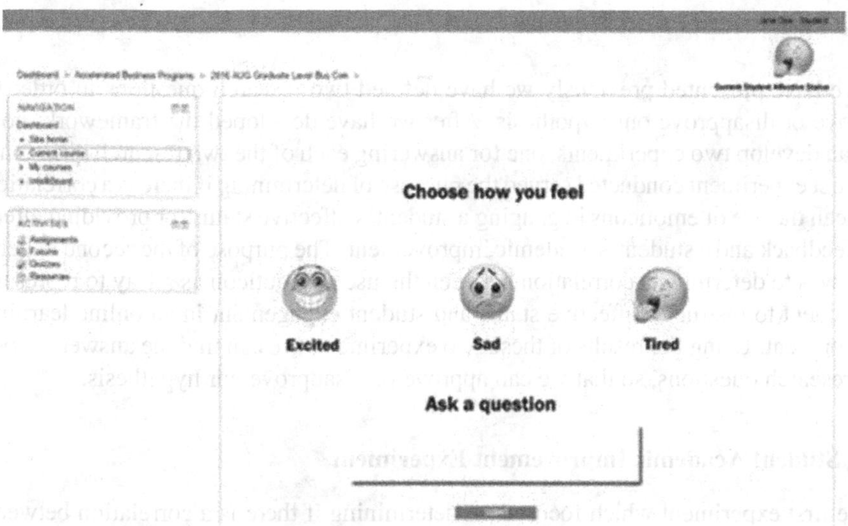

Fig. 3. Selecting affective status

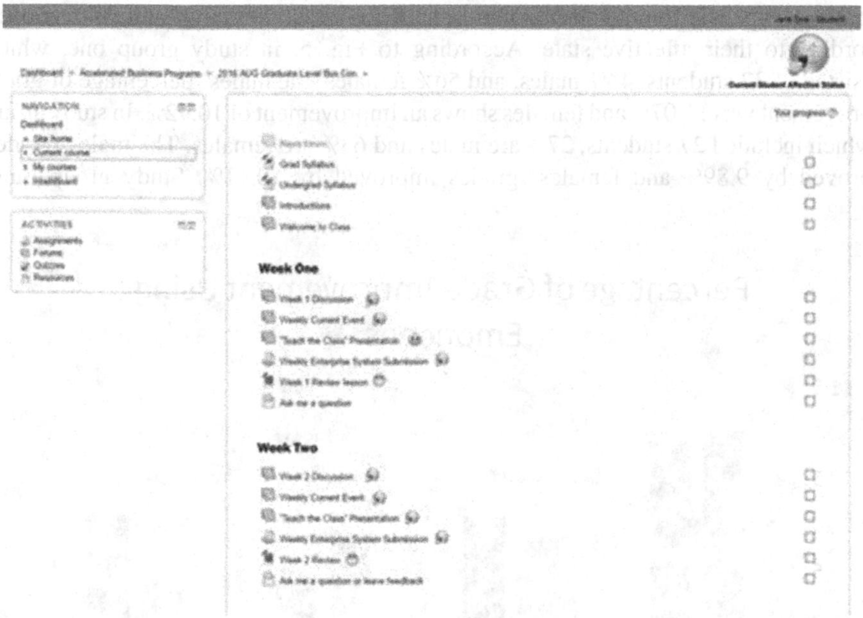

Fig. 4. Student's course dashboard

5   Experiments and Results

As we have presented previously we have defined two research questions in order to approve or disapprove our hypothesis. After we have developed the framework, now we can develop two experiments, one for answering each of the two research questions. The first experiment conducted served the purpose of determining if there is a correlation between the use of emoticons in gauging a student's affective status for providing effective feedback and a student's academic improvement. The purpose of the second experiment was to determine a correlation between the use of emoticon as a way to represent the student to instructor affective status and student engagement in an online learning environment. Using the results of these two experiments we can find the answers to our two research questions, so that we can approve or disapprove our hypothesis.

5.1   Student Academic Improvement Experiment

In the first experiment which focused on determining if there is a correlation between the use of emoticons and student academic improvement. The control group consisted of 105 students, which 61% were male and 49% were female. This group completed the course without the use of emoticons. There were four study groups, which the students in each group used emoticons to represent their affective status and as feedback according to their affective state. According to Fig. 5, in study group one, which consisted of 32 students, 44% males, and 56% females, the males' percentage of grade improvement was 11.07% and females shows an improvement of 10.92%. In study group 2, which included 27 students, 27% are males and 63% are females. The males' grades improved by 9.89% and females' grades improved by 10.11%. Study group three

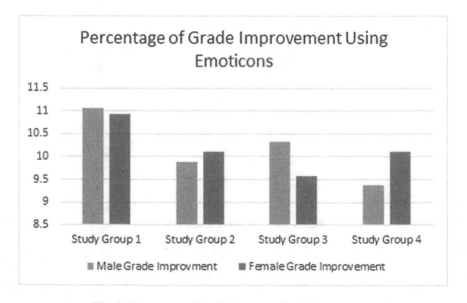

Fig. 5. Percentage of grade improvement using emoticons

displayed a wider margin in grade improvement between males and females. This group contained 28 students, which 43% were male and 57% were female. The males' grades improved by 10.33% and females by 9.58%. Study group four was comprised of 25 students, which 48% were male and 52% were female. Male's grades improved by 9.37% and females' grades improved by 10.11%.

The improvement of academic performance was measured by comparing the final calculated grade of students in the control group versus students of each study group and calculating the percentage of improvement from students in both the control and study groups. Furthermore, the average margin of improvement was 10.2% which extrapolates that student grades increased a letter grade with the use of emoticons. Therefore the results of the first experiment have clearly answered our first research question.

5.2 Student Engagement Experiment

The purpose of this correlational experiment was to investigate the possible relationship between the use of emoticons and the engagement of students in an online class. Any relationships found between the use of emoticons, and student engagement adds another tool for researchers, instructors, educators and educational leaders to consider when building course content. The categorical demographics of students in this study includes gender, age category and education level, where in the control group there were 120 students, 42% were males and 58% were females, and age range of 18–45 years old. The educational level of the students varied from some college to graduate studies. In the study group there were 21 females and nine males. The age of the participants varied from 18–45. Also, the education level varied from high school to graduate studies, with the most common having some college.

Based upon the student engagement score from the online classes containing students in the control group. The study group displayed a 20% increase in student engagement when using emoticons to interact with students. Furthermore, student course dropped rates decreased by 75% and student course incompletion rates decreased by 80%. The results also show there is no correlation between gender and the usage of emoticons in regards to student engagement, but results do show that students between the ages of 18–35 were more receptive to the use of emoticons in their online learning experience. Therefore the results of the second experiment have clearly answered our first research question.

6   Conclusion

In combine the results of two experiments, we have not only found the answers to our two research questions, but also approved our hypothesis.

Computer-mediated communication is replacing traditional face-to-face interactions, transforming the nature of information exchange. Emotions are often lost in digitalized communication. Research results in this study support an affective approach to providing effective feedback in a Cloud-based E-Learning environment using emoticons. Modern Cloud-based E-Learning systems should integrate emoticons which reflect the affective state of the interacting learners. Nearly three quarters (70%) of the respondents in this study were male, with females accounting for only 30%.

In reviewing the results of this study, majority of learners felt that instructors should be considerate of the emotional state of the learners before and after each assignment. The virtual environment is characterized by anonymity and for instructors; emoticons offer an easy and effective approach, particularly in the feedback processes. Stark and Crawford [11] affirm that, emoticons are more than a charming way of humanizing text information; they are a reminder on ways informational capital constantly seeks to monetize, analyze and standardize affect.

There is overwhelming correlation between academic success and emotions. Learners who are emotionally balanced are bound to be successful academically, with all respondents concurring with the sentiment. Affective factors influence the learner's motivation and subsequently impacts the learning process. Moreover, these results are also supportive of the need to adopt emoticons, as an effective tool in supporting instructors in a Cloud-based E-Learning environment.

Nonetheless, the use of emoticons is prevalent in social networking platforms, where messaging is spontaneous and users easily post their emotions more naturally. From this study, students expect the instructors to take the initiative on issues relating to academics and emotions. Students often use emoticons for informal communications and its related use in an education setting should be used by the instructors.

As a result of this study, students were able to express their level of understanding to their instructor by displaying their emotions, particularly during feedback after an assignment. This shows that instructors can therefore integrate emoticon functionalities into Cloud-based E-Learning. Detecting and managing student affective information can enable instructors to develop effective learning programs.

Acknowledgments. We thank our colleagues from Colorado Technical University and Strayer University who provided insight and expertise that assisted the research. Furthermore, we thank all participants of this research.

References

1. Morton, K., Qu, Y.: A feedback effectiveness oriented math word problem E-Tutor for E-Learning environment. In: 2015 IEEE 15th International Conference on Advanced Learning Technologies, pp. 301–302 (2015)
2. Dunlosky, J., Rawson, K.A., Marsh, E.J., Nathan, M.J., Willingham, D.T.: Improving students' learning with effective learning techniques: promising directions from cognitive and educational psychology. Psychol. Sci. Public Interest (PSPI) **14**, 4–48 (2013)
3. Rosenfield, S., Lou, Y., Dedic, H.: A feedback model and successful E-Learning. In: E-Learn: World Conference on E-Learning in Corporate, Government, Healthcare, and Higher Education, vol. 2002, pp. 1818–1821 (2002)
4. Park, J., Barash, V., Fink, C., Cha, M.: Emoticon style: interpreting differences in emoticons across cultures. In: ICWSM (2013)
5. Ortigosa, A., Martín, J.M., Carro, R.M.: Sentiment analysis in Facebook and its application to E-Learning. Comput. Hum. Behav. **31**, 527–541 (2014)

6. Swan, K.: Social presence and E-Learning. In: IADIS Virtual Multi Conference on Computer Science and Information Systems (MMCIS) (2005)
7. Shen, L., Wang, M., Shen, R.: Affective E-Learning: using 'Emotional' data to improve learning in pervasive learning environment. Educ. Technol. Soc. **12**, 176–189 (2009)
8. Attis, J.: An investigation of the variables that predict teacher E-Learning acceptance. In: Doctor of Education, Liberty University (2014)
9. Chen, G.-S., Lee, M.-F.: Detecting emotion model in E-Learning system. In: 2012 International Conference Machine Learning and Cybernetics (ICMLC), pp. 1686–1691 (2012)
10. Falloon, G.: Using avatars and virtual environments in learning: what do they have to offer? Br. J. Educ. Technol. **41**, 108–122 (2010)
11. Stark, L., Crawford, K.: The conservatism of emoji: work, affect, and communication. Soc. Media+Soc. **2015**, 1–11 (2015)
12. Meyer, A.K., Jones, J.S.: Do students experience "social intelligence," laughter, and other emotions online? J. Asynchronous Learn. Netw. **16**, 99–111 (2012)
13. Dunlap, J.C., Lowenthal, P.R.: The power of presence: our quest for the right mix of social presence in online courses. In: Life, R. (ed.) Distance Education: Case Studies in Practice. Information Age Publishing, Charlotte (2014)
14. Vogt, T., André, E., Bee, N.: EmoVoice—A framework for online recognition of emotions from voice. In: International Tutorial and Research Workshop on Perception and Interactive Technologies for Speech-Based Systems, pp. 188–199 (2008)
15. Huang, A.H., Yen, D.C., Zhang, X.: Exploring the potential effects of emoticons. Inf. Manag. **45**, 466–473 (2008)

Cloud Management Systems and Virtual Desktop Infrastructure Load Balancing Algorithms - A Survey

Micheal Ernest Taylor and Jian Shen[✉]

School of Computer and Software,
Nanjing University of Information Science and Technology,
Nanjing 210044, China
delen007@live.com, s_shenjian@126.com

Abstract. Cloud Computing Technology has hatched some fascinating services, including hosted file servers, applications on demand and business continuity solutions. The volume of data storage upsurges quickly in open environment. So, load balancing is a main challenge in cloud environment. Load balancing helps to distribute the dynamic workload across multiple nodes to ensure that no single node is overloaded. It helps in proper utilization of resources. It also improve the performance of the system. Cloud data center management is an essential problem due to the numerous and heterogeneous strategies that can be applied, ranging from the virtual machine location to the coalition with other clouds. Load Balancing is important for essential operations in cloud virtual environments. Many algorithms have been developed for allocating client's requests to available remote nodes. This paper presents a survey on load balancing algorithms in cloud management systems and virtual desktop infrastructure as well as properties of cloud computing. The survey also presents a comparative metrics on load balancing algorithms such as round robin, honey bee, ant colony, and active clustering and others as main the focus.

Keywords: Cloud computing · Virtualization · Algorithm · Load balancing

1 Introduction

The model of running shared desktops in virtual machines hosted on servers is a gripping proposition. In distinction to traditional desktop management strategies, these virtual desktops are easily maintained, upgraded and updated, and use of a variety of devices in various locations to access sensitive data without ever leaving the confines of the data center is highly possible for a user. This form of server-hosted desktops is known as virtual desktop infrastructure (VDI). However, instigating VDI has historically been a complex responsibility usually reserved for large enterprises due to demanding requirements for high-end server and storage hardware [5].

© Springer International Publishing AG 2017
X. Sun et al. (Eds.): ICCCS 2017, Part I, LNCS 10602, pp. 300–309, 2017.
https://doi.org/10.1007/978-3-319-68505-2_26

Cloud Computing Technology has hatched some fascinating services, including hosted file servers, applications on demand and business continuity solutions. Several vendors are now taking the technology to the next level, coalescing virtualization with cloud services [7]. A cloud-based VDI solution is a computing model where an end users system can access all the essential files and data virtually in spite of being alienated from the physical IT infrastructure. The VDI layer acts as an intermediary between backend and end-user application. Voluminous establishments use VDI technologies from vendors like Citrix and VMware to push virtual desktops out across their enterprises [7]. There are numerous existing issues in cloud computing. However, the key amongst them is load balancing. Load balancing is quite a new technique that accelerates networks and resources by providing a maximum throughput with minimum response time. Load balancing ensures efficient and fair distribution of computing resources to provide high satisfaction, better response time and utilization to users and prevent system bottlenecks which may occur due to load imbalance. Distributing the traffic between servers, data can be sent and received without high delay. Diverse types of algorithms are available that aids traffic loaded between available servers. Devoid of load balancing, users could experience delays, time-outs and possible long system responses. Load balancing solutions usually apply redundant servers which help a better distribution of the communication traffic so that the server availability is conclusively settled [6,9,11,14]. Due to this challenges of cloud computing its worthwhile to research in this area to improve on the existing load balancing algorithms and if possible an optimal solution provided. In this paper, a survey on related Load balancing algorithms in Cloud System and Virtual Desktop Infrastructure are presented.

The rest of the paper is organized as follows. In the second section, presents a literature review. The subsequent sections delineate in detail the architecture of Cloud Computing System, VDI, its pros and cons, and those of the platform that supports its services and methodology. This paper concludes with comments about the state of Cloud Computing and VDI and the likely component of the platform required for the support for business as a discussion of future work.

2   Related Works

The Cloud is made up of enormous resources. Management of these resources requires efficient planning. While planning an algorithm for resource provisioning on cloud the engineer should take into consideration the different existing cloud scenarios and must be aware of the issues that are to be resolved by the proposed algorithm. So, resource provisioning algorithm can be classified into different classes based on the environment, purpose and technique of proposed solution. Join-Idle Queue uses distributed dispatchers by first load balancing the idle processors across dispatchers and then assigning jobs to processors to reduce average queue length at each processor [8]. The disadvantage of this algorithm is that it is not scalable. Moharana [10] Proposed this load-balancing algorithm for dynamically scalable web services. It effectively reduces the system load, incurs no communication overhead at job arrivals and does not increase actual response time. It can perform close to optimal when used for web services.

Load balancing in cloud computing system [4] discussed on basic concepts of Cloud Computing and Load balancing and studied some existing load balancing algorithms, which can be applied to clouds. In addition to that, the closed-form solutions for minimum measurement and reporting time for single level tree networks with different load balancing strategies were also studied. The performance of these strategies with respect to the timing and the effect of link and measurement speed were studied. To maintain the load equilibrating in the cloud computing system, [1] proposed a scheduling algorithm. It combines the capabilities of both OLB (Opportunistic Load Balancing) [15] and LBMM (Load Balance Min-Min) [16] scheduling algorithms and are relatively more capable. Further, [1] gave an estimate to find the most beneficial cloud resource while regarding Cooperative Power aware Scheduled Load Balancing, a solution to the Cloud load balancing challenge.

In [2], the authors designed a load balancing algorithm based on round robin in Virtual Machine (VM) environment of cloud computing in order to achieve better response time and processing time. The load balancing algorithm is done before it reaches the processing servers the job is scheduled based on various parameters like processor speed and assigned load of Virtual Machine (VM) and etc. It maintains the information in each VM and numbers of request currently allocated to VM of the system. It identify the least loaded machine, when a request come to allocate and it identified the first one if there are more than one least loaded machine. In addition [12] projected a novel server-based load balancing policy for Internet servers that are distributed everywhere the world. The main contributions of this work are: (a) the evaluation of client-based server selection schemes in scenarios where several clients use the same schemes; and (b) the proposal of a new solution that outperforms existing ones by dynamically adapting the fraction of load each client submits to each server. In order to evaluate the solution, the author have implemented in a discrete event simulator framework using Java. The author has used the PackMime Internet traffic model [3] to generate HTTP traffic in the simulations. Pack Mime allows the generation of both HTTP/1.0 and HTTP/1.1 traffic.

3   Properties of Cloud Management Systems

3.1   Cloud Computing

The principal goal of Cloud Computing is to deliver on-demand computing services with high reliability, scalability, and availability in distributed environments. Despite this common goal, Cloud Computing [1] has been defined in many different ways [4] and no standard definition has been adopted until now.

A recently posted working definition of cloud computing by The Information Technology Laboratory at the National Institute of Standards and Technology (NIST) [9] states: "Cloud Computing is a model for enabling ubiquitous, convenient, on-demand network access to a shared pool of configurable computing resources (e.g. networks, servers, storage, applications, and services) that can be rapidly provisioned and released with minimal management effort or service provider interaction. This cloud model promotes availability and is composed of five essential characteristics (Rapid Elasticity, Measured Service, On-Demand Self-Service, Ubiquitous Network Access, Location-Independent Resource Pooling), three delivery models (Software as a Service, Platform as a Service, and Infrastructure as a Service), and four deployment models (Public Cloud, Private Cloud, Community Cloud and Hybrid Cloud)".

Theoretically, in Cloud Computing everything is anticipated as a service (XaaS) [1], such as TaaS (Testing as a Service), SaaS (Software as a Service), PaaS (Plat-form as a Service), HaaS (Hardware as a Service). To this end, a large number of cloud service providers and middleware suits have emerged, each providing different Cloud Computing services. These providers include Amazon EC2, Google App Engine (GAE), SalesForce.com (SFDC), Microsoft Azure, IBM Blue Cloud, 3Tera etc.

3.2 Virtualization

Virtualization refers to that which does not exist in real, but provides everything like it is real. Virtualization is the software implementation of a machine, which will execute different programs like a real machine. Through the virtualization, user can use the different applications or services of the cloud. Ostensibly, this is the main part of the cloud environment. There are different types of virtualization used in cloud environment. Two types of virtualization are:

- Full Virtualization: Full virtualization refers to when a complete machine is installed on another machine. That virtual machine provides all the function, which exists on the original machine. It facilities only when an actual machine is unavailable then the user can use the virtual machine.
- Para virtualization: Para virtualization refers to when the hardware allows multiple operating systems to run on single machine. It also allows efficient use of system resources such as memory and processor.

3.3 Virtual Desktop Infrastructure VDI

Virtual desktop infrastructure is a desktop virtualization approach in which a desktop operating system, typically Microsoft Windows, runs and is managed in a data center. The desktop image is delivered over a network to an endpoint device, which allows the user to interact with the OS and its applications as if they were running locally. The endpoint may be a traditional PC, thin client or even a mobile device. The term coined by VMware. Virtual desktop infrastructure (VDI) is a virtualization technology that hosts a desktop operating system on a centralized server in a data center. VDI is a variation on the client-server computing model, sometimes referred to as server-based computing [10]. Virtual desktop infrastructure or VDI is a computing model that adds a layer of virtualization between the server and the desktop PCs. By installing, this virtualization in place of a more traditional operating system, network administrators can provide end users with access anywhere capabilities and a familiar desktop experience, while simultaneously heightening data security throughout the organization [13].

3.4 VDI Architecture

VDI is an architecture requiring carefully crafted solutions that meet specific needs. All VDI solutions have virtualization of the users desktop in common. A complete VDI solution may also include other design elements that compliment, extend, or leverage the core features of VMware Infrastructure virtualization platform. A full spectrum VDI solution starts with the users access device and includes a number of logically sequential components spanning the full lifecycle of user activity [13]. VDI is the one of peer-to-peer solution that reduces IT management workload, in-creases security and increases control of end user access while lowering costs by centrally delivering desktop services. Though using a remote display protocol over the network, VDI clusters put desktop environments on cloud servers or local servers to deliver a desktop-centric service [14].

4   Load Balancing in Cloud Computing

Load balancing, as is shown in Fig. 1, is a new technique that provides high resource time and effective resource utilization by assigning the total load among the various cloud nodes [12], side by side; it solves the problem of overutilization and underutilization of virtual machines. Load balancing resolve problem of overloading, focuses on maximum throughput, optimizing resource utilization, and minimize response time. Load balancing is the prerequisite for maximizing the cloud performance and utilizing the resources efficiently. In utilization of clouds, there has been an improved resource allocation method using preemptible task

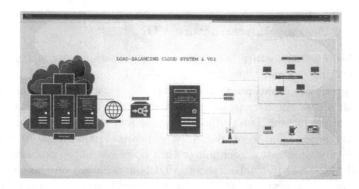

Fig. 1. Load balancing cloud system and VDI

execution. Adaptive resource allocation algorithm is presented for cloud system with preemptible tasks but this approach does not resolve the problem of response time and effective cost utilization.

4.1 Load Balancing Algorithms

In cloud computing, different load balancing algorithm have been proposed of which the main purpose is to achieve high throughput and minimum response time. Generally, load-balancing algorithm is of two types:

– A. Static load balancing algorithm
– B. Dynamic load balancing algorithm

The subsequent load balancing algorithms are currently prevalent in clouds.

4.2 Static Load Balancing Algorithm

The load does not depend on the current state of the system but it requires knowledge about the application and resources of the system. Static load balancing is a load balancing algorithms that distributes the workload based strictly on a fixed set of rules such as input workload. There are four different types of Static load balancing techniques: Round Robin algorithm, Central Manager Algorithm, Threshold algorithm and randomized algorithm.

– Round Robin Algorithm. It is one of the simplest scheduling algorithms that utilize the principle of time slices. Here, time is divided into multiple slices and each node is given a particular time interval. Each node is given a quantum and in this given quantum node has to perform its operations. If the user request completes within time quantum then user should not wait otherwise have to wait for its next slot. It means that this algorithm selects the load randomly, while in some case, some server is heavily loaded or someone is lightly loaded.
– Throttled Load Balancing Algorithm. This algorithm is totally based on the allocation of request to virtual machine. Here, client will first request the load balancer to check the right virtual machine, which access that load easily and performs the operations request by client or user. In this algorithm, the load balancer maintains an index table of virtual machines as well as their states (Available or Busy) [12]. Therefore, the client first requests the load balancer to find a suitable Virtual Machine to perform the required operations. These dynamic algorithms are being experimentally performed using the cloud analyst tool, which gives the output with respect to virtual machine

4.3 Dynamic Load Balancing Algorithm

Dynamic algorithms are more flexible than the static algorithm and do not rely on prior knowledge but depends on current state of the system. In a distributed system, dynamic load balancing has two different ways: distributed and non-distributed. In the distributed one, all nodes present in the system execute this algorithm and the task of load balancing is shared among these servers. The interaction among nodes to achieve load balancing can take two forms: cooperative and non-cooperative. In the first one, the nodes works side-by-side to achieve a common objective, which means is to improve the overall response time, etc. In the second form, each node works independently toward a goal local to it.

- Opportunistic Load Balancing Algorithm. This is static load balancing algorithm so it does not consider the current workload of the VM. It attempts to keep each node busy. This algorithm deals quickly with the unexecuted tasks in random order to the currently available node. Each task is assigned to the node randomly. It provides load balance schedule without good results. The task will process it slow in manner because it does not calculate the current execution time of the node.
- Min-Min Load Balancing Algorithm. The cloud manager identifies the execution and completion time of the unassigned tasks waiting in a queue. This is static load balancing algorithm so the parameters related to the job are known in advance. In this type of algorithm, the cloud manager first deals with the jobs having minimum execution time by assigning them to the processors according to the capability of complete the job in specified completion time. The jobs having maximum execution time has to wait for the unspecific period. Until all the tasks are assigned in the processor, the assigned tasks are updated in the processors and the task is removed from the waiting queue. This algorithm performs better when the numbers of jobs having small execution time is more than the jobs having large execution time. The main drawback of the algorithm is that it can lead to starvation.
- Max-Min Load Balancing Algorithm. Max-Min algorithm works similar to the Min-Min algorithm except the following: after finding out the minimum execution time, the cloud manager deals with tasks having maximum execution time. The assigned task is removed from the list of the tasks that are to be assigned to the processor and the execution time for all other tasks is updated on that processor. Because of its static approach the requirements are known in advance then the algorithm performed well. An enhanced version of max-min algorithm was proposed. It is based on the cases where meta-tasks contain homogeneous tasks of their completion and execution time. Improvement in the efficiency of the algorithm is achieved by increasing the opportunity of concurrent execution of tasks on resources.
- The Two Phase Scheduling Load Balancing Algorithm. It is the combination of OLB (Opportunistic Load Balancing) and LBMM (Load Balance Min-Min) Scheduling algorithms to utilize better execution efficiency and maintain the load balancing of the system. OLB scheduling algorithm keeps every node in working state to achieve the goal of load balance and LBMM scheduling algorithm is utilized to minimize the execution of time of each task on the node thereby minimizing the overall completion time. This algorithm works to enhance the utilization of resources and enhances the work efficiency.

- Ant Colony Optimization Based Load Balancing Algorithm. Aim of the ant colony optimization to search an optimal path between the source of food and colony of ant based on their behavior. This approach aims at efficiently distributing workload among the nodes. When request is initialized, the ant starts movement towards the source of food from the head node. Regional Load Balancing Node (RLBN) is chosen in Cloud Computing Service Provider (CCSP) as a head node. Ants keep records of every node they visit and record their data for future decision making. Ant deposits the pheromones during their movement for other ants to select next node. The intensity of pheromones can vary on the bases of certain factors like distance of food, quality of food etc. When the job gets successful the pheromones is updated. Each ant builds their own individual result set and later on built into a complete solution. The ant continuously updates a single result set rather than updating its own result set. By the ant pheromones trials, the solution set is continuously updated.
- Honeybee Foraging Load Balancing Algorithm. It is a nature inspired decentralized load balancing technique, which helps to achieve load balancing across heterogeneous virtual machine of cloud computing environment through local server action, and maximize the throughput. The current workload of the VM is calculated then it decides the VM states whether it is over loaded, under loaded or balanced according to the current load of VM they are grouped. The priority of the task is taken into consideration after it is removed from the overload VM, which are waiting for the VM. Then the task is schedule to the lightly loaded VM. The earlier removed task are helpful for the finding the lightly loaded VM. These tasks are known as scout bee in the next step. Honey Bee Behavior inspired Load Balancing technique reduces the response time of VM and reduces the waiting time of task.
- Active Clustering Load Balancing Algorithm. Active Clustering works based on grouping similar nodes and increases the performance of the algorithm the process of grouping is based on the concept of matchmaker node. Matchmaker node forms connection between its neighbors that is like the initial node. Then the matchmaker node disconnects the connection between itself and the initial node. The above set of processes is done repetitively. The performance of the system tends to increase because of high availability of resources, because of that, the throughput is propelled to also increase.

4.4   Motivation of Load Balancing Algorithms

There are countless reasons for coalescing cloud management systems with virtual desktop infrastructure of which the major is load balancing. Efficient load balancing algorithm provides efficient and dynamic workload across nodes. Research indicates the countless problems posed by this imbalance and inefficiency in these systems to provide these services to requesting nodes. Many cloud systems vendors keeps proliferating providing services to organizations hence the failure or imbalance of load distribution dynamically to various subscribers, therefore a critical reason which calls for thorough research in this area of study.

4.5   Analysis of Load Balancing Algorithms

Based on a collective and qualitative approach various documentations were reviewed relating to load balancing algorithms in cloud management systems and VDI. A comparison of the various existing load balancing algorithms were revisited. The table below presents the comparison table of the aforementioned. The table gives us detailed descriptions of the various mechanisms of load balancing algorithms which has been made simple with a TRUE and FALSE elaborating its capabilities and limitations individually in Table 1.

Table 1. Algorithm comparative metrics table

	ROUND ROBIN	OLB	MIN MIN	MIN MAX	TWO PHASE
Fault tolerance	F	F	F	F	F
Overhead	T	F	T	T	T
Throughput	T	F	T	T	T
Response time	T	F	T	T	T
Performance	T	T	T	T	T
Scalability	F	F	F	F	F
Resource utilization	T	T	T	T	
	ANT COLONY	HONEY BEE	ACTIVE CLUSTERING	BIASED RANDOM SAMPLING	
Fault tolerance	F	F	F	F	
Overhead	F	F	T	F	
Throughput	T	T	F	T	
Response time	F	F	F	F	
Performance	T	T	F	T	
Scalability	T	T	F	F	
Resource utilization	T	F	T	F	

5   Conclusion and Future Work

This paper has presented a survey on cloud computing and various algorithm for load balancing in cloud computing. It is no doubt that cloud computing is one of the most emerging technology in computer science but it also has some lapses and load balancing is one of the major lapses of the cloud. This issue can be resolved by using various load balancing algorithm that balances the workload. This paper reviews some of the various load balancing algorithms like Honey Bee, Round Robin, OLB, BRS, Active Clustering, Min-Min, Min-Max and Ant Colony Optimization. Further, the survey also highlights comparison of the parameters between algorithms under review and their distinguishing properties.

According to the survey, none of the algorithms seem to completely satisfy the comparative metrics to solve the lapses of load balancing in cloud computing, as such load balancing still remains a critical issue for scientific research.

References

1. Armbrust, M., Fox, A., Griffith, R., Joseph, A.D., Katz, R.H.: Above the clouds: a berkeley view of cloud computing. Commun. ACM **53**(4), 50–58 (2009). Eecs Department University of California Berkeley
2. Begum, S., Prashanth, C.S.R.: Review of load balancing in cloud computing. Int. J. Comput. Sci. Issues **10**(1), s536 (2013)
3. Cao, J., Cleveland, W.S., Gao, Y., Jeffay, K., Smith, F.D., Weigle, M.: Stochastic models for generating synthetic HTTP source traffic. In: Joint Conference of the IEEE Computer and Communications Societies, vol. 3, pp. 1546–1557 (2004)
4. Cavoukian, A.: Privacy in the clouds - a white paper on privacy and digital identity implications for the internet (2008). https://www.ipc.on.ca/wp-content/uploads/2008/05/privacyintheclouds.pdf
5. Dasilva, D.A., Liu, L., Bessis, N., Zhan, Y.: Enabling green it through building a virtual desktop infrastructure. In: Eighth International Conference on Semantics, Knowledge and Grids, pp. 32–38 (2012)
6. Daz, M., Martn, C., Rubio, B.: State-of-the-art, challenges, and open issues in the integration of internet of things and cloud computing. J. Netw. Comput. Appl. **67**(C), 99–117 (2016)
7. Liu, J., Lai, W.: Security analysis of VLAN-based virtual desktop infrastructure. In: International Conference on Educational and Network Technology, pp. 301–304 (2010)
8. Lu, Y., Xie, Q., Kliot, G., Geller, A., Larus, J.R., Greenberg, A.: Join-idle-queue: A novel load balancing algorithm for dynamically scalable web services. Perform. Eval. **68**(11), 1056–1071 (2011)
9. Mell, P., Grance, T.: The nist definition of cloud computing. Commun. ACM **53**(6), 50 (2009)
10. Moharana, S.S.: Analysis of load balancers in cloud computing. Int. J. Comput. Sci. Eng. **2**(2), 101–108 (2013)
11. Moura, J., Hutchison, D.: Review and analysis of networking challenges in cloud computing. J. Netw. Comput. Appl. **60**, 113–129 (2016)
12. Nakai, A.M., Madeira, E., Buzato, L.E.: Improving the QOS of web services via client-based load distribution. In: XXIX Simpósio Brasileiro de Redes de Computadores e Sistemas Distribuídos (2011)
13. Sharma, R., Kumar, A.: Load balancing in cloud computing system. AJES, 1(2) (2012)
14. Shimonski, R.: Windows server 2003 clustering & load balancing (ebook), 1st edn. Windows Server. McGraw-Hill Education (2003). ISBN-13: 978-0072226225, ISBN-10: 0072226226
15. Wang, S.C., Yan, K.Q., Liao, W.P., Wang, S.S.: Towards a load balancing in a three-level cloud computing network. In: IEEE International Conference on Computer Science and Information Technology, pp. 108–113 (2010)
16. Zhang, Z.P., Wen, L.J.: Loba-min-min: The grid resources scheduling algorithm based on load balance. Appl. Mech. Mater. **321–324**, 2507–2513 (2013)

IoT Applications

Design and Deployment of Wireless Sensor Networks for Flood Detection in Indonesia

Irfan Dwiguna Sumitra(✉), Rongtao Hou, and Sri Supatmi

School of Computer and Software, Nanjing University of Information Science and Technology, Jiangsu, China
irfan_dwiguna@unikom.ac.id

Abstract. Flood is one of the major of the natural disasters that cause casualties and infrastructure damage. The flood often happens in several regions in Indonesia caused by high rainfall during the rainy season. This paper describes the design and deployment of the system to detect the elevation of water level in the river automatically. Alert system of the surface water has been completed by employing an ultrasonic sensor-based microcontroller with communication via wireless, which will determine the water heights whether are below, normal or above states. The results of the implemented system have an accuracy of the ultrasonic sensor that generates mean error obtained of 0.97% and RMSE is 0.36 for each increase in 1 cm.

Keywords: Alert system · Flood · Ultrasonic sensor · Wireless sensor networks

1 Introduction

Flooding is one of the major disasters occurring in various parts of the world especially Indonesia. Flooding able to prevent by making a reasonable decision to the actions necessary to be performed using real-time monitored data such as flow, precipitation level or water level on an early warning system [1]. The main effects of flooding are material, human, economic and social losses in flooded areas, infection from waterborne diseases and contaminated water. Given this situation, the essential is the monitoring of river levels. However, carrying out monitoring as an isolated task will not put an end to the human and financial losses [2].

Indonesia has a tropical climate which is variable from area to area. The primary variable is not temperature or air pressure, but precipitation. The extreme variations in rainfall are sometimes connecting to changing the monsoons. Generally speaking, there is a dry season from June to September influenced by the Australian continental air masses, and a rainy season from December to March that is the result of mainland Asia and the Pacific Ocean air masses. Prevailing wind patterns interact with local topographic conditions to produce significant variations in rainfall throughout the archipelago. In general, western and northern parts of Indonesia experience the most precipitation, since the north- and westward-moving monsoon clouds are heavy with moisture by the time they reach these more distant regions. Western Sumatra, Java, Bali, the

© Springer International Publishing AG 2017
X. Sun et al. (Eds.): ICCCS 2017, Part I, LNCS 10602, pp. 313–325, 2017.
https://doi.org/10.1007/978-3-319-68505-2_27

interiors of Kalimantan, Sulawesi, and Papua are the most predictably damp parts of Indonesia, with rainfall measuring more than 2,000 mm per year [3].

Wireless Sensor Networks (WSNs) is a device that has low power and small size with a standard sensor which able to detect events such data and transmit the sensed data in more or less homogeneously in a geographical region. Detecting event or send the sensed data could using a two-tiered approach having clusters of short distance communicating nodes together with some nodes capable of communication over a wider range [4–6]. WSNs also using for real-time monitoring that has the capability to capture some object quickly, process, and transmit pf critical high-resolution data [6].

This research builds a system for detecting the floods in some flood-prone areas and warms the communities or stakeholder that responsibility with the flood warning to prevent them from the disaster. The system consists of Arduino nano as a microcontroller, an ultrasonic sensor as water level detection, buzzer and light emitting diode (LED) as notification as well as a personal computer for the network interface. Basically, the communication by wireless where the water level detection consists if two segments, receiver and transmitter.

2   Related Work

In [5], this paper only presents a forecasting model designed using WSNs to predict flood in rivers using a straightforward and fast calculation to provide real-time results. The simulation results present for the predicted water level compared to the actual water level. This research is only made simulation without implementation in a real environment using hardware component such as a sensor to detect the water level.

In [6], the research talked about detection of landslides system using WSNs. It was design, development, and deployment in a real environment. The research result showed useful capability, but there is any weakness: the cost of this investigation are expensive for small area development, unable to the optimal number of geophysical sensor and used more energy consumptions that affect the lifetime of WSNs.

In [7], proposed innovative framework to detect flood and send an alert to the local community that covers both wireless sensor networks components and Arduino-based technology. This paper only present the idea to detect the flood without implementation in the environment.

In [8], this paper present simulation and testing flooding/drought forecasting possibilities in wireless sensor networks based on flood/drought forecasting system (FDFS) to help authorities gain early information for Pakistan using Network Simulator (NS). This research only focuses on simulation for flooding/drought without implementing hardware system, e.g., sensors, microcontroller, real wireless sensor networks in the real environment.

In [9], this paper proposed a conceptual rainfall-runoff model to give flash flood warning system by Lorent/Gevers serves for the Truse absorption in Thuringia Germany. This research only present with respect to a theoretical for flood warning system and not implemented that theoretical in the environment.

The new contributions in this paper compared with [5–9] are summarized as follows:

1. For the first time, we proposed the design and deployment of the system to detect the water level in order that preparedness against the flood disaster in Indonesia with employing radio frequency (RF), where the alert system is absence in the real environment.
2. The design is made in a size of hardware that is quite small, low cost and low power, and capable of covering a large area.
3. Through rigorous analysis and experiments on the artificial water tank, our proposed systems are efficient and feasible to measure the water level.

3 Component Requirements

In this section describes the fundamental both hardware and software components to construction the system, such as Arduino Nano, ultrasonic sensor, buzzer, and RF-433 MHz as well as Arduino Integrated Development Environment (IDE).

The Arduino Nano is a small, complete, and bread-friendly board based on the ATmega328 as Arduino Nano 3.0. It lacks only a DC power jack and works with a Mini-B USB cable instead of a standard one. This Arduino is working in operating voltage with logic level 5 V. Input voltage from 7 V to 12 V. Have 14 pins of digital I/O. It also has flash memory 16 KB to 32 KB, and EEPROM from 512 bytes to 1 KB [10] (Fig. 1).

Fig. 1. Arduino Nano

The sensor utilized ultrasonic ranging module HC-SR04. This sensor module provides non-contact measurement function from 2 cm to 400 cm. The modules include ultrasonic transmitters, receiver, and control unit. The fundamental principle of work for this module is using an IO trigger for at least 10 μs high-level signals, automatically sends eight 40 kHz and detect whether there is a pulse signal back and if the signal back, through high level, time of high output IO duration is the time from sending ultrasonic to returning [11].

The physical characteristic of the ultrasonic wave appears as below:

$$r = \frac{(h_t \times v_s)}{2} \tag{1}$$

Where r is the range of ultrasonic, h_t is the high level time between sending trigger signal and receiving echo signal and v_s is the velocity of sound is 340 m/s (Fig. 2).

Fig. 2. Ultrasonic sensor module

A buzzer is a signaling device that converting electricity signal to sound signal. Buzzer consists of vibrator: thin metal plate and thick metal plate, have low-frequency tone around 2 kHz. Those metal plate conducted by voltage to working and make a sound [12]. In the proposed research, buzzer has a function to give notification if water level sensor is changing (Fig. 3).

Fig. 3. Buzzer

RF-433 MHz is a micro transceiver for high-speed transmission of data signals. It can package, detect the error and correct error of transmitted data. Components of RF-433 MHz are industry grade standard, small size, easy to install and are stable and reliable. It can apply to security alarm, wireless automatic meter reading, home and industrial automation, remote control, wireless data transmission and other systems [13] (Fig. 4).

Fig. 4. Radio frequency 433 MHz module

Specific software called Arduino IDE is available to program any Arduino compatible board with a C-like programming language. This software supplies a serial monitor which allows not only reading but also sending data through a serial connection. With growing number of product-specific libraries, Arduino offers useful tools for designs related to embedded systems [14].

4 System Design

The design of the alert system itself consists of two main parts namely hardware system and a data collection of the software system. The hardware is employing the microcontroller as data processing, an ultrasonic sensor as an input system, buzzer and LED as a notification system as well as radio frequency as wireless communication. On the other hand, applied to a personal computer for receiving the data from hardware system and send back the notification to enable the alert system when the flood occurs.

4.1 Design of Hardware

Global of system architecture consists of transmitter and receiver system. The transmitter is sending the data sensors to the receiver. Suppose there are two alert systems in the river as sensor 1 and sensor 2, respectively. After that, they will send the water height information to the personal computer as depicted in Fig. 5.

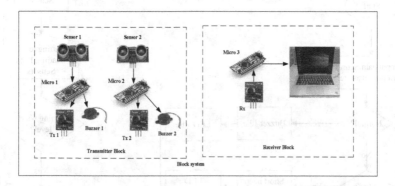

Fig. 5. Block system architecture

Figure 6 shown the design of the ultrasonic sensor. The ultrasonic sensor is placed at the top of the PVC pipe as the level gauge tube in the river. Each span of 5 cm from the bottom of the pipeline is used as an indicator of whether the water levels are normal, alert or danger states. This method works when ripple water submerges in pipes of small holes leading to the measurement.

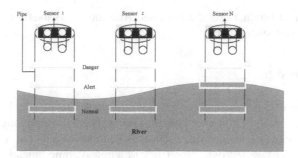

Fig. 6. Design of ultrasonic sensor in transmitter system

The ultrasonic which will continuously sense the water level data from the surface of the water. Otherwise, the result that wants to achieve is the height of water level from the bottom to the surface. To solve this problem using the algorithm in the microcontroller at the transmitter. The algorithm in Fig. 7(a) and (b) shown the transmitter and receiver that attached into the microcontroller.

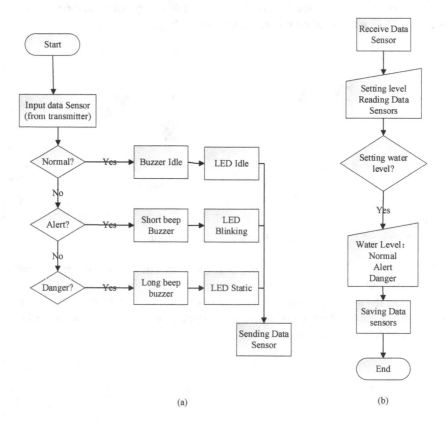

(a)   (b)

Fig. 7. The algorithm of (a) transmitter and (b) receiver program.

The communication between transmitter and receiver using wireless radio frequency. The radio frequency utilized amplitude shift keying (ASK) modulation. ASK modulation consists of modulator and demodulator. ASK Modulator applicable for converting the binary data from microcontroller to analog signal in ASK shown in Fig. 8 before sending through the transmitter. Due to the binary signal unable to communicate directly using analog modulation. Application in the personal computer able to read the demodulator ASK in use to converting the analog signal that receives from radio frequency to the binary data, and the data from the transmitter.

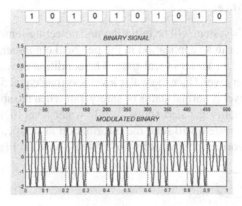

Fig. 8. Amplitude shift keying modulation

In the Fig. 9 shows overall system within the transmitter hand that the ultrasonic sensor has four pins: VCC, GND, Echo and Trigger. The VCC connects to 5 V in the microcontroller pin, GND connects to GND, Trigger to D9 and Echo to D8. After that

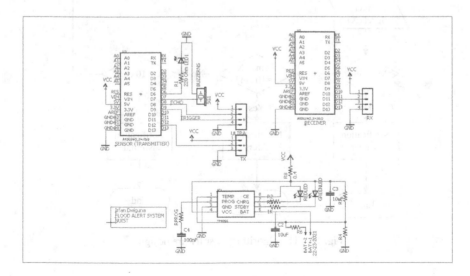

Fig. 9. Schematic of alert system

for notify system, our connected the resistor 220 Ω to LED in D6 and buzzer to D7. The RF-433 as a communication link to D12. The system can work with a supply voltage from 2 batteries of 2.4 V with a current of 1900 mAh. The DC converter is using to step up boost the voltage of 2.4 V to 5 V with 500 mA. The solar cell utilized as source power to batteries of the whole system. For charging the batteries through the solar cell using TP4056 so that the system more portable application. In the other hand, our connecting the RF-433 to D11 in the microcontroller.

4.2 Design of Software

Software design of this system will be initiating and detecting sensor of water elevation by the ultrasonic sensor in an application in the personal computer. The system will be showing the result of data sensor in real-time. The condition of water gives some notification for every water level. Once the water level less than equal 5 cm from the sensor, it is mean the water level is normal status or safety, but when the span of water level for 6 cm to 10 cm, then notify the alert status. While water level higher than 10 cm, it is potential to flood; the system will send the information as notification and display the danger status. The algorithm for this software system shown in Fig. 10.

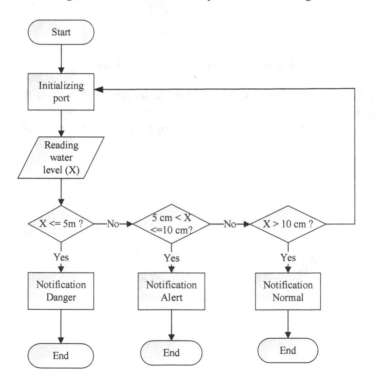

Fig. 10. The algorithm of software design

5 Result and Analysis

5.1 Calibration of Ultrasonic Sensor

Model calibration consists of adjusting the model of the ultrasonic sensor as an input parameter, the initial condition of water level and air temperature so that model simulates the alert system to the desired degree of accuracy. The calibration process involves matching water level, buzzer and LED changes as well as a range of communication.

The principal work of ultrasonic sensor within this experiment acquired with three conditions:

- State 1: water elevation less than equal 5 cm from the sensor is the normal state.
- State 2: water elevation more than 5 cm and less than equal 10 cm from the sensor is an alert state.
- State 3: water elevation more than 10 cm from the sensor is the danger state.

Table 1 demonstrates that all parameters in the alert system have been calibrated. As input parameter detected by the ultrasonic sensor, after that the output will notice through the LED and buzzer to warning the people when the water is overflow.

Table 1. Calibration of the sensors

Water level	Sensor	LED	Buzzer	Status
$x > 10$ cm	Detecting	Static	Long beep	Danger
10 cm $\geq x > 5$ cm	Detecting	Blinking	Short beep	Alert
$x \leq 5$ cm	Detecting	Idle	Idle	Normal

Fig. 11. Hardware of flood detection sensor

Figure 11 shown the complete hardware system consist of an ultrasonic sensor, microcontroller, RF module, and solar cell which able to provide supply to two batteries with specification voltage of 2.4 V and current capacity of 1900 mAh.

5.2 Experiment Result

In this section, we examined the water level through a personal computer via RF-433 MHz with low frequency. The ultrasonic sensor sends the data from a transmitter placed in a river to the receiver in every second and real-time. Tables 2 and 3 are lists the data of water level sensor.

Table 2. Result of experiment of sensor

Actual water level (cm)	Measure water level (cm)	Period (µs)	Error (%)	Status of water level
1	1	918	0.00	Normal
2	2	849	0.00	Normal
3	3	775	0.00	Normal
4	4	694	0.00	Normal
5	5	640	0.00	Normal
6	6	577	0.00	Alert
7	7	518	0.00	Alert
8	8	458	0.00	Alert
9	9	440	0.00	Alert
10	10	392	0.00	Alert
11	12	240	8.33	Danger
12	12	207	0.00	Danger
13	13	189	0.00	Danger
14	14	159	0.00	Danger
15	16	98	6.25	Danger

Table 3. Result of experiment of sensor within distance

Distance (m)	Water level (X in cm)	Average of period (µs)	Status of water level
5	$X \leq 5$	805	Normal
	$10 \leq X > 5$	473.2	Alert
	$X > 10$	196.8	Danger
10	$X \leq 5$	806	Normal
	$10 \leq X > 5$	473	Alert
	$X > 10$	196	Danger
15	$X \leq 5$	804	Normal
	$10 \leq X > 5$	473.1	Alert
	$X > 10$	195	Danger
20	$X \leq 5$	808	Normal
	$10 \leq X > 5$	473.5	Alert
	$X > 10$	197	Danger

In Table 2 contains the elevation from 1 cm to 15 cm, period and error of the ultrasonic sensing and the information status as well. The highest level of the water means that the surface water nearest with ultrasonic sensors and the lowest level means that the bottom of the water distant with an ultrasonic sensor.

Table 3 shown the experiment of water height for 1 cm to 15 cm with different range communication in the span of 5 m up to 20 m.

5.3 Analysis Results

The experiment performed to show that water level is affected by the echo and trigger of the ultrasonic sensors to sensing the water surface data and then transmitted the data to the computer screen and displayed the result of analyzed (numerical and graph). Figure 12 demonstrated the sensor required less time to detect the water level while the water level in the artificial tank increases.

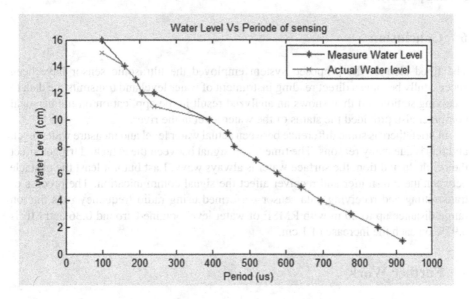

Fig. 12. Graphic of water level against time

The ultrasonic sensor has an error in sensing of water level, based on the root mean square error (RMSE) at the actual water level against the measure water level. The RMSE is defined by formula (2) as below:

$$RMSE = \sqrt{\frac{\sum_{i=1}^{k} \left\| h - \bar{h} \right\|}{k}} \tag{2}$$

Since h is actual of water height, $\bar{h}$ is a measure of water height, whereas k is a set of the water height.

The following Table 2, RMSE for the experiment obtain 0.36. It is mean that measured water level has the capability to minimize the error level so that its result more accurate even when the distance is farther away from the transmitter.

According to the experiment within Table 2, compared with the actual water level utilizing a ruler and measuring the water level sensing by ultrasonic sensor is obtained ME with the following formula:

$$ME(\%) = \frac{\sum_{i=1}^{n} \| A_w - M_w \|}{n} \times 100\% \tag{3}$$

Since n is a set to water level, Aw is an actual water level, and Mw is measured water level.

As formula (3) obtain ME is 0.97% on each water height of 1 cm. It is mean that measure water level sensing by ultrasonic sensor has high accuracy and the systems running properly.

6   Conclusion

The flood alert of the proposed system employed the ultrasonic sensor have been successfully become a direct reading instrument of water level and transmits the data to receiving station and then shows an analyzed result in the application on the personal computer also provided the status of the water level in the river.

In brief, there is some difference between actual water level and measure water level, and this is due many reasons. The time travel signal between the echo and trigger affect the result. In addition, the surface water is always wavy. Last but not least the obstacle between the transmitter and receiver affect the signal communication. The process of transmitting and receiving data sensor performed using radio frequency runs fine on range distance up to 20 m with RMSE of water level obtained around 0.36 and ME is 0.97% on each the increase of 1 cm.

7   Further Work

Further work of this experiment is by adding Global Positioning System (GPS) to aware with respect to location of the sensors more precision in an outdoor environment as well as implement security on data that can be sent to cloud computing according to the proposed schemes in [15–17].

Competing Interests. The author declares that there is no conflict of interests regarding the publication of this paper.

Acknowledgements. First of all, author thank Prof. Hou Rongtao and Prof. Shen Jian for their thoroughness, valuable advice, and patience. Also, the author would like to thank Sri Supatmi who always encourages and inspires with new ideas in our research.

References

1. Khedo, K.K.: Real-time flood monitoring using wireless sensor networks. J. Inst. Eng. Maurit. 59–69 (2013)
2. Degrossi, L.C., Do Amaral, G.G., De Vasconcelos, E.S.M., de Albuquerque, J.P., Ueyama, J.: Using wireless sensor networks in the sensor web for flood monitoring in Brazil. In: Proceedings of the 10th International ISCRAM Conference, Baden-Baden, Germany, pp. 458–462, May 2013
3. Frederick, W.H., Worden, R.L.: Indonesia: A Country Study:, GPO for the Library of Congress, Washington, US, (1993). http://countrystudies.us/indonesia/29.htm
4. Nugroho, R.B., Susanto, E., Sunarya, U.: Wireless sensor network for prototype of fire detection. In: 2nd International Conference on Information and Communication Technology (ICoICT) (2014)
5. Seal, V., Raha, A., Maity, S., Mitra, S.K., Mukherjee, A., Naskar, M.K.: A simple flood forecasting scheme using wireless sensor network. Int. J. Ad Hoc Sens. Ubiquit. Comput. (IJASUC) 3(1), 45–60 (2012)
6. Ramesh, M.V.: Design, development, and deployment of a wireless sensor network for detection of landslides. J. Ad Hoc Netw. 13, 2–18 (2014)
7. Vunabandi, V., Matsunaga, R., Markon, S., Willy, N.: Flooding sensing framework by Arduino and wireless sensor network in rural-rwanda. In: SNPD 2015, Takamatsu, Japan. IEEE, 1–3 June 2015
8. Khan, F., Memon, S., Jokhio, I.A., Jokhio, S.H.: Wireless sensor network based flood/drought forecasting system. IEEE (2015)
9. Linke, H., Karimanzira, D., Rauschenbach, T., Pfützenreuter, T.: Flash Flood prediction for small rivers. IEEE (2011)
10. Anonymous: Arduino Nano Datasheet. www.robomania.ro/datasheet/Arduino_Nano_ robomania.pdf. Accessed 20 Feb 2017
11. Anonymous: Ultrasonic Ranging Module HC-SR04. http://www.micropik.com/PDF/ HCSR04.pdf. Accessed 20 Feb 2017
12. Anonymous. Piezoelectric Buzzers Datasheet, May 2011. https://product.tdk.com/info/en/ catalog/datasheets/ef532_ps.pdf
13. Chunjiang, Y.: Development of a smart home control system based on mobile internet technology. Int. J. Smart Home 10(3), 293–300 (2016). http://dx.doi.org/10.14257/ijsh. 2016.10.3.28
14. Gokceli, S., Zhmurov, N., Karabulut Kurt, G., Ors, B.: IoT in action: design and implementation of a building evacuation service. J. Comput. Netw. Commun. 2017 (2017). Article ID 8595404. https://doi.org/10.1155/2017/8595404
15. Gu, B., Sheng, V.S.: A robust regularization path algorithm for v-support vector classification. IEEE Trans. Neural Netw. Learn. Syst. 28, 1241–1248 (2016)
16. Xia, Z., Wang, X., Zhang, L., Qin, Z., Sun, X., Ren, K.: A privacy-preserving and copy-deterrence content-based image retrieval scheme in cloud computing. IEEE Trans. Inf. Forensics Secur. 11(11), 2594–2608 (2016)
17. Fu, Z., Ren, K., Shu, J., Sun, X., Huang, F.: Enabling personalized search over encrypted outsourced data with efficiency improvement. IEEE Trans. Parallel Distrib. Syst. 27(9), 2546–2559 (2016)

An Android App Recommendation Approach by Merging Network Traffic Cost

Xin Su[1,2,3], Xuchong Liu[1,2,3], Jiuchuan Lin[4(✉)], and Yu Tong[1,2,3]

[1] Hunan Provincial Key Laboratory of Network Investigational Technology,
Hunan Police Academy, Changsha, China
[2] Key Laboratory of Network Crime Investigation of Hunan Provincial Colleges,
Hunan Police Academy, Changsha, China
[3] Department of Information Technology, Hunan Police Academy, Changsha, China
suxin@hnu.edu.cn, 14117874@qq.com, 867530256@qq.com
[4] Key Lab of Information Network Security of Ministry of Public Security,
The Third Research Institute of Ministry of Public Security, Shanghai, China
linjiuchuan@stars.org.cn

Abstract. A large amount and different types of mobile applications are being offered to end users via app markets. Existing mobile app markets generally recommend the most popular mobile apps to mobile users for purpose of facilitate the proper selection of mobile apps. However, these apps normally generate network traffic, which will consumes user mobile data plan and may even cause potential security issues. Therefore, more and more mobile users are hesitant or even reluctant to use the mobile apps that are recommended by the mobile app markets. To fill this crucial gap, we propose a mobile app recommendation approach which can provide app recommendations by considering both the app popularity and their traffic cost. To achieve this goal, we first estimate app network traffic score based on bipartite graph. Then, we propose a flexible approach based on *Benefit-Cost analysis*, which can recommend apps by maintaining a balance between the app popularity and the traffic cost concern. Finally, we evaluate our approach with extensive experiments on a large-scale data set collected from Google Play. The experimental results clearly validate the effectiveness and efficiency of our approach.

1 Introduction

With the explosive increase to the number of smartphones and tablets in recent years, the popularity and quantity of the mobile applications (apps) are also growing noticeably. However, mobile apps are highly different and often poorly understood, particularly for their activities and functions that are related to network traffic usage. Moreover, some malware or third-party advertisement (or ad) libraries may collect privacy information and send to remote servers [1], which may result in the potential security issues for users. Therefore, it is critical to develop mobile App recommender system that is aware of network traffic usage for the healthy development of the mobile App industry.

© Springer International Publishing AG 2017
X. Sun et al. (Eds.): ICCCS 2017, Part I, LNCS 10602, pp. 326–338, 2017.
https://doi.org/10.1007/978-3-319-68505-2_28

Recently, there have been several research efforts on network traffic analysis for mobile apps, and also mobile app recommendations. Some prior works focused on mobile app identification [2] or perform network traffic characterization of mobile apps [3]. However, little research effort has been made to investigate network traffic usage of mobile apps when they are running, which is important both for wisely using mobile data plan and also for security and privacy preservation. Meanwhile, in the area of mobile App recommendation, some prior research works studied the personalized App recommendation methods [4,5], and Appolicious ranks and recommends mobile apps using reviews, friend recommendations and the list of apps that are currently installed by the end user.

To address these limitations, we propose a mobile app recommendation approach merging network traffic cost. First, this approach is analyzes the generated network traffic in order to measure network traffic cost of each mobile app based on the random walk regularization with an *app-host bipartite graph*, which can learn the traffic cost of mobile apps automatically without relying on any predefined traffic cost function. Then, based on the *modern portfolio theory*, we develop a flexible optimization approach for recommending apps by considering both apps popularity and users concerns about traffic cost. Finally, we evaluate our mobile app recommendation approach with extensive experiments on a real-world data set collected from Google Play, which contains 2,200 Android apps. The experimental results clearly validate the effectiveness and efficiency of our approach in terms of different evaluation metrics.

In summary, the main contributions of this work are listed as following:

- We propose and implement a mobile app recommender system, which can recommend mobile app using three different kinds of criteria: app popularity, traffic cost and hybrid.
- We propose an approach to accurately estimate the network traffic cost score of each mobile app for ranking purpose, which does not rely on any predefined traffic cost function.
- We evaluate the recommender system with extensive experiments on a real-world data set, and the results of experiment show that our recommender system not only can recommend mobile app based on either app's popularity or traffic cost, but it also can recommend mobile app based on both of these two criteria.

The rest of this paper is organized as follows. Section 2 introduces a framework of the recommender system. Section 3 describes traffic cost score estimation. Section 4 discusses the details of mobile app rank. In Sect. 5, we evaluate our approach with real world mobile traffic traces. We summary the related work in Sect. 6, and conclude this paper in Sect. 7.

2   System Overview

Figure 1 shows the proposed recommendation framework, which consists of two stages. The *offline learning stage* automatically learns the traffic cost scores for

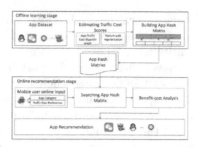

Fig. 1. Overview of app recommendation

apps by leveraging the random walk regularization with an *app-host bipartite graph*, and forms an *app hash matrix* from the app data set for efficiently managing apps. The *online recommendation stage* matches the given traffic cost and app categories according to the *app hash matrix*, ranks the candidate apps with respect to both apps popularity and traffic cost by leveraging the *Benefit-cost analysis* for recommendations.

3   Traffic Cost Score Estimation

In this section, we will explain how to estimate traffic cost score for mobile app, which reflect traffic cost level of a mobile app. The smaller the score is, the less traffic cost of the app is. We can know the traffic cost are essentially caused by the generated traffic and accessed different sources of apps, such as *original traffic* or *CDN+Cloud traffic*. Some of them are caused by third-party library, even malicious code, which are not necessary to an app. Thus, an intuitive approach for measuring the traffic cost of apps is to directly check traffic size of each kind of host when they access.

3.1   APP-TRAFFIC Cost Bipartite Graph

In this paper, we propose a regularization approach based on a bipartite graph [6], which can learn the traffic cost of mobile apps automatically without relying on any predefined traffic cost function. Particularly, we develop an app-traffic cost bipartite graph to build the connections between apps and traffic cost, which is defined as follows.

The graph can be denoted as $G = \{V, E, W\}$. $V = \{V^a, V^t\}$ is the node set, where $V^a = \{a_1, ..., a_M\}$ denotes the set of apps and $V^h = \{h_1, ..., h_N\}$ denotes the set of different kinds of hosts accessed by the apps. E is the edge set, where $e_{ij} \in E$ exists if and only if a_i access h_j during execution. W is the edge weight set, where each $w_{ij} \in W$ represents the weight of e_{ij} and denotes the probability that a_i will access h_j during execution.

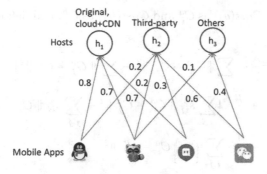

Fig. 2. An example of the bipartite graph

Figure 2 shows an example of app-traffic cost bipartite graph. Intuitively, the weight w_{ij} can be estimated by the traffic records of all Apps in a_i s category. Because traffic size of each kind of host accessed by the apps is different. Specifically, we can compute the weight by

$$w_{ij} = \frac{f_{ij}}{\sum_{e_{ik} \in E} f_{ik}} \times T$$

$$T = \frac{Trafficsize_{h_j}^{a_i}}{\sum_{i=1}^{N} Trafficsize_{h_j}^{a_i}}, (j = 1, ..., M) \tag{1}$$

where f_{ij} is the number of apps in category c ($a_i \epsilon c$) accessing host h_j, parameter T represents result of traffic size generated by each app accessed host h_j in category c divide the total traffic size generated by total apps accessed host h_j in category c. Furthermore, we can denote each app a_j and accessed hosts h_j as vectors $\boldsymbol{a_i} = w_{i1}, ..., w_{iN}$ and $\boldsymbol{h_j} = w_{1j}, ..., w_{Mj}$, respectively. Accordingly, we define the latent similarity between apps a_i and a_j by the Cosine distance,

$$s_{ij}^a = Cos(\boldsymbol{a_i}, \boldsymbol{a_j}) = \frac{\boldsymbol{a_i} \cdot \boldsymbol{a_j}}{\| \boldsymbol{a_i} \| \cdot \| \boldsymbol{a_j} \|} \tag{2}$$

Similarly, we define the latent similarity between accessed hosts h_i and h_j as $s_{ij}^h = Cos(\boldsymbol{h_i}, \boldsymbol{h_j})$.

3.2 Traffic Cost Score Estimation

To estimate app traffic cost score with app-traffic cost bipartite graph, we first define two traffic cost scores $Cost(a_i)$ and $Cost(h_j)$ for node $a_i \epsilon V^a$ and $h_j \epsilon V^h$, respectively. Intuitively, $Cost(a_i)$ is the objective app traffic cost score and $Cost(h_j)$ is the global host cost score. Second, we develop a regularization framework by regularizing the smoothness of the above two scores over the bipartite graph. We denote $Cost(a_i)$ as C_i^a and $Cost(h_j)$ as C_j^h, and define a cost function as follows,

$$\varrho(a, h) = \frac{\lambda}{2} \cdot \{\sum_i \| C_i^a - \tilde{C}_i^a \|^2 + \sum_j \| C_j^h - \tilde{C}_j^h \|^2\}$$
$$+ \frac{\mu}{2} \cdot \{\sum_{i,j} s_{ij}^a \| C_i^a - C_j^a \|^2 + \sum_{i,j} s_{ij}^h \| C_i^h - C_j^h \|^2\} \tag{3}$$
$$+ \frac{1}{2} \cdot \sum_{i,j} w_{ij}^a \| C_i^a - C_j^h \|^2$$

where λ and μ are the regularization parameters, $\tilde{C}_i^a$ and $\tilde{C}_j^h$ are the *prior traffic cost scores* derived from external knowledge.

Intuitively, this cost function is formed by three parts. The first part controlled by λ defines the constraint that the two traffic cost scores should fit prior knowledge. The second part controlled by μ defines the global consistency of the refined traffic cost scores over the graph. Specifically, it satisfies that, if two apps and their accessed hosts have high latent similarity, their traffic cost scores should be similar. The third part is the smoothness constraint between apps and accessed hosts, which guarantees that, if an app has high probability to access a specific kind of host, their traffic cost scores should be similar. Therefore, the problem of estimating traffic cost scores is converted to the optimization problem of finding optimal C_i^a and C_j^h to minimize the cost function ϱ. In this paper, we exploit the classic gradient descent method to solve this problem. Specifically, we first assign values to $C_i^a = \frac{1}{M}$ and $C_j^h = \frac{1}{N}$ and iteratively update them by setting the following differentiated results to zero.

$$\frac{\partial \varrho}{\partial a_i} = \lambda(C_i^a - \tilde{C}_i^a) + \mu \sum_j s_{ij}^a(C_i^a - C_j^a) + \sum_j w_{ij}(C_i^a - C_j^h),$$
$$C_i^a = \frac{\lambda \tilde{C}_i^a + \mu \sum_j s_{ij}^a C_j^a + \sum_j w_{ij} C_j^h}{\lambda + \mu \sum_j s_{ij}^a + \sum_j w_{ij}}. \tag{4}$$

$$\frac{\partial \varrho}{\partial h_j} = \lambda(C_j^h - \tilde{C}_j^h) + \mu \sum_j s_{ij}^h(C_j^h - C_i^h) + \sum_j w_{ij}(C_j^h - C_i^a),$$
$$C_j^h = \frac{\lambda \tilde{C}_j^h + \mu \sum_j s_{ij}^h C_j^h + \sum_j w_{ij} C_i^a}{\lambda + \mu \sum_j s_{ij}^h + \sum_j w_{ij}}. \tag{5}$$

After each iteration, all the values of C_i^a and C_j^h will be normalized again. i.e., $\| C^a \|_1 = 1$ and $\| C^h \|_1 = 1$. Finally, we can obtain the optimal traffic cost scores after the results converge.

According to the above Eqs. 3, 4 and 5, we notice that the key of estimating traffic cost scores is how to assign prior traffic cost scores $\tilde{C}_i^a$ and $\tilde{C}_j^h$ from external knowledge need to solve. In practice, some intuitive solutions include inviting domain experts for assigning traffic cost scores, building a traffic monitor through external traffic data reports, or exploiting state-of-the-art traffic models in relevant domains. In this paper, as an attempt, we leverage the Dempster-Shafer Theory for this task.

Dempster-Shafer Theory (DST) that uses a generalization of probabilities called beliefs to characterize confidence in evidence in support of a given hypothesis. According to the generated traffic of an app can divide into three kinds of traffic, namely original, CDN+Cloud traffic, third-party traffic and other traffic. We treat each kind of traffic generated by mobile app as an evidence in DST, and set the *Frames of discernment* in DS as $\Theta = \{original, CDN + Cloudtraffic, third - partytraffic, othertraffic\}$, and its *basic probability assignment (bpa)* is defined as $m_\Theta : 2^\Theta \rightarrow [0, 1]$. Based on Θ and *bpa*, the belief function of DST is defined as

$$For\ x \subseteq \Theta, Bel(x) = \sum m_\Theta(x) \tag{6}$$

where x is a proper subset of Θ, and m represents subjective probabilities are assigned to all subsets of Θ. Therefore, the traffic cost scores of host h_j can be estimated by $\tilde{C}_j^h = m(x), where\ x\epsilon\Theta$. DST has a combination method, the goal of which is to combine evidence for a hypothesis from multiple independent sources and calculate an overall belief for the hypothesis [7]. In general we have the following rule of combination known as the Dempster Rule.

$$Bel(A) = m_i(A) = \frac{1}{1-K}\cdot$$
$$\sum_{A_1\cap...\cap A_n = A\neq\emptyset} m_1(A_1)m_2(A_2)...m_n(A_n) \tag{7}$$
$$K = \sum_{A_1\cap...\cap A_n=\{\}} m_1(A_1)m_2(A_2)...m_n(A_n)$$

where K is a measure of the amount of conflict between the two m sets. Therefore, the traffic cost scores of app a_i can be estimated by $\tilde{C}_i^a = m_{1,2,3}(A)$. Note that, both $\tilde{C}_j^h$ and $\tilde{C}_i^a$ are normalized before learning our regularization framework. Although DST is a straightforward approach that cannot solve all the challenges mentioned before, its effectiveness on ranking traffic cost of apps has been well proved. Therefore, using DST as prior knowledge in our regularization framework is appropriate.

4 Mobile App Ranking

In this section, we plan to rank mobile app based on a hybrid criterion and build app hash matrix for purpose of mobile app searching. To achieve this, we first estimate traffic cost level for each mobile app. Then, we explain how to rank mobile apps based on app popularity and network traffic cost.

4.1 Traffic Cost Level Estimation

After estimating the traffic cost score for each mobile app, we can rank apps in ascending order with respect to their traffic cost scores for recommendations. Moreover, if some apps have the same traffic cost scores, they will be further ranked according to popularity scores (e.g., overall rating). However, for real-world app recommendation services, users may have difficulties to get clear perception about the traffic cost of ranked apps. A promising way to help users understand the different traffic cost of apps is to categorize the traffic cost into discrete levels (e.g., Low, Medium, High). Therefore, we propose a Coefficient Variation (CV) based approach to get an accurate and appropriate segmentation of apps with respect to their traffic cost scores due to the lack of appropriate criterion. We assume that two adjacent apps' traffic cost scores have big differences in the globally ranked list, which can be captured by the CV, e.g., $\frac{variation}{mean}$, of their traffic cost scores.

4.2 App Rank Based on Hybrid Criteria

Now, we can recommend apps for users. Intuitively, there are two types of ranking criteria for recommending apps.

- Popularity Criteria: We first rank app candidates in descending order by their popularity scores (e.g., overall rating), and apps have the same popularity scores will be further ranked by traffic cost scores.
- Traffic Cost Criteria: We first rank app candidates in ascending order by their traffic cost scores, and apps have the same scores will be further ranked by popularity scores (e.g., overall rating).

Furthermore, we need to strike a balance between users' traffic cost preferences and apps' popularity for recommendations. To achieve such a balance, we also propose a hybrid criteria for app recommendations, which is based on the Benefit-Cost Analysis [8]. This approach is a technique for evaluating a project or investment by comparing the economic benefits with the economic costs of the activity. In this paper, we treat a project as an app, the cost and benefit of projects can be regarded as traffic cost and popularity of apps. For example, government inverts a project which can bring maximum benefit and cause minimum cost. Specifically, a project ρ can be represented by a collection of n mobile apps with a corresponding weight w_i assigned to each app. According to the discussion in [9], the weight w_i represents attention the recommender system wants the target user to pay on the app a_i. Therefore, we first define the benefit of an app as $B(a)$, which can be computer by

$$B(a) = \sum_i^n \frac{w_i \cdot \triangle_i^{-1}}{1 + r_i}, \tag{8}$$

where $\triangle_i$ is the rank of app a_i in the popularity based ranked list $\Lambda^{(Pop)}$, r_i represents fluctuation ratio of app a_i rank. Also, we define the cost of the app as $C(\rho)$, which can computer by the following function [10],

$$C(a) = \sum_{i}^{n}(w_i^2 \nabla_i^{-2} + 2 \sum_{j=i+1}^{n} w_i w_j \nabla_i^{-1} \nabla_j^{-1} J_{ij}), \tag{9}$$

where ∇_i is the rank of app a_i in the traffic cost based ranked list $\Lambda^{(trafficcost)}$, and J_{ij} is the traffic cost correlation between apps a_i and a_j. In this paper, we estimate J_{ij} according to the similarity of generated traffic. For any two apps, the more common kind of traffic generated, the higher traffic cost similarity they have. We compute J_{ij} using Jaccard coefficient between apps a_i and a_j by,

$$J_{ij} = \frac{N_{ij}}{N_i + N_j - N_{ij}}, \tag{10}$$

where N_i is the number of different kinds of hosts accessed by app a_i, and N_{ij} is the number of common hosts accessed by two apps a_i and a_j.

The goal of recommendation based on hybrid criteria is to learn a maximum net profit (MNP) for maximizing the benefit and minimizing the cost the app that consists of recommendation candidates (app candidates). Based on the above definitions, we can formally define the MNP recommendation problem as follows.

Given a set of apps a_i, which have benefit $B(a)$, and cost $C(a)$. The MNP recommendation problem is to recommend a set of apps, which has the maximum net profit, i.e.,

$$arg_{max} \quad G(a) = B(a) - C(a), \tag{11}$$

the above optimization problem can be solved by the efficient frontier based approach introduced in [9], Specifically, we can obtain the MNP by obtain optimal weight w^* by

$$w^* = \frac{\begin{vmatrix} 1 & 1^T \sum^{-1} E \\ E^* & E^T \sum^{-1} E \end{vmatrix} \sum^{-1} 1 + \begin{vmatrix} 1^T \sum^{-1} 1 & 1 \\ E^T \sum^{-1} 1 & E^* \end{vmatrix} \sum^{-1} E}{\begin{vmatrix} 1^T \sum^{-1} 1 & 1^T \sum^{-1} E \\ E^T \sum^{-1} 1 & E^T \sum^{-1} E \end{vmatrix}}, \tag{12}$$

where $\sum_{ij} = \nabla_i^{-1} \nabla_j^{-1} J_{ij}$, $E = (\triangle_1^{-1}, ..., \triangle_n^{-1})^T$, and E^* can be computed by

$$E^* = \frac{(xz - y^2)^2 - 2b(xE - y1)^T \sum^{-1}(z1 - yE)}{2b(xE - y1)^T \sum^{-1}(xE - y1)}, \tag{13}$$

where $x = 1^T \sum^{-1} 1$, $y = 1^T \sum^{-1} E$, and $z = E^T \sum^{-1} E$.

5   Evaluation

5.1   Dataset

The experimental mobile app data set was collected from Google Play from December 2012 to January 2013. We downloaded 100 top popular (100 top rating score) mobile apps from each of 22 most popular categories, which cover most of the app categories which are defined in Google Play, such as Game, Book, etc. The reason why we choose the top 100 apps in each category is explained as follows. In Petsas et al. [11], the authors proved that the app popularity distribution follows a typical Pareto Principle, with 10% of the apps accounting for 70–90% of the total downloads. This phenomenon indicates that a small amount of popular apps are normally downloaded by the majority of users.

5.2 Results of App Ranking

We manually labeled 100 mobile apps with low traffic cost and 100 mobile apps with high traffic cost according to execute mobile apps as training data. For each app, we used its category, apk package name, and traffic cost as features to learn the ranking model. We also choose RankNet [12], RankBoost [13], ListNet [14], and compare with our approach. Figure 3 shows the compared results among NDCG@K, Precision@K, and ERR@K, where value of K from 1 to 100. We find that Mobile Recommendation based on Traffic Cost (MRTC) consistently outperforms previous approaches on for different K. Specially, we observe that MRTC outperforms other three approaches on NDCG and ERR. In terms of NDCG, we can observe that MRTC improves 6.01%, 1.96%, and 6.68% compare to RankNet, RankBoost, and ListNet on average, respectively. In terms of ERR, we can observe that MRTC improves 4.63%, 17.74%, 5.26% compare to RankNet, RankBoost, and ListNet, respectively. Table 1 shows comparison results among MRTC and three other ranking approaches based on metric of MAP. We find that our approach could achieve higher value of MAP than other three ranking approaches. Based on the results of four metrics, we find that our approach can achieve better ranking performance, and also is an appropriate approach for estimating mobile app traffic cost.

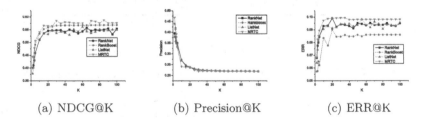

(a) NDCG@K   (b) Precision@K   (c) ERR@K

Fig. 3. The results of different ranking approach with different metrics

Table 1. Summary of traffic traces used in evaluation experiments

Metric	RankNet	RankBoost	ListNet	MRTC
MAP	0.4472	0.3962	0.4405	0.4673

5.3   Results of Mobile App Recommendation

Overall Performance. Because there is no ground truth for us to evaluate which recommendation results could satisfy users' needs. The goal of this evaluation is that check whether our recommendation approach can achieve a balance between mobile app popularity and user's traffic cost preferences. To achieve this goal, we still choose *NDCG* as evaluation metric to evaluate the performance of our recommendation approach. Specifically, there are three different ranking criteria in our recommendation approach, such as popularity, traffic cost and hybrid criteria. Given an app dataset and traffic cost level, each criterion can generate a ranked app list are the recommendation result. In this evaluation, we use two kinds of *NDCG* to evaluate the performance of each recommendation result. *NDCG_Pop* represents the recommendation result based on app popularity, *NDCG_TC* represents the recommendation result based on app traffic cost. If a recommendation result has higher *NDCG_Pop(NDCG_TC)*, which means the result focus more on app popularity(app traffic cost). Figure 4 shows the recommendation performance on three different traffic cost level based on three different ranking criteria. Level 1 contains mobile apps with the highest traffic cost, Level 3 contains the apps with medium traffic cost, and Level 5 contains the apps with the lowest traffic cost. From the results, we can obtain three observations. First, the result of recommend by pop recommends app with higher *NDCG_Pop* than *NDCG_TC* in each level. Second, the result of recommend by Traffic cost recommends app with higher *NDCG_TC* than *NDCG_Pop* in each level. Third, the hybrid recommendation approach can rank apps with a trade-off between popularity and traffic cost.

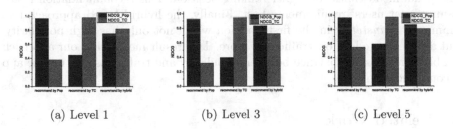

(a) Level 1   (b) Level 3   (c) Level 5

Fig. 4. The recommendation performances of different recommendation criteria on different traffic cost level

Similar Functionality Mobile App Recommendation. It is well known that Google Play provides a huge amount of Android apps for users to download. There are many apps that are not well-known, such as uninstaller app etc., and users do not have any preference on which specific app they should use to fulfill the functionality that they want. Moreover, based on our observations, these apps with similar functionality have different traffic cost when they are running. To further study evaluate the recommendation performances of our approach, we choose mobile apps with similar functionality as a case study. We choose 6 apps with similar functionality which are *EasyUninstaller(U1)*, *BatchUninstall(U2)*, *Uninstaller(U3)*, *GoUninstaller(U4)*, *AppUninstaller CacheCleaner(U5)*, *UninstallMaster(U6)*. Then, we rank the 6 apps based on app popularity (e.g., rating score, download times), traffic cost and hybrid, respectively. The recommendation results show in Table 2.

Table 2. App recommendation based on different recommendation criteria

Criterion	Recommendation
Popularity	EasyUninstaller, Uninstaller, GoUninstaller, UninstallMaster, BatchUninstall, AppUninstaller CacheCleaner
Traffic cost	AppUninstaller CacheCleaner, Uninstaller, UninstallMaster, BatchUninstall, GoUninstaller, EasyUninstaller
Hybrid	Uninstaller, AppUninstaller CacheCleaner,UninstallMaster, EasyUninstaller,GoUninstaller, BatchUninstall

In Table 2, Popularity represents mobile app recommendation based on app popularity (e.g., average rating, download times), Traffic cost means mobile app recommendation based on app traffic cost (e.g., traffic cost scores), and hybrid represents app recommendation based on our approach. From these results, we find that popularity based approach recommends *EasyUninstaller* in the first position which has the highest traffic cost score among the 6 apps. The traffic cost based approach would recommend some unpopular apps (e.g., lower rating or download times) in higher ranking position. This recommendation result cannot meet users' requirements best. Finally, the hybrid based approach recommends *Uninstaller* in the first position which not only has high popularity, but also generate has low traffic cost score. This result means that our approach is able to reach some balance between popularity and traffic cost for mobile app recommendation.

6   Related Work

There have been some previous works on mobile app recommendation, which aims to help mobile users pick apps more wisely. In [15], the authors introduce a novel context-aware collaborative filtering algorithm for implicit feedback data that is based on tensor factorization. They build a preference model in the absence of explicit feedback information from the user and incorporating real contextual information into a single recommendation model. In [16], the authors propose AppTrends, which incorporates a graph-based technique for application recommendation in the Android OS environment. They proposed a novel method for representing a users usage pattern as a graph where nodes are apps installed by the user and edges are distances of two connected apps. In [17], the authors proposed a functionality-based recommendation architecture that is able to provide more accurate and more diverse app recommendations by analyzing users functional requirements. In [18], the authors extract personal context-aware preferences from the context-rich device logs, and exploit these identified preferences for building personalized context-aware recommender systems. In [19], the authors present a novel framework that incorporates features distilled from version descriptions into app recommendation. This framework utilizes a semi-supervised variant of LDA that accounts for both text and metadata to characterize version features into a set of latent topics.

7 Conclusions

In this paper, we present study on app recommendations by merging network traffic cost. Specifically, we first propose a new recommendation approach to strike the balance between mobile apps' popularity and traffic cost. Our approach is scalable and automatic to estimate the traffic cost of mobile apps without relying on any predefined traffic cost functions. Moreover, we crawled a real-world dataset from Google Play and use it evaluate our method. The evaluation results demonstrate that our method achieves performance improvement over previous approaches. This implies that it is important to consider mobile app traffic cost on mobile app recommendations.

Acknowledgements. This work is supported by the Science and Technology Projects of Hunan Province (No.2016JC2074), the Research Foundation of Education Bureau of Hunan Province, China(No.16B085), the Open Research Fund of Key Laboratory of Network Crime Investigation of Hunan Provincial Colleges (No.2016WLFZZC008), the National Science Foundation of China(No.61471169), the Key Lab of Information Network Security, Ministry of Public Security (No.C16614).

References

1. Grace, M.C., Zhou, W., Jiang, X., Sadeghi, A.: Unsafe exposure analysis of mobile in-app advertisements. In: Proceedings of the Fifth ACM Conference on Security and Privacy in Wireless and Mobile Networks, pp. 101–112 (2012)
2. Dai, S., Tongaonkar, A., Wang, X., Nucci, A., Song, D.: NetworkProfiler: towards automatic fingerprinting of android apps. In: 2013 Proceedings IEEE INFOCOM, pp. 809–817 (2013)
3. Falaki, H., Lymberopoulos, D., Mahajan, R., Kandula, S., Estrin, D.: A first look at traffic on smartphones. In: Proceedings of the 10th ACM SIGCOMM Conference on Internet Measurement, pp. 281–287 (2013)
4. Yan, B., Chen, G.L.: AppJoy: personalized mobile application discovery. In: Proceedings of the 9th International Conference on Mobile Systems, Applications, and Services, pp. 113–126 (2011)
5. Fu, Z.J., Sun, X.M., Liu, Q., Zhou, L., Shu, J.G.: Achieving efficient cloud search services: multi-keyword ranked search over encrypted cloud data supporting parallel computing. IEICE Trans. Commun. **98**(1), 190–200 (2015)
6. Xie, H.R., Li, Q., Mao, X.D., Li, X.D., Cai, Y., Rao, Y.H.: Community-aware user profile enrichment in folksonomy. Neural Netw. **58**, 111–121 (2014)

7. Sentz, K., Ferson, S.: Combination of evidence in Dempster-Shafer theory. Technical report, Sandia National Laboratories (2014)
8. Cost-benefit analysis. http://en.wikipedia.org/wiki/Cost-benefit_analysis
9. Zhang, W.N., Wang, J., Chen, B.W., Zhao, X.X.: To personalize or not: a risk management perspective. In: Proceedings of the 7th ACM Conference on Recommender Systems (2013)
10. Luo, C.Y., Xiong, H., Zhou, W.J., Guo, Y.H., Deng, G.S.: Enhancing investment decisions in P2P lending: an investor composition perspective. In: Proceedings of the 17th ACM SIGKDD International Conference on Knowledge Discovery and Data Mining, pp. 292–300 (2011)
11. Petsas, T., Papadogiannakis, A., Polychronakis, M., Markatos, E.P., Karagiannis, T.: Rise of the planet of the apps: a systematic study of the mobile app ecosystem. In: Proceedings of the 2013 Conference on Internet Measurement Conference, pp. 277–290 (2013)
12. Chris, B., Tal, S., Erin, R., Ari, L., Matt, D., Nicole, H., Greg, H.: Learning to rank using gradient descent. In: Proceedings of the 22nd International Conference on Machine Learning, pp. 89–96 (2005)
13. Yoav, F., Raj, I., Robert, E.S., Yoram, S.: An efficient boosting algorithm for combining preferences. J. Mach. Learn. Res. 4, 933–969 (2005)
14. Cao, Z., Qin, T., Liu, T.Y., Tsai, M.F., Li, H.: Learning to rank: from pairwise approach to listwise approach. In: Proceedings of the 24th International Conference on Machine Learning, pp. 129–136 (2007)
15. Kong, Y., Zhang, M.J., Ye, D.Y.: A belief propagation-based method for task allocation in open and dynamic cloud environments. Knowl. Based Syst. 115, 123–132 (2017)
16. Bae, D., Han, K.J., Park, J., Yi, M.Y.: AppTrends: a graph-based mobile app recommendation system using usage history. In: International Conference on Big Data and Smart Computing, pp. 210–216 (2015)
17. Xu, X.Y., Dutta, K., Datta, A.: Functionality-based mobile app recommendation by identifying aspects from user reviews. In: Proceedings of the International Conference on Information Systems - Building a Better World through Information Systems, pp. 1–10 (2014)
18. Xie, H.R., Li, X.D., Wang, T., Chen, L., Li, K., Wang, F.L., Cai, Y., Li, Q., Min, H.Q.: Personalized search for social media via dominating verbal context. Neurocomputing 172, 27–37 (2016)
19. Liu, Q., Cai, W.D., Shen, J., Fu, Z.J., Liu, X.D., Linge, N.: A speculative approach to spatialtemporal efficiency with multiobjective optimization in a heterogeneous cloud environment. Secur. Commun. Netw. 9(17), 4002–4012 (2016)

A Virtual Grid-Based Routing Protocol
for Mobile Sink-Based WSNs

Qi Liu[1,2(✉)], Weixin Bu[2], Kai Zhang[2,3], Xiaodong Liu[4], and Nigel Linge[5]

[1] Jiangsu Collaborative Innovation Center of Atmospheric Environment and Equipment
Technology (CICAEET), Nanjing University of Information Science and Technology,
Nanjing, China
qrankl@163.com

[2] School of Computer and Software, Nanjing University of Information Science and Technology,
Nanjing, China
bwxhhjy@gmail.com

[3] Jiangsu Engineering Centre of Network Monitoring,
Nanjing University of Information Science and Technology,
Nanjing, China

[4] School of Computing, Edinburgh Napier University, 10 Colinton Road,
Edinburgh EH10 5DT, UK

[5] The University of Salford, Salford, Greater Manchester M5 4WT, UK

Abstract. In a non-uniform distributed network, data concentrating centers with sparse nodes deplete the battery energy faster, leading to the energy hole problem. To solve this problem, we proposed a virtual uneven grid-based routing protocol (VUGR), which divides these regions into smaller grid cells and makes them retire from the data concentrating center to decrease the energy consumption. Simulation results indicate that the VUGR protocol performs better than VGDRA in prolonging the network lifetime.

Keywords: Uneven grid · Sink mobility · Energy hole · Dynamic routes adjustment

1 Introduction

Typical wireless sensor networks (WSNs) consist of a lot of micro devices, which have the ability to perform many tasks, e.g., environment sensing, data processing and communicating [1]. Due to these features, smart micro devices are often applied into different domains, especially those dangerous or unattended physical environment, such as battle reconnaissance, forest fire monitoring and volcanic monitoring [2–4]. However, within these environments, supplying power for sensor devices is difficult. Hence, WSNs should be designed as energy efficient networks which can maximize the network lifetime.

In a multi-hop wireless sensor network, due to data convergecast property of traditional data transmission approaches resulting in higher data traffic around the static sink, these sensor nodes in the vicinity of the sink will consume more energy in packet

© Springer International Publishing AG 2017
X. Sun et al. (Eds.): ICCCS 2017, Part I, LNCS 10602, pp. 339–348, 2017.
https://doi.org/10.1007/978-3-319-68505-2_29

forwarding than other nodes in the distance, leading to the energy-hole problem. Sink mobility is proposed as a feasible solution to this problem [5, 6]. As mobile sinks move to the next sojourning position, the hotspots around the sinks will change, which helps acquiring uniform energy dissipation of nodes to extend the network lifetime.

Exploring sink mobility helps to mitigate the hotspot problem, thus balancing the node energy consumption and prolonging the network lifetime effectively; however, it also brings new challenges to data dissemination. Unlike static sink scenarios, the network topology becomes dynamic as mobile sinks change their locations continuously. How to keep fresh routes towards the sink on the move of mobile sinks is a core problem. The approach of overlaying a virtual infrastructure over the physical network has been proposed to enhance the data transmission efficiency as well as decrease node's energy dissipation in the case of mobile sinks [7]. In such virtual infrastructure based sensor networks, sensor nodes often play two roles. High-tier nodes are responsible for forwarding data packets generated from low-tier nodes to the sink.

In this paper, we propose an energy efficient routing protocol, called Virtual Uneven Grid-based Routing (VUGR). VUGR divides the network into several uneven grids, aiming to avoid formation of the energy hole due to non-uniform distribution of sensor nodes. A sensory data collection strategy with a single mobile sink is also developed to collect data from the network in the VUGR protocol.

The remainder of this paper is organized as follows. Section 2 reviews several virtual infrastructure-based routing protocols. In Sect. 3, the VUGR protocol is described in detail, including the virtual uneven grid construction approach and mobile sink-based sensory data collection scheme. Section 4 evaluates our proposed VUGR protocol. Finally, we conclude this paper in Sect. 5.

2   Related Work

Researchers have proposed many virtual infrastructure-based protocols in recent years intending to balance the node energy dissipation.

Two-Tier Data Dissemination (TTDD) is a scalable and efficient grid-based data dissemination approach that enables multiple mobile sinks to continuously receive data on the move [8]. TTDD limits flooding queries within a local cell, thus decreasing the overall energy dissipation. However, frequent grid construction overhead cannot be ignored.

It is obvious that TTDD is not suitable for periodic data reporting application because it needs to build a grid for all sources along the sink's trail. Virtual Grid-Based Dynamic Routes Adjustment Scheme (VGDRA) is a mobile-sink based algorithm, which only constructs one grid structure [9]. Cell-headers elected in each grid cell re-adjust their routes dynamically to maintain the latest location information of the mobile sink, thereby minimizing the communication cost. VGDRA shows good performance in alleviating the hotspot problem, however, in a non-uniform distributed network, the uniform gird construction approach causes different node densities in each grid cell. Grid cells with sparse nodes along the sink's moving trajectory will prematurely deplete all the node energy, leading to the energy hole.

To alleviate the hotspot problem, Prince et al. proposed an energy efficient uneven grid clustering based routing protocol (EEUGCR) [10], which divides the whole network into several rectangular grids of unequal size via the base station in a centralized approach. EEUGCR considers the distance between source nodes and the base station; however, in a non-uniform distributed network, this method may bring worse results if nodes around the base station is sparse. EEUGCR is limited by data collection methods.

Cluster-based network structure attracts the most researchers due to easy deployment and low complexity. Moreover, VGDRA and EEUGCR also combine with clusters. Member nodes in each grid only need to know the routing information to cell-headers and send the sensing data from the physical environment to cell-headers. Cell-headers only need to forward packets from low-tier nodes to the next hop based on the routing table, which stores the routing information between cell-headers.

Except the above two network structures, the line-based structure and ring-based structure are also respectively exploited in [6, 11]. In general, a successful virtual infrastructure-based routing protocol has an easily implemented hierarchical structure, which enables high-tier nodes to be aware of the latest routes towards the sink and low-tier nodes to acquire the latest position of high-tier nodes from the high-tier virtual infrastructure.

3 The Proposed VUGR Protocol

In this section, we propose the VUGR protocol, an energy-efficient uneven grid-based routing protocol with a mobile sink. Sensor nodes within the network are assigned three roles: regular nodes (RNs), main cell-headers (MCHs), assistant cell-headers (ACHs). These three roles are not constant. Cell-headers and regular nodes may switch roles due to some factors. The basis of the VUGR protocol is (*i*) virtual uneven grid construction, (*ii*) mobile-Sink based Sensory Data Collection Scheme.

Before we introduce the VUGR protocol in detail, some assumptions should be given:

- Sensor nodes with the same battery capacity are randomly distributed in the sensor field. They cannot move in the deployment area after deployed successfully.
- No obstacles in the external environment hinder communications between nodes.
- All sensor nodes know their own locations in the deployment area. These location information can be achieved by a positioning system or an energy-efficient positioning algorithm.

3.1 Virtual Uneven Grid Construction

Originally, VUGR divides the deployment area into several uniform grids with equal size. The number of grid cells is determined by the total number of sensor nodes in the deployment area. We consider 5% of the number of sensor nodes as the approximate optimal number of grid cells, which is used in [12]. Assuming K is the number of grid cells and N is the total number of sensor nodes. Equation 1 is adopted to divide the sensor field into uniform grid cells.

$$K = \begin{cases} 4 & N \times 0.05 \le 6; \\ 9 & 6 < N \times 0.05 \le 12; \\ 16 & 12 < N \times 0.05 \le 20; \\ \vdots & \vdots \end{cases} \qquad (1)$$

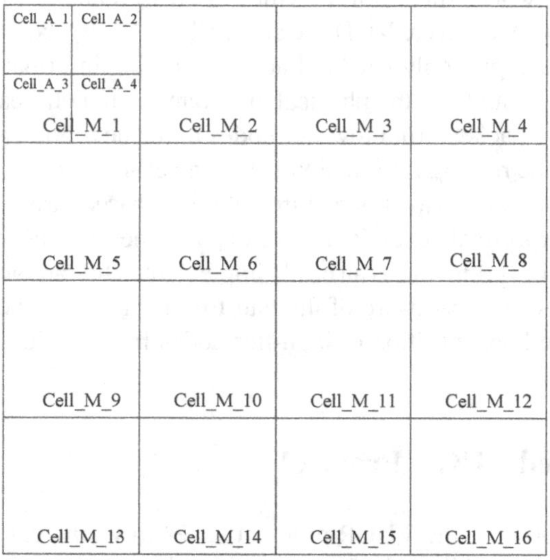

Cell_A_1 Cell_A_2 Cell_A_3 Cell_A_4 Cell_M_1	Cell_M_2	Cell_M_3	Cell_M_4
Cell_M_5	Cell_M_6	Cell_M_7	Cell_M_8
Cell_M_9	Cell_M_10	Cell_M_11	Cell_M_12
Cell_M_13	Cell_M_14	Cell_M_15	Cell_M_16

Fig. 1. Virtual uneven grid construction.

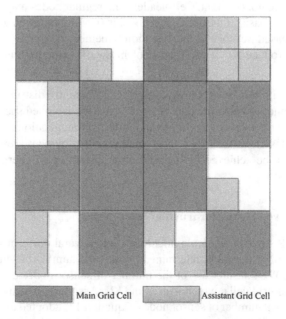

Main Grid Cell   Assistant Grid Cell

Fig. 2. Example of virtual uneven grid structure. (Color figure online)

After completing the network partition, every sensor node is aware of its own Cell_M_ID, based on its location information. Nodes closest to the mid-point of cells are elected as main cell-headers (MCHs).

Each grid cell is divided into four grid cells uniformly again as described in Fig. 1. Using the same method, grid cells are divided into smaller cells and cell-headers elected in the smaller cells are called assistant cell-headers (ACHs). Nodes elected as ACHs send a message to tell its MCHs, containing Cell_M_ID, Cell_A_ID, Num_RN, location information. If MCHs receive four status share packets from its ACHs, This main grid cell does not change. If not, this main grid cell is removed and all its existing assistant grid cells select a neighboring main grid cell to join. Figure 2 is a possible network structure after finishing all steps. Green cells represent main grid cells and yellow cells are assistant grid cells.

3.2   Mobile-Sink Based Sensory Data Collection Scheme

Routing between MCHs and ACHs

Nodes from assistant grid cells are only responsible to acquire information from the physical environment and generate packets. When a grid cell cannot find the next cell-headers, this grid cell should be partitioned into four smaller grid cell. The current cell-headers share this message with neighboring cell-headers. Neighboring cell-headers upon receiving this message return a confirmation. The cell-headers upon receiving the confirmation from its neighboring cell-headers check which neighboring cell-header is closer and become ACHS of this closest neighboring cell-header. Then ACHs send these packets to their corresponding MCHs. As shown in Fig. 3, ACHs do not participate in data forwarding.

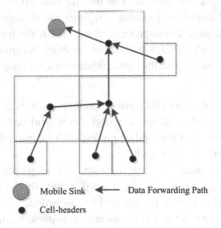

Fig. 3.   Local multi-hop routing.

Dynamic routes adjustment scheme

The mobile sink moves along horizontal and vertical directions around main grid cells. These main grid cells do not include those non-adjacent cells, e.g., main grid cell at the top-left corner in Fig. 4.

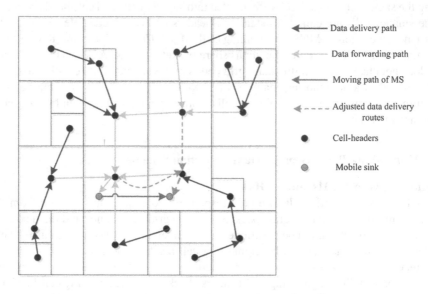

Fig. 4. Dynamic routes adjustment scheme.

When a MCH triggers the dynamic adjustment of grid cells, it will send a message to tell the mobile sink this information. The mobile sink upon receiving this message will delete this grid cell from its sojourning positions and change its moving path. After completing the dynamic adjustment process of grid cells, the mobile sink collects data along the new moving path. MCHs within the network follow some communication rules to facilitate the adjustment of the dynamic network topology. The specific process is as follows:

- **Step 1:** The mobile sink shares a location update packet with its surrounding MCHs periodically. If the mobile sink has reached a new grid cell, its current originating MCH will continue to share this update packet with its immediate MCHs, otherwise this update packet will be discarded.
- **Step 2:** MCHs upon receiving the location update packet check whether their previous next-hop is the sender. If not, this MCH will set the sender as its next-hop. Otherwise, this location update packet will be discarded.
- **Step 3:** MCHs continue to share the location update packet from the mobile sink with their downstream MCHs. Repeat Step 2 until all the downstream MCHs complete updating the latest routes towards the mobile sink.

3.3   Grid Maintenance

To ensure the normal operation of WSN, a grid maintenance scheme is necessary. The VUGR protocol rotates the role of cell-headers in every cell, which is similar to VGDRA. However, in the VUGR protocol, the node density is considered to participate in cell-header rotation.

The number of neighboring nodes is approximately indicated as node density. If the cell-header is located in the area of high density, it is obvious that more member nodes have shorter distance to their cell-headers. Such cell-header distribution also increases the number of nodes that communicate with the mobile sink directly when the mobile sink sojourns beside the cell-headers for data delivery. In the cell-header re-election process, the node that is relatively closer to the mid-point of grid cells and has more neighboring nodes and a higher energy level compared to other cell-header candidates is elected as the new cell-header. In order to protect high-level structure of the network, the current cell-header will share the information of the new cell-header with its member nodes and adjacent neighboring cell-headers. Moreover, nodes that have already served as the role of cell-headers no longer participate in the next cell-header rotation.

In the cell-header re-election process, only those nodes which are closer to the mid-point of the cell and have more residual battery energy, more neighboring nodes will be highly possible to be the next cell-headers. After a new cell-header is elected, the current cell-header shares information of the new cell-header with neighboring cell-headers and all its member nodes within the same cell.

4   Performance Evaluation

4.1   Simulation Environment

We use NS-2.34 to evaluate the performance of our proposed VUGR protocol in Ubuntu 10.10. 200 sensor nodes are randomly deployed in a region of 200 * 200 m^2. According to Eq. 1, the deployment area is divided into 9 cells. After completing uneven grid construction, the mobile sink moves at a constant speed within the net-work along horizontal and vertical directions around main grid cells. We consider the energy model used in VGDRA and assume the free space radio propagation model in NS2. Part of simulation parameters are listed in Table 1.

Table 1. Simulation parameters.

Parameter	Value
Simulation area	200×200 m^2
Number of nodes	200
Packet size	40 bits
E_{elec}	50 nJ/bit
E_{amp}	10 nJ/bit/m^2
Battery capacity	1 J

4.2 Results Analysis

We compared the VUGR protocol with VGDRA. VGDRA divides the deployment area into several uniform grids and utilizes a single mobile sink to move around the edge of the network to collect data. VGDRA exploits a dynamic routes adjustment scheme to significantly decrease routes reconstruction overhead. In VGDRA, grid cells around the edge of the network all can be data concentrating centers; however, if the grid cell with sparse nodes become the data concentrating center, it will deplete the energy fast, leading to the energy hole.

The VUGR protocol divides grid cells with sparse nodes into smaller grid cells and makes them attached to main grid cells. These smaller grid cells no longer become the data concentrating center, which helps prolonging the network lifetime. Therefore, the VUGR protocol has less failure nodes than VGDRA at the same time. Figure 5 demonstrates that the death nodes using the VUGR protocol are less than those using VGDRA.

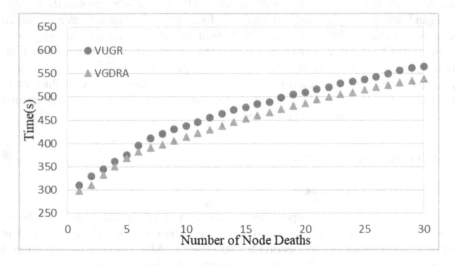

Fig. 5. Death time for first 30 nodes.

Network Lifetime is an important indicator to determine whether the VUGR protocol is an energy-efficient routing protocol. Figure 6 describes the energy consumption of VUGR and VGDRA in different rounds. Round indicates that all sensor nodes complete data delivery for one time. It is clear that The VUGR protocol shows better performance in prolong the network lifetime.

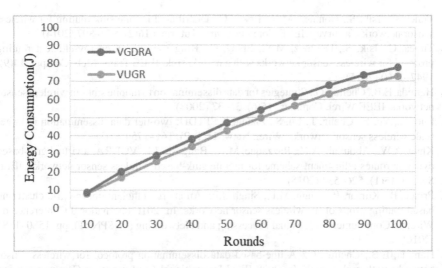

Fig. 6. Network lifetime.

5   Conclusions

In this paper, we propose an energy-efficient uneven grid-based routing protocol, called VUGR. VUGR aims to solve the energy-hole phenomenon appearing in grid cells with sparse nodes in a non-uniform distributed network using VGDRA. For those grid cells with sparse nodes, VUGR divides them into smaller cells. These smaller grid cells are attached to main grid cells and will not become data concentrating center, which helps prolonging the network lifetime.

Acknowledgments. This work is supported by Marie Curie Fellowship (701697-CAR-MSCA-IF-EF-ST), the NSFC (61300238 and 61672295), the 2014 Project of six personnel in Jiangsu Province under Grant No. 2014-WLW-013, and the PAPD fund.

References

1. Akyildiz, I.F., Su, W., Sankarasubramaniam, Y., Cayirci, E.: Wireless sensor network: a survey. Comput. Netw. **40**(8), 393–422 (2002)
2. Yick, J., Mukherjee, B., Ghosal, D.: Wireless sensor network survey. Comput. Netw. **52**(12), 2292–2330 (2008)
3. Wang, B., Gu, X., Ma, L., Yan, S.: Temperature error correction based on BP neural network in meteorological wireless sensor network. In: Sun, X., Liu, A., Chao, H.-C., Bertino, E. (eds.) ICCCS 2016. LNCS, vol. 10040, pp. 117–132. Springer, Cham (2016). doi: 10.1007/978-3-319-48674-1_11
4. Qu, Z., Keeney, J., Robitzsch, S., Zaman, F., Wang, X.: Multilevel pattern mining architecture for automatic network monitoring in heterogeneous wireless communication networks. Chin. Commun. **13**(7), 108–116 (2016)

5. Tunca, C., Isik, S., Donmez, M.Y., Ersoy, C.: Distributed mobile sink routing for wireless sensor networks: a survey. IEEE Commun. Surv. Tutorials **16**(2), 877–897 (2014)
6. Tunca, C., Isik, S., Donmez, M.Y., Ersoy, C.: Ring routing: an energy-efficient routing protocol for wireless sensor networks with a mobile sink. IEEE Trans. Mob. Comput. **14**(9), 1947–1960 (2015)
7. Hamida, E.B., Chelius, G.: Strategies for data dissemination to mobile sinks in wireless sensor networks. IEEE Wirel. Commun. **15**(6), 31–37 (2008)
8. Luo, H., Ye, F., Cheng, J., Lu, S., Zhang, L.: TTDD: two-tier data dissemination in large-scale wireless sensor networks. Wirel. Netw. **11**(1–2), 161–175 (2005)
9. Khan, A.W., Abdullah, A.H., Razzaque, M.A., Bangash, J.I.: VGDRA: a virtual grid-based dynamic routes adjustment scheme for mobile sink-based wireless sensor networks. IEEE Sens. J. **15**(1), 526–534 (2015)
10. Prince, B., Kumar, P., Singh, M.P., Singh, J.P.: An energy efficient uneven grid clustering based routing protocol for wireless sensor networks. In: 2016 International Conference on Wireless Communications, Signal Processing and Networking (WiSPNET), pp. 1580–1584 (2016)
11. Hamida, E.B., Chelius, G.: A line-based data dissemination protocol for wireless sensor networks with mobile sink. In: 2008 IEEE International Conference on Communications, Beijing, China, pp. 2201–2205 (2008)
12. Heinzelman, W.B., Chandrakasan, A.P., Balakrishnan, H.: An application-specific protocol architecture for wireless microsensor networks. IEEE Trans. Wireless Commun. **1**(4), 660–670 (2002)

Low-Energy Security-Enhanced Routing Protocol Based on DBSCAN Partition

Yating Hou[1,2]([⊠]), Feng Xu[1,2], and Ruilin Ding[1,2]

[1] College of Computer Science and Technology,
Nanjing University of Aeronautics and Astronautics, Nanjing, China
hyt11050@163.com, nuaaos@163.com, xuyunjie26@163.com
[2] Collaborative Innovation Center of Novel Software Technology and
Industrialization, Nanjing University of Aeronautics and Astronautics,
Nanjing, China

Abstract. The heterogeneity of node distribution of large-scale wireless sensor networks and its vulnerability to attack bring great challenges to the design of routing protocols. Under the uneven condition, balance network node energy consumption, prolong the network life cycle and improve the network security have become the main goal of designing routing protocols. In this paper, we propose a low-energy security-enhanced routing protocol based on DBSCAN partition (LESERP-DP). The DBSCAN algorithm is used to optimize the clustering in the case of non-uniform nodes distribution, and the key distribution mechanism is designed to enhance the anti-attack ability of the protocol. The simulation results show that the routing protocol is excellent in energy consumption and to a certain extent, reduces the threat of node capture to sensor networks.

Keywords: LS-WSNs · DBSCAN partition · Key management mechanism

1 Introduction

Wireless Sensor Networks (WSN) is a kind of distributed sensing network which makes data collection, data processing, and data transmission much easier. With the rapid development of microelectronics technology, the function of the sensor device is constantly improved, meanwhile the volume structure is becoming smaller and more integrated. The sensor network is developing towards larger and more complicated scale.

Large-scale WSN brings us convenience, but it brings tremendous challenges to routing protocol design. In LS-WSNs, the distribution of sensor nodes is generally non-uniform, which makes the large-scale wireless sensor network prone to the problem of local energy consumption imbalance, resulting in network structure rupture. What's more, when the wireless sensor network is getting larger and larger, its security needs are becoming more and more prominent.

© Springer International Publishing AG 2017
X. Sun et al. (Eds.): ICCCS 2017, Part I, LNCS 10602, pp. 349–360, 2017.
https://doi.org/10.1007/978-3-319-68505-2_30

Large-scale means that the collection of information becomes more comprehensive. Once the information is stolen, the listener can get more detailed privacy data. On the other hand, the size of the network becomes larger and the number of sensor nodes increases several times, which increases the difficulty of detecting malicious nodes. Most importantly, the addition of security mechanisms to the routing protocol will inevitably lead to a significant increase in energy consumption. Therefore, adopt an effective security strategy in the routing protocol, and to ensure that the network energy consumption will not be affected too much, which is our current purpose.

In order to achieve reasonable clustering under the node non-uniform distribution scene, enhance network security and adapt to large-scale networking application requirements, we propose an energy-saved and security-enhanced routing protocol based on DBSCAN partition. The rest of this paper is organized as follows: In the next section, the research work carried out related to the proposed approach is briefly explained. In Sect. 3, our proposed routing protocol is described in detail. In Sect. 4, experimental results and analysis of the proposed work are given. Finally, we conclude the paper with the some future work in Sect. 5.

2   Related Work

For large-scale wireless sensor networks, due to the expansion of application scope, many of studies [1–4] have a certain degree of inappropriate. In view of LS-WSNs, there are two effective ways to save energy, one is clustering optimization, and the other is routing optimization.

In recent years, researchers have proposed a variety of sensor networks clustering protocols. Heinzelman et al. [5] propose LEACH, a clustering-based protocol that utilizes randomized rotation to let the nodes take turns to be the cluster head. Soro et al. [6] adopt the idea of non-uniform clustering to balance energy consumption of CH nodes for the first time, and propose the UCS routing protocol. UCS adjusts the size of the cluster according to the expected forwarding load of the cluster head. Li et al. [7] present a novel routine protocol named EEUC. In EEUC, the cluster size is adjusted by controlling the competition radius of the cluster head so that the number of members of the cluster near the base station is relatively small. Logambigai et al. [8] propose a fuzzy logic based unequal clustering algorithm FBUC. FBUC calculates the node's competition radius through the fuzzy inference system, thus realizing non-uniform clustering.

As a result of the expansion of the wireless sensor network, optimizing the routing becomes an important means to extend the network life cycle. Commonly used measures include: event-triggered communication mechanism, multi-hop communication and cooperative communication [9–12]. Tran-Quang et al. [13] propose ARPEES routing protocol. They introduce the event triggering mechanism in the study, so that most of the nodes are in a dormant state until an event occurs. Farooq et al. [14] propose a multi-hop low-energy adaptive clustering hierarchical routing algorithm called MR-LEACH. In MR-LEACH, any node in the given layer will reach the BS in equal number of hops. Xu et al. [15] propose a low energy adaptive clustering multi-hop routing protocol based on fuzzy decision (FD-LEACH). In order to constitute a dynamic network routing structure, the protocol introduces the concept of fuzzy set and uses the theory of fuzzy decision to select excellent communication relay nodes.

With the maturity of various technologies and the wide application of wireless sensor networks, the security problem in the network has become a new main direction, and many security-oriented research work has arisen. Tanachaiwiwat et al. [16] propose a secure routing protocol based on location (TRANS). TRANS uses the concept of trust to select a secure path and avoid unsafe location. Zhou et al. [17] propose a security routing protocol based on intrusion tolerance named ITSRP. Li et al. [18] propose a new data fusion algorithm to protect privacy and integrity, which achieves integrity protection by adding homomorphic message verification code mechanism. Altisen et al. [19] propose a secure and flexible routing algorithm for wireless sensor networks (SR3), the algorithm uses lightweight encryption primitives to achieve data confidentiality. Alrajeh et al. [20] propose an adaptive routing protocol based on biological mechanism, it uses a distributed ant colony algorithm to select the two hop optimal path in order to maintain the security of routing.

The existing routing protocols generally consider only the energy consumption, or only consider the network security. How to extend the life cycle of the whole network in the wireless sensor network and realize the secure communication of the network becomes a hot spot in the current research. In order to solve the contradiction between "low energy consumption and high security", this paper proposes a low-energy security-enhanced routing protocol based on DBSCAN partition. Compared with the existing research work, the main contributions of this paper are as follows:

(1) We put forward a routing protocol, which is not only suitable for the scene with uniform distribution, but also can achieve remarkable energy conservation effect for the scene with uneven distribution. In the node heterogeneous distributed scenario, we use DBSCAN partitions and realize reasonable clustering.

(2) Considering the residual energy of the candidate route and energy cost for selecting the candidate route, an energy-efficient routing algorithm is designed for multi-hop data forwarding among cluster heads.

(3) An improved low-cost key management mechanism is proposed to enhance the security of routing protocol.

3   Low-Energy Security-Enhanced Routing Protocol Based on DBSCAN Partition

3.1   Protocol Thought

The distribution of large-scale sensor network node is relative random and complex. Therefore, LESERP-DP first designs a small strategy to determine whether the node distribution in the sensor network is uniform. In this paper, two kinds of different clustering algorithms are proposed to solve the problem of uniform and non-uniform distribution of the nodes in the sensor network. For non-uniform scene, we use the density based clustering method DBSCAN to operate partition. As a result, clustering structure can be improved. Taking into account the complexity of DBSCAN algorithm, clustering frequently will inevitably lead to the reduction of the efficiency of the protocol, at the same time, the network topological structure can not be changed greatly after only one round of data transmission. So in LESERP-DP, the method of determining the distribution of nodes in the network area is carried out for every ten rounds. In the process of multi-hop routing between cluster heads, LESERP-DP proposes the concept of candidate route set, and designs a routing algorithm which considers the residual energy as well as energy consumption. In order to enhance the security of the sensor network, a key management mechanism is also included.

3.2 DBSCAN Algorithm

DBSCAN (Density-Based Spatial Clustering of Applications with Noise) [21] is a representative density based clustering algorithm. The cluster is defined as the largest set of nodes connected by density, which can be divided into clusters with sufficiently high density, and can be used to find clusters of arbitrary shapes in the spatial database of noise. DBSCAN requires two parameters: the neighborhood range (ε) and the minimum number of points required to form a dense region (minPts). The main steps of the DBSCAN algorithm are as follows:

(1) Check all the object p that has not yet been checked in the samples set. If the point p has not been disposed (classified in a cluster or labeled as a noise point), check its ε-neighborhood, if the number of contained objects is not less than minPts, set up a new cluster C, add all of the objects to the candidate set N, these points become candidates for the next round; If the point p cannot be density reachable from any other object, thus, temporarily marking it as a noise point.
(2) For all the points p have not been disposed in the candidate set N, check its ε-neighborhood, if it contains at least minPts objects, these objects are added to the N; If the object q has not been included in any cluster, it can be added to the cluster C.
(3) Repeat step (2), to continue checking the unprocessed objects in N until the current candidate set N is empty.
(4) Repeat step (1)–(3) until all objects are grouped into a cluster or labeled as noise point.

3.3 Protocol Architecture

The protocol operation is divided into rounds similar to the EEUC [7] protocol. Each round has a setting up phase and a steady-state phase. In the setting up phase, cluster heads are elected, clusters are organized and multi-hop paths are constructed. Then, in the stable phase, the cluster heads are responsible for collecting data from the cluster nodes and then transferring data to the base station through a routing path.

3.3.1   Cluster Head Selection

In practical applications, the sensor nodes are deployed according to the actual requirements, so the distribution of nodes may be uniform or non-uniform. And as time goes on, some sensor nodes will fail because of energy depletion, resulting in changes in network topology. If the same clustering method is used for the uniform distribution of nodes and non-uniform distribution, it must lead to the irrationality of the clustering. Therefore, before the cluster head selection, we use a simple and effective way to judge the distribution of sensor nodes.

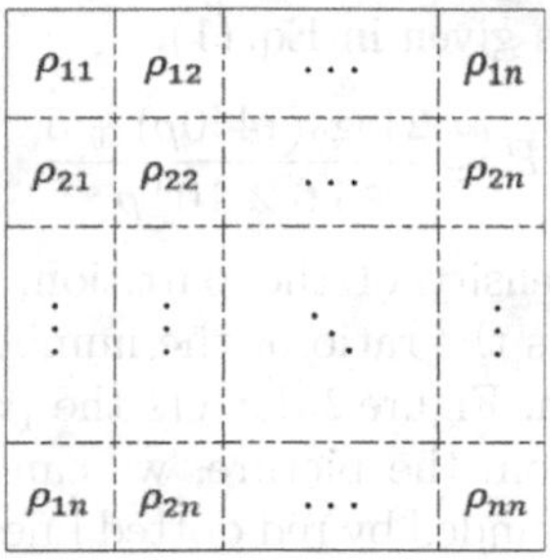

$$
\begin{array}{|c|c|c|c|}
\hline
p_{11} & p_{12} & \cdots & p_{1n} \\
\hline
p_{21} & p_{22} & \cdots & p_{2n} \\
\hline
\vdots & \vdots & \ddots & \vdots \\
\hline
p_{1n} & p_{2n} & \cdots & p_{nn} \\
\hline
\end{array}
$$

Fig. 1. Judgment method

As shown in Fig. 1, the whole network area is divided into N parts ($N = n * n$), the node density of each region is calculated separately. The node density of the region is the ratio of the number of nodes in the region and the whole network. Compare the node density of each region, if the density difference of any two regions exceeds a threshold DDT, which means the nodes in the network have been non-uniformly distributed.

For different scenarios, the specific cluster head campaign is as follows:

(1) Uneven distribution

When the nodes are distributed unevenly, the nodes should be firstly classified by DBSCAN algorithm, and then we use the classification results for partitioning. The use of DBSCAN algorithm for partitioning may cause some relatively isolated network nodes do not belong to any partition. In LESERP-DP, these isolated nodes do not participate in the campaign of cluster heads. Then cluster heads are chosen in each partition. In the selection of cluster head, we learn from the random selection strategy in LEACH protocol, each node generates a random number of a 0–1, if the random number is less than the threshold value of $T(n)$, the node is elected as cluster head. The threshold is set as:

$$T(n) = \begin{cases} \frac{P}{1 - P * (r \bmod \frac{1}{P})} & \text{if } n \in G \\ 0 & \text{otherwise} \end{cases}$$

where P is the desired percentage of cluster heads, r is the current round, and G is the set of nodes that have not been cluster-heads in the last $1/P$ rounds. On this basis, there are two small innovations. First, the residual energy of nodes is taken into consideration in the process of cluster head selection. In the proposed protocol, if the random number of a sensor node is less than the threshold, that node will not be immediately elected as a cluster head, but can become a candidate cluster head. Then according to the remaining energy level of the candidate cluster heads, select the top 50% candidate cluster heads as the final cluster heads. Second, instead of predefining the P value, we give the calculation formula of P value. And here, P presents the desired percentage of tentative cluster heads. The formula is given in Eq. (1):

$$P = \frac{2 \log_2(1440\rho) + 5}{3.6 \times 10^5 \, \rho} \tag{1}$$

where ρ means the node density of the partition. The node density of each partition can be expressed as the ratio of the number of nodes in the partition and the area of the partition. Figure 2 depicts the partitions obtained by using the DBSCAN algorithm. From the picture, we can see all the nodes in Cat.1 constitute the partition surrounded by red dotted lines. Nodes in Cat.2 constitute the partition surrounded by blue dotted lines. Nodes in Cat.3 constitute the partition surrounded by green dotted lines.

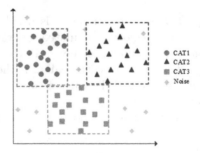

Fig. 2. The partition results using DBSCAN (Color figure online)

(2) Even distribution

When the nodes are evenly distributed, the method used for the cluster head election is similar to that used when the nodes are unevenly distributed. In this scenario, the cluster heads are selected in the whole network, and ρ is the node density of the whole network.

3.3.2   Clustering

The nodes that are selected as the cluster head nodes broadcast a message to the surrounding nodes. According to the received signal strength, each non-cluster head node chooses the nearest cluster to join, and sends a join message to notify the cluster head.

3.3.3   Multi-hop Path Construction

After clustering, a communication path from each cluster head to the base station is established. The process is given in great detail below.

First, each cluster head constructs a candidate route set $\{R_{CN}\}$. The selection rule of this set is that the nodes in the set are cluster heads whose distance from the cluster head which constructs this set is less than k times the coverage radius R_C of the cluster head. k is the smallest integer that makes the candidate route set non-null. R_C is the distance between the cluster head and its farthest cluster members.

The next, calculate the network energy overhead of cluster head S_i to each cluster head S_j in its candidate route set. The calculation of energy expenditure is shown in Eq. (2):

$$E_{ij} = d^2(S_i, S_j) + d^2(S_j, S_0) \tag{2}$$

where $d^2(S_i, S_j)$ is the distance from the cluster head S_i and the candidate route cluster head S_j, $d^2(S_j, S_0)$ is the distance from the candidate route cluster head S_j and the base station.

Finally, select the next hop route for each cluster head according to the following selection rules. If the candidate route set is empty, cluster head communicates directly with the base station; If the candidate route set has only one element, the candidate routing cluster head is directly elected as the next-hop routing; Otherwise, select two candidate nodes from the set with the least energy cost, compare their remaining energy, and the candidate routing cluster head with higher residual energy will act as the route.

3.3.4   Transmission Stable Stage

Firstly, the information is collected by the nodes in each cluster, and then, the nodes transmit the information to the cluster head nodes. Secondly, the cluster head node is responsible for integrating the information and then transmitting the information to the base station. Cluster heads go along with the routing path that is made by the protocol. They send the information to the relay node until reaching the base station.

3.4   Security Strategy

The traditional routing protocol is lack of the ability to defend various attacks from network layer effectively. In this paper, we add improved key distribution mechanism to LESERP-DP to improve the protocol security.

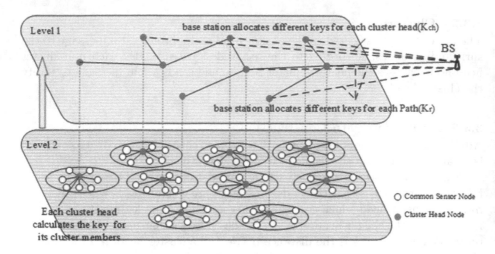

Fig. 3. Security policy model in LESERP-D

In general, LESERP-DP uses a key distribution mechanism with centralized management, the process needs to be carried out twice as shown in Fig. 3, one is at the cluster formation stage, and the other is at the inter-cluster routing selection stage.

After the cluster head is selected, the base station assigns a key to each cluster head. In order to ensure the security between different areas, the keys between any two cluster head must be not the same. So that even if a cluster head node is captured by the attacker, it will not affect the security of other areas. For each pair of key between cluster node and its cluster head is self-generated by the individual cluster head, rather than generated by the base station. In this way, cluster head do not have to allocate additional space for storing the key pairs, but only requiring a simple hash calculation. The key generation formula for each cluster node is as follows:

$$K_i = Hash\left(K_{ch}, ID_i\right) \tag{3}$$

In Eq. (3), K_i represents the key of node i, K_{ch} represents the key assigned by the cluster head node of the cluster, and ID_i represents the unique node label of i. The node label is sent when the nodes in each cluster send packets to the cluster head node when they are clustered. At the same time, in order to ensure the overall security of the key pair, the key for cluster head is not unchanged, but reallocated when a cluster head is selected every time. So the process will occur in each round of the algorithm.

At the stage of inter-cluster routing selection, each cluster head will build their own multi-hop path through the specific algorithm. In order to ensure the security of these paths, the base station need to assign a special transmission key for each path and the keys of each path should be different from each other. At the same time, in view of the overall security of the key, the two processes need to be carried out at the corresponding stage of each round. Since the assigned task is mainly borne by the base station, the cluster head only needs to calculate the corresponding hash value, it has little impact on network energy expenditure.

4   Experiment and Analysis

4.1   Security Analysis

By adding the key management mechanism to the LESERP-DP, the security of the network is improved to some extent, and some simple network attacks can be dealt with.

(1) Sybil attack: The so-called Sybil attacks need a fake identity, because of the introduction of key authentication mechanism, which blocks many of the attackers who can not capture nodes. And even if the attacker has captured the common node, as the key pair in each round will be redistributed, attack effect is very limited.

(2) HELLO flood attack: Because of the existence of key distribution mechanism, this kind of attack is invalid in most cases, or only works in one cycle. Besides, due to adopting the clustering structure, the impact of the attack is usually locked in one cluster without affecting other regions.

4.2   Energy Consumption Analysis

In this section, the simulation experiment is performed via Matlab software. The classical routing protocol LEACH and EEUC are used in the comparison experiment. In order to further enhance the contrast effect, MR-LEACH, a hierarchical routing protocol for large-scale WSNs is also introduced.

Some of the important parameters in the experiment are shown in the following Table 1:

Table 1. Parameter list

Parameters	Values
Network size $(xm * ym)$	$600 * 600\,\mathrm{m}^2$
Base station location $(sink.x, sink.y)$	$(300, 650)\,\mathrm{m}$
Number of sensor nodes (n)	1000 nodes
Initial energy of each sensor node (E_0)	0.5 J
Data packet length (DPL)	4000 bytes
Control packet length (CPL)	200 bytes
E_{elec}	50 nJ/bit
ε_{fs}	$10\,\mathrm{pJ/bit} \cdot \mathrm{m}^2$
ε_{mp}	$0.0013\,\mathrm{pJ/bit} \cdot \mathrm{m}^2$
Density difference threshold (DDT)	$1/400\,\mathrm{nodes/m}^2$

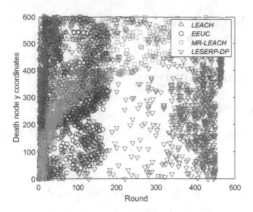

Fig. 4. Dead nodes in every round

We compared the four protocols from three aspects, the surviving nodes in the network, residual energy of the entire network and dead nodes in every round.

As can be seen from Figs. 4, 5 and 6, although the security mechanism is introduced, the protocol proposed in this paper, greatly extends the network life when compared to the traditional routing protocol LEACH and EEUC. Compared to the MR-LEACH, which is suitable for large-scale network, LESERP-DP also has its advantages. In the energy consumption rate, the performance of LESERP-DP is better than MR-LEACH, the energy consumption curve is relatively flat. From the distribution of death nodes, it can be seen that LESERP-DP is a good routing protocol that solves the energy hole problem and makes the energy consumption in the whole network more balanced.

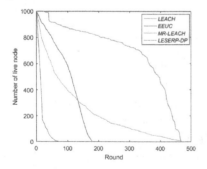

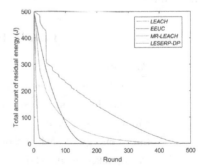

Fig. 5. Surviving nodes in the network

Fig. 6. Residual energy of the entire network

5 Conclusion

Through the above analysis, it is clear that the protocol proposed in this paper is able to adapt to a variety of complex environments and has broad application prospects. The protocol introduces the key management mechanism to enhance network security, but this does not affect its superiority in terms of energy saving. LESERP-DP can provide a better balance in energy consumption and significantly prolong network lifetime.

As the safe strategy used in LESERP-DP can only deal with simple network attack, in the next step, we will focus on the improvement of the security in Wireless Sensor Networks.

Acknowledgments. This work is supported by China Aviation Science Foundation (Grant No. 20101952021), Fundamental Research Funds for Central Universities (Grant No. NZ2013306) and Key Project supported by Medical Science and Technology Development Foundation, Nanjing Department of Health (Grant No. YKK15170).

References

1. Li, C., Zhang, H., Hao, B., et al.: A survey on routing protocols for large-scale wireless sensor networks. Sensors **11**(4), 3498–3526 (2011)
2. Gu, B., Sheng, V.S.: A robust regularization path algorithm for v-support vector classification. IEEE Trans. Neural Netw. Learn. **28**(5), 1241–1248 (2017)
3. Chen, Y., Hao, C., Wu, W., et al.: Robust dense reconstruction by range merging based on confidence estimation. Sci. China Inf. Sci. **59**(9), 092103 (2016)
4. Kong, Y., Zhang, M., Ye, D.: A belief propagation-based method for task allocation in open and dynamic cloud environments. Knowl. Based. Syst. **115**, 123–132 (2017)
5. Heinzelman, W.R., Chandrakasan, A., Balakrishnan, H.: Energy-efficient communication protocol for wireless microsensor networks. In: 32rd Hawaii International Conference on System Sciences, pp. 1–10. IEEE, Hawaii (2000)
6. Soro, S., Heinzelman, W.B.: Prolonging the lifetime of wireless sensor networks via unequal clustering. In: 19th IEEE International Parallel and Distributed Processing Symposium, p. 236. IEEE, Denver (2000)
7. Li, C., Chen, G., Ye, M., et al.: An uneven cluster-based routing protocol for wireless sensor networks. Chin. J. Comput. **30**(1), 27–36 (2007)
8. Logambigai, R., Kannan, A.: Fuzzy logic based unequal clustering for wireless sensor networks. Wirel. Netw. **22**(3), 945–957 (2016)
9. Al-Karaki, J.N., Kamal, A.E.: Routing techniques in wireless sensor networks: a survey. IEEE Wirel. Commun. **11**(6), 6–28 (2004)
10. Pan, Z., Lei, J., Zhang, Y., et al.: Fast motion estimation based on content property for low-complexity H. 265/HEVC encoder. IEEE Trans. Broadcast. **62**(3), 675–684 (2016)
11. Zhang, Y., Sun, X., Wang, B.: Efficient algorithm for k-barrier coverage based on integer linear programming. China Commun. **13**(7), 16–23 (2016)
12. Pan, Z., Zhang, Y., Kwong, S.: Efficient motion and disparity estimation optimization for low complexity multiview video coding. IEEE Trans. Broadcast. **61**(2), 166–176 (2015)

13. Quang, V.T., Miyoshi, T.: Adaptive routing protocol with energy efficiency and event clustering for wireless sensor networks. IEICE Trans. Commun. **91**(9), 2795–2805 (2008)

14. Farooq, M.O., Dogar, A.B., Shah, G.A.: MR-LEACH: multi-hop routing with low energy adaptive clustering hierarchy. In: 4th International Conference on Sensor Technologies and Applications, pp. 262–268. IEEE, Washington (2010)

15. Xu, F., Zhu, W., Xu, J., et al.: A low energy adaptive clustering multi-hop routing protocol based on fuzzy decision. J. Intell. Fuzzy Syst. **29**(6), 2547–2554 (2015)

16. Tanachaiwiwat, S., Dave, P., Bhindwale, R., et al.: Poster abstract secure locations: routing on trust and isolating compromised sensors in location-aware sensor networks. In: 1st International Conference on Embedded Networked Sensor Systems, pp. 324–325. ACM, Los Angeles (2003)

17. Zhou, J., Li, C., Cao, Q., et al.: An intrusion-tolerant secure routing protocol with key exchange for wireless sensor network. In: 2008 IEEE International Conference on Information and Automation, pp. 1547–1552. IEEE, Hunan (2008)

18. Wei, L., Geng, Y.: Energy-saving data aggregation algorithm for protecting privacy and integrity. J. Comput. Appl. **33**(9), 2505–2510 (2013)

19. Altisen, K., Devismes, S., Jamet, R., et al.: SR3: secure resilient reputation-based routing. Wirel. Netw. **19**(14), 1–23 (2013)

20. Alrajeh, N.A., Alabed, M.S., Elwahiby, M.S.: Secure ant-based routing protocol for wireless sensor network. Int. J. Distrib. Sens. Netw. **9**(6), 761–762 (2013)

21. Wang, W., Wu, Y., Tang, C., et al.: Adaptive density-based spatial clustering of applications with noise (DBSCAN) according to data. In: 17th International Conference on Machine Learning and Cybernetics, pp. 445–451. IEEE, Singapore (2015)

Power Consuming Activity Recognition in Home Environment

Xiaodong Liu and Qi Liu[✉]

School of Computing, Edinburgh Napier University, 10 Colinton Road,
Edinburgh EH10 5DT, UK
q.liu@napier.ac.uk

Abstract. This work proposed an activity recognition model which focus on the power consuming activity in home environment, to help residents modify their behavior. We set the IoT system with lower number of sensors. The key data for identifying activity comes from widely used smart sockets. It first took residents' acceptability into consideration to set the IoT system, then used a seamless indoor position system to get residents' position to help recognize the undergoing activities. Based on ontology, it made use of domain knowledge in daily activity and built an activity ontology. The system took real home situation into consideration and make full use of both electric and electronic appliances' data into the context awareness. The knowledge helps improve the performance of the data-driven method. The experiment shows the system can recognize the common activities with a high accuracy and have a good applicability to real home scenario.

Keywords: Activity recognition · Ontology · Second-order HMM

1 Introduction

Electric energy is one of the most widely used energy sources in the world. It is mainly used in industrial production, residential life, buildings, transportation and service industries. People's abuse of electricity, resulting in a lot of waste. Almost every activity in home need consumption of electricity, it is useful to recognize them for the conservation. As the Internet of Things (IoT) stimulates the development of the Smart Home (SH), SH uses the IoT technology to connect domestic devices together into the Internet, gets the status data of the devices, and provides smart control along with some related services. Activity recognition in home is more and more necessary for SH to offer the personal service. Activity recognition now has become a hot topic and received increasing attention from many fields, such as image processing, pattern identification, wireless sensor network and data mining. First we should distinguish between action and activity, action is a basic human motion or repeat of a kind of basic motion, e.g. stand, walk or sit. But activity is a combination of the basic human motion, e.g. watching TV can be decomposed into opening TV, sitting and watching it. So an activity is more complicated than an action. In home, lots of daily activities need power consumption. With the help of the activity recognition, we could find what activity consume some unnecessary power, and power feedback will have a good effect on end user to save

© Springer International Publishing AG 2017
X. Sun et al. (Eds.): ICCCS 2017, Part I, LNCS 10602, pp. 361–372, 2017.
https://doi.org/10.1007/978-3-319-68505-2_31

consumption [1]. So it can remind the residents to modify their behaviors and save the energy.

A lot of works have been done to this area, but to home environment, these works have encountered problems of one kind or another to real scenarios, such as privacy concern, installation complexity, residents' acceptance and so on. So our work focused on the real situation in home, took the residents and home environment's characteristic into consideration. Nearly every activity in home will have something to do with these appliances. So it makes sense that we use the domestic appliances to infer home activity. The proposed method used the intelligent sockets to collect the load data about the appliances, utilized smart phones to assist our indoor position system. We do not need too many additional sensors to construct the system. Depend on the load data of appliances, we can classify them for a fine-grain activities. The main contributions of this study are described below:

1. This study has made full use of existing equipment in home, we not only used the electric appliances but also the electronic appliances. Depend on residents' acceptance, users do not need to take any specific devices with them, and there is no risk of privacy concern. The system do not need too many additional sensors.
2. We proposed a domain knowledge based activity model, which can store necessary knowledge in our ontology model. The model is also helpful to the accuracy for the activity recognition.

2   Related Work

A lot of researchers have done many studies on this topic, recognition methods have different ways of data extraction and different activity models. According to the architecture proposed by Chen et al. [2], most recognition models have the following steps: data collection, data label, feature extraction and activity recognition.

According to the pattern of data collection, methods can be divided into four categories, one is depend on the video frame ([3] is a review for it), the second one is based on the wireless sensor networks, the third one is based on wearable sensors, and the last one is based on the wireless technology. Image-based method has the problem of the privacy concern, intrusive mood and installation cost and complexity. Also, this kind of approach suffers from the variability of human activity, complex background and ambient illumination, so it is limited in some specific circumstances, such as medical care [4, 5, 6] or security, and it is not desirable in home environment. Wireless sensor networks based on ambient sensors is able to collect the context aware information in indoor situation. The works like [7, 8, 9] utilized a large number of sensors to get the context, then used these data to infer the activity that the user is doing. It is inevitable that these methods need huge deployment and maintenance cost. Wearable sensors [10, 11, 12] have become a mature technology, more and more wearable products have been in mass production by the manufacturers. But these approaches require subjects to wear separated sensors on different parts of the body, so they need specific devices and these devices need charging and cannot be wore all the time. There are also lots of methods utilizing the accelerometer and gyroscope in smartphone [13, 14, 15] or RFID [16] to recognize activities. These methods all require users to take certain specific devices with them, the problem they brought is just like the wearable sensors. Recent years, the wireless technology have been a promising work, such as Wi-See [17] and Wi-Vi [18], but both of the works depend on specific platform, i.e. the USRP-N210 SDR system. The availability in home remains.

Few researchers worked on the domestic appliances to activity recognition. Lai [19] and Cho et al. [20] worked on this, and they calculated a relevance between devices and activities, then used a Naïve Bayes to classify the activity.

There are mainly two kinds of recognition methods: data-driven methods and knowledge-driven methods. The two most commonly used data-driven methods are hidden Markov model (HMM) [21] and Conditional random field (CRF) [22]. There are some variations of the two methods used to deal with the activity recognition. The other is knowledge-driven approaches [23], it can solve the cold start problem that data-driven methods have, make the model reusable.

3 Proposed System Architecture

Traditional activity recognition methods based on wireless sensor networks has several shortcomings. First, it need install a large number of sensors, which is difficult for user to accept. Second, to different home environments, it needs different sensors. Third, it assumes that the activity can only happen in a fixed room, but in fact, you can use your laptop in your bedroom or sitting room. Next we will introduce our system, it can solve the above problems.

3.1 Intelligent Sockets

People's life cannot be without appliances today, a large number of the indoor activities are connected to the appliances. So using domestic appliances is possible to recognize human activity in home. Now the smart meter and intelligent sockets are used more and

Fig. 1. Intelligent socket

more broadly by the residents, the construction of smart grids has also become goals for many countries. We designed our own intelligent sockets to get the load data of appliances. The system adopts the power measurement chip HLW8012 produced by Shenzhen Heliwei Technology Company, and the ESP8266 WIFI module produced by Shanghai Lexin technology company. The intelligent socket is show in Fig. 1. In our experiment, we detected 11 appliances and recognized 10 activities.

3.2   Indoor Seamless Positioning Module

Positioning based on the mobile phone Wi-Fi RSSI (Received Signal Strength Indication): With the increasing popularity of smart phones, smart phones increasingly become an indispensable device in people's lives, residents often carry mobile phones in home. In a modern home, a router is an indispensable device in many homes where the location is basically fixed and a router's signal cannot generally cover all parts of the home. So a home with more than one router is a normal phenomenon. In the system we do not need add more expensive equipment. Using the smartphone system SDK to access to the surrounding Wi-Fi hotspot (i.e. access point, AP) signal strength value, we can use the phone to detect the person's indoor location. At present, there are two main indoor positioning algorithms based on RSSI, one is the trigonometric positioning method and the other is the fingerprint localization algorithm.

Fingerprint algorithm needs to divide the indoor area into grids first. Because the temperature, humidity, multipath, occlusion of the object and the influence of shadow fading effect, RSSI values the receiver gets in the same position are also different at the same point, So a large number of samples are need (Usually 100 times) to represent the average RSSI value of the region, and then record the location and address of the AP. The experimental environment is a 60-square-meter single room, if using the fingerprint algorithm, it is necessary to sample 100 values in the range of $1 * 1$ m^2 to $1.5 * 1.5$ m^2, so the cost of sampling is very large and time consuming, so it is not recommended to be used in home environment.

Triangulation algorithm requires us to know the locations of the APs in advance. This is easy to do because the home AP (router) locations are fixed. Using the classic signal attenuation model, you can use less data points to get accurate distance. Finally, according to the calculated RSSI value, the distance of the smartphone to the AP access point is obtained, and the position is calculated according to the triangle centroid algorithm. RSSI signal strength and distance of the classical theoretical model:

$$RSSI = A - 10\,n\lg(d) \tag{3.1}$$

where A is the received signal strength value of the receiving end get per unit length. Equation (3.1) is a classical model for calculating the relationship between RSSI and distance d, where the parameters A and n are closely related to the AP access point hardware and the specific environment. Thus, in different home environments, parameters A and n are different. The parameter values of A and n in the current environment are calculated by the linear regression method through the actual measurement of multiple sets of test data. In our experiment, the relationship between distance d and RSSI is shown in Fig. 2, and A is -39.2 and n is 3.7.

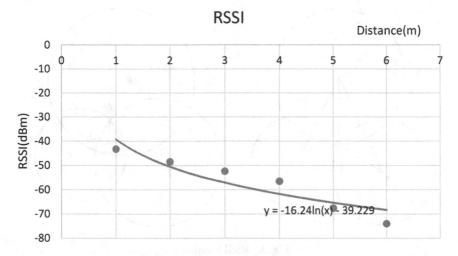

Fig. 2. RSSI ranging

Triangular centroid algorithm: We need to know the coordinates of 3 AP access points in advance, $A(x_a, y_a), B(x_b, y_b), C(x_c, y_c)$ and the measured distances d'_A, d'_B, d'_C, as Fig. 3 shows, we get the centroid by the following formula:

$$\begin{cases} \sqrt{(x_e - x_A)^2 + (y_e - y_A)^2} \le d'_A \\ \sqrt{(x_e - x_B)^2 + (y_e - y_B)^2} = d'_B \\ \sqrt{(x_e - x_C)^2 + (y_e - y_C)^2} = d'_C \end{cases} \qquad (3.2)$$

the coordinate of centroid D or D_1 is $\left(\dfrac{x_e + x_f + x_g}{3}, \dfrac{y_e + y_f + y_g}{3} \right)$, we can get the room level of the person location. But in home, people do not always take a mobile phone with them. We only determine the location of a person based on the phone when the smartphone is moving (that is, when a user is carrying it). According to the built-in three-axis accelerator, if $|G_{t-1} - G_t| > \varphi$, G_t is the acceleration taken at time t, φ is the preset threshold of 0.1 m/s^2.

Location of user with no device carried: Users can not always carry a smart phone at home, for example, when taking a bath. Two ultrasonic distance measuring sensors are installed on the door to detect the user's room level location when no device is being carried. The activation order of the two ultrasonic distance measuring sensors determines whether to enter the room or to exit the room. The whole seamless positioning system is shown in Fig. 4.

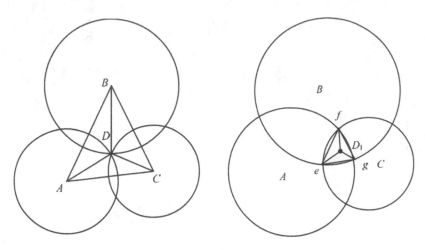

Fig. 3. RSSI location

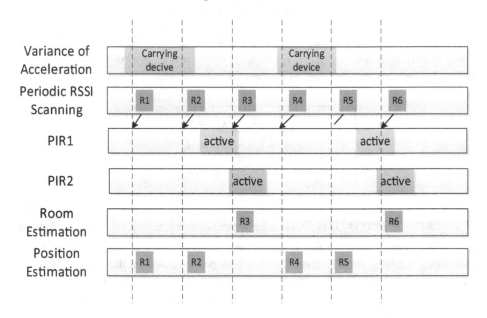

Fig. 4. Home seamless positioning

4 Activity Recognition

4.1 Activity Ontology Model

Ontology is a systematic explanation of objective reality, which is concerned with the abstract nature of objective reality. In 1993, Gruber gave one of the most popular definitions of Ontology: "Ontology is the clear specification of a conceptual model" [20].

Knowledge of domestic user activity. The activity model is based on the activity knowledge base in the family. With the knowledge of the user activity in the household, the model can judge the classification according to the current input context. Knowledge base is the storage location of semantic information in the domain. The concepts, attributes, rules and instances in the ontology model are stored in the knowledge base. The definition of the activity, person, appliances and locations are also stored in it.

Domestic users tend to conduct daily activities in a particular situation, that is, a specific time and a specific location to carry out an activity. For example, people usually brush teeth every morning and every night in the bathroom. It usually includes the use of toothpaste, toothbrushes, cups and faucets. This information is referred to as the contextual information for the corresponding activity. However, due to the particularity of the home environment, an activity can occur at any time of the day, or it can be repeated at any time. For example, brushing teeth can be done early in the morning, but if someone gets up in the afternoon, the brushing teeth behavior may be carried out in the afternoon, in view of this situation, we do not consider the time information dimension.

Because the user has a different way of life, habits and hobbies, the way of a person conduct a daily activity is different from the way that other people carry out the activity. For example, a person likes to use the computer every morning, while others like to use the computer every night. Even in the case of the same behavior, such as the use of computers, you can open the main chassis, then open the monitor, and then turn on the sound to start using the computer. Or open the sound first, then open the monitor, and then open the main chassis to start using the computer. Therefore, we do not consider occurrence order of the seed action.

And because of the particularity of the home environment, some activities can only occur in a fixed position, and some activities can occur in multiple locations, rather than a fixed location. For example, the user at home on the toilet, the bath can only be carried out in the toilet; and the use of the computer the event, the user can be carried out in the bedroom, you can also carry out in the living room, so we need to restrict the user to carry out certain activities, Define multiple locations where certain activities can be made. We call this knowledge rule 1, describe the rule in a standardized language:

Rule 1: Activity ∀ hasLocation (Balcony or Bathroom or Bedroom or Diningroom or Kitchen or Sittingroom or OutOfHome)

Activity ∃ hasLocation Locations

Rule 1 is to say that every activity must have a place to happen, and can be expressed as a The following matrix:

$$P_{ra} = \begin{bmatrix} 0 & 0 & 0 & 1 & 1 & 0 & 0 & 0 & 1 \\ 0 & 0 & 0 & 0 & 1 & 0 & 0 & 0 & 1 \\ 0 & 0 & 1 & 0 & 0 & 0 & 1 & 0 & 1 \\ 1 & 1 & 0 & 0 & 0 & 0 & 1 & 1 & 1 \\ 0 & 0 & 0 & 0 & 0 & 1 & 1 & 0 & 1 \end{bmatrix}$$

P_{ra} is a 5 * 9 matrix, the horizontal axis represents that five indoor rooms, from top to bottom are: kitchen, restaurant, bedroom, bathroom, living room. The vertical axis indicates nine activities, from left to right, respectively, toileting, bathing, sleeping, cooking, eating, watching TV, using the computer, grooming, and doing nothing. The matrix represents the activities that may occur in each room.

Activity model. Based on the nature and characteristics of domestic users' activity in the family, we use "who", "where", "what", "how" to describe our activity, including people, location, sensors, electrical and activity information dimensions.

In this paper, we use the OWL language as a descriptive language that describes the concepts and correlations between different information dimensions of household user activity. As mentioned above, we divided five dimensions according to user activity. According to these five dimensions, we construct the corresponding ontology model, and each ontology model corresponds to the respective information dimension. The semantic links are established between the various dimensions through abstract attribute relations. These attributes relate to an ontology and some physical entities and conceptual entities. Each attribute has its domain and scope, the domain refers to the subject of the property, scope refers to the object of the property. An attribute uses a text or an instance of another class to describe a class, so you can interconnect two classes.

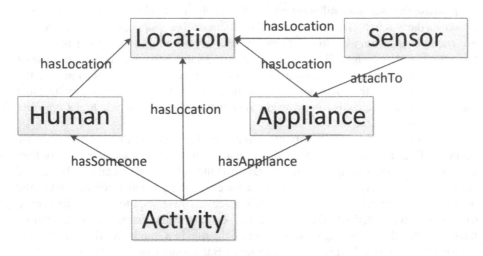

Fig. 5. Activity ontology model

Figure 5 shows the five ontology models and the links between these models. The ontology models are as follows: Sensor, Person, Location, Appliance, and Activity. These ontologies are interconnected by attributes. The sensor ontology is used to abstract and describe the attributes and performance of different sensors; the human ontology standardizes the user identity in the home environment; the position ontology abstracts and normalizes the location of user, appliance and sensor; the Appliance ontology is used to abstract and describe the appliance attributes; activity ontology used to abstract and describe the property of the activity.

4.2 HMM2

According to the actual situation, present activity is not only connected to the activity in previous state, the first-order assumptions are not very reasonable, so here we propose a second-order hidden Markov model, which also has two assumptions: a) The activity of time t is related not only to the activity of time t-1 but also to the activity of time t-2; b) The observed variable x_t at time t is related not only to the current state of the system but also to the previous state.

The second-order transition probability can be expressed as following:

$$a_{ijk} = P\left(y_t = s_k | y_{t-1} = s_i, y_{t-2} = s_j\right)$$

The second-order emission probability can be expressed as following:

$$b_{jk} = P\left(x_t | y_t = s_k, y_{t-1} = s_i\right)$$

Considering the initial condition, the HMM2's parameters are $\lambda = \left(\pi, A_1, A_2, B_1, B_2\right)$, where $\pi = \{\pi_i\}$; $A_1 = \{a_{ij}\}$; $A_2 = \{a_{ijk}\}$; $B_1 = \{b_k\}$; $B_2 = \{b_{jk}\}$, they represents the initial probability of the model, the first-order transition probability, the second-order transition probability, the first-order transmission probability and the second-order transmission probability respectively.

Second-order Viterbi algorithm with ontology knowledge. During each iteration of the Viterbi, we add our position information and the position-activity state matrix P_{ra}. According to the user location, there are only some activities can happen, so we do not need to search the whole activity space but to search some possible activities. It can be formally described as:

Loc = {kit,din,bed,toi,sit}, assume that kit = 1, din = 2, bed = 3, toi = 4, sit = 5, the search space is S' = S.*P_{ra}(Loc(n),:).

5 Experiment

Our experiment is carried in a single room, the configuration is shown in Table 1.

The volunteer said she has bought the Xiao MI intelligent socket before to control the water heaters on the way home. So she do not refuse to use more intelligent sockets. The annotation of the data is recorded by self-reporting.

Table 1. Details of the experiment environment

Number of people	1
Number of rooms	5
Duration	7 days
Activity detected	leave house, use toilet, take shower, go to bed, prepare food, eat food, watch TV, use computer, dressing, Idle

We first compared our method with the Naïve Bayes (NB) and HMM1, used "leave one day out" method to test the accuracy. The evaluation parameters we used are Precision, Recall, F-measure, Accuracy and Time. These can be calculated as following:

$$\text{Precision} = \frac{1}{C} \sum_{i=1}^{C} \frac{TP_{ii}}{NI_i}$$

$$Recall = \frac{1}{C} \sum_{i=1}^{C} \frac{TP_{ii}}{NT_i}$$

$$F1 = \frac{2 * precision * recall}{precision + recall}$$

$$\text{Accuracy} = \frac{\sum_{i=1}^{Q} TP_{ii}}{Total}$$

The performance comparison is shown in Table 2.

Table 2. Performance comparison

	Precision	Recall	F-measure	Accuracy	Time
NB	55.1	59.2	57.7	76.4	0.11
HMM	69.3	70.3	69.7	85.3	0.39
HMM2	70.4	71.8	71.1	88.0	0.51
HMM2 + Knowledge	79.9	84.2	82.0	95.8	0.27

As we can see, Hmm2's performance is slightly higher than HMM1's. It shows that higher order HMM may lead to better performance, but we cannot say that higher order can definitely lead to better performance, because in real situation, closer activity should have a bigger impact on the following activity. The domain knowledge help reduce the time cost, and improve the recognition accuracy. The fusion method has the best performance.

6   Conclusion and Future Work

In this work, we proposed a novel activity recognition system, it collected the load data to recognize the power consuming activity, and it also contained a seamless positioning and appliance recognition. With the improved system architecture, we can solve the problem that traditional wireless sensor network brings. First, the system can be used to any other home environment. Second, the acceptance of the user is good, because if no user admit the activity recognition system, it is useless. Last, our knowledge and data driven hybrid method could increase the accuracy of the activity recognition.

However, the method is only used for single resident and sequence activities, which should be expanded to multi-user situation. Next, we should consider the feedback about the behavior to help residents save the energy and we also want to find out the perform-ance of n-order HMM.

Acknowledgments. This work has received funding from the European Union's Horizon 2020 research and innovation programme under the Marie Sklodowska-Curie grant agreement No 701697.

References

1. Sarah, D.: The effectiveness of feedback on energy consumption. In: A Review for DEFRA of the Literature on Metering, Billing and Direct Displays, vol. 486 (2006)
2. Chen, C., Das, B., Cook, D.J.: A data mining framework for activity recognition in smart environments. In: The 6th International Conference on Intelligent Environments, pp. 80–83 (2010)
3. Poppe, R.: A survey on vision-based human action recognition. Image Vision Comput. **28**(6), 976–990 (2010)
4. Nappi, M., Piuri, V., Tan, T., Zhang, D.: Introduction to the special section on biometric systems and applications. IEEE Trans. Syst. Man Cybern. Syst. **44**(11), 1457–1460 (2014)
5. Peetoom, K.K.B., Lexis, M.A.S., Joore, M., Dirksen, C.D., De Witte, L.P.: Literature review on monitoring technologies and their outcomes in independently living elderly people. Disab. Rehabil. Assist. Technol. **10**(4), 271–294 (2015)
6. Liu, Q., Cai, W., Shen, J., Fu, Z., Liu, X., Linge, N.: A speculative approach to spatial-temporal efficiency with multi-objective optimization in a heterogeneous cloud environment. Secur. Commun. Netw. **9**(17), 4002–4012 (2016)
7. Wilson, D.H., Atkeson, C.: Simultaneous tracking and activity recognition (STAR) using many anonymous, binary sensors. In: Gellersen, H.W., Want, R., Schmidt, A. (eds.) Pervasive 2005. LNCS, vol. 3468, pp. 62–79. Springer, Heidelberg (2005). doi:10.1007/11428572_5
8. Tapia, E.M., Intille, S.S., Larson, K.: Activity recognition in the home using simple and ubiquitous sensors. In: Ferscha, A., Mattern, F. (eds.) Pervasive 2004. LNCS, vol. 3001, pp. 158–175. Springer, Heidelberg (2004). doi:10.1007/978-3-540-24646-6_10
9. Fu, Z., Huang, F., Sun, X., Vasilakos, A.V., Yang, C.-N.: Enabling semantic search based on conceptual graphs over encrypted outsourced data. IEEE Trans. Serv. Comput. (2016)
10. Shoaib, M., Bosch, S., Scholten, H., Havinga, P.J.M., Incel, O.D.: Towards detection of bad habits by fusing smartphone and smartwatch sensors. In: IEEE International Conference on Pervasive Computing and Communication Workshops (PerCom Workshops), pp. 591–596 (2015)
11. De, D., Bharti, P., Das, S.K., Chellappan, S.: Multimodal wearable sensing for fine-grained activity recognition in healthcare. IEEE Internet Comput. **19**, 26–35 (2015)
12. Xia, Z., Wang, X., Sun, X., Wang, B.: Steganalysis of least significant bit matching using multi-order differences. Secur. Commun. Netw. **7**(8), 1283–1291 (2014)
13. Abbate, S.: A smartphone-based fall detection system. Pervasive Mob. Comput. **8**(6), 883–899 (2012)
14. Kwapisz, J.R., Weiss, G.M., Moore, S.A.: Activity recognition using cell phone accelerometers. ACM SIGKDD Explor. Newslett. **12**(2), 74–82 (2010)
15. Zhang, Y., Sun, X., Baowei, W.: Efficient algorithm for K-barrier coverage based on integer linear programming. China Commun. **13**(7), 16–23 (2016)
16. Chen, M.: Towards smart city: M2M communications with software agent intelligence. Multimedia Tools Appl. **67**, 167–178 (2012)

17. Pu, Q., Gupta, S., Gollakota, S., Patel, S.: Whole-home gesture recognition using wireless signals. In: Proceedings of the ACM MOBICOM, pp. 27–38 (2013)
18. Adib, F., Katabi, D.: See through walls with WiFi!. In: Proceedings of the ACM SIGCOMM, pp. 75–86 (2013)
19. Lai, C.F., Lai, Y.X., Yang, L.T., Chao, H.C.: Integration of IoT energy management system with appliance and activity recognition. In: IEEE International Conference on Green Computing and Communications, pp. 66– 71 (2012)
20. Cho, W.T., Lai, Y.X., Lai, C.F., Huang, Y.M.: Appliance-aware activity recognition mechanism for IoT energy management system. Comput. J. **56**(8), 1020–1033 (2013)
21. Granovsky-Grisaru, S., Shaya, M., Diamant, Y.Z.: Recognizing independent and joint activities among multiple residents in smart environments. J. Ambient Intell. Humaniz. Comput. **1**(1), 57–63 (2010)
22. Nazerfard, E., Das, B., Holder, L.B., Cook, D.J.: Conditional random fields for activity recognition in smart environments. In: ACM International Health Informatics Symposium, pp. 282–286 (2010)
23. Chen, L., Nugent, C.D., Wang, H.: A knowledge-driven approach to activity recognition in smart homes. IEEE Trans. Knowl. Data Eng. **24**, 961–974 (2012)

A Pre-partition Based Uneven Clustering Multi-hop Routing Protocol

Yating Hou[1,2(✉)], Feng Xu[1,2], Mingming Su[1,2], and Kaibo Yu[1,2]

[1] College of Computer Science and Technology,
Nanjing University of Aeronautics and Astronautics, Nanjing, China
hyt11050@163.com, nuaaos@163.com, work_smm@163.com, 18338736315@163.com
[2] Collaborative Innovation Center of Novel Software Technology
and Industrialization, Nanjing, China

Abstract. So far, clustering multi-hop routing algorithm has employed in many wireless sensor network routing protocols to improve the network performance. However, unreasonable clustering can cause premature death of cluster head. Given this, in the paper, we propose a pre-partition based uneven clustering multi-hop routing protocol (PUCMR), which can conserve energy efficiently. In the protocol, explicit numerical calculations for hierarchy numbers and size of each layer are provided. Non-uniform layering is adopted to balance energy consumption of cluster heads in different layers and energy consumption of cluster heads in the same layer. Simulation results show that the proposed protocol can well adapt to the large-scale condition, and balance cluster-head energy consumption, so as to prolong the life cycle of the network.

Keywords: WSNs · Routing protocol · Pre-partition · Uneven clustering

1 Introduction

Wireless sensor network is a major technical progress in twenty-first Century, in recent years, the application of wireless sensor networks has become increasingly widespread, involving medical, environmental, family and other fields. However, the energy of sensor node is very limited, which hinders its development to a certain extent. How to design a new and more energy-efficient routing protocol to prolong the lifetime of sensor nodes has become one of the hot spots in wireless sensor network routing protocols.

For large-scale applications and achieve the purpose of saving energy, many wireless sensor network routing protocols use hierarchical structure based on clusters. Clustering method can reduce unnecessary data transmission and avoid the transmission energy consumption caused by redundant data. However, a disadvantage of the clustering routing protocol is the uneven energy consumption of cluster heads. To balance the energy consumption of cluster heads, non-uniform clustering method is often used, but the determination of cluster radius is still very difficult.

© Springer International Publishing AG 2017
X. Sun et al. (Eds.): ICCCS 2017, Part I, LNCS 10602, pp. 373–384, 2017.
https://doi.org/10.1007/978-3-319-68505-2_32

By analyzing classic clustering routing protocols, we propose the pre-partition based uneven clustering multi-hop routing protocol (PUCMR), which determines layer numbers, layer size and competition radius for each CH. Through this approach, the load imposed on the CH is alleviated and network lifetime is greatly extended.

2   Related Work

Researchers have put forward a variety of sensor network routing protocols.

Flat routing schemes are presented early. Classic flat routing protocol sequential assignment routing [1] builds tree by avoiding nodes with very low QoS and energy reserves, creates multiple paths from each node to the sink. However, with the increment of the network size, the early flat routing schemes cannot adapt to this change.

Afterwards, the uniform hierarchical management mechanism is introduced. There are many clustering protocols, like LEACH [2], MR-LEACH [3] and so on [4–6]. LEACH [2] performs the election of cluster-heads and the formation of clusters periodically, let all nodes in turn elected as cluster head. Both inter-cluster communication and communication in a cluster utilize single-hop communication paradigm. A shortcoming of LEACH is that it does not take into account the amount of energy left at the node when selecting cluster-head. Besides single-hop routing method leads to premature deaths of nodes far away from the base station. Farooq et al. [3] present MR-LEACH protocol. The CH election in MR-LEACH base on the available energy, and it partitions the network into different layers of clusters. CHs in each layer are responsible for relaying data for CHs at lower layers to transmit data to the BS.

While providing multi-hop routing with equal clustering, nodes close to the base station will die soon. Therefore, researchers put forward non-uniform clustering strategy to balance the energy consumption of the entire network. Wireless sensor network routing protocol based on non-uniform clustering put forward in recent years are EEUC [7], DEBUC [8], ACT [9], UCPIT [10], UCCGRA [11], UMBIC [12], and so on [13–15]. EEUC [7] is a typical uneven clustering routing protocol, the clusters closer to the BS have smaller sizes than those farther away from the sink, and thus the cluster-heads closer to the sink could save energy consumption in cluster for the inter-cluster data transmission. Paper [9] proposes a novel cluster-based routing protocol named ACT, which aims to equilibrium energy consumption by reducing the size of clusters near the base station. It also provides a method to arrange cluster size. UCPIT [10] protocol is also an unequal clustering method for WSNs, it optimizes the competition radius proposed in EEUC and adopts an inter-cluster routing protocol based on the improved SFLA (Shuffled Frog Leaping Algorithm). UCCGRA [11] sectionalizes sensor nodes into different unequal clusters in view of vote-based measure and the transmission power of these nodes. UMBIC [12] minimizes energy consumption, solves the hot spot problem by utilizing Unequal Clustering Mechanism (UCM) and the Multi-Objective Immune Algorithm (MOIA). This algorithm is applicable to small and large scale/homogeneous and heterogeneous wireless sensor networks with different densities.

The paper deeply analyzes the relationship between the size of the partition and the distance to the station. Based on EEUC algorithm [7], we present a pre-partition based uneven clustering multi-hop routing protocol (PUCMR). This protocol can not only effectively balance network load, obviously prolong the lifetime, but also avoid the excessive computation of the cluster size.

3   PUCMR: Pre-partition Based Uneven Clustering Multi-hop Routing

This section describes implementation mechanism of PUCMR. PUCMR protocol works in three phases, namely pre-partition by base station, establishment stage and stabilization stage. Among them, the establishment stage consists of three steps: CH election, route selection and cluster formation. Details of the protocol process are given in the following part.

3.1   Pre-partition

Previous studies have shown that multi-hop routing is more practical when cluster head needs to send data to the base station over a long distance. In this way, the cluster head, which is close to the base station, takes on the additional data forwarding task and expends more energy. In order to solve the problem that these energy-intensive sensors are early dead, PUCMR applies non-uniform partition. Partitioning is carried out at the beginning of the algorithm, and once the partition is determined, it will not be changed. Layer number is calculated based on optimal number of cluster heads in WSN.

3.1.1   The Optimal Number of Cluster Heads

The derivation of the optimal number of cluster heads (k) that makes the lowest energy consumption of the whole network is followed. Assumes that n sensor nodes are evenly deployed in the square field (M * M), and the network is divided into k clusters, network total energy consumption in a round can be expressed as Eq. (1):

$$E_{total} = \sum_{i=1}^{k} E_{cluster}(i) \tag{1}$$

where $E_{cluster}(i)$ is the energy spent in cluster i.

The energy usage of each cluster contains cluster head's and its cluster members' consumption. The total energy dissipation of a cluster head is:

$$E_{CH}(i) = E_{CH}^{r}(i) + E_{CH}^{f}(i) + E_{CH}^{t}(i) \tag{2}$$

where $E_{CH}^{r}(i)$ is the energy consumption of cluster node i for receiving data, $E_{CH}^{f}(i)$ is the energy consumption of cluster node i for data fusion, $E_{CH}^{t}(i)$ is the energy consumption of cluster node i for transmitting data. $E_{CH}^r(i)$, $E_{CH}^f(i)$, $E_{CH}^t(i)$ are calculated as follows:

$$
\begin{cases}
E_{CH}^r(i) = \left(\frac{n}{k} - 1\right) \times DPL \cdot E_{elec} + (relay(i) - 1) \times DPL \cdot E_{elec} \\
E_{CH}^f(i) = \frac{n}{k} \times DPL \cdot E_{DF} \\
E_{CH}^t(i) = relay(i) \times DPL \cdot E_{elec} + relay(i) \times DPL \cdot \varepsilon_{fs}(2r)^2
\end{cases}
\tag{3}
$$

where DPL is the packet length, $relay(i)$ is the number of packets forwarded by the cluster head i, $r = M/\sqrt{\pi k}$ means cluster coverage radius.

The energy dissipation of a cluster member node in a cluster is:

$$
E_{CMs}(i) = \left(\frac{n}{k} - 1\right) \times DPL \cdot E_{elec} + \left(\frac{n}{k} - 1\right) DPL \cdot \varepsilon_{fs}\, d_{toCH}^2
\tag{4}
$$

where $d_{toCH} = \sqrt{M^2/2\pi k}$ means expectation distance from cluster member node i to its corresponding cluster head.

Therefore, we rewrite Eq. (1) as:

$$
\begin{aligned}
E_{total} &= DPL\left[(2n - 3k)\,E_{elec} + n\,E_{DF} + (n - k)\,\varepsilon_{fs}\,d_{toCH}^2\right] \\
&\quad + DPL\sum_{i=1}^{k} relay(i) \cdot (2\,E_{elec} + \varepsilon_{fs}(2r)^2)
\end{aligned}
\tag{5}
$$

where, $\sum_{i=1}^{k} relay(i) = \left\lceil\sqrt{\frac{\pi k}{2}}\right\rceil (k/\lceil\pi k/2\rceil - 1)/2 \times k/\lceil\pi k/2\rceil$ means the total transfer amount of data. Eventually the optimal cluster number k in the network topology that makes the network total energy consumption obtain the minimum value can be Eq. (5).

3.1.2   Energy-Balancing Partition

Once figuring out the value of k, cluster head competition radius is also determined, and then we can be able to calculate the number of layers:

$$
L = \lceil M/(2r)\rceil
\tag{6}
$$

In the proposed algorithm, we hope to balance the energy consumption between layers. As layers closest to the base station spend more energy forwarding date delivered from lower layer, so non-uniform hierarchy is applied and partition area is small when closing to the BS. Denote layer nearest the sink as 1st level and then 2nd level, $\cdots$, Lth level. Formula derivation of partition size as followed.

The total energy dissipation of each level $i \in (1, L - 1)$ is:

$$
E_{level}(i) = E_{inter}(i) + E_{rece}(i) + E_{trans}(i)
\tag{7}
$$

where, $E_{inter}(i)$ represents the energy consumption in the ith level, which includes there parts of the energy consumption: energy consumption of the cluster members sending the collected data to the corresponding cluster heads, energy consumption of the cluster headers receiving the packets sent by the cluster members and energy consumption of the cluster headers performing data fusion operations. $E_{rece}(i)$ is the energy cost of receiving data from the $(i+1)$th level and $E_{trans}(i)$ is the transmission energy consumption from ith level to $(i-1)$th level. $E_{inter}(i)$, $E_{rece}(i)$ and $E_{trans}(i)$ are calculated as follows:

$$\begin{cases} E_{inter}(i) = \frac{nl_i}{M} \times \left(2DPL \cdot E_{elec} + DPL \cdot \varepsilon_{fs} \, d_{toCH}^2 + DPL \cdot E_{DF}\right) \\ E_{rece}(i) \approx \frac{k}{L} \times DPL \cdot E_{elec} \\ E_{trans}(i) \approx \frac{k}{L} \times DPL \cdot E_{elec} + \frac{k}{L} \times DPL \cdot \varepsilon_{fs}(2r)^2 \end{cases} \tag{8}$$

where l_i is partition height of layer i.

Because we hope the energy consumption of CHs in each level is similar, Eq. (9) is applied to calculate cluster radius in each level:

$$E_{level}(i) = E_{level}(i+1) \tag{9}$$

Based on Eqs. (7) and (8), Eq. (9) transforms into follows:

$$\begin{aligned} l_{i+1} - l_i \approx & \left[\frac{2k}{L} \times DPL \cdot E_{elec} + \frac{k}{L} \times DPL \cdot \varepsilon_{fs}(2r)^2\right] / \\ & \left[\frac{n}{M} \times \left(2DPL \cdot E_{elec} + DPL \cdot \varepsilon_{fs} \, d_{toCH}^2 + DPL \cdot E_{DF}\right)\right] \end{aligned} \tag{10}$$

Denote the right side of the formula by d. According to the arithmetic series summation formula, partition sizes can be calculated as Eq. (11).

$$\begin{cases} l_1 + l_2 + \ldots + l_L = M \\ l_{i+1} - l_i = d \end{cases} \tag{11}$$

3.2   Establishment Phase

3.2.1   Cluster Head Election Within Partition

In cluster-head election phase, we elect cluster heads in every layers. Each node broadcasts the HELLO message with its node $ID(i)$, node remaining energy $S(i).re$ and competition radius $S(i).rc$, which equals to the length of the region at which the node is located. Then neighbor node sets are constructed based on the received broadcast message. The neighbor nodes of the node i are set as: $S(i).N = \{S(j)|d(S(i), S(j)) < S(i).rc\}$, $d(S(i), S(j))$ is the distance between node i and node j. Aiming at network lifetime maximization, probability of the nodes with relatively higher residual energy selected as cluster head should be increased and that of nodes on the edge of the monitoring area should be reduced. Thence the probability of an ordinary node elected to be cluster head can be recorded as Eq. (12):

$$S(i).CFun = \alpha \frac{S(i).re}{E_0} + (1-\alpha)\frac{S(i).nn}{n} \tag{12}$$

where E_0 is initial energy of sensor nodes, $S(i).nn$ is the number of neighbor nodes of node i, α is a parameter factor which is given in the experimental part.

Node with greater elected probability than its entire adjacent nodes is finally selected as the cluster head node and its node status should be changed to "Cluster Head". Afterwards, the selected node broadcasts HEAD_MSG message to notify its neighboring nodes. Neighbor node receiving the message withdraws from the election and changes the status to "Member". This process continues until there is no "unknown" node in the layer.

3.2.2   Routing Selection

After selecting the cluster head, it is time to build the communication path to the base station for each cluster head. To reduce energy consumption of data transmission between clusters and avoid hot spots problem, cluster head determines feasible next hop according to the remaining energy of neighbor cluster-head node, the distance between cluster-head node and neighbor cluster-head node, and the distance between neighbor cluster-head node and base station. Specific rules are as follows:

(1) First of all, construct candidate routing node set of cluster-head i which is recorded as $S(i).R$.

$$S(i).R = \{j|j\ is\ a\ CH\&\&S(j).level = S(i).level - 1\&\&d(S(i),S(j)) < d_0\}$$

The selection function of the routing node is shown as Eq. (13).

$$S(j).RFun = \beta\frac{S(j).re}{E_0} + (1-\beta)\frac{d_{i\_BS}}{d_{i\_j}+d_{j\_BS}} \tag{13}$$

Where, d_{i_BS} is the distance from CH node i and BS, d_{i_j} is the distance from CH node i and CH node j, d_{j_BS} is the distance from CH node j and BS. β is a parameter factor which is given in the experimental part. CH node i chooses node with maximum RFun value as the next-hop node from $S(i).R$.

(2) If $S(i).R$ is empty collection and set $A = \{j|j\ is\ a\ CH\&\&S(j).level = S(i).level - 1\}$ is not null, then the cluster head closest to node i in set A is selected as the routing node.

(3) In PUCMR, cross-level data transmission to BS is allowed. When each sensor node in the $(S(i).level - 1)$st level can no longer serve as a CH, CHs in the $(S(i).level)$st level transmit data to BS directly.

3.2.3   Cluster Formation

In the clustering phase, each ordinary node starts with finding the nearest cluster head and participating in the cluster. Considering cluster heads not only collect data from their member nodes but also act as relying nodes for cluster heads at lower-layers, adaptive adjustment is required in the formed cluster.

The energy consumption of cluster head to accept and merge data sent by a cluster member is denoted as $E_{intra\_cluster}$, which can be calculated by using the following formula:

$$E_{intra\_cluster} = DPL \times E_{elec} + DPL \times E_{DF} \tag{14}$$

The approximate energy consumption of the cluster head to relay a data packet is recorded as $E_{inter\_cluster}$, and Eq. (15) calculate the about value.

$$E_{inter\_cluster} = 2DPL \times E_{elec} + DPL \cdot \varepsilon_{fs} \left[\left(\frac{l_L + l_{L-1}}{2} + \cdots + \frac{l_2 + l_1}{2} \right) / (L - 1) \right]^2 \quad (15)$$

Thus, overhead of cluster head forwarding a packet is equal to its cost on $E_{inter\_cluster} / E_{intra\_cluster}$ cluster members. With the node number = 1000, M = 400 scene as an example, $E_{inter\_cluster} / E_{intra\_cluster} \approx 3$.

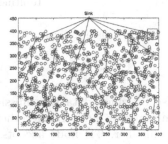

Fig. 1. Routing path (Color figure online)

Figure 1 depicts the routing path obtained according to the above steps. The two nodes, which are marked with red boxes, are both the first layer cluster heads. Data forwarding load on the left node is heavy, however, the right node does not need to collaborate with the adjacent nodes to transmit sensors data to the BS. This is bound to lead to uneven cluster-head energy consumption. In this paper, the settlement of the issue is further clustering in the cluster. Concrete implementation method can be summarized into three steps. At first, determine the cluster number (CN). The formula for calculation is shown as the following:

$$CN = round\left((CH\,(i)\,.members + CH\,(i)\,.RPN * 3) / (n/k) \right) \quad (16)$$

where $CH\,(i)\,.members$ is the number of members belonging to CH i, $CH\,(i)\,.RPN$ is the number of packets forwarded by the CH i. Secondly, if $CN > 1$, we should select another $CN - 1$ cluster heads in the original cluster. The rule that new cluster-head chosen here is merely upon residual energy. The $CN - 1$ nodes with the highest residual energy are elected as cluster head and then each non-cluster-head node decides the cluster to join based on the received signal strength of the advertisement. The last step, adjust routing strategy is adopted. As seen in Fig. 2(a), cluster-head C transmits X packages to A, cluster-head D transmits Y packages to A. We assume cluster-head A demands an extra cluster head to distribute its load, and the newly elected cluster head node denoted as B. Then after adjusting path, the final routing path is as shown in Fig. 2(b), cluster-head C delivers $\lceil X/2 \rceil$ packets to A and $\lfloor X/2 \rfloor$ packets to B, meanwhile, cluster-head D delivers $\lceil Y/2 \rceil$ packets to A and $\lfloor Y/2 \rfloor$ packets to B.

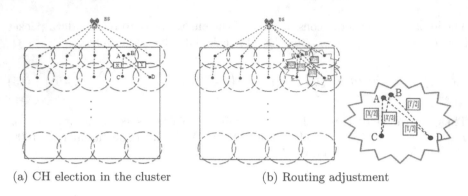

(a) CH election in the cluster   (b) Routing adjustment

Fig. 2. Cluster adjustment

3.3 Stable Phase

Stabilization phase can also be called data transmission phase. In this phase, cluster members gather information and transfer them to the corresponding cluster head by single-hop manner. CH node accepts the data sent from the cluster member and merges data into a fixed length data packet. Finally, the CH node transmits the fused data packet together with data packets receiving from the lower layer to the base station along the routing path that is made by the protocol.

Define the threshold of CH power as T (15% of initial energy). When the remaining power of a CH is under T, construction phase is needed, otherwise, another round of data transmission is conducted directly.

4   Experiment and Analysis

In the research, we conduct performance analysis and evaluation of PUCMR with three state of the art protocols. The simulation experiment is implemented on MATLAB platform. Firstly, we describe the simulation settings. Then, we focus on verifying the energy efficiency and stability of our proposed protocol.

4.1   Simulation Settings

To make a fair comparison of the energy efficiency of each protocol, LEACH and MR-LEACH apply data fusion method like PUCMR in the process of simulation experiment. The general parameters of the protocols used in the experiment are shown in Table 1. The energy consumption model related parameters are taken from the literature [2].

The other parameters are acquired by running the experiment many times to find out the optimal value. Finally, parameter α in cluster-head probability formula is set to 0.9 and parameter β in routing selection function is 0.5. In specific environment where 1000 nodes are uniformly distributed in the monitoring area of 400 * 400, the optimum number of cluster heads k is 32.

Table 1. Parameter list

Parameters	Values
Network size $(xm * ym)$	$400 * 400 \, \mathrm{m}^2$
Base station location $(sink.x, sink.y)$	$(200, 450) \, \mathrm{m}$
Number of sensor nodes (n)	1000 nodes
Initial energy of each sensor node (E_0)	0.5 J
Data packet length (DPL)	4000 bytes
E_{elec}	50 nJ/bit
ε_{fs}	$10 \, \mathrm{pJ}/(\mathrm{bit} \cdot \mathrm{m}^2)$
ε_{mp}	$0.0013 \, \mathrm{pJ}/(\mathrm{bit} \cdot \mathrm{m}^2)$
E_{DF}	5 nJ/bit

4.2   Cluster Head Analysis

The number of cluster heads is an important index to evaluate the protocol. If the number is too small, some nodes in the network have to transmit their data very far to reach the cluster-head, causing the global energy in the system to be large. While the number is too large causes less data compression, and increases the number of data packages need to be transferred. The number of cluster heads can also react to the stability of the algorithm. Under the condition of the fixed network topology, a stable clustering protocol should generate compared consistent number of cluster heads. From each clustering protocol simulation

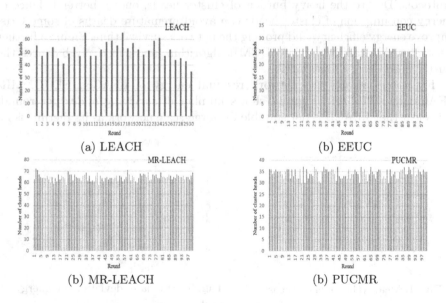

(a) LEACH   (b) EEUC

(b) MR-LEACH   (b) PUCMR

Fig. 3. Cluster adjustment

experiment, randomly select 100 rounds (For LEACH, we select 30 rounds, as its lifetime is only 62 rounds), the distributions of the number of cluster heads are shown in Fig. 3.

Seen from Fig. 3, the number of cluster heads changes very large every round in LEACH. The reason must be the cluster head selection is random in LEACH. EEUC, MR-LEACH and PUCMR consider the coverage of cluster heads, effectively control the number of cluster heads, therefore, the number of cluster head is very concentrated. However, the number of cluster heads of EEUC compared to the optimal cluster head slightly smaller, while the number of MR-LEACH cluster heads is too much. Overall, the number of cluster head generated by PUCMR is optimal and stable. Thus, PUCMR protocol is proved of high reliability.

4.3   Energy Efficiency

Since cluster-heads are the critical nodes in the network, we should minimize their energy use as far as possible, avoiding exhausting their power so quickly. Hence, the average energy consumption of cluster heads in one round is compared firstly. Ten rounds randomly selected from the experiment, the average energy consumption of the cluster heads in each protocol is recorded. Observing Fig. 4, we find the consumption of cluster heads in MR-LEACH, and that in PUCMR are fairly few, and the two are quite consistent. This is because both protocols use a very efficient routing strategy. However, operating efficiency of MR-LEACH is quite low.

Next, we study on energy consumption balancing of cluster heads of the four protocols. Due to the heavy burden of cluster heads, only a better balance of energy consumption of cluster heads can avoid premature deaths of some CHs, improve energy efficiency, and prolong the network survival time. Figure 5 further illustrates the stability of the PUCMR algorithm, and effectively balances the cluster head energy consumption.

Figure 6 compares the network residual energy of LEACH, EEUC, MR-LEACH and PUCMR. Figure 7 shows number of surviving nodes per round. It is clear that LEACH is not suitable for large-scale network as its lifetime is no

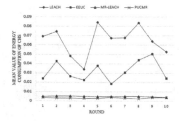

Fig. 4. Mean value of energy cost

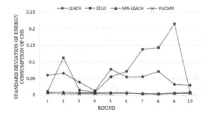

Fig. 5. Standard deviation of energy cost

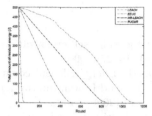
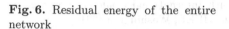
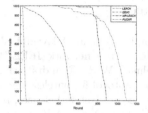

Fig. 6. Residual energy of the entire network

Fig. 7. Surviving nodes in the network

more than 100 rounds. Compared with LEACH, the network using EEUC algorithm is not so fast failure, but the result is still not satisfactory. Compared with MR-LEACH, at the very beginning, MR-LEACH outperforms our method. This may be because MR-LEACH algorithm chooses a large number of cluster heads, sharing the transmission task, so that the cluster head will not die directly at first, but the total energy expenditure in a round is still larger than PUCMR. Whats more, MR-LEACH is evenly layered, node near base station is easy to die and results "energy hole". As a result, PUCMR extends the overall lifetime by approximately 200 rounds as compared to MR-LEACH.

5   Summary and Outlook

Aiming at the characteristics of large-scale wireless sensor networks, this paper analyzes the existing problems and deficiencies of the current classical routing protocols. On the basis of the research on these protocols, we propose a pre partition based uneven clustering multi-hop routing protocol (PUCMR). Kernel idea of our algorithm is to resolve hot spot problem by organizing the network into clusters of non-uniform size using an energy-saving uneven clustering method. Also, efforts are made in the derivation process of the hierarchical size relation, which reducing the calculation of the cluster size. Our simulations show that, under the same conditions, PUCMR outperforms LEACH, EEUC, MR-LEACH in terms of energy dissipation, and system lifetime of the network.

Wireless sensor network as a hot research topic today, is also the focus of the development of science and technology in the future. The proposed algorithm is just a little improvement in energy consumption, without considering QoS, security and other factors in the practical application of wireless sensor networks. We will devote energies to approach the solutions to these problems.

Acknowledgments. This work is supported by China Aviation Science Foundation (Grant No. 20101952021), Fundamental Research Funds for Central Universities (Grant No. NZ2013306) and Key Project supported by Medical Science and Technology Development Foundation, Nanjing Department of Health (Grant No. YKK15170).

References

1. Sohrabi, K., Gao, J., Ailawadhi, V., Pottie, G.J.: Protocols for self-organization of a wireless sensor network. IEEE Pers. Commun. **7**(5), 16–27 (2000)
2. Heinzelman, W.R., Chandrakasan, A., Balakrishnan, H.: Energy-efficient communication protocol for wireless microsensor networks. In: 32nd Hawaii International Conference on System Sciences, pp. 1–10. IEEE, Hawaii (2000)
3. Farooq, M.O., Dogar, A.B., Shah, G.A.: MR-LEACH: multi-hop routing with low energy adaptive clustering hierarchy. In: 4th International Conference on Sensor Technologies and Applications, pp. 262–268. IEEE, Washington (2010)
4. Gu, B., Sheng, V.S.: A robust regularization path algorithm for v-support vector classification. IEEE Trans. Neural Netw. Learn. Syst. **28**(5), 1241–1248 (2017)
5. Xia, Z., Wang, X., Zhang, L., et al.: A privacy-preserving and copy-deterrence content-based image retrieval scheme in cloud computing. IEEE Trans. Inf. Forensic Secur. **11**(11), 2594–2608 (2016)
6. Fu, Z., Ren, K., Shu, J., et al.: Enabling personalized search over encrypted outsourced data with efficiency improvement. IEEE Trans. Parall. Distr. **27**(9), 2546–2559 (2016)
7. Li, C., Chen, G., Ye, M., et al.: An uneven cluster-based routing protocol for wireless sensor networks. Chin. J. Comput. **30**(1), 27–36 (2007)
8. Jiang, C., Shi, W., Tang, X., et al.: Energy-balanced unequal clustering routing protocol for wireless sensor networks. J. Softw. **23**(5), 1222–1232 (2012)
9. Lai, W., Fan, C., Lin, L.: Arranging cluster sizes and transmission ranges for wireless sensor networks. Inf. Sci. **183**(1), 117–131 (2012)
10. You, Z., Cao, X., Wang, Y.: An unequal clustering strategy for WSNs based urban intelligent transportation system. J. Inf. Comput. Sci. **12**(10), 4001–4012 (2015)
11. Xia, H., Zhang, R., Yu, J., et al.: Energy-efficient routing algorithm based on unequal clustering and connected graph in wireless sensor networks. Int. J. Wireless Inf. Netw. **23**(2), 141–150 (2016)
12. Sabor, N., Abo-Zahhad, M., Sasaki, S., et al.: An unequal multi-hop balanced immune clustering protocol for wireless sensor networks. Appl. Soft Comput. **43**, 372–389 (2016)
13. Chen, Y., Hao, C., Wu, W., et al.: Robust dense reconstruction by range merging based on confidence estimation. Sci. China Inf. Sci. **59**(9), 092103 (2016)
14. Pan, Z., Lei, J., Zhang, Y., et al.: Fast motion estimation based on content property for low-complexity H. 265/HEVC encoder. IEEE Trans. Broadcast. **62**(3), 675–684 (2016)
15. Ma, T., Zhou, J., Tang, M., et al.: Social network and tag sources based augmenting collaborative recommender system. IEICE Trans. Inf. Syst. **98**(4), 902–910 (2015)

A Credibility Evaluation Method in Opportunistic Networks

Jinxia Dou[1,2], Wenbin Yao[1,2(✉)], and Dongbin Wang[3]

[1] Beijing Key Laboratory of Intelligent Telecommunications Software and Multimedia,
Beijing University of Posts and Telecommunications, Beijing 100876, China
doujinxia450460@163.com, yaowenbin_cdc@163.com

[2] National Engineering Laboratory for Mobile Network Security, Beijing University of Posts and
Telecommunications, Beijing 100876, China

[3] Key Laboratory of Ministry of Education for Trustworthy Distributed Computing and Service,
Beijing University of Posts and Telecommunications, Beijing 100876, China

Abstract. There are lots of misbehaving nodes in opportunistic networks which
can cause severe performance downgrade. Those misbehaving nodes contains
malicious nodes and selfish nodes. Selfish nodes don't cooperate in routing and
forwarding. Malicious nodes drop data packets or forward lots of garbage packets
hindering the normal process of data forwarding. In order to improve network
performance, a credibility evaluation method is proposed in this paper, named
FICT. According to the FICT, familiar degree, intimate degree and contribution
degree are defined to describe the social attributes of nodes. We use the number
of contacts, connect time and PLR to calculate the value of the credibility of nodes.
Just when the value of credibility is greater than or equal to the threshold, the
node is selected to forward data packets. We performed simulation experiments
with FICT method on the ONE. The simulation results show that by using the
FICT method, the success rate of message delivery increases and the average
latency of message delivery reduces. Especially when the number of misbehaving
nodes becomes large, the FICT method can improve the performance of the
networks significantly.

Keywords: Opportunistic networks · Social trust · Credibility evaluation

1 Introduction

The concept of opportunistic networks [1] (OppNets) comes from delay tolerant
networks (DTN) and Mobile Ad-hoc Networks (MANETs). Compared to the traditional
DTNs, the information and messages can be transmitted by encounter opportunities
between different nodes. Moreover, in opportunistic networks no end-to-end path exist
between the source node and the destination node which is an implicit assumption in
the MANETs [2]. All nodes forward messages with the "store-carry-and-forward"
mode, which is an opportunistic behavior.

© Springer International Publishing AG 2017
X. Sun et al. (Eds.): ICCCS 2017, Part I, LNCS 10602, pp. 385–397, 2017.
https://doi.org/10.1007/978-3-319-68505-2_33

Most researches in opportunistic networks depend on the hypothesis that each individual node always wants to help with relaying messages for other nodes [3]. However, the fact is that owing to the lack of energy, storage and computing resources lots of nodes present to be selfish [4] or malicious [5]. Selfish nodes make use of the network but do not cooperate with other nodes. Selfish nodes save battery life for their own communications, and do not intend to directly damage other nodes. On other hand, malicious nodes aim at damaging other nodes by causing network outrage by partitioning while saving battery life is not a priority. Malicious nodes may deliberately exaggerate the probability of encountering the destination node to intercept the data packets that should be sent to normal nodes, forming "the black hole attack" [6]. In addition, malicious nodes could pretend to be certain nodes so as to execute identity fraud [7], and it could produce lots of irrelevant data packets during the forwarding process wasting bandwidth resources and reducing the success rate of message delivery at the same time. The existing studies have shown that those misbehaving nodes may make network severe performance downgrade and cause it disastrous damage, even put the entire networks in danger. Consequently, it is necessary to propose evaluation methods of trust to avoid the bad influence of misbehaving nodes.

Up to now, lots of evaluation methods of trust have been put forward for opportunistic networks. Generally, the evaluation methods can be classified into four types: the first type is based on feedback information, liking incentive mechanism of rewards and punishments; the second type is based on peer to peer evaluation; the third type is based on the history of interactions; type 4 is based on topology and hop counts. Nevertheless, the feedback information cost too much time to transfer, and the update frequency of the credibility is very low. The complexity of these methods is high. For these reasons, there is an increasing need in designing succinct evaluation methods for opportunistic networks with considerable challenges.

In this paper, we present a credibility evaluation method named FICT, which is designed to avoid the bad influence of misbehaving nodes. In this method, familiar degree, intimate degree and contribution degree of social trust is used to quantify the value of credibility. Nodes forward data packets only when the value of credibility is greater or equal to the defined threshold. By this way, we can ensure nodes involved in forwarding process are not misbehaving nodes.

The remainder of this paper is organized as follows: in Sect. 2, an overview is given of related work which has been put to evaluate the credibility of nodes. Section 3 illustrates the evaluation method FICT. In Sect. 4, we performed simulations to test the method and analyze the results. The conclusion of this paper is presented in Sect. 5.

2 Related Works

In recent years, lots of evaluation methods of trust have been put forward for opportunistic networks. Conti [8] proposed that social relationships can be formed by different social attributes in opportunistic networks, and the trust degree of nodes can be reflected by relationships. Sacha [9] proposed an approach to build a trust model based on social trust, which describes the trust degree of nodes from two aspects. The first part of the trust is measured by the network topology and hop distance, the second part of the trust is evaluated by the historical interaction records between nodes. The final trust value of the node is obtained by combining these two parts above.

In [10], a trust model is established from the point of view of node cooperation to ensure that the data in the network can be transmitted from the source node to the destination node safely and efficiently. Firstly, popular nodes are selected by the degree of cooperation. Secondly, using common interests, common friends, common distance among the relay nodes to measure nodes' trust, and chose the most-trusted path evaluated by the relay nodes between the source node and the destination node. The proposed trust model can help the data to be transmitted safely, but it can cause long time delay in a large scale opportunistic networks.

In [11], a trusted data forwarding algorithm in opportunistic networks was proposed, this algorithm introduced friends into the social networks, and evaluated the credibility by the number of common friends, the more common friends they have the higher credibility they own. Combining the prediction and forwarding mode of opportunistic network and the node popularity algorithm, this algorithm improved the efficiency and reliability of data forwarding. However, it takes a long time to establish the relationship between nodes during the process of application.

Selfish nodes are identified by the social relations among the nodes in [12], and the corresponding incentive mechanism is used to encourage selfish nodes to participate in the data forwarding processes. The credibility of intermediate nodes comes from the feedback information of the source node and the destination node. The system can effectively solve the problem that selfish nodes refuse to transmit data. However, the destination node takes a long time to send back its feedback information which can slow update speed and poor accuracy of the network.

Based on the predicted forwarding, Guptain [13] used trust mechanisms and node cooperation methods to resisted the black hole attack. The routing protocol evaluates the credibility of nodes by the similarity and the hop count with the source node. On the basis of the proposed trust evaluation algorithm, the trust degree of nodes on the forwarding path decreases with the increase of hop distance, so as to prevent black hole nodes from posing as the high trust node to obtain the forwarding data. However, this method cannot completely avoid the black hole attack. Some black hole nodes can still pretend to be trust nodes to get the forwarding data.

In [14], a data forwarding algorithm based on reputation management is proposed in the opportunistic network with malicious nodes and selfish nodes. When the data packet arrived at the destination node, the destination node will send back an ACK packet through the routing path to acknowledge the source node, meanwhile the source node updates the credibility of nodes which took part in the data forwarding process. For the malicious nodes and selfish nodes, its reputation value will only be maintained at a low level because that they do not help with the data forwarding process. The normal nodes in the subsequent data forwarding process will gradually refuse to send data to these nodes. However, it takes a long time to identify malicious nodes and selfish nodes, and the delay time that the source node receives ACK packets can be too long.

3   The Credibility Evaluation Method

In the process of interpersonal social interactions, when members want to interact with another unfamiliar member, the first and foremost thing is to judge whether he/she is trustworthy. In social networks, social trust is the phenomenon that members in social group trust each other and receive recognition from others and communicate sincerely with each other [15]. Due to the influence of human social behaviors, nodes in opportunistic networks have certain social attributes the same as people in real society. Therefore, social trust in social networks can be introduced into the opportunistic networks. Nodes in opportunistic networks can establish trust relationship to avoid the bad influence of misbehaving nodes.

Based on those theories above, we proposed a credibility evaluation method called FICT. In the FICT, familiar degree, intimate degree and contribution degree are used as social attributes of nodes to build trust relationships in opportunistic networks.

3.1   Familiar Degree

In real society, if two people can meet each other very often, we rank that they are familiar with each other and they have built trust relationships in a certain sense. Nodes in opportunistic networks work in a self-organizing manner, and different nodes have different trajectories and behaviors in the moving process. Thus, we can use contact times between nodes to calculate the familiar degree, and choose the familiar nodes to forward data packets. The definition of familiar degree is as follows:

$$\text{famiDegree}_{i,j} = \frac{\text{ConTimes}_{i,j}}{\sum_{k=0}^{n} \text{ConTimes}_{i,k}} \tag{1}$$

In this formulation, $famiDegree_{i,j}$ represents the familiar degree between node i and node j, and $famiDegree_{i,j} \in [0, 1]$. $ConTimes_{i,j}$ is the contact times between node i and node j in their historical interactions, $\sum_{k=0}^{n} ConTimes_{i,k}$ represents the summation of contact times between node i and all nodes around i within its communication range.

3.2   Intimate Degree

Social psychology holds that social trust is established through communications among social members [9]. The more time they used to communicate, the more intimate their relationships are. Similarity in opportunistic networks, if two nodes are in contact with each other for a long time, we rank that the trust relationships have been built between them. For opportunistic networks, malicious nodes may improve their familiar degree by contacting with other nodes frequently. Therefore, we define intimate degree as the formulation shows:

$$intiDegree_{i,j} = \frac{ConnectTime_{i,j}}{\sum_{k=0}^{n} ConnectTime_{i,k}} \tag{2}$$

In this formulation, $intiDegree_{i,j}$ represents the intimate degree between node i and node j, and $intiDegree_{i,j} \in [0, 1]$. $ConnectTime_{i,j}$ is the connect time between node i and node j in their historical interactions, $\sum_{k=0}^{n} ConnectTime_{i,k}$ represents the summation of connect time between node i and all nodes around i within its communication range.

3.3 Contribution Degree

In real society, we can infer one's credibility by his or her contributions during the process of cooperation intuitively. High contribution degree in the social cooperation environment indicates high reliability. In opportunistic networks nodes forward data packets to transfer messages only by cooperating with other nodes. Normal nodes take part in cooperation forwarding processes while those misbehaving nodes make less contribution or even do harm to these processes. Thus, in the process of data forwarding, nodes with greater contribution can be more trustful than those nodes which made less contribution.

In opportunistic networks, the number of data packets forwarded by one node has a positive correlation with its contribution degree. We can use the packet loss rate (PLR) to calculate the contribution degree.

$$PLR'_{i,j} = \frac{N_{received} - N_{sent}}{N_{received}} \tag{3}$$

In this formulation, $N_{received}$ represents the number of data packets node j received in the historical interactions. N_{sent} represents the number of data packets node j sent in the historical interactions. We can analyze $PLR'_{i,j}$ in four cases:

i. $PLR'_{i,j} < 0$. The number of data packets node j received is smaller than the number node j sent to next hop. We can infer that node j added irrelevant data packets during the data forwarding process. Under this circumstance, the $contriDegree_{i,j}$ is inversely proportional to $PLR'_{i,j}$;
ii. $PLR'_{i,j} = 0$. Under this circumstance, all data packets were forwarding successfully to the next hop. we use a constant number C to represent it, and $C \in (0, 1]$;
iii. $0 < PLR'_{i,j} < 1$. Node j lost some data packets during forwarding process, so the $contriDegree_{i,j}$ is inversely proportional to $PLR'_{i,j}$;
iv. $PLR'_{i,j} = 1$. Under this circumstance, $N_{sent} = 0$ and all data packets that node j received has been dropped or deleted, so the $contriDegree_{i,j} = 0$;

To summarize, we can use a piecewise function to describe the relationship between contribution degree and the $PLR'_{i,j}$:

$$\text{contriDegree}_{i,j} = \begin{cases} \dfrac{1}{\left|\text{PLR}'_{i,j}\right|}, & \text{PLR}'_{i,j} < 0 \\ C, & \text{PLR}'_{i,j} = 0 \\ \dfrac{C}{\text{PLR}'_{i,j}}, & 0 < \text{PLR}'_{i,j} < 1 \\ 0, & \text{PLR}'_{i,j} = 1 \end{cases} \quad (C \text{ is a constant, } C \in (0,1]) \qquad (4)$$

In this formulation, $\text{contriDegree}_{i,j}$ represents the contribution degree of node j has for node i, and $\text{contriDegree}_{i,j} \in (0,1]$. $\text{contriDegree}_{i,j}$ is not necessarily equal to $\text{contriDegree}_{j,i}$. $\text{PLR}'_{i,j}$ represents the packet loss rate of node j for node i.

3.4 Calculation of Credibility

We describe the social trust structure of nodes from three aspects: familiar degree, intimate degree and contribution degree. Because social trust is a combination of different social attributes, so the calculation of social trust takes the form of weighted summation, as shown in the following formulation:

$$T_{i,j} = \alpha \, \text{contriDegree}_{i,j} + \beta \, \text{famiDegree}_{i,j} + \gamma \, \text{intiDegree}_{i,j} \qquad (5)$$

In this formulation, $T_{i,j}$ represents the credibility of node i relative to node j, α, β, γ represent the different weight of familiar degree, intimate degree and contribution degree. $\alpha \in (0,1]$, $\beta \in (0,1]$ and $\gamma \in (0,1]$, besides $\alpha + \beta + \gamma = 1$. The formulation of weight distribution is as follows:

$$\beta = \frac{\text{famiDegree}_{i,j}}{\text{famiDegree}_{i,j} + \text{intiDegree}_{i,j}}(1 - \alpha) \qquad (6)$$

$$\gamma = \frac{\text{intiDegree}_{i,j}}{\text{famiDegree}_{i,j} + \text{intiDegree}_{i,j}}(1 - \alpha) \qquad (7)$$

In order to reflect the subjectivity of trust evaluation processes, we firstly set the value of α to calculate the value of β, γ, because contribution degree plays an important role among these three attributes. If one node made a great contribution to the transfer of messages, its possibility to be a misbehaving node can be very low. By this way with the contribution degree we can distinguish normal nodes from misbehaving nodes gradually. Then the contact times and the connection time can tell the difference among nodes. Therefore, due to the different degree of emphasis on familiar degree and intimate degree, we use familiar degree and intimate degree to calculate β, γ.

4 Simulation and Analysis

4.1 Simulation Environment

To test the FICT method, we used the Opportunistic Networking Environment Simulator (The ONE) version 1.5.1 with Helsinki street scene as the simulation scene. Helsinki is the capital city of Finland. There are 200 nodes in the simulation area, all nodes use Bluetooth to communicate with each other, and the communication radius is 10 m, the data transfer rate is 200 Kbps. The specific parameters of experiments are as Table 1 shows:

Table 1. The specific parameters of experiments

The specific parameters	Values
Coverage area	4500 m * 3500 m
Total number of nodes	200
Number of misbehaving nodes	20, 40, 160
Moving type of nodes	SPMBM
Moving speed of nodes	1–3 m/s
Data transfer rate	200 Kbps
Communication approach of nodes	Bluetooth
Size of data packet	50 kb
Survival time of data packet	3600 s
Generation frequency of data packet	30 s
Memory capacity of nodes	30 M
Simulation time	360 min

4.2 Simulation Process

In this simulation process, we named the data forwarding type used FICT method as FICT-Epidemic. Nodes in opportunistic networks make a usage of the FICT to evaluate the credibility of the next hop before forward data packets. According to the value of credibility, nodes decide whether to deliver data packets to the next hop. In order to distinguish normal nodes from misbehaving nodes as soon as possible, we use θ as the initial trust value, and update the credibility according to the behaviors of nodes. The specific process is described in the following subsections:

i. We set the initial trust value for all nodes to θ;

ii. If node i needs to forward data packets to node j for the first time, according to the initial trust value, node i forwards data packets to node j directly;

iii. If it is not the first interaction between node i and node j, node i calculates the value $T_{i,j}$ according to the FICT method as the credibility of node j and update the value of credibility to $T_{i,j}$;

iv. If $T_{i,j} \geq \theta$, the node j is considered as a credible node and node i forwards data packets to node j, if $T_{i,j} < \theta$, the node j is considered as a misbehaving node and node i refuses to forward data packets to node j. θ is the threshold of credibility.

4.3 Simulation Results

In this paper, we measure the effectiveness of the credibility evaluation method proposed in this paper in two ways: success rate of message delivery and average latency of message delivery. These two evaluation parameters are the key indexes to validate the routing algorithm.

In our experiments, we performed simulations with Epidemic Routing, Binary Spray and Wait Routing and FICT-Epidemic. We have simulated data packets forwarding processes with different number of misbehaving nodes. In the first experiment, we set the number of normal nodes to 140, about 70% of the total nodes. The results are shown in Fig. 1.

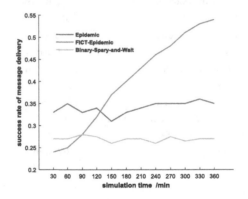

Fig. 1. Success rate of message delivery with 70% of normal nodes

In the second experiment, the number of normal nodes was set to 60, about 30% of the total nodes, and other conditions are the same as the first experiment. The statistics data forms the line graph the Fig. 2.

From the Fig. 1 we can see that at the beginning of the experiment the success rate of message delivery with FICT-Epidemic is lower than the Epidemic and Binary Spray and Wait. The reason of this phenomenon is that trust relationships between nodes has not yet been established at the beginning of the experiment. Some misbehaving nodes are temporarily misjudged as normal nodes. With the simulation processes carried on, the interaction times between nodes increased, the credibility of those misbehaving nodes become lower and lower. When the credibility of nodes is lower than the threshold, these nodes are isolated and not be allowed to participate in the forwarding processes. Later more and more malicious nodes and selfish nodes were isolated, meanwhile most nodes participating in the interaction process are trustworthy. Therefore, the success rate

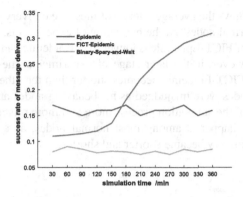

Fig. 2. Success rate of message delivery with 30% of normal nodes

of message delivery increased rapidly. However, with the establishment of trust relationships among nodes, the success rate of message delivery grows slowly after most misbehaving nodes being isolated.

Figures 1 and 2 show similar trends, but due to the increase of the proportion of those misbehaving nodes, the success rate of message delivery reduced. Compared with Epidemic and Binary Spray and Wait, FICT-Epidemic has higher success rate of message delivery when the number of misbehaving nodes increased.

The success rate of message delivery of different proportion of normal nodes is shown in Fig. 3. With the proportion of normal nodes reduced, the trend of FICT-Epidemic becomes slow down compared with Epidemic and Binary Spray and Wait. When the proportion of normal nodes is greater than 70%, the success rate of message delivery becomes greater than Epidemic and Binary Spray and Wait. This is because malicious nodes and selfish nodes dropped or deleted lots of data packets while forwarding, and trust relationships were established among nodes. Before the forwarding process, they chose trustworthy nodes to forward data packets.

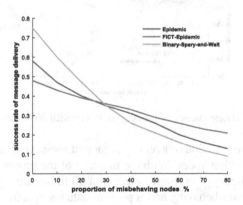

Fig. 3. Success rate of message delivery with different proportion of misbehaving nodes

Figures 4 and 5 shows the average latency of message delivery with 70% of normal nodes and 30% of normal nodes. At the beginning of experiments, the average latency of message delivery of FICT-Epidemic is longer than Epidemic and shorter than Binary Spray and Wait. However, in the later stage of experiments, the average latency of message delivery of FICT-Epidemic becomes shorter than the other two types. This is because that some nodes were misjudged as misbehaving nodes at the beginning, and with the continuous of the simulation process more and more misbehaving nodes were isolated. Interactions happened among most normal nodes, as a result, the average latency of message delivery became shorter and shorter.

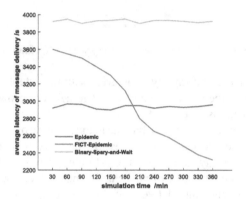

Fig. 4. Average latency of message delivery with 70% normal nodes

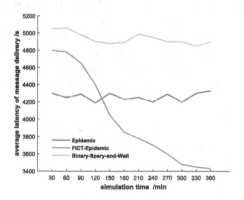

Fig. 5. Average latency of message delivery with 30% normal nodes

Figure 6 shows the variation of average latency of message delivery under different proportion of misbehaving nodes. With the increase of the proportion of misbehaving nodes, the average latency of message delivery of all these three types increased. This is because that lots of misbehaving nodes prevent data packets from reaching the destination node, the probability that data packets sent to the destination node reduces and the average latency of message delivery increases. However, the average latency of message delivery of FICT-Epidemic increased slower than Epidemic and Binary Spray and Wait. Even when the proportion of misbehaving nodes is more than 35%, the average latency of message delivery of FICT-Epidemic becomes lower than Epidemic and Binary Spray and Wait. The reason is that when the proportion of misbehaving nodes is more than 35%, trust relationships were established among nodes.

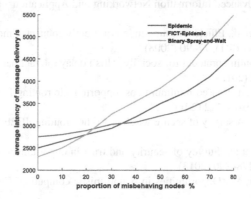

Fig. 6. Average latency of message delivery with different proportion of misbehaving nodes

5 Conclusions

This paper focuses on how to calculate the credibility of nodes in opportunistic networks, and proposes a new method based on social trust named FICT. The FICT evaluation method calculates the credibility of nodes according to familiar degree, intimate degree and contribution degree of nodes. It mainly solves these problems like misbehaving nodes refusing cooperation, dropping data packets or adding irrelevant data packets. The simulation experiments proved that the FICT method could increase the success rate of message delivery and reduce the average latency of message delivery. Especially, the higher the proportion of misbehaving nodes is, the more obvious the effect is. Therefore, the proposed method FICT could evaluate the credibility of nodes effectively.

Acknowledgements. This work was partly supported by the NSFC-Guangdong Joint Found (U1501254) and National key research and development program (2016YFB0800302) and the Co-construction Program with the Beijing Municipal Commission of Education and the Ministry of Science and Technology of China (2012BAH45B01) and the Director's Project Fund of Key Laboratory of Trustworthy Distributed Computing and Service (BUPT), Ministry of Education (Grant No. 2017ZR01) and the Fundamental Research Funds for the Central Universities (BUPT2011RCZJ16, 2014ZD03-03) and China Information Security Special Fund (NDRC).

References

1. Xiong, Y.P., Sun, L.M., et al.: Opportunistic networks. J. Softw. **20**(1), 124–137 (2009)
2. Huang, C.M., Lan, K.C., et al.: A survey of opportunistic networks. In: International Conference on Advanced Information Networking and Applications, pp. 1672–1677. IEEE (2008)
3. Spyropoulos, T., et al.: Efficient routing in intermittently connected mobile networks. IEEE/ACM Trans. Netw. **16**(1), 77–90 (2008)
4. Li, Q., et al.: A routing protocol for socially selfish delay tolerant networks. Ad Hoc Netw. **10**(1), 1619–1632 (2012)
5. Wang, B., et al.: Trust-based minimum cost opportunistic routing for Ad hoc networks. J. Syst. Softw. **84**, 2107–2122 (2011)
6. Hu, Y., Perrig, A.: A survey of secure wireless Ad hoc routing. IEEE Secur. Priv. **2**(3), 28–39 (2004)
7. Wu, Y., Li, J.H., et al.: Survey of security and trust in opportunistic networks. J. Comput. Res. Dev. **50**(2), 278–290 (2013)
8. Conti, M., Kumar, M.: Opportunities in opportunistic computing. Computer **43**(1), 42–50 (2010)
9. Trifunovic, S., Legendre, F., et al.: Social trust in opportunistic networks. In: INFOCOM IEEE Conference on Computer Communications Workshops, pp. 1–6. IEEE (2010)
10. Mtibaa, A., Harras, K.A.: Social-based trust in mobile opportunistic networks. In: Proceedings of IEEE Simna (2011)
11. Becker, C., Schlinga, S., et al.: Trustful data forwarding in social opportunistic networks. In: 2013 IEEE 10th International Conference on Ubiquitous Intelligence and Computing, and 10th International Conference on Autonomic and Trusted Computing (UIC/ATC), pp. 430–437. IEEE (2013)
12. Bigwood, G., Henderson, T.: IRONMAN: using social networks to add incentives and reputation to opportunistic networks. In: 2011 IEEE Third International Conference on Privacy, Security, Risk and Trust (PASSAT), and 2011 IEEE Third International Conference on Social Computing (Social Com), pp. 65–72. IEEE (2011)
13. Gupta, S., Dhurandher, S.K., et al.: Trust-based security protocol against black hole attacks in opportunistic networks. In: 2013 IEEE 9th International Conference on Wireless and Mobile Computing, Networking and Communications (WiMob), pp. 724–729. IEEE, Lyon (2013)
14. Premalatha, S., Mary Anita Rajam, V.: Reputation management for data forwarding in opportunistic networks. In: 2014 International Conference on Computer Communication and Informatics (ICCCI), pp. 1–7. IEEE, Coimbatore (2014)
15. Grabner-Kräuter, S., Bitter, S.: Trust in online social networks: a multifaceted perspective. Forum Soc. Econ. **44**, 48–68 (2013). doi:10.1080/07360932.2013.781517
16. Gu, B., Sheng, V.S.: A robust regularization path algorithm for v-support vector classification. IEEE Trans. Neural Netw. Learn. Syst. **28**, 1241–1248 (2017). doi:10.1109/TNNLS.2016.2527796
17. Xia, Z., Wang, X., Zhang, L., Qin, Z., Sun, X., Ren, K.: A privacy-preserving and copy-deterrence content-based image retrieval scheme in cloud computing. IEEE Trans. Inf. Forensics Secur. **11**, 2594–2608 (2016). doi:10.1109/TIFS.2016.2590944
18. Fu, Z., Ren, K., Shu, J., Sun, X., Huang, F.: Enabling personalized search over encrypted outsourced data with efficiency improvement. IEEE Trans. Parallel Distrib. Syst. **27**, 2546–2559 (2016). doi:10.1109/TPDS.2015.2506573

19. Gu, B., Sheng, V.S., Tay, K.Y., Romano, W., Li, S.: Incremental support vector learning for ordinal regression. IEEE Trans. Neural Netw. Learn. Syst. **26**, 1403–1416 (2015). doi: 10.1109/TNNLS.2014.2342533

20. Chen, Y., Hao, C., Wu, W., Wu, E.: Robust dense reconstruction by range merging based on confidence estimation. Sci. China Inf. Sci. **59** (2016). doi:10.1007/s11432-015-0957-4

21. Kong, Y., Zhang, M., Ye, D.: A belief propagation-based method for task allocation in open and dynamic cloud environments. Knowl. Based Syst. **115**, 123–132 (2017). doi:10.1016/j.knosys.2016.10.016

Unsupervised Energy Disaggregation of Home Appliances

Kondwani M. Kamoto[1], Qi Liu[2(✉)], and Xiaodong Liu[3]

[1] Jiangsu Collaborative Innovation Center of Atmospheric Environment and Equipment Technology (CICAEET), Nanjing University of Information Science and Technology, Nanjing, China
k_kamoto@yahoo.co.uk

[2] School of Computer and Software, Jiangsu Engineering Centre of Network Monitoring, Nanjing University of Information Science and Technology, Nanjing, China
qrank1@163.com

[3] School of Computing, Edinburgh Napier University, 10 Colinton Road Edinburgh EH10 5DT, UK
x.liu@napier.ac.uk

Abstract. Energy management is a growing concern especially with the increasing growth of smart appliances within the home. Energy disaggregation is an ongoing challenge to discover the appliance usage by examining the energy output of a household or building. Unsupervised NILM presents the additional challenge of energy disaggregation without any reliance on training data. A key issue to address in Unsupervised NILM is the discovery of appliances without a priori information. In this paper we present a new approach based on Competitive Agglomeration (CA) which incorporates the good qualities of both hierarchical and partitional clustering. Our proposed energy disaggregation algorithm makes use of CA in order to discover appliances without prior information about the number of appliances. Validation with experimental data from the Reference Energy Disaggregation Dataset (REDD), and comparison with recent state of the art Unsupervised NILM indicates that our proposed algorithm is effective.

Keywords: Home energy management · Unsupervised energy disaggregation · Unsupervised non-intrusive load monitoring

1 Introduction

The growth of devices has increased the energy consumption of households as shown in [1], and placed a greater stress on energy demand [2]. This situation can be partially attributed to the advent of the Internet of Things and the increasing number of smart devices in homes. Given this, there is greater importance on the efficiency of energy usage, especially within the home. To this end there has been ongoing work to enable people to be better informed about their household energy usage. Feedback has been shown to have a positive impact on the livelihood of a household as shown in [3, 4], and a study [5] has presented findings that indicate that people are showing greater concern towards their energy consumption and protecting the environment.

© Springer International Publishing AG 2017
X. Sun et al. (Eds.): ICCCS 2017, Part I, LNCS 10602, pp. 398–409, 2017.
https://doi.org/10.1007/978-3-319-68505-2_34

The first works on NILM were conducted by Hart in the 1980s and 1990s, and presented in [6]. In his work Hart defined the total load model as follows:

$$P(t) = \sum_{i=1}^{n} P_i + e(t) \tag{1}$$

where $P(t)$ is the total power load as seen at time t, and $e(t)$ is a small noise or error term. This model is used as the basis for the energy disaggregation problem.

NILM classifies appliances as either Type I ON/OFF, Type II Finite State Machines (FSMs), or Type III Continuously Variable Devices (CVDs). Uncovering the composition of a total load is done through the use of appliance signatures, with steady-state signatures being preferred since they don't require complex extraction methods. Work in NILM typically involves extracting the data from the source and transforming it into an appropriate format for analysis. Events or changes in energy usage are then detected and then clustered placing similar events together. The next steps are then to build models of the appliances and track the energy usage through the models, and lastly provide feedback through the appliance models and their corresponding usage. There has been a wide range of approaches to the Unsupervised NILM problem, but practical solutions that can be applied in real world situations are of greater value. We aim to introduce one such practical approach with the research work presented in this paper.

2   Related Works

One of the most recent works in Unsupervised NILM is [7] which builds on the emerging Graph Signal Processing (GSP) concepts to develop a novel, blind, unsupervised low-rate NALM approach. Based on the results from disaggregating aggregate loads measured from 4 real houses, they show that their training-less GSP-based NALM approach has comparable performance with the supervised GSP-based NALM approach. [8] presents a Bayesian approach to obtain the disaggregation of the loads where only active power measurements are available at a sampling rate of a few seconds. The proposed method requires the prior availability of appliance information which are obtained using unsupervised learning. The results indicated that the appliances are disaggregated with a greater accuracy when the appliance ratings are distinct and those appliances with closely placed ratings have a poorer results. Also the possibility of some load combination power matching another appliance also affects the disaggregation results. Henao et al. [9] use transformed active power transitions as features. The proposed approach is based on the Subtractive Clustering and the Maximum Likelihood Classifier. The validation results with six commonly found ON/OFF residential appliances indicate that the proposed approach is effective. In addition, the obtained results from a Monte Carlo simulation suggest that this approach is less sensitive to power grid noise than a K-mean-based NIALM method. An unsupervised load disaggregation approach is proposed in [10] that works without a priori knowledge about appliances. The proposed algorithm works autonomously in real time. The number of used appliances and the corresponding appliance models are learned in operation and are progressively updated. The proposed algorithm considers each useful and suitable detected power state, and tries to detect power states corresponding to ON/OFF appliances as well as to multi-state appliances based on active power measurements in 1 s resolution. In [11] Jia et all present a fully unsupervised NILM framework based on Nonparametric Factorial Hidden Markov Models. They also propose a criterion, Generalized State Prediction Accuracy, to properly evaluate the overall performance for methods targeting at both appliance number detection and load disaggregation. Using low frequency power measurements from real world, they have showed that their framework outperforms the other Factorial Hidden Markov Model (FHMM) approaches, and is very computationally efficient. The aforementioned works show that the active power signature can be effectively used for unsupervised energy disaggregation.

Various approaches have also been used to address the challenge of discovering the number of appliances present in the load. [12] focuses on Stochastic Modeling and energy disaggregation based on Conditional Random Fields (CRFs) using real-world energy consumption data. The proposed disaggregation method uses a clustering method and histogram analysis to detect the ON/OFF states of selected types of energy-using devices in the home. Long spans of data from 21 households were used in a binary classification experiment, in which an 86.1% average classification accuracy was achieved. The proposed method was also evaluated using Hidden Markov models (HMMs), but significantly higher accuracy was obtained when CRFs were applied. In [13] a Heuristic Unsupervised Clustering algorithm is presented and evaluated to enable autonomous partitioning of appliances signature space (i.e. feature space) for applications in electricity consumption disaggregation. The algorithm is based on Hierarchical Clustering and uses the characteristics of a cluster binary tree to determine the distance threshold for pruning the tree without a priori information. The algorithm determines the partition of a feature space recursively to account for multi-scale nature of the binary cluster tree. [14] presents research on an unsupervised NILM system which consists of the typical stages of an event-based NILM system with the difference that only unsupervised algorithms are utilized in each stage eliminating the need for a pre-training process and providing wider applicability. They make use of Grid-Based Clustering algorithm for the event detection and Mean-Shift Clustering algorithm on the features extracted from the detected events. The system is tested on the publicly available Building-Level Fully Labeled Electricity Disaggregation Dataset (BLUED) and shows event detection and clustering accuracy more than 98%. The system also shows possible disaggregation up to 92% of the energy of phase A of the BLUED dataset. From our research work, there is no unsupervised NILM literature that makes use of our proposed approach for feature clustering, so we are justified in stating that our algorithm uses a new approach to energy disaggregation.

Additional literature on Unsupervised NILM algorithms including a listing of summary of the state of the art contribution performance can be found in [15].

The work presented in [16] first introduced a new clustering algorithm called Competitive Agglomeration (CA). CA minimizes an objective function that incorporates the advantages of both hierarchical and partitional clustering. The objective function has two components. The first component, is the sum of squared distances to the prototypes weighted by constrained memberships. This component allows for control of the shapes and sizes of the clusters and to obtain compact clusters. The second component is the sum of squares of the cardinalities of the clusters which allows us to control the number of clusters. When both components are combined and α is chosen properly, the final partition will minimize the sum of intra-cluster distances, while partitioning the data set into the smallest possible number of clusters. The clusters which are depleted as the algorithm proceeds will be discarded. The objective function of the CA algorithm is defined as follows:

$$J(B, U, X) = \sum_{i=1}^{C} \sum_{j=1}^{N} (u_{ij})^2 d^2 (x_j, \beta_i) - \alpha \sum_{i=1}^{C} \left[\sum_{j=1}^{N} u_{ij} \right]^2 \tag{2}$$

Subject to

$$\sum_{i=1}^{C} u_{ij} = 1, \ for \ j \in \{1, \ldots, N\} \tag{3}$$

where $X = \{x_j | j = 1, \ldots, N\}$ is a set of N vectors in an n-dimensional feature space with coordinate axis labels $(x_1, \ldots, x_n)$, and $B = \{\beta_1, \ldots, \beta_c\}$ represents a C-tuple of prototypes each of which characterizes one of the clusters. $d^2(x_j, \beta_i)$ represents the distance from feature vector x_j to the prototype β_i, u_{ij} represents the degree of membership of feature point x_j in cluster β_i, and $U = [U_{ij}]$ is a C x N matrix called a constrained fuzzy C-partition matrix. Equation 2 is constrained to Eq. 3, which states that the total membership for each cluster must be equal to 1.

3   Algorithm Design

3.1   Problem Definition

The NILM problem can be defined using Eq. (1). The goal is to find each individual appliance usage $P_i(t)$ that the total load is comprised of. The additional challenge of Unsupervised NILM is that we solve Eq. (1) without reliance on training data. Our algorithm makes use of active power as features, and thus the problem we aim to address can be stated as follows

$$P_{t_i} = \sum_{j=1}^{n} P_{jt_i} + e_{t_i} \tag{4}$$

where P_{t_i} is the total active power as seen at time t_i, P_{jt_i} is an individual appliance's active power contribution to the total active power, and e_{t_i} is a small noise or error term.

3.2   Goal and Objectives

The goals of the algorithm can be stated as follows:

1. Given a total load at time t decompose it into the individual energy usage events using the active power feature
2. Group similar features together and use these groups to build appliance models

3. Recognize the presence of appliances using the appliance models
4. Reconstruct the total load at time t by matching it with a set of appliances models.

The assumptions made with this algorithm are that:

1. the total load is sampled at a low-rate
2. only one device will change within the given window of time t.

3.3   Algorithm Overview

Our proposed algorithm is comprised of five modules: Feature Extraction, Feature Clustering, Appliance Modeling, Appliance Recognition, and Load Reconstruction.

Feature Extraction
Given a total load, the variations of the active power between given time windows can indicate the presence of an event, which would represent some form of change of state of an appliance. In order to determine appliance usage, we need to find the significant events that would indicate that an appliance could be in use. To do this we define a threshold value and make use of Eq. (5).

$$\Delta P_{t_i} = \left(P_{t_{i+1}} - P_{t_i}\right) > 0\,\mathrm{W} \tag{5}$$

where ΔP_{t_i} is a significant change in active power between two event windows.

Once all the significant events have been detected and the features extracted, they are then passed on to the Feature Clustering module.

Feature Clustering
Each feature is placed in a cluster that has features similar in value to itself magnitude-wise, resulting in a set of positive and negative clusters. The feature clustering module is based on the CA algorithm. We provide the CA algorithm with the extracted features and initialize the initial overspecified clusters (Cmax) to a fixed value. The CA algorithm iteratively groups similar features together. Once the algorithm has stabilized or run the maximum number of iterations, it outputs a set of feature clusters. The final number of clusters is determined automatically which is in line with our requirement of not depending on knowledge of the number or types of appliances in use.

The next step is to define appliance models which will serve as representations of actual appliances.

Appliance Modeling
Due to the simplicity of modeling transitions for Type I appliances, we make use of them here. In order to perform the modeling the set of positive and negative clusters will be split into two groups, one containing the positive clusters (C_P), and the other containing the negative clusters (C_N). The appliance models will be defined by first examining the set of positive clusters and doing the following:

1. given a positive cluster search the set of negative clusters for a cluster that is similar
2. if there is a match then the two clusters form a pair representing a cycle of state changes, and the clusters will be removed from their respective sets

We make use of the following equation for the appliance modeling:

$$M_i = \left\{ C_{P_i}, min\left(\left\| C_{p_i} - C_{N_j} \right\|^2 \right) \right\} \tag{6}$$

where M_i is the appliance model, C_{P_i} is the positive cluster, C_{N_j} is the negative cluster, $min\left(\left\| C_{p_i} - C_{N_j} \right\|^2 \right)$ is the negative cluster with the smallest Euclidean distance to the positive cluster, for $i = 1, \ldots, C_{p_n}$, and $j = 1, \ldots, C_{N_n}$.

The process stated above will be run until all the positive clusters have been examined and the result will be a set of paired clusters that each represent a cycle of events. Any unmatched positive and/or negative clusters will be discarded as we only consider matched pairs of clusters for Type I appliance models. This set of paired clusters will form the basis for determining the appliance usage and reconstructing the load.

Appliance Recognition
With the appliance models defined the next part is to use them to recognize their presence as part of the total load. The appliance recognition steps are as follows

1. given ΔP_{t_i} check if there is an appliance model that matches it, and record a value of true if there is a match
2. otherwise record a value of false

The appliance recognition can be defined as in Eq. (7) for step-up transitions and Eq. (8) for step-down transitions.

$$Match \; if \; rnd\left(\Delta P_{t_i} \right) = rnd\left(M_{j_P} \right) \tag{7}$$

$$Match \; if \; rnd\left(\Delta P_{t_i} \right) = rnd\left(M_{j_N} \right) \tag{8}$$

where M_{j_P} is the ON value of the appliance model, and M_{j_N} is the OFF value of the appliance model, for $i = 1, \ldots, n$, and $j = 1, \ldots, M_n$. If there is no close matching appliance model then the ΔP_{t_i} will be recorded as not being recognized.

Load Reconstruction
The Load Reconstruction module pieces together the appliance usage into an aggregate load. In order to do this we first examine the total load and for each time window t we take the following steps:

1. if there is a significant change, and if this significant change was detected, then we take note of the appliance usage
2. if there is a significant change, but the change wasn't detected then we don't take note of the appliance usage

The significant events that were matched will be used to reconstruct the signal. This is done by connecting the detected significant events together into one whole signal. The output will be a time series indicating the usage of appliances.

4   Validation with Experimental Data from REDD Database

In order to validate our proposed algorithm we make use of energy data from Reference Energy Disaggregation Dataset (REDD) [17], which is a commonly cited open access data set for energy data.

4.1   Validation Context and Scenario

To enable for a like-for-like comparison with the state of art FHMM approach [18] and the latest GSP-based approach [7] we made use of energy data from Houses 1, 2, and 6 of the REDD. We considered a three day period for each of the houses, from 28 to 30 April 2011 for Houses 1 and 2, and 28 to 30 May 2011 for House 6 (Fig. 1).

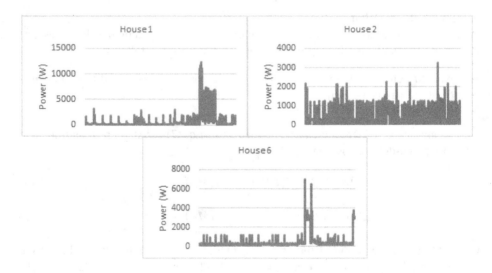

Fig. 1. Aggregate loads for REDD Houses 1, 2, and 6

4.2   Evaluation Metrics

In this paper we make use of Precision (P), Recall (R), and F-measure (f_1) NILM metrics, which are defined as:

$$P = \frac{TP}{TP + FP} \tag{9}$$

$$R = \frac{TP}{TP + FN} \tag{10}$$

$$f_1 = \frac{2 \cdot P \cdot R}{P + R} \tag{11}$$

where the true positive (TP) presents the correct claim that the appliance was used, false positive (FP) represents an incorrect claim that an appliance was used, and false negative (FN) indicates that the correct appliance was not identified.

We also make use of the Disaggregation Accuracy metric for the household which is defined as:

$$\text{DAcc.} = 1 - \frac{\sum_{i=1}^{n} \sum_{m \in M} \left| \hat{P}_{m_{t_i}} - P_{mt_i} \right|}{2 \sum_{i=1}^{n} \overline{P}_{t_i}} \tag{12}$$

4.3   Results and Discussion

We evaluated our proposed algorithm using the energy data from each of the aforementioned houses. We extracted features from each of the loads, shown in Fig. 2.

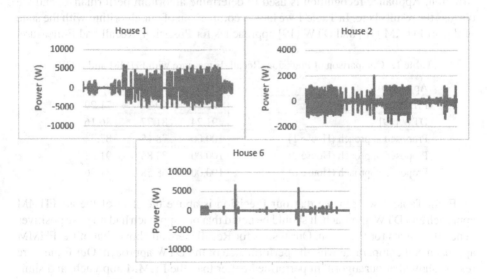

Fig. 2. Extracted features for REDD Houses 1, 2, and 6

The extracted features were then grouped together using the Feature Clustering module and the resulting clusters were used for Type I appliance modeling. The models are shown in Fig. 3.

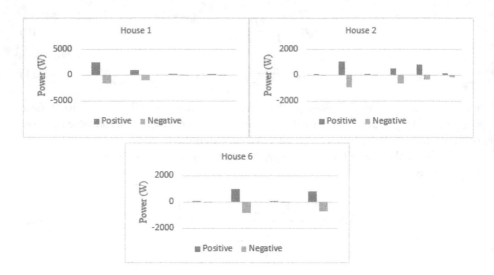

Fig. 3. Appliance models for REDD Houses 1, 2, and 6

The appliance models were then used for appliance recognition and load reconstruction. Appliance recognition is used to determine algorithm performance, and we discuss the results here. In Table 1 we have a comparison of our algorithm with the state of the art FHMM [18] and DTW [19] approaches for Precision, Recall and F-measure.

Table 1. Comparison of Precision, Recall, F-measure with FHMM and DTW

Approach	P (%)	R (%)	f_1 (%)
FHMM [18]	82.70	60.30	71.29
DTW [19]	91.24	81.77	86.16
Proposed approach (House 1)	100.00	78.15	87.74
Proposed approach (House 2)	100.00	83.86	91.22
Proposed approach (House 6)	100.00	68.58	81.36

From Table 1 we can see that our Precision is above the state of the art FHMM approach and DTW approach. It should be noted that our approach had no false positives hence the values for Precision. Our results for Recall were all above that of the FHMM approach and comparable with the performance of the DTW approach. Our F-measure results show that our algorithm performed better than the FHMM approach, and similarly with Recall it was comparable with the performance of the DTW approach.

Table 2 shows the disaggregation accuracies for the GSP-based approach and its benchmarks, alongside our proposed approach. It should be noted that the Expectation Maximization FHMM (EM-FHMM), Factorial Hierarchical Dirichlet Process HMM (F-HDP-HMM), and F-HDP Hidden Semi-Markov Model (F-HDP-HSMM) approaches [20] only considered the 5 top consuming appliances when performing the disaggregation. Additionally the GSP-based approach also used a pre-processing step to denoise the energy data which we did not do in this work.

Table 2. Disaggregation accuracy comparison with GSP-based and benchmarks

Approach	DAcc. (%)
Proposed approach	71.00
GSP-based [7]	77.20
EM FHMM [20]	50.80
F-HDP-HMM [20]	70.70
F-HDP-HSMM [20]	84.80
FHMM (without interaction) [21]	65.80
FHMM (with interaction) [21]	66.50

Table 2 shows that our algorithm outperforms the EM-FHMM, FHMM (without interaction), and FHMM (with interaction) approaches. It has similar performance with the F-HDP-HMM approach, and is slightly worse than the GSP-based and F-HDP-HSMM approaches. The result of F-HDP-HSMM approach could be due to the fact that it only considered the 5 top consuming appliances, whereas our approach, the GSP-based approach, and the two FHMM-based approaches used 7 appliances.

From the validation we saw that our theoretical framework for the proposed unsupervised energy disaggregation is justified to a certain extent. Our algorithm provides a means to disaggregate energy data without prior knowledge of the number or types of appliances. We were able to extract features from an aggregate load, group similar features together without knowledge of the actual clusters, and define appliance models that were used to recognize appliance usage in the aggregate load.

Our approach has some limitations. Due to the fact that we model Type I appliances it means that we cannot provide information regarding the actual appliances that the aggregate load is comprised off. We also made use of fixed values for the threshold for denoting significant events and the Cmax value in the feature clustering process. These limitations will serve as part of future work for this algorithm.

5 Conclusion

5.1 Conclusion and Future Works

In this paper we introduced a new approach to unsupervised energy disaggregation based on Competitive Agglomeration (CA) and the active power signature. Our proposed algorithm incorporates the goals of NILM and is able to disaggregate energy data, all without knowledge of the number of actual appliances in use. We validated the design of our algorithm with experimental data from the Reference Energy Disaggregation Data Set (REDD), and the results of this validation indicates that our unsupervised energy disaggregation algorithm is indeed effective. Additionally comparison of our algorithm with recent state of the art Unsupervised NILM algorithms shows that our work outperforms some of these works but also has slightly worse performance for others. Overall the comparison indicates that our algorithm has good performance.

In our future work we aim to overcome the identified limitations of the algorithm, and will focus on improvements to the appliance modeling and appliance recognition modules in order to gain better disaggregation performance.

Acknowledgements. This work is supported by the NSFC (61300238, 61300237, 61232016, 1405254, and 61373133); Marie Curie Fellowship (701697-CAR-MSCA-IF-EF-ST); the 2014 Project of six personnel in Jiangsu Province under Grant No. 2014-WLW-013; the 2015 Project of six personnel in Jiangsu Province under Grant No. R2015L06, and the PAPD fund.

References

1. Chen, J., Wang, X., Steemers, K.: A statistical analysis of a residential energy consumption survey study in Hangzhou, China. Energy Build. **66**, 193–202 (2013). Science Direct
2. Zheng, X., Wei, C., Qin, P., Guo, J., Yihua, Yu., Song, F., Chen, Z.: Characteristics of residential energy consumption in China: findings from a household survey. Energy Policy **75**, 126–135 (2014). Science Direct
3. Liu, Q., Cooper, G., Linge, N.: DEHEMS: creating a digital environment for large-scale energy management at homes. IEEE Trans. Consum. Electron. **59**(1), 62–89 (2013)
4. Lynham, J., Nitta, K., Saijo, T., Tarui, N.: Why does real-time information reduce energy consumption? Energy Econ. **54**, 173–181 (2016). Science Direct
5. Deloitte: Deloitte Resources 2016 Study – Energy Management: Navigating the Headwinds, pp. 7–17 (2016)
6. Hart, G.W.: Nonintrusive appliance load monitoring. Proc. IEEE **80**(12), 1870–1891 (1992)
7. Zhao, B., Stankovic, L., Stankovic, V.: On a training-less solution for non-intrusive appliance load monitoring using graph signal processing. IEEE Access **4**, 1784–1799 (2016)
8. Srinivasarengan, K., Goutam, Y.G., Chandra, M.G., Kadhe, S.: A framework for non-intrusive load monitoring using Bayesian inference. In: 2013 Seventh International Conference on Innovative Mobile and Internet Services in Ubiquitous Computing, pp. 427–432 (2013)
9. Henao, N., Agbossou, K., Kelouwani, S., Dubé, Y., Fournier, M.: Approach in nonintrusive type I load monitoring using subtractive clustering. IEEE Trans. Smart Grid **PP**(99) (2015)
10. Egarter, D., Elmenreich, W.: Autonomous load disaggregation approach based on active power measurements. In: 2015 IEEE International Conference on Pervasive Computing and Communication Workshops (PerCom Workshops), pp. 293–298 (2015)
11. Jia, R., Gao, Y., Spanos, C.J.: A fully unsupervised non-intrusive load monitoring framework. In: 2015 IEEE International Conference on Smart Grid Communications (SmartGridComm) (2015)
12. Heracleous, P., Angkititrakul, P., Kitaoka, N., Takeda, K.: Unsupervised energy disaggregation using conditional random fields. In: IEEE PES Innovative Smart Grid Technologies, Europe, pp. 1–5 (2014)
13. Jazizadeh, F., Becerik-Gerber, B., Berges, M., Soibelman, L.: An unsupervised hierarchical clustering based heuristic algorithm for facilitated training of electricity consumption disaggregation systems. Adv. Eng. Inform. **28**, 311–326 (2014). Elsevier
14. Barsim, K.S., Streubel, R., Yang, B.: An approach for unsupervised non-intrusive load monitoring of residential appliances. In: 2nd Non-Intrusive Load Monitoring (NILM) Workshop 2014, Austin (2014)

15. Bonfigli, R., Squartini, S., Fagiani, M., Piazza, F.: Unsupervised algorithms for non-intrusive load monitoring: an up-to-date overview. In: 2015 IEEE 15th International Conference on Environmental and Electrical Engineering (EEEIC), pp. 1175–1180 (2015)
16. Frigui, H., Krishnapuram, R.: Clustering by competitive agglomeration. Pattern Recogn. **30**(7), 1109–1119 (1997)
17. Zico Kolter, J., Johnson, M.J.: REDD: a public data set for energy disaggregation re-search. In: Proceedings of the SustKDD workshop on Data Mining Applications in Sustainability (2011)
18. Kolter, J.Z., Jaakkola, T.: Approximate inference in additive factorial HMMs with application to energy disaggregation. In: AISTATS. JMLR Proceedings, vol. 22, pp. 1472–1482 (2012)
19. Jing, L., Elafoudi, G., Stankovic, L., Stankovic, V.: Power disaggregation for low-sampling rate data. In: Proceedings of the 2nd International Workshop on Non-Intrusive Load Monitoring (2014)
20. Johnson, M.J., Willsky, A.S.: Bayesian nonparametric hidden semi-markov models. J. Mach. Learn. Res. **14**(1), 673–701 (2013)
21. Aiad, M., Lee, P.H.: Unsupervised approach for load disaggregation with devices interactions'. Energy Build. **116**, 96–103 (2016)

Planar-Based Visual Positioning for a Mobile Robot with Monocular Vision

Yang Guo, Zheng Xiao$^{(\boxtimes)}$, Hui Chen, and Ling Huang

College of Computer Science and Electronic Engineering, Hunan University,
Changsha, Hunan, China
{guoyang,zxiao,chui}@hnu.edu.cn, huangling951026@163.com

Abstract. Positioning is a fundamental component in many applications such as mobile robot. In this field, vision-based positioning becomes a popular way. This paper proposes an approach of positioning in the planar scene through monocular vision considering its high accuracy and low cost. The accuracy of monocular vision methods depends on the calibration when locating by use of the image of a single camera. The I-C transformation model substitutes arc for edge to reduce approximation error. Furthermore, the C-W transformation model is designed aiming at the absolute coordinates in the planar scene frame with two points as a prior knowledge. A physical testbed is constructed and experimental results reveal that 82% of the error in distances of the I-C transformation model is less than 1 cm and the average is 0.6591 cm. And a theoretical analysis is executed for the worst case performance of the C-W transformation model.

Keywords: Monocular vision · Plane-based · Absolute coordinate · Pinhole imaging

1 Introduction

Positioning is a fundamental component in many applications, such as mobile robot and aerospace, by which to avoid obstacle and do path planning has been a very hot direction. Therefore, it is an indispensable step to obtain the relative position and the absolute coordinate of the object [1,2].

Nowadays, absolute positioning is widely applied in real world because of some place with the need of absolute coordinate, such as do path planning for robot and rescue supplies for earthquake. So far, there is a lot of literature research on it. The widely used technologies include global positioning system (GPS), map matching technique landmarks navigation method. GPS uses 24 satellites to calculate the position information of receiver. However, it may not practical when the places are covered [3]. Map matching technique uses sensor to create a local location map, and then compares the local map with a pre-stored global map. But it is challenge to carry out map matching [4]. Landmarks navigation method locates the sensor by the relative position with the fixed or known landmarks, and its accuracy depends to a large extent on the landmarks [5,6].

© Springer International Publishing AG 2017
X. Sun et al. (Eds.): ICCCS 2017, Part I, LNCS 10602, pp. 410–421, 2017.
https://doi.org/10.1007/978-3-319-68505-2_35

A great quantity of information can be exploited from positioning by sensors. And there are many kinds of sensor applied in real world, like ultrasonic sensors, laser range finder and camera. The reason why the camera is so popular is that it makes control entity more humane and the secondary development more convenient. In addition, it is completely different from traditional sensors with single mode and low flexibility. And according to the number of cameras, vision-based positioning methods are divided into the following categories [7–9]: the binocular vision positioning method is mostly applied in extremely harsh environments; the omnidirectional vision positioning method is mainly applied in some indoor robots; in contrast, the monocular vision positioning method does not have to figure out the most optimal distance of many cameras or match marked points in the binocular vision positioning, and it never confront great distortion which happens in the omnidirectional vision positioning.

At present, there are many ways to use monocular vision for absolute positioning. The point feature and the line feature are the most common features, so they are frequently used for positioning [10–12]. The typical method is the PnP method, which obtains absolute position through several locating points and their corresponding points in image. Nevertheless, for different n, it may get several different solutions, so it is essential to add some other constraints to get the unique solution. And the most common methods are P3P, P4P and P5P [13–16]. In Reference [17], it mixed the point and line features to do monocular vision positioning. The problem is transformed into a quadratic equation problem. In Reference [18], it framed the mapping relation between the image point and the target point based on pinhole imaging, established the geometric relationship model and got the revised position information of the target point. Most of the above methods need multiple iterations to determine the unique solution, or have complex matrix calculation.

Therefore, it is necessary to find a simple way to get the unique position of the target point. The main purpose of this paper is to achieve the goal with a simple and fast speed method, and it focuses on the planar scene. It get the extrinsic parameters though the linear calibration, get the relative position information based on triangle similarity theorem, and according to robot kinematics get the absolute coordinate of the target point. In order to facilitate the introduction of the method, this paper takes mobile robot as an example to describe the method in detail. Simultaneously, it is worth noting that the method is general and can be widely applied in many other applications.

The rest of this paper is organized as follows. In Sect. 2, monocular vision system for mobile robot is introduced. In Sect. 3, it introduces the I-C transformation model that calculates distance between mobile robot and target and the C-W transformation model which calculates absolute coordinate of target. In Sect. 4, experiments and results are provided and meanwhile theoretical analysis. Finally, this paper is concluded in Sect. 5.

2   Monocular Vision System

2.1   Configuration and Frame Assignment

It is assumed that a camera is fixed on the top of a mobile robot moving on flat ground. This monocular vision system involves three different frames as Fig. 1 shows.

Image Frame $(O_i - X_i - Y_i)$: It is assigned to the image from camera, whose origin is at the bottom left corner of the image, X_i-axis is vertical upward and Y_i-axis is horizontal right. And its unit is pixel.

Camera Frame $(O_c - X_c - Y_c - Z_c)$: Its origin sits at the projection point on the ground of the optical center of camera, whose X_c-axis and Y_c-axis are parallel to X_i-axis and Y_i-axis respectively and Z_c-axis is perpendicular to ground. Once camera moves, the origin moves and orientation of this frame also changes.

World Frame $(O_w - X_w - Y_w - Z_w)$: Symbol Ow is the origin of this frame, while X_w-axis, Y_w-axis and Z_w-axis are the three orthogonal axes. Generally, it is static and provides the absolute coordinates. Because our method focuses on planar world, Z_w-axis can be ignored.

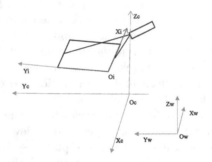

Fig. 1. Frames in monocular vision system.

There are two kinds of locating points in this system.

Marked point: Its coordinate in camera frame or in world frame is known. Quite a few such points scatter on the plane. They help obtain the absolute coordinates.

Target point: It is the very point to be positioned.
Positioning is divided into two stages.

Relative positioning: Its main goal is to get the relative position of the target point and camera, that is, the coordinate of the target point in camera frame.

Absolute positioning: It can obtain the coordinate of the target point in world frame.

This paper focuses on absolute positioning and it obtains absolute coordinate of the target point referring to marked points nearby. Meanwhile, relative positioning is its foundation.

2.2 Calibration

The goal of calibration is to determine some parameters of monocular vision system, which facilitate transformation from image frame to camera frame. In this paper, we use the linear calibration method based on pinhole imaging due to its fast speed [19].

The calibration is based on camera frame as shown in Fig. 2. The ellipse is the potential view field of the camera, and the rectangle is the area the image covers. Note that when calibrating, camera keeps still, that is, some parameters are fixed such as pitch angle $\angle KGO_c$ and height GO_c.

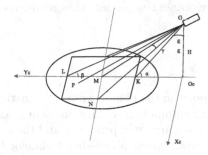

Fig. 2. Linear calibration for monocular vision positioning.

In our model, the following six parameters need to be calibrated. Table 1 gives their notations and definitions. H is measured manually.

Table 1. Calibrated parameters in our model.

Notations	Definition
H	Height from the camera's optical geometric center to its projection point on the ground
Sx	The number of horizontal pixels of the image from camera
Sy	The number of vertical pixels of the image from camera
α	The view angle of the nearest vertical point the image covers, i.e., GKOc
β	The view angle of the farthest vertical point the image covers, i.e., GLOc
γ	The view angle of the broadest horizontal point the image covers, i.e., NGM

If coordinates of K, L, and N in camera frame are known, it is easy to obtain α, β and γ. The coordinate of K is calibrated as $({}^cX_K, {}^cY_K, {}^cZ_K)$, where ${}^cX_K = {}^cZ_K = 0$.

$$\alpha = \arctan(\frac{H}{{}^cY_K}). \tag{1}$$

By analogy, β can be computed by Eq. 2 if the coordinate of L is known as $({}^cX_L, {}^cY_L, {}^cZ_L)$.

$$\beta = \arctan(\frac{H}{{}^cY_L}). \tag{2}$$

${}^cX_N$ of the coordinate of N needs to be calibrated, but ${}^cY_N$ can be determined based on K and L, that is, ${}^cY_N = ({}^cY_K + {}^cY_L)/2$. And we have ${}^cX_K = {}^cX_L$. So there is

$$\gamma = \arctan(\frac{{}^cX_N}{\sqrt{H^2 + (\frac{{}^cY_K + {}^cY_L}{2})^2}}). \tag{3}$$

At the same time, we obtain the vertical view angle $\alpha - \beta$, and the horizontal view angle 2γ.

3   Positioning

Assume P is the target point in the planar scene. Our method tries to retrieve its coordinate in world frame automatically. This problem is solved by three steps as Fig. 3 shows. The solid boxes are main processes and the dashed boxes are intermediate input/output. First, image processing technology is used to recognize the locating points. The intermediate output is the coordinate ${}^IP$ of P in image frame. Then, relative positioning (the I-C transformation model) transforms the pixel coordinate in image frame into coordinate in camera frame, based on the aforementioned calibration. Finally, absolute positioning (the C-W transformation model) transforms the coordinate in camera frame into coordinate in world frame, referring to two marked points. The three processes present a progressive relationship.

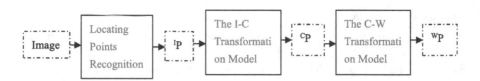

Fig. 3. The proposed positioning approach.

3.1 Relative Positioning

The I-C transformation model is the implementation of relative positioning, which transforms the pixel coordinate of the target point in image frame into the coordinate in camera frame with the calibrated data.

As shown in Fig. 4, according to the edge r in the two right angled triangles is equal and there is

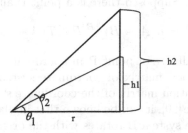

Fig. 4. The I-C transformation model.

$$\frac{h_1}{\tan(\theta_1)} = \frac{h_2}{\tan(\theta_2)}. \tag{4}$$

Then using θ_2 to express θ_1:

$$\theta_1 = \arctan(\frac{h_1}{h_2}\tan(\theta_2)). \tag{5}$$

Next step is putting the theory into the I-C transformation model. Supposed pixel coordinate of the target point P in image frame is $(^iX, {}^iY)$, and coordinate in camera frame is $(^cX, {}^cY)$. Consequently, in right angled triangle $\triangle GPO_c$, the projection angle of $\angle PGO_c$ in plane GO_cX_c is $\arctan(\frac{{}^iX-Sx/2}{Sx/2})\tan(\frac{\gamma}{2})$, and in plane GO_cY_c is $\frac{PI}{2} - \alpha + \frac{\alpha-\beta}{2} + \arctan(\frac{{}^iY-Sy/2}{Sy/2}\tan(\frac{\alpha-\beta}{2}))$. Therefore

$$^cY = H\tan(\frac{PI}{2} - \alpha + \frac{\alpha-\beta}{2} + \arctan(\frac{{}^iY-Sy/2}{Sy/2}\tan(\frac{\alpha-\beta}{2})))). \tag{6}$$

$$^cX = {}^cY\tan(\arctan(\frac{{}^iX-Sx/2}{Sx/2})\tan(\frac{\gamma}{2})). \tag{7}$$

Finally, we can further calculate distance d_1 between the target point and the origin of camera frame.

$$d_1 = \sqrt{^cX *^c X +^c Y *^c Y}. \tag{8}$$

3.2   Absolute Positioning

In this paper, our final goal is to get the absolute position of object. Therefore, in this subsection we introduce how to obtain absolute coordinate of the target point in world frame by the C-W transformation model based on the transformation matrix. So far absolute positioning is completed.

According to robot kinematics in planar world, there is a relationship between any two frames: One of the two can be completely coincident with another by rotation and translation. Supposed there is a point P and we have

$$^AP = R(A \to B) *^B P + T(A \to B). \tag{9}$$

where ^AP denotes coordinate of point P in coordinate system A, so does ^BP, $R(A \to B)$ is the rotation matrix of coordinate system B relative to A, and $T(A \to B)$ is the translation matrix of the coordinate system B relative to A.

By reading Reference [20], it can be known that in planar world where Z-axis is zero, when coordinate system B rotates with the origin of coordinate system A as rotation center, the rotation matrix and the translation matrix can be expressed as Eqs. 10 and 11.

$$R(A \to B) = \begin{pmatrix} \cos(\varphi) & -\sin(\varphi) & 0 \\ \sin(\varphi) & \cos(\varphi) & 0 \\ 0 & 0 & 1 \end{pmatrix}. \tag{10}$$

$$T(A \to B) = \begin{pmatrix} ^BX & ^BY & 0 \end{pmatrix}. \tag{11}$$

where φ is rotation angle, ^BX and ^BY are the translation coordinates of coordinate system B relative to coordinate system A in X-axis and Y-axis, respectively.

$$T(A \to B) = {}^AP - R(A \to B) *^B P. \tag{12}$$

The most important step to solve $R(A \to B)$ in Eq. 12 is to get rotation angle φ, which has a great effect on the four parameters in rotation matrix. In this paper, we put a novel method to get value of φ between camera frame and world frame.

There are two marked points M_1, M_2. As shown in Fig. 5, the two vectors $\overrightarrow{mw}$ and $\overrightarrow{mc}$ consist of coordinates of M_1 and M_2 in world frame and coordinates in camera frame, respectively (Noted that the value of the Z-axis is zero). In other word, there are $\overrightarrow{mw} = {}^wM_1 - {}^w M_2$ and $\overrightarrow{mc} = {}^cM_1 - {}^c M_2$. The angle between the two vectors is exactly the rotation angle between the two frames, and it is φ. Therefore, we have

$$\overrightarrow{mw} \cdot \overrightarrow{mc} = |\overrightarrow{mw}| * |\overrightarrow{mc}| * \cos(\varphi). \tag{13}$$

$$\overrightarrow{flag} = |\overrightarrow{mw}| \times |\overrightarrow{mc}|. \tag{14}$$

The $\overrightarrow{flag}$ is cross product between $\overrightarrow{mw}$ and $\overrightarrow{mc}$, and if Z-component of $\overrightarrow{flag}$ is negative, the corresponding φ is positive; on the contrary, φ is positive.

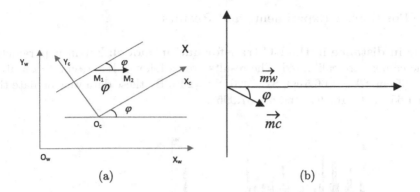

Fig. 5. The C-W transformation model.

By marked points M_1 and M_2, it is very easy to get values of $R(A \to B)$ by Eqs. 13 and 14 and to obtain $T(A \to B)$ with Eq. 12. So far, we get the position of the mobile robot in world camera, which can directly be used for applications such as path planning. In addition, we can further obtain absolute coordinate of any the point of camera frame by use Eq. 9. And if we want to transform pixel coordinate of image frame into absolute coordinate, we can use the I-C transformation model at first. Combined with the two transformation model, we can easily apply mobile to the harsh environment with the need of absolute positioning. For example, we may use robot for positioning in forest in order to carry fire rescue.

4   Experiments and Results

The testbed is composed by two parts, where the hardware part includes a calibration board, a mobile car, a camera and the software is composed of the image processing software OpenCV and the programming environment VS2010. The camera was mounted on the top of the mobile car, whose pitch angle and height are fixed in one measurement.

4.1   Experiment Procedure

The procedure of experiment is described as follows.

(1) The parameters of the camera are calibrated.
(2) Through the following image processing, we can extract the target points in the image and display coordinate: graying extracting edge with canny operator finding outline drawing outline calculating pixel coordinate of the target point.
(3) The coordinates of the target point in camera frame and world frame are calculated with the approach described in Sect. 3.

4.2 Positioning Experiments and Results

Error in distance in the I-C transformation model: Extrinsic parameters of the camera are calibrated. The results are as follows: $H = 19$ cm, $^cY_K = 9$ cm, $^cY_L = 65$ cm, $^cX_N = 66.5$ cm, $Sx = 320$, $Sy = 240$. By these data we calculate that $\alpha = 64.654°$, $\beta = 16.294°$ and $\gamma = 57.995°$.

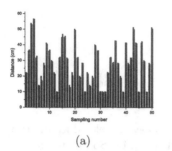   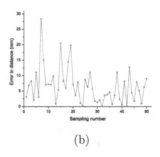

(a)   (b)

Fig. 6. The results about distance on the I-C transformation model

The experiments on the I-C transformation model were carried out on 50 sets of data. As shown in Fig. 6(a), it includes 50 sets of data of actual distance and measured distance, which is the distance between the target point and the origin of camera frame, in Fig. 6(b) it is the error in distance between actual distance and measured distance, and the Table 2 shows the statistics results of Fig. 6(b). According to these, we know that error in distance of 41 sets of data is not more than 1.0 cm, accounting for 82%, and there is a group of errors more than 2.4 cm, which is most likely caused by the measurement errors or image processing. The average error in distance is 0.6591 cm and the experimental result on the I-C transformation model is pretty good in general.

Table 2. The statistics result about distance on the I-C transformation model.

Error in distance(cm)	Number	Proportion(%)
≥ 2.4	1	2
≤ 1.2	44	88
$1.2 \sim 2.4$	5	10

Distance accuracy comparison on relative positioning: In Reference [21], it transforms the target position in image frame into the position in camera frame through the triangular transformation formula. Its relative errors distance on the X-axis and Y-axis are 3.5009% and 1.7658% respectively, while the relative error of the whole distance of the I-C transformation is 2.3369%. Therefore, the results show that the performance of the I-C transformation model is pretty good and its accuracy is much better than other geometric method. In Reference [18], it conducted 10 set of experimental data, and its average error in distance is 0.72 cm while its maximum relative error in distance is 1.75%. The most possibility is that it revised the distortion caused by the cameras lenses.

Error in distance in the C-W transformation model: The analytical expression of the C-W transformation model is theoretically correct if we directly use it. However, in most practical applications, it is necessary to take output of the I-C transformation model as input, and there is error accumulation of the I-C transformation model. Table 3 shows output results of the C-W transformation model with 7 group data, where angle is rotation angle, measured coordinate is calculated by the I-C transformation model and the C-W transformation model.

Table 3. The result on the transformation model.

The angle φ (°)	Actual coordinate(cm,cm)	Measured coordinate(cm,cm)	Error in distance(cm)
−0.190043	(10,0)	(9.32376,1.71709)	1.845453496
−2.54625	(20,50)	(21.1715,50.4825)	1.266972178
0.0951015	(30,10)	(30.5841,11.1484)	1.288408076
3.03648	(40,60)	(38.3265,60.6817)	1.807018854
1.63329	(50,30)	(49.4988,30.7205)	0.877679719
0.350292	(60,0)	(61.4248,2.03431)	2.483640919
2.09696	(50,60)	(50.7748,57.9989)	2.145860259

Error in distance is the distance between actual coordinate and measured coordinate, most of which are distributed around 1.2 cm. The upper limit is less than 2.5 cm and the average is 1.67 cm. The results are relatively stable distribution.

Error analysis in angle of the C-W transformation model: From the above results, we can know error in distance of the I-C transformation model will result in error accumulation of the C-W transformation model. Here by making an analysis about the upper limit of error in rotation angle, we will know how much error is accumulated.

In Fig. 7, the two center points of the two circles are the exactly position where the two marked points M_1, M_2 in world frame should be. But since 82% error in distance can be less than 1 cm in the I-C transformation model, we give input data 1 cm error range. That is to say radius of the two circles are 1 cm. $\overrightarrow{pw_1}$ is the correct vector composed by the two marked points in world frame, $\overrightarrow{pc_1}$ and $\overrightarrow{pc_2}$ denote the two extreme cases under consideration of the input error, and the final result of these two cases obviously produces a big gap. As a result of in experiments, distance between the marked points is at least 9 cm. Let the maximum error angle be ω, there is

$$\omega = \arcsin(\frac{1\,\text{cm}}{9\,\text{cm}/2}) = 12.84°. \tag{15}$$

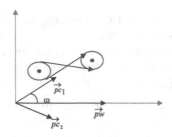

Fig. 7. The error analysis of the C-W transformation model.

That is to say, if the error in distance of the I-C transformation model is set at 1 cm, the upper limit of the error in rotation angle in the C-W transformation model is 12.84°. This error is so large and unbearable in positioning. But it needs to know that the situation is very rarely, because it must meet the three conditions at the same time: error in distance of the I-C transformation model is about 1 cm, wrong direction of the marked points is absolutely opposite and distance between the two is 9 cm.

5   Conclusion

Our main contribution is that we develop a relative to the cameras positioning model under the linear calibration and according to robot kinematics propose a absolute position transformation model, which is based on monocular vision and independent of the camera. In this paper, we make an analysis in detail about obtaining the coordinate of the target point in two-dimensional space, introduce positioning procedure, and through experiments prove that the proposed method is feasible. The positioning approach consists of three main parts: the calibration, the I-C transformation model and the transformation model. The calibration measures the initial parameters of the mobile robot in camera frame. The I-C transformation model obtains the coordinate of the target point in camera frame and of course we can know the distance between the object and mobile robot. Finally the C-W transformation model gets the absolute coordinate of the target point.

Therefore, on the one hand we will pay attention to the aspects in improving the accuracy, such as considering camera distortion or further combining with other positioning methods. On the other hand, because the research in this paper is just about positioning and it is a foundation technology, we will focus on further research, such as doing path planning and tracking moving target.

References

1. Wen, X., Guo, H., Nanchang University: Study of indoor self-localization method for mobile robots. Sci. Surv. Mapp. (2016)
2. Tiche, F., Ghai, N.S., Hgli, H.: Self-positioning and localization of a mobile robot using vision-based behaviors. In: Proceeding of Mecatronics, Europe-Asia Congress on Mechatronics (2009)
3. Ma, W.-Z., Li, L., Jiang, L.: Identification of common molecular subsequences. Electron. Technol. Softw. Eng. **21**, 61 (2014). (in Chinese)
4. Hinkel, R., Knieriemen, T.: Environment perception with a laser radar in a fast moving robot. Robot Control 271–277 (1989)
5. An, X.: Research on Binocular Vision Absolute Localization Method for Indoor Robot Based on Natural Landmarks. Jilin University (2016). (in Chinese)
6. Xu, M.: Research on Object Recognition and Location for Mobile Robot System Based on Monocular Vision. South China University of Technology (2014). (in Chinese)
7. Li, H., Chen, Y.L., Chang, T., Wu, X.: Binocular vision positioning for robot grasping. In: IEEE International Conference on Robotics and Biomimetics, pp. 1522–1527 (2011)
8. Feng, W., Liu, Y., Cao, Z.: Omnidirectional vision tracking and positioning for vehicles. In: International Conference on Natural Computation, pp. 183–187 (2008)
9. Beijing: Study on monocular vision method used for camera positioning. Acta Optica Sinica (2001)
10. Xu, D., Han, L., Tan, M., Li, Y.F.: Ceiling-based visual positioning for an indoor mobile robot with monocular vision. IEEE Trans. Ind. Electron. **56**(5), 1617–1628 (2009)
11. Lee, J.M., Son, K., Man, H.L., Choi, J.W.: Localization of a mobile robot using the image of a moving object. IEEE Trans. Ind. Electron. **50**(3), 612–619 (2003)
12. Desouza, G.N., Kak, A.C.: Vision for mobile robot navigation: a survey. IEEE Trans. Pattern Anal. Mach. Intell. **24**(2), 237–267 (2002)
13. Li, R., Lu, L., Jin, G.: Research overview of location method for monocular vision. Modern Comput. **11**, 9–12 (2011). (in Chinese)
14. Xu, D., Li, Y.F., Tan, M.: A general recursive linear method and unique solution pattern design for the perspective-n-point problem. Image Vis. Comput. **26**(6), 740–750 (2008). (in Chinese)
15. Wei, Z., Yu, J., Xu, D., Min, T.: Monocular vision measurement system based on ARM microprocessor. Control Eng. China **17**(4), 509–512 (2010)
16. Tang, J., Chen, W.S., Wang, J.: A novel linear algorithm for P5P problem. Appl. Math. Comput. **205**(2), 628–634 (2008)
17. Liu, C., Zhu, F., Xia, R.B.: Monocular pose determination from coplanar two points and one line features. Appl. Res. Comput. **8**, 3145–3147 (2012)
18. Li, F., Zhou, L., Miao, G.: Target distance measurement based on monocular vision system. In: 2012 East China Six Provinces and One City Automation Society 2012 Academic Annual Meeting (2012). (in Chinese)
19. Han, Y.-X., Zhang, Z.-S., Dai, M.: Monocular vision system for distance measurement based on feature points. Opt. Precis. Eng. **19**(5), 1082–1087 (2011)
20. Cai, Z.: Robotics Foundation. Machinery Industry Press, Norwalk (2015). (in Chinese)
21. Fang, Y., Zushu, L., Niu, W.: New method for autonomous soccer monocular lsion position determination. Comput. Meas. Control **15**(12), 1781–1784 (2007). (in Chinese)

Energy Efficient MAC Protocol for Wireless Sensor Networks: A Survey

Zichun Wang$^{(\boxtimes)}$, Meng Feng, Tiantian Miao, Wei Jiang, and Jian Shen

School of Computer and Software, Nanjing University of Information Science and Technology,
Nanjing 210044, China
wzc@nuist.edu.cn

Abstract. Wireless Sensor Networks (WSNs) has gained tremendous popularity in various practical applications, in which sensors are fundamentally battery-powered and significantly resource-limited. Well-designed Medium Access Control (MAC) protocols can make great contribution on the performance of the networks. In this paper, we present a survey on some typical or newly proposed MAC protocols which aims at enhancing energy efficiency of the networks. The classification and beneficial characteristics of MAC protocols are discussed. Furthermore, we analyze the protocols' performance in various fields, and point out the open research issue.

Keywords: WSNs · MAC protocols · Energy efficient

1 Introduction

Wireless Sensor Networks (WSNs) has been under worldwide concentration in recent years, thanks to the expansion in Micro-Electro-Mechanical System (MEMS) technology which has made the development of integrated smart sensors feasible [1]. The sensor nodes in the network establish communication by using the wireless medium, which may be either radio frequency waves, infrared medium or any other media in which there is no use of the wires is done [2]. These nodes are capable of monitoring physical or environmental conditions, such as temperature, sound, pressure, etc. Nodes can also cooperatively pass their data through the network to a main location. There are four top basic functions that must be performed by wireless sensor networks: sensing, processing, storage of data, and communication.

Fundamentally, the number of the sensor nodes that are involved in functional WSNs is large, due to the small size and resource limitation of sensor nodes. Nodes depend on limited battery power as their primary power resource, which may get depleted easily due to the complex operations these nodes have to perform. Additionally, hostile deployment regions make it unrealistic to recharge or replace the batteries frequently. Therefore, the main challenge in WSNs is to reduce the energy consumption and maximize network's lifetime. Major sources of energy waste in WSNs are basically of five types [3, 4], which are shown as follows.

© Springer International Publishing AG 2017
X. Sun et al. (Eds.): ICCCS 2017, Part I, LNCS 10602, pp. 422–429, 2017.
https://doi.org/10.1007/978-3-319-68505-2_36

- Collision: When a transmitted packet is corrupted because of interference, it has to be discarded and retransmitted by the sender when available. This causes wastage in both sender and receiver as it expands energy without any benefit [5]. Collision also increases latency which adversely affects the network transmission speed.
- Overhearing: When node receives a packet that is not destined to it, "overhearing" or "on-listening" happens [6]. This received packet must be discarded and the whole process, receiving and discarding the packet, ends up with a waste of energy.
- Packet Overhead: In WSNs, packet header and other additional overheads (like control messages) occupy a large proportion of the medium, while data packets are normally small in size. Sending minimal number of control packets will decrease energy wastage [5].
- Idle Listening: It appears when node listens to an idle channel in order to receive possible traffic, and is particularly costly in energy in the case of applications that do not require virtually a large data exchange [6]. Due to the fact of WSNs' low traffic loads, idle listening is regarded as the major energy wastage in a sensor node [5].
- Over Emitting: "Over emitting" or "on-emission" happens when receiver node is not ready for receiving data which has been sent already by sender node.

Many researches aiming at this topic have been conducted for proposing energy efficient Medium Access Control (MAC) protocols. MAC protocols can directly regulate the communication module, which can significantly affect the performances of WSNs in many perspectives.

In this paper, we investigate some MAC protocols that are broadly utilized in applications for WSNs. The remainder of this paper is structured as follows. Section 2 summarizes the characteristics of MAC protocols. Section 3 categorizes and surveys some typical MAC protocols and their features. Section 4 gives a comparative analysis of the protocols' performance. Section 5 concludes the paper.

2 Characteristics of MAC Protocols

Medium Access Control (MAC) protocol is used to establish and regulate data communication [8]. MAC is the sub-layer of data link layer, the second layer in Open Systems Interconnection (OSI) model. MAC plays an important role in making decision when a node can access the shared medium, framing, addressing and flow control etc. It also ensures that nodes share the communication medium fairly and efficiently. Some major characteristics of MAC Protocol for WSNs are discussed below.

- Energy Efficiency: Energy is a scarce resource for WSNs, due to the limited battery power and the difficulty of recharging or replacing the battery. As MAC layer regulates the activities of the radio layer, which consumes the most energy, then we can deduce that the MAC protocol can avoid energy wastage, hence reach the goal of energy efficiency.
- Adaptability: In most applications of WSNs, traffic density varies significantly over time and from part of the network to another [9, 10]. This network is dynamic in

many aspects, such as size, density and topology. In this case, MAC protocol designers must take these uncertain factors into consideration.

- Latency: Many applications of WSNs require delay-bounded delivery of data, such as target tracking and precise data monitoring. In these applications, the detected events must be reported to the sink node in real time, and in this way the appropriate action could be taken immediately [7, 11].
- Throughput: This is the total data amount that successfully transmitted between a transmitter and a receiver in a definite time. Data throughput requirement can be a crucial feature in applications that process a large amount of data.
- Fairness: In many applications of WSNs, it is necessary to ensure sink nodes to receive information from all sensor nodes fairly [11]. This property remains very important in conventional wireless networks in the fact that each node wants the same chance as other nodes for transmitting or receiving data.

3   Classification of MAC Protocols

MAC protocols are generally divided into two categories – schedule based and contention based MAC protocol. Schedule based protocol can avoid collisions, overhearing and idle listening by making transmit & listen periods scheduled. This collision-free protocol is efficient in terms of energy, but requires strict time synchronization [11]. The contention based protocol, also known as unscheduled protocol [12], has relax time synchronization requirement, and can easily adjust to the topology changes as some new nodes may join and other may die few years after deployment [13, 16].

3.1   Schedule Based MAC Protocols

These protocols access the medium by defining a schedule for the transmission, reception or being idle by the nodes in the network. Nodes communicate during specific allotted time slot and stay idle otherwise. Some widely used protocols are discussed as follows.

(1) **Low-Energy Adaptive Clustering Hierarchy Protocol (LEACH).** LEACH protocols involve different characteristics for communication in WSNs [14, 17]. LEACH is the initial and most popular energy efficient hierarchical clustering protocol for WSNs that was developed for reducing energy waste [15]. Clustering is an energy efficient communication algorithm utilized when sensor nodes broadcast the sensed data to the sink nodes. Every cluster has a special node which is responsible for managing the data transmission activities of other nodes in this cluster, called cluster head. Data transfer from a lower clustered layer to a higher one, and the hierarchical structure precedes the data faster to the base station. LEACH protocol fully takes this advantage. Moreover, cluster head rotation prolongs the network lifetime by equilibrating the rate of energy usage by all the nodes in network [8]. It also enhances the scalability and reliability in the network by limiting different communication inside the different local clusters [11]. LEACH

is a crucial and fundamental one of the clustering hierarchical MAC protocols in WSN [1].

(2) **Traffic Adaptive MAC Protocol (TRAMA).** The traffic adaptive medium access [15] is a TDMA based protocol that has been designed for reducing the energy consumption by means of avoiding collision in WSN. Switching nodes to low-power sleeping state when they are idle also contributes to the network's energy efficiency. This protocol is composed of three main parts:

- The Neighbor protocol is for gathering the corresponding information about the neighboring nodes.
- Schedule Exchange Algorithm plays its role in transmitting information and schedule between the two-hop neighbors.
- Referring to the neighborhood and schedule information, the Adaptive Election Algorithm decides the transmitting and receiving nodes for the current time slot. The other nodes in the same slot are switched into low power mode, reducing idle listening effectively.

Although TRAMA protocol successfully achieves the goal of energy efficiency, the latency it brings is considerable compared to the other contention based MAC protocols [11]. This protocol is suitable for applications that require high energy efficiency and throughput.

(3) **Wise-MAC Protocol.** Wise-MAC protocol uses "Preamble Sampling" mechanism to minimize the energy loss due to passive listening [6]. In this mechanism, receiver nodes listen to the channel periodically during relatively short periods to detect activities on the channel. If the channel is busy, the receiver node continues listening, waiting for a packet intended for itself, until the channel returns to free state [20]. As for the transmitter, a "Wake up" preamble is transmitted before each message to activate the receiver, in this way the message can be successfully received. To avoid collisions, Wise-MAC randomly chooses the "Wake up" preamble with a non-persistent CSMA technique, hence reduces energy waste. However, the transmission of preambles will consume energy either at the transmitter level or the receiver one. In order to remedy this energy loss, Wise-MAC dynamically determines the length of the preambles so that is as small as possible [20].

(4) **Bitmap-assisted Efficient and Scalable TDMA-based MAC Protocol (BEST-MAC).** BEST-MAC is proposed for adaptive traffic in hierarchical WSNs that can be deployed in the smart cities [21]. It can flexibly handle the varying amount of data traffic by using large number of small size data slots. The implementation of Knapsack optimization technique significantly reduces sensor nodes' job completion time, thus decreasing the average packet delay. The link utilization of the networks is also well enhanced due to these aforementioned attributes. Nevertheless, this protocol enables nodes to be identified by a unique 1 byte short address, which reduces the control overhead and minimizes energy consumption.

3.2 Contention Based MAC Protocols

In contention based MAC protocols the medium access is distributed, and there is no central coordination for nodes to access the medium [3, 18]. These protocols mostly follow the operational model of CSMA, incorporating handshaking signals and a back-off mechanism to avoid collisions [19]. Some protocols are discussed here.

(1) **Sensor MAC Protocol (S-MAC).** Sensor MAC protocol is specifically designed for WSNs with the purpose of reducing energy losses [22]. Locally managed synchronizations and periodic active-asleep schedules based on these synchronizations form the basic idea behind the S-MAC protocol [23]. In this protocol, sensor node periodically goes to the fixed listen/sleep cycle. A time frame is basically divided into two parts: one for listening session and the other for a sleeping session [25]. Only for a listen period, sensor nodes can communicate with other nodes and send control packets, such as SYNC, RTS (Request to Send), CTS (Clear to Send) and ACK (Acknowledgement). Specially, by exchanging SYNC packet all neighboring nodes can synchronize together, and by using RTS/CTS exchange two nodes can communicate with each other.
S-MAC protocol effectively saves energy by utilizing sleep and wake up technique. It also simplifies the network's implementation and prevents time synchronization overhead with sleep schedule announcements. However, the sleep and listen periods are predefined and constant, which lowers the transmission efficiency under variable traffic condition.

(2) **TimeOut MAC Protocol (T-MAC).** T-MAC adopts contention-based scheme that lays on improvement of S-MAC protocol by enabling active nodes to have adaptive duty-cycles for the operation [22]. In T-MAC, nodes wake up to broadcast with its nearby nodes and then switch to sleep mode until the next frame starts. The listen period ends when no activation event has occurred for a time threshold TA, whose decision is presented along with some solutions to the early sleeping problem defined in [22, 24]. This protocol can deal with variable traffic load due to active/asleep schedule and high energy efficiency for low data rate applications. The handicap of this protocol is that T-MAC has higher transmission latency as compared to the S-MAC protocol.

(3) **Berkeley MAC.** Berkeley MAC refers to Berkeley Medium Access Control for low-power sensor networks [26], is highly configurable and can be implemented with a small code and memory size. It mainly consists of three parts: clear channel assessment (CCA), packet back-off and link layer acknowledgements [13]. When a node is ready to transmit packet, it has to wait during a back-off period before the operation of CCA. If the channel is accessible, the node transmits its packet, or a second back-off begins. Every node must check the channel regularly by using low-power listening (LPL) [8]. If the channel is found free and the node has no packet to transmit, then the node goes to sleep state [26]. The B-MAC protocol does not use a RTS-CTS scheme, which is utilized in many ad-hoc networks and causes considerable overhead. However, the adaptive preamble of the B-MAC protocol inevitably results in overhead, which may lower its energy efficiency [26].

(4) **Priority-based Adaptive MAC Protocol (PA-MAC).** In this protocol, the fixed dedicated beacon channel (BC) is assigned for the beacon, while the rest of the communication operates through the data channel (DC) [27]. The data traffic is prioritized by using a priority-guaranteed carrier-sense multiple access with collision avoidance (CSMA/CA) procedure in the contention access period (CAP). In contention free period (CPF), continuous and massive data packets are transmitted to the coordinator. This traffic prioritization scheme, along with the classification of the data transfer procedure, lowers the contention complexity and avoids collision and retransmission of the packets effectively. In this way, PA-MAC protocol can highly rise the quality of service and energy efficiency of WSNs.

4 Comparative Analysis

We compare the typical state-of-art MAC protocols for WSNs proposed so far in the literature. First, we categorize the MAC protocols to two types, schedule based and contention based. Then we analyze the performance of every protocol in various aspects, such as latency, adaptivity, QoS, robustness, and most important of all, energy efficiency. Table 1 summarizes the comparison result of MAC protocols.

Table 1. Comparison of MAC protocols

Protocol	Type	Energy efficiency	Latency	Adaptivity	Robustness	Quality of service
LEACH	Schedule based	Low	Low	Normal	High	Low
TRAMA	Schedule based	High	High	High	Normal	Low
Wise-MAC	Schedule based	High	Low	High	Normal	Low
BEST-MAC	Schedule based	High	Very low	Normal	High	High
S-MAC	Contention based	Low	High	High	High	Low
T-MAC	Contention based	Normal	Normal	High	Normal	Low
Berkeley MAC	Contention based	High	High	High	Normal	Low
PA-MAC	Contention based	High	Low	High	High	Very high

From this comparison table and our comparative analysis, some conclusive comments can be drawn. BEST-MAC outperforms other schedule based MAC protocols due to its extremely low transmission latency. As for contention based MAC protocols, PA-MAC can be implemented by application calls for rigidly guaranteed quality of service.

In summary, every aforementioned MAC protocol takes energy efficiency into consideration specifically, and accomplishes this goal by optimizing different property of the networks. Due to the advancement of algorithm and technology, the newly proposed MAC protocol can outperform the typical ones in many aspects apparently.

5   Conclusion

In WSNs, sensor nodes are basically supported by energy-constraint batteries, so increasing energy efficiency becomes the paramount goal for many applications. A well designed medium access control protocol can contribute to this by regulating the distribution of the medium and the activity of sensor nodes. In this paper, we have provided a brief introduction of WSNs, and analyze the main sources of energy waste. We have discussed some typical MAC protocol suitable for WSNs and their characteristics. According to comparison, choice of MAC protocol depends on the requirements of applications.

Acknowledgments. This work is supported by the National Science Foundation of China under Grant No. 61300237, No. U1536206, No. U1405254, No. 61232016 and No. 61402234, the National Basic Research Program 973 under Grant No. 2011CB311808, the Natural Science Foundation of Jiangsu province under Grant No. BK2012461, the research fund from Jiangsu Technology & Engineering Center of Meteorological Sensor Network in NUIST under Grant No. KDXG1301, the research fund from Jiangsu Engineering Center of Network Monitoring in NUIST under Grant No. KJR1302, the research fund from Nanjing University of Information Science and Technology under Grant No. S8113003001, the 2013 Nanjing Project of Science and Technology Activities for Returning from Overseas, the 2015 Project of six personnel in Jiangsu Province under Grant No. R2015L06, the CICAEET fund, and the PAPD fund.

References

1. Kaur, J., Sahni, V.: Survey on hierarchical cluster routing protocols of WSN. Int. J. Comput. Appl. **130**(17), 18–22 (2015)
2. Pant, S., Naveen, C., Prashant, K.: Effective cache based policies in wireless sensor networks: a survey. Int. J. Comput. Appl. **11**(10), 17–21 (2010)
3. Wei, Y., Heidemann, J., Estrin, D.: An Energy-efficient MAC protocol for wireless sensor networks. In: IEEE Global Telecommunications Conference, pp. 1567–1576. IEEE (2012)
4. Tijs, V., Langendoen, K.: An Adaptive energy-efficient MAC protocol for wireless sensor networks. International Conference on Embedded Networked Sensor Systems, pp. 171–180. ACM (2003)
5. Rai, A., Deswal, S., Singh, P.: MAC protocols in wireless sensor network: a survey. Int. J. New Innovations Eng. Technol. **5**(1), 95–101 (2016)
6. Ridha, A.: Energy consumption and fault tolerance in the MAC protocols for WSN. J. Comput. Commun. **3**(6), 118–130 (2015)
7. Fu, Z.: Enabling personalized search over encrypted outsourced data with efficiency improvement. IEEE Trans. Parallel Distrib. Syst. **27**(9), 2546–2559 (2015)
8. Ritesh, K., Rai, K.: A survey on MAC protocols in WSN. Int. J. Eng. Trends Technol. 10–11 (2014)
9. Akyildiz, I.: Wireless sensor networks: a survey. Comput. Netw. Int. J. Comput. Telecommun. Netw. **38**(4), 393–422 (2002)

10. Pottie, J., Kaiser, J.: Wireless integrated network sensors. Wireless Integr. Netw. Sens. Next Gener. **43**(5), 51–58 (1999)
11. Yadav, R., Varma, S., Malaviya, N.: A survey of MAC protocols for wireless sensor networks. UbiCC J. **4**(3), 827–833 (2009)
12. Nukhet, S.: An energy efficient MAC protocol for cluster based event driven WSN applications. In: International Conference on Software, Telecommunications and Computer Networks IEEE Xplore, pp. 76–81 (2010)
13. Patil, U., Modi, S., Suma, J.: A survey: MAC layer protocol for wireless sensor networks. Int. J. Emerg.Technol. Adv. Eng. **3**(9), 203–211 (2013)
14. Heinzelman, B., Chandrakasan, P., Balakrishnan, H.: An application-specific protocol architecture for wireless microsensor networks. IEEE Trans. Wireless Commun. **1**(4), 660–670 (2000)
15. Heinzelman, L.: Energy-efficient communication protocol for wireless microsensor networks. Adhoc & Sensor Wireless Netw. **18**(10), 18–27 (2000)
16. Fu, Z.: Enabling semantic search based on conceptual graphs over encrypted outsourced data. IEEE Trans. Serv. Comput. p. 99 (2016)
17. Kaur, R., Sharma, D., Kaur, N.: Comparative analysis of leach and its descendant protocols in wireless sensor network. Int. J. P2P Netw. Trends Technol. **3**(1), 51–55 (2013)
18. Rajendran, V., Obraczka, K., Garcia-Luna-Aceves, J.: Energy-efficient, collision-free medium access control for wireless sensor networks. Wireless Netw. **12**(1), 63–78 (2006)
19. Bao, L., Garcia-Luna-Aceves, J.: A new approach to channel access scheduling for Ad Hoc networks. In: International Conference on Mobile Computing and NETWORKING, pp. 210–221. ACM (2001)
20. El-Hoiydi, A., Decotignie, J.-D.: WiseMAC: an ultra low power MAC protocol for multi-hop wireless sensor networks. In: Nikoletseas, S.E., Rolim, J.D.P. (eds.) ALGOSENSORS 2004. LNCS, vol. 3121, pp. 18–31. Springer, Heidelberg (2004). doi:10.1007/978-3-540-27820-7_4
21. Alvi, N.: BEST-MAC: bitmap-assisted efficient and scalable TDMA-based WSN MAC protocol for smart cities. IEEE Access **4**, 312–322 (2016)
22. Tijs, V., Langendoen, K.: An Adaptive energy-efficient MAC protocol for wireless sensor networks. In: International Conference on Embedded Networked Sensor Systems, pp. 171–180. ACM (2003)
23. Ye, W., Heidemann, J., Estrin, D.: Medium access control with coordinated adaptive sleeping for wireless sensor networks. IEEE/ACM Trans. Netw. **12**(3), 493–506 (2004)
24. Zhang, Y., Sun, X., Wang, B.: Efficient algorithm for K-barrier coverage based on integer linear programming. China Commun. **13**(7), 16–23 (2016)
25. Ye, W., Heidemann, J., Estrin, D.: An energy-efficient MAC protocol for wireless sensor networks. In: IEEE Global Telecommunications Conference, pp. 1567–1576. IEEE (2012)
26. Joseph, K., Calle, M.: MAC protocols used by wireless sensor networks and a general method of performance evaluation. Int. J. Distrib. Sensor Netw. **2012**(1), 285–288 (2012)
27. Sabin, B., Sangman, M.: A priority-based adaptive MAC protocol for wireless body area networks. Sensors **16**(3), 401 (2016)

A Particle Swarm Optimization and Mutation Operator Based Node Deployment Strategy for WSNs

Jin Wang[1], Chunwei Ju[1], Huan Ji[1], Geumran Youn[2], and Jeong-Uk Kim[2(✉)]

[1] School of Information Engineering, Yangzhou University, Yangzhou, China
{jinwang,huanji}@yzu.edu.cn, jvchunwei@163.com
[2] Department of Electrical Engineering, Sangmyung University, Seoul, Korea
{gryoun,jukim}@sum.ac.kr

Abstract. Coverage control is one of the most critical issues for wireless sensor networks (WSNs), which is closely related to the sensor network performance. Generally, sensor nodes are randomly and massively deployed in targeted area, this densely deployment will give rise to communication overhead. In order to fully utilize sensor nodes in target area, we consider the problem of maximizing the lifetime of network with fewer nodes. In this paper, we propose a novel algorithm based on particle swarm optimization and mutation operator. We first give a mathematic model to calculate network coverage rate. Then, premature phenomenon judgment is given and a mutation operator is introduced. Finally, we utilize mutation operator to improve particle swarm optimization in particle search process. Simulation results show that compared with traditional particle swarm algorithm, our algorithm can effectively increase the coverage rate.

Keywords: Wireless sensor network · Coverage · Particle swarm optimization · Mutation operator

1 Introduction

Wireless sensor networks (WSNs) [1, 2] are low-power and self-organized networks, which consist of a great deal of tiny sensors and a remote sink node (or a base station). Owing to the low cost of sensor nodes, WSNs can be applied to massive deployment environments, such as battlefield monitoring [3], disaster detection [4] etc. Sensor nodes are energy constrained since their batteries are usually non-replaceable. Thus, energy efficiency for WSNs can directly impact network lifetime.

Generally, sensor nodes are randomly and massively deployed to fully cover the target area [5]. This kind of deployment can lead to coverage redundancy and give rise to interference of data transmission [6]. Thus, coverage control is an important technique for WSNs. With the aim to achieve the maximum network coverage with limited sensor nodes, each sensor needs to be scheduled very effectively, so that we can ensure that all sensing areas can be monitored with better quality of service.

© Springer International Publishing AG 2017
X. Sun et al. (Eds.): ICCCS 2017, Part I, LNCS 10602, pp. 430–437, 2017.
https://doi.org/10.1007/978-3-319-68505-2_37

Swarm intelligence algorithms is becoming more and more popular in recent research, such as ant colony optimization (ACO) [8] and particle swarm optimization (PSO) [11–13]. In PSO algorithm, once a particle finds a current best position, other particles move close to it. This can restrain the global search capability of particles and give rise to premature phenomenon. So, we should make some improvement before utilizing this algorithm.

In this paper, we propose a novel particle swarm optimization and mutation operator based node deployment algorithm for WSNs. Firstly, we give a mathematical model as per coverage rate calculation. Then, we introduce premature phenomenon judgment and explain mutation operator in detail. Finally, the improved particle swarm optimization is proposed for nodes deployment in WSNs.

The rest of this paper is organized as follows. Section 2 provides some related work. Section 3 presents the system model. Section 4 gives our proposed algorithm in detail. Simulation results are given in Sects. 5 and 6 concludes the paper.

2 Related Work

Recently many scholars have put research effort to the coverage control problems. Bartolini et al. presented a virtual force (VF) based mobile sensor deployment algorithm [7]. The authors introduced an attack called opportunistic movement, and analyze its efficiency in traditional VF approach. They found that this attack can reduce more than 50% of coverage rate. Thus, they presented two improved algorithms (DRM and Secure VF) to counteract this attack. DRM (Density based Random Movement) is a simple algorithm that can reposition nodes in overcrowded areas, secure VF is a much more complex algorithm which can detect malicious sensors. These algorithms do not consider mobile sensor nodes' residual energy and influence the network performance.

Lee et al. presented an ant colony optimization (ACO) based coverage algorithm [8], and energy efficiency coverage is addressed in this research. But ant colony optimization requires large calculations and gives rise to extra energy cost. Authors in [9, 10] proposed a coverage algorithm based on genetic algorithm (GA) for sensor networks. However, GA is easy to fall into premature phenomenon in space search, and it requires lots of time for calculation.

The authors in [11–13] try to utilize particle swarm optimization for coverage optimization. In [11], the authors introduced an improved PSO to achieve a balance energy consumption and coverage. Simulation results show that the proposed algorithm can effectively cover the network with fewer nodes. In [12], the authors presented a chaotic particle swarm optimization coverage control algorithm. This algorithm utilizes the chaotic algorithm to optimize PSO function. Simulation results show that this algorithm can get be energy efficient as well as get good performance in coverage quality. In [13], the authors proposed a particle swarm optimization based clustering algorithm with mobile sink for WSNs, where virtual clustering technique is performed during routing process by using PSO algorithm. The residual energy and position of the nodes are the primary parameters to select cluster head.

Gu et al. presented a new equivalent dual formulation for v-SVC (v-support vector classification) in [14], and proposed a robust v-SvcPath. Experimental results also show that their proposed v-SvcRPath fits the entire solution path with fewer steps and less running time than v-SvcPath does. In [15], the authors proposed a scheme that supports CBIR (content-based image retrieval) over encrypted images without leaking the sensitive information to the cloud server. The security analysis and the experiments show the security and efficiency of the proposed scheme. The authors in [16] built a user interest model for individual user with the help of semantic ontology WordNet, and proposed two PRSE schemes to solve two limitations (the model of "one size fit all" and keyword exact search) in most existing searchable encryption schemes. Simulation results show that their proposed solution is very efficient and effective.

Ma et al. proposed two recommendation approaches fusing user-generated tags and social relations in [17]. The authors compare experimental results with two baseline methods: user-based CF (collaborative filtering) and user-based CF. Experimental results show that their methods can get high accuracy. Authors in [18] proposed an early reference frame decision algorithm. Experimental results show that the proposed algorithm can efficiently improves the coding efficiency. In [19], the authors presented a fast motion estimation (ME) method to reduce the encoding complexity of the H.265/HEVC encoder. Experimental results show high efficiency of the proposed method.

3 System Model

3.1 Network Model

Wireless sensor network can be viewed as a directed graph $G = <V_{node} \cup V_{sink}, E>$, where V_{node} and V_{sink} represents the set of sensor nodes and sink nodes respectively. E represents the set of all links $l(i,j)$, where i and j are neighboring sensor nodes. In this paper, we consider that all sensor nodes are randomly deployed in initial deploy phase. We make some assumptions as follows:

(1) Sensors are homogenous.
(2) Sensors have same initial energy.
(3) Sensors have same sensing radius.

3.2 Coverage Rate

We deploy N sensor nodes in the network and the sensing radius of each node is r. All sensor nodes forms a set $G = \{g_1, g_2, \ldots, g_n\}$, where $g_i (i = 1, 2, \ldots, n)$ and its coordinate is (x_i, y_i), the coverage area of node i is the circle which sensing radius is r. Assuming that the coordinate of pixel P is (x_P, y_P), then the distance between pixel P and sensor node g_i is $d(g_i, P) = \sqrt{(x_i - x_P)^2 + (y_i - y_P)^2}$. The sensing rate $p(g_i, P)$ for pixel P to be covered by node g_i can be expressed:

$$p(g_i, P) = \begin{cases} 1 & d(g_i, P) \leq r \\ 0 & d(g_i, P) > r \end{cases} \tag{1}$$

Generally, a pixel can be covered by several sensor nodes at the same time. The sensing rate $p(G, P)$ for pixel P to be covered by set G is shown below:

$$p(G, P) = 1 - \prod_{g_i \in G} [1 - p(g_i, P)] \, (i = 1, 2, \ldots, n) \tag{2}$$

If sensing rate $p(G, P)$ is 1, then pixel P is covered by sensor nodes. Otherwise, pixel P is not covered by sensor nodes. Thus, the number of pixels covered by sensors can be calculated in formula (3):

$$SUM(P) = \sum_{P \in m \times n} p(G, P) \tag{3}$$

$SUM(p)$ denotes the total number of pixels covered by sensors. The coverage rate of target area $R(G)$ is shown in formula (4):

$$R(G) = \frac{\sum\limits_{P \in m \times n} p(G, P)}{m \times N} \tag{4}$$

4   Our Proposed Algorithm

4.1   Mutation Operator

Traditional particle swarm optimization algorithm is easy to fall into premature phenomenon in space search. To alleviate this problem, we introduce a combination with PSO and mutation operator in vector speed update process.

When a PSO algorithm fall into premature phenomenon, all particle are concentrate at one point, this makes it difficult to find the optimal value. Thus, we introduce mutation operator to tackle this issue. Firstly, we judge whether this algorithm has fallen into local optimum. Group fitness standard deviation of particles can be calculated as shown in formula (5):

$$S = \sqrt{\frac{1}{k} \sum_{i=1}^{k} (R_i - R_{avg})^2} \tag{5}$$

where S is group fitness standard deviation, k is the number of particles, R_i is the coverage rate of particle i and R_{avg} is the average coverage rate. R_{avg} can be calculated as in formula (6):

$$R_{avg} = \frac{1}{n} \sum_{i=1}^{k} R_i \tag{6}$$

where $S \rightarrow 0$ means the algorithm converge at a global optimum or a local optimum. Then, we check the predefined number of iteration t ($t < 1000$). If the current iteration number $t_c < t$, mutation begins. The mutation probability p_m ($0 \leq p_m \leq 0.3$), p_m is a predefined number.

4.2   The Improved PSO Algorithm

Step 1:   We initialize k particles $X^0 = (x_1^0, x_2^0, \ldots, x_k^0)$, the state of particle i moves in N-dimensional space at iteration t is show as follows:

Position: $x_i^t = (x_{i1}^t, x_{i2}^t, \ldots, x_{in}^t)$. $x_i^t \in [L_n, U_n]$, where $[L_n, U_n]$ is the search interval.
Speed: $v_i^t = (v_{i1}^t, v_{i2}^t, \ldots, v_{in}^t)$. $v_i^t \in [v_{min}, v_{max}]$, where $[v_{min}, v_{max}]$ is the speed interval.
Individual optimal position coverage rate: $R_i^t = (R_{i1}^t, R_{i2}^t, \ldots, R_{in}^t)$.
Global optimal position coverage rate: $R_g^t = (R_{g1}^t, R_{g2}^t, \ldots, R_{gn}^t)$.

Step 2:   The number of iteration k add 1. Update particles' position and speed.
Step 3:   Calculate current coverage rate of the network.
Step 4:   Compare current position coverage rate R_c^t with global optimal position coverage rate R_g^t. If $R_c^t > R_g^t$, $R_g^t = R_c^t$; otherwise, continue.
Step 5:   If $S \neq 0$ and $t \leq t_{max}$, go to step 2; If $S = 0$ and $t_c \leq t$, conduct mutation operation, go to step 2; otherwise end step.

In mutation operation, according to mutation probability p_m, the number of mutation particles are $\lfloor p_m \cdot k \rfloor$. We select these particles and randomly initialize their current position and speed.

After iteration is finished, global optimal position is the best solution. Sensor nodes update their positions and then node deployment is finished.

5   Performance Evaluation

To evaluate the performance of our proposed PSO-MO algorithm, we compare it with common particle swarm optimization algorithm in literature [11], and simulation is conducted in Matlab. In this paper, we assume that the target area is 50 m*50 m and there are [10–50] sensor nodes randomly deployed in the network. The sensing range of each node is [3–8] m, and the communication range is twice as sensing range. Parameters of PSO-MO algorithm are $p_m = 0.2$, $t = 800$, $k = 20$.

When sensing range is 8 m, the relationship between sensor number and coverage rate is shown in Fig. 1.

It can be seen that in the beginning, the number of sensors is small and the coverage rate is similar. As the number of nodes increased, our proposed PSO-MO algorithm shows better performance. It can get 10% coverage improvement compared with traditional PSO algorithm. We can see that sensor nodes cannot effectively cover WSN since their number is not enough. As their number increased, the network coverage rate can be increased. When the number of sensor nodes comes to certain degree, the coverage rate trends to be stable.

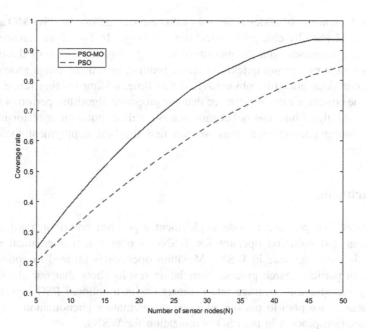

Fig. 1. Comparison of coverage rate along with nodes

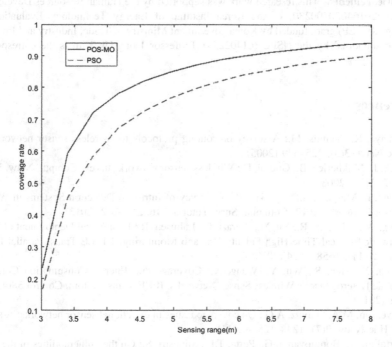

Fig. 2. Comparison of coverage rate along with sensing range

When the number of nodes is 50, we evaluate coverage rate of PSO-MO algorithm and traditional PSO by changing nodes' sensing range. In Fig. 2 we can see that the coverage rate increases with the growth of sensing range. For both of the two algorithms, coverage rate grows quickly in the beginning, as sensing range grows to 8 m, coverage rate does not grow obviously. At this time, adding sensing range has little effect on the coverage rate. We can see that our proposed algorithm performs well than common PSO algorithm, this is because that we utilize mutation operator in PSO to avoid premature phenomenon, thus we can find the best deployment locations for sensor nodes.

6 Conclusion

In this paper, we propose a node deployment algorithm based on particle swarm optimization and mutation operator for WSNs. We give a mathematical model to calculate the coverage rate in WSNs. Mutation operator is utilized to optimize PSO algorithm in particle search process. Simulation results show that our algorithm can effectively increase the coverage rate compared with traditional PSO algorithm. For future research, we plan to put our attention on premature phenomenon judgment as well as variation process in the PSO optimization for WSNs.

Acknowledgements. This research work was supported by the Human Resources Development Program (20164030300230) of the Korea Institute of Energy Technology Evaluation and Planning (KETEP) grant funded by Korea government Ministry of Trade, Industry and Energy. It was also supported by the NSFC (61402234). Professor Jeong-Uk Kim is the corresponding author.

References

1. Akkaya, K., Younis, M.: A survey on routing protocols for wireless sensor networks. Ad Hoc Netw. **3**(3), 325–349 (2005)
2. Yick, J., Mukherjee, B., Ghosal, D.: Wireless sensor network survey. Comput. Netw. **52**(12), 2292–2330 (2008)
3. Butun, I., Morgera, S.D., Sankar, R.: A Survey of Intrusion Detection Systems in Wireless Sensor Networks. IEEE Commun. Surv. Tutorials **16**, 266–282 (2013)
4. Song, W.Z., Huang, R., Xu, M., Shirazi, B., Lahusen, R.: Design and Deployment of Sensor Network for Real-Time High-Fidelity Volcano Monitoring. J IEEE Trans. Parallel Distrib. Syst. **21**(11), 1658–1674 (2010)
5. Wang, X., Han, S., Wu, Y., Wang, X.: Coverage and Energy Consumption Control in Mobile Heterogeneous Wireless Sensor Networks. IEEE Trans. Autom. Control **58**(4), 975–988 (2013)
6. Guvensan, M.A., Yavuz, A.G.: On coverage issues in directional sensor networks: A survey. Ad Hoc Netw. **9**(7), 1238–1255 (2011)
7. Bartolini, N., Bongiovanni, G., Porta, T.L., Silvestri, S.: On the vulnerabilities of the virtual force approach to mobile sensor deployment. IEEE Trans. Mob. Comput. **13**(11), 2592–2605 (2014)

8. Lee, J.W., Lee, J.J.: Ant-colony-based scheduling algorithm for energy-efficient coverage of WSN. IEEE Sens. J. **12**(10), 3036–3046 (2012)

9. Hu, X.M., Zhang, J., Yu, Y., Chung, S.H., Li, Y.L., Shi, Y.H.: Hybrid genetic algorithm using a forward encoding scheme for lifetime maximization of wireless sensor networks. J. IEEE Trans. Evol. Comput. **14**(5), 766–781 (2010)

10. Kalayci, T.E., Yildirim, K.S., Ugur, A.: Maximizing coverage in a connected and k-covered wireless sensor network using genetic algorithms. J. Int. J. Appl. Math. Inf. **1**(3), 123–130 (2007)

11. Cong, C.: A coverage algorithm for WSN based on the improved PSO. In: International Conference on Intelligent Transportation, Big Data and Smart City, pp. 12–15. EEE (2015)

12. Xiao, J., Zhang, Y., Xu, F., Li, J.: Research of chaotic PSO coverage control algorithm based on energy balance. In: IEEE International Conference on Robotics and Biomimetics, pp. 2077–2082. IEEE (2011)

13. Wang, J., Cao, Y., Li, B., Kim, H.J., Lee, S.: Particle swarm optimization based clustering algorithm with mobile sink for WSNs. Future Gener. Comput. Syst. **76**, 452–457 (2016)

14. Gu, B., Sheng, V.S.: A robust regularization path algorithm for v-support vector classification. IEEE Trans. Neural Netw. Learn. Syst. **99**, 1–8 (2016)

15. Xia, Z., Wang, X., Zhang, L., Qin, Z., Sun, X., Ren, K.: A privacy-preserving and copy-deterrence content-based image retrieval scheme in cloud computing. IEEE Trans. Inf. Forensics Secur. **11**(11), 2594–2608 (2016)

16. Fu, Z., Ren, K., Shu, J., Sun, X., Huang, F.: Enabling personalized search over encrypted outsourced data with efficiency improvement. IEEE Trans. Parallel Distrib. Syst. **27**(9), 2546–2559 (2016)

17. Ma, T., Zhou, J., Tang, M., Tian, Y., Aldhelaan, A., Alrodhaan, M.: Social network and tag sources based augmenting collaborative recommender system. IEICE Trans. Inf. Syst. **98**(4), 902–910 (2015)

18. Pan, Z., Jin, P., Lei, J., Zhang, Y., Sun, X., Kwong, S.: Fast reference frame selection based on content similarity for low complexity HEVC encoder. J. Vis. Commun. Image Represent. **40**, 516–524 (2016)

19. Pan, Z., Lei, J., Zhang, Y., Sun, X., Kwong, S.: Fast motion estimation based on content property for low-complexity H. 265/HEVC encoder. IEEE Trans. Broadcast. **62**(3), 675–684 (2016)

A Distributed Sparse Signal Reconstruction Algorithm in Wireless Sensor Network

Zhi Zhao, Peng Pin, and WeiYu Yu$^{(\boxtimes)}$

School of Electronic and Information Engineering,
South China University of Technology, Guangzhou, China
Zhaozhi.perfect@163.com, 610466608@qq.com,
yuweiyu@scut.edu.cn

Abstract. We propose a distributed sparse signal reconstruction algorithm in the full Bayesian framework by using Variational Bayesian(VB) with embedded consensus filter. Specifically, each node execute one-step average-consensus with its neighbors per VB step and thus reach a consensus on estimate of sparse signal finally. The proposed approach is ease of implementation and scalability to large networks. In addition, due to the observability of nodes can be enhanced by average-consensus, the number of measurements for each node can be further reduced and not necessary to satisfy lower bound required by CS. Simulation results demonstrate that the proposed distributed approach have good recovery performance and converge to their centralized counterpart.

Keywords: Compressive sensing · Sparse signal · Variational Bayesian · Consensus filter · Wireless sensor networks

1 Introduction

The recently developed compressive sensing(CS) theory [1, 2] is a new sampling paradigm that can achieve acquisition of information contained in a large-scale data using only much fewer samples than that required by Nyquist sampling theorem. Indeed, advances in electronics and digital communications have made wireless sensor networks (WSNs) the predicted panacea for solving a variety of large-scale decision and information-processing tasks [3–6]. Hence, CS is a promising technique for WSNs in saving bandwidth and energy. However, most of CS reconstruction algorithms operate in centralized manner where all the measurements need to be concentrated for processing. It can be seen that the practical application of these centralized approaches are not strong. Due to the high fault tolerance and scalability, distributed processing are becoming increasingly popular in the WSNs applications. Recently, many researchers have attempted to discuss the distributed sparse signal recovery problems [7–9] for WSN applications when a centralized approach is not possible or desirable, for example, Iterative Hard Thresholding (IHT) [7], Basis Pursuit (BP) [8], Least Absolute Shrinkage and Selection Operator (Lasso) [9], etc. However, these aforementioned works based on convex optimization usually require one or more practically unknown parameters, e.g., the noise statistics, the regularization parameters, etc. In addition, a main issue of these deterministic method is that the uncertainty of signal reconstruction

© Springer International Publishing AG 2017
X. Sun et al. (Eds.): ICCCS 2017, Part I, LNCS 10602, pp. 438–449, 2017.
https://doi.org/10.1007/978-3-319-68505-2_38

is generally obscure. Therefore, Sparse Bayesian learning (SBL) was introduced in [10] and has become a popular method for sparse signal recovery in CS [11]. Moreover, An alternative approach to SBL is the variational rendition of SBL (VSBL) with several advantages compared to SBL [12]. However, the VSBL algorithm is a centralized method, and apply the several ADMM procedure in each expectation maximization (EM). Compared with ADMM technique, average-consensus strategies naturally lead to an equalization effect across the sensors without complexity [13].

Motivated by all of the above, this paper aims to propose a distributed algorithm for sparse signal reconstruction in the full Bayesian framework by using variational approximation and average-consensus techniques. We employed average-consensus as a diffusion strategy for acquiring three global information quantities which extracted from centralized approach; particularly, the average-consensus step only needs to be performed once among neighbors in each fixed point iteration of variational SBL for saving communication resource and energy.

2 Problem Statement and System Model

Consider a network composed of K nodes whose connectivity is described by an undirected graph $\mathcal{G} = (\mathcal{V}, \mathcal{E}, \mathcal{A})$ of the order K. Accordingly, node $k \in \mathcal{V}$ represents a sensor and can communicate with node $l \in \mathcal{V}$ if the edge (k, l) in the set $\mathcal{E} \subseteq \mathcal{V} \times \mathcal{V}$, and the adjacency matrix $\mathcal{A} = [a_{kl}]_{K \times K}$ with nonnegative adjacency element a_{kl}, namely, $a_{kl} > 0 \Leftrightarrow (k, l) \in \mathcal{E}$. Node l is called a neighbor of node k if $(k, l) \in \mathcal{E}$ and $l \neq k$. The neighborhood set of node k is denoted by $\mathcal{N}_k$. The degree of vertex k is set as $d_i = |\mathcal{N}_k|$, and the maximum degree is $d_{max} = \max_k d_k$. Each node is able to process the local data and collaborate with its single-hop neighbors.

Assume that each node k is interested in reconstructing an unknown sparse signal $\mathbf{x} \in \mathbb{R}^N$ from m_k local noisy measurements $\mathbf{z}_k \in \mathbb{R}^{m_k}$. Thus, the sensing model at node k is

$$\mathbf{z}_k = \mathbf{A}_k \mathbf{x} + \mathbf{w}_k, \ 1 \leq k \leq K \tag{1}$$

where $\mathbf{A}_k \in \mathbb{R}^{m_k \times N}$ is the local sensing matrix for node k, and $\mathbf{w}_k \in \mathbb{R}^{m_k}$ is the zero-mean Gaussian noise with covariance $\beta^{-1} \mathbf{I}_{m_k}$. Let M be the total number of measurements from all the nodes, i.e., $M = \sum_{k=1}^{K} m_k$. We have the global measurement, $\mathbf{Z} \in \mathbb{R}^M$, the global sensing matrix, $\mathbf{A} \in \mathbb{R}^{M \times N}$, and the global measurement noise $\mathbf{W} \in \mathbb{R}^M$ as follows

$$\mathbf{Z} = \begin{bmatrix} \mathbf{z}_1 \\ \vdots \\ \mathbf{z}_K \end{bmatrix}, \mathbf{A} = \begin{bmatrix} \mathbf{A}_1 \\ \vdots \\ \mathbf{A}_K \end{bmatrix}, \mathbf{W} = \begin{bmatrix} \mathbf{w}_1 \\ \vdots \\ \mathbf{w}_K \end{bmatrix} \tag{2}$$

Then the global sensing model is given by

$$\mathbf{Z} = \mathbf{Ax} + \mathbf{W} \tag{3}$$

The construction of $\mathbf{A}$ satisfies so-called restricted isometry property (RIP) imposed in the design of compressive sensing schemes, i.e., the elements of $\mathbf{A}$ are drawn from $\mathcal{N}(0, 1/M)$. From the sensing model (3) and noise statistics, the measurements likelihood function is given by

$$
\begin{aligned}
p(\mathbf{Z}|\mathbf{x}, \beta) &= \prod_{k=1}^{K} p(\mathbf{z}_k|\mathbf{x}, \beta) \\
&= \prod_{k=1}^{K} \frac{\beta^{m_k/2}}{(2\pi)^{m_k/2}} \exp\left[-\frac{\beta}{2}\|\mathbf{z}_k - \mathbf{A}_k\mathbf{x}\|^2\right]
\end{aligned}
\tag{4}
$$

Moreover, as stated previously, the estimate of $\mathbf{x}$ is constrained to be sparse. To this end, the likelihood should be complemented by suitable conjugate priors over $\mathbf{x}$ and β. Specifically, a Gamma prior with parameters c and d is selected for precision β

$$p(\beta|c, d) = G(\beta|c, d) = \frac{d^c \beta^{c-1} exp[-d\beta]}{\Gamma(c)} \tag{5}$$

From a probabilistic point of view, a heavy-tailed distribution is well-suited to reflect prior knowledge about sparsity of signal. Here, two level prior is set for our Baysian model. For the first level, a Gaussian distribution is adopted for x similar to SBL, i.e.,

$$
\begin{aligned}
p(x|\alpha) &= N(x|0, \Lambda^{-1}) = \prod_{i=1}^{N} p(x_i|\alpha_i) \\
&= \prod_{i=1}^{N} (2\pi)^{-1/2} \alpha_i^{1/2} exp\left[-\frac{1}{2}x_i^2\alpha_i\right]
\end{aligned}
\tag{6}
$$

where $\alpha = [\alpha_1, \alpha_2, \ldots, \alpha_N]^T$ and $\Lambda = \text{diag}(\alpha)$. In the second level, a Gamma distribution is selected for the precision parameters α_i s

$$p(\alpha_i|a_i, b_i) = G(\alpha_i|a_i, b_i) = \frac{b_i^{a_i} \alpha_i^{a_i-1} exp[-b_i\alpha_i]}{\Gamma(a_i)} \tag{7}$$

Heretofore, the Baysian system model is developed for sparse signal reconstruction in WSN. Based on the proposed Baysian model, our goal is to recover the sparse signal

x at each node using distributed processing. Next, we firstly derive centralized variational Bayesian method to facilitate the distributed algorithm design.

3 Variational Bayesian Approximation for Centralized Sparse Signal Reconstruction

In this section, we briefly review the variational approximation technique and derive the centralized VSBL for aforementioned full Bayesian model. For ease of notation, we define $\boldsymbol{\psi} = [x_1, \ldots, x_N, \beta, \alpha_1, \ldots, \alpha_N]^T$ as the unknown parameters and hidden variables of the model which are referred to as unknown variables, and $\boldsymbol{\theta} = [a_1, \ldots, a_N, b_1, \ldots, b_N, c, d]^T$ as the hyperparameters of the imposed prior. Based on the Bayesian model previous, variational Baysian is to approximate the posterior of $\boldsymbol{\psi}$, $p(\boldsymbol{\psi}|\mathbf{Z})$, by a more tractable distribution $Q(\boldsymbol{\psi})$. To this end, the hyperparameters $\boldsymbol{\theta}$ is inferred by maximizing the following log-likelihood

$$\ln p(\mathbf{Z}|\boldsymbol{\theta}) = F(Q(\boldsymbol{\psi})) + KL(Q(\boldsymbol{\psi}) \parallel p(\boldsymbol{\psi}|\mathbf{Z}, \boldsymbol{\theta})) \tag{8}$$

where F is the free energy

$$F(Q(\boldsymbol{\psi}), \boldsymbol{\theta}) = \int Q(\boldsymbol{\psi}) \ln\left(\frac{p(\mathbf{Z}|\boldsymbol{\psi})p(\boldsymbol{\psi}|\boldsymbol{\theta})}{Q(\boldsymbol{\psi})}\right) d\boldsymbol{\psi} \tag{9}$$

and

$$KL(Q(\boldsymbol{\psi})\|p(\boldsymbol{\psi}|\mathbf{Z}, \boldsymbol{\theta})) = \int Q(\boldsymbol{\psi}) \log\left(\frac{Q(\boldsymbol{\psi})}{p(\boldsymbol{\psi}|\mathbf{Z}, \boldsymbol{\theta})}\right) \tag{10}$$

is the Kullback-Leibler (KL) divergence between the posterior $p(\boldsymbol{\psi}|\mathbf{Z}, \boldsymbol{\theta})$ and a tractable distribution $Q(\boldsymbol{\psi})$. In Eq. (8), since the KL divergence is non-negative and the log-likelihood $\ln p(\mathbf{Z}, \boldsymbol{\theta})$ is fixed with respect to $Q(\boldsymbol{\psi})$, the variational free energy can be viewed as lower bound for $lnp(\mathbf{Z}, \boldsymbol{\theta})$. Therefore, minimizing the KL divergence is equivalent to maximizing the variational free energy. From an optimization point of view, the model parameters of $Q(\boldsymbol{\psi})$ is well-suited selected so that the lower bound can be minimized. In order to make it tractable, we resort to a simpler variational free form $Q(\boldsymbol{\psi})$ to approximate the posterior based on the mean-field theory from statistical physics. Specifically, $Q(\boldsymbol{\psi})$ can be factorized into a family of q-distribution w.r.t. some partitions $\boldsymbol{\psi} = \{\boldsymbol{\psi}_1, \ldots, \boldsymbol{\psi}_L\}$ as follows

$$Q(\boldsymbol{\psi}) = \prod_{j=1}^{L} q_j(\boldsymbol{\psi}_j) \tag{11}$$

i.e., each partition $\boldsymbol{\psi}_j$ of the unknown variables is mutually independent given the measurements. In fact, if we let $\boldsymbol{\psi}_i$ denote the j-th partition of the vector $\boldsymbol{\psi} = [x_1, \ldots, x_N, \beta, \alpha_1, \ldots, \alpha_N]^T$ containing the parameters of the Bayesian hierarchical model, and ψ_{-j} refers to the other parameters after removing j-th partition. Maximizing the free energy in Eq. (9) is realized by taking functional derivatives with respect to each of the $q(\cdot)$ distributions while fixing the other distributions and setting $\partial F(q)/\partial q(\cdot) = 0$ [14]. Furthermore, the computation of $\partial F(q)/\partial q(\cdot) = 0$ can be expressed as

$$\ln q^*(\psi_j) \propto E_{q(\psi_{-j})}[\ln(p(Y|\psi)p(\psi|\theta))] \tag{12}$$

where $E_{q(\psi_{-j})}$ denotes the expectation w.r.t. $\prod_{i \neq j} q(\psi_i)$. From Eq. (12), it is noted that q^* don't represent explicit solution since it depends on the other factors $q(\psi_i)$ for $i \neq j$. Thus, the optimum solution $q^*(\psi_j)$ is sought by first initializing all the $q(\psi_j)$ appropriately and then cycling through the factors and replacing each in turn with updated estimate given by Eq. (12) using current estimates for all of the other factors. Since the lower bound is convex w.r.t. $q(\psi_j)$, the convergence is guaranteed.

By applying the variational bayesian techniques to our model, we first take the following logarithm of the joint distribution over $\mathbf{Z}$ and all unknown variables ψ

$$\begin{aligned}
\ln(p(\mathbf{Z}|\psi)p(\psi|\theta)) = & \sum_{k=1}^{K} \ln p(\mathbf{z}_k|\mathbf{x}, \beta) + \sum_{i=1}^{N} \ln p(x_i|\alpha_i) \\
& + \sum_{i=1}^{N} \ln p(\alpha_i|a_i, b_i) + \ln p(\beta|c, d)
\end{aligned} \tag{13}$$

For each factor, averaging w.r.t. those variables not in that factor by making use of (12), we can express the re-estimation equations for the factors analytically, namely

$$\ln q(\mathbf{x}) \propto E_{q(\alpha)q(\beta)}[\ln(p(\mathbf{Z}|\psi)p(\psi|\theta))] \propto N(\mathbf{x}|\mu, \Gamma) \tag{14}$$

$$\ln q(\beta) \propto E_{q(\mathbf{x})q(\alpha)}[\ln(p(\mathbf{Z}|\psi)p(\psi|\theta))] \propto G(\beta|\tilde{c}, \tilde{d}) \tag{15}$$

$$\ln q(\alpha) \propto E_{q(\mathbf{x})q(\beta)}[\ln(p(\mathbf{Z}|\psi)p(\psi|\theta))] \propto G(\alpha_i|\tilde{a}_i, \tilde{b}_i) = G(\alpha|\tilde{a}, \tilde{b}) \tag{16}$$

From Eqs. (14)–(16), we recognize that $q(\mathbf{x})$ is Gaussian distribution, $q(\beta)$ and $q(\alpha)$ are Gamma distributions, i.e., $q(\mathbf{x}) = N(\mathbf{x}|\mu, \Gamma)$, $q(\beta) = G(\beta|\tilde{c}, \tilde{d})$ and $q(\alpha) = G(\alpha|\tilde{\mathbf{a}}, \tilde{\mathbf{b}})$. where

$$\Gamma = \left(\text{diag}(\mathbb{E}[\alpha_i]) + \sum_{k=1}^{K} \mathbb{E}[\beta] A_k^T A_k \right)^{-1} \tag{17}$$

$$\mu = \sum_{k=1}^{K} \mathbb{E}[\beta] \Gamma A_k^T \mathbf{z}_k$$

$$\tilde{a}_i = a + \frac{1}{2} \tag{18a}$$

$$\tilde{b}_i = b + \frac{E[x_i^2]}{2} \tag{18b}$$

$$\tilde{c} = c + \frac{M}{2} \tag{18c}$$

$$\tilde{d} = d + \frac{1}{2} \sum_{k=1}^{K} \mathbf{z}_k^T \mathbf{z}_k - \sum_{k=1}^{K} E[\mathbf{x}]^T \mathbf{A}_k^T \mathbf{z}_k$$
$$+ \frac{1}{2} \text{Tr} \left(\sum_{k=1}^{K} \mathbf{A}_k^T \mathbf{A}_k \cdot (\mathbf{\Gamma} + \boldsymbol{\mu}^T \boldsymbol{\mu}) \right) \tag{18d}$$

In the above, the required moments can be easily computed as follows

$$E[\mathbf{x}] = \boldsymbol{\mu}$$

$$E[x_i^2] = \Gamma_{ii} + \mu_i^2$$

$$E[\alpha_i] = \tilde{a}_i / \tilde{b}_i \tag{19}$$

$$E[\beta] = \tilde{c} / \tilde{d}$$

The variational optimization proceeds by iteratively updating Eqs. (14)–(18d) until convergence to stable hyperparameters θ. From the aforementioned formulas, it is noted that a fusion center is required to gather all the measurements and then reconstruct the sparse signal. However, there is no fusion center in the distributed scenario and formulas derived above can't be implemented directly. In order to develop the distributed counterpart, we attempt to reformulate the centralized formulas which will be presented in the following section.

4 Distributed Variational Sparse Bayesian Learning Algorithm

In this section, we propose a distributed variational Bayesian algorithm for jointly reconstructing sparse signal, which is developed from the previous variational Bayesian inference. Hereinafter, the distributed algorithm will be referred to as DVSBL. It is assumed that each node performs the inference severally and has no knowledge of other nodes' measurement matrices and measurements. Therefore, by inspecting the former equations, we define the following global information quantities

$$\mathcal{I}^{(1)} = \sum_{k=1}^{K} \mathbf{A}_k^T \mathbf{A}_k$$

$$\mathcal{I}^{(2)} = \sum_{k=1}^{K} \mathbf{A}_k^T \mathbf{z}_k$$

$$\mathcal{I}^{(3)} = \sum_{k=1}^{K} \mathbf{z}_k^T \mathbf{z}_k \qquad (20)$$

and define the following local quantities

$$\mathcal{I}_k^{(1)} = \mathbf{A}_k^T \mathbf{A}_k$$

$$\mathcal{I}_k^{(2)} = \mathbf{A}_k^T \mathbf{z}_k$$

$$\mathcal{I}_k^{(3)} = \mathbf{z}_k^T \mathbf{z}_k \qquad (21)$$

so the Eqs. (17) and (18d) can be reformulated as follows

$$\mathbf{\Gamma} = \left(\mathrm{diag}(E[\alpha_i]) + E[\beta]\mathcal{I}^{(1)} \right)^{-1} \qquad (22)$$

$$\mathbf{\mu} = E[\beta]\mathbf{\Gamma}\mathcal{I}^{(2)} \qquad (23)$$

$$\tilde{d} = d + \frac{1}{2}\mathcal{I}^{(3)} - E[\mathbf{x}]^T \mathcal{I}^{(2)} + \frac{1}{2}\mathrm{Tr}\left(\mathcal{I}^{(1)} \cdot (\mathbf{\Gamma} + \mathbf{\mu}^T \mathbf{\mu}) \right) \qquad (24)$$

It is obvious that the calculation of required parameters involves three global quantities. However, each sensor only interacts solely with its neighbors in the distributed scenario, thus the global quantities $\mathcal{I}^{(1)}, \mathcal{I}^{(2)}, \mathcal{I}^{(3)}$ cannot be calculated locally. It is noted that these global information quantities can also be redetermined by averaging the local quantities from all nodes in Eq. (21).

$$\bar{\mathcal{I}}^{(1)} = \frac{1}{K}\sum_{k=1}^{K} \mathcal{I}_k^{(1)}$$

$$\bar{\mathcal{I}}^{(2)} = \frac{1}{K}\sum_{k=1}^{K} \mathcal{I}_k^{(2)}$$

$$\bar{\mathcal{I}}^{(3)} = \frac{1}{K}\sum_{k=1}^{K} \mathcal{I}_k^{(3)} \qquad (25)$$

Note that the redefinition of global quantities has no impact on the parameter approximation in Eqs. (17) and (18d). To obtain the global average at each node, an average consensus filter suggested in [15] can be employed to approximate the global information quantities defined in Eq. (25). Particularly, the local information quantities possessed by each node are interchanged with their neighbors, then the global average is approximated asymptotically at each node depending upon the local information quantities input from others by using consensus filer. Hence, the DVSBL algorithm can be developed by employing such average consensus filter.

According to [15], a consensus filter can be formulated by following continuous compact form

$$\dot{\xi}_k = \sum_{l\in\mathcal{N}_k} (\xi_l - \xi_k) + \sum_{l\in\mathcal{N}_k\cup k} (u_l - \xi_k) \tag{26}$$

where ξ_k is the filter state of node k, which approximates the filter input u_l. The discrete-time form of consensus filter suggested in [15] is as follows:

$$\xi_k^{t+1} = \xi_k^t + \eta^t \left[\sum_{l\in\mathcal{N}_k} (\xi_l^t - \xi_k^t) + \sum_{l\in\mathcal{N}_k\cup k} (u_l^t - \xi_k^t) \right] \tag{27}$$

where the superscript t denotes the number of iteration; η is the updating rate and should be

$$\eta^t \le \frac{1}{d_{max}}$$

$$\sum_{t=1}^{\infty} \eta^t = \infty$$

$$\sum_{t=1}^{\infty} (\eta)^2 < \infty \tag{28}$$

Equation (28) is the stableness condition of the discrete consensus filter according to the Gershgorin theorem[16]. Thus, the filtering algorithm can be carried out in a distributed manner if the averages Eq. (25) can be obtained by every node. Before the distributed algorithm is presented, we use $u_k^t = \{\mathcal{I}_k^{(1)}, \mathcal{I}_k^{(2)}, \mathcal{I}_k^{(3)}\}$ to denote the local information quantities in the node k, and ξ_k^t denote the estimated global information quantities. Here, both u_k^t and ξ_k^t are referred as vector. In particular, the vector factors $\xi_k^t(1)$, $\xi_k^t(2)$, $\xi_k^t(3)$ are the approximations of $\bar{\mathcal{I}}^{(1)}, \bar{\mathcal{I}}^{(2)}, \bar{\mathcal{I}}^{(3)}$. The consensus filter in node k takes the local quantities u_k and neighbors' approximated global quantities ξ_l^t as inputs. The filter states asymptotically converge to

$$\xi_k^t(1) \rightarrow \frac{1}{K}\sum_{k=1}^{K} \mathcal{I}_k^{(1)}$$

$$\xi_k^t(2) \rightarrow \frac{1}{K}\sum_{k=1}^{K} \mathcal{I}_k^{(2)}$$

$$\xi_k^t(3) \to \frac{1}{K}\sum_{k=1}^{K}\mathcal{I}_k^{(3)} \tag{29}$$

Simultaneously, the hyperparameters $\{\tilde{a}_{k,i}, \tilde{b}_{k,i}, \tilde{c}_k, \tilde{d}_k, \Gamma_k, \mu_k\}$ at each node will be approached by their estimates $\{\hat{a}_{k,i}, \hat{b}_{k,i}, \hat{c}_k, \hat{d}_k, \hat{\Gamma}_k, \mu_k\}$, as the exact global information quantity vector is quantity vector approached by its estimated value. Thus

$$\hat{\Gamma}_k^t = \left(\text{diag}(E[\alpha_{k,i}^t]) + E[\beta_k^t]K\xi_k^t(1)\right)^{-1} \tag{30a}$$

$$\hat{\mu}_k^t = E[\beta_k^t]\,\hat{\Gamma}_k^t\,K\xi_k^t(2) \tag{30b}$$

$$\hat{a}_{k,i}^t = a + \frac{1}{2} \tag{30c}$$

$$\hat{b}_{k,i}^t = b + \frac{E[x_{k,i}^2]}{2} \tag{30d}$$

$$\hat{c}_k^t = c + \frac{M}{2} \tag{30e}$$

$$\begin{aligned}\hat{d}_k^t &= d + \frac{1}{2}K\xi_k^t(3) - E[\mathbf{x}_k]^T K\xi_k^t(2)\\ &\quad + \frac{1}{2}\text{Tr}\left(K\xi_k^t(1)\cdot\left(\hat{\Gamma}_k^t + \hat{\mu}_k^{t^T}\hat{\mu}_k^t\right)\right)\end{aligned} \tag{30f}$$

where the according moments are given by

$$E[\mathbf{x}_k] = \hat{\mu}_k^t$$

$$E[x_{k,i}^2] = \hat{\Gamma}_{ii}^t + \hat{\mu}_i^{t^2}$$

$$E[\alpha_{k,i}^t] = \hat{a}_{k,i}^t / \hat{b}_{k,i}^t \tag{31}$$

$$E[\beta_k^t] = \hat{c}_k^t / \hat{d}_k^t$$

Heretofore, the DVSBL algorithm has been developed above.

5   Simulations

In this section, to verify the performance of the proposed algorithm for distributed WSNs, without loss of generality, we consider a network with 6 nodes, which is represented by an undirected graph $\mathcal{G} = (\mathcal{V}, \mathcal{E}, \mathcal{A})$ with the set of nodes $\mathcal{A} = (1, 2, 3, 4, 5, 6)$, the set of edges

$E = \{(1,2),(1,4),(1,6),(2,3),(2,5),$
$(3,4),(3,6),(4,1),(4,5),(5,2),(5,6),(6,1),(6,3)\}$, and the adjacency matrix

$$
\mathcal{A} = \begin{bmatrix}
0 & 1 & 0 & 1 & 0 & 1 \\
1 & 0 & 1 & 0 & 1 & 0 \\
0 & 1 & 0 & 1 & 0 & 1 \\
1 & 0 & 1 & 0 & 1 & 0 \\
0 & 1 & 0 & 1 & 0 & 1 \\
1 & 0 & 1 & 0 & 1 & 0
\end{bmatrix}
\tag{32}
$$

In this example, the signal $\mathbf{x} \in \mathbb{R}^{256}$ is assumed to be sparse itself. There are altogether 10 non-zero elements $\mathbf{x}\{i\} \neq 0$ in the sparse signal, where i is the index of support and $\mathbf{x}\{i\}$ denote the value of support. Here, the index and value are unknown and sampled over $i \sim U_i[1, 256]$ and $\mathbf{x}\{i\} \sim \mathcal{N}(0, 5^2)$, respectively. We randomly generate a set of 12×256 measurement matrices $\{\mathbf{A}_k, k = 1, 2, \ldots, 6\}$ from the standard independent and identically distributed (iid) Gaussian ensemble. Then, we generate the local measurements $\{\mathbf{z}_k, k = 1, 2, \ldots, 6\}$ for each node. The received measurements are corrupted by additive zero-mean Gaussian noise to yield signal noise ratio(SNR), i.e., $\frac{\|\mathbf{A}_k \mathbf{x}_k\|_2^2}{\|\mathbf{w}_k\|_2^2}$, of 20 dB. the updating rate of the consensus filter is chosen as $\eta = \frac{1}{d_{max} + \tau t}, 0 < \tau < 1$.

The convergence rate of algorithm is given in Figs. 1 and 2, which show the local quantity $\mathcal{I}_k^{(3)}$ versus the number of iteration and Normalized MSE(i.e., $\|\mathbf{x} - \hat{\mathbf{x}}_k\|_2 / \|\mathbf{x}\|_2$) versus iteration, respectively. As expected, our numerical simulation results confirm that all the nodes reach a consensus on the local quantity and estimate of sparse signals as the iteration increasing. Moreover, it is easy to see that both the NMSE and local quantity have almost identical convergence rate.

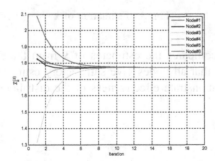

Fig. 1. Evolution of global information quantity $I_k^{(3)}$

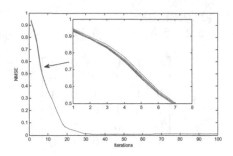

Fig. 2. Normalized MSE versus iteration

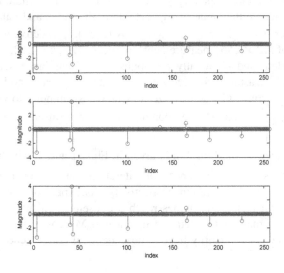

Fig. 3. Estimation of **x**

In addition, Fig. 3 compares the estimates of **x** from three nodes using DVSBL algorithm. It is obvious that all nodes give satisfactory estimates of the actual sparse signal. These results demonstrate effectiveness of the distributed sparse signal reconstruction algorithm.

6   Conclusion

In this paper, we tackle the sparse signal reconstruction in WSNs, where all the nodes cooperate and interact with each other without centralized coordination. A distributed variational Bayesian algorithm is proposed for full Bayesian system model. First, we have addressed the centralized scenario, where all node measurements are available at fusion center. In this case, a centralized approach is derived to facilitate the design of distributed counterpart. Next, a distributed reconstruction algorithm is obtained by means of consensus filter due to its efficiency and low-complexity. In particular, there exists merely one-step average-consensus iteration in each VB update. To evaluate the effectiveness of the proposed algorithm, the numerical simulations on both synthetic and real data demonstrate that the proposed algorithm has comparable recovery performance and convergence properties.

References

1. Donoho, D.L.: Compressed sensing. IEEE Trans. Inf. Theor. **52**(4), 1289–1306 (2006)
2. Baraniuk, R.G., Candes, E., Nowak, R., Vetterli, M., et al.: Compressive sampling. IEEE Sig. Process. Mag. **25**(2), 12–13 (2008)
3. Brunelli, D., Caione, C.: Sparse recovery optimization in wireless sensor networks with a sub-nyquist sampling rate. Sensors **15**(7), 16654–16673 (2015)
4. Shen, J., Tan, H.W., Wang, J.W., et al.: A novel routing protocol providing good transmission reliability in underwater sensor networks. J. Internet Technol. **16**(1), 171–178 (2015)
5. Xie, S.D., Wang, Y.X.: Construction of tree nework with limited delivery latency in homogeneous wireless sensor networks. Wirel. Pers. Commun. **78**(1), 231–246 (2014)
6. Weng, Y., Xiao, W.D., Xie, L.H.: Diffusion-based EM algorithm for distributed estimation of gaussian mixtures in wireless sensor networks. Senosrs **11**(6), 6297–6316 (2011)
7. Patterson, S., Eldar, Y., Keidar, I.: Distributed compressed sensing for static and time-varying networks. IEEE Trans. Sig. Process. **62**(19), 4931–4946 (2013)
8. Mota, J.F.C., Xavier, J.M.F., Aguiar, P.M.Q., et al.: Distributed basis pursuit. IEEE Trans. Sig. Process. **60**(4), 1942–1956 (2012)
9. Mateosm, G., Bazerquem, J.A., Giannakism, G.B.: Distributed sparse linear regression. IEEE Trans. Sig. Process. **58**(10), 5262–5276 (2010)
10. Tipping, M.E.: Sparse bayesian learning and the relevance vecotor machine. J. Mach. Learn. Res. **1**(3), 211–244 (2001)
11. Ji, S., Xue, Y., Carin, L.: Bayesian compressive sensing. IEEE Trans. Sig. Process. **56**(6), 2346–2356 (2008)
12. Bishop, C.M., Tipping, M.E.: Variationnal relevance vector machines. In: Proceedings of the Sixteenth Conference on Uncertainty in Artificial Intelligence, vol. 28, no. 3, pp. 46–53 (2000)
13. Sayed, A.H.: Adaptive networks. In: Proceedings of the IEEE, vol. 102, pp. 460–497 (2014)
14. Zhu, H., Leung, H., He, Z.: State estimation in unknown non-gaussian measurement noise using variational bayesian technique. IEEE Trans. Aerosp. Electron. Syst. **49**(4), 2601–2614 (2013)
15. Kingston, D., Beard, R.W.: Discrete-time average-consensus under switching network topologies. In: American Control Conference, p. 6 (2006)
16. Horn, R.A., Johnson, C.R.: Matrix Analysis. Cambridge University Press, Cambridge (1986)

An Energy-Efficiency Routing Scheme Based on Clusters with a Mobile Sink for WSNs

Xiaodong Liu and Qi Liu[✉]

School of Computing, Edinburgh Napier University, 10 Colinton Road,
Edinburgh EH10 5DT, UK
q.liu@napier.ac.uk

Abstract. With the development of microelectronic devices and the radio, the application of WSN is more popular and can be applied in the various areas, which has attracted scholars. However, the requirements of performance for WSNs are becoming great in terms of reducing the energy consumption and prolonging the network lifetime. In the paper, an energy-efficiency routing scheme based on clusters with a mobile sink which consist of six parts is proposed. Through the simulation, we have demonstrated that the proposed routing algorithm has a higher performance which can reduce energy consumption on WSNs.

Keywords: Energy-efficiency · Routing algorithm · WSN · Sink

1 Introduction

A wireless sensor network can be reviewed as a large-scale, self-organization and multi-hops communication network. It consists of a large number of sensor nodes which are small and cheap. Development of the microelectronic devices and the radio make the application of WSN [1] become broad which can be applied in military, healthcare, environmental [2], traffic and other civilian areas [3].

However, it also has grown a higher requirements on the performance of WSN in term of energy efficiency, the network lifetime and the rate of the packets delivered successfully [4]. Many scholars making the research on WSN have been a breakthrough continuously, though these constraints restrict the development of WSN, and make the WSN become more prefect [5]. We briefly introduce many changes of the way of data transmission in WSN below.

On the WSNs, there are two categories which are the traditional methods and the layered approaches on data transmission. Traditionally, sensor node only transfer the data to base station or user with a form of single hop. Although the source can transfer directly to the base station (BS), the energy consumption of the nodes is more serious, and these nodes are prone to fail, so it has a significant influence on the performance of WSN. Therefore, the communication mode of multi-hops is introduced that data is transmitted from source to BS indirectly. Compared with the traditional mode, the mode is more energy-efficient and can prolong the network life. For the further improvements, the sink which has more energy than general nodes is introduced into WSN. The sink

X. Sun et al. (Eds.): ICCCS 2017, Part I, LNCS 10602, pp. 450–459, 2017.
https://doi.org/10.1007/978-3-319-68505-2_39

is responsible for collecting the data from sources and aggregating the data, and then transmitting these aggregated data to BS or user. This kind of transmission mode can obviously save energy and prolong the network lifetime. It is can be said that the introduction of the sink is a significant breakthrough for WSNs. With the further research, the mode of the sink which can move in the network is proposed [6], so that it can save energy compared with the static sink in the network. For the movement of the sink [7], the assumption is that the sink move with a constant speed and along the predetermined routing at the beginning. The source can predict [8] the mobile trajectory of the sink and transmit data to the position predicted [9] advance, when the sink moves near the position, it can receive the data directly. These modes of data transmissions can save energy to a great extent. With the through research, the approach that multi sinks [10] can be used in network is proposed which can significantly increase the efficiency of data transmission and reduce the delay.

In the paper, we propose an energy-efficiency routing algorithm based on clusters with a mobile sink. In our scheme, data transmission is in the communication mode of multi-hops and sensor nodes are deployed at random in an environment of rectangular. The optimal routing will be acquired through our scheme. Compared with other routing algorithms [11–13], our proposed algorithm can improve the efficiency of data transmission on WSNs.

The rest of the paper is organized as follows. The system model is described in Sect. 2. Section 3, we describe our proposed algorithm in detail. Then the simulation and evaluation are presented in Sects. 4 and 5 concludes our paper.

2   System Model

In the section, the system model that we used in our scheme is introduced. First, many basic assumptions of the system model are introduced, then the network model is presented, finally we describe the energy model.

2.1   Basic Assumption

Before describing the network and energy model, many assumptions in our scheme are proposed as follows:

- All sensor nodes are randomly deployed in a regular rectangle network.
- For distinguishing with sensor nodes, each node has the unique identifier.
- In our scheme, the energy consumption of data transmission between the sink and the BS can be ignored.
- In the same region, if one node is selected as the relay node, then it cannot be the major node.
- In the first round of the routing, the energy of the whole nodes is enough to support data transmission of this round.

2.2 Network Model

The WSN is formed through randomly deploying the sensor nodes into a rectangle, which is expressed as a graph 'G = <V, K>' where V represents the each node and K represents the weight between two adjacent nodes. For example, k(i, j) represent the distance between the node i and it's adjacent node j. Then, the network will be divided into several regions and the regulation of classification will be introduced in detail in Sect. 3.

2.3 Energy Model

In our scheme, the first radio energy model is adopted. Then, many parameters used in our proposed algorithm are introduced and their meaning as showing in the following Table 1.

Table 1. The parameters and their descriptions

Notation	Description
E_0	The initial energy of general sensor node
E_{elec}	The energy consumption of running the radio device (nj/bit)
L	The length of data transmission(bit)
N	The total number of sensor nodes
V	The speed of the mobile sink
d_{ij}	The distance between node i and node j
d_0	A distance threshold that we set

The energy consumption of data transmission is based on the distance between the node i and the node j, so we set up a distance threshold called d_0, if the distance between the node i and the node j is less than the d0, then a free space model is adopted to calculate the energy consumption by the d_{ij}^2, otherwise we adopt the multi-path fading channel model to calculate the energy consumption by the d_{ij}^4. So the energy consumption of data transmission can be expressed as follows based on the distance between two nodes.

$$E_{Tx}(l, d) = \begin{cases} lF_{elec} + l\varepsilon_{fs}d^2, & d < d_0 \\ lE_{elec} + l\varepsilon_{mp}d^4, & d >= d_0 \end{cases} \tag{1}$$

And the energy consumption of receiving data can use the following formula to express.

$$E_{Rx}(l) = lE_{elec} \tag{2}$$

Hence, the total energy consumption of transmission and receiving data can be expressed as

$$E = E_{Tx} + E_{Rx} \tag{3}$$

3 Our Proposed Algorithm

In the paper, an energy-efficiency routing algorithm based on clusters with a mobile sink is proposed. In this section, our proposed scheme is described in detail as follows, which consists of six parts.

3.1 Network Partition

In this part, the regulation of network partition is described and it is a reference to [12]. In our paper, the number of the regions which is said to k is determined by the 5% of the sensor nodes and k can be expressed as the following formula:

$$k = \begin{cases} 4, & N \times 5\% <= 5 \\ 9, & 5 < N \times 5\% <= 10 \\ 16, & 10 < N \times 5\% <= 15 \\ 25, & 15 < N \times 5\% <= 20 \\ \cdots\cdots\cdots \end{cases} \tag{4}$$

3.2 Mobile Strategy of the Sink

The sink moves at the fixed speed along the predetermined routing in the deployed sensor networks. The sink can receive data request from the base station, and then begins to select the relay node. When the relay node is determined, the sink will sojourn at position near the relay node and collects the data from the source according to 3.6.

3.3 Selection of Relay Node

In our scheme, the selection of the relay node has two stages, the first stage is to select these nodes of the distance inside r0 between the sink and it adjacent node through the signal strength of nodes with the RSSI, the second is to select the maximum residual energy node as the relay node among these nodes according to the first stage. If the residual energy of nodes is the same, the node with the minimum identifier is as the relay node.

3.4 Selection of Major Node

Selection of the major node is dependent on the residual energy and the identifier of the node. First, the node which near to the center of the region can be regarded as the major node, and then it broadcasts a data packet which includes residual energy and identifier to neighbors. It needs to compare the residual energy and the identifier with neighbors for selecting the most suitable major node. If the residual energy of neighbor nodes is less than it, then it continues to compare with other adjacent nodes until all the nodes are involved in the comparison.

3.5   Routing Determining

In this part, the routing determining is described. When relay node is determined by the sink, the sink will broadcast the data packet named that which has the data to the whole network through the relay node. The data packet includes not only the requested data information, but also the current position of the sink. If a node receives the data packet, it will reply the packet of 'I have the packet' to the relay node along the reverse path and record the location of the relay node. At this time, it can be regarded as the source.

Since the source is determined, it sends a packet to next hop which is determined by the following regulation on the direction of the relay node according to the location of the relay node and itself.

The regulation of the routing is as follows:

1. Calculating the distance between the source and it adjacent node to determine which node is the nearest to the source according to the signal strength of RSSI, then adding the identifier of the node that is nearest to the source into the routing table;
2. Considering the node according to (1), the source sends a packet to the node which concludes updated information. the node also calculate the distance between the node and adjacent nodes to judge which node is closest to the node, then adding the identifier of new node in to the routing table;
3. Considering the new node according to (2), the node sends the packet to the new node which concludes the latest hop count, the distance and the routing table;
4. Repeating 2 and 3, until taking the all node on the direction of the relay node into account. At this time, the relay node sends a data packet of conformation which is set as OK along the reverse of the routing to show that the relay node has known the routing and the source can transmit the data to the relay node along the routing.

3.6   Data Transmission

In this part, the regulation of data transmission for our scheme is detailed described from the source to the sink as follows:

(1) When the region which the sink sojourns at and the region that the source located is the same, the major node is responsible for collecting the data from the source and aggregating them in together. Then the shortest routing is constructed from the major node to the relay node. The aggregated data is transmitted from the major node to the relay node along the routing, finally the data is transmitted to the sink by the relay node;
(2) When the region which the sink sojourns at and the region that the source located is not the same, but the two regions are adjacent. First the major node of the region which the source locates in collects the data from the source and aggregate them. There are two kinds ways of next data transmission which are shown on Figs. 1 and 2;
  - With major node: first is that the major node directly transmits the aggregated data to the major node of the region which the relay node locates in. When the major node of the region which the relay node locates in receives the aggregated data, then the sink collects these data.

- Without major node: second is that data transmission is without the major node of the region where the relay node located. It is means that the relay node directly collects the data from the major node. In this case, the data is directly transmitted from the major node to the relay node, and finally is sent to the sink.

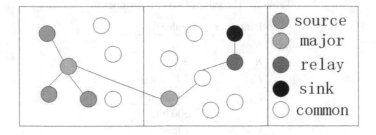

Fig. 1. Data transmission with major node

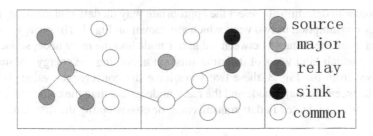

Fig. 2. Data transmission without major node

(3) When the region which the sink sojourns at and the region that the source located is not the same, but the two regions are not adjacent. First for the each region, the major node of these regions collects the data from the source and aggregates them together. Then the routing is constructed by these major nodes in addition to the major node of the region which the relay node located. The aggregated data is transmitted from the first major node to the major node of the last hop region which the relay node located. Finally, the sink collects the aggregated data according to (2).

4   Performance Evaluation

In this section, the simulation is conducted on the MATLAB and the experimental results is evaluated and analyzed for the performance of the routing scheme.

4.1 Simulation Environment

In our experiment, the number of the sensor nodes is set to 500, and then the value of several parameters we used is shown on the Table 2

Table 2. The value of several parameters

Parameter	Value
N	500
R	300 m
E_0	2 J
E_{elec}	50 nJ/bit
l	500 bits
v	1 m/s

4.2 Performance Evaluation

Here, in order to determine to select the appropriate way on data transmission, through the energy consumption of two ways which are shown on Fig. 3. The energy consumption depends on the distance between the major node and the relay node, so judging to how to use which kind ways of data transmission according the energy consumption. We can see from the Fig. 3, these two ways have the convergence value. When the distance between the major node and the relay node is less than the convergence value, the second way is adopted in data transmission, or else adopting the first way.

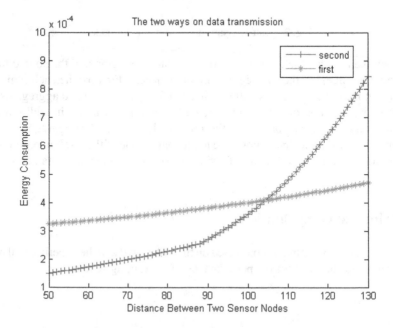

Fig. 3. The two ways on data transmission

For our scheme, these constraints of the residual energy in our proposed algorithm are compared with that of the MEAR [11], VGDRA [12] and IAR [13], since these factors are important for evaluating the performance of the network.

The residual energy of four algorithms is compared which are shown on Fig. 4. The residual energy is determined through the rounds of the data transmission.

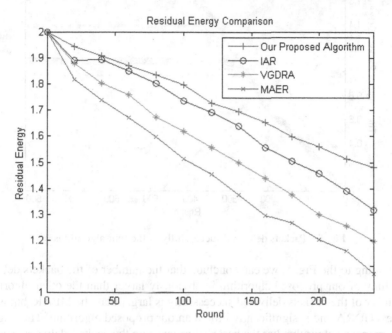

Fig. 4. Residual energy of the four algorithms

Through the Fig. 4, we can see that the residual energy of nodes that we proposed algorithm is more than residual energy of other algorithms. That is means the energy consumption on the network for our proposed algorithm is less compared with other algorithms. It is obviously that the energy consumes faster than our proposed algorithm for the MEAR.

The Fig. 5 shows the comparison of the packets delivered successfully for the four algorithms. The number of packets delivered successfully also is an important factor to measure the performance of the network. Here, through judging the number of the packets delivered successfully after many rounds of data transmission, to compare the four algorithms on the performance of the network.

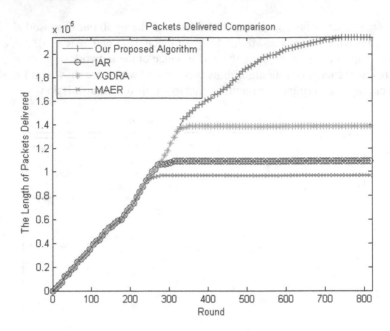

Fig. 5. Packets delivered successfully of the four algorithms

According to the Fig. 5, we can conclude that the number of the packets delivered successfully of our proposed algorithm is obviously larger than the other algorithms. The number of the packets delivered successfully is larger than the MEAR, but is little than the VGDRA and is significantly little than our proposed algorithm. This suggests that our proposed algorithm has the best performance on the packets delivered successfully compared with other algorithms.

5   Conclusion

In this paper, the energy-efficiency routing scheme based on clusters with a mobile sink for WSNs is proposed. Compared with other algorithms, our proposed scheme has the less energy consumption. So it is effective to improve the performance on the sensor network.

However, it is not enough for conducting the evaluation in an ideal environment. We ignore several factors and many parameters. In the future, we will try our best to take these factors into account for the further research.

Acknowledgment.   This work has received funding from the European Union's Horizon 2020 research and innovation programme under the Marie Sklodowska-Curie grant agreement No 701697.

References

1. Zhiguo, Q., John, K., Sebastian, R., Faisal, Z., Xiaojun, W.: Multilevel pattern mining architecture for automatic network monitoring in heterogeneous wireless communication networks. China Commun. **13**(7), 108–116 (2016)
2. Qianping, W., Yan, Z., Yu, S., Hongmei, L., Ke, W.: A routing algorithm based on mobile agent for mine monitoring. In: IEEE Computer Society, pp. 16–21 (2009)
3. Jin, W., Yue, Y., Jianwei, Z., Sungyoung, L., Robert, S.S.: Mobility based energy efficient and multi-sink algorithms for consumer home networks. IEEE Trans. Consum. Electron. **59**(1), 77–84 (2013)
4. Xiaobing, W., Guihai, C.: Dual-sink: using mobile and static sinks for lifetime improvement in wireless sensor networks. In: 16th International Conference on Computer Communications and Networks, Honolulu, Hawaii, USA, pp. 1297–1302 (2007)
5. Chufu, W., Jau-Der, S., Bohan, P., Tinyu, W.: A network lifetime enhancement method for sink relocation and its analysis in wireless sensor networks. IEEE Sens. J. **14**(6), 1932–1943 (2014)
6. Azadeh, L., Abolfazl, H., Arash, E.: Extending directed diffusion routing algorithm to support sink mobility in wireless sensor networks. In: 9th IEEE Malaysia International Conference on Communications, pp. 541–546 (2009)
7. Hyungjoo, L., Jeongcheol, L., Ssungmin, O., Sangha, K.: Data dissemination scheme for wireless sensor networks with mobile sink groups. In: IEEE International Symposium on Personal Indoor & Mobile Radio Communications, vol. 45(2), pp. 1911–1916 (2010)
8. Hamidreza, S., Kwanwu, C., Fazel, N.: An energy-efficient mobile-sink path selection strategy for wireless sensor networks. IEEE Trans. Veh. Technol. **63**(5), 2407–2419 (2014)
9. Bin, G., Victor, S.: A robust regularization path algorithm for v-support vector classification. IEEE Trans. Neural Netw. Learn. Syst. **28**(5), 1241–1248 (2017)
10. Dongliang, X., Xiaojie, W., Dan, L., Jia, S.: Multiple mobile sinks data dissemination mechanism for large scale wireless sensor network. China Commun. **11**(13), 1–8 (2014)
11. Elhadi, S., Xinyu, X., Haroon, M.: Mobile agent for efficient routing among source nodes in wireless sensor networks. In: International Conference on Autonomic & Autonomous Systems, Athens, Greece, pp. 39–39 (2007)
12. Abdul, W.K., Hanan, A., Mohammad, A.R., Javed, B.: VGDRA: a virtual grid-based dynamic routes adjustment scheme for mobile sink-based wireless sensor networks. IEEE Sens. J. **15**(1), 526–534 (2015)
13. Jae-Wan, K., Jeong-Sik, I., Kyeong, H., Jin-Woo, K., Doo, S.E.: An intelligent agent-based routing structure for mobile sinks in WSNs. IEEE Trans. Consumer Electron. **56**(4), 2310–2316 (2010)

Energy-Efficient Power Control and Resource Allocation for D2D Communications in Underlaying Cellular Networks

Xiaoxiao Guan[(⊠)], Xiangping Zhai, Jiabin Yuan, and Hu Liu

College of Computer Science and Technology,
Nanjing University of Aeronautics and Astronautics, Nanjing, China
{gxiaoxiao,blueicezhaixp,ok,liuhu}@nuaa.edu.cn

Abstract. In this paper, we investigate the energy-efficient power control and resource allocation problem in the context of underlaying device-to-device (D2D) communication, which aims to maximize the energy efficiency (EE) of D2D users with power and subchannel optimized while providing the quality of service (QoS) provisioning of the cellular users. We formulate it as a non-convex optimization problem in fractional form and transform it from power of all users to the joint power and subchannel allocation of D2D users. By the properties of fractional programming, we then transfer it into subtractive form and propose an energy-efficient iterative algorithm. To optimize the power and subchannel, we divide the subchannel allocation into two cases, which could be solved by penalty function approach and dual decomposition as well as sub-gradient method respectively. Accordingly, we propose a dual-based algorithm. Numerical results demonstrate that the proposed algorithms outperform a conventional algorithm in terms of energy efficiency.

Keywords: D2D communication · Energy efficiency · Power and subchannel allocation · Fractional programming

1 Introduction

The forecast in [1] indicates that 90% of the world's population will have mobile coverage by 2018. It is essential for us to consider that in the years to come, not only everyone but also everything is expected to be connected and to communicate by Internet of Things (IoT). However, the exponential growth of wireless users and their traffic demand have triggered the shift towards the fifth generation (5G) mobile network, which is envisioned to have potential advantages such as improved energy efficiency, high data rate, reduced latency, etc. To this end, the promising technique termed D2D takes this responsibility [2–7].

D2D communication enables that the two devices in close proximity can communicate directly without traversing the central base station and it gains various benefits in contrast to the typical infrastructure-based system with the mobile services based on proximity increase exponentially. First, it offloads the

© Springer International Publishing AG 2017
X. Sun et al. (Eds.): ICCCS 2017, Part I, LNCS 10602, pp. 460–471, 2017.
https://doi.org/10.1007/978-3-319-68505-2_40

proximal traffic and frees both the uplink and downlink from the core network. Second, the short transmission link brings about lower transmit power, reduced interference as well as battery power savings among devices. Further, the end-to-end delay and the performance of the cellular network such as throughput and energy efficiency can be enhanced. Third, as the D2D data are not conveyed via Internet clouds but on the intended services, it provides the inherent security. Last but not the least, D2D communication can extent the coverage of cellular network [8,9]. Generally, D2D communication can be divided into two parts: outband D2D communication and inband D2D communication. The former uses unlicensed spectrum and the latter occurs on the licensed band, which can be further categorized as overlay and underlay [10,11]. However, paramount challenges needed to be dealt with for taking full advantage of D2D communication. The environment concerns as well as battery constraints become the motivation of green wireless communication networks. To this end, there are some related works focus on green design in D2D-based networks. The authors in [12] presented a joint algorithm to minimize power consumption in OFDMA-based wireless networks with D2D communications. In [13], the authors explored the maximum sum rate through minimum transmit power in D2D communication underlaying single-cell cellular networks. However, one of the main design concerns of making D2D communication efficient and reliable is to improve the energy efficiency. The authors in [14] put forward a distributed interference-aware algorithm to maximize the EE of individual D2D and cellular user. The resource and power are optimized to maximize the EE of overall D2D communications in [15]. In [16], the authors addressed the minimum weighted EE maximization problem of D2D links by three resource allocation algorithms with different complexity.

Motivated by the aforementioned reviews, we address the EE maximization problem of all D2D users with power and resource optimized. It is formulated as a non-convex problem in fractional and transformed into subtractive form further. Then an iterative energy-efficient algorithm is presented. We discuss the subchannel allocation into one-to-one and one-to-many policies, which could be solved by penalty function approach and dual decomposition as well as sub-gradient method respectively. We then propose a dual-based algorithm. The remainder of this paper is organized as follows: In Sect. 2, we describe the system model of D2D communication underlaying cellular network. In Sect. 3, the energy-efficient power control and resource allocation scheme is presented. Section 4 gives the simulation results, followed by the conclusion in Sect. 5.

2   System Model and Problem Formulation

2.1   System Scenario

In this paper, we consider the uplink resource allocation scenario of a single-cell system, which is composed of the base station, multiple cellular users (CUs) and D2D users, where by one D2D user we mean a transmitter-receiver pair. All users are typically hand-held services with limited battery life. The D2D users operate as an underlay and we assume that the spectrum resource of CUs are allowed to be reused by D2D users. The CUs are assigned orthogonal subchannels to eliminate the co-channel interference between them. Besides, the interference level from D2D user to base station tends to be very low due to the low transmit power of the D2D transmitter and the distance between them, so we don't take it into account here.

Let $\mathcal{M} = \{1, \cdots, M\}$, $\mathcal{N} = \{1, \cdots, N\}$, $\mathcal{L} = \{1, \cdots, L\}$ denote the sets of the CUs, the D2D users as well as the orthogonal subchannels and $M = |\mathcal{M}|$, $N = |\mathcal{N}|$, $L = |\mathcal{L}|$ represent the numbers of them in the considered single cell, respectively. Here $|\mathcal{S}|$ denotes the cardinality of the set $\mathcal{S}$ and $N \leq M = L$. We label the CUs, D2D users and orthogonal subchannels by lower-case letters m, n and l ($\forall m \in \mathcal{M}, \forall n \in \mathcal{N}, \forall l \in \mathcal{L}$) respectively. We assume that the subchannel allocation for CUs has been predetermined and without loss of generality, the m-th CU occupies the l-th orthogonal subchannel. We are interested in the energy-efficient power control and resource allocation for the D2D users.

The power vector of all users is $\mathbf{p} = [\mathbf{p}_c, \mathbf{p}_d]$, where $\mathbf{p}_c = [p_{c1}^1, \cdots, p_{cM}^L]$ for M CUs and $\mathbf{p}_d = [\mathbf{p}_{d1}, \cdots, \mathbf{p}_{dN}]$ for N D2D users. Here, $\mathbf{p}_{dn} = [p_{dn}^1, \cdots, p_{dn}^L]$. The p_{cm}^l and p_{dn}^l denote the transmit power allocations of the m-th CU and the n-th D2D user on the l-th subchannel, respectively. The subchannel allocation vector for all D2D users is $\mathbf{x} = [\mathbf{x}_1, \cdots, \mathbf{x}_N]$, where the $\mathbf{x}_n = [x_n^l, \cdots, x_n^L]$ describes the subchannel allocation decisions for the n-th D2D user and $x_n^l \in \{0,1\}$. Here, $x_n^l = 1$ represents that the l-th subchannel is allocated to the n-th D2D user and $x_n^l = 0$, otherwise. The following notations are related to the Signal-to-Interference-and-Noise Ratio (SINR), which is defined as the ratio of the received signal power to the sum of the interference signal power and additive noise power:

- h_{mm}^l: channel gain from the m-th CU to the m-th CU on the l-th subchannel.
- h_{mn}^l: interference channel gain from the m-th CU to the receiver of the n-th D2D user on the l-th subchannel.
- h_{nm}^l: interference channel gain from the transmitter of the n-th D2D user to the m-th CU on the l-th subchannel.
- h_{nn}^l: channel gain from the transmitter to the receiver of the n-th D2D user on the l-th subchannel.
- σ^l: white Gaussian noise power at the user on the l-th subchannel, which is assumed to be same for all.

Then, the SINR of the m-th CU and the n-th D2D user on the l-th subchannel can be written respectively as:

$$\text{SINR}_{cm}^l(\mathbf{p}, \mathbf{x}) = \frac{p_{cm}^l h_{mm}^l}{\sum\limits_{n \in \mathcal{N}} x_n^l p_{dn}^l h_{nm}^l + \sigma^l}, \quad \text{SINR}_{dn}^l(\mathbf{p}, \mathbf{x}) = \frac{p_{dn}^l h_{nn}^l}{p_{cm}^l h_{mn}^l + \sigma^l}, \quad (1)$$

where the $\sum\limits_{n \in \mathcal{N}} x_n^l p_{dn}^l h_{nm}^l$ is the interference to CU due to the D2D users reusing this subchannel, and the $p_{cm}^l h_{mn}^l$ is the interference to D2D user from the CU.

Therefore, based on the Shannon capacity formula, the achievable data rates normalized by the subchannel bandwidth of them can be given respectively as:

$$R_{cm}^l(\mathbf{p}, \mathbf{x}) = \log_2\left(1 + \mathsf{SINR}_{cm}^l(\mathbf{p}, \mathbf{x})\right), \quad R_{dn}^l(\mathbf{p}, \mathbf{x}) = \log_2\left(1 + \mathsf{SINR}_{dn}^l(\mathbf{p}, \mathbf{x})\right).$$
(2)

The total power consumption of the n-th D2D user including two parts: the transmission power and the circuit power. It can be expressed as:

$$P_{dn}^{total}(\mathbf{p}_d, \mathbf{x}) = \frac{1}{\eta}\sum_{l\in\mathcal{L}} x_n^l p_{dn}^l + 2P_{cir},$$
(3)

where the $0 < \eta < 1$ is a factor reflecting the compensation for the power amplifier loss. The P_{cir} accounts for the circuit power, which is a power offset independent on radiated power and incurred by all circuit blocks along the signal path and battery backup of both the transmitter and receiver of D2D user. Without loss of generality, we assume they are same for all D2D users.

2.2   Problem Formulation

Optimization Objective. Let U_{EE} denote the EE of all D2D communications, which is the ratio of sum throughput to total power consumption of D2D users. We assume that $P_{dn}^{total}(\mathbf{p}_d, \mathbf{x}) > 0$ without loss of generality, and we have:

$$U_{EE} = \frac{\sum\limits_{n\in\mathcal{N}}\sum\limits_{l\in\mathcal{L}} x_n^l R_{dn}^l(\mathbf{p}, \mathbf{x})}{\sum\limits_{n\in\mathcal{N}} P_{dn}^{total}(\mathbf{p}_d, \mathbf{x})}.$$
(4)

Constraints. We consider the EE optimization with the following constraints.

(1) Subchannel Allocation Variable Constraint: The subchannel allocation variables are required to be binary, i.e.,

$$x_n^l \in \{0, 1\}, \forall n \in \mathcal{N}, \forall l \in \mathcal{L}.$$
(5)

To limit the interference from D2D users to CUs and guarantee the performance of the CUs, we assume that each subchannel cannot be shared by more than one D2D user. To guarantee the quality of communication of D2D users, we assume that each D2D user can reuse at least one subchannel. So we have:

$$\sum_{n\in\mathcal{N}} x_n^l \leq 1, \forall l \in \mathcal{L}.$$
(6)

$$\sum_{l\in\mathcal{L}} x_n^l \geq 1, \forall n \in \mathcal{N}.$$
(7)

(2) Minimum Data Rate Constraint: It is required to maintain the minimum data rate R_{cm}^{min} of the m-th CU on its l-th allocated subchannel, i.e.,

$$R_{cm}^l(\mathbf{p}, \mathbf{x}) \geq R_{cm}^{min}, \forall m \in \mathcal{M}, \forall l \in \mathcal{L}.$$
(8)

(3) Maximum Transmit Power Constraint: We utilize the non-negative and peak transmit power constraints for individual CU and D2D user respectively:

$$0 \leq p_{cm}^l \leq P_{cm}^{max}, \forall m \in \mathcal{M}, \forall l \in \mathcal{L}, \tag{9}$$

$$0 \leq \sum_{l \in \mathcal{L}} x_n^l p_{dn}^l \leq P_{dn}^{max}, \forall n \in \mathcal{N}, \tag{10}$$

where P_{cm}^{max} and P_{dn}^{max} are the maximum transmit powers of the m-th CU and the n-th D2D user separately, which are assumed to be same without loss of generality. Besides, (10) implies that the assigned power of the n-th D2D user to one subchannel cannot go beyond this threshold naturally, i.e., $0 \leq p_{dn}^l \leq P_{dn}^{max}$.

Optimization Problem. So far, the EE maximization problem of overall D2D users can be mathematically formulated as:

$$\max_{\mathbf{p}, \mathbf{x}} \quad U_{EE} \tag{11}$$

$$\text{s.t.} \quad (5), (6), (7), (8), (9), (10).$$

3   Power Control and Resource Allocation Scheme

The optimization problem (11) falls into the scope of non-linear fractional programming [17] with non-convexity and non-smoothness, thus is hard to solve. Moreover, given the integer assignment variables x_n^l, it is more complicated. To obtain an insight into it, we first investigate the relationship between the CUs with rate requirement satisfied and D2D users. Then we transform the initial problem (11) from the feasible domain $(\mathbf{p}, \mathbf{x})$ to $(\mathbf{p}_d, \mathbf{x})$ for simplicity.

Lemma 1. *If the n-th D2D user reuses the l-th subchannel, then its transmit power on this channel can be expressed as* $p_{dn}^l = \frac{1}{h_{nm}^l}\left(\frac{p_{cm}^l h_{mm}^l}{2^{R_{cm}^{min}} - 1} - \sigma^l\right)$, *where*

$$0 \leq p_{dn}^l \leq \bar{P}_{dn}^{max}, \quad \bar{P}_{dn}^{max} \triangleq \min\left\{P_{dn}^{max}, \frac{1}{h_{nm}^l}\left(\frac{P_{cm}^{max} h_{mm}^l}{2^{R_{cm}^{min}} - 1} - \sigma^l\right)\right\}. \tag{12}$$

Proof. As the min-rate constraint (8) of individual CU must be met at equality and the peak power constraint (9) must be satisfied, we complete the proof [16].

Then, the data rate R_{dn}^l can be rewritten as $\bar{R}_{dn}^l(\mathbf{p}_d) = \log_2$ $\left(1 - \frac{p_{dn}^l}{s_{mn} + t_{mn}p_{dn}^l}\right)$, where $s_{mn} \triangleq \frac{(2^{R_{cm}^{min}} - 1)h_{mn}^l \sigma^l}{h_{mm}^l h_{nn}^l} + \frac{\sigma^l}{h_{nn}^l}$, and $t_{mn} \triangleq \frac{(2^{R_{cm}^{min}} - 1)h_{mn}^l h_{nm}^l}{h_{mm}^l h_{nn}^l}$. Now, we transform the problem (11) into an equivalent fractional form in term of $(\mathbf{p}_d, \mathbf{x})$:

$$\max_{\mathbf{p}_d, \mathbf{x}} \quad \frac{\sum\limits_{n \in \mathcal{N}} \sum\limits_{l \in \mathcal{L}} x_n^l \bar{R}_{dn}^l(\mathbf{p}_d)}{\sum\limits_{n \in \mathcal{N}} P_{dn}^{total}(\mathbf{p}_d, \mathbf{x})} \tag{13}$$

$$\text{s.t.} \quad (5), (6), (7), (9), (10), (12).$$

The objection function in (13) is still in fractional form, so it has no closed-form solution [14]. In order to solve it, we next transform it into an equivalent subtractive form. Let $q^\star$ denote the maximum EE of all D2D users, i.e., $q^\star = \max\limits_{\mathbf{P}_d, \mathbf{x}} \dfrac{\sum\limits_{n \in \mathcal{N}} \sum\limits_{l \in \mathcal{L}} x_n^l \bar{R}_{dn}^l(\mathbf{p}_d)}{\sum\limits_{n \in \mathcal{N}} P_{dn}^{total}(\mathbf{p}_d, \mathbf{x})}$. Let $\mathbf{p}_d^\star$ and $x^\star$ represent the optimal policy of power and subchannel allocations respectively, we have:

Theorem 1. *The maximum EE $q^\star$ is achieved if and only if:*

$$
\max_{\mathbf{P}_d, \mathbf{x}} \left[\sum_{n \in \mathcal{N}} \sum_{l \in \mathcal{L}} x_n^l \bar{R}_{dn}^l(\mathbf{p}_d) - q^\star \sum_{n \in \mathcal{N}} P_{dn}^{total}(\mathbf{p}_d, \mathbf{x}) \right]
$$
$$
= \sum_{n \in \mathcal{N}} \sum_{l \in \mathcal{L}} x_n^{l\star} \bar{R}_{dn}^l(\mathbf{p}_d^\star) - q^\star \sum_{n \in \mathcal{N}} P_{dn}^{total}(\mathbf{p}_d^\star, \mathbf{x}^\star) = 0. \tag{14}
$$

Proof. Such equivalence has been proved and utilized by some previous studies on non-linear fractional programming, please referring to [18,19] for its proof.

It can be seen from Theorem 1 that there exits an equivalent objective function in subtractive form for the initial problem in fractional form in the considered case. Here, it reveals that we can solve (13) via (14) by finding the root for non-linear equation $F(q^\star) = 0$. Moreover, it is clear that $F(q)$ is generally a continuous but non-differential function with respect to q due to the discrete integer variable $\mathbf{x}_n^l$ [19]. An iterative energy-efficient algorithm solving problem (13) based on the solution (14) and Dinkelbach [17] method is proposed here. Let i denote the number of iterations, q_i represent the temporary EE and ε be the convergence threshold. The Algorithm 1 iteratively solves problem (14) for a given q_i and updates it until convergence. The remaining challenge is how to solve problem (14) and obtain the power and resource allocation policy. Our idea is to discuss the subchannel allocation into two cases according to the constraint (7). Note that there is at least one subchannel assigned to each individual D2D user, so the problem can be simplified if each D2D user can only use one subchannel as shown in Fig. 1(a), i.e., $\sum\limits_{l \in \mathcal{L}} x_n^l = 1$ ($\forall n \in \mathcal{N}$). On the contrary, Fig. 1(b) describes the most general case given in (7). We will give the details in the next part.

Special Case. Assume that each D2D user can choose the subchannel with the interference from CU sharing this resource within an acceptable range. Taking constraints into account and by penalty function method, we transform the optimization problem in each iteration into an equivalent form as:

$$
\max_{\mathbf{P}_d, \mathbf{x}} \left\{ \sum_{n \in \mathcal{N}} \left[\sum_{l \in \mathcal{L}} x_n^l \bar{R}_{dn}^l(\mathbf{p}_d) - q \sum_{l \in \mathcal{L}} \frac{1}{\eta} x_n^l p_{dn}^l \right] + \theta_1 g_1 \right\}, \tag{15}
$$

where θ_1 represents the penalty factor, which should be set as large as possible, and $g_1 = \sum\limits_{n \in \mathcal{N}} \sum\limits_{l \in \mathcal{L}} x_n^l \min\{0, \bar{P}_{dn}^{max} - p_{dn}^l\}$. Then (15) can be rewritten as

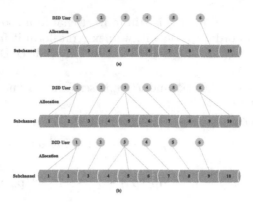

Fig. 1. An illustration of the subchannel allocation policies for D2D users.

Algorithm 1. Iterative Energy-Efficient Algorithm

---

1 **Initialization:** $i = 1$, $q_i = 0$, $\varepsilon = 10^{-3}$.
2 **repeat**
3 $\quad$ For given q_i, solve $F(q_i) = \max\limits_{\mathbf{P}_d, \mathbf{x}} \left[\sum\limits_{n \in \mathcal{N}} \sum\limits_{l \in \mathcal{L}} x_n^l \bar{R}_{dn}^l(\mathbf{P}_d) - q_i \sum\limits_{n \in \mathcal{N}} P_{dn}^{total}(\mathbf{P}_d, \mathbf{x}) \right]$;
4 $\quad$ Obtain $\mathbf{p}'_d$ and $\mathbf{x}'$;
5 $\quad$ Set $q_i = \dfrac{\sum\limits_{n \in \mathcal{N}} \sum\limits_{l \in \mathcal{L}} x_n^{l'} \bar{R}_{dn}^l(\mathbf{p}'_d)}{\sum\limits_{n \in \mathcal{N}} P_{dn}^{total}(\mathbf{p}'_d, \mathbf{x}')}$;
6 $\quad$ **if** $|F(q_i)| \geq \varepsilon$ **then**
7 $\quad\quad$ $\lfloor$ set $i = i + 1$;
8 **until** $|F(q_i)| \leq \varepsilon$;
9 $\mathbf{p}_d^\star = \mathbf{p}'_d$, $\mathbf{x}^\star = \mathbf{x}'$ and $q^\star = q_i$;
10 Output $\mathbf{p}_d^\star$, $\mathbf{x}^\star$ and $q^\star$.

$\max\limits_{\mathbf{P}_d, \mathbf{x}} \sum\limits_{n \in \mathcal{N}} \sum\limits_{l \in \mathcal{L}} x_n^l f_n^l(p_{dn}^l)$, where $f_n^l(p_{dn}^l) = \bar{R}_{dn}^l - \frac{q}{\eta} p_{dn}^l + \theta_1 \min\{0, \bar{P}_{dn}^{max} - p_{dn}^l\}$.
Leveraging the constraint $\sum\limits_{l \in \mathcal{L}} x_n^l = 1$ and referring to [15], we have:

Theorem 2. *The optimal solution p_{dn}^l to $\max\limits_{\mathbf{P}_d, \mathbf{x}} \sum\limits_{n \in \mathcal{N}} \sum\limits_{l \in \mathcal{L}} x_n^l f_n^l(p_{dn}^l)$ must be the*
optimal solution to optimization problem $\max\limits_{\mathbf{P}_d} \sum\limits_{n \in \mathcal{N}} f_n^{l(n)}(p_{dn}^{l(n)})$, which can be
further expressed into equivalent N independent optimization problems as
$\max\limits_{\mathbf{P}_d} f_n^l(p_{dn}^l)$.

Proof. The proof is similar to the one in [15].

Therefore, a two-phase separate power control and resource allocation optimization problem is developed. First, by taking the derivative of $f_n^l(p_{dn}^l)$ in term of p_{dn}^l and let it equal to zero, we could obtain the corresponding optimal transmit power $p_{dn}^{l\star}$, which could guide the resource allocation next. Second, according to the one-to-one subchannel allocation policy, the preceding optimization problem can be further rewritten into a classical resource-allocation problem as:

$$\max_{\mathbf{x}} \quad \sum_{n \in \mathcal{N}} \sum_{l \in \mathcal{L}} x_n^l f_n^l(p_{dn}^{l\star})$$

$$\text{s.t.} \quad (5), (6), \sum_{l \in \mathcal{L}} x_n^l = 1 (\forall n \in \mathcal{N}), \tag{16}$$

which can be solved optimally. Hence, the special case which is a one-to-one subchannel allocation policy has been solved with low complexity and a centralized approach is assumed, which would incur the signal overhead. Next, we discuss the most general case.

General Case. Here, we solve the problem in each iteration by the dual decomposition and sub-gradient approach. The Lagrangian associated with it is:

$$L_d(\mathbf{p}_d, \mathbf{x}, q, \boldsymbol{\lambda}) = \sum_{n \in \mathcal{N}} \sum_{l \in \mathcal{L}} x_n^l \bar{R}_{dn}^l(\mathbf{p}_d) - q \sum_{n \in \mathcal{N}} \left(\frac{1}{\eta} \sum_{l \in \mathcal{L}} x_n^l p_{dn}^l + 2P_{cir} \right)$$
$$+ \sum_{n \in \mathcal{N}} \lambda_n \left(P_{dn}^{max} - \sum_{l \in \mathcal{L}} x_n^l p_{dn}^l \right), \tag{17}$$

where the vector $\boldsymbol{\lambda} = [\lambda_1, \cdots, \lambda_N]$ represents the corresponding dual variable or Lagrangian multiplier vector. Then, the dual problem and dual function can be written respectively as:

$$\bar{L}_d(q) = \min_{\boldsymbol{\lambda} > 0} \max_{\mathbf{p}_d, \mathbf{x}} L_d(\mathbf{p}_d, \mathbf{x}, q, \boldsymbol{\lambda}), \tag{18}$$

$$\hat{L}_d(q, \boldsymbol{\lambda}) = \max_{\mathbf{p}_d, \mathbf{x}} L_d(\mathbf{p}_d, \mathbf{x}, q, \boldsymbol{\lambda}). \tag{19}$$

Here, the dual function (19) can be decomposed into N individual resource allocation problems where the one for $n \in \mathcal{N}$ is:

$$\hat{L}_d^{l(n)}(q, \boldsymbol{\lambda}) = \max_{\mathbf{p}_d, \mathbf{x}} \left\{ \sum_{l \in \mathcal{L}} x_n^l \left[\bar{R}_{dn}^l(\mathbf{p}_d) - \left(\frac{q}{\eta} + \lambda_n \right) p_{dn}^l \right] + \lambda_n P_{dn}^{max} - 2qP_{cir} \right\}. \tag{20}$$

Now, we have $p_{dn}^{l\star} = \arg \max f_n^l(p_{dn}^l)$, where $f_n^l(p_{dn}^l) = \bar{R}_{dn}^l(\mathbf{p}_d) - \left(\frac{q}{\eta} + \lambda_n \right) p_{dn}^l$. Then, by taking the first order derivative towards $f_n^l(p_n^l)$ with respect to p_n^l, we could compute the optimal transmit power by addressing $\frac{\partial f_n^l(p_n^l)}{\partial p_{dn}^l} = 0$, which is equivalent to find the root of the quadratic equation $A_{mn}(p_{dn}^l)^2 + B_{mn}p_{dn}^l + C_{mn} = 0$, and we have:

$$A_{mn} \triangleq t_{mn}(t_{mn} + 1), \quad B_{mn} \triangleq 2s_{mn}t_{mn} + s_{mn}, \quad C_{mn} \triangleq s_{mn}^2 - \frac{\eta s_{mn}}{q + \eta \lambda_n},$$

$$\triangle_{mn} = (B_{mn})^2 - 4A_{mn}C_{mn}, \quad p_{dn}^{l\star} = \left[\frac{-B_{mn} + \sqrt{\triangle}}{2A_{mn}} \right]_0^{P_{dn}^{max}},$$

$$\tag{21}$$

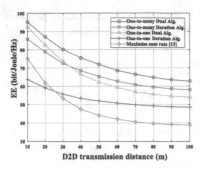

(a) An illustration of the topology.

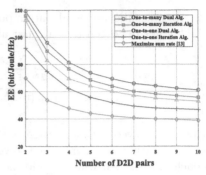

(b) EE versus number of D2D pairs.

Fig. 2. Simulation result.

where $[x]_a^b = b$ if $x > b$, $[x]_a^b = a$ if $x < a$, otherwise, $[x]_a^b = a$ $(b > a)$. Therefore, the optimal subchannel allocation $x_n^{l\star}(\forall n \in \mathcal{N}, \forall l \in \mathcal{L})$ can be readily obtained:

$$x_n^{l\star} = \begin{cases} 1, & if \ n = \arg\max_{n \in \mathcal{N}} f_n^l(p_{dn}^{l\star}) \\ 0. & otherwise \end{cases} \tag{22}$$

We update the dual variable $\boldsymbol{\lambda}$ according to the sub-gradient method [20]:

$$\lambda_n^{(i+1)} = \left[\lambda_n^{(i)} + \varphi_{n,\lambda}^{(i)}\Big(\sum_{l \in \mathcal{L}} x_n^{l\star}p_{dn}^{l\star} - P_{dn}^{max}\Big)\right]^+, \forall n \in \mathcal{N}, \forall l \in \mathcal{L}, \tag{23}$$

where i is the iteration index and $[x]^+ = \max\{0, x\}$ denotes the projection onto the non-negative orthant to guarantee the feasibility constraint $\lambda_n^{(i+1)} > 0$. The $\varphi_{n,\lambda}^{(i)}$ is positive step size, which can be chosen appropriately to ensure the convergence of the iterative updates [20]. Here, the general case which is a one-to-many subchannel allocation policy has been solve through the dual decomposition as well as sub-gradient techniques and a distributed implementation is assumed, which could potentially reduce the burden of the base station and the signal overhead. Accordingly, we propose the dual-based algorithm to solve the optimization problem (13).

4   Numerical Results

In this section, the performance of proposed algorithms are evaluated via simulations. The values of simulation parameters are inspired by [14–16] for $\forall n \in \mathcal{N}, \forall l \in \mathcal{L}$ as: the cell radius is 500 m, the number of CUs, D2D users, subchannel is $M = 15$, $N = 6$ and $L = 15$ respectively, the maximum transmit power of CUs and D2D users is same as $P_{cm}^{max} = P_{dn}^{max} = 0.5$ W, the minimum data rate of all cellular users is same as $R_{cm}^{min} = 1$ bit/s/Hz, the maximum D2D

Algorithm 2. Dual-Based Algorithm

---

1 **repeat**
2   **Initialization:** q^{miin}, q^{max}.
3      $q = \dfrac{1}{2}\left(q^{min} + q^{max}\right)$, $\lambda_n^{(0)} = \frac{1}{N}$.
4   **repeat**
5   Compute the optimal transmit power by (21);
6   Compute the optimal resource allocation by (22);
7   Update the dual variables $\boldsymbol{\lambda}$ by (23);
8   **until** *Convergence*;
9   Compute $F(q_i) = \max\limits_{\mathbf{P}_d, \mathbf{x}}\left[\sum\limits_{n \in \mathcal{N}}\sum\limits_{l \in \mathcal{L}} x_n^l \bar{R}_{dn}^l(\mathbf{P}_d) - q_i \sum\limits_{n \in \mathcal{N}} P_{dn}^{total}(\mathbf{P}_d, \mathbf{x})\right]$
10   **if** $|F(q_i)| \geq 0$ **then**
11   set $q_{min} = q$;
12   **else**
13   set $q_{max} = q$;
14 **until** *Convergence of q*;
15 Output $\mathbf{p}_d^*$, $\mathbf{x}^*$ and q^*.

---

transmission distance is $D2Dmax = 50\,\text{m}$, the circuit power is $P_{cir} = 0.1\,\text{W}$, the power amplifier efficiency is $\eta = 0.35$, and the noise power is $\sigma^l = 10^{-8}\,\text{W}$.

Figure 2(a) shows how the distance between the users in one D2D pair affects the EE with 6 D2D pairs of the proposed scheme, compared with the scheme in [13], which is rate adaptive. Obviously, our proposed scheme has a better performance than the scheme in [13] in terms of the EE criterion. It can be observed that the EE decreases with the increase of the distance between the D2D transmitter and receiver. The reason why this downward trend appears is that D2D communication will lose its lower transmit power and higher data rate properties with the distance increases. Hence, the transmission distance within D2D have a great impact on the proposed scheme. Moreover, the one-to-many subchannel allocation policy outperforms the one-to-one policy. There are two reasons count for this decline. First, the former takes full use of subchannels. Second, the interference has been well managed in our proposed scheme. Furthermore, it is obvious that the dual-based algorithm surpasses the general iterative algorithm in terms of the same resource allocation. Note that the complexity of Algorithm 2 is $O(NL)$ as the dual decomposition method solves problem (14) for given q with complexity of $O(NL)$, and the iterative update required of q has complexity of $O(1)$. So our proposed scheme has polynomial complexity with regard to problem scale N and L, which facilitates the practical implementation. Figure 2(b) describes that the achieved EE of D2D users versus the number of D2D pairs compared with the scheme in [13], which shows that the EE decreases as the number of D2D pairs increases. It comes from the fact that as the system supports more D2D users, the available resources for each D2D user become scare, which correspondingly leads to the decrease in the achieved EE of D2D users.

5   Conclusion

In this work, the issue of maximizing the energy efficiency of D2D users while optimizing power and subchannel assignments and guaranteeing the minimum data rates of cellular users in D2D-based cellular network has been addressed. The iterative and dual-based energy-efficient power and resource allocation algorithms were proposed. In particular, we divided the subchannel allocation policy into two cases and gave the corresponding methods to solve the problem. Simulation results verified that the proposed algorithms outperform a conventional algorithm in terms of EE.

Acknowledgments. The work in this paper was partially supported by the Natural Science Foundation of Jiangsu Province (No. BK20140835), and the Postdoctoral Foundation of Jiangsu Province (No. 1401018B).

References

1. Unit, E.: Ericsson energy and carbon report: on the impact of networked society. Ericsson (2013). http://www.ericsson.com/res/docs/2013/ericsson-energy-and-carbon-report.pdf
2. Gupta, A., Jha, R.: A survey of 5G network: architecture and emerging technologies. IEEE Access **3**, 1206–1232 (2015)
3. Al-Fuqaha, A., Guizani, M., Mohammadi, M., Aledhari, M., Ayyash, M.: Internet of things: a survey on enabling technologies, protocols, and applications. IEEE Commun. Surv. Tutorials **17**(4), 2347–2376 (2015)
4. Whitmore, A., Agarwal, A., Daxu, L.: The internet of things-a survey of topics and trends. Inf. Syst. Front. **17**(2), 261–274 (2015). Springer
5. Fu, Z., Sun, X., Ji, S., Xie, G.: Towards efficient content-aware search over encrypted outsourced data in cloud. In: Proceedings of the 35th Annual IEEE International Conference on Computer Communications, pp. 1–9. IEEE INFOCOM, San Francisco (2016)
6. Chen, Y., Hao, C., Wu, W., Wu, E.: Robust dense reconstruction by range merging based on confidence estimation. Sci. China Inf. Sci. **59**(9), 1–11 (2016). Springer
7. Kong, Y., Zhang, M., Ye, D.: A belief propagation-based method for task allocation in open and dynamic cloud environments. Knowl.-Based Syst. **115**, 123–132 (2017). Elsevier
8. Sambo, Y., Shakir, M., Qaraqe, K., Serpedin, E.: Energy efficiency improvements in HetNets by exploiting device-to-device communications. In: Signal Processing Conference, pp. 151–155. IEEE (2014)
9. Xu, Y.: Energy-efficient power control scheme for device-to-device communications. Wirel. Pers. Commun. **94**, 481–495 (2015). Springer
10. Bhadauria, S., Vishwakarma, S.: Energy efficient D2D application for increasing battery usage of smartphones. Int. J. Hybrid Inf. Technol. **9**(2), 311–328 (2016)
11. Xu, Y.: A mode selection scheme for D2D communication in heterogeneous cellular networks. In: Global Communications Conference, pp. 1–6. IEEE (2016)
12. Gao, C., Sheng, X., Tang, J., Zhang, W., Zou, S., Guizani, M.: Joint mode selection, channel allocation and power assignment for green device-to-device communication. In: International Conference on Communications, pp. 178–183. IEEE (2014)

13. Yu, C., Tirkkonen, O., Doppler, K., Ribeiro, C.: Power optimization of device-to-device communication underlaying cellular communication. In: International Conference on Communications, pp. 1–5. IEEE (2009)

14. Zhou, Z., Dong, M., Ota, K., Wu, J., Sato, T.: Distributed interference-aware energy-efficient resource allocation for device-to-device communications underlaying cellular networks. In: Global Communications Conference, pp. 4454–4459. IEEE (2014)

15. Jiang, Y., Liu, Q., Zheng, F., Gao, X., You, X.: Energy-efficient joint resource allocation and power control for D2D communications. IEEE Trans. Veh. Technol. **65**(8), 6119–6127 (2016). IEEE

16. Hoang, T., Le, L., Le-Ngoc, T.: Energy-efficient resource allocation for D2D communications in cellular networks. IEEE Trans. Veh. Technol. **65**(9), 6972–6986 (2016). IEEE

17. Dinkelbach, W.: On nonlinear fractional programming. Manage. Sci. **13**(7), 492–498 (1967)

18. Ng, D., Lo, E., Schober, R.: Energy-efficient resource allocation in SDMA systems with large numbers of base station antennas. In: International Conference on Communications, pp. 4027–4032. IEEE (2012)

19. Xiao, X., Tao, X., Lu, J.: QoS-aware energy-efficient radio resource scheduling in multi-user SDMA systems. Commun. Lett. **17**(1), 75–78 (2013). IEEE

20. Boyd, S., Xiao, L., Mutapcic, A.: Subgradient methods. In: Lecture Notes of EE392o, Stanford University, Autumn Quarter, vol. 2004, pp. 1–21 (2003)

Virtual Machine Placement Based on Metaheuristic for IoT Cloud

Shih-Yun Huang[1], Chen-Chi Liao[2], Yao-Chung Chang[3(✉)], and Han-Chieh Chao[1,2,4]

[1] Department of Electrical Engineering, National Dong Hwa University, Hualien, Taiwan, Republic of China
deantt67@gmail.com
[2] Department of Computer Science and Information Engineering, National Ilan University, Yilan, Taiwan, Republic of China
einstein0320@gmail.com
[3] Department of Computer Science and Information Engineering, National Taitung University, Taitung, Taiwan, Republic of China
ycc@nttu.edu.tw
[4] College of Computer and Software, Nanjing University of Information Science and Technology, Nanjing, China
hcchao@gmail.com

Abstract. Recently, the technology of smart home devices is very attractive. Hence, the development of Internet of thing (IoT) becomes more important. The data center through the devices collected the data with user information. At the transmission rush hour with many devices send the data to center. Moreover, the amount of data will be enormous, and it needs to analysis immediately. The cloud services will be very helpful for this situation because it provides powerful computing power let processed data very quickly. This study uses the cloud computing to solve this problem. However, at the off-peak time does not need the computing power of the cloud, it is too much and waste. How to dynamic adjustment the computing power is a major issue. Considered this problem, this study proposes the metaheuristic algorithm to adjust the virtual machine for a rush hour or off-peak time. Moreover, our method needs to guarantees the final virtual machine place is optimum, and the resource consumption is minimal. The simulation result shows our method can be effectively reduced a waste of resource and deal with more data.

Keywords: Internet of thing (IoT) · Metaheuristic algorithm · Virtual machine placement

1 Introduction

Internet of thing (IoT) is a critical technology in our life; more and more application using the smart devices with a wireless network to collects the data, as well as know the situation or some information at that time. For example, the IoT can be used on the smart grid [1, 2]. Due to the future of IoT that can be an important technique to the smart grid. There has more research focus on the how to using IoT combined the smart grid to reduce

© Springer International Publishing AG 2017
X. Sun et al. (Eds.): ICCCS 2017, Part I, LNCS 10602, pp. 472–482, 2017.
https://doi.org/10.1007/978-3-319-68505-2_41

the energy consumption and the energy used can be efficient. At the same time, the application of IoT with smart grid has the benefit with economic. Due to the power company will be utilized the history to doing strategy if the user does not need too much energy, the company can allocate the more energy to needs a user. However, the research of IoT almost studies the security and lifetime of the device. As the security issue, because the IoT usually embedded the smart appliance, like smart home or smart car system. If attacker hacks in the instrument, the personal information or password may be changed. On the other hand, to live time for devices, the most devices are using to collects the data for information; the devices can not charge when these devices or sensors has been deployment, the energy consumption is a key point for this wireless IoT network. However, consider the situation in IoT, there are more different applications are using IoT to calculate the information, the number of heterogeneous data will be large, or we can call big data [3] when it wants to analyze data in real-time the computing power is not enough. The cloud computing perhaps is a method can help us. At the same time, the [11] also highlight the relationship with cloud computing and IoT. Considerate this, the data center needs to analyze the amount of the primary heterogeneous data, how to deal with at the real time is a big problem.

The cloud computing supports many services to help some issues solved the problem that can apply in cloud computing for the encryption algorithm or identification for image and data [13–16]. In fact, the application of cloud computing is the main research issue in the future. Moreover, there are many other issues should be solved, for example how to build the robust path. The cloud computing can help to decide the better path [17]. Therefore, the cloud computing may be a solution to our problem. The cloud computing can provide powerful computing power, as well as it can achieve the energy saving. That is cloud data center will use the technique of virtualization. Because this reason, many application can provide the high-quality service. On the other side, the most important thing is the concept of virtualization that virtual machine (VM) can adjust the state (on/off) dynamically. For example, if the computing power is not enough, the decision policy need to decide how many numbers of VMs should be aware and which physical machine (PM) put it in. However we also need to think about this, the VMs can using the full resource of PM or not [4]. In addition to the cloud service has to care the crash. If the user sends the request with the amount of large number, or the number of data needs to deal, the resource of PM that can use is full, and this is why the cloud service is unstable [5, 6]. This entire problem has to studies necessary. Due to the advantage of cloud computing, we can combine the IoT and cloud computing to analysis the real-time data. However, the only problem is the when transmission data at the rush hour or off-peak time, the computing power is enough or not?

For IoT, the most research almost focuses on the network lifetime and the security of information. However, how to process the data immediately is a critical issue that cannot ignore. In [1] also lists the many problems in the IoT. In this paper, we proposed the using the cloud computing to process the IoT real-time data. Consider the transmission rush hour and off-peak time the computing power we need must be different, how to efficiently doing the VMs placement is a key point. Here we are using the metaheuristic algorithm to find the optimum position for VMs and the number of VMs in each PMs. The solution needs to guarantees the resource cost is minimal and can deal with the most data. There are many studies to efficient improved the resource allocation of cloud data center. They also considerate the allocated the number of VMs in PM, but will ignore the live data that increases at one little time slot. This work also focuses on the consumption of link, not just only the resource of physical. For improving the ability to deal with the data, the proposed algorithm can use the least time to find the best solution.

This paper is structured as follows: Sect. 2 denotes the problem in the cloud computing and the methods to solve the virtual machine placement. Section 3 presents our environment and problem definition. The description of the proposed method and detail algorithm are described in Sect. 4. The simulation results are demonstrated in Sect. 5. Finally, conclusions of this work are marked in Sect. 6.

2   Related Work

This paper is used the powerful computing power of the cloud to help smart grid for real-time data processing. In this article, we will show the research with virtual machines placement and physical device management. In [7], the authors considerate the load balancing between physical machines, the virtual machine migration is a key point, so to achieve this goal, they proposed the using hybrid VM migration and multi-objects optimization algorithm. Moreover, authors also defined the three metrics, these are inter-HM load unevenness, intra-HM load disequilibrium, and the hybrid live VM migrations cost. However, we think about in our environment the real-time data need to be processed immediately, and associated with the VMs placement adjustment should be quick.

At the [8, 9] is using the method of the agent to doing the PMs and VMs placement. [8] the authors think about in the large scale data center, the multi-agent is a method that VMs placement maybe quickly. For this reason, they proposed the using multi-agent and the allocated algorithm, and this algorithm is contained in the CloudSim toolkit. This way reduced the response time when the number of VMs wants to add. In the other hand, the [9] is using the method of multi-agents. However, it combined the machine learning, called Cooperative Fuzzy Q-Learning (CO-FQL). The authors consider the distributed dynamic virtual machine consolidation (DDVMC) is dependent the decision-making process, although it is one of the methods, can optimize the placement of virtual machines, the dynamic adjustment not so good.

Liu et al. [10] authors consider the resource allocation of energy efficiently for VMs in the cloud data center. The solution of genetic algorithm (GA) and simulated annealing algorithm (SA) are nearest the optimal solution, but still, need to improve. Therefore they proposed combined the mechanism of GA and SA to get the optimal placement of VMs and achieved the best energy efficiency. Finally, in the [12], the link between PMs will be the cost, and most researchers do not consider that, the authors proposed the method of link-aware virtual machine placement (LAVMP) to calculate the cost to link.

3   Problem Definition

For apparently know the problem with this paper, the environment and network architecture are defined in this section. Figure 1 shows our environment and network architecture, when a user using the smart device or the sensor is power on, the devices start collecting the data, here we need to know the different type of application in IoT, the time of collecting the data and update is different. For example, if IoT network just to sensing the temperature or humidity, the sensor may start with per hour. However, the smart car system needs to collect the data and analysis immediate. In our environment, we assume these devices need to collect the data and doing analysis anytime. When devices have been collecting the data, it will transmit the data to the data center through wireless method, if the distance is long, the wireless network can be cellar network or LTE, else it can be using the unlicensed band, like Wi-Fi. However, the different type of application, the collect the data are different too, deal with heterogeneous data is more complicated than the single model data. To ensure the data center processed the real-time data can be fast, we using the cloud computing to help us. In the part of the cloud, the resource of PM is limited, in other words, the one PM just have the fixed number of VMs. Also the connecting is existing between two PMs, the PMs in the different domain through the gateway to connect, the gateway can be responsible the fixed number of PMs at the same time.

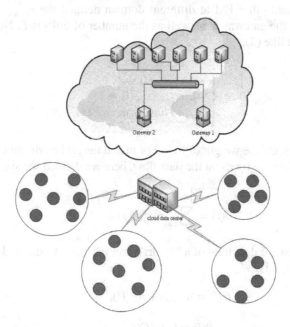

Fig. 1. The environment and network architecture

When we defined our environment, the problem is how to place our virtual machines at the rush hour and off-peak time. First, we assume in our environment has a number of devices N, then $N = \{1, 2, ..., n\}$.. Next we, defined the two sets $I = \{1, 2, ..., i\}$,

$J = \{1, 2, \ldots, j\}$, the I present the number of VMs, and the J is number of PMs. Know we assume the specification with VM are all same to help us to defined problem. Using this assumption we can show the current CPU energy consumption in this paper,

$$u_{cpu}(j) = p_{cpu}\left(c_{cputotal}(j) - c_{cpuidle}(j)\right),$$ (1)

the $u_{cpu}(j)$ presents the CPU energy consumption in j^{th} PM, p_{cpu} is a unit with energy consumption of CPU, as well as we defined the $c_{cputotal}(j)$ is how many CPU resource can be used in j^{th} PM and $c_{cpuidle}(j)$ is the remainder CPU resource can be used in j^{th} PM. However for clearly to know how many CPU resource are remainder, must to calculated the $c_{cpuidle}(j)$, so we defined the (2) to get the residual resource. At this function, $c_{cpu}^{vm}(i)$ presents the ith VM used how many CPU resource.

$$c_{cpuidle}(j) = \sum_{i=1}^{i} C_{cpu}^{vm}(i).$$ (2)

In actually, the cloud data center building with many PMs, the connecting between PMs is necessarily, and the gateway just can service fixed number of PMs. So we must consider the consumption with a link. For this reason, we defined the link consumption between j^{th} PM and other PM in the same domain is $c_{PMcon}(j)$, if the link consumption between j^{th} PM and other PM at different domain defined the $c_{Gatewaycon}(j)$. We also assume there has the gateway K as well as the number of links is L. Now presents the link consumption like (3),

$$u_{con}(j) = \begin{cases} w_1, & c_{PMcon}(j) = 1 \\ w_2, & c_{Gatewaycon}(j) = 1 \\ 0, & no\ link\ between\ PMs \end{cases},$$ (3)

the w_1 and w_2 presents the weight of link. For match the real environments the w_2 must bigger then w_1. Now we focus on the data flow, here we defined the size of data flow at time t is $\emptyset$,

$$\emptyset(t) = \sum_{n=1}^{n} \emptyset_{n\_meter}(t),$$ (4)

the $\emptyset_{n\_meter}$ denoted the data flow of nth smart meter at time t. Combined (1), (3) and (4) get the cost function is

$$C(j) = u_{cpu}(j) + u_{con}(j),$$ (5)

$$P(j) = \emptyset(t)/C(j).$$ (6)

So far, follow the assumption we can define our problem is to get the minimum resource consumption to avoid the unnecessarily waste, also can guarantee to have enough computing power to process the data. Table 1 is our relevant symbol list, and Table 2 is our linear programming Model.

Table 1. The symbol list.

Symbol	Definition
N	Number of smart meters
K	Number of Gateways
L	Number of link between PMs
i	i^{th} VMs
j	j^{th} PMs
$u_{cpu}(j)$	CPU energy consumption in j^{th} PM
p_{cpu}	The unit with CPU energy consumption
$c_{cputotal}(j)$	The total CPU resource can be used in j^{th} PM
$c_{cpuidle}(j)$	The remainder CPU resource in j^{th} PM
$c_{cpu}^{vm}(i)$	The CPU resource has been used for VM i
$c_{PMcon}(j)$	The link between PM j and other PM at same gateway
$c_{Gatewaycon}(j)$	The link between PM j and other PM at different gateway
$u_{con}(j)$	The consumption for link
$w_1,$ w_2	Weight of link
$\emptyset(t)$	The total data flow at time t
$\emptyset_{n\_meter}$	The data flow of nth smart meter at time t
$P(j)$	The performance with PM j

Table 2. ILP.

$$\text{Maximize } \sum_{j=1}^{j} P(j)$$

s.t.
$$i, j \in R$$
$$i, j \geq 1$$
$$w_1, w_2 \neq 0$$

4   The SA-Based Data Flow Algorithm

According to the future of IoT, the data center will know the information via has been collecting data. However, consider the need to processed real time data will be large at transmission rush hour. At this time, the cloud computing can help data center to deal with it. Whatever the number of data at IoT not fixed, it will change anytime; the data center only can through history record to guesses needs the computing power. If this computing power cannot adjustment dynamic will be let computing power overloading or under loading. In this paper, we proposed the using the data flow to watching the computing power. For the optimization, we combined the simulated annealing algorithm (SA) to find the optimal VMs placement.

For example, the transmission state is off-peak time now. We assume there have the set of PM denoted $G = \{PM_1, PM_2, \ldots, PM_j\}$, and the $PM_j = \{VM_1, VM_2, \ldots, VM_i\}$, we defined the power on or shutdown of VM_i is

$$VM_i = \begin{cases} 1, & VM\ power\ on \\ 0, & VM\ shutdown \end{cases},$$ (7)

then the state of G can be show in (8)

$$G = \begin{cases} 0\ 0\ 0 & 0\ 0 \\ 0\ 1\ 0 & 0\ 0 \\ \vdots\ \vdots\ \vdots\ \ldots\ \vdots\ \vdots \\ 1\ 1\ 1 & 0\ 0 \\ 1\ 1\ 1 & 1\ 0 \end{cases}.$$ (8)

According to our proposed method, we defined the θ is threshold, when $\emptyset(t)$ is bigger then θ, the VMs should be replacement again when the computing power is enough. If $\emptyset(t)$ small then $\theta/2$, also need to replacement VM too, because it maybe waste the computing power and increased the power consumption.

Next step in the proposed method we use the simulated annealing algorithm to find the position for VMs placement. The Algorithm 1 is SA-based data flow algorithm. First, the system will decide the data flow $\emptyset(t)$ is bigger then threshold or small then $\theta/2$. If yes, will initial the state of PM and randomly generator the number of VM in each PM. At this time, the solution we denoted the optimal solution $Sol_{optimal}$. Next step will choices the PM randomly and changed the number of VM, it can find the other solution Sol. Compared these two solution, if new solution is the best it will replaced the old solution become $Sol_{optimal}$, or the temperature small then threshold of SA, it can replaced too. This represent it have the probability get worse solution let system can be find the optimum solution quickly.

Algorithm 2. The SA-based data flow algorithm

Algorithm 3: The SA-based data flow algorithm
1.   Input: n, i, j
2.   Output: $Sol_{optimal}$
3.   Parameter: T, $\Psi = e^{(-\frac{Sol_{optimal}-Sol}{T})}$, w_1, w_2
4.   Randomly generator the $\emptyset$
5.   If $\emptyset < \theta$ or $\emptyset > \theta/2$
6.   Maintain the status
7.   Else if
8.   Initial the resource of PM
9.   The randomly put the VM into the PM j. $PM_j = \{VM_1, VM_2, ..., VM_i\}$
10. Calculated the solution and this solution is $Sol_{optimal}$
11. Randomly choices the PM and change the number of VM.
12. Calculated the solution Sol
13. If $Sol > Sol_{optimal}$ or T<Ψ
14. $Sol_{optimal} = Sol$
15. Else if
16. Return
17. T=T*α
18. End
19. End

5   Simulation and Result

5.1   Simulation Setting

In this paper, simulation is using MATLAB to simulate the problem and the proposed method. Moreover, our simulation environment and network architecture are shown in Fig. 1. Table 3 is our setting with parameters.

Table 3. Simulation parameter list

Parameter	Number
i	10
j	20
Iteration	1000
T	1000°
α	0.95

5.2   Result

The simulation of this work compares with the greedy algorithm. Because existing algorithm can find the optimal solution, it has the chances spend so many time that placement of PMs and VMs do not have instantaneity. The unit with CPU energy consumption and weight of link we set is the generation randomly. The Fig. 3 shows the actions of a different number of data, and the value of Y-axis in the unit of resource consumption can deal with how many numbers of evidence. When the number of data is 10,000–14,000, the performance of the greedy algorithm is better than our method. That is it will use the full resource can be used in PM, but in our process, the VM not full in PM, as well as the number of VM may be bigger than using a greedy algorithm. That is to say; the single VM will remain the computing power. When the data need to process more and more, the greedy algorithm has to add the number of VM. It will increase the resource consumption. On the other hand, the computing power of VM has remained, the cost increases not so dark than the greedy algorithms. The metaheuristic algorithm needs to consider the iteration for the computing time (Fig. 2).

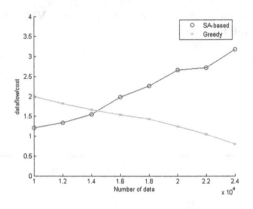

Fig. 2. Comparison of the *data flow/Cost* between Greedy and SA-based dataflow

Finding the metaheuristic algorithm needs many computing time, it will lead to adjust the placement of VM not so quickly, and the Fig. 3 is SA-based data flow algorithm with periods of iteration. The times of iteration is 16 is convergence. Moreover, we set the number of data is 24,000. It can show our proposed method can handle this problem.

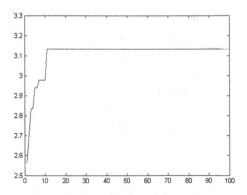

Fig. 3. The times of iteration curve

6   Conclusion

The IoT technology becomes necessary in our daily life, especially the development of a smart application with IoT. When the devices in IoT network start collect the real-time data and need to analysis at transmission rush hour, the IoT network computing power not so enough, therefore the cloud computing combined the IoT is one of the solutions. In this paper, we proposed the SA-based algorithm with data flow to help the Placement of VM to cloud. The simulation shows using this method can achieve the used minimal resource consumption to deal with the maximal data. In the future work, the [18] highlights another point which is the task allocation in a dynamic cloud environment. We will add this concept to our structure and solve this issue.

Acknowledgments. This research was partly funded by the National Science Council of the R.O.C. under grants MOST 105-2221-E-197 -010 -MY2 and MOST 105-2221-E-143 -001 -MY2.

References

1. Shah, S.H., Yaqoob, I.: A survey: internet of things (IoT) technologies, application and challenges. In: Smart Energy Grid Engineering (SEGE), pp. 381–385. IEEE Press, Canada (2016)
2. Arasteh, H., Hosseinnezhad, V., Loia, V., Tommasetti, A., Troisi, O., Shafie-khah, M., Siano, P.: IoT-based smart cities: a survey. In: IEEE 16th International Conference on Environment and Electrical Engineering (EEEIC). IEEE Press, Italy (2016)
3. Sharma, S.K., Wang, X.: Live data analytics with collaborative edge and cloud processing in wireless IOT networks. IEEE Access 5, 4621–4635 (2017)
4. Colman-Meixner, C., Develder, C., Tornatore, M., Mukherjee, B.: A survey on resiliency techniques in cloud computing infrastructures and applications view document. IEEE Commun. Survey. Tutorials 18(3), 2244–2281 (2016)
5. Amoon, M.: Adaptive framework for reliable cloud computing environment. IEEE Access 4, 9469–94787 (2016)
6. Vijayalakshmi, M., Yakobu, D., Veeraiah, D., Rao, N.G.: Automatic healing of services in cloud computing environment. In: International Conference on Advanced Communication Control and Computing Technologies (ACCCT), India, pp. 740–745 (2016)
7. Li, R., Zheng, Q., Li, X., Wu, J.: A novel multi-objective optimization scheme for rebalancing virtual machine placement. In: International Conference on Cloud Computing (CLOUD), USA, pp. 710–717 (2016)
8. Al-Ou'n, A., Kiran, M., Kouvatsos, D.D.: Using agent–based VM policy. In: International Conference on Future Internet of Things and Cloud, Italy, pp. 272–281 (2015)
9. Masoumzadeh, S.S., Hlavacs, H.: A cooperative multi agent learning approach to manage physical host nodes for dynamic consolidation of virtual machines. In: IEEE Fourth Symposium on Network Cloud Computing and Applications (NCCA), pp. 43–50. IEEE Press, Germany (2015)
10. Liu, D., Sui, X., Li, L.: An energy-efficient virtual machine placement algorithm in cloud data center. In: International Conference on Natural Computation, Fuzzy Systems and Knowledge Discovery (ICNC-FSKD), China, pp. 719–723 (2016)
11. Babu, S.M., Lakshmi, A.J., Rao, B.T.: A study on cloud based Internet of things: CloudIoT. In: Global Conference on Communication Technologies (GCCT), India, pp. 60–65 (2015)

12. Tseng, F.-H., Jheng, Y.-M., Chou, L.-D., Chao, H.-C., Leung, V.C.M.: Link-aware virtual machine placement for cloud services based on service-oriented architecture. IEEE Trans. Cloud Comput. (2017)

13. Xia, Z., Wang, X., Zhang, L., Qin, Z., Sun, X., Ren, K.: A privacy preserving and copy deterrence content based image retrieval scheme in cloud computing. IEEE Trans. Inf. Forensics Secur. 11(11), 2594–2608 (2016)

14. Fu, Z., Ren, K., Shu, J., Sun, X., Huang, F.: Enabling personalized search over encrypted outsourced data with efficiency improvement. IEEE Trans. Parallel Distrb. Syst. 27(9), 2546–2559 (2016)

15. Fu, Z., Sun, X., Liu, Q., Zhou, L., Shu, J.: Achieving efficient cloud search services: multi keyword ranked search over encrypted cloud data supporting parallel computing. IEICE Trans. Commun. E98B(1), 190–200 (2015)

16. Zhou, Z., Wang, Y., Wu, Q.M.J., Yang, C.N., Sun, X.: Effective and efficient global context verification for image copy detection. IEEE Trans. Inf. Forensics Secur. 12(1), 48–63 (2017)

17. Bin, G., Sheng, V.S.: A robust regularization path algorithm for v-support vector classification. IEEE Trans. Neural Netw. Learn. Syst. 28, 1241–1248 (2016)

18. Kong, Y., Zhang, M., Ye, D.: A belief propagation based method for task allocation in open and dynamic cloud environments. Knowl. Based Syst. 115, 123–132 (2016)

A Novel Kalman Filter Based NLOS Localization Method for Wireless Sensor Networks

Long Cheng[1,2(✉)], Yuchao Shao[1], and Yan Wang[1]

[1] Department of Computer and Communication Engineering,
Northeastern University, Qinhuangdao 066004, China
chenglong8501@gmail.com
[2] School of Information Science and Engineering,
Northeastern University, Shenyang 110819, China

Abstract. Wireless sensor networks (WSNs) have the focus of research in recent years. Moreover, positioning is very important for wireless sensor networks. However, the positioning accuracy still has large error in the case of non-line-of-sight. In this paper, we propose an improved Kalman filter algorithm to reduce the influence of NLOS error. For the case of NLOS, the measurement residual $E_i(k)$ is updated firstly. This method can effectively reduce the NLOS error, which makes the positioning result more accurate. The simulation results show that the proposed localization algorithm can accurately apply to the normal NLOS location problem.

Keywords: Wireless sensor networks · Localization · Non-line-of-sight · Kalman filter

1 Introduction

The accuracy of global position system (GPS) will drastically decrease when the receiver of the positioning system is in large buildings. So in recent years, the research interest of wireless sensor network (WSN) has been growing rapidly. Wireless sensor nodes are usually a miniature embedded system. Wireless sensor network that consist of thousands of distributed sensors is setting, and the node position can be changed at any time. What's more, it can be wired or wirelessly connected with the Internet. The WSN based localization strategy has the features of well flexibility, convenient maintenance and low cost. Therefore, it is widely used in military, intelligent transportation, environment monitoring, medical and health or other fields [1–3].

There are many common localization methods based on WSN. Among them, the four most classic methods to estimate the indoor location are time of arrival (TOA), time difference of arrival (TDOA), angle of arrival (AOA) and received signal strength indicator (RSSI). TOA method estimates the position of nodes based on the propagation time of the signal. In TDOA method, the transmitting node simultaneously transmits two kinds of wireless signals with different propagation speed, and the receiving node calculates the position of the node according to the arrival time

© Springer International Publishing AG 2017
X. Sun et al. (Eds.): ICCCS 2017, Part I, LNCS 10602, pp. 483–494, 2017.
https://doi.org/10.1007/978-3-319-68505-2_42

difference of the two signals. AOA method is located by measuring the direction of arrival of the node signal. RSSI method has established the signal transmission model to calculate the distance between the anchor node and the unknown node. And then the unknown node position information is calculated by combining the above measurement methods such as TOA, TDOA or AOA.

When there is a line-of-sight (LOS) propagation among the beacon nodes and the mobile node, accurate location estimation can be obtained by using techniques such as Kalman filtering. However, in the real station, especially in the indoor area, the complex indoor environment leads to the non-line-of-sight (NLOS) and the direct path is blocked by the obstacle. At this time, the NLOS effect will lead to large positioning error. As a result, research under the NLOS environment remains the biggest challenge for the precise positioning of WSN.

In this paper, the main contribution is given as follows.

(1) The propagation condition of beacon nodes can be identified by the NLOS identification method. When the propagation condition is NLOS, we choose to update the measurement residual, and when the propagation condition is LOS, it is not need to be updated.
(2) For the NLOS error, this paper combines the Kalman filter algorithm and maximum likelihood localization method to predict, recognize and update the unknown nodal coordinates. And at last, a more accurate coordinate position is obtained to reduce the NLOS error.
(3) The algorithm in this paper can be measured by using the TOA method. What's more, it can be easily extended to other methods such as TDOA and RSSI.

The rest of paper is organized as follows. The related works are provided in Sect. 2. Some of the basic system models used in this paper are presented in Sect. 3. There is our proposed strategy in LOS/NLOS conditions which is mentioned in Sect. 4. The simulation results are shown in Sect. 5. And the conclusions are described in Sect. 6.

2   Related Works

A number of positioning methods have been proposed in NLOS environment. When it comes to cooperative positioning of mobile stations in LOS and NLOS environment, in [4], the authors develop a multi-sensor multi-model filter using the interaction multiple model (IMM) method and the extended Kalman filter (EKF) technique, and transmit the position estimate derived from the anchor sensor measurements to generate the predicted cooperative measurements in the EKF. In [5], the authors propose a mobile localization strategy based on Kalman filter to identify and mitigate NLOS. The advantage of this method is that it doesn't require a priori knowledge of the NLOS error, and it is independent of the physical measurement mode. In [6], considering the characteristics of NLOS errors, this paper proposes a localization algorithm based on voting mechanism to filter distance measurements and to retain reliable measurements. Then, through the modified probability data association algorithm and the linear least squares algorithm finally determines the location of the mobile node. And in [7], the authors propose Gaussian mixed model based non-metric Multidimensional (GMDS) to perform location estimation without providing a priori knowledge. This method has higher precision in indoor mixed LOS/NLOS positioning.

In [8], they develop a novel robust optimization approach to source localization using time-difference-of-arrival (TDOA) measurements that are collected in NLOS environments, and it doesn't need to know the distribution or statistics of NLOS errors. To improve accuracy and reduce the time required for WSN to locate in harsh environments, in [9], they perturb Edge-based SDP (ESDP) relaxation and add several constraints to the optimization problem so that they can make this method robust against large number of error in distance measurement. In [10], a novel cooperative localization algorithm with the ability to mitigate NLOS propagation based on semi-definite programming (SDP) is proposed. In [11], a progressive localization scheme is proposed, which doesn't need any cluster, and it can greatly improve the location accuracy even in the presence of channel noise. Due to the frequent stochastic transition of LOS/NLOS environments, the authors propose an indoor mobile localization scheme with REE measurements in mixed LOS/NLOS conditions in [12].

3 System Model

In this section, this paper will briefly introduce the signal model used. In a variety of distance-based positioning methods, this paper chooses the positioning method based on time of arrival (TOA). In the method based on TOA, when the propagation velocity of the signal is known, the distance between the unknown node and the beacon node can be calculated from the propagation time of the signal which is measured. And then, we can get the exact position of the unknown node according to the trilateration algorithm. In this case, supposing that the time between two nodes is exactly synchronized, when the transmitting node sends a signal sequence, the corresponding module notify the receiving node to prepare the detection signal through the synchronization message.

The corresponding scene design is as follows: the coordinates of M beacon nodes are $\psi_i = (x_i, y_i)^T$, $i = 1, \ldots, M$, and the nodes are randomly placed at specific coordinates in complex site. The locations of obstructions in the site are also randomly distributed. The position of the unknown node moving randomly at time k in the field is $(x(k), y(k))$. In this paper, the movement of unknown position in two-dimensional is introduced, and the motion of position in three-dimensional can be deduced accordingly.

At time k, the true distance between the unknown node and the ith bacon node is:

$$d_i(k) = \sqrt{(x(k) - x_i)^2 + (y(k) - y_i)^2} \tag{1}$$

Under the line-of sight propagation condition (LOS), the distance estimation of ith bacon node at time k is as follows:

$$\hat{d}_i(k) = d_i(k) + n_i \tag{2}$$

where n_i is the Gaussian white noise with zero mean and variance σ_i^2.

Under the non-line-of-sight propagation condition (NLOS), because the process of propagation encountered obstacles, the signal does not spread along the straight line. Therefore, the distance estimation of the ith beacon node at time k is as follows:

$$\hat{d}_i(k) = d_i(k) + n_i + n_{NLOS} \tag{3}$$

where n_{NLOS} is the NLOS error independent of noise n_i. Since the propagation path in NLOS is longer than the LOS situation, n_{NLOS} is positive. n_{NLOS} obeys Gaussian, Uniform or Exponential distribution. And when the environment changes, its parameter characteristics also change.

The probability density function of n_i is:

$$f(n_i) = \frac{1}{\sqrt{2\pi\sigma_i^2}} \exp\left(-\frac{n_i^2}{2\sigma_i^2}\right) \tag{4}$$

When n_{NLOS} obeys the Gaussian distribution, its probability density function can be expressed as follows:

$$f(n_{NLOS}) = \frac{1}{\sqrt{2\pi\sigma_{NLOS}^2}} \exp\left(-\frac{(n_{NLOS} - \mu_{NLOS})^2}{2\sigma_{NLOS}^2}\right) \tag{5}$$

When n_{NLOS} obeys the Uniform distribution, its probability density function is described by:

$$f(n_{NLOS}) = \begin{cases} \frac{1}{u_{max} - u_{min}}, & u_{min} \leq n_{NLOS} \leq u_{max} \\ 0, & else \end{cases} \tag{6}$$

In addition, the probability density function is given as follows when n_{NLOS} obeys the Exponential distribution:

$$f(n_{NLOS}) = \begin{cases} \lambda^{-1} e^{-n_{NLOS}/\lambda}, & n_{NLOS} \geq 0 \\ 0, & n_{NLOS} < 0 \end{cases} \tag{7}$$

4 Proposed Method

4.1 Kalman Prediction

Since the ith beacon node obtains N measurements over time slot $[k - \delta, k + \delta]$, the measured value $\hat{\mathbf{d}}_i(k)$ in time slot k can be described as the expression $\hat{\mathbf{d}}_i(k) = [\hat{d}_i^1(k), \hat{d}_i^2(k), \ldots, \hat{d}_i^N(k)]$. And the average value of $\hat{\mathbf{d}}_i(k)$ is given as $\eta_i(k) = (1/N) \sum_{n=1}^{N} \hat{d}_i^n(k)$. Therefore, the state vector of the ith beacon node is described as follows:

$$\mathbf{X}_i(k) = [\eta_i(k), \dot{\eta}_i(k)]^T, k = 1, \ldots, K \tag{8}$$

where $\dot{\eta}_i(k)$ is the moving velocity of the unknown node.

When the propagation condition of the signal is constant (LOS/NLOS), the state equation and the measurement equation of the ith beacon node are shown in Eqs. (9) and (10).

$$\mathbf{X}_i(k) = \mathbf{F}\mathbf{X}_i(k - 1) + \mathbf{C}w_i(k - 1) \tag{9}$$

$$Z_i(k) = d_i(k) + N_{LOS/NLOS} \tag{10}$$

where $\mathbf{F} = \begin{bmatrix} 1 & \Delta t \\ 0 & 1 \end{bmatrix}$, $\mathbf{C} = \begin{bmatrix} \Delta t^2/2 \\ \Delta t \end{bmatrix}$, $\Delta t = 1$ is the sample period of this method. $w_i(k - 1)$ is the noise in the process and it obeys the distribution $N\left(0, \sigma_{w,i}^2\right)$. When under the NLOS environment, N_{NLOS} contains the measurement noise n_i and NLOS error n_{NLOS}. When in the NLOS condition, $N_{NLOS} = n_i$.

In this section, the method presented in this paper will be described in detail. Firstly, the prediction state and the covariance matrix are calculated using the Kalman prediction of the time slot k. Secondly, the NLOS recognition algorithm is used to identify the type of signal propagation condition (LOS/NLOS). If the propagation condition is LOS, the measurement residual $E_i(k)$ of Kalman filter is applied directly. If the propagation condition is NLOS, the measurement residual $E_i(k)$ is updated. And the rest of the steps are similar. The flow chart of the proposed algorithm is shown specifically in Fig. 1.

From the Kalman filter model we can see, the predicted state and prediction covariance are given by:

$$\hat{\mathbf{X}}_i(k|k - 1) = \mathbf{F}\hat{\mathbf{X}}_i(k - 1|k - 1) \tag{11}$$

$$\mathbf{P}_i(k|k - 1) = \mathbf{F}\mathbf{P}_i(k - 1|k - 1)\mathbf{F}^T + \sigma_i^2 \mathbf{C}\mathbf{C}^T \tag{12}$$

where $\hat{\mathbf{X}}_i(k|k - 1)$ and $\hat{\mathbf{X}}_i(k - 1|k - 1)$ are the predicted and updated state estimate at time slot k − 1, $\mathbf{P}_i(k - 1|k - 1)$ and $\mathbf{P}_i(k|k - 1)$ are the updated and predicted covariance at time slot k − 1, respectively.

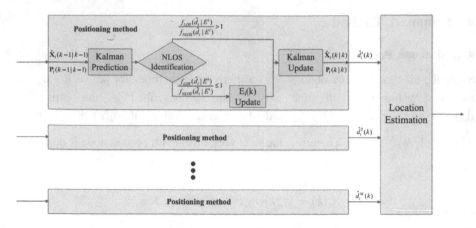

Fig. 1. The flowchart for the proposed method

The measurement residual is described as follows (where $\mathbf{H} = [10]$):

$$E_i(k) = Z_i(k) + \hat{Z}_i(k|k-1) \tag{13}$$

$$\hat{Z}_i(k|k-1) = \mathbf{H}\hat{\mathbf{X}}_i(k|k-1) \tag{14}$$

$$S_i(k) = \mathbf{H}\mathbf{P}_i(k|k-1)\mathbf{H}^T + \mathbf{Q} \tag{15}$$

where $\mathbf{Q}$ is the covariance matrix of measurement error.

Finally, the gain of Kalman is as follows:

$$\mathbf{K}_i(k) = \mathbf{P}_i(k|k-1)\mathbf{H}^T(S_i(k))^{-1} \tag{16}$$

4.2   NLOS Identification

If the propagation of the signal is identified as LOS, the range measurement by the ith beacon node is modeled as Eq. (17), which as shown in the TOA model in Sect. 3. And on the contrary, if the propagation of the signal is identified as NLOS, the range measurement by the ith beacon node is modeled as Eq. (18).

$$\hat{d}_i = d_i + n_i \tag{17}$$

$$\hat{d}_i = d_i + n_i + n_{NLOS} \tag{18}$$

where n_i obeys the distribution $N\left(0, \sigma_{w,i}^2\right)$ and n_{NLOS} obeys the distribution $N\left(\mu_{NLOS}, \sigma_{NLOS}^2\right)$.

Assuming that under the LOS environment, the probability density function of $\hat{d}_i$ is shown in Eq. (19). And similarly, when under the NLOS environment, the probability density function of $\hat{d}_i$ is expressed in Eq. (20).

$$f_{LOS}(\hat{d}_i) = \frac{1}{\sqrt{2\pi\sigma_i^2}} \exp\left(-\frac{(\hat{d}_i - d_i)^2}{2\sigma_i^2}\right) \tag{19}$$

$$f_{NLOS}(\hat{d}_i) = \frac{1}{\sqrt{2\pi(\sigma_i^2 + \sigma_{NLOS}^2)}} \exp\left(-\frac{(\hat{d}_i - d_i - \mu_{NLOS})^2}{2(\sigma_i^2 + \sigma_{NLOS}^2)}\right) \tag{20}$$

Comparing Eqs. (19) and (20), if Eq. (21) is satisfied, the signal propagation condition is LOS. And if Eq. (22) is satisfied, the condition of signal propagation is NLOS.

$$\frac{f_{LOS}(\hat{d}_i|E^i)}{f_{NLOS}(\hat{d}_i|E^i)} > 1 \tag{21}$$

$$\frac{f_{LOS}(\hat{d}_i|E^i)}{f_{NLOS}(\hat{d}_i|E^i)} \leq 1 \tag{22}$$

4.3   Kalman Update

In the NLOS identification in Sect. 2, if the signal propagation condition is LOS, the Kalman filter is applied directly without updating, and the measurement residual $E_i(k)$ is shown in Eq. (13). Conversely, if the condition of the signal propagation is NLOS, we choose to carry out the Kalman update, and $E_i(k)$ update equation is as follows:

$$E_i(k) = Z_i(k) - \hat{Z}_i(k|k-1) - \mu_{NLOS} \tag{23}$$

Therefore, the Kalman update equations can be described as follows:

$$\hat{X}_i(k) = \hat{X}_i(k) - K_i(k)E_i(k) \tag{24}$$

$$P_i(k) = P_i(k|k-1) - K_i(k)S_i(k)(K_i(k))^T \tag{25}$$

So the estimated distance of the ith beacon node can derived from the estimated state vector $\hat{X}_i(k|k)$ as follows:

$$\tilde{d}_i(k) = D\hat{X}_i(k|k), D = [1,0] \tag{26}$$

The position of the unknown node can be derived from the filter distance calculated by Eq. (26) in the above.

4.4   Maximum Likelihood Localization Method

At last, we use maximum likelihood localization method for location estimation in this section. In the maximum likelihood localization method, the positions of beacon nodes are $[(x_1, y_1), (x_2, y_2), ..., (x_M, y_M)]$, and the estimated position of unknown node at time k is $U(k) = [\hat{x}(k), \hat{y}(k)]^T$, which is the output of the method in Sect. 3. So the maximum likelihood equation is as follows:

$$\begin{cases} (x_1 - \hat{x}(k))^2 + (y_1 - \hat{y}(k))^2 = (\tilde{d}_1(k))^2 \\ \quad\quad \vdots \\ (x_M - \hat{x}(k))^2 + (y_M - \hat{y}(k))^2 = (\tilde{d}_M(k))^2 \end{cases} \tag{27}$$

When A and B are as follows, the above equation can be converted to $AU(k) = B$.

$$A = 2 \begin{bmatrix} (x_1 - x_2) & (y_1 - y_2) \\ (x_1 - x_3) & (y_1 - y_3) \\ \vdots & \vdots \\ (x_1 - x_M) & (y_1 - y_M) \end{bmatrix} \tag{28}$$

$$B = \begin{bmatrix} [\hat{d}_2(k)]^2 - [\hat{d}_1(k)]^2 - (x_2^2 + y_2^2) + (x_1^2 + y_1^2) \\ [\hat{d}_3(k)]^2 - [\hat{d}_1(k)]^2 - (x_3^2 + y_3^2) + (x_1^2 + y_1^2) \\ \vdots \\ [\hat{d}_M(k)]^2 - [\hat{d}_1(k)]^2 - (x_M^2 + y_M^2) + (x_1^2 + y_1^2) \end{bmatrix} \tag{29}$$

Finally, the coordinate matrix of unknown node can be obtained after calculation can be given as follows:

$$U(k) = (A^T A)^{-1} A^T B \tag{30}$$

5   Simulation

In this section, we present simulation and experiment results for the improved Kalman filter algorithm for mobile localization in the nonlinear line of sight environment. Through the simulation and experimental results, the effectiveness of the proposed algorithm is evaluated.

Figure 2(a) shows that the filtered distance using proposed when compared with the measurement distance and true distance. It can be observed that the proposed method could not mitigate the error obviously in the first twenty steps, but the filtered distance curve is approaching to the true distance curve gradually after twenty steps.

Figure 2(b) indicates the comparison between the filtered error and measurement error in each time step. It can be observed that the proposed method has a smaller error compared with the measurement error.

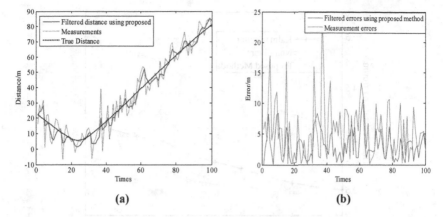

Fig. 2. (a) The comparison of distance. (b) The filter error in time step

Figure 3 provides the relationship between the standard deviation of measurement noise and the localization error. At the beginning, the localization error of the three methods is not obvious. With the increase of the standard deviation of measurement noise, the superiority of the method proposed in this paper began to reflect. It can be observed that the proposed method is more advantageous than Kalman filter.

In Fig. 4, when the mean of NLOS error is 1, the localization error of the proposed method reduces 34.24%, 4.37% compared with non filter and Kalman filter method. And when the mean of NLOS error is 6, the localization error of the proposed method reduces 43.53%, 18.91% compared with non filter and Kalman filter method. With the increase of the mean of NLOS error, the localization error of the method proposed is smaller obviously.

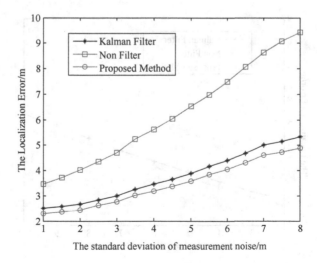

Fig. 3. The standard deviation of measurement noise versus the localization error

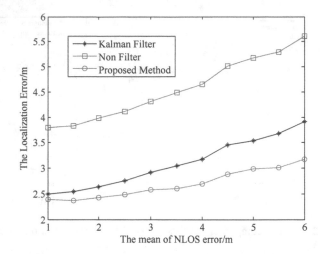

Fig. 4. The mean of NLOS error versus the localization error

Figure 5 shows the relationship between the standard deviation of NLOS error and the localization error. The results demonstrate that the advantage of proposed method increase obviously with the increase of the standard deviation of NLOS error. On average, the localization accuracy of the proposed method improves 38.36%, 6.99% when compared with non filter and Kalman filter method.

To further evaluate the proposed method, we compared the number of beacon nodes and the localization error in Fig. 6. It shows that the localization accuracy will been greatly improved with the increasing number of beacon nodes. When the number of beacon nodes is 4, the localization accuracy of the proposed method improves

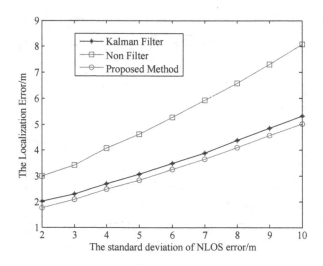

Fig. 5. The standard deviation of NLOS error versus the localization error

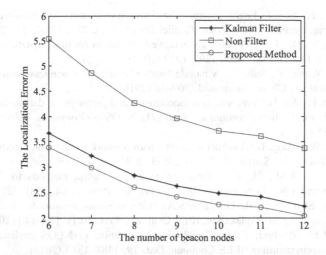

Fig. 6. The number of beacon nodes versus the localization error

38.81%, 7.74% when compared with non filter and Kalman filter method. When the number of beacon nodes is 12, the localization accuracy of the proposed method improves 39.48%, 8.64% when compared with non filter and Kalman filter method.

6 Conclusions

Due to the complex environment, non-line-of-sight signal transmission can cause great measurement. Therefore, in this paper, we propose an improved Kalman filter. In this method, the measurement residuals are updated in mixed LOS/NLOS cases. At last, simulation and experimental results show that the proposed method can effectively reduce the influence of NLOS error, and can achieve higher positioning accuracy than Kalman filter algorithm.

Acknowledgements. This work was supported by the National Natural Science Foundation of China under Grant No. 61403068; Natural Science Foundation of Hebei Province under Grant No. F2015501097 and F2016501080; Scientific Research Fund of Hebei Provincial Education Department under Grant No. Z2014078; NEUQ internal funding under Grant No. XNB2015009 and XNB2015010.

References

1. Bin, G., Sheng, S.: A robust regularization path algorithm for ν-Support Vector Classification. IEEE Trans. Neural Netw. Learn. Syst. **28**, 1241–1248 (2016)
2. Xia, Z., Wang, X., Zhang, L., Qin, Z.: A privacy-preserving and copy-deterrence content-based image retrieval scheme in cloud computing. IEEE Trans. Inf. Forensics Secur. **11**, 2594–2608 (2016)

3. Fu, Z., Ren, K., Shu, J.: Enabling personalized search over encrypted outsourced data with efficiency improvement. IEEE Trans. Parallel Distrib. Syst. **27**, 2546–2559 (2016)
4. Li, W., Jia, Y., Du, J.: TOA-based cooperative localization for mobile stations with NLOS mitigation. J. Franklin Inst. **353**, 1297–1312 (2016)
5. Cheng, L., Wang, Y., Sun, X.: A mobile location strategy for wireless sensor network in NLOS conditions. China Commun. **13**, 69–78 (2016)
6. Hu, N., Liu, P., Wu, H.: Vote selection mechanisms and probabilistic data association-based mobile node localization algorithm in mixed LOS/NLOS environments. Telecommun. Syst. **62**, 641–655 (2016)
7. Li, B., Cui, W., Wang, B.: A robust wireless sensor network localization algorithm in mixed LOS/NLOS scenario. Sensor **15**, 23536–23553 (2015)
8. Wang, G., So, A.M., Li, Y.: Robust convex approximation methods for TDOA-based localization under NLOS conditions. IEEE Trans. Sig. Process. **64**, 3281–3296 (2016)
9. Ghari, P.M., Shahbazian, R., Ghorashi, S.A.: Wireless sensor network localization in harsh environments using SDP relaxation. IEEE Commun. Lett. **20**(1), 137–140 (2016)
10. Vaghefi, R.M., Buehrer, R.M.: Cooperative localization in NLOS environments using semidefinite programming. IEEE Commun. Lett. **19**, 1382–1385 (2015)
11. Banerjee I., Chatterjee M., Samanta T.: Sensor localization using received signal strength measurements for obstructed wireless sensor networks with noisy channels. In: Wireless Communications and Networking Conference Workshops (WCNCW), pp. 47–51 (2015)
12. Cai Z., Shang L., Gao D.: Indoor mobile localization in mixed environment with RSS measurements. In: IEEE 21st International Symposium on Personal, Indoor and Mobile Radio Communications Workshops, pp. 1–13 (2015)

An Improved Localization Algorithm
for Anisotropic Sensor Networks

Xiaoyong Yan[1,2,3](✉), Zhong Yang[3], Yu Liu[4], Zhong Su[5],
and Huijun Li[6]

[1] School of Computer, Nanjing University of Posts and Telecommunications,
Nanjing, China
[2] Jiangsu High Technology Research Key Laboratory for Wireless Sensor
Networks, Nanjing University of Posts and Telecommunications, Nanjing, China
[3] School of Intelligence Science and Control Engineering,
Jinling Institute of Technology, Nanjing, China
{xiaoyong_yan,yz}@jit.edu.cn
[4] School of Computer Engineering,
Jinling Institute of Technology, Nanjing, China
ayu987@jit.edu.cn
[5] Center of Information Construction and Management,
Jinling Institute of Technology, Nanjing, China
suzhong@jit.edu.cn
[6] School of Instrument Science and Engineering,
Southeast University, Nanjing, China
lihuijun@seu.edu.cn

Abstract. Aiming at the problem that the multi-hop range-free wireless
localization algorithm is sensitive to the influence of the anisotropic sensor
network factors, we propose a new approach for localization in wireless sensor
networks based on regularization algorithm. We first construct the mapping
model using the hop-counts and the distance between anchors, and regularization algorithm is used to describe the optimal linear transformations between the
hop-counts and the distance. We then use the hop-counts of no-anchors to
anchors and this mapping model to the locations of the non-anchors. We
evaluate our algorithm under irregular distribution of nodes and the uneven
deployment of nodes, and analyze its performance. We also compare our
approach with several existing approaches, and demonstrate our proposed
algorithm can effectively avoid the network anisotropy.

Keywords: Wireless sensor networks · Multi-hop range-free localization ·
Anisotropic network · Regularized algorithm

1 Introduction

With the development of wireless sensor networks (WSNs) technology and mature
products, wireless sensor network with its own unique advantages, began to gradually
replace the traditional wired sensor products, and infiltrated into various fields and
sectors of society [1]. Location information plays a crucial role in most practical

© Springer International Publishing AG 2017
X. Sun et al. (Eds.): ICCCS 2017, Part I, LNCS 10602, pp. 495–507, 2017.
https://doi.org/10.1007/978-3-319-68505-2_43

applications of WSNs [2–4]. The most convenient way to obtain the location information is to add a satellite localization system module on the nodes of WSNs. The satellite localization system directly communicates with the receiving terminal through the satellite, which forms one-hop localization system, but the satellite localization system has high cost and high power consumption, and it can only be used in outdoor environment without obstacles. However, in a study about human activity habits found that people spend more than 80% of their life and work time in the closed housing conditions [5, 6]. In addition to, this study also found that 95% of the social production activities are completed in this kind of environment [5] in closed environments, satellite signals suffer not only from severe attenuation and multipath but from complex variations thereof. For example, the typically GPS L1 C/A code signal receiving power is set to at least −160 dBW for elevation angles between 5x and 90x (ICD 2000) [7]. However, signals received do not meet this minimum under these environments.

With the emergence of new technologies such as sensor networks, Internet of things, etc., one-hop localization mode has gradually upgraded to the multi-hop localization mode [8, 9]. In terms of whether the distance information is measured among nodes in localization process, the multi-hop localization algorithms can be roughly divided into the range-based (as shown in Fig. 1a) and range-free ones (as shown in Fig. 1b) [2, 3, 10].

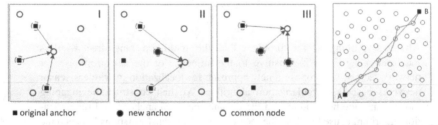

(a) Range-based multi-hop localization

(b) Range-free multi-hop localization

Fig. 1. Multi-hop localizations.

Among them, range-free multi-hop techniques attracts much more attentions due to the fact that it does not need special hardware and low costly but just needs connectivity information among nodes. In this paper, we propose LocRR, a novel range-free multi-free localization algorithm that provides accurate location estimates in anisotropic WSNs.

As shown in Fig. 2, node A send a HELLO message to node B. If the nodes are well-distributed, then the distance of per-hop distance is basically the same (as shown Fig. 2a). However, if there is an obstacle or coverage missing in the deployment area, then the per-hop distance deviating the physical distance (as shown Fig. 2b).

In this paper, we study the irregular distribution of nodes, which lead to the anisotropic problem in wireless sensor networks. This paper presents a new wireless

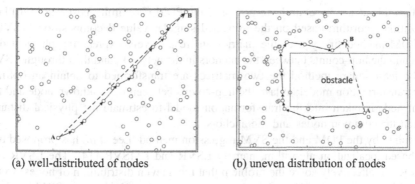

(a) well-distributed of nodes   (b) uneven distribution of nodes

Fig. 2. Well-distributed and uneven distribution.

localization method based on regularized regression, namely LocRR (Localization by regularized regression), which effectively solves the influence of the anisotropy network on the localization performance.

The rest of this paper is organized as follows: In Sect. 2, related work about multi-hop range-free localization algorithms in wireless sensor networks is described. In Sect. 3, the motivation of this paper is explained and the new multi-hop range-free localization method is proposed. In Sect. 4, various simulations are conducted and the results of the proposed methods are compared with those of previous methods. Finally, conclusions are drawn in Sect. 5.

2 Related Work

After years of exploration and development, several researchers have proposed a large number of multi-hop range-free localization approaches. Typical implementations range-free multi-hop techniques include DV-hop [11], Amorphous [12], *etc.* All of them assume that the sensor networks are isotropic and nodes all are uniformly distributed, so that hop count represents the real distance. First, DV-hop and Amorphous measure the internode hop-counts and linearly convert them to the average per-hop distance. Then, localization algorithms calculate the estimated distances between common nodes and anchors using hop-counts multiplied by the average per-hop distance. Last, based on the estimated distances to the anchors, the common nodes estimate themselves position by the multilateration. However, in the real environment, the sensor networks may be anisotropic and the distribution of nodes is not uniform. If sensor networks are anisotropic, the per-hop distance may not fix. Hence, it will introduce huge errors by using fixed per-hop distance represents the physical distance among nodes.

In recent years, building a localization model with the help of machine learning methods has become one of the research hotspots. Using the relationship between party nodes with known location information in the network, these methods find the location dependent relationship between the nodes to be located and the anchors, and makes use of the dependencies to predict the location of the non-anchors as accurately as possible.

Based on this idea, Lim et al. have proposed the PDM (Proximity Distance Map) [13] localization algorithm based on the truncated singular value decomposition (TSVD). The PDM method firstly uses the matrices to respectively express the physical distances and the hop-counts between the anchors in the network; and then through TSVD and the least square method the two matrices are transformed to obtain an optimal linear transformation model; at last, the hop-counts between the unknown node and the known node is taken into the transformation model to estimate the physical distance between the common nodes and the anchors.

Inspired by the PDM and the SVM-regression method, Lee *et al.* has proposed two SVR-based localization algorithm, namely LSVR and LMSVR [14]. The LSVR and LMSVR can effectively solve the problem that the uneven distribution of nodes, so the adaptability of the network environment is stronger than that of the PDM method. However, the SVR-based method involves more parameters [15–17], and often needs to employ cross-validation or the grid search method, resulting in high computational complexity, so that it is not appropriate for the applications of wireless sensor networks.

The proposed LocRR method employs the regularized regression which is similar to the TSVD regularization in the PDM method to construct the mapping model between hop-counts and distances. In fact, TSVD deletes the unreliable parts of the hop-counts matrix, but doing so will damage the accuracy of location estimation. Different from TSVD in the PDM method, a filter factor is added to the high frequency component in the regularized regression, which can damp or filter out the noise in the high frequency component to ensure the stability and accuracy of the solution. In addition, before constructing the mapping model between hop-counts and distances, carry out the centralized processing for the matrix of hop-counts and distances. Thus the scale between hop-counts and distances mismatch problem in the process of the transformation is eliminated.

3   LocRR: Localization by Regularized Regression

3.1   Statement of the Localization Scene

Given n sensor nodes $\{S_i\}_{i=1}^{n}$ are deployed in a two-dimensional plane area, where the first $m(m \ll n)$ nodes $\{S_i\}_{i=1}^{m} \in A$ are the anchors with know their positions a priori, while the remaining $n - m$ nodes $\{S_i\}_{i=m+1}^{n} \in U$ are common nodes with unknown positions. The coordinates of nodes can be expressed by the formula (1):

$$\mathbf{cor}(S_i) = (x_i, y_i)^T \; for \; i = 1, \cdots m, \cdots, n \tag{1}$$

The physical distance from the node S_i to the node S_j can be represented by the formula (2):

$$d(S_i, S_j) = \|cor(S_i) - cor(S_j)\|$$
$$= \sqrt{(x_i - x_j)^2 + (x_i - x_j)^2} \in \mathbb{R}^2 \tag{2}$$

After a period of communication time, the anchor $S_i \in \mathbf{B}$ has collected two sets of data: the minimum hop-count vector between the anchors, denoted as $\mathbf{h}_i = [h_{i,1}, \cdots, h_{i,m}]^T$, which denotes the minimum hop counts between the reference node S_i and the rest $m - 1$ anchors. Corresponding, the physical distance vector between the anchors is denoted as $\mathbf{d}_i = [d_{i,1}, \cdots, d_{i,m}]^T$, which be the physical distance vector between the anchor node $S_i \in \mathbf{B}$ and the other anchors. The minimum hop-count matrix between the corresponding anchors is $\mathbf{H} = [\mathbf{h}_1, \cdots, \mathbf{h}_m]$. Similarly, the physical distance matrix is $\mathbf{D} = [\mathbf{d}_1, \cdots, \mathbf{d}_m]$.

In network, the common nodes can obtain the hop-counts to the connected anchors, so the objective of multi-hop range-free wireless localization problem is to recover the locations of sensors $S_{m+1}, \cdots, S_n$ solely on the basis of the hop-counts. Thus, the multi-hop range-free wireless localization problem can be formulated as the formula (3),

$$\begin{aligned} &\text{Estimate } \mathbf{cor}(S_k) \\ &\text{Given } \mathbf{cor}(S_i),\, d(S_i, S_j),\, and\, h(S_i, S_k) \end{aligned} \tag{3}$$

where $S_i, S_j \in \mathbf{B}$, $S_k \in \mathbf{U}$, and $h(S_i, S_k)$ is the hop-count between the anchor S_i and the non-anchor S_k.

Thus, the mapping relation between the hop-counts and the physical distances can be obtained:

$$\mathbf{D} = \mathbf{H}\mathbf{T} + \mathbf{E} \tag{4}$$

where $\mathbf{D}, \mathbf{H}$ are respectively the physical distance matrix and the hop count matrix between the related nodes; $\mathbf{T}$ is the mapping relationship between the hop-counts and the distances; $\mathbf{E}$ is the random error.

3.2   Localization Algorithm

The process of LocRR is roughly divided into three stages: the measure stage, the model building stage and the location estimation stage.

1. The measure stage

Using the distance vector routing exchange protocol by drawing lessons from the DV-hop method, and after a period of time of communication among nodes, all nodes in the network can obtain the shortest hop-count to the anchors. The specific process is: each anchor transmits a broadcast information packet with its own location information to the rest nodes within the communication radius. The packet at least contains the identify field of the anchor (ID), the location information of the coordinates (X axis and Y axis) and the hop-counts field (the initial value is 1). The packet format is as follows:

ID	X	Y	Hop_counts

After receiving the packet information, each node records the minimum hop-count to the connected anchor, meanwhile incrementing the field value of Hop_counts in the packet by 1. When the value of Hop_counts received from the same anchor is not the minimum, the procedure automatically ignores the packet. Using the above method, all the nodes record the minimum hop-counts to their connected anchors in the network.

The distance between the anchors can be obtained by the physical distance formula (2) based on their own coordinates.

2. The model building stage

After obtaining the least hop-count matrix and the physical distance matrix between the anchors, the mapping relationship can be constructed by using the formula (4). Each column vector t_i of T can be obtained by minimizing the mean square error of the errors:

$$v_i = \sum_{k=1}^{m} (d_{ik} - h_k t_i)^2 = \|d_i - Ht_i\|^2 \tag{5}$$

It is easy to get that the least square solution of the column vector t_i is:

$$t_i = (H^T H)^{-1} H^T d_i \tag{6}$$

In order to avoid the problem of "the big data eat the little data" caused by the level of number difference in the transformation process of the relationship between the hop count and the distance, in the actual operation process the centralized processing will be carried out for the hop count and the distance. So, the formula (4) is turned into $\tilde{D} = \tilde{H}T + E$, where $\tilde{D}$, $\tilde{H}$ are the centralized distances matrix and the centralized hop-counts matrix, respectively. At this point, the matrix solution corresponding to the formula (6) is:

$$\hat{T} = (\tilde{H}^T \tilde{H})^{-1} \tilde{H}^T \tilde{D} \tag{7}$$

In the process of the transformation between the hop-counts and the distances, there exist serious multiple correlations between hop-count vectors and the case that the number of the sample points in H is less than the number of variables. At the moment, since the data does not have enough information to obtain the optimal solution, it is not wise to try to calculate forcibly. The above mentioned problem is also called the ill-posed problem, which can be effectively solved by the regularization method [18].

Consider the general form of the Regularized Regression criterion, the mapping relationship between the hop-counts and the distances can be written as

$$\hat{T} = (\tilde{H}^T \tilde{H} + \xi I)^{-1} \tilde{H}^T \tilde{D} \tag{8}$$

where, $\xi(\xi > 0)$ is known as the regularization parameter, which defines the trade-off between norm and loss, it controls the grade of regularization. I is a $m \times m$ dimension identity matrix.

From the formula (8), it is obvious that the key to solving $\hat{T}$ lies in the selection of the regularization parameter ξ. If the regularization parameter ξ is very small (like $\xi \to 0$), the formula (8) will be very close to the solution of the original problem, and at this moment the solution will cause the oscillation. On the contrary, if the regularization parameter ξ is too large, it will introduce too much human disturbance to the equation. Therefore, choosing a compromise value of ξ is the key to solving this problem. In general, the most well-known way to obtain optimal regularization parameter by the cross-validation [19], L-curve [20] and the discrepancy principle [18], etc.

3. The location estimation stage

An unknown node $S_t \in U$ can obtain the hop-counts matrix H_t to all anchors. It then obtains the predict the physical distance matrix D_{pred} by multiplying H_t with $\hat{T}$:

$$D_{pred} = \tilde{H}_{test}\hat{T}_{train} + repmat(\tilde{h},n) \tag{9}$$

where $\tilde{H}_{test}$ is the matrix after the centralized processing on H_t; $\tilde{h}$ is the column mean of H; $repmat(\tilde{h},n)$ is the stack of n rows of $\tilde{h}$.

Finally, each common node employ multilateration to localize its own position.

4 Simulation Results

Multi-hop range-free wireless localization methods are often suitable for large-scale applications, which have the characteristics of many nodes. In addition, the validation of the localization algorithm is sometimes required to adjust the different parameters in the same scene. The above reasons will result in the problem of the verification work difficult to continue under the condition of insufficient funds and limited experimental conditions. Therefore, based on these reasons, the simulation software is usually used to verify the localization performance in the multi-hop range-free wireless localization researches. In order to verify the performance of the LocRR algorithm, a series of experiments are carried out with the aid of the simulation software matlab2013b. In the simulation, non-anchors and anchors are even deployed in a 600-by-600 unit region and two kinds of node distribution are set up in anisotropic network: (1) nodes are randomly placed in C-shaped network, Z-shaped network and G-shaped network and (2) nodes are regularly placed in C-shaped network, Z-shaped network and G-shaped network. Two kinds of distributions and three topologies are shown in Table 1.

Table 1. Distribution of nodes in anisotropic networks

	C-shaped	Z-shaped	G-shaped
randomly distributed			
uniformly distributed			

4.1 Localization Results with Randomly Deployed Sensors

In this group of experiments, 500 sensor nodes are randomly deployed in C-shaped, G-shaped and Z-shaped region, the anchors are also randomly deployed too. Table 2 shows the localization results for each node in the network with 40 anchors.

Table 3 gives the root mean square error (RMS) with four multi-hop range-free localization methods under different topology in the randomly deployed sensor network.

Figure 3 describes the performance of five multi-hop range-free localization with 40 anchors under different topology in the randomly deployed sensor network. In order to reduce the influence of one single experiment on the result in randomly deployed situations, simulations were carried out several times are performed in the same network. We collect 50 results of simulations, and take the mean value of RMS as the evaluation criteria. We can see that the performance is significantly difference under same deployment environment. This demonstrates that the proposed algorithm can gain a better performance under anisotropic network.

4.2 Localization Results with Uniformly Deployed Sensors

In this set of experiments, 405, 464 and 487 sensor nodes are uniformly deployed in the distance of 20 C-shaped, G-shaped and Z-shaped region respectively. Table 4 shows the localization results for each node in the network with 40 anchors.

For the uniformly placed sensor network, we also compare our algorithm with the other algorithms (i.e., DV-hop, Amorphous, PDM, LSVR) under same deployment scenario. Table 5 gives the root mean square error with four multi-hop range-free

Table 2. Location results for randomly deployed sensor network.

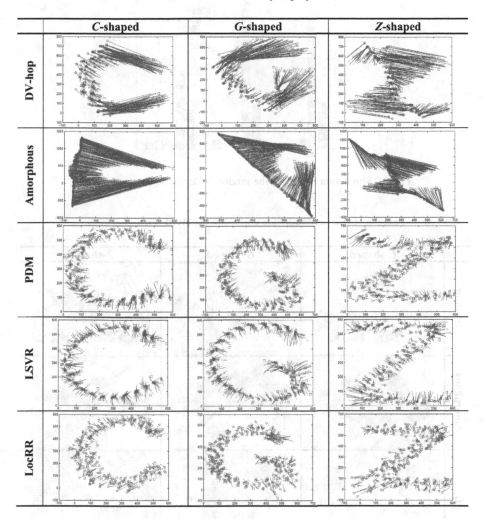

Table 3. RMS of different methods in the randomly deployed sensor network.

	C-shaped	G-shaped	Z-shaped
DV-hop	204.4	220.24	162.23
Amorphous	551.69	610.06	338.92
PDM	37.71	45.58	38.89
LSVR	37.3	44.42	36.14
LocRR	29.48	41.6	34.98

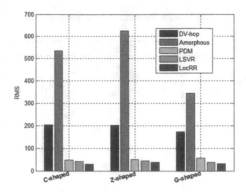

Fig. 3. Simulation results of the randomly deployed sensor network

Table 4. Location results for uniformly deployed sensor network.

	C-shaped	*G*-shaped	*Z*-shaped
DV-hop			
Amorphous			
PDM			
LSVR			
LocRR			

Table 5. RMS of different methods in the uniformly deployed sensor network.

	C-shaped	G-shaped	Z-shaped
DV-hop	183.65	202.72	225.45
Amorphous	448.81	650.30	450.72
PDM	45.61	63.81	43.48
LSVR	38.72	60.13	32.73
LocRR	34.42	43.31	28.43

localization methods under different topology in the uniformly deployed sensor network.

Figure 4 describes the performance of five multi-hop range-free localization with 40 anchors under different topology in the uniformly deployed sensor network. We can find that our algorithm always achieve the low RMS under difference anisotropic network.

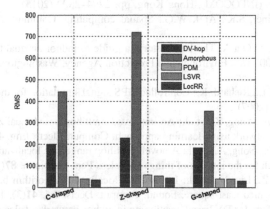

Fig. 4. Simulation results of the uniformly deployed sensor network

5   Conclusion

In this paper, a multi-hop range-free localization method based on the regularized regression is proposed. After centralizing the data of the hop-counts and the physical distances, the method uses the regularized regression to construct the mapping model between the hop-counts and the distances. The method based on the regularized regression can effectively solve the anisotropic problem caused by the uneven distribution and irregular deployment of nodes. Compared with other similar researches, it has some advantages, such as easy to design parameters, low computational complexity, high localization accuracy, stable performance and adapting to the complex environment.

Acknowledgements. The paper is sponsored by the NSF of China (61403080, 61572261, 61373139), National Natural Science Foundation of Jiangsu Province (BK20140641, BK20150868), China Postdoctoral Science Foundation (2014M551635, 2016M601861), Postdoctoral Fund of Jiangsu Province (1302085B), Natural Science Foundation of the Jiangsu Higher Education Institutions of China (15KJB520009) and the Open Project Program of Jiangsu Key Laboratory of Remote Measurement and Control (YCCK201603).

References

1. Akyildiz, I.F., Vuran, M.C.: Wireless Sensor Networks. Wiley, New York (2010)
2. Yang, Z., Wu, C., Liu, Y.: Location-Based Computing: Localization and Localizability of Wireless Networks, pp. 48–57. Tsinghua University Press, Beijing (2014)
3. Liu, Y., Yang, Z.: Location, Localization, and Localizability Location-Awareness Technology for Wireless Networks. Springer, New York (2011)
4. Xiao, F., Sha, C., Chen, L., et al.: Noise-tolerant localization from incomplete range measurements for wireless sensor networks. In: 2015 IEEE Conference on Computer Communications (INFOCOM), Hong Kong, pp. 2794–2802 (2015)
5. Shekhar, S., Feiner, S.K., Aref, W.G.: Spatial computing. Commun. ACM **59**(1), 72–81 (2016)
6. Radiation U S E O O a A: The Inside story: a guide to indoor air quality. Technical report EPA 402-K-93-007.U.S. Environmental Protection Agency, Washington, D.C. http://goo.gl/RkZUBU
7. Tao, H., Gérard, L., Richard, K.: Controlled GPS signal simulation for the indoors. J. Navig. **60**(2), 265–280 (2007)
8. Yan, X., Song, A., Yang, Z., et al.: An improved multihop-based localization algorithm for wireless sensor network using learning approach. Comput. Electr. Eng. **48**, 247–257 (2015)
9. Yan, X., Yang, Z., Song, A., et al.: A novel multihop range-free localization based on kernel learning approach for the internet of things. Wireless Pers. Commun. **87**(1), 269–292 (2016)
10. Yan, X., Yang, Z., Liu, Y., et al.: Incremental localization algorithm based on regularized iteratively reweighted least square. Found. Comput. Decis. Sci. **41**(3), 183–196 (2016)
11. Niculescu, D., Nath, B.: DV based positioning in ad hoc networks. Telecommun. Syst. **22**(1–4), 267–280 (2003)
12. Nagpal, R., Shrobe, H., Bachrach, J.: Organizing a global coordinate system from local information on an ad hoc sensor network. In: Zhao, F., Guibas, L. (eds.) IPSN 2003. LNCS, vol. 2634, pp. 333–348. Springer, Heidelberg (2003). doi:10.1007/3-540-36978-3_22
13. Lim, H., Hou, J.C.: Distributed localization for anisotropic sensor networks. ACM Trans. Sensor Netw. (TOSN) **5**(2), 1–26 (2009)
14. Lee, J., Chung, W., Kim, E.: A new kernelized approach to wireless sensor network localization. Inf. Sci. **243**(2013), 20–38 (2013)
15. Gu, B., Sheng, V.S.: A robust regularization path algorithm for v-support vector classification. IEEE Trans. Neural Netw. Learn. Syst. **28**(5), 1241–1248 (2017)
16. Xia, Z., Wang, X., Zhang, L., Qin, Z., Sun, X., Ren, K.: A privacy-preserving and copy-deterrence content-based image retrieval scheme in cloud computing. IEEE Trans. Inf. Forensics Secur. **11**(11), 2594–2608 (2016)
17. Fu, Z., Ren, K., Shu, J., Sun, X., Huang, F.: Enabling personalized search over encrypted outsourced data with efficiency improvement. IEEE Trans. Parallel Distrib. Syst. **27**(9), 2546–2559 (2016)
18. Bickel, P.J., Li, B.: Regularization in statistics. Test **15**(2), 271–344 (2006)

19. Hansen, P.C.: Regularization tools: a matlab package for analysis and solution of discrete ill-posed problems. Numer. Algorithms **6**(1), 1–35 (1994)
20. Zhang, L., Hua, C., Tang, Y., et al.: Ill-posed echo state network based on L-curve method for prediction of blast furnace gas flow. Neural Process. Lett. **43**(1), 97–113 (2016)

Further Results on Finite-Time Stability of Switched Static Neural Networks

Zhihua Diao, Chunying Diao, Xiaoliang Qian, and Yuanyuan Wu$^{(\boxtimes)}$

College of Electric and Information Engineering,
Zhengzhou University of Light Industry, Zhengzhou 450002, China
diaozhua@163.com, diaochunying1@163.com, wyuanyuan82@163.com

Abstract. This paper deals with the finite-time stability problem for switched static neural networks with time-varying delay. By employing the Lyapunov-like functional method and the average dwell time approach, a sufficient criterion is obtained, which can guarantee the finite-time stability of the concerned networks. Moreover, the derived conditions can be simplified into linear matrix inequalities conditions for convenient use. Finally, a numerical example is given to show the validity of the proposed results.

Keywords: Finite-time stability · Switched static neural networks · Time-varying delay · Lyapunov-like functional · Average dwell time

1 Introduction

In the past few years, neural networks (NNs) have been found successful applications in many areas, such as signal processing, image processing, pattern classification, associative memories, solving certain optimization problems, and so on. According to whether neuron states (the external states of neurons) or local fields states (the internal states of neurons) are selected as basic variables, neural networks can be classified as static neural networks or local field neural networks [1], and the two models are not always equivalent [2]. Actually, the static neural networks have been widely used to solve various optimization problems, such as some linear variational inequality problems. Compared with the extensive investigation of the stability problem of local field neural networks, the static neural networks have got less attention [3–9].

As a special class of hybrid system, switched systems consist of a family of subsystems and a switched rule, and have attracted considerable attention for its success in practical applications during the past decade. Considering the switched happened in neural networks, switched neural networks are proposed, and some results have been put forward on the stability analysis of the switched neural networks [10,11]. Furthermore, the stability and passivity analysis are considered for switched neural networks with time-varying delay in [12,13], and the stability analysis is investigated for discrete-time switched neural networks in [14–16]. The global exponential stability is concerned for switched stochastic

© Springer International Publishing AG 2017
X. Sun et al. (Eds.): ICCCS 2017, Part I, LNCS 10602, pp. 508–518, 2017.
https://doi.org/10.1007/978-3-319-68505-2_44

neural networks with time-varying delays in [17]. The synchronization control is studied for switched neural networks with time delay in [18,19]. As well known, integration and communication delays are unavoidably encountered in neural networks, then it is important and valuable to study the switched neural networks with time delay.

As far as the stability problem is concerned, most existing literatures are focused on the classical Lyapunov stability, which is the stability in an infinite-time interval. In many practical applications, the dynamical behavior over a fixed finite time interval is paid more attention for a system. For example, the property that the state does not exceed a certain threshold in a finite time interval with a given bound on the initial condition, which is corresponding to the finite-time stability. Now, concepts of finite-time stability have been proposed for several decades [20,21], and the definition of finite-time stability has been extended to the definition of finite-time bounded by taking the presence of external disturbances into account [22]. Meanwhile, many relevant results have been reported [23–26]. Most recently, several valuable results have been proposed for the finite-time problems of neural networks. The finite-time boundedness stability is studied for neural networks with parametric uncertainties in [27], and for uncertain neural networks with Markovian jumps in [28,29]. The problem of finite-time state estimation is investigated for neural networks with time-varying delays in [30]. To the best of the authors' knowledge, there is few work on the finite-time stability of static neural networks.

Motivated by the above analysis, this paper considers finite-time stability of the switched static neural networks (SSNNs) with time-varying delay. First, the concept of finite-time stability is extended to switched static neural networks. Then, employing the proper model transformation and Lyapunov-like functional, a sufficient condition is presented for the finite-time stability of switched static neural networks. In the rest of this paper is organized as follows. In Sect. 2, the switched static neural networks model with time-varying delay is formulated and some preliminaries are given. The sufficient condition of finite-time stability is obtained in Sect. 3. Section 4 provides a numerical example to illustrate the effectiveness of the proposed method. Some conclusions are made in Sect. 5.

Notation. Throughout this paper, the superscript "T" stands for the transpose of a matrix. R^n and $R^{n \times n}$ denote the n-dimension Euclidean space and set of all $n \times n$ real matrices, respectively. A real symmetric matrix $P > 0 (\geq 0)$ denotes P being a positive definite (positive semi-definite) matrix. $\lambda_{max}(P)$ and $\lambda_{min}(P)$ represent for the maximum and minimum eigenvalues of the matrix P respectively. Matrices, if not explicitly stated, are assumed to have compatible dimensions. The symmetric terms in a symmetric matrix are denoted by $*$.

2   Problem Statement and Preliminaries

Consider the following switched static neural networks with time-varying delay:

$$\begin{cases} \dot{x}(t) = -A_{\sigma(t)}x(t) + f(W_{\sigma(t)}x(t - \tau(t)) + J), \\ x(t) = \varphi(t), \quad -\tau \leq t \leq 0, \end{cases}$$

where $x(\cdot) = [x_1(\cdot), x_2(\cdot), \cdots, x_n(\cdot)]^T \in \mathbb{R}^n$ is the neuron state vector, $f(x(\cdot)) = [f_1(x_1(\cdot)), f_2(x_2(\cdot)), \cdots, f_n(s_n(\cdot))]^T \in \mathbb{R}^n$ represents the neuron activation function, and $J = [j_1, j_2, \cdots, j_n]^T \in \mathbb{R}^n$ is a constant input vector. $\sigma(t) : [0, +\infty) \longrightarrow \mathbb{N} = \{1, 2, \cdots, N\}$ is a piecewise constant switching signal, e.g. when $\sigma(t) = r \in \mathbb{N}$, it implies that the rth subnetworks is activated, where $\mathbb{N}$ is a finite set. For $\forall r \in \mathbb{N}$, $A_r = diag\{a_{r1}, a_{r2}, \cdots, a_{rn}\} \in \mathbb{R}^{n \times n}$ is a positive diagonal matrix, and $W_r = [W_{r1}^T, W_{r2}^T, \cdots, W_{rn}^T]^T \in \mathbb{R}^{n \times n}$ is the delayed connection weight matrix. $\tau(t)$ is a time-varying delay with $0 \leq \tau(t) \leq \tau$ and $\dot{\tau}(t) \leq \mu$, and $\varphi(t)(-\tau \leq t \leq 0)$ is the initial condition. In this paper, we assume:

Assumption 1. The each neuron activation function in system (2) is assumed to be bounded and satisfy

$$l_i^- \leq \frac{f_i(x) - f_i(y)}{x - y} \leq l_i^+, \quad \forall x, y \in R, x \neq y, \ i = 1, 2, \cdots, n, \tag{1}$$

where l_i^- and l_i^+ are some known constants. Define $l_i = \max\{|l_i^-|, |l_i^+|\}$, and let $\underline{L} = diag\{l_1^-, l_2^-, \cdots, l_n^-\}, \overline{L} = diag\{l_1^+, l_2^+, \cdots, l_n^+\}$, and $L = diag\{l_1, l_2, \cdots, l_n\}$.

Remark 1. Assume that W_β is invertible and $W_\beta A_\beta = A_\beta W_\beta$ holds, then (2) can be easily transformed to the following local neural networks by $y(t) = W_\beta x(t) + J$,

$$\dot{y}(t) = -A_\beta y(t) + W_\beta f(y(t - \tau(t))) + A_\beta J.$$

However, in many application, the two models are not equivalent. Therefore, it is necessary to study the switched static neural network (2).

Under Assumption 1, there is an equilibrium x^* of (2). For simplicity, let $z(\cdot) = x(\cdot) - x^*$, then system (2) can be transformed into

$$\dot{z}(t) = -A_{\sigma(t)}z(t) + g(W_{\sigma(t)}z(t - \tau(t))),$$
$$z(t) = \psi(t), \quad -\tau \leq t \leq 0. \tag{2}$$

where $z(\cdot) = [z_1(\cdot), z_2(\cdot), \cdots, z_n(\cdot)]^T$ is the state vector of the transformed system (4), $\psi(t) = \varphi(t) - x^*$ is the initial condition, and the transformed neuron activation functions is $g(W_k z(\cdot)) = [g_1(W_{\beta 1} z(\cdot)), g_2(W_{\beta 2} z(\cdot)), \cdots, g_n(W_{\beta n} z(\cdot))]^T = f(W_\beta z(\cdot) + W_\beta x^* + J) - f(W_\beta x^* + J)$. It is clear that $g_i(\cdot)$ satisfy:

$$l_i^- \leq \frac{g_i(x)}{x} \leq l_i^+, \quad \forall x \in R, x \neq 0, \ i = 1, 2, \cdots, n. \tag{3}$$

Based on the analysis above, we know that the stability analysis of system (2) on equilibrium is changed into the zero stability problem of system (4). We are now to introduce the notion of the finite-time stability for the system (4).

Definition 1. *Given a positive matrix R, three positive constants c_1, c_2, T with $c_1 < c_2$, the switched static neural networks (4) is said to be finite-time stable with respect to (c_1, c_2, T, R), if for any switched rule,*

$$\sup_{\theta \in [-\tau, 0]} z^T(\theta) R z(\theta) \leq c_1 \Longrightarrow z^T(t) R z(t) < c_2, \forall t \in [0, T].$$

Before giving the main results, we will address an employed lemma as follows:

Lemma 1 *(The Jensen Inequality). For any constant matrix* $R = R^T \geq 0$, *scalar* $\tau > 0$ *and vector function* $x(\cdot) : [-\tau, 0] \to \mathbb{R}^n$ *such that the following integrals are well defined, then*

$$-\tau \int_{t-\tau}^{t} x^T(s)Rx(s)ds \leq -\left[\int_{t-\tau}^{t} x(s)ds\right]^T R\left[\int_{t-\tau}^{t} x(s)ds\right]. \tag{4}$$

3   Main Results

In this section, we will present the finite-time stability criteria for the considered SSNNs (4).

Theorem 1. *Under the Assumption 1, the SSNNs (4) is finite-time stable with respect to* (c_1, c_2, T, R), *if there exists a scalar* $\alpha > 0$, *matrices* $P > 0$, $Q > 0$, $T > 0$, $S > 0$, *and diagonal matrix* $U \geq 0$ *such that the following inequalities hold for* $k = 1, 2, \cdots, N$:

$$\Xi_i = \begin{bmatrix} \Gamma_{11}^i & S_i & \Gamma_{13}^i \\ * & \Gamma_{22}^i & \Gamma_{23}^i \\ * & * & \Gamma_{33}^i \end{bmatrix} < 0, \tag{5}$$

$$\omega_2 c_1 < \omega_1 c_2 e^{-\alpha T}, \tag{6}$$

and the average dwell-time T_a *of the switching signal* σ *satisfies*

$$T_a > T_a^* = \frac{T \ln(v)}{\ln(\omega_1 c_2) - \ln(\omega_2 c_1) - \alpha T} \tag{7}$$

where

$\Gamma_{11}^i = -P_i A_i - A_i P_i + Q_i + \tau^2 A_i S_i A_i - S_i - \alpha P_i,$

$\Gamma_{22}^i = -(1 - \mu e^{\alpha \tau})Q_i - S_i - 2W_i^T \underline{L} U_i \overline{L} W_i,$

$\Gamma_{13}^i = -\tau^2 A_i S_i + P_i, \quad \Gamma_{23}^i = W_i^T \underline{L} U_i + W_i^T \overline{L} U_i,$

$\Gamma_{33}^i = \tau^2 S_i - 2U_i,$

$\omega_1 = \min_{\lambda \in \mathbb{N}}(\lambda_{min}(R^{-\frac{1}{2}} P_\lambda R^{-\frac{1}{2}})),$

$\omega_2 = \max_{\lambda \in \mathbb{N}}(\lambda_{max}(R^{-\frac{1}{2}} P_\lambda R^{-\frac{1}{2}})) + \tau e^{\alpha \tau} \max_{\lambda \in \mathbb{N}}(\lambda_{max}(R^{-\frac{1}{2}} Q_\lambda R^{-\frac{1}{2}}))$

$\qquad + 2\tau^3 e^{\alpha \tau} \max_{\lambda \in \mathbb{N}}(\lambda_{max}(R^{-\frac{1}{2}} A_\lambda S_\lambda A_\lambda R^{-\frac{1}{2}}) + \lambda_{max}(R^{-\frac{1}{2}} W_\lambda^T LS_\lambda LW_\lambda R^{-\frac{1}{2}}))$

$v = \max\{\dfrac{\max\limits_{\lambda \in \mathbb{N}}(\lambda_{max}(P_\lambda))}{\min\limits_{\lambda \in \mathbb{N}}(\lambda_{min}(P_\lambda))}, \dfrac{\max\limits_{\lambda \in \mathbb{N}}(\lambda_{max}(Q_\lambda))}{\min\limits_{\lambda \in \mathbb{N}}(\lambda_{min}(Q_\lambda))}, \dfrac{\max\limits_{\lambda \in \mathbb{N}}(\lambda_{max}(S_\lambda))}{\min\limits_{\lambda \in \mathbb{N}}(\lambda_{min}(S_\lambda))}\}.$

with $\bar{P} = R^{-\frac{1}{2}} P R^{-\frac{1}{2}}$, $\bar{Q} = R^{-\frac{1}{2}} Q R^{-\frac{1}{2}}$, $\bar{T}_k = R^{-\frac{1}{2}} W_k^T LTLW_k R^{-\frac{1}{2}}$, $\bar{S}_k^1 = R^{-\frac{1}{2}} A_k SA_k R^{-\frac{1}{2}}$, *and* $\bar{S}_k^2 = R^{-\frac{1}{2}} W_k^T LSLW_k R^{-\frac{1}{2}}$.

Proof. Now, choose a Lyapunov-like functional candidate for system (9) as:

$$V_{\sigma(t)}(z(t)) = V_{1\sigma(t)}(t) + V_{2\sigma(t)}(t) + V_{3\sigma(t)}(t) + V_{4\sigma(t)}(t), \tag{8}$$

where

$$V_{1\sigma(t)}(t) = z^T(t)P_{\sigma(t)}z(t),$$

$$V_{2\sigma(t)}(t) = \int_{t-\tau(t)}^{t} e^{\alpha(t-s)}z^T(s)Q_{\sigma(t)}z(s)ds,$$

$$V_{3\sigma(t)}(t) = \tau \int_{-\tau}^{0} \int_{t+\theta}^{t} e^{\alpha(t-s)}\dot{z}^T(s)S_{\sigma(t)}\dot{z}(s)dsd\theta.$$

with $\sigma(t) \in \mathbb{N}$, $P_{\sigma(t)}$, $Q_{\sigma(t)}$, $S_{\sigma(t)}$ are symmetric positive-definite matrices, and α is a scalar parameter. At the switching instant t_k, we assume $\sigma(t_k) = i$, $\sigma(t_k^-) = j$ $(i, j \in \mathbb{N})$. When $t \in [t_k, t_{k+1})$, then $\sigma(t) = i$, and the derivative of V_{ki} $(k = 1, 2, 3, 4)$ along the trajectory of system (9) can be calculated respectively as follows

$$\dot{V}_{1i}(t) = 2z^T(t)P_i[-A_iz(t) + g(W_iz(t - \tau(t)))], \tag{9}$$

and

$$\dot{V}_{2i}(t) \leq \alpha \int_{t-\tau(t)}^{t} e^{\alpha(t-s)}z^T(s)Q_iz(s)ds + z^T(t)Q_iz(t)$$
$$- (1 - \mu e^{\alpha\tau})z^T(t - \tau(t))Q_iz(t - \tau(t)). \tag{10}$$

Using Lemma 1, it can be deduced that

$$\dot{V}_{3i}(t) \leq \alpha\tau \int_{-\tau}^{0} \int_{t+\theta}^{t} e^{\alpha(t-s)}\dot{z}^T(s)S_i\dot{z}(s)dsd\theta + \tau^2\dot{z}^T(t)S_i\dot{z}(t)$$
$$- \tau(t)\int_{t-\tau(t)}^{t} \dot{z}^T(s)S_i\dot{z}(s)ds$$
$$\leq \alpha\tau \int_{-\tau}^{0} \int_{t+\theta}^{t} e^{\alpha(t-s)}\dot{z}^T(s)S_i\dot{z}(s)dsd\theta + \tau^2[-A_iz(t)$$
$$+ g(W_iz(t - \tau(t)))]^T S_i[-A_iz(t) + g(W_iz(t - \tau(t)))]$$
$$- [z(t) - z(t - \tau(t))]^T S_i[z(t) - z(t - \tau(t))]. \tag{11}$$

From the inequality condition (5), we know that there exists a diagonally matrix $U_i \geq 0$ such that:

$$2[g(W_iz(t - \tau(t))) - \underline{L}W_iz(t - \tau(t))]^T U_i[\overline{L}W_iz(t - \tau(t)) - g(W_iz(t - \tau(t)))] \geq 0. \tag{12}$$

Considering (11)–(16), then we can obtain

$$\dot{V}_i(z(t)) \leq \eta_i^T(t)\Xi_i\eta_i(t) + \alpha V_i(z(t)), \tag{13}$$

It is clear that the inequality (7) in Theorem 1 can guarantee

$$\dot{V}_i(z(t)) \leq \alpha V_i((z(t)). \tag{14}$$

Multiplying the above inequality (18) by $e^{\alpha t}$, and then integrating it from 0 to t, with $t \in [0, T]$, we have

By integrating from t_k to t, the inequality (3.13) reduces to

$$V_i(t) \leq e^{\alpha(t-t_k)}V_i(t_k), \tag{15}$$

On the other hand, since $P_i > 0$, then for $\forall z \in \mathbb{R}^n$, it yields

$$z^T(t)P_i z(t) \leq \lambda_{max}(P_i)z^T(t)z(t)$$
$$\leq \frac{\max\limits_{\lambda \in N}(\lambda_{max}(P_\lambda))}{\min\limits_{\lambda \in N}(\lambda_{min}(P_\lambda))} z^T(t)P_j z(t).$$

Let $\upsilon_1 = \frac{\max\limits_{\lambda \in N}(\lambda_{max}(P_\lambda))}{\min\limits_{\lambda \in N}(\lambda_{min}(P_\lambda))}$, then the above inequality becomes $z^T(t)P_i z(t) \leq \upsilon_1 z^T(t)P_j z(t)$. According to the definition of V_{1i}, one can have that

$$V_{1i}(t) < \upsilon_1 V_{1j}(t). \tag{16}$$

By similar estimation method, the following inequalities hold.

$$V_{2i}(t) \leq \upsilon_2 V_{2j}(t), \quad V_{3i}(t) \leq \upsilon_3 V_{3j}(t), \tag{17}$$

where $\upsilon_2 = \frac{\max\limits_{\lambda \in N}(\lambda_{max}(Q_\lambda))}{\min\limits_{\lambda \in N}(\lambda_{min}(Q_\lambda))}$ and $\upsilon_3 = \frac{\max\limits_{\lambda \in N}(\lambda_{max}(S_\lambda))}{\min\limits_{\lambda \in N}(\lambda_{min}(S_\lambda))}$.

Denote $\upsilon = \max\{\upsilon_1, \upsilon_2, \upsilon_3\}$, then it follows that $V_i(t) \leq \upsilon V_j(t)$, which means that

$$V_{\sigma(t_k)}(t_k) \leq \upsilon V_{\sigma(t_k^-)}(t_k^-). \tag{18}$$

Let N be the number of switching on the time period $[0, T)$, and T_a be the average dwell time, then $N \leq \frac{T}{T_a}$. Notice that $\upsilon \geq 1$, then for any $t \in [0, T)$, the following inequalities hold by iterative method.

$$V_{\sigma(t)}(t) \leq e^{\alpha T} \upsilon^{\frac{T}{T_a}} V_{\sigma(0)}(0). \tag{19}$$

Estimating $V_{\sigma(0)}(0)$ and $V_{\sigma(t)}(t)$ according to the corresponding definition (3.6), it gives that

$$V_{\sigma(t)}(t) \geq \min\limits_{\lambda \in N}(\lambda_{min}(R^{-\frac{1}{2}}P_\lambda R^{-\frac{1}{2}}))z^T(t)Rz(t), \tag{20}$$

and

$$
\begin{aligned}
V_{\sigma(0)}(0) \le{}& z^T(0)P_{\sigma(0)}z(0) + \int_{-\tau}^{0} e^{-\alpha s}z^T(s)Q_{\sigma(0)}z(s)ds \\
&+ \tau\int_{-\tau}^{0}\int_{\theta}^{0} e^{-\alpha s}\dot{z}^T(s)S_{\sigma(0)}\dot{z}(s)ds \\
\le{}& \max_{\lambda\in\mathbb{N}}(\lambda_{max}(R^{-\frac{1}{2}}P_\lambda R^{-\frac{1}{2}}))z^T(0)Rz(0) \\
&+ \tau e^{\alpha\tau}\max_{\lambda\in\mathbb{N}}(\lambda_{max}(R^{-\frac{1}{2}}Q_\lambda R^{-\frac{1}{2}}))\sup_{-\tau\le\theta\le0} z^T(\theta)Rz(\theta) \\
&+ 2\tau^3 e^{\alpha\tau}\max_{\lambda\in\mathbb{N}}(\lambda_{max}(R^{-\frac{1}{2}}A_\lambda S_\lambda A_\lambda R^{-\frac{1}{2}}) + \lambda_{max}(R^{-\frac{1}{2}}W_\lambda^T LS_\lambda LW_\lambda R^{-\frac{1}{2}})) \\
&\sup_{-\tau\le\theta\le0} z^T(\theta)Rz(\theta),
\end{aligned}
\tag{21}
$$

where L_3 is defined before in Sect. 2. Denote $\omega_1 = \min\limits_{\lambda\in\mathbb{N}}(\lambda_{min}(\bar{P}_\lambda))$ and $\omega_2 = \max\limits_{\lambda\in\mathbb{N}}(\lambda_{max}(\bar{P}_\lambda)) + \tau e^{\bar{\alpha}\tau}\max\limits_{\lambda\in\mathbb{N}}(\lambda_{max}(\bar{Q}_\lambda)) + \tau e^{\bar{\alpha}\tau}\max\limits_{\lambda\in\mathbb{N}}(\lambda_{max}(\bar{Z}_\lambda))$ with $\bar{P}_\lambda = R^{-\frac{1}{2}}P_\lambda R^{-\frac{1}{2}}, \bar{Q}_\lambda = R^{-\frac{1}{2}}Q_\lambda R^{-\frac{1}{2}}, \bar{Z}_\lambda = R^{-\frac{1}{2}}L_3 Z_\lambda L_3 R^{-\frac{1}{2}}$, then the above inequalities (3.19) and (3.20) yield that

$$
V_{\sigma(t)}(t) \ge \omega_1 z^T(t)Rz(t),
\tag{22}
$$

$$
V_{\sigma(0)}(0) \le \omega_2 \sup_{-\tau\le\theta\le0} z^T(\theta)Rz(\theta).
\tag{23}
$$

Combining the inequalities (3.18), (3.21) and (3.22), the following inequalities are true.

$$
z^T(t)Rz(t) \le \frac{1}{\omega_1}V_{\sigma(t)}(t) \le \frac{1}{\omega_1}e^{\alpha T}v^{\frac{T}{T_a}}\omega_2 \sup_{-\tau\le\theta\le0}(z^T(\theta)Rz(\theta)).
\tag{24}
$$

Assume that $\sup_{-\tau\le\theta\le0}(z^T(\theta)Rz(\theta)) < c_1$, then the conditions (3.4) and (3.5) in Theorem 3.1 can guarantee that

$$
\frac{\omega_2 c_1}{\omega_1}e^{\alpha T}v^{\frac{T}{T_a}} < c_2.
\tag{25}
$$

Therefore, under the conditions in Theorem 3.1, for all $t \in [0,T]$, $z^T(t)Rz(t) < c_2$. That is, the uncertain switched static neural networks (3.1) is finite-time bounded. Now, the proof follows.

Remark 2. Clearly, Theorem 1 are independent on the switching rule. That is, Theorem 1 holds for any switching rule. Furthermore, the conditions in Theorem 1 are delay-dependent. Generally speaking, delay-dependent conditions are less conservative than delay-independent ones especially when the size of the delay is small.

Remark 3. It can be seen that the conditions in Theorem 1 are not standard linear matrix inequalities (LMIs). From a viewpoint of computation, once we have fixed a value of α, the condition (7) can be turned into LMIs and then solved by Matlab LMI toolbox. Especially, when $\alpha = 0$, the finite-time stability turns to be the asymptotical stability.

On the other hand, we can easily check that the condition (8) in Theorem 1 can be guaranteed by the following LMIs conditions:

$$\gamma_1 I < P < \gamma_2 I, \ Q < \gamma_3 I, \ T < \gamma_4 I, \ S < \gamma_5 I, \tag{26}$$

$$-c_2 \gamma_1 \pi_1 e^{-\alpha T} + c_1 [(\gamma_2 + \gamma_3)\pi_1 + (\gamma_4 + \gamma_5)\pi_2 + \gamma_5 \pi_3] < 0, \tag{27}$$

where $\gamma_i (i = 1, 2, 3, 4, 5)$ are positive scalars and $\pi_j (j = 1, 2, 3)$ is defined as

$$\pi_1 = \lambda_{max}(R^{-1}), \ \pi_2 = \max_{k \in \mathbb{E}}(\lambda_{max}(R^{-\frac{1}{2}} W_k^T LLW_k R^{-\frac{1}{2}})),$$

$$\pi_3 = \max_{k \in \mathbb{E}}(\lambda_{max}(R^{-\frac{1}{2}} A_k^T A_k R^{-\frac{1}{2}})).$$

4   A Numerical Example

In this section, a numerical example is given to illustrate the validity of the proposed results. Consider SSNNs (9) with the following parameters:

$$A_1 = \begin{bmatrix} 1.2 & 0 \\ 0 & 2.1 \end{bmatrix}, \ A_2 = \begin{bmatrix} 1.1 & 0 \\ 0 & 1.9 \end{bmatrix},$$

$$W_1 = \begin{bmatrix} 2.5 & 1.1 \\ -1.1 & 3.1 \end{bmatrix}, \ W_2 = \begin{bmatrix} 2.1 & 0.9 \\ -1.1 & 3.2 \end{bmatrix},$$

The activation functions are defined as $g_1(t) = \tanh(0.3t)$, $g_2(t) = \tanh(0.5t)$, and the time-varying delay is $\tau(t) = 0.3 + 0.2\sin(t)$. It means that

$$\tau = 0.5, \ \mu = 0.2, \ \underline{L} = 0, \ L = \overline{L} = \begin{bmatrix} 0.3 & 0 \\ 0 & 0.5 \end{bmatrix}.$$

The other parameters are chosen as $c_1 = 0.5$, $c_2 = 10$, $T = 10$ and $R = I$. By Matlab LMI toolbox, solving the inequalities (7), (23) and (24) for $\alpha = 0.001$ gives the feasible solutions:

$$P_1 = \begin{bmatrix} 0.7174 & -0.0078 \\ -0.0078 & 0.5642 \end{bmatrix}, \ P_2 = \begin{bmatrix} 0.7335 & -0.0225 \\ -0.0225 & 0.5427 \end{bmatrix},$$

$$Q_1 = \begin{bmatrix} 0.8145 & -0.0389 \\ -0.0389 & 1.0844 \end{bmatrix}, \ Q_2 = \begin{bmatrix} 0.7636 & -0.0632 \\ -0.0632 & 0.9631 \end{bmatrix},$$

$$S_1 = \begin{bmatrix} 0.5375 & -0.0070 \\ -0.0070 & 0.5510 \end{bmatrix}, \ S_2 = \begin{bmatrix} 0.5400 & -0.0095 \\ -0.0095 & 0.5410 \end{bmatrix},$$

$$U_1 = \begin{bmatrix} 0.6880 & 0 \\ 0 & 0.3430 \end{bmatrix}, \ U_2 = \begin{bmatrix} 0.7324 & 0 \\ 0 & 0.2987 \end{bmatrix},$$

which satisfy the condition (8). According to Theorem 1, we can conclude that the concerned SSNNs is finite-time stable with respect to $(1, 10, 10, I)$, and the average dwell time satisfies that $T_a > 2.4468$. See simulation results in Figs. 1 and 2.

Remark 4. Notice that the conditions (23) and (24) are dependent on the size of c_2, then we can also get the optimal lower bound of c_2 to guarantee the finite-time stability by solving a simple optimal problem. For example, we can obtain the optimal lower bound of c_2 is 3.9351.

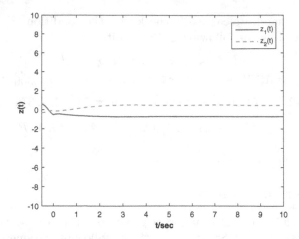

Fig. 1. State responses of the closed-loop networks in the numerical example

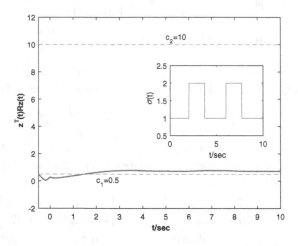

Fig. 2. Time history of $\mathbf{e}^T(t)Re(t)$ of the closed-loop networks in the numerical example

5   Conclusions

This paper has studied the problem of finite-time stability for switched static neural networks. The Lyapunov-like function method and LMIs technique are developed to derive a sufficient criterion, which can guarantee the finite-time stability of SSNNs. In the end, a numerical example is provided to show the effectiveness of our proposed theoretical results. In the further investigations, we will search the other analysis technique to obtain the less conservative results, and consider some control problems of SSNNs in finite-time sense.

Acknowledgments. This work was funded by the National Natural Science Foundation of China under Grants 61603350 and 61501407.

References

1. Xu, Z.B., Qiao, H., Peng, J., Zhang, B.: A comparative study on two modeling approaches in neural networks. Neural Netw. **17**, 73–85 (2004)
2. Qiao, H., Peng, J., Xu, Z.B., Zhang, B.: A reference model approach to stability analysis of neuralnetworks. IEEE Trans. Syst. Man Cybern. Part B **33**, 925–936 (2003)
3. Liang, J.L., Cao, J.D.: A based-on LMI stability criterion for delayed recurrent neural networks. Chaos Solitons Fractals **28**, 154–160 (2006)
4. Shao, H.Y.: Delay-dependent stability for recurrent neural networks with time-varying delays. IEEE Trans. Neural Netw. **19**, 1647–1651 (2008)
5. Shao, H.Y.: Delay-dependent approaches to globally exponential stability for recurrent neural networks. IEEE Trans. Circ. Syst. II Express Briefs **55**, 591–595 (2008)
6. Zheng, C.D., Zhang, H., Wang, Z.: Delay-dependent globally exponential stability criteria for static neural networks: an LMI approach. IEEE Trans. Circ. Syst. II **56**(56), 605–609 (2009)
7. Huang, H., Feng, G., Cao, J.D.: State estimation for static neural networks with time-varying delay. Neural Netw. **23**, 1202–1207 (2010)
8. Li, X., Gao, H., Yu, X.: A unified approach to the stability of generalized static neural networks with linear fractional uncertainties and delays. IEEE Trans. Syst. Man Cybern. Part B **41**, 1275–1286 (2011)
9. Xiao, J., Zeng, Z.G., Wu, A.L.: New criteria for exponential stability of delayed recurrent neural networks. Neurocomputing **134**, 182–188 (2014)
10. Huang, H., Qu, Y., Li, H.: Robust stability analysis of switched Hopfield neural networks with time-varying delay under uncertainty. Phys. Lett. A. **345**, 345–354 (2005)
11. Yuan, K., Cao, J.D., Li, H.: Robust stability of switched Cohen Grossberg neural networks with mixed time-varying delays. IEEE Trans. Syst. Man Cybern. Part B **36**, 1356–1363 (2006)
12. Li, P., Cao, J.: Global stability in switched recurrent neural networks with time-varying delay via nonlinear measure. Nonlinear Dynam. **49**, 295–305 (2007)
13. Hu, M.F., Cao, J.D., Yang, Y.Q., Hu, A.H.: Passivity analysis for switched generalized neural networks with time-varying delay and uncertain output. IMA J. Math. Control Inf. **30**, 407–422 (2013)
14. Hu, M.F., Cao, J.D., Hu, A.H.: Mean square exponential stability for discrete-time stochastic switched static neural networks with randomly occurring nonlinearities and stochastic delay. Neurocomputing **129**, 476–481 (2014)
15. Hou, L., Zong, G., Wu, Y.: Robust exponential stability analysis of discrete-time switched Hopfield neural networks with time delay. Nonlinear Anal. Hybrid Syst. **5**, 525–534 (2011)
16. Arunkumar, A., Sakthivel, R., Mathiyalagan, K., Anthoni, S.M.: Robust stability criteria for discrete-time switched neural networks with various activation functions. Appl. Math. Comput. **218**, 10803–10816 (2012)
17. Wu, X.T., Tian, Y., Zhang, W.B.: Stability analysis of switched stochastic neural networks with time-varying delays. Neural Netw. **51**, 39–49 (2014)
18. Yang, X.S., Cao, J.D., Zhu, Q.X.: Synchronization of switched neural networks with mixed delays via impulsive control. Chaos Solitons Fractals **44**, 817–826 (2011)
19. Yu, W.W., Cao, J.D., Lu, W.L.: Synchronization control of switched linearly coupled neural networks with delay. Neurocomputing **73**, 858–866 (2010)

20. Dorato, P.: Short time stability in linear time-varying systems. In: Proceeding of the IRE International Convention Record Part 4, pp. 83–87 (1961)
21. Orlowski, P.: Methods for stability evaluation for linear time varying, discrete-time system on finite time horizon. Int. J. Control **79**, 249–262 (2006)
22. Amato, F., Ariola, M., Dorate, P.: Finite-time control of linear systems subject to parameteric uncertainties and disturbances. Automatica **37**, 1459–1463 (2001)
23. Du, H.B., Lin, X.Z., Li, S.H.: Finite-time boundedness and stabilization of switched linear systems. Kybernetika **46**, 870–889 (2010)
24. Liu, H., Shen, Y., Zhao, X.D.: Finite-time stabilization and boundedness of switched linear system under state-dependent switching. J. Franklin Inst. **350**, 541–555 (2013)
25. Chen, G.P., Yang, Y.: Finite-time stability of switched positive linear systems. Int. J. Robust Nonlinear Control **24**, 179–190 (2014)
26. Zhang, J.F., Yang, Y.: Robust finite-time stability and stabilisation of switched positive systems. IET Control Theory Appl. **8**, 67–75 (2014)
27. Shen, Y.J., Li, C.C.: LMI-based finite-time boundedness analysis of neural networks with parametric uncertainties. Neurocomputing **71**, 502–507 (2008)
28. He, S.P., Liu, F.: Finite-time boundedness of uncertain time-delayed neural network with Markovian jumping parameters. Neurocomputing **103**, 87–92 (2013)
29. Zhang, Y.Q., Shi, P., Nguang, S.K., Zhang, J.H., Karimi, H.R.: Finite-time boundedness for uncertain discrete neural networks with time-delays and Markovian jumps. Neurocomputing **140**, 1–7 (2014)
30. Cheng, J., Zhong, S.M., Zhong, Q.S., Zhu, H., Du, Y.H.: Finite-time boundedness of state estimation for neural networks with time-varying delays. Neurocomputing **129**, 257–264 (2014)

An Improved Artificial Immune Network
Based on the Secondary Immune Mechanism
for Data Clustering

Yangyang Li[1(✉)], Xiaoju Hou[1], Licheng Jiao[1], and Yu Xue[2]

[1] Key Laboratory of Intelligent Perception and Image Understanding
of Ministry of Education, International Research Center for Intelligent Perception
and Computation, Joint International Research Laboratory of Intelligent
Perception and Computation, Xidian University, Xi'an 710071, Shanxi, China
yyli@xidian.edu.cn
[2] School of Computer and Software,
Nanjing University of Information Science and Technology (NUIST),
Nanjing, China

Abstract. Data clustering is a typical method in data mining. As a effective algorithm for clustering, the Artificial Immune Network is inspired by natural immune system can reflect the structure of the given dataset, filter redundancy and cluster datasets without the number of clusters, so far it is widely used. However, it can't effectively identify the noise nodes, the running time is long and too much parameters are set in improved algorithms. In order to shorten running time and reduce the impact of parameters, this paper proposes an improved artificial immune network based on the secondary immune mechanism. The Clone operator and Mutation operator are replaced by Competition Selection operator and Competition Selection strategy, which are inspired by the resource limited artificial immune system. Because the algorithm can reach a stable convergence only through two times, so it greatly reduce the running time; and can effectively identify the noise nodes due to the introduction of stimulation level. A number of datasets including artificial datasets and real-world datasets are used to evaluate the performance of the proposed algorithm and the other existing clustering algorithms, such as K-means, FCM, SC, aiNet and FCAIN. The simulation results indicate that the proposed artificial immune network algorithm is an effective and efficient method in data clustering.

Keywords: Artificial immune network · Data clustering · Competition selection operator · Secondary immune mechanism

1 Introduction

Asan unsupervised classification process, clustering [1] doesn't need to provide the sample labels as prior knowledge, which can give the rational division only through the degree of similarity between samples. Clustering pays more attention to find the underlying structure of samples and collects the similar samples into the same cluster.

© Springer International Publishing AG 2017
X. Sun et al. (Eds.): ICCCS 2017, Part I, LNCS 10602, pp. 519–530, 2017.
https://doi.org/10.1007/978-3-319-68505-2_45

Artificial immune system [2, 3] is one of the important achievements in the field of artificial intelligence. It is inspired by the natural immune system and has been widely applied to engineering optimization [4], intrusion detection [5], data mining and so on. There are three classical theories in artificial immune system: clonal selection [6, 7], immune network [8, 9] and negative selection [10].

In Spectral Clustering algorithm (SC) [11], as an important clustering algorithm, the samples are regarded as the vertices and the level of similarity between the samples are regarded as the weighted edges. Corresponding, the clustering problem can be resolved by graph partitioning problem. SC is a good way to deal with non-diffuse datasets. However, SC requires the number of clusters as prior knowledge. In the case of real environment, the number of clusters is usually unknown, so this method is not practical sometimes. K-means [12] is the most popular algorithm for clustering, due to its simplicity, facility to implement and quick convergence. However, it is sensitive to the initialization of clustering center and converges to local optima solutions. Fuzzy C-Means Clustering Algorithm (FCM) [13] is another classical algorithm. Each sample has a degree belonging to different clusters rather than belonging to just one cluster. Thus, points on the edge of a cluster may have a lower degree than points in the center of the cluster. It is more objective to reflect the real world, however, the number of clusters is also needed in FCM.

Under the efforts of researchers, a lot of achievements have been put forward in artificial immune network [14]. The artificial immune network algorithm (aiNet) [15] and resource limited artificial immune system (RLAIS) [16] have become the most famous models. They are able to filter redundancy and reveal the potential structure. However, many parameters defined in aiNet. So it needs high computational cost, and it is sensitive to noise nodes. The improved artificial immune network clustering algorithm based on forbidden clone (FCAIN) [17] is proposed to improve weak denoising ability. However, it still needs to define many parameters and cannot shorten running time.

This paper proposes a new artificial immune network based on the secondary immune mechanism [18, 19] (SIMAIN), which can obtain the accurate network structure and shorten the running time. The competition selection strategy is employed to guide the process and reduce the number of iterations.

The remainder of this paper is arranged as follows. Section 2 not only reviews the significant aiNet algorithm, but also simply introduces the minimum spanning tree (MST) [20]. Section 3 gives technical details of the proposed SIMAIN. Then, some experimental results are discussed in Sect. 4 compared with other clustering algorithms. Section 5 draws some conclusions.

2   Related Works

2.1   Artificial Immune Network Algorithm

Artificial immune network [21, 22] is divided into antibody network and memory network [23, 24]. The datasets to be clustered is considered antigens, the obtained network nodes are treated as antibodies. The memory network is the basis of the immune response, which is made of selected antibodies. When antibody network is invaded by the antigens, it updates antibodies and adjusts the memory network.

After the learning process, the antibodies in the memory network represent internal images of the antigens. The aiNet algorithm aims at building a memory collection which recognizes and represents the data structure. In general, this algorithm is universal. However, there are still some shortcomings, such as the large number of the parameters, and the high calculation cost.

2.2   Minimum Spanning Tree

After getting the final memory network, we can get a simple network structure through the connection of the network nodes. Because the minimum spanning tree (MST) can describe and analyze the structure of the clustering network, we use the minimum spanning tree to obtain the relationship between the network nodes.

When the dimension of network nodes is less than or equal to two, the clustering structure obtained by MST directly. However, when the dimension of network nodes is equal to or more than three, the distances between network nodes will be obtained through the mapping diagram (bar chart) of the MST. If the performance of the algorithm is good, we can get the distance threshold from the bar chart obviously, and then classify the network nodes.

3   The Proposed SIMAIN Algorithm

3.1   Secondary Immune Mechanism

To cluster the datasets automatically and efficiently, an improved artificial immune network [25, 26] algorithm based on secondary immune mechanism is proposed.

According to the principles of immune mechanism, especially the immune memory and the secondary response. In the immune system, when antigens invade body, the antibodies will be produced to recognize antigens. When the same type antigens invade the body again, existing antibodies can recognize the antigens, and the memory cells will respond quickly and secrete the antibodies to remove antigens rapidly though immune memory. The process is known as the secondary immune response. This mechanism is named as Secondary Immune Mechanism (SIM).

In our algorithm, the clone operator and mutation operator are replaced by competition selection operator and competition selection strategy. Because the clone operator is used to clone antibodies with high affinity and increase the ability to search the optimal solution; and the mutation operator is used to expand the scope of search space. But, these evolutionary operators need multiple iterations and lead to low efficiency. However, our competition selection strategy can recognize antigens quickly through the choice of antibodies with high affinity, and increase the ability to identify antigens by stimulation degree. The higher the stimulation degree the better the ability to identify the antigens. Then, we can obtain the memory network only through selecting the antibodies with high stimulation degree.

The stimulation degree is inspired by the resource limited artificial immune system, it can identify noise nodes effectively and acquire accurate structure of datasets. The stimulation level (SL) is used to reveal the degree that the immune recognition ball (ARB) is stimulated by antigens. The ARB with higher stimulation level can acquire more resources, so the survival rate is high; on the contrary, the ARB with lower stimulation level will be eliminated due to lacking resources. The lower the antigen density around ARB, the lower the stimulation level, thus the eliminated ARBs are the noise nodes. Our algorithm is not only useful for simple structure of artificial datasets, but also useful for complex datasets and real-world datasets. Memory cells in the final memory network can almost know all specificities of the antigens after two iterations. So under the help of the secondary immune mechanism, the running time is greatly reduced.

3.2   The Introduction of SIMAIN

And then we analyze the SIMAIN algorithm step by step in detail (Fig. 1).

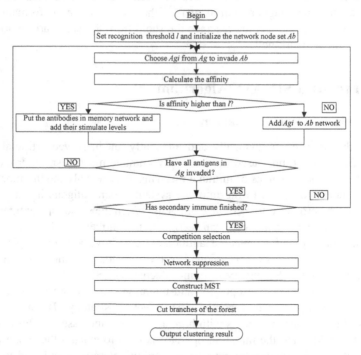

Fig. 1. Flow chart of SIMAIN

(1) Set recognition threshold l and initialize the network node Ab: The affinity recognition threshold l between antibodies and antigens is set reasonable. If the affinity is higher than l, the antibodies can recognize the antigens. Otherwise they can't recognize each other. The network node Ab which has the same number of columns as Ag is generated randomly.

(2) Choose Ag_i form Ag to invade Ab: Ag_i as an antigen selected from Ag randomly invades antibody network Ab.

(3) Calculate the affinity: Calculate the affinity $f_{ij}(j = 1, 2, \ldots, N_{ab})$ between Ag_i and each antibody in the current network Ab, which is based on distance D_{ij} as follows:

$$D_{1,2} = \sqrt{\sum_{d=1}^{m} (x_{1d} - x_{2d})^2} = \|x_1 - x_2\| \tag{1}$$

$$D_{ij} = \|Ag_i - Ab_j\| \tag{2}$$

$$f_{ij} = 1/D_{ij} \tag{3}$$

Where N_{ab} is the number of the current network Ab. When the D_{ij} is equal to zero, the f_{ij} is equal to infinity. Where $D_{1,2}$ is the Euclidean distance between two samples, d is the dimension of sample. For any two nodes, the smaller their distance, the greater their affinity.

(4) Is affinity higher than l?

(a) Put the antibody Ab_j whose affinity is higher than l in memory network M as memory cell, and then add its stimulate level N;

$$M \leftarrow [M; Ab_j] \tag{4}$$

$$N = N + 1 \tag{5}$$

(b) Add the antigen whose affinity is less than l to the antibody network Ab as an antibody;

$$Ab \leftarrow [Ab; Ag_i] \tag{6}$$

(5) Have all antigens in Ag invaded?: Insure all antigens have invaded antibody network Ab.

(6) Has secondary immune finished?: Insure the process has completed the second cycle, namely secondary invasion.

(7) Competition selection: Rank network nodes according to stimulate levels N and select the prior $n\%$ network nodes.

(8) Network suppression: Eliminate the antibody nodes whose affinity are higher than the recognition threshold $l1$ until all antibody nodes can't recognize each other in

memory network M. The recognition threshold controls the specificity level of the antibodies, the clustering accuracy and network plasticity.

(a) Calculate the affinity f_{ik} among all the antibody nodes in memory network M.

$$f_{ik} = \frac{1}{\|M_i - M_k\|}, M_i \in M, M_k \in M, \forall i, k \tag{7}$$

(b) Eliminate the antibody nodes in memory network M whose f_{ik} is higher $l1$, where $l1$ is the affinity recognition threshold between antibody nodes.

(9) Construct MST: Construct minimum spanning tree according to network nodes in memory network.

(a) After the algorithm, a collection of antibody nodes in memory network $M = \{M_1, M_2, \ldots, M_m\}$ can be obtained, and m is the number of antibody nodes.
(b) Construct a complete graph:

$$G = (M, D) \tag{8}$$

$$D = \{D(M_i, M_j) | D(M_i, M_j) = \|M_i - M_j\|, i, j \in [1\, m]\} \tag{9}$$

(c) Construct MST and draw bar chart according to the distances between the adjacent network nodes.

(10) Cut branches of the forest: The threshold which can separate categories is obtained, then cut branches of the forest according to the obtained threshold.
(11) Output clustering result.

4 Experimental Results and Discussions

This section gives some comparative experiments and the related results. Several algorithms are used to compare with the proposed SIMAIN algorithm, such as K-mcans [27], FCM, SC, aiNet and FCAIN. These algorithms were coded in Mat-labR2013b. The corresponding simulations have been carried out on a personal computer with Inter(R) M 370 2.4 GHz, 6 GB RAM, and Windows 7.

4.1 Experimental Datasets

In order to verify the clustering performance of proposed SIMAIN, two real-world datasets and seven artificial datasets are used. The real-world datasets are from UCI datasets. In order to avoid the instability of the experimental results, each dataset of each algorithm will be carried out 30 times and the experimental results are averaged. And we can see the stability level through the variance.

These artificial datasets represent different types. The Sticks and Spiral are non-convex. The AD_20_2 belongs to sphere distribution. The Sizes5 is diffuse. The Data9 is three-dimensional. The Data18 is 18-dimensional whose distribution is Gaussian distribution. The Data100 is 100-dimensional whose distribution is also Gaussian distribution. More details about the real-world and artificial datasets are described in Table 1.

Table 1. The details about datasets.

Dataset	Number of samples	Number of dimensions	Number of clusters
Artificial dataset			
Sticks	512	2	4
Spiral	1000	2	2
AD_20_2	1000	2	20
Sizes5	1000	2	4
Data9	600	3	3
Data18	1000	18	5
Data100	1000	100	5
Real-world dataset			
Vote	435	16	2
Wine	178	13	3

4.2 Parameter Setting

For the K-means, FCM and SC, the number of clusters is known in advance. And the scale parameter is specified in SC. For FCAIN, the threshold of forbidden clone is initialized.

We can obtain that the SIMAIN algorithm doesn't need to define a lot of parameters and large number of iterations compared with FCAIN and aiNet. We only need to define the natural death threshold l, the suppression threshold ll, and the simulation degree in our algorithm. So, our algorithm reduces the dependence on parameters. And, two iterations is helpful to shorten running time.

4.3 Evaluation Index

In order to evaluate the clustering accuracy of SIMAIN, Clustering Accuracy (CA) [28], and Adjusted Rand Index (ARI) [29] are employed. It needs to be stated that the labels are used only for evaluation, the proposed algorithm doesn't need the labels when clustering.

CA: It is the rate of correct labels, through comparing the true label of each sample with the label obtained by algorithm clustering results. It is defined as follows, where n_i represents the number of wrong samples which should belong to label i, and n is the number of all samples. CA is a value in the interval of [0, 1], and the bigger the value, the better the clustering effect.

$$CA = 1 - \frac{\sum_{i=1}^{k} n_i}{n} \qquad (10)$$

ARI: It is defined as follows, where n_{lk} represents the number of samples which belong to both cluster l and cluster k ($l \in T, k \in S$). T is the true cluster, and S is the obtained cluster. The ARI is also a value in the interval [0, 1], and the bigger value, the better the clustering effect.

$$ARI = R(T, S) = \frac{\sum_{lk} \binom{n_{lk}}{2} - [\sum_l \binom{n_{l*}}{2} * \sum_k \binom{n_{*k}}{2}] / \binom{n}{2}}{1/2 [\sum_l \binom{n_{l*}}{2} + \sum_k \binom{n_{*k}}{2}] - [\sum_l \binom{n_{l*}}{2} * \sum_k \binom{n_{*k}}{2}] / \binom{n}{2}} \qquad (11)$$

4.4   Simulation Results and Discussions

In order to reflect the advantages of our algorithm specifically, We can visually see the experimental results from the Fig. 2, and more details are described in Tables 2, 3 and 4.

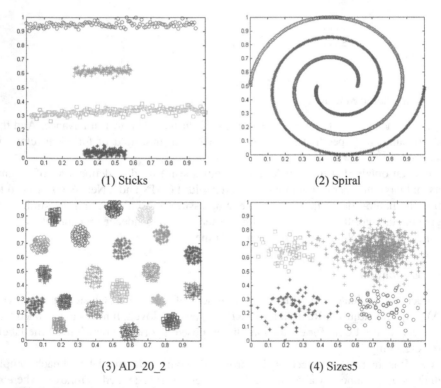

(1) Sticks

(2) Spiral

(3) AD_20_2

(4) Sizes5

Fig. 2. The visualization results of some artificial datasets on the SIMAIN algorithm

Table 2. The results of clustering about CA index.

Datasets	CA	K-means	FCM	SC	aiNet	SIMAIN
Sticks	Mean	0.6592	0.7449	0.9371	**1**	**1**
	Std	0.0739	0.0135	0.1406	**0**	**0**
Spiral	Mean	0.5966	0.5901	0.6020	**1**	**1**
	Std	9.3218e−04	7.3030e−04	2.2584e−04	**0**	**0**
AD_20_2	Mean	0.8085	0.8750	0.8440	0.8594	**0.9050**
	Std	0.0573	0.0590	0.0643	**0.0360**	0.1039
Sizes5	Mean	0.8611	0.6218	**0.9668**	0.7390	0.9540
	Std	0.1647	**0.0164**	0.0452	0.0665	0.0436
Data9	Mean	0.8347	0.9383	0.9679	**1**	**1**
	Std	0.0646	5.6460e−04	0.1222	**0**	**0**
Data18	Mean	0.7762	**1**	0.9257	**1**	**1**
	Std	0.1784	**0**	0.1287	**0**	**0**
Data100	Mean	0.8047	**1**	0.9450	0.2312	**1**
	Std	0.1814	**0**	0.1230	0.0982	**0**
Vote	Mean	0.8571	0.8621	**0.8696**	0.2736	0.8341
	Std	0.0525	4.5168e−04	**0.0046**	0.2330	0.0571
Wine	Mean	**0.6961**	0.6854	0.2511	0.2685	0.6378
	Std	0.0338	**0**	0.0663	0.1198	0.2650

Table 3. The results of clustering about ARI index.

Datasets	ARI	K-means	FCM	SC	aiNet	SIMAIN
Sticks	Mean	0.5038	0.4897	0.9239	**1**	**1**
	Std	0.0393	0.0236	0.1702	**0**	**0**
Spiral	Mean	0.0364	0.0315	0.0407	**1**	**1**
	Std	7.2410e−04	5.3804e−04	0	**0**	**0**
AD_20_2	Mean	0.8279	0.8759	0.8554	0.8938	**0.9468**
	Std	**0.0539**	0.0564	0.0649	0.0565	0.0564
Sizes5	Mean	0.7547	0.3904	**0.9429**	0.6094	0.9390
	Std	0.2375	**0.0041**	0.0449	0.2681	0.0227
Data9	Mean	0.6502	0.8325	0.9630	**1**	**1**
	Std	0.0476	5.6460e−04	0.1409	**0**	**0**
Data18	Mean	0.7857	**1**	0.9188	**1**	**1**
	Std	0.1661	**0**	0.1406	**0**	**0**
Data100	Mean	0.8134	**1**	0.9445	0.4751	**1**
	Std	0.1701	**0**	0.1242	0.0408	**0**
Vote	Mean	0.5189	0.5233	**0.5453**	0.1174	0.4570
	Std	0.0974	**0**	0.0137	0.0884	0.1297
Wine	Mean	0.3700	0.3539	0.0019	0.1873	**0.6049**
	Std	0.0059	**1.6938e−16**	0.0079	0.1760	0.1672

Table 4. The results of clustering about time.

Datasets	SC	aiNet	FCAIN	SIMAIN
Sticks	0.8594	18.7574	29.6600	**0.5328**
Spiral	1.6506	37.0046	29.0705	**0.7067**
AD_20_2	1.9187	48.8031	33.4139	**1.6194**
Sizes5	1.7088	322.0864	44.2509	**11.4227**
Data9	3.4934	39.2272	39.2949	**3.4206**
Data18	2.3469	144.1856	3256.1494	**0.6646**
Data100	**1.6424**	60.4152	7384.6405	3.2125
Vote	0.6728	12.9028	319.3132	**0.0733**
Wine	0.3249	5.7454	51.0142	**0.1280**

It can be seen from Fig. 2 that our algorithm obtains good clustering results as a whole, and gets the clear cluster distribution.

From above Tables 2 and 3, we can obtain that the proposed SIMAIN has the best clustering results in these datasets as a whole. For Sticks, Spiral, Data9, Data18, and Data100, we can acquire the correct clustering results because our algorithm inherit the performance of the artificial immune network. For AD_20_2, the results of our algorithm is the best. For Sizes5 and Vote, although the results of our algorithm are not the best, but just a little worse than the best sometimes, and much better than the aiNet obviously. Because the structure of Sizes5 is diffuse, so that our algorithm can recognize the noise nodes. For Wine, although the effect of our algorithm is worse than SC algorithm about CA index, but the effect is the best about ARI index. And the stability of the clustering results of some datasets has been improved. So, it shows that our algorithm has made great progress.

From the Table 4, although the time is not always the shortest, but our algorithm is much better than aiNet and FCAIN. So, it proves that our algorithm has made great improvement in terms of time performance.

In general, the SIMAIN is a better algorithm not only can recognize the noise nodes and cluster datasets whose distribution is special, but also can shorten the running time to solve the disadvantage of the evolutionary algorithm.

5 Conclusions

This paper proposed an improved artificial immune network clustering algorithm based on secondary immune mechanism. The SIMAIN algorithm introduces the simulation level based on RLAIS and the secondary immune mechanism to improve the efficiency and accuracy of data clustering. The simulation results indicate that our algorithm is good at clustering datasets whose distribution is special and effectively recognize the noise nodes. Besides it enhances the ability to analyze the datasets whose boundaries of the distribution are not clear. On the basis of aiNet, the improved artificial immune network clustering algorithm also doesn't need the number of clusters as prior knowledge. Most important of all, it reduces the number of input parameters and shortens the running time compared with aiNet and FCAIN. Therefore, it can be concluded that SIMAIN is an effective and efficiency algorithm for data clustering.

We will analyze datasets with high dimension or large-scale by using this algorithm in the next stage.

Acknowledgments. This work was supported by the National Natural Science Foundation of China (Nos. 61272279, 61272282, 61371201, and 61203303), the National Basic Research Program (973 Program) of China (No. 2013CB329402), the Program for Cheung Kong Scholars and Innovative Research Team in University (No. IRT_15R53), and the Fund for Foreign Scholars in University Research and Teaching Programs (the 111 Project) (No. B07048).

References

1. Zhao, W., Ying, X., Ping, L.: Research on clustering analysis and its application in customer data mining of enterprise. Int. J. Technol. Manag. **9**, 16–19 (2014)
2. Malim, M.R., Halim, F.A.: Immunology and artificial immune systems. Int. J. Artif. Intell. Tools **21**(6), 1250031-1–1250031-27 (2013)
3. Dasgupta, D., Ji, Z., Gonzalez, F.: Artificial immune system (AIS) research in the last five years. In: The 2003 Congress on Evolutionary Computation (CEC 2003), vol. 1, pp. 123–130. IEEE Xplore (2004)
4. Xue, Y., Jiang, J., Zhao, B., Ma, T.: A self-adaptive artificial bee colony algorithm based on global best for global optimization. Soft Comput. 1–18 (2017)
5. Sifei, W., Xu, J.: An artificial immune clustering approach to unsupervised network intrusion detection. In: International Symposium on Data, Privacy, and e-Commerce, pp. 511–513. IEEE (2007)
6. De Castro, L.N., Von Zuben, F.J.: Learning and optimization using the clonal selection principle. IEEE Trans. Evol. Comput. **6**(3), 239–251 (2002)
7. Castro, L.N.D., Zuben, F.J.V.: The clonal selection algorithm with engineering applications. In: Workshop Proceedings, GECCO 2002, pp. 36–37 (2001)
8. Castro, L.N.D., Zuben, F.J.V.: An evolutionary immune network for data clustering. In: Brazilian Symposium on Neural Networks, pp. 84–89. IEEE (2000)
9. Yue, X., Chi, Z., Hao, Y.: Incremental clustering algorithm of data stream based on artificial immune network. In: World Congress on Intelligent Control and Automation, pp. 4021–4025. IEEE (2006)
10. Gonzalez, F., Dasgupta, D., Kozma, R.: Combining negative selection and classification techniques for anomaly detection. In: Congress on Evolutionary Computation, vol. 1, No. 11, pp. 705–710. IEEE (2002)
11. Ng, A.Y., Jordan, M.I., Weiss, Y.: On spectral clustering: analysis and an algorithm. In: Proceedings of Advances in Neural Information Processing Systems 14, pp. 849–856 (2002)
12. Kuo, R.J., Chen, S.S., Cheng, W.C.: Integration of artificial immune network and K-means for cluster analysis. Knowl. Inf. Syst. **40**(3), 541–557 (2014)
13. Chang, C.T., Lai, J.Z.C., Jeng, M.D.: A fuzzy K-means clustering algorithm using cluster center displacement. J. Inf. Sci. Eng. **27**(3), 995–1009 (2011)
14. Li, Z., Fang, X., Zhou, J.: Optimal data clustering by using artificial immune network with elitist learning. In: China Control and Decision Conference, pp. 5192–5197 (2014)
15. Nunes, L., José, F., Zuben, V.: aiNet: an artificial immune network for data analysis. In: Data Mining a Heuristic Approach (2002)

16. Timmis, J., Neal, M.: A resource limited artificial immune system for data analysis. Knowl.-Based Syst. **14**(3), 121–130 (2001)
17. Li, J.: Study on New Algorithm of Fuzzy Clustering Based on Natural Computing. Xidian University (2004)
18. Qing, J., Liang, X., Bie, R.: A new clustering algorithm based on artificial immune network and K-means method. In: International Conference on Natural Computation, pp. 2826–2830 (2010)
19. Hu, X., Liu, X., Li, T.: Dynamically real-time intrusion detection algorithm with immune network. J. Comput. Inf. Syst. **11**(2), 587–594 (2015)
20. Laszlo, M., Mukherjee, S.: Minimum spanning tree partitioning algorithm for microaggregation. IEEE Trans. Knowl. Data Eng. **17**(7), 902–911 (2005)
21. Shi, X., Feng, Q.: An optimization algorithm based on multi-population artificial immune network. In: Fifth International Conference on Natural Computation, pp. 379–383. IEEE Computer Society (2009)
22. Castro, L.N.D., Timmis, J.: An artificial immune network for multimodal function optimization. In: Congress on Evolutionary Computation (CEC 2002), pp. 289–296. IEEE (2005)
23. Potter, M.A., De Jong, K.A.: The coevolution of antibodies for concept learning. In: Eiben, A.E., Bäck, T., Schoenauer, M., Schwefel, H.-P. (eds.) PPSN 1998. LNCS, vol. 1498, pp. 530–539. Springer, Heidelberg (1998). doi:10.1007/BFb0056895
24. Wu, L., Peng, L., Ye, Y.L.: An evolutionary immune network based on kernel method for data clustering. In: International Conference on Machine Learning and Cybernetics, pp. 1759–1764. IEEE Xplore (2007)
25. Karimi-Majd, A.M., Fathian, M., Amiri, B.: A hybrid artificial immune network for detecting communities in complex networks. Computing **97**(5), 483–507 (2015)
26. Shang, R., Li, Y., Jiao, L.: Co-evolution-based immune clonal algorithm for clustering. Soft Comput. **20**(4), 1503–1519 (2016)
27. Jiang, P., Zhang, C., Guo, G.: A K-means approach based on concept hierarchical tree for search results clustering. In: Sixth International Conference on Fuzzy Systems and Knowledge Discovery, FSKD 2009, vol. 1, pp. 380–386 (2009)
28. Das, S., Abraham, A., Konar, A.: Automatic kernel clustering with a multi-elitist particle swarm optimization algorithm. Pattern Recogn. Lett. **29**(5), 688–699 (2008)
29. Handl, J., Knowles, J.: An evolutionary approach to multiobjective clustering. IEEE Trans. Evol. Comput. **11**(1), 56–76 (2007)

Analysis of User's Abnormal Behavior Based on Behavior Sequence in Enterprise Network

Haichao Guan, Huakang Li, and Guozi Sun[✉]

School of Computer Science and Technology, School of Software,
Jiangsu Key Lab of Big Data and Security and Intelligent Processing,
Nanjing University of Posts and Telecommunications, Nanjing 210003, China
{1015041023,huakanglee,sun}@njupt.edu.cn

Abstract. There are many abnormal user behavior in the enterprise network environment, how to monitor it effectively is a hot research hotspot. At present, the analysis of abnormal behavior is mainly through the means of traffic monitoring, but there is no precise definition and related research on the behavior of enterprise network users. Therefore, the paper propose a model to analyze the abnormal behavior of enterprise network users. First, the data from the monitoring log of enterprise network should be pre-processing and the user behavior are serializing; then, for each user behavior sequence in sequence databases, calculating the user behavior similarity and correlation coefficient in a week by the improved algorithm; finally, comparing the similarity and the correlation coefficient between users and finding the user abnormal behavior. In this paper, we use the model to verify the feasibility of the internal network of the company, and find out the user's abnormal behavior.

Keywords: Behavior sequence · Abnormal behavior analysis · Behavior similarity

1 Introduction

User behavior analysis refers to get the relevant network flow data from network port and the web site, and process the data with statistical method. From the results, it can find user's regular pattern of visiting the website and sum up the user's behavior habits. Be able to grasp the user behavior habits has important significance to predict the user Internet behavior and abnormal behavior. There is a series of problems in the user behavior analysis now. Yang proposes the analysis of network user behavior with the abnormal traffic generated by online based on traffic identification [1], but the definition of user behavior is not perfect. Farraposo provides a user behavior analysis method based on the IPFIX protocol [2], the method can detect most of abnormal traffic behavior in the network, but it cannot detect the network traffic with little influence of the internet. Leland and Psxon find that the traffic is self-similarity based on the analysis of the traffic flow in different networks [3,4], and detect the traffic abnormal with the self-similarity

© Springer International Publishing AG 2017
X. Sun et al. (Eds.): ICCCS 2017, Part I, LNCS 10602, pp. 531–541, 2017.
https://doi.org/10.1007/978-3-319-68505-2_46

of network traffic. Barford uses the wavelet analysis to detect the abnormal traffic behavior on different scales of network traffic [5]. Xu detect the network abnormal based on the macroscopic analysis of network traffic [6]. These methods provide a solid theoretical basis for research and analysis of abnormal traffic behavior, but there are some questions, such as these methods can only detect the abnormal which change the natural structure and difficult to meet the real-time requirements. The problem of defining the user network traffic behavior, the problem of reducing the dimension of describing the user network behavior, and the problem of analysing the individual user behavior effective from big data and other problems have not been solved very well.

As the user access behavior is dynamically variable, but some of the above methods did not take the time or path sequence into account. Therefore, this paper proposed an analysis method of abnormal behavior based on user behavior and time sequence and extracted the enterprise network users from the preprocessing network traffic data after data cleaning and user identification, then serialize the user behavior by time. The user behavior sequence can reflect the user's behavior effectively, so the user behavior similarity was calculated by the sequence similarity algorithm. The similarity of user behavior reflects the similarity between users browsing path in the internet. The paper introduces the concept of user behavior correlation coefficient to reflect the similarity between users online behavior. Finally, through the detection of different time windows, we find out the users abnormal coefficient of correlation coefficient in a certain time window, and judge the abnormal behavior.

2   Research Framework

The model of user abnormal behavior analysis established in this paper is mainly divided into four modules as Fig. 1.

1. Data preprocessing module: grabbing data from the enterprise server or the communication link and analyzing the pcap packet, then cleaning the raw data and distinguish the users by the data, the data are processed into a sequence at the last.
2. Sequential pattern mining module: the sequence should be stored in the sequence database, and the behavior sequence of each user is generated based on the time so that the longest common subsequence of the user is obtained.
3. Similarity algorithm module: the results obtained from the sequential pattern mining module can get the behavior similarity and the correlation coefficient between the users by week.
4. Behavior analysis module: compare the change of behavior similarity between users of each week and days, find out the significant change of the user and judge the abnormal behavior.

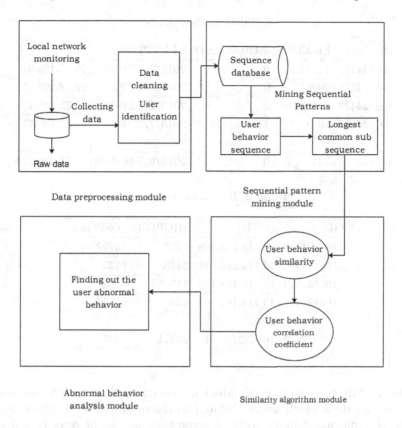

Fig. 1. The model of user abnormal behavior analysis.

3 Data Preprocessing Module

3.1 The Raw Data

The paper uses the original data from the monitoring log of one enterprise network, the time span of 7 weeks, a total of about 2000000 lines of records. Network monitoring system is deployed in the network of the enterprise, it can monitor all the packet data transmit with the main line. It records the following information: ID (record number), FILELEN (the network connection of the total length of the transmission data), ISCRACKED (whether the package is damaged), STARTTIME (start time), SRCIP (source IP), DSTIP (destination IP), SRCPORT (source port), DSTPORT (destination port). Tables 1 and 2 shows the raw data.

3.2 Data Cleaning and User Identification

Data preprocessing refers to some of the processing steps of the original data before use the data [7], including data cleaning and user identification. Data

Table 1. Raw data

ID	FILELEN	ISCRACKED	STARTTIME	SRCIP
166124419	14232	0	2015/7/22 0:00	10.52.128.2
166124478	2008	0	2015/7/22 0:00	10.67.220.27
166124423	4490	0	2015/7/22 0:00	10.52.140.75
166124424	4628	1	2015/7/22 0:00	10.52.140.75
...	...	...	...	...
172872627	731	0	2015/9/9 9:59:00	10.71.216.221

Table 2. Raw data (continued)

ID	DSTIP	SRCPORT	DSPORT
166124419	10.118.163.108	1433	3799
166124478	10.145.216.221	2445	135
166124423	10.118.163.105	445	1534
166124424	10.118.163.105	445	1534
...	...	...	...
172872627	10.67.220.221	23321	445

cleaning mainly to solve the redundant information [8], error information and user behavior data which are not related to the original data in the raw data. Due to the machine failure, artificial error such as loss of records and input errors, for these data, it should be screened and deleted. The procedure of data cleaning as Fig. 2.

First, we get the raw data from the pcap package. Then, after the data analysis, the redundant data, some of the erroneous information of the original data, and some of the missing attribute data are deleted. We want to study user behavior in enterprise network so we have to study the connection information of each host in the network. Due to the topology network is not clear, so we must identify the host user and server first.

In this paper, all of the IP addresses in the data set were used to represent the force diagram which expresses the communication of the host in internal networks as Fig. 3, and the node means the host. The line indicated that there is communication between two hosts, so there are some hosts which have many connections with other hosts from the figure, and the flow is greater than most of the host so that we can judge that the host is the server. Then finding the host which may be the host, as shown in the black square of the figure. At the same time, the cleaning conversion rules abandoned the host which the number of connections were less, because there are little record of user network behavior and little possibility of detecting the abnormal behavior, so it is difficult to study the behavior similarity between this user with other users, and the similarity may be infinitely close to zero. After data cleaning, the final data were fitted

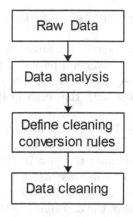

Fig. 2. The model of data cleaning.

with the requirements of the research, not only reduced the confusion of the algorithm of the model and the computational complexity, but also increased the computational efficiency of the model.

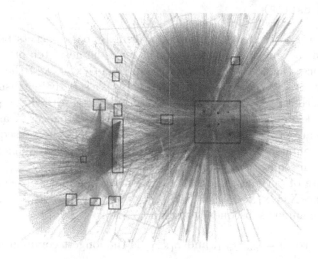

Fig. 3. The force diagram of connections of the host.

4   Sequential Pattern Mining Module

Sequential pattern mining refers to excavate the pattern which compared with time or other things with high frequency [9], but the sequence patterns of the model in this paper is not a typical mining sequence mining algorithm. For the user behavior sequence in the enterprise internal network, we can get the longest common subsequence between every users with the longest common subsequence algorithm.

The paper defines the user behavior: assume that the active host 1, 2, 3, and the purpose host A, B, C $\cdots$, in a certain period of time (assuming a week), the user 1 has access to the purpose host with the series of A, B, D, C, and the user 2 has access to the purpose host with the series of B, A, D. So, the series is the user behavior.

The paper uses the method of Python dictionary to number the host IP. Assuming that there are n IP: 127.0.0.1, 127.0.0.2, $\cdots$, 127.0.0.n, for the above IP address serialization, and number the first IP address appears the first time. Pseudo-code can be expressed as follows: use a python dictionary to preserve sequence IP serialization values, it means that the value of keys of the dictionary is the IP address, and the value of the dictionary is the number of the IP address.

How to number the host IP

```
dst={}, i =1
for every access:
    if not dst.has_key:(IP)
       i=i+1;
    else
       return dst(IP)
```

After the data is processed, the route that sent by data packets be processed, and generated the single user access sequence for the next step of work.

Subsequence: there is a sequence $X = (x_1, x_2, \cdots, x_m)$, and the meaning of another sequence $Z = (z_1, z_2, \cdots, z_m)$ is that there is a strictly increasing sequence $(i_1, i_2, \cdots, i_m)$ that make every $j = 1, \cdots, k$, and $Z_j = x_{i_j}$ with the sequence of X.

The longest common subsequence: there are two sequences X and Y, when another sequence of Z is both the subsequence of X and the subsequence of Y, then Z is the common subsequence of X and Y. The longest sequence of Z is the longest common sequence of X and Y.

The feature of optimal substructure of longest common subsequence: there are two sequence $X = (x_1, x_2, \cdots, x_m)$ and $Y = (y_1, y_2, \cdots, y_m)$, $Z = (z_1, z_2, \cdots, z_m)$ is the longest common subsequence of X and Y [10].

1. If $x_m = y_n$, so $Z_k = x_m = y_n$, and $Z_{(k-1)}$ is the longest common subsequence of $X_{(m-1)}$ and $Y_{(n-1)}$;
2. If $x_m \neq y_n$, so $Z_k \neq x_m$, and Z is the longest common subsequence of $X_{(m-1)}$ and Y;
3. If $x_m \neq y_n$, so $Z_k \neq y_n$, and Z is the longest common subsequence of X and $Y_{(n-1)}$ [11];

The process of solving a common subsequence can be obtained by the characteristic of the optimal substructure as Fig. 4:

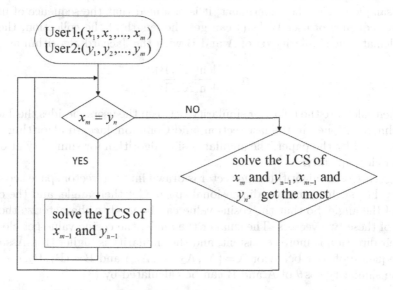

Fig. 4. The process of calculating the longest common sub sequence.

The longest common subsequence of $X = (x_1, x_2, \cdots, x_m)$ and $Y = (y_1, y_2, \cdots, y_m)$ is saved in $c[i][j]$, so:

$$c[i][j] = \begin{cases} 0 & \text{if } i = 0 \text{ or } j = 0 \\ c[i-1][j-1] & \text{if } i, j > 0 \text{ and} \\ & x_i = y_j \\ max\{c[i][j-1], c[i-1][j-1]\} & \text{if } i, j > 0 \text{ and} \\ & x_i \neq y_j \end{cases} \quad (1)$$

So we can get the longest common subsequence of two users.

5   Similarity Algorithm Module

5.1   Common_Jaccard Algorithm

With each user's behavior sequence, we can get the users behavior similarity and relationship by calculating the similarity between the users, so the similarity is the basis of the whole model. Now the algorithm of computing the sequence similarity between the users is based on the intersection of the collection of operations [12], such as Jaccard algorithm, the angular cosine algorithm, etc. This paper presents an improvement algorithm based on the Jaccard algorithm, which can represent the accuracy of the user more accurately after the experiment.

Jaccard algorithm: Jaccard coefficient is mainly used to calculate the similarity between the individual symbol metric or Boolean metric [13,14]. Jaccard coefficient is equal to the ratio of the intersection of the sample set and the union of the sample set. In the experiment, it is assumed that the sequence of user A and the sequence of user B, len() can get the length of the collection, then we can calculate the similarity α_j of A and B with the Jaccard algorithm as (2).

$$\alpha_j = \frac{\text{len}(A \cap B)}{\text{len}(A \cup B)} \tag{2}$$

When calculate the behavior similarity between the users, besides the Jaccard algorithm mentioned in the last section, and Common_Jaccard algorithm which was proposed by the paper, the angular cosine algorithm for similarity also used in research frequently.

Angular Cosine algorithm: the vector is drawn into the vector space according to the value, such as the two-dimensional space. Get their angle, and the cosine value of the angle. So that the cosine value can be used to characterize the similarity of these two vectors. The smaller the angle, the cosine value get closer to '1', their direction is more consistent, and the similarity is higher [15]. Assuming that sequence of user behavior $A = (A_1, A_2, \cdots, A_m)$ and $B = (B_1, B_2, \cdots, B_m)$, and the similarity $\cos \theta$ of A and B can be calculated by (3).

$$\cos \theta = \frac{\sum_{i=1}^{n}(A_i \times B_i)}{\sqrt{\sum_{i=1}^{n} A_i^2} \times \sqrt{\sum_{i=1}^{n} B_i^2}} \tag{3}$$

Common_Jaccard algorithm: assuming that the sequence of user A and the sequence of user B, len() can get the length of the collection, C is the longest common subsequence of A and B, then we can calculate the similarity α_{cj} of A and B with the Common_Jaccard algorithm as (4).

$$\alpha_{cj} = \frac{\text{len}(C)}{\text{len}(A \cup B)} \tag{4}$$

5.2 Comparing the Accuracy of the Algorithms

The original data time span of two months, the paper gets the first six weeks of data as a training set, the seventh week of data as a test set. First of all, the paper presents the concept of accuracy to measure the accuracy of three algorithms. Assuming that there are user A and user B, for the first six weeks of data, the similarity α of A and B every weeks were calculated, and then calculate the average similarity α_{avg} and the variance of the similarity α_{dx} of first six weeks. So that the range of similarity prediction of the seventh week can be calculated by (5).

$$\alpha_{avg} \pm \alpha_{dx} \tag{5}$$

For the set of the host IP in the original data, using the Jaccard algorithm, the angular cosine method, Common_Jaccard algorithm to calculate the accuracy rate, the results as Table 3:

Table 3. Table of the accuracy rate of similarity algorithm

Algorithm	The accuracy rate
Jaccard	0.662863964927
Angular cosine method	0.768421052632
Common_Jaccard	0.836257309942

By the experimental results, the Common_Jaccard algorithm proposed in this paper can be more effective in response to the behavior of users. Therefore, the following experiments are based on Common_Jaccard algorithm.

5.3 Correlation Coefficient of User Behavior

Based on the Common_Jaccard algorithm, which is a better way to describe the behavior similarity between users, the similarity between all users with each other in two months has been obtained. In this paper, the concept of correlation coefficient is proposed: by analyzing the change of similarity of a period of time (n weeks), we can get the set of user which surfing track was most closely in the period of time. The average similarity α_{avg} is larger, the change of the similarity is smaller, and the relationship between these two users is more similar. This feature can be expressed by the correlation coefficient of RC. If the variance is α_{dx}, RC can be calculated by (6).

$$RC = \frac{\alpha_{avg}}{\alpha_{dx}} \qquad (6)$$

So, the higher RC between the two users, the more similar between the behavior of the two users. With the similarity α and the correlation coefficient RC, we can describe the behavior between the user and the degree of similarity accurately and lay the foundations for looking for abnormal behavior.

6 Behavior Analysis Module

Abnormal behavior analysis module find out the users who may have the abnormal behavior based on the results of the previous modules. The set of host generated by the original data may contain 1000 users span seven weeks. Set the time window for one week for the following steps.

1. Set the first six weeks as a training set, and the seventh week as a test set.
2. Calculate the correlation coefficient and the similarity of a week between all users of the training set, get the average correlation coefficient RC_{avg} and correlation coefficient variance RC_{dx}. If the correlation coefficient RC between the relative application of the test set is within the range of $RC_{avg} + RC_{dx}$, it can be regarded as a stable user combination. Conversely, it will be regarded as a combination of suspected abnormal users.

3. Compare the variation degree of similarity between the combination of suspected abnormal user and the other users, if the variation degree of similarity of a user in a suspected abnormal user combination is larger, it can be judged as an abnormal user, so it should be added into the set of abnormal user.
4. Set every one week of the first six weeks as the test set and the rest as the training set, repeat the step of 2 and 3.

According to the above steps, the abnormal user set can be obtained by programming calculation, but we can only judge the abnormal user in one week but we dont know the precise days. Therefore, the method changes the time window as one day so that we can judge the day which user abnormal behavior was generated. Comparing the final test results with the original data set, the correct rate of finding abnormal behavior can reach 90%, indicating that the method has a positive influence of finding abnormal user behavior in enterprise network.

7 Conclusions

The model of analysis of user abnormal behavior in enterprise network considering the factor such as time and research based on user behavior sequence, the model can describe the user behavior in enterprise network effectively and verified using the original data of one company. However, the data spans two months and the results may not be perfect, and there may be one algorithm which describes the user behavior similarity more accurate when calculate the user behavior similarity. For a longer time span of the data sets and different companies data to consider further research work, and try to use more algorithm of behavior similarity, not only in the sequence, but also vector similarity, text similarity algorithm can be considered. At the same time, more features were added to the user sequence, so that more factors affect the similarity between users.

Acknowledgments. This work was supported by the NSFC (No. 61502247, 11501302, 61502243, 91646116), China Postdoctoral Science Foundation (No. 2016M600434), Natural Science Foundation of Jiangsu Province (BK20140895, BK20150862), Scientific and Technological Support Project (Society) of Jiangsu Province (No. BE2016776), Postdoctoral Science Foundation of Jiangsu Province (1601128B), and the Project of Natural Science Research in Universities of Jiangsu Province (14KJB520028).

References

1. Yang, Z.: Analysis of network user behavior based on traffic identification. Chongqing University (2009)
2. Farraposo, S., Owezarski, P., Monteiro, P.: A multi-scale tomographic algorithm for detecting and classifying traffic anomalies. In: Proceedings of IEEE International Conference on Communications, pp. 363–370. IEEE Press, Glasgow (2007)

3. Leland, W.E., Taqqu, M.S., Willinger, W., Wilson, D.V.: On the self-similar nature of Ethernet traffic. In: ACM SIGCOMM Conference, San Francisco, pp. 183–193 (1993)
4. Psxon, V., Floyd, S.: Wide-area traffic: the failure of Poisson modeling. In: ACM SIGCOMM Conference, San Francisco, pp. 257–268 (1993)
5. Barford, P., Kline, J., Plonka, D.: A signal analysis of network traffic anomalies. In: Proceedings of the 2nd ACM SIGCOMM Internet Measurement Workshop, Marseille, pp. 71–82 (2002)
6. Xu, X.D., Zhu, S.R., Sun, Y.M.: Anomaly detection algorithm based on fractal characteristics of large-scale network traffic. J. Commun. **30**, 43–53 (2009)
7. Gu, B., Sun, X.M., Sheng, V.S.: Structural minimax probability machine. IEEE Trans. Neural Netw. Learn. Syst. **28**, 1646–1656 (2016)
8. Yang, F.X., Liu, Y.C., Duan, Z.H.: An overview of data cleaning. Appl. Res. Comput. **3**, 8–11 (2007)
9. Zhang, C.H., Kong-Fa, H.U., Chen, L.: Research on sequential pattern mining algorithms. J. Yangzhou Univ. **10**, 41–46 (2007)
10. Zheng, C.L.: Analysis and implementation of longest common subsequence algorithm. J. Wuyi Coll. **2**, 44–48 (2010)
11. Yu, H.Y.: The comparison of the LCS algorithm with the GST algorithm in strings similarity metrics. Electron. Sci. Technol. **3**, 101–103 (2011)
12. Fan, D., Stefan, S., Sergej, Z.: Efficient Jaccard-based diversity analysis of large document collections. In: 21st ACM International Conference on Information and Knowledge Management, Maui, pp. 1402–1411 (2012)
13. Gu, B., Sheng, V.S., Keng, Y.T., Romano, W., Li, S.: Incremental support vector learning for ordinal regression. IEEE Trans. Neural Netw. Learn. Syst. **26**, 1403–1416 (2015)
14. Pan, L., Lei, Y., Wang, C., Xie, J.: Method on entity identification using similarity measure based on weight of Jaccard. J. Beijing Jiaotong Univ. **34**, 141–145 (2009)
15. Luo, L., Zhang, K., Xia, Z.: Study on the user behavior of digital library with Cosine Similarity Algorithm. In: IEEE International Symposium on It in Medicine and Education, Xiameng, pp. 369–374 (2008)

An Efficient Speeding up Algorithm of Frobenius Based Scalar Multiplication on Koblitz Curves for Cloud Computing

Yunqi Dou[1](✉), Chuangui Ma[2], Yanbin Li[2], and Fushan Wei[1]

[1] State Key Laboratory of Mathematical Engineering and Advanced Computing,
Zhengzhou, China
douyunqi@126.com
[2] Department of Basic, Army Aviation Institution, Beijing, China

Abstract. With the rapid development of wireless sensor network, cloud computing and Internet of Things, the problems of security and privacy are becoming more and more serious. Elliptic curve cryptography as a public key cryptography plays an important role to solve the security issues, in which scalar multiplication is the most important and time-consuming operation. Koblitz curve is a special class of elliptic curve over binary field, Frobenius endomorphism can be used to accelerate the scalar multiplication. By converting single scalar multiplication into simultaneous multiple scalar multiplication, GLV method can use Straus-Shamir trick to calculate the scalar multiplication. In this paper, we combine the idea of Frobenius endomorphism and GLV method to speed up the scalar multiplication on Koblitz curve. Our algorithm can efficiently convert scalar multiplication into multi-scalar multiplication to reduce the cost of point additions and Frobenius operations. Theoretical analysis results show that: Compared with τ-and-add algorithm, our 2-dimensional implementation provides a speedup over 19%, 3-dimensional implementation speeds up over 29%. Finally, a parallel scalar multiplication algorithm for Koblitz curve is designed, which can flexibly select the dimension of the parallel algorithm based on the number r of processing unit. Compared with the standard τ-and-add algorithm, this algorithm can achieve a speedup of almost r times.

Keywords: Koblitz curve · GLV method · Scalar multiplication · Frobenius endomorphism · Parallel algorithm

1 Introduction

Recently, wireless sensor networks, cloud computing and Internet of things (IoT) have been widely researched and applied. They cover many applications in different areas, such as environmental monitoring, medical and healthcare systems, building and home automation and so on. These technologies bring us much convenience both in life and work, however, they also bring more security risks

© Springer International Publishing AG 2017
X. Sun et al. (Eds.): ICCCS 2017, Part I, LNCS 10602, pp. 542–551, 2017.
https://doi.org/10.1007/978-3-319-68505-2_47

at the same time. As an alternative to RSA and other cryptographic schemes on finite field, Elliptic curve cryptography [1,2] plays a crucial role to overcome security problems by providing such services as encryption, authentication and key establishment. Under the same security level, elliptic curve cryptography has faster processing speed and requires less storage and bandwidth, which is especially suitable for low-end processors and resource constrained devices such as smart cards. Scalar multiplication is the most important and time-consuming operation in elliptic curve cryptography. The calculation speed of scalar multiplication determines the performance and practicality of elliptic curve cryptosystems. How to speed up the scalar multiplication has always been a hotspot in elliptic curve cryptography.

The Koblitz curves [3] is a special class of elliptic curves defined over the binary field. The main advantage of Koblitz curves is that the Frobenius endomorphism $\tau(x,y) = (x^2, y^2)$, which is much cheaper than doubling. To calculate kP, the classical double-and-add algorithm requires $\log_2 k$ doublings and $\frac{\log_2 k}{2}$ additions on average. If the scalar k is given as τ-adic expansion, the scalar multiplication kP can be computed with τ-and-add algorithm, which is similar to the double-and-add algorithm except that point doublings are replaced with cheaper Frobenius endomorphisms. Because doublings are no longer required, Koblitz curves offer more efficient scalar multiplication than general binary curves. At present, Koblitz curves have been widely used in many industry standards, such as the five Koblitz curves recommended by NIST standard [4] and elliptic curve cryptography cipher suite for TLS [5,6].

Solina [7] generalized the NAF (non-adjacent form) and w-NAF methods to the τ-adic expansion, and the corresponding scalar multiplication algorithms require on average $\frac{\log_2 k}{3}$ and $\frac{\log_2 k}{w+1}$ point additions, respectively. In [8], Avanzi et al. combined point halving [9] with τ-adic NAF approach and proposed a new scalar multiplication algorithm without precomputation. Their algorithm can reduce the number of point additions from $\frac{\log_2 k}{3}$ to $\frac{2\log_2 k}{7}$. Okeya et al. [10] embed the precomputation process in the scalar multiplication to reduce the memory consumption of the scalar multiplication algorithm. For hardware implementation, their algorithm is as fast as the 5-NAF but requires only one auxiliary point instead of seven. Avanzi et al. [11] and Dimitrov et al. [12] propose sublinear scalar multiplication algorithm on Koblitz curves using the double-base and triple-base number presentation, respectively. In 2016, Oliveira et al. [13] designed the fast and timing attack resistant scalar multiplication algorithm on a Koblitz curve defined over finite field F_4 for the first time. In order to adapt to the implementation of scalar multiplication algorithms on high-performance servers, a variety of parallel scalar multiplication algorithms are proposed [14–16].

In 2001, Gallant et al. [17] proposed GLV method to accelerate the scalar multiplication on elliptic curves with efficiently computable endomorphisms. Let E be an elliptic curve over finite field F_p and $P \in E(F_p)$ a point of large prime order n such that $\phi(P) \in \langle P \rangle$, the computation of kP can be decomposed as $k_1 P + k_2 \phi(P)$ where $|k_1|, |k_2| \approx \sqrt{n}$. Therefore, this immediately eliminates about half of all doublings by using the Straus-Shamir trick for simultaneous scalar multiplication. In 2009, Galbraith et al. [18] presented a method to construct an efficiently computable endomorphism on elliptic curve $E(F_{p^2})$ by exploiting the action of Frobenius map, and generalized the GLV method to a large class of elliptic curves over F_{p^2} (a.k.a GLS curves). In [19], Hankerson et al. considered the GLS elliptic curves defined over binary fields, and presented the 2-dimensional GLV method on such curves.

In this paper, we focus on Koblitz curves and consider whether the Frobenius endomorphism can be combined with the GLV method to accelerate the scalar multiplication. We firstly show that the GLV method cannot be applied directly to Koblitz curve. Although the scalar multiplication kP can be decomposed as $k_1P + k_2\tau(P)$ with $|k_1|, |k_2| \approx \sqrt{n}$ using the GLV method, the length of the τ-adic expansion for k_1 and k_2 cannot be controlled, which will increase the computational cost of scalar multiplication. Since the scalar k can be divided using τ^s, we can convert flexibly a single scalar multiplication into simultaneous multiscalar multiplication. Although Frobenius endomorphism is less expensive than the multiplication on finite field, it is not negligible. The cost of endomorphism τ^s is significantly smaller than s consecutive Frobenius map τ. Our algorithm can reduce the number of point additions and Frobenius endomorphism τ at the same time. Theoretical analysis results show that: Compared with τ-and-add algorithm, our 2-dimensional implementation provides a speedup over 19%, 3-dimensional implementation speeds up over 29%. Finally, a parallel algorithm for Koblitz curve scalar multiplication is designed, which can flexibly select the dimension of the parallel algorithm based on the number r of processing unit. Compared with the standard τ-and-add algorithm, this algorithm can achieve a speedup of almost r times.

The rest of this paper is organized as follows. Section 2 presents some preliminaries about Koblitz curves and basis representation. Section 3 analyzes the GLV method on Koblitz curve. Our new scalar multiplication algorithms on Koblitz curve are described in Sect. 4. Finally, we draw our conclusions in Sect. 5.

2 Preliminaries

2.1 Koblitz Curves

Koblitz curves are the elliptic curves defined over F_2:

$$E_a : y^2 + xy = x^3 + ax^2 + 1, \text{with } a \in \{0,1\}. \tag{1}$$

Let $d|m$, then $E_a(F_{2^d})$ is a subgroup of $E_a(F_{2^m})$ and $\#E_a(F_{2^d})|\#E_a(F_{2^m})$. In particular, $\#E_0(F_2) = 4, \#E_1(F_2) = 2$, so $4|\#E_0(F_{2^m}), 2|\#E_1(F_{2^m})$. If $\#E_a(F_{2^m}) = hn$ where n is prime and h satisfies

$$h = \begin{cases} 4 & \text{if } a = 0, \\ 2 & \text{if } a = 1. \end{cases}$$

then $\#E_a(F_{2^m})$ is almost prime and h is called the cofactor. NIST recommends five Koblitz curves over binary fields $m = 163, 233, 283, 409, 571$.

The Frobenius endomorphism is defined by

$$\tau : \begin{cases} E(F_{2^m}) \to E(F_{2^m}) \\ (x, y) \mapsto (x^2, y^2) \end{cases}$$

Since squaring in F_{2^m} is relatively inexpensive, the Frobenius endomorphism can be computed efficiently. It has been shown that $(\tau^2 + 2)P = \mu\tau(P)$ for every point $P \in E_a(F_{2^m})$, where $\mu = (-1)^{1-a}$. Therefore, the Frobenius map can be seen as a complex number $\tau = (\mu + \sqrt{-7})/2$ which satisfies $\tau^2 - \mu\tau + 2 = 0$. If the scalar is represented as τ-adic expansion

$$k = \sum_{i=1}^{l-1} a_i\tau^i, a_i \in \{0, \pm 1\}, \tag{2}$$

then point doublings can be replaced by the efficiently computable Frobenius endomorphism in scalar multiplication. In order to take advantage of this property, it is required that the τ-adic expansion is short and sparse. Solinas [7] generalized the NAF method to τ-adic expansion, and presented an efficient algorithm to compute the τ-adic NAF.

Similar to the classical NAF, every positive integer k has a unique τ-adic NAF, whose average density is $1/3$. $\mathbb{Z}[\tau] = \{a + b\tau | a, b \in \mathbb{Z}\}$ is Euclidean domain. Due to norm $N(k) = k^2$ and $N(\tau) = 2$, the length of τ-adic NAF for k is approximately $2\log_2 k$, which is twice the length of NAF. If we replace the ordinary NAF by the τ-adic NAF, we have to double the number of point additions. Let $\delta = (\tau^m - 1)/(\tau - 1)$, $\rho \equiv k \mod \delta$, then $kP = \rho P$ for every point $P \in E_a(F_{2^m})\backslash E_a(F_2)$. Solinas also presented an efficient algorithm to compute the τ-adic NAF of ρ, whose length is at most $m + a + 3$. Algorithm 1 presents the τ-and-add algorithm using reduced τ-adic NAF above.

Algorithm 1. τ-and-add algorithm on Koblitz curves

Input: $k \in \mathbb{Z}, P \in E_a(F_{2^m})\backslash E_a(F_2)$

Output: kP

1: compute the reduced τ-adic NAF $k = \sum_{i=1}^{l-1} a_i\tau^i, a_i \in \{0, \pm 1\}$
2: $R \leftarrow \mathcal{O}$
3: For i from $l - 1$ downto 0 do
4:     $R \leftarrow \tau R$
5:     if $a_i \neq 0$ then $R \leftarrow R + a_i P$
6: return R

2.2 Basis Representation

F_{2^m} can be viewed as a m-dimensional vector space over F_2, so there exists a basis $\{\alpha_0, \alpha_1, \cdots, \alpha_{m-1}\}$. Then every element $\alpha \in F_{2^m}$ can be represented uniquely as $\alpha = a_0\alpha_0 + a_1\alpha_1 + \cdots + a_{m-1}\alpha_{m-1}$, where $a_1, \cdots, a_{m-1} \in F_2$. From the perspective of implementation, two types of basis are usually considered: polynomial bases and norm bases. Let $f(x) \in F_2[x]$ be an irreducible polynomial of degree m over F_2, and β be a root of $f(x)$ in F_{2^m}, then $\{1, \beta, \beta^2, \cdots, \beta^{m-1}\}$ is a polynomial basis of F_{2^m} over F_2, and $\{\beta, \beta^2, \cdots, \beta^{2^{m-1}}\}$ is a normal basis of F_{2^m} over F_2. In normal basis, squaring is simply a right cyclic shift: Let $\alpha = a_0\beta + a_1\beta^2 + \cdots + a_{m-1}\beta^{2^{m-1}} = (a_0, a_1, \cdots, a_{m-1})$, then

$$\alpha^2 = a_{m-1} + a_0\beta^2 + \cdots + a_{m-2}\beta^{2^{m-1}} = (a_{m-1}, a_0, \cdots, a_{m-2}).$$

However, normal basis multiplications are slow. In polynomial basis, squaring on F_{2^m} is a linear operation [23], which is much faster than the multiplication. The normal basis is suitable for hardware implementation, while the polynomial basis is more suitable for software implementation.

3   Analysis of GLV Method on Koblitz Curve

For Koblitz curve E_a, Frobenius map τ is a trivial endomorphism, whose characteristic polynomial is $x^2 - \mu x + 2 = 0$ with $\mu = (-1)^{1-a}$. Let $P \in E_a(F_{2^m})$ be a point of prime order n, then $\tau(P) = \lambda P$, where λ is a root of $x^2 - \mu x + 2 = 0 \mod n$. Using the method in [17], we can decompose the scalar $k = k_1 + k_2\lambda \mod n$, with $max\{|k_1|, |k_2|\} = O(\sqrt{n})$. Therefore, the scalar multiplication kP can be replaced by the multi-scalar multiplication $kP = k_1P + k_2\tau(P)$. In order to take advantage of τ-and-add algorithm, we need to compute the reduced τ-adic NAF of k_1 and k_2. However, the length of the τ-adic expansion for k_1 and k_2 cannot be controlled, their length is still about $m + a + 3$. An example is given below for the Koblitz curve K-163 recommended by NIST.

Let $m = 163$, $F_{2^m} = F_2[x]/(f(x))$, where $f(x) = x^{163} + x^7 + x^6 + x^3 + 1$. Considering the Koblitz curve $E_1 : y^2 + xy = x^3 + x^2 + 1$ over F_{2^m}, then $\#E_1(F_{2^m}) = 2n$, where n is a large prime

$n = $ 0x400000000000000000000020108A2E0CC0D99F8A5EF (163 bits).

$P = (x, y)$ is point of order n, where

$x = $ 0x6419A48E7599E6BC72EC0CFF374C0FE460AB0B2E,

$y = $ 0x3D71ED7855592ABCCB1D10F03E5E9057232987E97.

Then $\lambda =$ 5124886332546225921918603466361262992169187649242 is a root of equation $x^2 - \mu x + 2 = 0 \mod n$ and satifies $\lambda P = \tau(P)$.

Suppose $k =$ 2563738480479344601191691557472330766150714787288, then

$$k = k_1 + k_2\lambda \mod n,$$

where

$$k_1 = 398219958404448976648888,$$

$$k_2 = 1099031975179646102400891.$$

$\delta = (\tau^m - 1)/(\tau - 1) = 1824026374634505274957943 + 755360064476226375461$
594τ.

Due to $max\{|k_1|, |k_2|\} = O(\sqrt{n})$, the reduced τ-adic NAF is of no practical significance in this case and the length of k_1 and k_2 is about m bits. Specifically, the τ-adic NAF of k_1 and k_2 are as follow:

$k_1 = 100\bar{1}0010100\bar{1}0010\bar{1}010\bar{1}0\bar{1}0001010001001010010\bar{1}010\bar{1}0\bar{1}0010\bar{1}010\bar{1}00\bar{1}00\bar{1}0$
$10\bar{1}01000\bar{1}00000100100\bar{1}00\bar{1}001000\bar{1}0\bar{1}001000010100\bar{1}00001001001010000\bar{1}0100$
$10\bar{1}0100101000\bar{1}000101000$ (157 bits)
$k_2 = 1001000101001001001001001000\bar{1}01010000\bar{1}000\bar{1}00\bar{1}00000\bar{1}00100010000101001001010010$ (162 bits)
where $\bar{1}$ represents -1.

4   Efficient Scalar Multiplication on Koblitz Curves

4.1   New Scalar Multiplication Algorithm

For every integer $s \in \mathbb{Z}$, the endomorphism τ^s can also be computed efficiently. Suppose the τ-adic NAF of scalar k is

$$k = \sum_{i=0}^{l-1} a_i\tau^i, a_i \in \{0, \pm 1\},$$

where $l \leq m + a + 3$. Let $s = \lceil \frac{l}{r} \rceil$, then the τ-adic NAF above can be divided into r segments of the same length (if l/r is not an integer, padding a few 0s at the most significant bit)

$$k = \sum_{i=0}^{s-1} a_i\tau^i + \sum_{i=s}^{2s-1} a_i\tau^i + \cdots + \sum_{i=(r-1)s}^{rs-1} a_i\tau^i$$

$$= \sum_{i=0}^{s-1} a_i\tau^i + \tau^s \sum_{i=0}^{s-1} a_{i+s}\tau^i + \cdots + \tau^{(r-1)s} \sum_{i=0}^{s-1} a_{i+(r-1)s}\tau^i$$

Let $\phi = \tau^s$, $k_1 = \sum_{i=0}^{s-1} a_i\tau^i, k_2 = \sum_{i=0}^{s-1} a_{i+s}\tau^i, \cdots, k_r = \sum_{i=0}^{s-1} a_{i+(r-1)s}\tau^i$, then

$$kP = k_1P + k_2\tau^s(P) + \cdots + k_r\tau^{(r-1)s}(P)$$
$$= k_1P + k_2\phi(P) + \cdots + k_r\phi^{(r-1)}(P) \quad (3)$$

Therefore, we can compute the scalar multiplication kP using the Straus-Shamir trick for simultaneous scalar multiplication. Algorithm 2 presents the new

548   Y. Dou et al.

scalar multiplication algorithm. The dimension r of multi-scalar multiplication in Algorithm 2 can be chosen flexibly. When $r = 1$, Algorithm 2 is the τ-and-add algorithm. When $r \geq 2$, the Algorithm 2 can reduce the number of τ from m to $\lceil m/r \rceil$. On the other hand, Algorithm 2 can also reduce the number of point additions. For example, the number of point additions is reduced from $m/3$ to $5m/18$ for the case $r = 2$.

Algorithm 2. New scalar multiplication algorithm on Koblitz curve

---

Input: $k \in \mathbb{Z}, P \in E_a(F_{2^m}) \backslash E_a(F_2)$, dimension r
Output: kP
1: compute the reduced τ-adic NAF $k = \sum_{i=1}^{l-1} a_i \tau^i, a_i \in \{0, \pm 1\}$
2: precompute $i_1 P + i_2 \phi(P) + \cdots + i_r \phi^{r-1}(P), i_1, \cdots, i_n \in \{0, \pm 1\}$
3: write k as $k_1 \| k_2 \| \cdots \| k_r$, where each k_i is a $\{0, \pm 1\}$-string of length s,
   $k_{i,j}$ denotes the j-th bit of k_i.
4: $R \leftarrow \mathcal{O}$
5: For i from $s - 1$ downto 0 do
6:    $R \leftarrow \tau R$
7:    $R \leftarrow R + (k_{1,i} P + \cdots + k_{r,i} \phi^{r-1}(P))$
8: return R

4.2 Performance Estimate

In this subsection, we evaluate the efficiency of the Algorithm 2 for specific curves. Two Koblitz curves recommended by NIST are considered: K-163 and K-233. The multiplication and squaring on finite field F_{2^m} can be implemented efficiently using the polynomial basis. Let M, S and I denote the cost of field multiplication, field squaring and field inversion. We ignore the costs of field addition, field subtraction and multiplication by small constants. According to the literatures [20, 21], $S \approx \frac{1}{7.5}M, I \approx 8M$ when $m = 163$, and $S \approx \frac{1}{9}M, I \approx 10M$ when $m = 233$. In addition, the cost of exponentiation to 2^s is about $1/6$ that of s consecutive squaring [22].

To implement the point operations on elliptic curve over binary filed, we choose to use López-Dahab projective coordinates [23], which can prevent field inversions in affine formulae. The projective point $(X : Y : Z)$ corresponds to the affine point $(X/Z, Y/Z^2)$. In this case, the cost of point addition (ADD) is 13M+4S, the cost of mixed point addition (mADD) is 8M+5S, the cost of point doubling (DBL) and Frobenius endomorphism is 3M+5S and 3S, respectively.

Since the length of τ-adic NAF for scalar k is about $m+a+3$, the cost of τ-and-add algorithm is about $\frac{m+a+2}{3}$ADD$+(m+a+2)\tau$. In Algorithm 2, precomputation are required: when $r = 2$, precomputing points $P \pm \phi(P)$ needs 2 point addition and $1\ \tau^s$; when $r = 3$, precomputing $P \pm \phi(P), P \pm \phi^2(P), P \pm \phi(P) \pm \phi^2(P)$ needs 6 point additions and $2\ \tau^s$. When $r = 2$, the average density of $\binom{k_1}{k_2}$ is $\frac{5}{9}$, the cost of τ^s is about $\frac{m+a+2}{4}$S, then the cost of Algorithm 2 is $\frac{5(m+a+2)}{18}$ADD$+\frac{m+a+2}{2}\tau^s$. With the increase of dimension r, the number of point additions in the main loop of Algorithm 2 will reduce. However, the precomputation increases exponentially at the same time. For the random point scalar multiplication, $r = 3$ is the optimal choice. Finally, the projective coordinates will be converted into affine coordinates, whose cost is 1I+2M+1S. Table 1 presents the evaluation results of Algorithm 2. For the case of $m = 163$, it represents a speedup of about 19.4% over original τ-and-add algorithm when $r = 2$, a speedup of 29.6% when $r = 3$. For the case of $m = 233$, it represents a speedup of about 20.1% and 33.5%, respectively.

Table 1. Performance estimation on Algorithm 2

m	a	τ-and-add algorithm	Algorithm 2 ($r = 2$)	speedup	Algorithm 2 ($r = 3$)	speedup
163	1	556.1M	465.8M	19.4%	429.1M	29.6%
2333	0	760.6M	633.4M	20.1%	569.9M	33.5%

4.3 Parallel Scalar Multiplication Algorithm on Koblitz Curve

The basic strategy of our parallel scalar multiplication algorithm is to rewrite formula (3) as

$$kP = k_1 P + k_2 \phi(P) + \cdots + k_r \phi^{(r-1)}(P)$$
$$= k_1 P + \phi(k_2 P) + \cdots + \phi^{(r-1)}(k_r P) \tag{4}$$

where r can be chosen flexibly according to the number of processors. From the formula (4), we can obtain Algorithm 3 below. The algorithm divides the scalar multiplication into r irrelevant parts and does not require precomputation. For those designs where r processing units are affordable, our parallel algorithm is able to achieve a speedup close to r.

Algorithm 3. New scalar multiplication algorithm on Koblitz curve

---

Input: $k \in \mathbb{Z}, P \in E_a(F_{2^m})\backslash E_a(F_2)$, integer r
Output: kP
1: compute the reduced τ-adic NAF $k = \sum_{i=1}^{l-1} a_i \tau^i, a_i \in \{0, \pm 1\}$
2: write k as $k_1 \| k_2 \| \cdots \| k_r$, where each k_i is a $\{0, \pm 1\}$-string of length s,
   $k_{i,j}$ denotes the j-th bit of k_i
3: $R \leftarrow \mathcal{O}, R_1 \leftarrow \mathcal{O}, R_2 \leftarrow \mathcal{O}, \cdots, R_r \leftarrow \mathcal{O}$

4: For i from $s - 1$ downto 0 do	4: For i from $s - 1$ downto 0 do
5: $R_1 \leftarrow \tau R_1$	5: $R_r \leftarrow \tau R_r$
6: if $k_{1,i} \neq 0$ then	6: if $k_{r,i} \neq 0$ then
7: $R_1 \leftarrow R_1 + k_{1,i}P$ $\cdots$	7: $R_r \leftarrow R_r + k_{r,i}P$
8: $R_1 \leftarrow R_1$	8: $R_r \leftarrow \phi^{r-1}R_r$

9: $R \leftarrow R_1 + R_2 + \cdots + R_r$
10: return R

---

5   Conclusions

In this paper, the Frobenius endomorphism τ is combined with the GLV method to design the scalar multiplication algorithm on Koblitz curve. Our algorithm can efficiently convert scalar multiplication into multiple scalar multiplication so that the number of point additions and Frobenius operations is reduced. For the curves K-163 and K-233 recommended by NIST, 2-dimensional implementation achieves a speedup above 19%, 3-dimensional implementation achieve a speedup above 29%. Compared with GLV scalar decompostition, this method is more flexible and simpler. In addition, the method can also be generalized to scalar multiplication algorithm based on the τ-adic w-NAF. Finally, we propose a parallel scalar multiplication algorithm on Koblitz curve, which can flexibly select the dimension of the parallel algorithm according to the number r of processing units. Compared with the standard τ-and-add algorithm, this algorithm is able to achieve a speedup close to r.

Acknowledgments. The authors would like to thank the anonymous referees for their helpful comments. This work is supported by the National Natural Science Foundation of China (No. 61379150, 61309016, 61602512), the Funding of Science and Technology on Information Assurance Laboratory (No. KJ1302) and Key Scientific and Technological Project of Henan Province (No. 122102210126, 092101210502).

References

1. Miller, V.S.: Use of elliptic curves in cryptography. In: Williams, H.C. (ed.) CRYPTO 1985. LNCS, vol. 218, pp. 417–426. Springer, Heidelberg (1986). doi:10.1007/3-540-39799-X_31
2. Koblitz, N.: Elliptic curve cryptosystems. Math. Comput. **48**(177), 203–209 (1987)
3. Koblitz, N.: CM-Curves with Good Cryptographic Properties. In: Feigenbaum, J. (ed.) CRYPTO 1991. LNCS, vol. 576, pp. 279–287. Springer, Heidelberg (1992). doi:10.1007/3-540-46766-1_22
4. National Institute of Standards and Technology. Recommended elliptic curves for federal government use. NIST Special Publication (1999). http://csrc.nist.gov/groups/ST/toolkit/documents/dss/NISTReCur.pdf
5. Dierks, T., Rescorla, E.: The transport layer security (TLS) protocol version 1.2. RFC 5246. Internet Engineering Task Force (IETF) (2008). https://tools.ietf.org/html/rfc5246
6. Blake-Wilson, S., Bolyard, N., et al.: Elliptic curve cryptography (ECC) cipher suites for transport layer security (TLS). RFC 4492. Internet Engineering Task Force (IETF) (2006). https://tools.ietf.org/html/rfc4492
7. Solinas, J.: Efficient arithmetic on Koblitz curves. Des. Codes Crypt. **19**(2), 195–249 (2000)
8. Avanzi, R.M., Ciet, M., Sica, F.: Faster scalar multiplication on Koblitz curves combining point halving with the Frobenius endomorphism. In: Bao, F., Deng, R., Zhou, J. (eds.) PKC 2004. LNCS, vol. 2947, pp. 28–40. Springer, Heidelberg (2004). doi:10.1007/978-3-540-24632-9_3
9. Knudsen, E.W.: Elliptic scalar multiplication using point halving. In: Lam, K.-Y., Okamoto, E., Xing, C. (eds.) ASIACRYPT 1999. LNCS, vol. 1716, pp. 135–149. Springer, Heidelberg (1999). doi:10.1007/978-3-540-48000-6_12

10. Okeya, K., Takagi, T., Vuillaume, C.: Short memory scalar multiplication on Koblitz Curves. In: Rao, J.R., Sunar, B. (eds.) CHES 2005. LNCS, vol. 3659, pp. 91–105. Springer, Heidelberg (2005). doi:10.1007/11545262_7

11. Avanzi, R., Sica, F.: Scalar multiplication on Koblitz curves using double bases. In: Nguyen, P.Q. (ed.) VIETCRYPT 2006. LNCS, vol. 4341, pp. 131–146. Springer, Heidelberg (2006). doi:10.1007/11958239_9

12. Dimitrov, V.S., Järvinen, K.U., Jacobson, M.J., Chan, W.F., Huang, Z.: FPGA implementation of point multiplication on Koblitz curves using Kleinian integers. In: Goubin, L., Matsui, M. (eds.) CHES 2006. LNCS, vol. 4249, pp. 445–459. Springer, Heidelberg (2006). doi:10.1007/11894063_35

13. Oliveira, T., López, J., Rodríguez-Henríquez, F.: Software implementation of Koblitz curves over quadratic fields. In: Gierlichs, B., Poschmann, A.Y. (eds.) CHES 2016. LNCS, vol. 9813, pp. 259–279. Springer, Heidelberg (2016). doi:10.1007/978-3-662-53140-2_13

14. Mishra, P.K.: Pipelined computation of scalar multiplication in elliptic curve cryptosystems. IEEE Trans. Comput. 55(8), 1000–1010 (2006)

15. Ahmadi, O., Hankerson, D., Rodríguez-Henríquez, F.: Parallel formulations of scalar multiplication on Koblitz curves. J. Univ. Comput. Sci. 14(3), 481–504 (2008)

16. Wu, K., Li, H., Zhu, D.: Fast and scalable parallel processing of scalar multiplication in elliptic curve cryptosystems. Secur. Commun. Netw. 5(6), 648–657 (2012)

17. Gallant, R.P., Lambert, R.J., Vanstone, S.A.: Faster point multiplication on elliptic curves with efficient endomorphisms. In: Kilian, J. (ed.) CRYPTO 2001. LNCS, vol. 2139, pp. 190–200. Springer, Heidelberg (2001). doi:10.1007/3-540-44647-8_11

18. Galbraith, S.D., Lin, X., Scott, M.: Endomorphisms for faster elliptic curve cryptography on a large class of curves. J. Cryptol. 24(3), 446–469 (2011)

19. Hankerson, D., Karabina, K., Menezes, A.: Analyzing the Galbraith-Lin-Scott point multiplication method for elliptic curves over binary fields. IEEE Trans. Comput. 58(10), 1411–1420 (2009)

20. Hankerson, D., López Hernandez, J., Menezes, A.: Software implementation of elliptic curve cryptography over binary fields. In: Koç, Ç.K., Paar, C. (eds.) CHES 2000. LNCS, vol. 1965, pp. 1–24. Springer, Heidelberg (2000). doi:10.1007/3-540-44499-8_1

21. Fong, K., Hankerson, D., López, J., Menezes, A.: Field inversion and point halving revisited. IEEE Trans. Comput. 53(8), 1047–1059 (2004)

22. Taverne, J., Faz-Hernández, A., Aranha, D.F., Rodríguez-Henríquez, F., Hankerson, D., López, J.: Software implementation of binary elliptic curves: impact of the carry-less multiplier on scalar multiplication. In: Preneel, B., Takagi, T. (eds.) CHES 2011. LNCS, vol. 6917, pp. 108–123. Springer, Heidelberg (2011). doi:10.1007/978-3-642-23951-9_8

23. Hankerson, D., Menezes, A., Vanstone, S.: Guide to Elliptic Curve Cryptography. Springer, New York (2004)

Consensus of Multi-agent Systems with State Constraints

Qingling Wang$^{(\boxtimes)}$

School of Automation, Southeast University, Nanjing 210096, China
qlwang@seu.edu.cn

Abstract. This paper is devoted to the consensus problem of single-integrator agents with state constraints. The state of agents under consideration is subject to saturation nonlinearities. Some necessary and sufficient conditions of consensus with state constraints are first proposed based on investigating the unique achievable equilibrium and employing an integral Lyapunov function. With the proposed necessary and sufficient condition, the consensus problem of single-integrator agents can be solved under an undirected and connected graph. In addition, some properties of the unachievable consensus are discussed. Finally, simulation examples are given to show the validity of the theoretical results.

Keywords: Consensus · State constraints · Multi-agent systems

1 Introduction

In recent decades, the consensus problem has received considerable attention due to its wide applications [1–3,5,8,14,15,18,21,24]. By using local neighborhood information, the main task of consensus is to design distributed protocols to achieve global motions [7,11,17]. For instance, consider a group of N first-order agents

$$\dot{x}_i = \sum_{j=1}^{N} a_{ij}(x_j - x_i), \quad i = 1, 2, \ldots, N,$$

where $x_i \in \mathbb{R}$ is the agents' state. As we know [13], the agents can achieve consensus over a connected graph. In fact, the consensus is reached only on the occasion that each agent can get the exact measurement of states of its neighbors.

In real applications, as the measurement units may have nonlinearities due to the usage of digital sensors, it is rather difficult to get the exact measurement of agents' states. However, it is easy to get bounded information of these exact measurements of agents' states. Therefore, the study of consensus problem with bounded nonlinearities has widely appeared. For example, the consensus problem with input saturation has been well studied in [6,16,20,22,23,25]. However, fewer results have been received for the consensus problem with state constraints. It is worth pointing that the consensus with state constraints may not be reached due to bounded nonlinearities, such as the discarded consensus in [12], which

X. Sun et al. (Eds.): ICCCS 2017, Part I, LNCS 10602, pp. 552–560, 2017.
https://doi.org/10.1007/978-3-319-68505-2_48

discards the neighbor's state if the agents' state is outside the saturation constraint. However, the assumption in [12] is that the initial state of each agent should be bounded, and only a sufficient condition is obtained. Furthermore, the conditions in [9,19] are for the multi-agent systems with output saturation. In this paper, the sufficient and necessary condition of multi-agent systems with state constraints is investigated, without the assumption that the initial state of each agent is bounded.

We consider the dynamics of agents as identical single-integrators under the undirected graph. Firstly, we analyze the consensus with state constraints under the undirected and connected graph. By employing an integral Lyapunov function, we provide the necessary and sufficient condition for achieving consensus with investigating the unique achievable equilibrium. We next discuss some properties of the unachievable consensus case. It is worth pointing out that the main contributions are twofold. Firstly, some necessary and sufficient conditions for achieving consensus of single-integrator agents with state constraints are first obtained. Secondly, to let the results for necessary and sufficient conditions on consensus be more general, the magnitude saturation functions are considered.

Notation: The sign function sign(y) takes the value $+1$ if $y \geq 0$ and -1 if $y < 0$. Let diag$\{\omega_1, \omega_2, \ldots, \omega_n\}$ be a diagonal matrix whose diagonal entries are $\omega_i, i = 1, 2, \ldots, n$, and $P > 0$ (≥ 0) denotes that P is a real symmetric positive (semi-positive) definite matrix.

2   Problem Formulation

In the beginning, the graph theory will be introduced. A graph $\mathcal{G}$ can be defined as a three-tuple $(\mathcal{V}, \mathcal{E}, \mathcal{A})$, where $\mathcal{V}$ denotes the set of nodes, $\mathcal{E} \subseteq \mathcal{V} \times \mathcal{V}$ denotes the set of edges, and $\mathcal{A} = [a_{ij}] \in \mathbb{R}^{N \times N}$, where a_{ij} is the underlying weighted adjacency matrix defined as $a_{ij} > 0$ if $(i,j) \in \mathcal{E}$, and $a_{ij} = 0$ otherwise. The Laplacian matrix of the graph is defined as $L = \mathcal{D} - \mathcal{A}$, where $\mathcal{D} = \text{diag}(\mathcal{A}1_N) \in \mathbb{R}^{N \times N}$, where $1_N = \begin{bmatrix} 1 & 1 & \ldots & 1 \end{bmatrix}^T$ is an vector with multiplicity 1. For any pair of vertices (i,j), if $a_{ij} = a_{ji}$, the graph is called an undirected graph. In this case, $\mathcal{G}$ is connected if there is a directed path between any pair of distinct nodes; otherwise, it is termed a directed graph. For a directed graph, L is no longer to be symmetric, and the eigenvalues of L have non-negative real part. A directed path of length l is defined as a sequence of edges in a directed graph of the form $((i_1, i_2), (i_2, i_3), \ldots, (i_l, i_{l+1}))$ in which $(i_j, i_{j+1}) \in \mathcal{E}$ for $j = 1, \ldots, l$ and $i_j \neq i_k$ for $j, k = 1, \ldots, l$ and $j \neq k$.

In this paper, we consider a network of N single-integrator dynamics, labeled from 1 to N. Let $x_i \in \mathbb{R}$ be the state of agent i, and it has the following dynamics,

$$\dot{x}_i = \sum_{j=1}^{N} a_{ij}(x_j - x_i), \quad i = 1, 2, \ldots, N. \tag{1}$$

As we know [13], the agents (1) can achieve consensus over a connected graph. It is observed from (1) that each agent can get the exact measurement of states of its neighbors. However, in practice, the measurement part may have bounded nonlinearities or saturation constraints due to sensor limitations. Therefore, in this paper, the consensus problem with state constraints will be considered. That is, we consider the agents with the following dynamics,

$$\dot{x}_i = \sum_{j=1}^{N} a_{ij} \left(\mathrm{sat}_M \left(x_j \right) - \mathrm{sat}_M \left(x_i \right) \right), \tag{2}$$

where the function $\mathrm{sat}_M \left(\cdot \right)$ is described as a saturated characteristic given by

$$\mathrm{sat}_M \left(x \right) = \begin{cases} x, & \text{if } |x| \leq M \\ M \mathrm{sign} \left(x \right), & \text{if } |x| > M \end{cases},$$

where $M > 0$ is the saturation limit.

Definition 1. *Consider a dynamical network of N agents, whose communication topology is described by a graph $\mathcal{G}$. The consensus is said to be achieved for the group of agents (2), if*

$$\lim_{t \to \infty} \left(x_i(t) - x_j(t) \right) = 0, \tag{3}$$

for all initial conditions $x_i(0) \in \mathbb{R}, i = 1, 2, \ldots, N$.

It is worth pointing that the consensus of agents (2) may not be achieved due to the saturation function on the states [10]. Therefore, the problem is under what conditions the consensus is achieved. This motivates us to find some necessary and sufficient conditions, under which the agents can achieve consensus.

3   Main Results

We consider in this section the consensus with state constraints under the undirected graph, and the following theorem is obtained.

Theorem 1. *Suppose that the undirected graph $\mathcal{G}$ is connected. The consensus problem of agents (2) is solved if and only if*

$$\left| \frac{1}{N} \sum_{i=1}^{N} x_i(0) \right| \leq M. \tag{4}$$

Furthermore, the final consensus state is $\lim_{t \to \infty} x_i(t) = \frac{1}{N} \sum_{i=1}^{N} x_i(0)$.

Proof. Let $\xi(t) = \frac{1}{N} \sum_{i=1}^{N} x_i(t)$, and it is proved that $\dot{\xi}(t) = \frac{1}{N} \sum_{i=1}^{N} \dot{x}_i(t) = \frac{1}{N} 1_N^T L \mathrm{sat}_M(x) = 0$, where $x = \begin{bmatrix} x_1 \ x_2 \ \ldots \ x_N \end{bmatrix}^T$ and $1_N = \begin{bmatrix} 1 \ 1 \ \ldots \ 1 \end{bmatrix}^T$ is the right eigenvector of L corresponding to eigenvalue 0 with multiplicity 1. Therefore, $\xi(t)$ is time-invariant for agents (2), which implies the final consensus state is $\frac{1}{N} \sum_{i=1}^{N} x_i(0)$ if the consensus is reached.

(The sufficiency part): Let $\xi = \frac{1}{N}\sum_{i=1}^{N} x_i(0)$, and consider the following Lyapunov function

$$V_1 = \sum_{i=1}^{N} \int_{\xi}^{x_i} (\mathrm{sat}_M(s) - \mathrm{sat}_M(\xi))\, ds.$$

Since $\xi = \frac{1}{N}\sum_{i=1}^{N} x_i(0)$ and $\left|\frac{1}{N}\sum_{i=1}^{N} x_i(0)\right| \leq M$, it can be proved that $\mathrm{sign}(\mathrm{sat}_M(s) - \mathrm{sat}_M(\zeta)) = \mathrm{sign}(s - \zeta)$. That is, $\frac{\mathrm{sat}_M(s) - \mathrm{sat}_M(\zeta)}{s - \zeta} > 0$ for any $s \neq \zeta \in \mathbb{R}$, which implies there exists a constant $\epsilon > 0$ such that $1 \geq \frac{\mathrm{sat}_M(s) - \mathrm{sat}_M(\zeta)}{s - \zeta} \geq \epsilon$. Then, we have

$$V_1 \geq \epsilon \sum_{i=1}^{N} \int_{\xi}^{x_i} (s - \xi)\, ds = \frac{\epsilon}{2} \sum_{i=1}^{N} (x_i - \xi)^2 \geq 0. \tag{5}$$

It is clear that $V_1 = 0$ only when $x_i = \xi, i = 1, 2, \ldots, N$. That is, $V_1 = 0$ only when $x_i = x_j, i, j = 1, 2, \ldots, N$. Then, the time derivative of V_1 is given by

$$\dot{V}_1 = \sum_{i=1}^{N} (\mathrm{sat}_M(x_i) - \mathrm{sat}_M(\xi))\, \dot{x}_i$$

$$= \sum_{i=1}^{N} \sum_{j=1}^{N} a_{ij} (\mathrm{sat}_M(x_i) - \mathrm{sat}_M(\xi))$$

$$\times (\mathrm{sat}_M(x_j) - \mathrm{sat}_M(x_i)).$$

Let $\bar{x}_i = \mathrm{sat}_M(x_i) - \mathrm{sat}_M(\xi)$, and we have

$$\dot{V}_1 = \sum_{i=1}^{N} \sum_{j=1}^{N} a_{ij}\bar{x}_i \left(\bar{x}_j - \bar{x}_i\right)$$

$$= -\frac{1}{2} \sum_{i=1}^{N} \sum_{j=1}^{N} a_{ij} \left(\bar{x}_i - \bar{x}_j\right)^2$$

$$\leq 0, \tag{6}$$

where we have $\sum_{i=1}^{N} \sum_{j=1}^{N} a_{ij}\varepsilon_i (\zeta_i - \zeta_j) = \frac{1}{2}\sum_{i=1}^{N} \sum_{j=1}^{N} a_{ij} (\varepsilon_i - \varepsilon_j)(\zeta_i - \zeta_j)$ for any $\varepsilon_i, \zeta_i \in \mathbb{R}, i = 1, 2, \ldots, N$ under the undirected and connected graph. Since $\xi = \frac{1}{N}\sum_{i=1}^{N} x_i(0)$ and $\left|\frac{1}{N}\sum_{i=1}^{N} x_i(0)\right| \leq M$, we know that $V_1 = 0$ only when $\bar{x}_i = \bar{x}_j$, that is, $\mathrm{sat}_M(x_i) - \mathrm{sat}_M(\xi) = \mathrm{sat}_M(x_j) - \mathrm{sat}_M(\xi)$. Therefore, the consensus can be reached and the final consensus state is $\xi = \frac{1}{N}\sum_{i=1}^{N} x_i(0)$ if $\mathrm{sat}_M(x_i) = \mathrm{sat}_M(x_j), i, j = 1, 2, \ldots, N$ implies $x_i = x_j, i, j = 1, 2, \ldots, N$.

Note that $\mathrm{sat}_M(x_i) = \mathrm{sat}_M(x_j), i, j = 1, 2, \ldots, N$ only under the conditions that $x_i \geq M$ or $x_i \leq -M$, and $|x_i| \leq M$ with $x_1 = x_2 = \ldots = x_N$. Since

$\xi = \frac{1}{N} \sum_{i=1}^{N} x_i(0)$ and $\left| \frac{1}{N} \sum_{i=1}^{N} x_i(0) \right| \leq M$, then the condition that $x_i \geq M$ or $x_i \leq -M$ is not satisfied. Therefore, $\mathrm{sat}_M(x_i) = \mathrm{sat}_M(x_j)$ only when $x_i = x_j$, which implies that $V_1 = 0$ only when $x_i = x_j, i, j = 1, 2, \ldots, N$. In summary, we have $\lim_{t \to \infty} x_i(t) - x_j(t) = 0$ and the the final consensus state is $\frac{1}{N} \sum_{i=1}^{N} x_i(0)$.

(The necessity part): Since the consensus is reached with the condition that $\left| \frac{1}{N} \sum_{i=1}^{N} x_i(0) \right| \leq M$, we prove this part by using a contradiction. Without loss of generality, to avoid the trivial result, we assume that there exists $i \neq j$, where $i, j = 1, 2, \ldots, N$, such that $x_i(0) \neq x_j(0)$.

Suppose that the consensus is reached with $\frac{1}{N} \sum_{i=1}^{N} x_i(0) > M$ or $\frac{1}{N} \sum_{i=1}^{N} x_i(0) < -M$, which implies the final state $\xi > M$ or $\xi < -M$. In what follows, the proof will be divided into two cases. At first, we consider the case that the consensus is reached with the condition $\xi > M$. Since the consensus is reached with $\xi > M$, which means the final value of states is larger than M. It is reasonable to know that there exists a time $t_c \geq 0$ (For example, very close to the time of achieving consensus) such that $x_i(t_c) \geq M, i = 1, 2, \ldots, N$, which means the consensus is not reached at time t_c. However, at the time t_c, we have $\dot{x}_i(t_c) = \sum_{j=1}^{N} a_{ij} (\mathrm{sat}_M(x_j(t_c)) - \mathrm{sat}_M(x_i(t_c))) = 0, i, j = 1, 2, \ldots, N$, which implies the consensus is achieved at time t_c. This is a contradiction. For the case $\frac{1}{N} \sum_{i=1}^{N} x_i(0) < -M$, a similar contradiction can be obtained by following the same process, which completes the proof.

In what follows, we discuss some properties of the unachievable consensus case, and the definition of the unbounded interactions graph will be introduced.

Definition 2. *A graph $\mathcal{G} = (\mathcal{V}, \mathcal{E}, \mathcal{A})$ is called the unbounded interactions graph if the following conditions are satisfied: (1) each $a_{ij}(\cdot)$ is a nonnegative and measurable function; (2) $a_{ii}(t) = 0$ for all i, and $\int_0^\infty a_{ij}(t)dt = \infty$ for $(j, i) \in \varepsilon$.*

Then, the following assumption and lemma from [4] will be needed.

Assumption 1 *(Cut-balance).* There exists a constant $K \geq 1$ such that for all t, and any nonempty proper subset S of $\{1, 2, \ldots, N\}$, we have

$$K^{-1} \sum_{i \in S, j \notin S} a_{ji}(t) \leq \sum_{i \in S, j \notin S} a_{ij}(t) \leq K \sum_{i \in S, j \notin S} a_{ji}(t).$$

Lemma 1. *Suppose that Assumption 1 (cut-balance) holds. Let $x : \mathbb{R}^+ \to \mathbb{R}^N$ be a solution to the system of integral equations*

$$x_i(t) = x_i(0) + \int_0^t \sum_{j=1}^{N} a_{ij}(\tau)(x_j(\tau) - x_i(\tau)) d\tau, \qquad (7)$$

for $i = 1, 2, \ldots, N$. If the graph $\mathcal{G}$ is the unbounded interactions graph, we have
(a) The limit $x_i^* = \lim_{t \to \infty} x_i(t)$ exists, and $x_i^* \in [\min_j x_j(0), \max_j x_j(0)]$, for all i.

(b) For every j and i, we have $\int_0^\infty a_{ij}(t)|x_j(t) - x_i(t)| < \infty$. Furthermore, if i and j belongs to the same connected component, then $x_i^* = x_j^*$.

It is easy to know that the undirected graph is the unbounded interactions graph, and it satisfies the Assumption 1. Furthermore, the integral equations of (2) are given as

$$x_i(t) = x_i(0) + \int_0^t \sum_{j=1}^N a_{ij}(\tau)$$
$$\times \left(\text{sat}_M\left(x_j(\tau)\right) - \text{sat}_M\left(x_i(\tau)\right)\right) d\tau. \tag{8}$$

In view of (8), it can be proved that

$$x_i(t) = x_i(0) + \int_0^t \sum_{j=1}^N a_{ij}(\tau)$$
$$\times \left(\text{sat}_M\left(x_j(\tau)\right) - \text{sat}_M\left(x_i(\tau)\right)\right) d\tau$$
$$\leq x_i(0) + \int_0^t \sum_{j=1}^N a_{ij}(\tau)\left(x_j(\tau) - x_i(\tau)\right) d\tau.$$

According to Lemma 1, since $\lim_{t\to\infty} x_i(t) = x_i^* \in [\min_j x_j(0), \max_j x_j(0)]$ exists for the system of integral equation (7), then, for the integral equation (8), we have $x_i^* = \lim_{t\to\infty} x_i(t)$ exists, and $x_i^* \in [\min_j x_j(0), \max_j x_j(0)]$, for all i. That is, the final states of agents (2) are bounded in $[\min_j x_j(0), \max_j x_j(0)], j = 1, 2, \ldots, N$.

As discussed above, some properties of the unachievable consensus are summarized as follows.

Theorem 2. Suppose that the graph $\mathcal{G}$ is undirected. Let $x : \mathbb{R}^+ \to \mathbb{R}^N$ be a solution to the integral equations of (2) such that

$$x_i(t) = x_i(0) + \int_0^t \sum_{j=1}^N a_{ij}(\tau)\left(\text{sat}_M\left(x_j(\tau)\right) - \text{sat}_M\left(x_i(\tau)\right)\right) d\tau,$$

for $i = 1, 2, \ldots, N$. Then, we have that the limit $x_i^* = \lim_{t\to\infty} x_i(t)$ exists, and $x_i^* \in [\min_j x_j(0), \max_j x_j(0)]$ for all i.

4   Simulation Examples

In the simulation, we use one example to demonstrate our findings of multi-agent systems on an undirected graph.

We consider a group of 10 single-integrator agents, whose topology is undirected and connected, and the saturation limit is $M = 3$. The initial conditions are randomly distributed and belongs to the interval $[-20, 20]$. Figure 1 shows

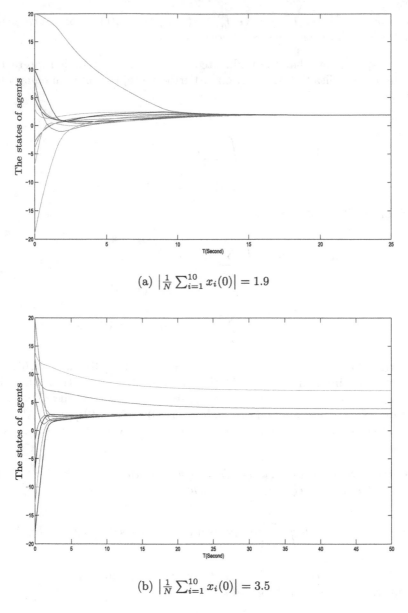

(a) $\left|\frac{1}{N}\sum_{i=1}^{10} x_i(0)\right| = 1.9$

(b) $\left|\frac{1}{N}\sum_{i=1}^{10} x_i(0)\right| = 3.5$

Fig. 1. Consensus with state constraints for 10 agents on the undirected graph

the simulation results under different initial conditions, where Fig. 1(a) shows when the absolute final value is $\left|\frac{1}{10}\sum_{i=1}^{10} x_i(0)\right| = 1.9 \leq M = 3$, which satisfies the condition (4), and then the agents can achieve consensus. However, the absolute final value is $\left|\frac{1}{10}\sum_{i=1}^{10} x_i(0)\right| = 3.5 > M = 3$ in Fig. 1(b), which does not satisfy the condition (4), and thus the consensus can not be reached. But it can be verified that the final states are bounded.

5 Conclusions

In this paper, we have studied the first-order consensus problem with state constraints. Due to the existence of saturation functions, the agents may not achieve consensus. Therefore, we have investigated the conditions for achieving consensus with state constraints. The general magnitude saturation function has been considered in this paper. By investigating the equilibrium and employing an integral Lyapunov function, some necessary and sufficient conditions for achieving consensus have been provided. Additionally, some properties of the unachievable consensus were discussed. Finally, simulation examples illustrated the effectiveness of the proposed conditions.

Acknowledgements. This work was partially supported by the National Natural Science Foundation of China (61503079), the Jiangsu Natural Science Foundation (BK20150625), the Fundamental Research Funds for the Central Universities, and a project funded by the Priority Academic Program Development of Jiangsu Higher Education Institutions.

References

1. Chen, Z., Zhang, H.: Analysis of joint connectivity condition for multiagents with boundary constraints. IEEE Trans. Cybern. **43**(2), 437–444 (2013)
2. Dong, X., Shi, Z., Lu, G., Zhong, Y.: Formation-containment analysis and design for high-order linear time-invariant swarm systems. Int. J. Robust Nonlinear Control **25**(17), 3439–3456 (2015)
3. Dong, X., Zhou, Y., Ren, Z., Zhong, Y.: Time-varying formation control for unmanned aerial vehicles with switching interaction topologies. Control Eng. Pract. **46**, 26–36 (2016)
4. Hendrickx, J., Tsitsiklis, J.: Convergence of type-symmetric and cut-balanced consensus seeking systems. IEEE Trans. Autom. Control **58**(1), 214–218 (2013)
5. Hong, Y., Hu, J., Gao, L.: Tracking control for multi-agent consensus with an active leader and variable topology. Automatica **42**(7), 1177–1182 (2006)
6. Li, Y., Xiang, J., Wei, W.: Consensus problems for linear time-invariant multiagent systems with saturation constraints. IET Control Theory Appl. **5**(6), 823–829 (2011)
7. Li, Z., Duan, Z., Chen, G., Huang, L.: Consensus of multiagent systems and synchronization of complex networks: a unified viewpoint. IEEE Trans. Circuits and Systems (I) **57**(1), 213–224 (2010)
8. Li, Z., Zhao, Y., Duan, Z.: Distributed robust consensus of a class of lipschitz nonlinear multi-agent systems with matching uncertainties. Asian J. Control **17**(1), 3–13 (2015)
9. Lim, Y.: Consensus of multi-agent systems with saturation constraints. Ph.D. thesis, Gwangju Institute of Science and Technology (2016)
10. Liu, X., Chen, T., Lu, W.: Consensus problem in directed networks of multi-agents via nonlinear protocols. Physica-A **373**(35), 3122–3127 (2009)

11. Liu, Y., Jia, Y.: Adaptive consensus protocol for networks of multiple agents with nonlinear dynamics using neural networks. Asian J. Control **14**(5), 1328–1339 (2012)

12. Liu, Z., Chen, Z.: Discarded consensus of network of agents with state constraint. IEEE Trans. Autom. Control **57**(11), 2869–2874 (2012)

13. Olfati-Saber, R., Murray, R.: Consensus problems in networks of agents with switching topology and time-delays. IEEE Trans. Autom. Control **49**(9), 1520–1533 (2004)

14. Qiu, J., Feng, G., Gao, H.: Fuzzy-model-based piecewise static-output-feedback controller design for networked nonlinear systems. IEEE Trans. Fuzzy Syst. **18**(5), 919–934 (2010)

15. Qiu, J., Feng, G., Gao, H.: Observer-based piecewise affine output feedback controller synthesis of continuous-time t-s fuzzy affine dynamic systems using quantized measurements. IEEE Trans. Fuzzy Syst. **20**(6), 1046–1062 (2012)

16. Su, H., Chen, M., Lam, J., Lin, Z.: Semi-global leader-following consensus of linear multi-agent systems with input saturation via low gain feedback. IEEE Trans. Circuits Syst. (I) **60**(7), 1881–1889 (2013)

17. Sun, W., Li, Y., Li, C., Chen, Y.: Convergence speed of a fractional order consensus algorithm over undirected scale-free networks. Asian J. Control **13**(6), 936–946 (2011)

18. Wang, J., Cheng, D., Hu, X.: Consensus of multi-agent linear dynamic systems. Asian J. Control **10**(2), 144–155 (2008)

19. Wang, Q., Sun, C.: Conditions for consensus in directed networks of agents with heterogeneous output saturation. IET Control Theory Appl. **10**(16), 2119–2127 (2016)

20. Wang, Q., Yu, C., Gao, H.: Semiglobal synchronization of multiple generic linear agents with input saturation. Int. J. Robust Nonlinear Control **24**(18), 3239–3254 (2014)

21. Wang, Y., Wu, Q.: Distributed robust H_∞ consensus for multi-agent systems with nonlinear dynamics and parameter uncertainties. Asian J. Control **17**(1), 352–361 (2015)

22. Wen, G., Duan, Z., Yu, W., Chen, G.: Consensus in multi-agent systems with communication constraints. Int. J. Robust Nonlinear Control **22**(2), 170–182 (2012)

23. Yang, T., Meng, Z., Dimarogonas, D., Johansson, K.: Global consensus for discrete-time multi-agent systems with input saturation constraints. Automatica **50**(2), 499–506 (2014)

24. Ye, Z., Chen, Y., Zhang, H.: Distributed consensus of delayed multi-agent systems with nonlinear dynamics via intermittent control. Asian J. Control **18**(3), 964–975 (2015). doi:10.1002/asjc1172

25. Zhao, Z., Lin, Z.: Semi-global leader-following consensus of multiple linear systems with position and rate limited actuators. Int. J. Robust Nonlinear Control **25**(13), 2083–2100 (2015)

Author Index